CARIBBEAN INTEGRATION LAW

Caribbean Integration Law

DAVID S BERRY

OXFORD
UNIVERSITY PRESS

OXFORD
UNIVERSITY PRESS

Great Clarendon Street, Oxford, OX2 6DP,
United Kingdom

Oxford University Press is a department of the University of Oxford.
It furthers the University's objective of excellence in research, scholarship,
and education by publishing worldwide. Oxford is a registered trade mark of
Oxford University Press in the UK and in certain other countries

First Edition published in 2014
Impression: 1

Published in the United States of America by Oxford University Press
198 Madison Avenue, New York, NY 10016, United States of America

British Library Cataloguing in Publication Data
Data available

Library of Congress Control Number: 2013952975

ISBN 978–0–19–967007–9

Printed and bound in Great Britain by
CPI Group (UK) Ltd, Croydon, CR0 4YY

To Nicola and Alec, my two muses.

Acknowledgments

This book could not have been written without the encouragement and assistance of a large number of persons, to all of whom I express my gratitude. The Hon Mr Justice Andrew Burgess must be thanked for pushing me to develop a more active interest in Caribbean integration when he assigned me to teach a new course in 1998 called 'Caribbean Integration Law'. A decade and a half of students have continuously re-energized my interest in the field and, through their persistent questioning, have encouraged me to work harder to master the topic. A number of researchers helped me develop my course materials over the years and one, Jeffrey Foreman, particularly assisted in updating Caribbean statutory references and in providing further research on the history and economics of the region. I also thank the staff of the CARICOM Secretariat for their hospitality during my week of research at their Headquarters in August 2012. Safiya Ali, the General Counsel of CARICOM, was especially helpful in providing clear and informed views of the internal workings of CARICOM and the status of various treaties and instruments. Several persons provided comments on earlier drafts of the book and I would like to thank Dr Chantal Ononaiwu and Professor Alina Kaczorowska-Ireland for their constructive, critical readings of several chapters. I of course take full responsibility for any errors or omissions.

Finally, I would like to thank most of all my wife, Nicola Berry, and father, Edward Berry, for their constant encouragement. Without the exacting proofreading of my father, the book would lack clarity and precision in many areas. Without the sacrifice of Nicola, the book probably would not exist.

Contents

III. THE LEGAL SYSTEMS

IV. SUBSTANTIVE RULES AND POLICIES

Table of Cases

CARIBBEAN (DOMESTIC)

EUROPEAN UNION

INTERNATIONAL AND REST OF WORLD

UNITED KINGDOM

Table of Legislation

Table of Treaties

List of Abbreviations

ACCP	Assembly of Caribbean Community Parliamentarians
CARICOM	Caribbean Community
CCJ	Caribbean Court of Justice
CCJ Agreement	Agreement Establishing the Caribbean Court of Justice
CET	Common External Tariff
COFAP	Council for Finance and Planning
COFCOR	Council for Foreign and Community Relations
COHSOD	Council for Human and Social Development
Community Council	Community Council of Ministers
Conference	Conference of Heads of Government
COTED	Council for Trade and Economic Development
CSME	CARICOM Single Market and Economy
DSA	Dispute Settlement Annex to the Revised Treaty of Basseterre Establishing the Organisation of Eastern Caribbean States Economic Union
ECJ	European Court of Justice
EU	European Union
GDP	Gross domestic product
ICJ	International Court of Justice
OECS	Organisation of Eastern Caribbean States
PCIJ	Permanent Court of International Justice
RTB	Revised Treaty of Basseterre Establishing the Organisation of Eastern Caribbean States Economic Union
RTC	Revised Treaty of Chaguaramas Establishing the Caribbean Community Including the CARICOM Single Market and Economy
TEU	Treaty on European Union
TFEU	Treaty on the Functioning of the European Union
UN	United Nations
VCLT	Vienna Convention on the Law of Treaties, 1969

PART I

FUNDAMENTALS OF CARIBBEAN INTEGRATION

1
Introduction

The natural state of our Caribbean is fragmentation.

Shridath Ramphal[1]

Fragmentation ought not to be our natural state. Our fragmentation is the result of a calculated colonial practice that exploited our geography, producing an instinct of insularity and isolation instead of a culture of co-operation and collaboration.

Kenny D. Anthony[2]

The Caribbean region hosts two of the most successful and long-standing regional integration movements in the developing world: the Caribbean Community (CARICOM) and the Organisation of Eastern Caribbean States (OECS). These two regional organizations overlap in membership and share similar goals, but diverge in interesting ways so as to best reflect the particular needs of their members. This book introduces the reader to the legal systems of CARICOM and the OECS. It locates them in their historical and theoretical contexts and engages in a detailed exploration of their treaty structures, texts, and legal practices. It also introduces the reader to fundamental concepts of international institutional law and the law of treaties and offers comparisons with similar developments in the European Union.

This book is expressly comparative. In each section the rules and institutional structures of the two regional organizations are described, compared, and contrasted and, where helpful, analysed in light of the rules and practices of other institutions, both regional and international. For such an analysis the relevance of public international law, the law of international institutions, and precedents and rules of the European Union legal system cannot be seriously questioned. Although Caribbean integration has its own unique organizations, organs, and processes, it must be remembered that the legal rules of CARICOM and the OECS are grounded in public international law and the law of international institutions. Both regional organizations are founded upon treaties, and these constituent instruments are governed by the customary international law of treaties.

[1] As reproduced in Christoph Müllerleile, *CARICOM Integration: Progress and Hurdles—A European View* (Kingston, Jamaica: Kingston Publishers, 1996) 31.

[2] Kenny D Anthony, 'Caribbean Integration: The Future Relationship between Barbados and the OECS' (1998) 23(1) *Journal of Eastern Caribbean Studies* 35–50, at 37.

The relevance of the EU raises more interesting questions. Of course there can be no exact comparison between Caribbean and European regional organizations, and it would be deeply problematic to impose the practices and procedures of other organizations upon the Caribbean. The histories of the two regions, the nature of the members, and the powers and competences that have been allocated to each organization are clearly different. However there are certain striking parallels that cannot be overlooked. There are, for example, clear similarities in the texts of the EU and Caribbean treaties. In some cases the wordings of the treaty articles are almost, or are, identical. This is no accident. Caribbean legal drafters did not reinvent the wheel. Rather, they carefully selected and incorporated into their own treaties useful phrases and concepts which have evolved in the EU system. As a result, the role of the European Union as a comparator must be accepted, albeit with some caution. This is reflected in academic and institutional writings, and the judgments of at least one regional court, the Caribbean Court of Justice.[3]

Nevertheless two caveats must be urged upon the reader at this point. Firstly, it should always be kept in mind that Caribbean states and Caribbean legal drafters did not intend to create a replica of the European Union. Even if the same words are used in places, the two Caribbean legal systems which were created differ, and were meant to differ, in important and fundamental ways from the EU. As a result any parallels between the texts of the treaties of the two regions cannot be used to definitively resolve questions for Caribbean integration. Secondly, the institutional structures of the two regional models must be carefully distinguished, even if, in the case of the OECS, there is some similarity in the nomenclature used to describe the organs. This is because the various organs possess substantially different competences and the organizations as a whole place their organs in unique and interdependent relationships. A limitation in competence of one organ, for example, can have a ripple effect on the competences of other organs or the organization as a whole.

Another issue that should be addressed is the heavy reliance of this book on the texts of the constituent documents of CARICOM and the OECS. Those with intimate inside knowledge of the processes of both regional organizations may be frustrated by such a strong focus on formal texts. However this focus is both inevitable and necessary. It is inevitable because of the overwhelming tendency of Caribbean regional organizations to classify and otherwise restrict access to fundamental documentation, including basic decisions of organs. This practice has been described as being part of a 'culture of confidentiality' by the authors of a recent report, a culture in which the 'Secretariat's default setting is that documents and information are classified'.[4] Although calls for declassification are being made, this

[3] See eg *Trinidad Cement Ltd and TCL Guyana Inc v Guyana*, Judgment, [2009] CCJ 5 (OJ) 20 August 2009 [24] (citing and applying principles from European Court of Justice cases in the context of state liability).

[4] Richard Stoneman, Justice Duke Pollard, and Hugo Inniss, 'Turning Around CARICOM: Proposals to Restructure the Secretariat', Landell Mills Ltd/Final Report/January 2012, as available at <http://www.caricom.org/jsp/communications/caricom_online_pubs/Restructuring%20the%20Secretariat%20-%20Landell%20Mills%20Final%20Report.pdf> (9 February 2013) p 67.

culture is unlikely to change quickly.[5] Until these documents are declassified they cannot be cited in this book.

A textual focus is also necessary because the text shows us the meaning and potential of the treaties. The text tells us not only what should be done, but what can be done. In other words, a strict textual interpretation of the Revised Treaty of Chaguaramas and the Revised Treaty of Basseterre must guide any sound legal analysis of regional integration because it allows us to hold regional organizations to their assigned functions and competences. It also allows us to remind them of their future potential. Under a textual analysis the question therefore becomes not 'what happens in practice', but rather 'what does the text, in its context and in light of its object and purpose, allow'.

As a further note to the reader, it should be highlighted that this book seeks to explore the legal rules and texts related to Caribbean regional organizations at a variety of levels, given its assumed readership. Explanations of basic legal concepts and translations of Latin terms are provided for students, who will also be aided by the list of abbreviations. Detailed and at times exhaustive analysis of the texts of the constituent treaties is provided for attorneys at law who may seek guidance on particular legal problems. The index has been specifically designed to assist these readers. The comprehensive textual analysis of the treaties is also tailored to the reader who seeks a holistic overview of the current CARICOM and OECS legal systems. For ease of comprehension the pattern of the analysis in the following chapters is to describe the texts, analyse their strengths and weaknesses, examine their regional judicial interpretations, and, where possible, compare similar texts and interpretive practices from outside the Caribbean. The latter, comparative analysis of EU law and international legal developments is provided for scholars in the fields of regional integration and international institutional law, and for policy makers and judges, who will be required both to interpret the texts of the treaties and to shape the direction of CARICOM and OECS law.

The chapters that follow are divided into six parts, examining the fundamentals of Caribbean integration, the institutional frameworks of CARICOM and the OECS, their legal systems, dispute settlement procedures, and potential future developments. In Part I the present introductory chapter is followed by a chapter setting out the geographical, economic, historical, and theoretical contexts for the two regional organizations. Chapter 2 briefly traces the evolutionary trajectory of regional integration in the Caribbean, and comments on some of the factors influencing institutional design, including the EU model, the law of treaties, and the rules of international institutional law. In providing a brief overview of theories and concepts related to integration and the rules of international institutional law, it offers practical guidance to those seeking to understand the complex relations between, and applicability of, international law and regional law.

Chapter 3 initiates an examination of the institutional frameworks of CARICOM and the OECS, the focus of Part II, starting with the status of their respective

[5] Stoneman, Pollard, and Inniss, 'Turning Around CARICOM' (n 4).

treaties and of the organizations more generally. It also provides an overview of the objects and purposes of the organizations, and examines questions related to membership and other forms of participation. Chapter 4 analyses the structure, competences, and decision-making processes of the main and secondary organs of the organizations. It seeks to help the reader understand the institutional structure within which integration issues will be addressed, including questions related to which organ might have competence to address a particular issue, and how that organ can create and implement rules in the broader organizational context. Chapter 5 looks at the issues related to personality, legal capacity, privileges and immunities, and the final provisions of the treaties of CARICOM and the OECS.

Part III examines the general legal systems of the two regional organizations. Chapter 6 looks at the bases through which legal obligations are created, implemented, and enforced in CARICOM and the OECS. In examining the general exceptions to legal obligations in the treaties and under international law, it reveals both the concrete building blocks for, and challenges to, the uniformity of Community and OECS Economic Union obligations. It also examines the interaction of international law and domestic law in the context of the creation of binding obligations under the CARICOM and OECS treaty regimes. It sets out the practical consequences of the common law requirement for transformation of treaty obligations into domestic law, and the interpretive issues which arise as from the incorporation of Caribbean regional treaties. Chapter 7 introduces the concept of general principles of law, examining its meaning and scope in legal theory, international law, and EU law. Chapter 8 explores several general principles that have a potential basis in the treaties of the two regional organizations, either express or implicit. It compares them with general principles and other foundational concepts that have emerged in EU law, suggesting that the latter may also arise in the law of CARICOM and the OECS either as general principles, or through the interpretation of the texts of the regional treaties.

Part IV examines the substantive rules and policies set out in the constituent instruments of the two organizations. Chapter 9 focuses upon three of the four freedoms—movement of persons (including via the right of establishment), services, and capital—and their restrictions and limitations. Chapter 10 examines the core economic provisions of the two treaty frameworks related to the fourth freedom, the free movement of goods. It surveys the complex and detailed rules governing everything from the enforcement of the Common External Tariff (CET), to the abolition of duties, to the restriction of discriminatory internal taxes and unauthorized quantitative restrictions. It also examines the regimes related to subsidies and anti-dumping. These rules are complex and interdependent, and in order to clearly comprehend and apply them one must understand both the process of their creation (since some of the cross-referencing in the Revised Treaty of Chaguaramas is incorrect), and the models from which they were derived, including EU treaty models. Chapter 11 offers a very brief overview of the competition and consumer protection rules established in the two treaties, and explains the general framework in which these rules will operate. Chapter 12 rounds off Part IV by briefly surveying the policy regimes established in the two treaties, including policies related to sectoral development, common supportive measures and development.

Chapter 13 opens the dispute settlement analysis of Part V. It examines all of the dispute settlement mechanisms, except adjudication, established in the treaties of the two regional organizations. It looks at the dispute settlement functions of the central organs of CARICOM and the OECS, and the ad hoc binding and non-binding mechanisms made available in Chapter IX of CARICOM's treaty and the Dispute Settlement Annex and Protocol to the OECS treaty. Chapter 14 focuses on the two regional courts which assist in the regional integration process, the Caribbean Court of Justice and the Eastern Caribbean Court of Appeal. It provides an overview of their competences, including the different bases on which they may take jurisdiction over a treaty-related dispute, and their remedial powers. It also examines the early jurisprudence of these courts, including the several original jurisdiction decisions of the Caribbean Court of Justice—decisions which already reveal the important role that the Court will play in the regional integration process.

Part VI contains the final chapter, which offers brief conclusions and suggestions about the legal developments that may be required to assist in moving the integration processes forward. Countering pessimistic predictions about the potential demise of CARICOM or the OECS, Chapter 15 expresses an optimistic view about the continued legal viability, even vibrancy, of the Caribbean regional integration project. The revised treaties of CARICOM and the OECS offer sound legal frameworks and create the potential for deeper regional integration. Moreover, the creation, and active use, of at least one of the two final and binding legal integration tribunals—the Caribbean Court of Justice—offers considerable hope for determinate and uniform interpretation and enforcement of treaty obligations.

2

Foundations of Caribbean Integration

The present chapter introduces the context of Caribbean integration, examining the geographical, economic, and political factors that have shaped the regional integration movement. It provides a brief overview of the history of regional integration from the pre-independence period until the present. It also introduces readers to the theoretical and legal tools necessary to understand regional integration, by briefly examining economic models, the rules of treaty interpretation, and specific legal concepts related to regional and international organizations. The reader familiar with these latter concepts may wish to skip the final section of the chapter.

2.1 Overview

The focus of the present book is on the regional integration developments related to the primarily English-speaking islands and mainland territories of the Caribbean, spanning the entire Caribbean Basin area. These territories extend from Belize, located in Central America, all of the way along the Caribbean island chain to Guyana, on the South American continent. Two non-English speaking members of the Caribbean Community, namely, Dutch-speaking Suriname and French-speaking Haiti, also fall within the scope of the present study. These territories are illustrated on the map reproduced in Figure 2.1.

2.1.1 CARICOM membership

All of the territories studied are bordered, or surrounded by, the Caribbean Sea and fall within the ecosystem of the Wider Caribbean Region.[1] Falling primarily between the Tropic of Cancer and the Equator, Caribbean territories benefit from idyllic climates and scenery, but also are susceptible to hurricanes, tsunamis, and other natural disasters. Given their geography, CARICOM states rely almost exclusively upon sea and air transportation and depend heavily upon the sea for fisheries, shipping, and tourism. Subject to the two exceptions of Haiti and Suriname, which were former French and Dutch colonies, all of the

[1] For the scope and complexity of the Wider Caribbean Region from a marine ecosystem perspective see Lucia Fanning et al, 'A Large Marine Ecosystem Governance Framework' (2007) 31 *Marine Policy* 434–43, 435–6.

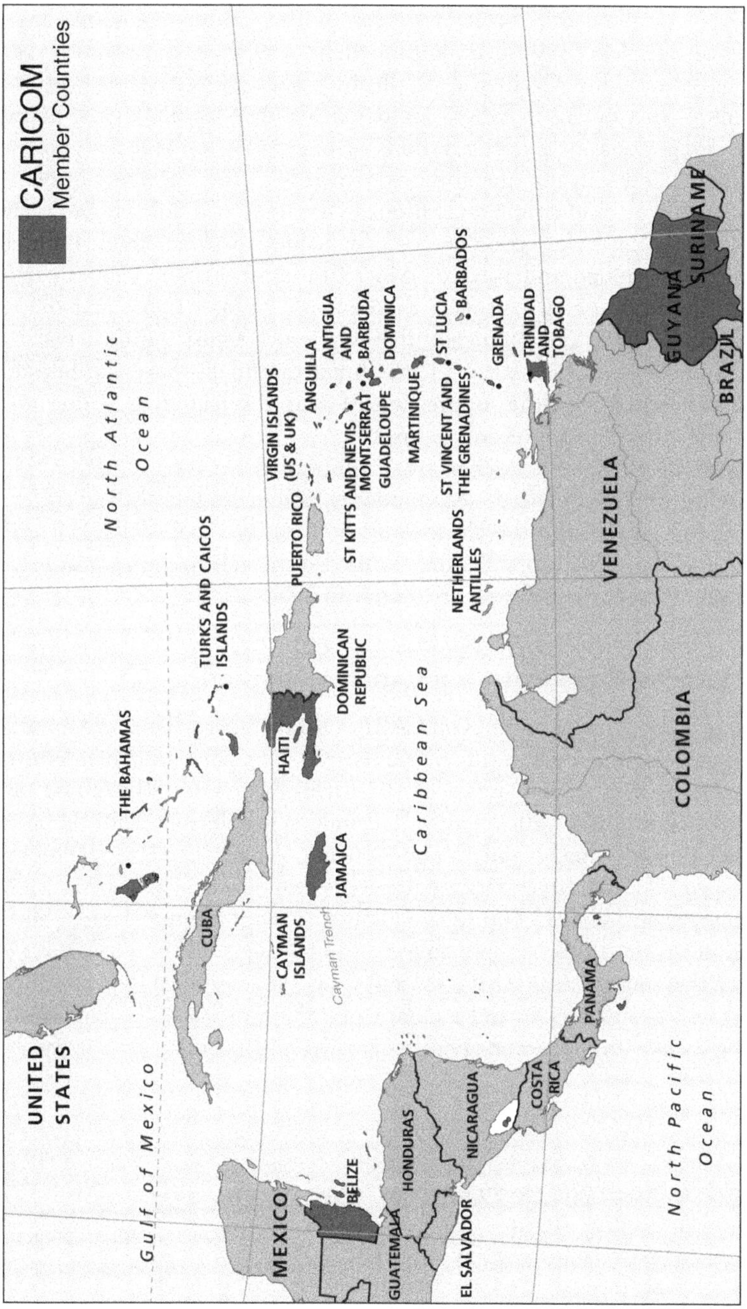

Figure 2.1 Map illustrating CARICOM membership[2]

[2] Map has been adapted from Ben Bowling, *Policing the Caribbean: Transnational Security Cooperation in Practice* (Oxford: Oxford University Press, 2010).

territories examined are former colonies of the United Kingdom and share a common law legal system underpinned by a written constitution. Most of the English-speaking Caribbean territories have enjoyed stable, broad-based democratic rule, especially when compared to other regions of the developing world.[3] Exceptions include the periods of one-party, left leaning governments in Suriname and Guyana, the authoritarian rule of the Duvaliers in Haiti, and the attempted or brief coups/revolutions in Trinidad and Tobago and Grenada.[4] Racial, ethnic, and class conflict pose challenges to some states, especially in Guyana and Trinidad and Tobago.[5] Most Commonwealth Caribbean states are generally acknowledged to respect fundamental human rights and the rule of law. However, since geographically they serve as a transit point between Latin America and North America, or Latin America and Europe, Caribbean states remain concerned with the suppression of drug trafficking and other forms of illicit trade, and the suppression of poverty.[6]

As with all of the territories in the Caribbean Basin Area, CARICOM states have been strongly influenced—economically, politically, socially, and culturally—by European powers and the United States.[7] Most of the CARICOM territories studied also share small populations, limited territorial size, and relatively small economies. Comparative figures are set out in Table 2.1.

2.1.2 General characteristics of Caribbean territories

As seen in Table 2.1, the statistics on CARICOM member states reveal some significant differences. The tiniest territory, Montserrat, has a population of approximately 5,200 persons in a territorial area of 102 square kilometres. The largest in terms of population is Haiti, with roughly 10.2 million inhabitants, with the next largest—Jamaica and Trinidad and Tobago—coming in at 2.7 and 1.3 million inhabitants, respectively. The largest territorial space is held by Guyana, possessing a surface area of approximately 215,000 square kilometres, with the next largest, Suriname, possessing a surface area of approximately 164,000 square kilometres. It is notable, however, that most of the CARICOM and OECS states studied have populations of fewer than 500,000 persons and a surface area of less than 1,000 square kilometres, bringing them within the category of the smallest independent states in the world.

[3] See eg Thomas J D'Agostino, 'Caribbean Politics' in Richard S Hillman and Thomas J D'Agostino (eds), *Understanding the Contemporary Caribbean*, 2nd edn (Boulder, CO: Lynne Rienner Publishers, 2009) 87–132.

[4] D'Agostino, 'Caribbean Politics' (n 3). See also Jacqueline Anne Braveboy-Wagner, 'International Relations' in Richard S Hillman and Thomas J D'Agostino (eds), *Understanding the Contemporary Caribbean*, 2nd edn (Boulder, CO: Lynne Rienner Publishers, 2009) 161–90.

[5] See eg Norman Girvan, 'Reinterpreting the Caribbean', in Brian Meeks and Folke Lindahl (eds), *New Caribbean Thought: A Reader* (Kingston, Jamaica: University of the West Indies Press, 2001) 3–23 at 16.

[6] See eg Girvan, 'Reinterpreting the Caribbean' (n 5).

[7] For a brief overview of influences, including the more recent role of Venezuela, see Jacqueline Anne Braveboy-Wagner, 'International Relations' (n 4).

Table 2.1 Statistics regarding subject Caribbean territories (2012)[8]

Country or Territory	Membership	Population, total	Surface area (sq. km)	GDP (current US$)	GDP per capita (current US$)	GNI per capita, PPP (current int'l $)	HDI Rank
Antigua and Barbuda	*CARICOM, OECS*	89,069	**440**	1,176,348,888	13,207	19,260	67
The Bahamas	CARICOM	371,960	**13,880**	8,149,004,000	21,908	**29,740**	49
Barbados	CARICOM	283,221	**430**	**3,685,000,000**	**13,076**	18,400	38
Belize	CARICOM	324,060	**22,970**	**1,447,500,000**	4,577	**6,880**	96
Dominica	*CARICOM, OECS*	71,684	**750**	479,638,820	6,691	12,190	72
Grenada	*CARICOM, OECS*	105,483	**340**	789,542,404	7,485	10,300	63
Guyana	CARICOM	795,369	**214,970**	2,850,572,407	3,584	3,400	118
Haiti	CARICOM	10,173,775	**27,750**	7,843,484,458	771	1,240	161
Jamaica	CARICOM	2,712,100	**10,990**	14,839,858,411	5,472	Not available	85
Montserrat	*CARICOM, OECS*	5,189 (July 2013 est.)	**102**	43.78 million (2006 est., PPP)	8,500 (2006 est., PPP)	Not available	Not available
St. Kitts and Nevis	*CARICOM, OECS*	53,584	**260**	748,492,572	13,969	17,280	72
St. Lucia	*CARICOM, OECS*	180,870	**620**	1,186,225,298	6,558	11,020	88
St. Vincent and the Grenadines	*CARICOM, OECS*	109,373	**390**	712,589,074	6,515	10,810	83
Suriname	CARICOM	534,541	**163,820**	4,738,181,820	8,864	8,500	105
Trinidad and Tobago	CARICOM	1,337,439	**5,130**	23,985,710,493	17,934	22,400	67

Key						
	Bold	2011 data	*Italic*	Membership in *both* regional organizations	GNI	Gross national income
	Underline	2009 data	GDP	Gross domestic product	PPP	purchasing power parity

[8] All country data, except that related to Montserrat and for Human Development Index rankings, is from the World Bank, 'World DataBank—World Development Indicators' database, as available through <http://databank.worldbank.org/>. Montserrat data is from the CIA (US), *The World Factbook* 2013–14 (Washington, DC: Central Intelligence Agency, 2013) at 143, as available through <https://www.cia.gov/library/publications/the-world-factbook/index.html>. Human development index rankings are from the UNDP, *2013 Human Development Report—The Rise of the South: Human Progress in a Diverse World* (New York,

Montserrat, as an Overseas Territory of the United Kingdom, is not an independent state and relies upon the UK for the conduct of external affairs. Montserrat's full membership and dependent status have interesting consequences for both CARICOM and the OECS. As discussed later, because of Montserrat's membership, both constituent treaties fall outside of the scope of the 1969 Vienna Convention on the Law of Treaties (VCLT).[9] In addition, the ability of Montserrat to participate fully in both regional organizations requires consent (entrustment) from the United Kingdom.

2.1.3 Economies

The gross domestic product (GDP) figures range from as little as US $43.8 million for Montserrat to close to US $24 billion for Trinidad and Tobago. Per capital GDP figures reveal different extremes, with Haitians producing US $771 per capita on the one end, in contrast with Bahamians producing close to US $22,000 per capita on the other. The gross national income figures, converted to international dollars using purchasing power parity rates, reveal a similarly wide range, with the same countries varying from US $1,240 to US $29,740.

The forms of economic activity undertaken by CARICOM's member states, combined with their small geographic and market sizes, have influenced regional integration. In the 1940s to 1950s Caribbean economies were largely focused on export of agricultural products and natural resources, although some efforts were also made to attract foreign investment to encourage industrialization.[10] In the 1950s to 1960s several Caribbean states turned to tourism, with some success.[11] However the end result, as highlighted by Payne and Sutton, was that most CARICOM countries competed in the same market with the same products:

[T]he structure of post-war development strategy had actually served to exacerbate, rather than ameliorate, divisions within the region. Caribbean economies had in effect become competitor economies in this period: they produced broadly the same commodities, they

NY: United Nations Development Program, 2013) at 143, as available at <http://hdr.undp.org/en/reports/global/hdr2013/download/>. Definitions and explanations regarding the data are available, respectively, from the 'metadata links' on the World Bank website, the 'Notes and Definitions' page on the World Factbook site and at p 147 of the *Human Development Report*. All websites were accessed on 2 July 2013. Unless otherwise indicated, all data is for the 2012 period.

[9] Because the RTC and RTB allow non-state parties they do not fall under the terms of the Vienna Convention on the Law of Treaties (adopted 23 May 1969, in force 27 January 1980) 1155 UNTS 331 (VCLT) which only governs international legal agreements between states: Art 2(1)(a) VCLT. However Art 3 of the VCLT does not exclude the application of the rules of the VCLT to other treaties or to the relations between states in a treaty involving non-states parties. In addition, many of the rules of the VCLT reflect the current customary international legal position, and thus may be relied upon as representing that customary international law. On the customary status of the VCLT rules regarding interpretation see Richard Gardiner, *Treaty Interpretation* (Oxford: Oxford University Press, 2008) 12–13; on the customary status of the *VCLT* more generally see Anthony Aust, *Modern Treaty Law and Practice* (Cambridge: Cambridge University Press, 2000) 10–11.

[10] See eg Anthony Payne and Paul Sutton, *Charting Caribbean Development* (London: MacMillan Education Ltd, 2001) 2–6.

[11] Payne and Sutton, *Charting Caribbean Development* (n 10).

wanted to attract the same foreign investors, and they appealed to the same would-be tourists. There was thus no easy route to development to be found simply by making a regional connection.[12]

Current economic focuses of CARICOM member states include: agriculture (eg rice, sugar, and bananas); fisheries, natural resource extraction and processing (eg oil and natural gas from Trinidad and Tobago, oil refining in The Bahamas, and bauxite in Jamaica and Guyana); foreign direct investment (eg Barbados, Guyana, Jamaica and Trinidad and Tobago); offshore financial services (eg Antigua and Barbuda, The Bahamas, Barbados, Cayman Islands, St Vincent and the Grenadines); export processing zones (eg Jamaica); manufacturing (eg Trinidad and Tobago); tourism (eg Jamaica, Barbados, The Bahamas, and increasingly the OECS countries); eco-tourism (eg Guyana, Belize, Dominica); and other service industries.[13] Interestingly, for over two thirds of CARICOM member states for which data is available, the services sector accounts for over 50 per cent of the value added percentage of gross domestic product (GDP), as illustrated in Table 2.2.

Table 2.2 Value added by different economic sectors as percentage of GDP[14]

Country	Data Year	Agriculture	Industry	Manufacturing	Services, etc
Antigua and Barbuda	2011	2.3	18.2	1.8	79.5
The Bahamas	2012	2.1	17.9	4.5	80
Barbados	2009	3	23.2	–	73.8
Belize	2008	12.1	22.7	14.3	65.2
Dominica	2011	13.8	15.8	2.5	70.4
Grenada	2011	5.3	16.6	4.6	78.1
Guyana	2011	21.3	33.7	3.8	44.9
Haiti	*(not available)*				
Jamaica	2011	6.5	21.5	9.2	71.9
St Kitts and Nevis	2011	1.8	22.8	6.6	75.4
St Lucia	2011	3.4	16.9	3.8	79.7
St Vincent and the Grenadines	2011	6.3	19.5	5.8	74.2
Suriname	2011	9.7	38.3	23.3	52
Trinidad and Tobago	2011	0.6	57	4.5	42.4

[12] Payne and Sutton, *Charting Caribbean Development* 6.

[13] See eg Payne and Sutton, *Charting Caribbean Development* 2–6; Roger Hosein, 'Trade Policy in the Caribbean' in Caribbean Development Bank, *Growth and Development Strategies for the Caribbean* (St Michael, Barbados: Caribbean Development Bank, 2009) 151–83; Dennis A Pantin and Marlene Attzs, 'The Economies of the Caribbean' in Richard S Hillman and Thomas J D'Agostino (eds), *Understanding the Contemporary Caribbean*, 2nd edn (Boulder, CO: Lynne Rienner Publishers, 2009) 133–60.

[14] All data is from the World Bank, 'World DataBank—World Development Indicators' database, as available through <http://databank.worldbank.org/> (6 Jul 2013). In the 'View Metadata'

2.1.4 Value of sectors

Many of these sectors continue to experience significant challenges. In terms of tourism, Caribbean territories are competing against one another with nearly the same product, which is very expensive to maintain given the demands of primarily North American and European tourists for first world amenities.[15] The nearly complete demise of preferential arrangements with the UK and Europe has dramatically affected agriculture. Overfishing, environmental challenges, and climate change have posed challenges for fisheries.[16] Offshore banking has been threatened by OECD regulatory requirements, and mining and other extractive industries have been affected by changes in natural resource prices.[17]

In terms of trade, according to World Bank data all CARICOM states except Belize and Trinidad and Tobago display a significant trade imbalance, importing a greater value of goods and services than they export. This continues to pose significant challenges to the ability of states to maintain adequate foreign exchange reserves.[18] Foreign direct investment has had a minimal effect in softening this trade imbalance, with most CARICOM states experiencing a net inflow of foreign direct investment of less than 10 per cent of their GDP. St Vincent and the Grenadines and St Kitts and Nevis are the exceptions, with over 15 per cent of their GDP being attributable to foreign direct investment. These figures are set out in Table 2.3.

sections of the World Bank website the definitions of these terms include the following information: '*Agriculture* corresponds to International Standard Industrial Classification (ISIC) divisions 1–5 and includes forestry, hunting, and fishing, as well as cultivation of crops and livestock production. *Industry* corresponds to ISIC divisions 10–45 and includes manufacturing. It comprises value added in mining, manufacturing (also reported as a separate subgroup), construction, electricity, water, and gas. *Manufacturing* refers to industries belonging to ISIC divisions 15–37. *Services* correspond to ISIC divisions 50–99 and they include value added in wholesale and retail trade (including hotels and restaurants), transport, and government, financial, professional, and personal services such as education, health care, and real estate services. Also included are imputed bank service charges, import duties, and any statistical discrepancies noted by national compilers as well as discrepancies arising from rescaling' (emphasis added).

[15] See eg Brenda Lange, *Global Organizations: The Caribbean Community* (New York, NY: Chelsea House Publishers, 2009) 45–8.

[16] Lange, *Global Organizations* (n 15) 48–52.

[17] Lange, *Global Organizations* 52–3.

[18] Current account balances are in deficit for all CARICOM Member States except Suriname and Trinidad and Tobago. Data from the World Bank, 'World DataBank—World Development Indicators' database, as available through <http://databank.worldbank.org/> (6 Jul 2013), sets out the following current account balances, expressed as a percentage of their GDP (year of data in brackets): Antigua and Barbuda, -10.7 (2011), The Bahamas, -13.9 (2011), Barbados, -5.3 (2010), Belize, -1.4 (2011), Dominica, -17.8 (2011), Grenada, -27.8 (2011), Guyana, -7.1 (2010), Haiti, -4.6 (2011), Jamaica, -14.3 (2011), St Kitts and Nevis, -8.1 (2011), St Lucia, -23.4 (2011), St Vincent and the Grenadines, -30.0 (2011), Suriname, 5.8 (2011), Trinidad and Tobago, 20.2 (2010). See also International Monetary Fund, 'Regional Economic Outlook: Western Hemisphere', World Economic and Financial Surveys (Washington, DC: International Monetary Fund, 2013), available through <http://www.imf.org/external/pubs/ft/reo/reorepts.aspx> (11 Jul 2013).

Table 2.3 Trade statistics and foreign direct investment as percentage of GDP[19]

State	Data Year	Trade	Trade in services	Imports of goods and services	Exports of goods and services	Foreign direct investment, net inflows (2011 data)
Antigua and Barbuda	2011	105.0	63.2	57.3	47.7	5.1
The Bahamas	2011	101.0	49.5	57.4	43.6	7.6
Barbados	2010	99.7	57.7	52.4	47.3	9.1
Belize	2011	130.8	35.3	65.3	65.6	6.6
Dominica	2011	89.6	42.3	54.7	34.9	7.2
Grenada	2011	73.8	31.2	50.2	23.6	5.3
Guyana	2005	203.8	42.3	119.2	84.6	6.4
Haiti	2011	68.8	18.9	55.1	13.7	2.5
Jamaica	2011	84.7	31.7	53.8	30.9	1.2
St Kitts and Nevis	2011	72.6	36.2	42.1	30.5	15.2
St Lucia	2011	114.1	48.4	67.9	46.2	6.7
St Vincent and the Grenadines	2011	82.9	34.0	55.9	26.9	15.9
Suriname	2012	120.8	17.7 [2011 data]	62.1	58.7	3.4
Trinidad and Tobago	2010	91.9	6.1	33.3	58.6	2.4

[19] All data is from the World Bank, 'World DataBank—World Development Indicators' database, as available through <http://databank.worldbank.org/> (6 Jul 2013). Data for trade in services for Suriname is 2011 data; all foreign direct investment data is for the year 2011. In the 'View Metadata' sections of the World Bank website the definitions of these categories include the following information: '*Trade* is the sum of exports and imports of goods and services measured as a share of gross domestic product. *Trade in services* is the sum of service exports and imports divided by the value of GDP, all in current U.S. dollars. *Imports of goods and services* represent the value of all goods and other market services received from the rest of the world. They include the value of merchandise, freight, insurance, transport, travel, royalties, license fees, and other services, such as communication, construction, financial, information, business, personal, and government services. They exclude compensation of employees and investment income (formerly called factor services) and transfer payments. *Exports of goods and services* represent the value of all goods and other market services provided to the rest of the world. They include the value of merchandise, freight, insurance, transport, travel, royalties, license fees, and other services, such as communication, construction, financial, information, business, personal, and government services. They exclude compensation of employees and investment income (formerly called factor services) and transfer payments. *Foreign direct investment* are the net inflows of investment to acquire a lasting management interest (10% or more of voting stock) in an enterprise operating in an economy other than that of the investor. It is the sum of equity capital, reinvestment of earnings, other long-term capital, and short-term capital as shown in the balance of payments. This series shows net inflows (new investment inflows less disinvestment) in the reporting economy from foreign investors, and is divided by GDP' (emphasis added).

2.1.5 Trade and foreign direct investment

In terms of trade within CARICOM, a 2012 consultancy report notes that in the Caribbean region the cost of moving people and goods between mainly island-based territories is significant and discourages intra-regional trade.[20] Likewise, with a total population of roughly 6 million persons (excluding Haiti which is not yet an effective actor in the CSME), the Caribbean Community is limited in terms of its economic capacity.[21] Due to such factors intra-regional trade was less than 15 per cent of CARICOM's total trade in the period 2001–2007, and intra-regional imports and exports amounted to over 17 per cent and 12 per cent, respectively.[22]

As illustrated in Table 2.1, the independent states that make up CARICOM also fall within the full range of rankings in the United Nations Human Development Index. Only Barbados is ranked in the 'Very High Human Development' category. A number of states fall within the 'High Human Development Category', namely, Antigua and Barbuda, The Bahamas, Dominica, Grenada, Jamaica, St Kitts and Nevis, St Lucia, St Vincent and the Grenadines, and Trinidad and Tobago. Belize, Suriname, and Guyana fall within the 'Medium Human Development' category, and Haiti falls within the 'Low Human Development' category.

This wide variation in human development scores mirrors the diversity of the broader Caribbean. As noted by Fanning et al, the Wider Caribbean Region, which extends from the Northeast coast of Brazil to the south of Florida (and thereby includes states in addition to those studied), 'is one of the most geopolitically complex regions in the world. Its countries range from among the largest to the smallest, the richest to the poorest and the most to the least developed. There is a complex colonial legacy from European countries, including five official languages in the region (English, Spanish, French, Dutch, and Portuguese) as well as indigenous cultural elements.'[23]

[20] Richard Stoneman, Justice Duke Pollard, and Hugo Inniss, 'Turning Around CARICOM: Proposals to Restructure the Secretariat', Landell Mills Ltd/Final Report/January 2012, at 19–20, as available at <http://www.caricom.org/jsp/communications/caricom_online_pubs/Restructuring%20the%20Secretariat%20-%20Landell%20Mills%20Final%20Report.pdf> (9 Feb 2013).

[21] Stoneman, Pollard, and Inniss, 'Turning Around CARICOM' (n 20). In a 2011 interview the CARICOM Secretary General indicated that COTED had agreed to allow Haiti to trade on a non-reciprocal basis with the Caribbean Community, as a temporary arrangement to help stimulate the economy: Ricky Jordan, 'Let's Put People at the Centre: New CARICOM Chief's Call', *Sunday Sun* (Barbados), 13 November 2011, 12A–13A.

[22] See Norman Girvan, 'Caribbean Community: The Elusive Quest for Economic Integration' in Caribbean Development Bank, *Growth and Development Strategies for the Caribbean* (St Michael, Barbados: Caribbean Development Bank, 2009) 199–218.

[23] Fanning et al, 'A Large Marine Ecosystem Governance Framework' (n 2) 434–43, 435–6.

2.2 Historical Underpinnings[24]

2.2.1 Colonial origins

The early history of the Caribbean provides insight into the potential origins of many of the tensions that continue to impede integration in the region in the twenty-first century.[25] Both the peoples and islands of the Caribbean were shaped by the territorial and commercial ambitions of a number of European powers, including the Spanish, Portuguese, French, English, Dutch, Danish, and Americans. The colonial empires of Europe both unified and divided Caribbean islands, through their centralized, but separate, administrative regimes, which frequently employed a 'divide and conquer' strategy of rule. Historically, most of the CARICOM economies were founded on sugar plantations, slavery, and slave trading, the latter of which are now accepted as two of the most fundamental violations of the rules of international law, breaching *jus cogens* obligations.[26] The horrors of the institution of slavery, under which approximately 15 million Africans were captured, enslaved, and shipped to the New World, left a deep and permanent imprint upon the peoples and countries of the region. Such historical experiences, combined with long-standing colonial oppression, have helped to produce a strong sovereignty-independence discourse in the politics of the region.[27]

Early attempts at regional integration, concentrated around the end of the nineteenth century, were at the hands of the British colonial authorities, who wished to impose regional structures that would allow them to more efficiently administer the region.[28] Such attempts were unsuccessful, primarily as a result of rejection by the existing plantocracy in the region.[29] In the early twentieth century the Colonial Office again investigated the possibility of political union for the British Caribbean colonies, but this was rejected as impractical.

[24] For a succinct overview of the history of Caribbean integration from just before the Second World War until the end of the twentieth century see eg Christoph Müllerleile, *CARICOM Integration: Progress and Hurdles—A European View* (Kingston: Kingston Publishers, 1996) [hereafter 'Müllerleile'].

[25] For an overview, see eg John H Parry, Philip M Sherlock, and Anthony P Maingot, *A Short History of the West Indies*, 4th edn (London: MacMillan Education, 1987). For a brief analysis of the international legal history of the region see David S Berry, 'The Caribbean' in Bardo Fassbender et al (eds), *The Oxford Handbook of the History of International Law* (Oxford: Oxford University Press, 2012) 579–603.

[26] For a decision of the Inter-American Court of Human Rights finding slavery to violate *jus cogens* rules, see the case of *Aloeboetoe et al v Suriname, Reparations (Art. 63(1) American Convention on Human Rights)*, I-A Ct HR, Judgment of 10 September 1993, Series C, No 15, at [57].

[27] For a historical analysis of the primarily inter-governmental nature of regional integration in the Caribbean, from the time of the West Indies Federation to the present, see Derek O'Brien, 'CARICOM: Regional Integration in a Post-Colonial World' (2011) 17 *European Law Journal* 642–60.

[28] See eg Hugh W Springer, 'Reflections on the Failure of the First West Indian Federation', Occasional Papers in International Affairs No 4 (Cambridge, MA: Harvard University Center for International Affairs, 1962) 1–3 [hereafter 'Springer'].

[29] Müllerleile (n 24) 32–3.

2.2.2 Beginnings of indigenous integration

Some early twentieth-century indigenous developments had an impact upon regional integration. The drive for greater independence on the part of colonies in the Caribbean was felt from the 1930s, coinciding with the labour unrest in the region.[30] Labour agitation did not have an immediate effect upon regional integration, but the rise of labour unions in the Caribbean, and the strong influence of several dynamic regional leaders, ushered in the beginnings of pan-Caribbean organization. A Conference of Unofficial Caribbean Leaders was held in 1932, which called for a Federation, universal adult suffrage, and dominion status for the Caribbean territories. This call for dominion status combined with federalism was repeated in 1945 when the Caribbean Labour Congress was formed.[31]

Integrationist tendencies heightened during the Second World War. Military imperatives required closer cooperation from the islands of the region.[32] The US and UK linked Caribbean defence efforts, with the British military authority in the region eventually yielding to that of the US. In addition, several regional bodies, including The University of the West Indies, were established shortly after the end of the Second World War.[33]

2.2.3 West Indies Federation

The most important early attempt at regional integration began after the end the Second World War, again at the initiative of British colonial authorities.[34] The British called a conference at Montego Bay in 1947 of all of its Caribbean territories to explore the possibility of regional federalism.[35] This drive was motivated by self-interest, since the war effort had weakened the UK and its colonies were increasingly seen as burdensome. The planned Federation of ten territories was to include Trinidad and Tobago, Barbados, Jamaica, Antigua, Dominica, Grenada, Montserrat, St Kitts-Nevis-Anguilla, St Lucia, and St Vincent. The British Honduras, British Guiana, and the British Virgin Islands did not wish to take part, with the former two voicing fears of mass immigration. The agreement to federate was signed in 1956, but it took another two years for the Federal Government to come into existence.[36]

The structure of the West Indies Federation included a constitution, which provided for an Executive Council, two Houses of Parliament, a Prime Minister, and a Governor-General. The latter was to be appointed by the British and was provided with nearly absolute authority, similar to the French President. All financial control was retained by the UK and the Federation was based in Trinidad. The Federation had an official flag, made up of four horizontal wavy bars against a blue

[30] Springer (n 28) 3–8. [31] Müllerleile (n 24) 34. [32] Springer (n 28) 6–7.
[33] Müllerleile (n 24) 33.
[34] See generally Müllerleile (n 29) 34–9. See also Hans J Geiser, Pamela Alleyne, and Carroll Gajraj, *Legal Problems of Caribbean Integration: A study of legal aspects of CARICOM* (Leyden: Sijthoff, 1976) 11 [hereafter 'Geiser et al'].
[35] Springer (n 28) 7–8. [36] Springer (n 28) 12.

background with an orange sun in the middle (representing the sun and sea of the region), and was granted a coat-of-arms, which contained the wording 'To Dwell Together in Unity'.[37]

It should be noted that from the outset this federal model was subject to stringent criticism, especially from Jamaica and Trinidad and Tobago, which were concerned with its financial implications. Jamaica, perhaps because of its more limited ties with the rest of the region, also displayed less enthusiasm for integration.[38] But all ten territories decided to participate in the federal experiment, primarily because it provided a means for greater independence from the British colonial authorities. In fact, Caribbean leaders appear to have taken the pragmatic view that the Federation would either itself provide greater independence, or serve as the impetus for independence if it failed.

The elections for the Federation took place in 1958 and were subject to considerable difficulties. The West Indies Federal Labour Party (WIFLP), headed by Jamaica's Norman Manley and supported by Trinidad's Dr Eric Williams, did not secure a clear majority in the polls and in fact lost in both Jamaica and Trinidad. The Democratic Labour Party, led by Alexander Bustamante, was the main opponent. It was only as a result of strong voting support in the Eastern Caribbean that the WIFLP was able to assume leadership in the Federal Parliament. Barbadian Sir Grantley Adams was chosen as the Prime Minister of the Federal Government, which was established in April 1958.

The functioning of the Federal Parliament was immediately hampered by differences in view between some of the Caribbean territories. Jamaica, for example, resisted federal control, whereas Trinidad urged for a strengthening of the Federation.[39] Dissatisfaction was also expressed over the disproportionate benefits received by the small Eastern Caribbean territories, both in terms of political representation and budgetary contributions. Proposals for change to the Federal Constitution were discussed.

However in Jamaica Alexander Bustamante astutely exploited the perceived illegitimacy of Manley and Williams during the elections, and suggested that Jamaica should move to independence without the Federation. A referendum was held in Jamaica on the Federation in 1961, with the opposition vote emerging victorious—54 per cent voted in favour of leaving.[40] After such disapproval Manley called a snap election in 1962, and was defeated by Bustamante. Following his victory, Bustamante immediately began independence negotiations with the UK. This lead was quickly followed by Trinidad and Tobago and both countries became independent in 1962.

At this point the question was whether the Federation could survive without Jamaica. Williams, in Trinidad, responded categorically: 'One from ten leaves

[37] For images of both the flag and coat-of-arms see eg the University of the West Indies, Cave Hill Campus, 'W.I. Federal Archives Centre' [pamphlet], as available at <http://www.cavehill.uwi.edu/research/resources/FedArchives2.pdf> (10 Aug 2013).

[38] For an overview of political developments, including those surrounding the West Indies Federation, see eg D'Agostino, 'Caribbean Politics' (n 3) 87–132.

[39] Springer (n 28) 15–17.

[40] Springer (n 28) 34.

zero.'[41] Efforts by the remaining eight territories to continue the federation without Jamaica and Trinidad, either as a unitary state, or as a 'Federation of the Eight', also failed.[42]

Several reasons have been advanced for the failure of the West Indies Federation. The rationales underpinning federation were inconsistent.[43] Some regional figures appear to have held romantic views of West Indian unity, whereas others simply sought greater access to the world economy. Different actors, like Manley and Williams, also had strongly divergent views about the mechanics of Federation, including how power, and responsibilities, should be distributed. They chose to focus their energies outside of the Federal structure and attended more to national politics, thereby creating tensions between local and federal levels of government. The Colonial Office, in contrast, sought greater efficiency for its regional administration.[44] The United Kingdom also sought to divest itself of its colonies. The Federation itself suffered from a lack of general, public support. It was not strongly promoted, nor were its structures and goals clearly explained to the people of the region. Fears related to migration and economic strength also played their part. Larger territories were concerned about mass migration, whereas smaller ones feared that their economies would be overwhelmed by their neighbours. Concerns were expressed about the levels of contribution to the Federation by certain member states, with Jamaica and Trinidad and Tobago being dissatisfied with having to contribute together more than three quarters of the budget.[45] The development of strong nationalism from the labour movements of the 1930s also played its part in some territories.[46]

Perhaps the most important factor in the failure of the West Indies Federation was its colonial origin and nature.[47] The Federation was from the start a colonial project. It did not bring significantly greater independence for its ten territorial units and was institutionally and financially controlled by Britain. West Indian leaders were naturally dissatisfied with such a system and sought further independence. Importantly, they believed that they could achieve independence either through, or without, federation. As a result, once it was demonstrated that West Indians could achieve independence outside of the Federation, they had little incentive to stay within it.

2.2.4 The attempted Federation of the Eight

As noted earlier, immediately after the failure of the West Indies Federation there was an attempt to preserve a smaller federation of the eight remaining territories

[41] As quoted in Müllerleile (n 24) at 36.

[42] See Arthur Lewis, 'The Agony of the Eight' (1998) 23(1) *Journal of Eastern Caribbean Studies* 6–26 (reprinting of original 1965 essay).

[43] See generally Müllerleile (n 24) 36–7; Lange, *Global Organizations* (n 15) 22–8; Springer (n 28).

[44] Geiser et al (n 34) 11.

[45] Müllerleile (n 24) 36–7. See also Kenny D Anthony, 'Caribbean Integration: The Future Relationship between Barbados and the OECS' (1998) 23 *Journal of Eastern Caribbean Studies* 35–50.

[46] Springer (n 28) 36–9.

[47] See eg Müllerleile (n 24) 37 and Geiser et al (n 34) 11.

of the Eastern Caribbean and Barbados, the 'Little Eight', as an Eastern Caribbean Federation.[48] Even though a constitution for the new 'Federation of the Eight' was agreed by May 1962, delays by the British Treasury eventually caused enthusiasm for the idea to dissipate.[49] The attempted Federation of the Eight also was frustrated because Barbados and the Eastern Caribbean territories were either tempted to join the newly independent Caribbean states (ie Grenada to join Trinidad and Tobago), or to become independent on their own, or for other reasons did not accept a new form of the Federation.[50] As a result, the remnants of the West Indies Federation adjourned in 1965.[51]

2.2.5 Shift in focus to economic integration

After the collapse of the West Indies Federation the regional integration movement faltered and changed course. Whereas in the Federation model integration had been politically oriented, following its demise leaders and technocrats turned towards an economically centred model.[52] Or more subtly, after 1962 there were two differing views. One group believed that economic integration was the most that could and should be achieved; the second group still sought a deeper, political model of integration, but saw this as only being possible through the gradual strengthening of functional and economic cooperation. Almost all agreed that by settling on a mainly economic agenda, integration could be achieved in a more rational, less politically divisive, way. Two economic models were considered at the time, a free trade model and an 'integration of production' model. Both could be utilized, but the free trade model was perceived as easier to achieve than trying to harmonize production.[53]

Some regional institutions survived the collapse of the West Indies Federation, including the West Indies Shipping Corporation, the Caribbean Meteorological Service, and the University of the West Indies. These institutions retained a core of the Federation's functional cooperation.[54]

2.2.6 Caribbean Free Trade Association

Plans for some form of further economic cooperation were aired even at the time of the collapse of the Federation. The outcome, following on the heels of a free trade zone between British Guiana (now Guyana) and Barbados, was the creation

[48] See eg Arthur Lewis, 'The Agony of the Eight' (n 42), Vaughn A Lewis, 'Political Integration in the Caribbean: A Policy Approach' in Caribbean Development Bank, *Growth and Development Strategies for the Caribbean* (St Michael, Barbados: Caribbean Development Bank, 2009), 219–59.

[49] See Arthur Lewis, 'The Agony of the Eight' 15–18.

[50] See generally Arthur Lewis, 'The Agony of the Eight'. See also Müllerleile (n 24) 43. Interestingly, as recently as 1988 the Prime Minister of Barbados, Owen Arthur, argued in favour of a Confederation between Barbados and the OECS states: Owen S Arthur, 'Prospects for Caribbean Political Unity' (1998) 23 *Journal of Eastern Caribbean Studies* 27–34, at 33–4. See also Kenny D Anthony, 'Caribbean Integration (n 45) 35–50.

[51] Müllerleile (n 24) 44.

[52] Müllerleile (n 24) 39. See also Geiser et al (n 34) 12.

[53] Müllerleile (n 29) 39–40.

[54] Müllerleile (n 24) 40.

of the Caribbean Free Trade Association (CARIFTA) in 1965.[55] Interestingly, the CARIFTA negotiations were started by Barbados, Guyana, and eventually, Antigua in 1965, but only became effective for those states and Trinidad and Tobago in 1968. This was in part because of the debates about what form the integration movement should take and the two sides that emerged. Business leaders preferred a free trade arrangement, but some economists at the University of the West Indies preferred a sectoral approach.[56] The agreement of 1965 was used as the basis for the CARIFTA Agreement, which entered into force in May 1968.[57] Dominica, Grenada, St Kitts-Nevis-Anguilla, St Lucia, St Vincent, Jamaica, Montserrat, and Belize all joined. A regional Secretariat was established in Georgetown, Guyana, and the Caribbean Development Bank was founded and located in Barbados. The objectives of CARIFTA were economic in nature and included the broadening of regional markets, the creation of a customs union, and economic community in the Caribbean.[58] CARIFTA was accepted by the contracting parties to the GATT in October 1971.[59]

2.2.7 Eastern Caribbean

Shortly after the collapse of the West Indies Federation a smaller structure was set up by the British authorities in the Eastern Caribbean: the West Indies Associated States. The West Indies Associated States Council of Ministers was formed in 1966, involving a loose administrative grouping of seven territories in the Eastern Caribbean, and it was joined by the Eastern Caribbean Common Market in 1968.[60] Other institutions that came into existence at this time in the sub-region include: the East Caribbean Currency Authority (which created a common currency, the Eastern Caribbean Dollar), the West Indies Associated States Supreme Court, and the East Caribbean Tourist Association.

Various proposals were aired for some sort of overt political federation. James Mitchell of St Vincent and the Grenadines put forward some detailed plans for the region, and, interestingly, saw the possibility of a federation by incremental means (ie a few states joining, followed by others).[61] Several Heads of Government in the Eastern Caribbean even met and established concrete plans (the Grenada Declaration). The hopes for this structure were dashed, however, by the lack

[55] Müllerleile (n 24) 41. The constituent treaties for CARIFTA were the Dickenson Bay Agreement Establishing the Caribbean Free Trade Association (adopted 15 Dec 1965, in force 1 May 1968) 772 UNTS 3, and the Supplementary Agreement Under Article 31(3) of the Agreement for the Establishment of the Caribbean Free Trade Association signed at Dickenson Bay, Antigua, on 15 December 1965 (adopted and entered into force 18 Mar 1968) 772 UNTS 66. CARIFTA entered into a headquarters agreement with Guyana in 1970: Agreement between the Government of Guyana and the Council of the Caribbean Free Trade Association Regarding the Headquarters of the Association (adopted and entered into force 25 Nov 1970) 2324 UNTS 399.

[56] See the discussion in Geiser et al (n 34) 12–13.

[57] Geiser et al (n 34) 13.

[58] Müllerleile (n 24) 41.

[59] Geiser et al (n 34) 15–16. For a tentative analysis of the compatibility of the CARICOM Treaty and Annex with GATT see pp 59–69.

[60] See eg Müllerleile (n 24) 44. See also Geiser et al (n 34) 14.

[61] Müllerleile (n 24) 45–6.

of interest shown by the larger states of the Caribbean, including Trinidad and Tobago and Barbados.[62] In 1972 Hugh Wooding and Arthur Lewis drafted the Tobago Declaration, again setting out plans for a new West Indies Federation. This proposal did not come to fruition. Eric Williams, Prime Minister of Trinidad and Tobago, set forth a similar plan in 1973, for a new Federation of the Commonwealth Caribbean.[63] Williams' plan included very strong policing and security features, but likewise, was not widely embraced.[64]

Later explicit proposals for political mergers in the Eastern Caribbean were aired, as was a spontaneous joint-independence proposal by the leaders of St Vincent and St Kitts-Nevis-Anguilla.[65] A constitutional commission also made proposals for political integration in conjunction with independence of some of the smaller states.[66] All of these proposals came to naught, primarily because the territories in the sub-region sought political independence, not political integration.[67] The most that could be agreed upon was closer economic cooperation.

2.2.8 CARICOM

At the broader regional level the Heads of Government decided to transform CARIFTA into the Caribbean common market and to create the Caribbean Community, through their decision at the Seventh Conference of Heads of Government in 1972.[68] The historical context of CARICOM's emergence is noteworthy. CARICOM's formation followed closely the Jamaican elections in 1972, which brought into power the pro-integration government of Manley. It was formed in the period immediately following the independence of the majority of Commonwealth Caribbean states. It was prompted by concerns from less developed countries about the effectiveness of CARIFTA to address their needs.[69] It also emerged at a time when fears were emerging about the potential consequences for the region of the UK's accession to the European Economic Community.[70]

CARICOM was formalized by the signing at the Eighth Heads of Government Conference in 1973 of the Treaty Establishing the Caribbean Community (the 'Treaty') and the Annex to the Treaty—The Caribbean Common Market (the 'Annex').[71] This double-treaty arrangement created two distinct, but potentially overlapping, treaty regimes: a state could become a party to the Treaty, and not the Annex, but not vice versa.[72] This double-treaty arrangement represented a

62 Müllerleile (n 34) 46.
63 Müllerleile (n 24) 46–7.
64 Müllerleile (n 24) 47.
65 Müllerleile (n 24) 48.
66 Müllerleile (n 24) 48–9.
67 Müllerleile (n 24) 49.
68 Müllerleile (n 24) 41.
69 Geiser et al (n 34) 16–17.
70 See eg Payne and Sutton, *Charting Caribbean Development* (n 10).
71 See the Georgetown Accord, adopted at the Eighth Conference of Heads of Government of Commonwealth Caribbean Countries, Georgetown, Guyana, 9–12 April 1973. The Accord, which has been described as an 'international treaty' by Geiser et al (n 34) at 54, provided a schedule for the dissolution of CARIFTA and the entry into force of the CARICOM Treaty and Annex. See also the Treaty Establishing the Caribbean Community (adopted 4 Jul 1973, in force 1 Aug 1973) 949 UNTS 17.
72 Art 32 of the 1973 Treaty provided that the 'The Annex and Schedule to this Treaty shall form an integral part of this Treaty.' On the double nature of the CARICOM Treaty regimes see Geiser et al (n 34) 4. On the need to be at least a party to the Treaty, see p 105.

compromise between the different goals of regional integration.[73] Rather than create two completely separate treaties, the Treaty-Annex compromise preserved a strong, formal link to ensure coherence. It also allowed some separation, so that a state such as The Bahamas could join the Caribbean Community without joining the common market.[74]

The Treaty created the regional organization called the Caribbean Community and set out its institutional structure. It provided for, amongst other things, the organization's membership, objectives, organs (including their competences and voting rules), dispute settlement procedures, legal capacity, privileges and immunities, and the accession arrangements. The Annex created the Caribbean common market and set out its institutional structure, including membership, objectives, organs (including a Secretariat shared with the Caribbean Community), dispute settlement procedures, legal capacity, privileges and immunities, and the accession arrangements. In economic terms, the Annex created a customs union which included provisions on trade liberalization, the right of establishment, the provision of services, the movement of capital, a common external tariff, the coordination of economic policies and development planning, and a regime of protections for less developed countries. Although the Treaty of Chaguaramas contained some non-economic elements, it did not embrace any serious form of political integration. Rather the Treaty set up a system of state-centred or perhaps, more accurately, government-centred decision-making that prioritized national economic and political action at the regional level.[75]

2.2.9 OECS

After achieving independence, the original six Eastern Caribbean states (Antigua and Barbuda, Dominica, Grenada, St-Kitts-Nevis-Anguilla, St Lucia, and St Vincent and the Grenadines), were joined by Montserrat, a dependent territory, and on 2 July 1981 formed the Organisation of Eastern Caribbean States (OECS).[76] The Organisation superseded both the West Indies Associated States and the East Caribbean Common Market (ECCM), with the former's Secretariat becoming the Central Secretariat and the functions of the ECCM Secretariat being incorporated into the OECS Economic Affairs Secretariat (now merged with the Central Secretariat).

The OECS is based in St Lucia and demonstrates a high level of integration. Its members and one associate member, Anguilla, share a single currency, the Eastern

[73] See Geiser et al (n 34) 33–4. [74] cf Geiser et al (n 34) 33–4 and 103–4.

[75] See eg Payne and Sutton, *Charting Caribbean Development* (n 10) 174. It must be recalled that at the time of the formation of CARICOM three different types of territorial entities were Members: sovereign states, 'associated states' (having control over internal affairs but with the United Kingdom exercising foreign defence and external affairs), and colonies. See Geiser et al (n 34) 21–9.

[76] Treaty Establishing the Organisation of Eastern Caribbean States (adopted 18 Jun 1981, in force 2 Jul 1981) 1338 UNTS 97 and Agreement Establishing the East Caribbean Common Market (adopted 11 Jun 1968, in force 1 Jul 1968) 1338 UNTS 55.

Caribbean Dollar, which is overseen by the Eastern Caribbean Central Bank.[77] They also share a common judiciary—the Eastern Caribbean Supreme Court—which is divided into a High Court of Justice and Court of Appeal. High Court judges are based in each member state but the judges of the Court of Appeal reside in St Lucia and travel to the different territories to hear appeals. Some members also participate in OECS joint diplomatic missions.[78]

The OECS to some extent mirrored CARICOM at this early stage. As a result the casual observer may query the need for the creation of a distinct sub-regional organization in the Eastern Caribbean. A strong impetus lay in the need for a harmonizing body to represent the interests of the smaller states in the region, both with respect to the region, and with respect to the outside world.[79] Protectionism had started to emerge on the part of some of the larger Caribbean states and the OECS countries quickly realized that they needed a stronger organization to protect their interests. OECS members also realized that their smaller size and economic vulnerability required closer cooperation. The OECS allows for economies of scale and collaboration in the areas of foreign policy and security.

2.2.10 Obstacles and delays

From the end of the 1970s to the mid-1980s the Caribbean, as with most of the rest of the world, suffered a period of economic difficulty.[80] These challenges, including the oil crisis, dramatically slowed regional integration. Intra-regional trade, which had increased nearly 700 per cent under the Common Market Annex, fell dramatically.[81] Caribbean states focused on their own priorities and economic survival.[82] Conservative governments, with less of an ideological interest in Caribbean unity, also came to power in this period and they sought to restrict regional institutions to achieving limited economic goals. As noted by Hall, economics, not politics, dominated the regional agenda:

> At the very instance of its birth, CARICOM was threatened by economic not political forces.... [T]he world economic crisis hit the Community hard and compelled major adjustments by the Community itself and individual Member States. Accordingly, between 1973 and 1989 there was an evident preoccupation with economic matters.[83]

[77] The British Virgin Islands, an Associate Member, uses the US dollar.

[78] See the OECS website at <http://www.oecs.org/> (19 Sep 2011).

[79] Although note that Vaughan Lewis, in 'The OECS and Closer Political Union', in Kenneth O Hall (ed), *The Caribbean Community: Beyond Survival* (Kingston, Jamaica: Ian Randle Publishers, 2001) 301–14 at 306–7, highlights that the optimal framework for protection of OECS country interests globally would remain that of the larger regional organization, CARICOM.

[80] See eg Müllerleile (n 24) 50–2.

[81] Kenneth Hall, *Re-Inventing CARICOM: The Road to a New Integration* (Kingston, Jamaica: Ian Randle Publishers, 2003) xvi.

[82] See eg Payne and Sutton, *Charting Caribbean Development* (n 10) 177–200.

[83] Kenneth Hall, *Re-Inventing CARICOM* (n 81) 33.

Institutional factors also challenged CARICOM. The post of the Secretary General was vacant for a period of fifteen months between 1977 and 1978.[84] Several states also sought to enter into relations with Latin American countries, thus potentially diluting the strength of CARICOM and the OECS.

Following the mid-1980s, however, some further proposals for political integration emerged, mainly within the Eastern Caribbean sub-region. James Mitchell, for example, proposed a plan for an East Caribbean Republic.[85] The OECS itself briefly contemplated a closer political union of its member countries.[86] But all such proposals, and even the more limited ones which aimed to strengthen the economic aspects of CARICOM and the OECS, were either ignored or postponed.

In 1989, however, at their Tenth Meeting the Heads of Government of the Caribbean Community issued the 'Grand Anse Declaration', pledging to fulfil all of the remaining treaty obligations of the *Treaty of Chaguaramas* by 4 July 1993.[87] The Grand Anse Declaration further pledged to create a single market and economy, to establish an Assembly of Caribbean Community Parliamentarians, to establish an Independent West Indian Commission for Advancing the Goals of the Treaty of Chaguaramas, to eliminate the requirement of passports for CARICOM travel, and to eliminate the requirement for work permits for CARICOM nationals for certain occupations.[88] These goals were repeated in the West Indian Commission's 1992 Report, *Time for Action*, which also suggested additional developments, including strengthening of the Community's legislative process, providing for independent Community financing, and creating a CARICOM Commission, a CARICOM Assembly, a CARICOM Charter of Civil Society, and a CARICOM Supreme Court.[89] In the Rose Hall Declaration the Conference agreed in principle to the creation of a CARICOM Commission, similar to the European Commission, and for the automatic financing of Community institutions.[90] Neither of these suggestions from the Rose Hall Declaration has grown to fruition.

[84] See eg Payne and Sutton, *Charting Caribbean Development* (n 10) 177–200.

[85] Müllerleile (n 24) 53–66. Notice that one of the key reasons suggested for the failure of James Mitchell's plans was the lack of inclusion of Opposition views.

[86] See eg Vaughan Lewis, 'The OECS and Closer Political Union' (n 79) 301–14.

[87] Grand Anse Declaration and Work Programme for the Advancement of the Integration Movement, Grand Anse, Grenada, 7 July 1989, as available at <http://www.caricom.org/jsp/communications/meetings_statements/grand_anse_declaration.jsp?menu=communications> (7 Jul 2013). See also CARICOM Secretariat, 'Communiqué Issued at the Conclusion of the Tenth Meeting of the Conference of Heads of Government of the Caribbean Community', 3–7 July 1989, Grand Anse, Grenada, as available at <http://www.caricom.org/jsp/communications/communiques/10hgc_1989_communique.jsp> (7 Jul 2013). See also the later CARICOM Secretariat, 'Consensus of Chaguaramas', Issued at the Seventh Special Session of the Conference of Heads of Government, Chaguanas, Trinidad and Tobago, 26–27 October 1999, as available at <http://www.caricom.org/jsp/secretariat/legal_instruments/consensuschag.jsp?menu=secretariat> (7 Jul 2013).

[88] Grand Anse Declaration (n 87).

[89] See West Indian Commission, *Time for Action: Report of the West Indian Commission* (Black Rock, Barbados: The West Indian Commission, 1992) 474–501. For a critical reaction to this report see Peter Wickham, 'More Shadow than Substance', in Kenneth O Hall (ed), *The Caribbean Community: Beyond Survival* (Kingston, Jamaica: Ian Randle Publishers, 2001) 234–51.

[90] CARICOM Secretariat, 'Rose Hall Declaration on Regional Governance and Integrated Development', Adopted on the Occasion of the Thirtieth Anniversary of the Caribbean Community at the Twenty-Fourth Meeting of the Conference of Heads of Government of CARICOM, 2–5 July

Nevertheless, it had become clear by the late 1990s that the Treaty of Chaguaramas required an overhaul. The Mills Report, for example, identifies a number of problems:

> Continuing progress has been recorded in specific areas of non-economically-oriented institutions and programme areas of functional co-operation. On the other hand, the record is disappointing in economic areas which are considered the kernel of the integration movement: weaknesses in decision-making and implementation; weaknesses inherent in the Treaty itself; organisational problems; resource insufficiency and communications problems are some of the factors identified as constraints to the effective functioning of CARICOM in achieving the goals prescribed in the Treaty.[91]

Such concerns were echoed in the later Report of the West Indian Commission, which noted succinctly that 'it is not that the regional machinery for implementation [of CARICOM decisions] has broken down or is otherwise inadequate to its task; it is simply non-existent'.[92]

CARICOM and its member states responded by drafting a series of nine Protocols amending the original Treaty of Chaguaramas, which were adopted in the period between 1997 and 2000.[93] The decision to revise the original Treaty incrementally, using a number of protocols, was taken for a number of reasons. As noted by Pollard, the incremental approach allowed for the possibility of extensive national, in-country consultations alongside the meetings of the Inter-Governmental Task Force; it also would 'facilitate external donor funding from various sources for each

2003, Montego Bay, Jamaica, as available at <http://www.caricom.org/jsp/communications/meetings_statements/rose_hall_declaration.jsp?menu=communications> (7 Jul 2013). In paras A.3 and A.6, the Heads of Government agree in principle to:

> 3. The establishment of a CARICOM Commission or other executive mechanism, whose purpose will be to facilitate the deepening of regional integration in the areas of responsibility specified in the next following paragraph. The Commission's function will be to exercise full-time executive responsibility for furthering implementation of Community decisions in such areas as well as to initiate proposals for Community action in any such area. [. . .]
>
> 6. The adoption of the principle of automatic resource transfers for the financing of Community institutions, certainly on the establishment of any new tier of governance.

[91] Gladstone Mills et al, *Report on a Comprehensive Review of the Programmes, Institutions and Organisations of the Caribbean Community* (Georgetown, Guyana: Caribbean Community Secretariat, 1990) vi [10].

[92] West Indian Commission, *Time for Action: Report of the West Indian Commission* (Black Rock, Barbados: The West Indian Commission, 1992) 463.

[93] See Protocol amending the Treaty Establishing the Caribbean Community Signed At Chaguaramas on 4 July 1973 (Protocol I) (adopted 19 Feb 1997, not yet in force); Protocol Amending the Treaty Establishing the Caribbean Community (Protocol II: Establishment, Services, Capital) (adopted 1 Jul 1997, not yet in force); Protocol Amending the Treaty Establishing The Caribbean Community (Protocol III: Industrial Policy) (adopted 30 Jun 1998, not yet in force); Protocol Amending the Treaty Establishing The Caribbean Community (Protocol IV: Trade Policy) (adopted 4–7 Jul 1999, not yet in force); Protocol Amending the Treaty Establishing The Caribbean Community (Protocol V: Agricultural Policy) (adopted 13 Jun 1998, not yet in force); Protocol Amending the Treaty Establishing The Caribbean Community (Protocol VI: Transport Policy) (adopted 4–7 Jul 1999, not yet in force); Protocol Amending the Treaty Establishing the Caribbean Community (Protocol VII: Disadvantaged Countries, Regions and Sectors) (adopted 4–7 Jul 1999, not yet in force); Protocol Amending the Treaty Establishing the Caribbean Community (Protocol VIII: Competition Policy, Consumer Protection, Dumping and Subsides) (adopted 13–14 Mar 2000, not yet in force); and Protocol Amending the Treaty Establishing the Caribbean Community (Protocol IX: Disputes Settlement) (adopted 13–14 Mar 2000, not yet in force).

phase of the exercise'.[94] None of the Protocols entered into force, but most were provisionally applied from the date of their signature by a large number of member states.[95] These Protocols laid the foundation for, but were not identical to, the subsequent Revised Treaty of Chaguaramas Including the CARICOM Single Market and Economy. The Revised Treaty was preceded by the Agreement Establishing the Caribbean Court of Justice, adopted in February 2001, which created a regional appellate and treaty-interpreting tribunal.[96] As will be demonstrated throughout this book, the Protocols remain relevant to the interpretation of the Revised Treaty, especially for the purposes of assisting in the resolution of textual anomalies, such as cross-referencing problems.

It was only in 2001, in the Revised Treaty of Chaguaramas Including the CARICOM Single Market and Economy, that member states were able to formally commit themselves to fundamentally transform the institutional and legal structures of CARICOM.[97] They did so in a context where their two main trading partners were themselves involved in ever deepening integration processes, the US under NAFTA and Europe under the Treaty on European Union (the Treaty of Maastricht), and where WTO pressures to remove trade preferences had increased.[98] The influence of the collapse of the Soviet Union and fall of the Berlin Wall was also felt in the Caribbean.[99]

The Revised Treaty merges the two previous regimes of the original Treaty and Annex. It dramatically decreases the number of organs, strengthens their decision-making and dispute resolution structures, updates the regional trade regime towards a single market model, establishes a wide variety of policies, and imposes competition law obligations.[100] Although the Revised Treaty has been greeted with some scepticism from economists and political scientists, it has been argued by Owen Arthur, former Prime Minister of Barbados, to be the 'first realistic initiative' for allowing smaller states to escape 'the constraints imposed by

[94] Duke Pollard, 'Amending the Treaty of Chaguaramas', in Kenneth O Hall (ed), *The Caribbean Community: Beyond Survival* (Kingston, Jamaica: Ian Randle Publishers, 2001) 252–6 at 252.

[95] All nine Protocols were capable of being provisionally applied by those parties which declared their intention to do so. Protocols I and III–VII attracted a substantial number of declarations of provisional application. Protocols VIII and IX only attracted the declarations of Belize. Interestingly, there is no record of a declaration in relation to Protocol II. Information on declarations was obtained from the CARICOM Secretariat, *Matrix of Agreements*, last updated July 2012 (Georgetown, Guyana: CARICOM Secretariat, 2012).

[96] (Adopted 14 Feb 2001, entered into force 23 Jul 2002) 2255 UNTS 319.

[97] It should be noted in this context, however, that delays in obtaining sufficient ratifications to allow treaties to enter into force should not be equated with reluctance to commit to the treaty obligations in question. According to Safiya Ali, General Counsel of the CARICOM Secretariat, CARICOM Member States have tended to take actions in accordance with treaties far in advance of their ratification and entry into force, from as early as the time a decision is made to create an agreement, to the time it is signed but has not yet entered into force: Interview with Safiya Ali, General Counsel, CARICOM Secretariat, Georgetown, Guyana (6 Aug 2012).

[98] See eg Brenda Lange, *Global Organizations* (n 15) 53–7.

[99] Kenneth Hall and Myrtle Chuck-A-Sang (eds), *CARICOM Single Market and Economy: Challenges, Benefits, Prospects* (Kingston, Jamaica: Ian Randle Publishers, 2007) 12.

[100] For a commentary on the changes to the institutional structures, see David S Berry, 'The New Caribbean Community: An Introduction to the Institutional Changes in the *Revised Treaty of Chaguaramas*' (2002) 7(1) *Caribbean Law Bulletin* 1–58.

smallness in land, market and population sizes, and by limited natural resources'.[101] The creation of the Caribbean Court of Justice has been greeted with enthusiasm as an important engine to assist CARICOM's regional integration project, since its compulsory and binding role in enforcement of the Revised Treaty may help to overcome some of the serious challenges that faced the original 1973 Treaty regime.[102]

2.2.11 Other Caribbean regional organizations

Two other regional integration developments may be briefly noted here, although falling outside the scope of the present work, namely, the two broadly-based regional bodies of the Caribbean Forum of African, Caribbean and Pacific States (CARIFORUM) and the Association of Caribbean States (ACS).

CARIFORUM was created in 1993 to help coordinate positions in relation to trade negotiations between the African, Caribbean and Pacific States (ACP), and the European Union (EU). Its membership comprises the original independent member states of CARICOM plus Haiti (then a non-member) and the Dominican Republic and it has two organs, a Secretariat and a Programming Unit. The Secretariat is headed by a Secretary General, which post is filled by the CARICOM Secretary General. In October 2008 CARIFORUM concluded an Economic Partnership Agreement with the EU, which has been provisionally applied since 29 December 2008.[103]

The Association of Caribbean States (ACS) brings together states and territories from the broader Caribbean and Latin American region. Following the recommendations of the West Indian Commission's report Time for Action, the Convention Establishing the Association of Caribbean States was signed in 1994. The ACS has twenty-five members and four associate members, representing the entire Caribbean Basin region.[104] The ACS seeks to promote economic and functional cooperation in

[101] As quoted in Kenneth Hall and Myrtle Chuck-A-Sang (eds), *CARICOM Single Market and Economy. Challenges, Benefits, Prospects* (Kingston, Jamaica: Ian Randle Publishers, 2007) 31. See generally ch 2.

[102] Duke E Pollard, in *The Caribbean Court of Justice: Closing the Circle of Independence* (Kingston, Jamaica: The Caribbean Law Publishing Company, 2004) at 40, suggests that a key reason for failures under the original CARICOM regime was the lack of a binding judicial mechanism to enforce it:

> The experience of the Caribbean Community and Common Market established by the original Treaty of Chaguaramas (1973) would appear to confirm that the absence of credible mechanisms for disputes settlement and sanctioning non-compliance with obligations, encourage deviant conduct by participants in the regime and, ultimately, the frustration and nullification of benefits expected to arise from the operation of the integration arrangements.

[103] Office of Trade Negotiations, Caribbean Community (CARICOM) Secretariat, 'CARIFORUM Economic Partnership Agreement (EPA) Negotiations', as available at <http://www.crnm.org/index.php?option=com_content&view=article&id=276&Itemid=76> (19 Sep 2011).

[104] The following are ACS Member States: Antigua and Barbuda, Bahamas, Barbados, Belize, Colombia, Costa Rica, Cuba, Dominica, Dominican Republic, El Salvador, Grenada, Guatemala, Guyana, Haiti, Honduras, Jamaica, Mexico, Nicaragua, Panama, St Kitts and Nevis, St Lucia, St Vincent and the Grenadines, Suriname, Trinidad and Tobago, and Venezuela. The following are

the region and its purposes include promoting economic integration, regional coordination, cooperation, environmental preservation, and friendly relations.[105] The inaugural meeting of the ACS was held in August 1995 in Trinidad and Tobago, and the twin island Republic is also the site of the ACS headquarters. The ACS has three main organs: the Meeting of Heads of State, the Ministerial Council (which oversees a number of Special Committees), and the Secretariat.[106]

Both of these broader groupings demonstrate the willingness of Caribbean states to join together and to form strategic alliances to promote regional objectives. However neither demonstrates the cohesiveness required to found a strong regional integration movement. Thus they have been excluded from the scope of the present work.

2.2.12 Parallels between the Caribbean and Europe

Before leaving this brief historical introduction it may be useful to compare these developments with some of those that occurred in the context of European regional integration. A few clear commonalities emerge. Firstly, both integration movements started in earnest in nearly the same time period, after the Second World War. But a key difference lies in the originating impulses of both movements. The European process was initiated by independent states, whereas the Caribbean movement was initiated by the UK on behalf of its colonies. As previously noted, the colonial nature of the West Indies Federation may have been the most important cause of its failure.

Secondly, both integration movements have had periods of difficulty. During the global economic downturn of the 1970s and early 1980s states in Europe and the Caribbean did not have the stomach for major changes or developments. In Europe many of the treaty developments during this period were limited, in some cases merely serving to keep the integration process from stopping completely.[107] However a major difference between the European and Caribbean integration movements, during these periods and up until very recent times, was that in the EU there existed two strong, independent organs that could strengthen and push the process forward, namely, the European Commission and European Court of Justice. In the Caribbean there are now two courts to serve a role similar to the European Court of Justice—the Caribbean Court of Justice and the Eastern Caribbean Court of Appeal. Today the OECS also has a Commission in some ways similar to the European Commission; but CARICOM has no such organ. These two independent organs played an important role in European integration, by

Associate Members: Aruba, France (on behalf of French Guiana, Guadeloupe, and Martinique), the Netherlands Antilles, and Turks and Caicos.

[105] Convention Establishing the Association of Caribbean States (adopted 24 Jul 1994, in force 4 Aug 1995) 1985 UNTS 3; also available at <http://www.acs-aec.org/About/ACS_convention/convention.htm> (1 Nov 2011) Art III(2).

[106] Convention Establishing the Association of Caribbean States (n 105) Arts VII and VIII.

[107] For a general history of the EU, see Desmond Dinan, *Ever Closer Union? An Introduction to the European Community* (Boulder, Colorado: Lynne Rienner, 1994).

pushing the European project forward even in the face of resistance from member states. CARICOM and the OECS, in contrast, have not had the help of these engines of integration until very recently. The lack of an independent organ like a Commission in CARICOM may further stall its development. In light of this, it will be very interesting to observe the functioning of the OECS Commission, and to see what effect it has upon sub-regional integration.

Finally, both regional integration movements have faced fierce resistance from certain key states. The UK and France posed serious challenges to the function of the European movement at various stages of its development. In the Caribbean, the collapse of the West Indies Federation, and the failure to create a second, smaller federal structure, were in large part due to antagonisms between the two largest states, and larger and smaller states more generally. For this reason it is particularly useful when studying Caribbean integration not to romanticize the European experience or to downplay its challenges. European integration, like Caribbean integration, has been filled with disagreements, stalling tactics, and outright power struggles.

2.3 Motivations for Caribbean Integration

Having briefly examined the historical context, let us explore some of the motivations that have pushed towards integration in the Caribbean region. Integration can be defined as the coordinated effort to further the cooperation of sovereign states towards the end of unity, whether political or economic.[108] Some of the motives guiding, or rationales underpinning, the Caribbean integration movement include: preservation of a regional Caribbean identity; strengthening the effectiveness of sovereignty through concerted regional action; increasing economic prosperity by pooling scarce resources and small economies; enhancing foreign policy and security capabilities; and increasing the potential for drawing quality leaders, who will have greater political possibilities in a regional context.[109]

These motives are largely focused on national, rather than regional, imperatives. This fact has certainly shaped CARICOM. Payne and Sutton argue that for this reason CARICOM should not be identified as an integration movement, properly speaking:

> CARICOM is not an integration movement at all, if the term integration is considered to be a process in which countries have to be prepared to accept that the greater regional good must predominate over national concerns even to the point when, on occasion, their national interests are damaged. For good or ill, this has never been the case with CARICOM. It has simply not been concerned with integration in that sense; it is a structure created by

[108] cf Müllerleile (n 24) 31 (defining integration in terms of political unity).

[109] On historical motivations underpinning integration in the context of the Caribbean see eg Arthur Lewis, 'The Agony of the Eight' (n 42) 6–26.

national governments to make nationalist policies more effective by pursuing them within a regional framework.[110]

This criticism is perhaps too strong. Integration movements globally tend to be instrumental in nature, and CARICOM and the OECS are no different. Integration is a means to a variety of ends, including economic, social, cultural, political, and legal ones. For regional movements, integration has not generally been an end in itself.

2.3.1 Forms of economic integration

As highlighted by Balassa, although a dictionary might define '"integration" [as] the bringing together of parts into a whole,' the meaning of the term in economic literature is less clear.[111] He defines 'economic integration' as 'a process and as a state of affairs. Regarded as a process, it encompasses measures designed to abolish discrimination between economic units belonging to different national states; viewed as a state of affairs, it can be represented by the absence of various forms of discrimination between national economies.'[112] He further distinguishes between integration, on the one hand, and cooperation, on the other.[113] Integration is more active, more comprehensive. When we integrate, we may have to remove current restrictions, such as trade barriers.[114] Integration therefore involves greater intervention into existing domestic laws than mere cooperation.

According to El-Agraa a number of terms can be used to describe the different kinds of integration movements, from more limited free trade areas to complete political unions.[115] A *free trade area* exists where member states remove all trade impediments between themselves, but reserve complete freedom in their dealings with the outside world. A *customs union* is created when member states remove all trade impediments between themselves and conduct and pursue common external commercial relations, such as through adopting a Common External Tariff. A *common market* exists where there is both a customs union and free factor mobility across national member frontiers, including free movement of capital, labour, technology, and enterprises. Common markets would include the four freedoms

[110] Payne and Sutton, *Charting Caribbean Development* (n 10) 174. Similarly, the West Indian Commission was keen to de-emphasize the impact of its recommendations upon sovereignty in *Time for Action: Report of the West Indian Commission* (Black Rock, Barbados: The West Indian Commission, 1992) at 466:

> Our proposals are rooted instead in the concept of CARICOM as a Community of sovereign states who by treaty agree to the pooling of certain of their sovereignties and to exercising them collectively in very specific respects. It is the same sharing of the exercise of sovereignty, not a transfer of it, that is involved in the integration process.

[111] Bela Balassa, *The Theory of Economic Integration* (London: George Allen and Unwin Ltd, 1961) 1.

[112] Balassa, *The Theory of Economic Integration* (n 111).

[113] Balassa, *The Theory of Economic Integration* (n 111) 2.

[114] Balassa, *The Theory of Economic Integration* (n 111) 2.

[115] See Ali M El-Agraa (ed) *The European Union: Economics and Policies*, 8th edn (Cambridge: Cambridge University Press, 2007) 1–3. See also Balassa (n 111) 2.

that underpin EU law: free movement of goods, persons, services, and capital. A *complete economic union* exists where there is a common market that requires the complete unification of monetary and fiscal policies. A *complete political union* exists when two or more states become a single state (such as occurred in the unification of the two Germanies).

Using this terminology, it could be argued that CARICOM is moving closer to, but has not yet achieved, the status of a common market. The OECS is closer, demonstrating features of a free trade area, customs union, and common market, and some aspects of an economic union.[116] The European Union is closest to a complete economic union and possesses supranational authority capable of making decisions binding upon members.[117] Importantly, although it is tempting to see these terms as reflecting a scale along which regional organizations must progress, one step at a time, El-Agraa makes clear that this is not the case.[118] States can simply agree to move right into a common market without passing through other stages.

It is also useful to distinguish between negative and positive integration.[119] *Negative* integration simply refers to the removal of impediments to, or restrictions on, trade. So, for example, negative integration entails states repealing laws that would restrict trade. *Positive* integration, on the other hand, requires the modification of existing rules or the creation of new rules so as to enable the market to function properly. Examples of both positive and negative integration may be found in the constituent treaties establishing CARICOM, the OECS, and the EU. In Europe, for example, negative integration has been achieved through application of the principle of non-discrimination and use of the market access test, whereas positive integration has been encouraged through harmonization.[120] Because these two forms of integration require different action, the responsibilities for negative and positive integration may be assigned to different bodies. A regional organization, for example, may be assigned a larger role in developing and implementing positive integration, whereas its member states may play a more important role in implementing negative integration (subject, of course, to supervision by regional organs).

A contrast may be made between the free market form of integration (*laissez faire*) and a state-centred view. But Balassa points out that both positions are extreme. Rather, the choice must lie somewhere in the middle, with only the level of emphasis differing. He argues that 'the question is not whether government

[116] The OECS Secretariat, in its publication *Economic Union Treaty—Frequently Asked Questions* (Castries: OECS Secretariat, April 2008) as available at <http://www.oecs.org/doc-lib/economic-union> (20 Sep 2011) summarizes at p 11: 'The OECS countries demonstrate features of a Free Trade Area, a Customs Union, a Common Market and lastly an Economic Union. The latter is because of the single currency (EC dollar) and a common monetary policy.'

[117] For an application of these kinds of models to analyse the position of the EU see Catherine Barnard, *The Substantive Law of the EU: The Four Freedoms*, 3rd edn (Oxford: Oxford University Press, 2010) 8–14.

[118] El-Agraa (ed) *The European Union* (n 115) 1–3.

[119] See eg El-Agraa (ed) *The European Union* (n 115).

[120] See eg Catherine Barnard, *The Substantive Law of the EU* (n 117) 17–29.

intervention is needed or not in an integrated area, but whether economic integration results in a more intensive participation of the state in economic affairs or in a more intensive reliance on market methods'.[121] In addition, free market methods may be more suitable in developed economies, with developing ones requiring more state intervention.[122]

In thinking about the benefits that may flow from integration, Balassa points out that the success of any integration movement ultimately must be judged by its ability to increase social welfare. The most basic test is that found in Pareto's condition that 'an increase in one man's welfare leads to an increase in social welfare only if there is no reduction in the welfare of any other members of the group'.[123] Some indicators of a change in social welfare include changes in: the quantity of goods produced in a region, the consumer's choice between local and foreign goods, the redistribution of income between countries (poorer states getting richer), the redistribution of income within a country (higher GDP, higher income levels), and the dynamic efficiency of economies (ie nations become more competitive).[124]

Finally, it is useful to note that integration can develop in either a holistic or sectoral manner. Taking a holistic approach, states can decide to implement a particular level of integration (free trade) across the entire spectrum of their economies. In contrast, if states choose a sectoral approach they can decide to open up specific areas of their economies, while keeping other areas closed. Some, like Balassa, are critical of the sectoral approach as a piecemeal form of integration.[125] However in practice this sectoral model tends to be used by regional organizations, which integrate particular sectors at different stages of their development. Europe, for example, started with coal and steel and then gradually expanded its integration project to include many other areas. CARICOM and the OECS more strictly regulate certain economic areas, and leave the remainder within the substantial control of their member states.

A number of benefits may flow from deepening and strengthening regional economic integration, including the increased efficiencies generated by specialization, economies of scale, intensified competition between firms, improvements and advancements in technology, and a collective bargaining position with respect to the outside world. Further, if a region is able to achieve integration beyond the level of a customs union, added benefits arise, from higher national incomes to cost reductions and better income distribution.[126] In the EU during the ten-year period from 1993 it is estimated that the adoption of the Single Market package boosted the EU's GDP 2.2 per cent (or €223 billion), increased employment by 1.4 per cent, reduced consumer price-cost margins and increased price convergence, increased intra-EU manufacturing trade by approximately 13

[121] Balassa, *The Theory of Economic Integration* (n 111) 9.
[122] Balassa, *The Theory of Economic Integration* (n 111) 10.
[123] Balassa, *The Theory of Economic Integration* (n 111) 10–11.
[124] Balassa, *The Theory of Economic Integration* (n 111) 10–13.
[125] See Balassa, *The Theory of Economic Integration* 15–17.
[126] See eg El-Agraa (ed) *The European Union* (n 115) 17.

per cent, increased foreign direct investment from €23 billion in 1992 (EU-15) to a projected €145 billion in 2006 (EU-25), and reduced the number of customs clearance documents by 60 million per year.[127] The estimated savings from the introduction of the EU's internal market reforms from 1992 until 2010 include a 70 per cent drop in mobile phone prices and a 40 per cent drop in airline ticket prices.[128]

In order for states to understand the imperative of deeper integration, however, they must be driven not only by enlightened idealism, but also by simple economic necessity. This is demonstrated by the history of the European Union, where the removal of a large number of physical, technical, and fiscal barriers was impelled in large part by economic necessity. The cost of *not integrating* was simply too high. A study referred to in the House of Lords, for example, showed that the cost of one single barrier to trade—a tax on Scottish whiskey over a period of three to four years—was 'four times as much as the British annual net contribution to the Community budget'.[129] This shows the amazing potential for waste that can arise as a result of barriers to trade.

2.4 Ground Rules from International Institutional Law

This section reviews some of the basic rules regarding the law of treaties and the rules applicable to international institutions. Both sets of rules underpin the constituent treaties of regional organizations such as CARICOM and the OECS.

2.4.1 Introduction to rules of treaty interpretation

An international organization is generally formed by means of a treaty, termed the constituent instrument, which must be interpreted and applied during its life. Such interpretation requires reference to the specific rules of the international law of treaties. Although the RTC and RTB do not fall within the terms of the 1969 Vienna Convention on the Law of Treaties (VCLT), since they were concluded between state and non-states parties, they may nevertheless be analysed using the VCLT framework.[130] This is because Article 3 of the VCLT does not exclude the application of its rules to other treaties or to the relations between states in a

[127] See eg European Commission DG Enterprise and Industry, 'Facts and Figures', in *Single Market for Goods Information Pack* (European Union, 2007) as available through <http://bookshop.europa.eu/en/single-market-for-goods-pbNB7807452/?CatalogCategoryID=_z0KABstpR4AAAEjr5AY4e5L> (1 Nov 2011) [no page numbering].

[128] See eg European Commission Internal Market and Services, *Your Single Market? Single Market Act for a highly competitive social market economy* (European Union, Luxembourg, 2010) as available at <http://ec.europa.eu/internal_market/smact/docs/brochure-web_en.pdf> (1 Nov 2011) 4.

[129] H Schmitt von Sydow, 'Basic Strategies of the Commission's White Paper', as reproduced in Stephen Weatherill, *Cases & Materials on EU Law*, 9th edn (Oxford: Oxford University Press, 2010) 267.

[130] The VCLT only governs international legal agreements between states: Art 2(1)(a) VCLT.

treaty involving non-states parties.[131] Moreover, many of the rules of the VCLT also reflect the current customary international legal position.[132] As a result one could rely upon the VCLT rules as codifying the applicable customary international law, even if the VCLT itself does not, strictly speaking, apply to the treaty in question.[133] For such reasons Articles 31–32 of the VCLT have been expressly relied upon by parties arguing before the CCJ, and by the CCJ itself, when issues involving the interpretation of the meaning of the RTC have arisen.[134]

There are three main approaches to treaty interpretation under the general law of treaties and under the 1969 VCLT, namely, the textual, the subjective, and the teleological schools.[135] The *textual* approach towards treaty interpretation is the dominant one and involves interpreting a treaty and its provisions in good faith in accordance with the ordinary meaning to be given to the terms in their context.[136] The benefit of this approach is that when the text is clear it can be applied according to its ordinary meaning, and such application will respect the written text of the treaty. As noted by the International Court of Justice in its Advisory Opinion on the Competence of the General Assembly:

> [T]he first duty of a tribunal which is called upon to interpret and apply the provisions of a treaty, is to endeavour to give effect to them in their natural and ordinary meaning in the context in which they occur. If the relevant words in their natural and ordinary meaning make sense in their context, that is the end of the matter.[137]

[131] Art 3 VCLT provides:

> The fact that the present Convention does not apply to international agreements concluded between States and other subjects of international law or between such other subjects of international law, or to international agreements not in written form, shall not affect:
> (a) the legal force of such agreements;
> (b) the application to them of any of the rules set forth in the present Convention to which they would be subject under international law independently of the Convention;
> (c) the application of the Convention to the relations of States as between themselves under international agreements to which other subjects of international law are also parties.

[132] See eg *Territorial Dispute (Libyan Arab Jamahiriya/Chad)* [1994] ICJ Rep 6, at pp 21–2 [41]; *LaGrand (Germany v United States of America)* [2001] ICJ Rep 466, at p 501 [99]; *The Effect of Reservations on the Entry Into Force of the American Convention on Human Rights (Arts 74 and 75)*, I-A Ct HR, Advisory Opinion OC-2/82 of 24 September 1982, Series A, No 2; *Interpretation of the American Declaration of the Rights and Duties of Man Within the Framework of Article 64 of the American Convention on Human Rights*, I-A Ct HR, Advisory Opinion OC-10/89 of 14 July 1989, Series A, No 10.

[133] On the customary status of the VCLT rules regarding interpretation see Richard Gardiner, *Treaty Interpretation* (n 9) 12–13. On the customary status of the VCLT more generally see Anthony Aust, *Modern Treaty Law and Practice* (n 9) 10–11.

[134] *Trinidad Cement Ltd and TCL Guyana Inc v Guyana*, Judgment [2009] CCJ 1 (OJ), (2009) 74 WIR 302, 15 January 2009, at [10]–[11].

[135] See generally, PK Menon, *An Introduction to the Law of Treaties* (Cave Hill, Barbados: UWI/USAID Caribbean Justice Improvement Project, 1992) ch 7; Anthony Aust, *Modern Treaty Law and Practice* (n 9) ch 13; Richard Gardiner, *Treaty Interpretation* (n 9).

[136] See VCLT Art 31(1); Anthony Aust, *Modern Treaty Law and Practice* (n 9) 184–206; Richard Gardiner, *Treaty Interpretation* (n 9) 161–77. See also PK Menon, *An Introduction to the Law of Treaties* (UWI/USAID Caribbean Justice Improvement Project, 1992) 56–9.

[137] *Competence of the General Assembly Regarding Admission to the United Nations* (Advisory Opinion) [1950] ICJ Rep 4, at p 8.

Unfortunately, however, in many cases this clarity may be illusory since even the simplest words can have many meanings and it may be difficult to establish whether a treaty is meant to encompass a particular fact situation.

The *subjective* approach looks to the intention of the parties.[138] This approach emphasizes the importance of ascertaining the *original* intentions of the creators of a treaty in order to interpret how it should be applied. Thus the subjective method requires us to search out the real intention of the drafters of the treaty by looking at, for example, evidence of the negotiations.[139] The problem with the subjective approach is that it assumes an ascertainable common intention, one that may not in fact exist. This is because in negotiations parties may agree to compromise on the wording of a particular treaty provision when each has a different position on the matter. Also, certain events may simply not have been contemplated by the drafters and thus it will be impossible to ascribe a common intention. Finally, in modern multilateral treaties, given the wide range of parties, no common intention may in fact exist.[140]

The *teleological* approach, sometimes called the purposive approach, interprets treaties in light of their aims, objects, or purposes.[141] Rather than looking closely at the particular provisions of the treaty, the teleological approach tries to situate the treaty in a broad context to see what it is seeking to accomplish. Thus, 'matters such as the general tenor and atmosphere of the treaty, the circumstances in which it was concluded', and its role in international society are important.[142] This approach also allows the interpreter to look at developments that have occurred subsequent to the making of the treaty in order to help ascertain the object and purpose of the treaty.[143]

The teleological approach is different from the subjective approach because it is not concerned solely with the original intent; it looks at subsequent developments. The teleological approach differs from the textual approach because it is not closely rooted to the specific wording of the treaty. The problem with the teleological approach, however, is that any interpreter applying it may be seen as *usurping* the role of the treaty makers and substituting her or his own preferences for those of the states parties.[144]

Although the textual form of treaty interpretation is most widely employed, with the subjective and teleological approaches having lesser prominence, in the area of the law of international organizations, or international institutional law, the teleological approach is sometimes favoured.[145] As noted by the International Court of Justice, although the general rules of treaty interpretation apply to the

138 See generally PK Menon *An Introduction to the Law of Treaties* (n 136) 53–6.
139 Menon *An Introduction to the Law of Treaties* (n 136) 53.
140 Menon *An Introduction to the Law of Treaties* (n 136) 55.
141 Menon *An Introduction to the Law of Treaties* (n 136) 59–60.
142 Menon *An Introduction to the Law of Treaties* (n 136) 59.
143 Menon *An Introduction to the Law of Treaties* (n 136) 59.
144 cf Menon *An Introduction to the Law of Treaties* (n 136) 60.
145 eg Anthony Aust, *Modern Treaty Law and Practice* (n 9) 188.

constituent document of an international organization, such documents also have special characteristics:

> [T]he constituent instruments of international organizations are also treaties of a particular type; their object is to create new subjects of law endowed with a certain autonomy, to which the parties entrust the task of realizing common goals. Such treaties can raise specific problems of interpretation owing, *inter alia*, to their character which is conventional and at the same time institutional; the very nature of the organization created, the objectives which have been assigned to it by its founders, the imperatives associated with the effective performance of its functions, as well as its own practice, are all elements which may deserve special attention when the time comes to interpret these constituent treaties.[146]

This view makes sense when one considers that the treaty in question—the constituent document of the organization—must serve as the institutional foundation for the existence and continued growth of the organization, in a similar way that a constitution sustains the development of a nation state. Moreover, as the organization develops new questions will arise that cannot be answered definitively by consulting either the wording of the text of the treaty or the expressed intentions of the treaty drafters. The teleological approach can in such cases be employed to fill in the gaps in the treaty. The Caribbean Court of Justice has already employed the teleological form of treaty interpretation.[147]

The VCLT primarily follows the textual school, looking to the words of the treaty and reading them in their ordinary meaning. But Articles 31–32 of the VCLT provide a basis for use of all three forms of interpretation, as highlighted next:

> Article 31
>
> *General rule of interpretation*
>
> 1. A treaty shall be interpreted in good faith in accordance with the *ordinary meaning to be given to the terms of the treaty* in their context and in the light of its *object and purpose.*
> 2. The context for the purpose of the interpretation of a treaty shall comprise, in addition to the text, including its preamble and annexes:
>   (a) any agreement relating to the treaty which was made between all the parties in connexion with the conclusion of the treaty;
>   (b) any instrument which was made by one or more parties in connexion with the conclusion of the treaty and accepted by the other parties as an instrument related to the treaty.
> 3. There shall be taken into account, together with the context:
>   (a) any subsequent agreement between the parties regarding the interpretation of the treaty or the application of its provisions;

[146] *Legality of the Use by a State of Nuclear Weapons in Armed Conflict* (Advisory Opinion) [1996] ICJ Rep 66, at p 75.

[147] See *Trinidad Cement Ltd and TCL Guyana Inc v Guyana*, Judgment [2009] CCJ 1 (OJ), (2009) 74 WIR 302, 15 January 2009, at [38].

(b) any subsequent practice in the application of the treaty which establishes the agreement of the parties regarding its interpretation;
(c) any relevant rules of international law applicable in the relations between the parties.

4. A special meaning shall be given to a term if it is established that the parties so intended.

Article 32

Supplementary means of interpretation

Recourse may be had to supplementary means of interpretation, including the *preparatory work of the treaty and the circumstances of its conclusion*, in order to confirm the meaning resulting from the application of article 31, or to determine the meaning when the interpretation according to article 31:
(a) leaves the meaning ambiguous or obscure; or
(b) leads to a result which is manifestly absurd or unreasonable.[148]

Article 31(1) authorizes use of both the textual and teleological forms of treaty interpretation, and Article 32 permits use of the subjective form. Article 31(1) also sets out four general rules and principles of treaty interpretation, namely, those related to (1) good faith, (2) ordinary meaning, (3) context, and (4) object and purpose.[149]

Good faith is a requirement flowing from the most fundamental rule of the law of treaties, *pacta sunt servanda*.[150] This rule can be expressed as 'treaties are binding and must be observed in good faith'.[151] Good faith applies to all aspects of the treaty, including its interpretation, so that, for example, parties are not allowed to rely upon what are clearly drafting errors to escape treaty obligations. As seen later in this book—particularly in Part IV, dealing with the substantive rules and policies of CARICOM and the OECS—this good faith requirement in relation to drafting errors is of tremendous importance because the RTC is riddled with cross-referencing errors. The phrase '*ordinary meaning*' clearly emphasizes the textual approach to interpretation: the text is to be read so as to accord with its ordinary meaning. Nevertheless, this meaning is not to be determined in the abstract, and Article 31 makes clear that attention must also be paid to the context in which the terms are set, and the object and purpose of the treaty.[152] Reference to a treaty's *context* in Article 31 allows the interpreter to go beyond the plain treaty text and to look at related instruments. Thus, one may look at any agreements between the treaty parties directly related to the treaty, as well as subsequent agreements meant to help interpret or apply the treaty. One may also look at any subsequent practice of the parties, and the general international law rules applicable to the parties that might affect the treaty. Note in this regard that Article 31 expressly refers to agreements and practice of the treaty parties.

[148] Emphasis added. [149] See generally Gardiner, *Treaty Interpretation* (n 9) ch 5.
[150] See Gardiner, *Treaty Interpretation* (n 9) 148–50. [151] See VCLT Art 26.
[152] See eg Gardiner, *Treaty Interpretation* (n 9) 162–4.

It thereby sets out two requirements: firstly, there must be an agreement; secondly, the agreement must be between *parties*.[153]

As a result, the judgments of a regional court or the practice of the organs of the organization may not, strictly speaking, be appropriate for determining context. However if those judgments, or even the practices of organs, are expressly accepted by the states parties (for example, through reliance upon that jurisprudence or practice in subsequent actions), then they may appropriately fall under the category of context.[154] This is a contentious point, however, since often the practice of organs or regional courts may not be accepted by member states.[155]

The reference to *object and purpose* in Article 31(1) allows the teleological method of interpretation, but perhaps in a more limited manner than possible under the general rules of treaty interpretation. This is because the phrase 'object and purpose' is expressly linked to the terms of the treaty. It is not employed in a separate subsection of, or even separate sentence in, Article 31; it is inextricably linked to the text itself. Moreover, Article 31 uses cautious phrasing. One is instructed to interpret the text 'in the light of' its object and purpose, rather than, for example, 'in accordance with' it. Thus, although the teleological approach may allow the filling of gaps in the treaty, and the implying of new powers to the international organization from existing powers, under the rules of the 1969 VCLT the teleological approach will not usually be employed to overrule the specific wording of the treaty text. This may be so even if the text itself is deficient and yields an unpalatable result.[156] The

[153] Anthony Aust, in *Modern Treaty Law and Practice* (n 9) at p 195, makes clear that real agreement must be ascertained:

> It is not necessary to show that each party has engaged in a practice, only that all have accepted it, albeit tacitly. But, if a clear difference of opinion between the parties exists, the practice may not be relied upon as a supplementary means of interpretation.

The International Law Commission, in its 'Draft Articles on the Law of Treaties with Commentaries' (1966) *Yearbook of the International Law Commission, 1966*, Vol II, at p 222, makes clear that that the relevant practice must be consistent between the parties:

> The text provisionally adopted in 1964 spoke of a practice which 'establishes the understanding of all the parties'. By omitting the word 'all' the Commission did not intend to change the rule. It considered that the phrase 'the understanding of the parties' necessarily means 'the parties as a whole'. It omitted the word 'all' merely to avoid any possible misconception that every party must individually have engaged in the practice where it suffices that it should have accepted the practice.

[154] Note that the ICJ in *Legality of the Use by a State of Nuclear Weapons in Armed Conflict* (Advisory Opinion) [1996] ICJ Rep 66, at p 75 [19], implicitly accepts that the practice of the UN might be relevant to interpreting the Charter of the United Nations. But James Crawford, in *Brownlie's Principles of Public International Law*, 8th edn (Oxford: Oxford University Press, 2012) at p 187, notes in this context that 'Article 31(3)(b), is not, however a perfect analogue, referring impliedly as it does to the practice of states parties to the treaty rather than that of the organization itself.'

[155] For an example of acceptance by states of the practice of an organization not supported by the text of the treaty—an abstention being counted as a 'concurring vote'—see *Legal Consequences for States of the Continued Presence of South Africa in Namibia (South West Africa) notwithstanding Security Council Resolution 276 (1970)* (Advisory Opinion) [1971] ICJ Rep 16, at p 22 [22].

[156] See eg *Interpretation of Peace Treaties with Bulgaria, Hungary and Roumania* (Second Phase) [1950] ICJ Rep 221, *Competence of the General Assembly Regarding Admission to the United Nations*, (Advisory Opinion) [1950] ICJ Rep 4.

remedy in such cases is for the parties simply to accept the weakness of the treaty, or to agree to its amendment.

Article 32 allows use of the subjective form of treaty interpretation by providing for limited circumstances in which an interpreter may refer to the 'preparatory work of the treaty and the circumstances of its conclusion'. This preparatory work, usually described with the French term '*travaux préparatoires*', would include previous drafts of the treaty and any records regarding the debates on its terms.[157] However use of the *travaux préparatoires* is expressly limited under Article 32 of the VCLT to two situations, namely, either (1) to confirm an interpretation that has already been made under Article 31, or (2) to determine the meaning of the text where an Article 31 interpretation remains ambiguous or leads to an absurd result. In such circumstances it becomes clear that the subjective form of interpretation is supplementary to the normal means of interpretation under Article 31.

As a final point, it should be noted that many treaties have official texts in several languages, and the VCLT has rules that cover interpretative problems that may arise from these different languages.[158] Most of these treaties will state which language is the authoritative one. But where the treaty does not do so, Article 33 of the VCLT provides that the text in each language is equally authoritative. If there is a conflict between the two languages, the means of interpretation set out in Articles 31 and 32 are applied to decide which meaning is correct. If there is still a problem, then Article 33 also allows one to look at the overall object and purpose of the treaty to decide which language is correct.[159] These rules regarding pluralingualism of treaties may not be important to CARICOM at present, but given the inclusion of Haiti and Suriname in its membership, and the potential future inclusion of the Dominican Republic, they may become increasingly important.

2.4.2 Rules and principles related to international organizations

Four general concepts in international institutional law also should be highlighted briefly. These are the rules related to autointerpretation, international legal personality, implied powers, and the doctrine of ultra vires.

Autointerpretation

The term 'autointerpretation' applies to a situation where the organization, or organ, interprets its own constituent document. As Schermers and Blokker succinctly state, '[w]hoever applies a rule in the first instance will also interpret it.'[160] An act of autointerpretation may be authoritative if the first interpretation is accepted as correct by the other organs of the organization and its member

[157] See generally Gardiner, *Treaty Interpretation* (n 9) ch 8.

[158] See generally Gardiner, *Treaty Interpretation* (n 9) ch 9.

[159] For an example of this approach see the *LaGrand Case (Germany v USA)* [2001] ICJ Rep 466.

[160] Henry G Schermers and Niels M Blokker, *International Institutional Law* 4th edn (Boston: Martinus Nijhoff, 2003) 839 (§1344).

states. However it may also be challenged or disputed. Such disputes will generally be resolved within the organization or by a third party (such as an international tribunal).[161] Upon their resolution the correct meaning of the term or rule will be established. In other words, autointerpretation alerts us to the fact that in international organizations, as in many areas of international life, the actors themselves will first interpret the rules, and only if there is disagreement will another party be asked to help interpret them.[162]

The principle of autointerpretation also applies to member states when interpreting how the rules of international organizations apply to themselves.[163] If these rules have not already been authoritatively interpreted, it will be up to each state, in the first instance, to interpret how it is to be applied to itself.[164] National courts of states will also have to interpret any law of an international organization that is invoked before them. However in some cases such a law will be considered akin to an act of a foreign state and thus fall outside of the jurisdiction of the national court.[165] Under the RTC, specific provision is made to exclude the jurisdiction of national courts to interpret the RTC, which falls under the CCJ's exclusive jurisdiction.[166]

These many levels of autointerpretation can lead to inconsistencies unless the organization has mechanisms to publicize and promote uniform interpretations or there is available a formal body with authority to decide such matters with finality.[167] The member states of the EU, for example, are by and large made aware of the actions of national courts of each state in interpreting the various treaties of the EU, and guidance is also provided by the various directives issued by European authorities. The European Court of Justice, like the Caribbean Court of Justice

[161] See eg Crawford, *Brownlie's Principles of International Law* (n 154) 184–6.

[162] See eg *Certain Expenses of the United Nations* (Advisory Opinion) [1962] ICJ Rep 151, 168, where the ICJ held in relation to the question of whether peacekeeping expenses were 'expenses of the Organisation' under the UN Charter:

> In the legal systems of States, there is often some procedure for determining the validity of even a legislative or governmental act, but no analogous procedure is to be found in the structure of the United Nations. Proposals made during the drafting of the Charter to place the ultimate authority to interpret the Charter in the International Court of Justice were not accepted; the opinion which the Court is in course of rendering is an *advisory* opinion. As anticipated in 1945, therefore, each organ must, in the first place at least, determine its own jurisdiction. If the Security Council, for example, adopts a resolution purportedly for the maintenance of international peace and security and if, in accordance with a mandate or authorization in such resolution, the Secretary-General incurs financial obligations, these amounts must be presumed to constitute 'expenses of the Organization'.

The Court concluded that the peacekeeping expenses were expenses of the UN: *Certain Expenses* pp 179–80.

[163] Schermers and Blokker, *International Institutional Law* (n 160) 846–7 (§1351).

[164] Schermers and Blokker, *International Institutional Law* (n 160) 846–7 (§1351).

[165] Schermers and Blokker, *International Institutional Law* (n 160) 849–52 (§1353–4).

[166] Art 211(1) of the RTC gives the CCJ 'compulsory and exclusive jurisdiction to hear and determine disputes concerning the interpretation and application of the Treaty'. Art 214 bolsters this exclusive jurisdiction by requiring national courts seised of an issue requiring interpretation of the RTC to refer such questions to the CCJ, under its referral jurisdiction. See further Chapter 14.

[167] On the role of judicial organs see Schermers and Blokker, *International Institutional Law* (n 160) 857–65 (§1363–78).

and Eastern Caribbean Court of Appeal, also serves as an authoritative body to resolve such matters.

International legal personality

The phrase 'international personality' is merely another way to say subject of international law.[168] All subjects of international law have international personality of some form. Historically, states were the only real subjects of international law, the only actors in the international sphere. Even today only one subject of international law has unlimited international personality: in principle, the state is the only entity that automatically possesses all international rights and obligations. All other actors in the international sphere that have personality have limited forms of it. This came out clearly in the *Reparation for Injuries Case* when the International Court of Justice explicitly stated that the UN will not automatically have all of the powers of states, and definitely cannot be considered to be a 'super state'.[169]

Crawford suggests three criteria for the attribution of international legal personality to international organizations: '(1) a permanent association of states, with lawful objectives, equipped with organs; (2) a distinction, in terms of legal powers and purposes, between the organisation and its member states; and (3) the existence of legal powers exercisable on the international plane and not solely within the national systems of one or more states.'[170]

Some entities will have certain features of international personality, but not others. As a result, the focal question in the area of international personality in relation to any entity is simply whether that personality includes the particular international capacity that the entity seeks to exercise.[171] In other words, does the international personality of *X* mean that it can do *Y*? Understood in this way, international legal personality refers to the capacity of an entity to do certain acts in certain contexts. For example, a particular international organization may be able to make certain claims against its member states that it cannot make against non-members.

In order to deal with such a varied notion of international personality, in addition to the normal methods of treaty interpretation, international institutional law has developed a functional test for the personality of international organizations. Under a functional approach the question narrows to that of whether a particular component or attribute of personality is *necessary* for the organization to carry out its intended functions. To answer this question one could in some cases ask an advisory opinion of an international or regional judicial body. But the more frequent means of resolving it will simply be for the organ concerned to decide for itself whether it has such personality and act accordingly. In such cases, other organs of the organization or the states parties themselves remain free to challenge

[168] See generally Schermers and Blokker, *International Institutional Law* (n 160) ch 11.

[169] *Reparation for Injuries Suffered in the Service of the United Nations* (Advisory Opinion) [1949] ICJ Rep 174, at p 179.

[170] Crawford, *Brownlie's Principles of International Law* (n 154) 169.

[171] See eg DP O'Connell, *International Law*, 2nd edn (London: Stevens, 1970) Vol 1, 80–2.

the right of the organ to so act, either through internal processes or by reference to international judicial bodies.[172]

The types of powers that may be possessed by an international organization as a consequence of its international personality include: the power to bind member states to its decisions; exceptionally (ie the UN Security Council acting under Chapter VII) the power to bind non-member states to its decisions; the power to make treaties with member states, non-member states, and other international organizations; the power to have legal standing and legal capacity under the national law of member states; and the power to make claims against persons, states, and other international organizations at either international law or national law.[173] In addition, the United Nations has the exceptional competences of being able to maintain an international force (under Article 43 agreements, and possibly by implication as a result of peacekeeping developments); exercise jurisdiction over, and even administer, a territory; authorize use of force; and exercise the functional capacity to protect its agents.[174] Moreover any power not prohibited by international law could be assigned to an international organization. In this sense, international personality may be extended to the extent of the aspirations of the member states.

The scope of international personality for any international organization will be limited by a variety of things including the general rules of international law, the terms of the constituent treaty, the extent of the organization's overall purpose and function, the breadth of its membership and the jurisdictional competences of its member states. Regarding the limitation imposed by breadth of membership, it is useful to remember that most international organizations will exercise powers in relation to their member states and may not be able to influence non-members.[175] With respect to jurisdictional competence, all international organizations will be allocated specific competences and the remainder will be left with the member states. This is termed the 'principle of conferral' in European Union law, and has been read robustly to mean that the European Union legislation must both fall within the scope of the treaties and be enacted under the correct treaty provisions.[176] The United Nations is also specifically prohibited by Article 2(7) of the UN Charter from intervening 'in matters which are essentially within the domestic jurisdiction of any state'.[177]

[172] The *Effects of Awards of Compensation Made by the UN Administrative Tribunal* (Advisory Opinion) [1945] ICJ Rep 47, falls in this category, since the UN went ahead and set up a compensation tribunal, and only after this had been accomplished did states protest about the organization's competence to do so. This involved a question of international personality because the UN was binding its member states to certain expenditures against their will.

[173] See generally Crawford, *Brownlie's Principles of International Law* (n 154) 179–84.

[174] See eg Crawford, *Brownlie's Principles of International Law* 119–20, 179–84, 757–68; *Reparation for Injuries* (n 169).

[175] But see the comments in Crawford, *Brownlie's Principles of International Law* (n 154) 191, suggesting that Art 2(6) of the UN Charter may bind non-parties.

[176] See eg TC Hartley, *The Foundations of European Union Law*, 7th edn (Oxford: Oxford University Press, 2010) 110–16. See also the analysis of the principle of conferral in Chapter 8.

[177] Charter of the United Nations (adopted 26 Jun 1945, in force 24 Oct 1945) 1 UNTS xvi, 39 AJIL Supp 190, Art 2(7).

The most controversial powers falling under international personality are those that might affect non-member states. These powers can only exist if the international organization has 'objective' international personality. Objective international personality should not be possible for an international organization under the basic rules of treaty law, which establish the general rule that a treaty cannot bind third parties against their will.[178] Since public international organizations are products of treaties, any attempt to bind a non-member to accept any legal aspect of the international organization would be an attempt to bind a non-party to the treaty. Nevertheless under international institutional law objective international personality has been found to exist.

The *Reparation for Injuries Case* established that the UN has objective international personality, at least to the extent of having the capacity to bring claims against non-members. The International Court of Justice held:

> [T]he Court's opinion is that fifty States [the original members], representing the vast majority of the Members of the international community, had the power, in conformity with international law, to bring into being an entity possessing objective international personality, and not merely personality recognized by them alone, together with capacity to bring international claims.[179]

This passage is striking because the court expressly stated that such objective international personality must arise 'in conformity with international law' without providing any insight regarding how objective international personality is compatible with the rule against treaties having binding effect upon third parties without their consent.[180] The likely justification for the court's position would be that the objective international legal personality of the United Nations arose by means of customary international law, outside of the UN Charter, or through other doctrines, such as acquiescence.[181]

Implied powers

Under the law of international institutions an international or regional organization may be deemed to have implied powers. Implied powers either arise by implication from the text of the treaty establishing the organization, or from its general objects and purposes. In international institutional law there are various bases upon which these implied powers can be grounded, ranging from the doctrine of *effet utile* (ie required for 'effectiveness' and arising through treaty interpretation), to the functions and objectives of the organization (the power arising out of 'necessary intendment'), to the inherent powers doctrine.[182]

[178] eg Art 34 of the VCLT provides: 'A treaty does not create either obligations or rights for a third State without its consent.'

[179] *Reparation for Injuries* (n 169) at p 185.

[180] See VCLT Arts 34–37.

[181] Art 38 of the VCLT expressly provides for this possibility, stating 'Nothing in articles 34 to 37 precludes a rule set forth in a treaty from becoming binding upon a third State as a customary rule of international law, recognized as such.'

[182] See generally Jan Klabbers, *An Introduction to International Institutional Law* (Cambridge: Cambridge University Press, 2002) ch 4; Schermers and Blokker, *International Institutional Law* (n 160) 175–83 [§232–6].

The most acceptable basis for implied powers is that of 'necessary intendment.' The clearest statement of this principle is found in a passage of the dissenting judgment of Judge Hackworth in the *Reparation for Injuries Case*, in which he stated:

> Powers not expressed cannot freely be implied. Implied powers flow from a grant of express powers, and are limited to those that are 'necessary' to the exercise of the powers expressly granted.[183]

Thus implied powers must be (a) derived from express powers and (b) limited to those necessary for the exercise of those express powers.

The doctrine of implied powers has become a fundamental pillar supporting the growth of many international organizations. This is for the simple reason that the drafters of the constituent document are unable to plan for all future developments related to the organization, which must grow and develop in response to changing conditions. Textual and subjective forms of interpretation may be inadequate to provide the organization with the necessary competences. Further, the usual processes of treaty amendment and revision are particularly cumbersome in the context of multilateral, broad-based international institutions, since such changes would require the formal support of the entire membership.

The *Reparation for Injuries Suffered in the Service of the United Nations* Advisory Opinion is famous for its approach towards the question of implied powers.[184] In that case the International Court of Justice was asked whether the United Nations had the power to bring claims on behalf of its staff in the event of their injury or death. The UN Charter had no specific provision authorizing the UN to do so. The Court held that although the Charter was silent on the matter, the UN must nevertheless be deemed to have those powers arising by means of necessary implication:

> The Charter does not expressly confer upon the Organization the capacity to include, in its claim for reparation, damage caused to the victim or to persons entitled through him. [...] Under international law, the Organization must be deemed to have those powers which, though not expressly provided in the Charter, are conferred upon it by necessary implication as being essential to the performance of its duties.[185]

In determining whether such a necessary implication existed in the context of diplomatic protection, the Court held that the UN must have such a capacity in order for it to function effectively. In order for agents of the UN to perform their duties independently and without fear, they must be able to rely upon the protection of the UN, and not some other source. If protection came from the agents' states of nationality their independence would be compromised, and this would conflict with Article 100 of the UN Charter. Also, the agent should be equally protected when working on behalf of the UN, regardless of the strength of her or his state of nationality, or its sympathy with her or his task. As a result, in the words of the Court, 'the capacity of the Organisation to exercise a measure of functional protection of its agents

[183] *Reparation for Injuries* (n 169) p 198 (Hackworth J, dissenting).

[184] *Reparation for Injuries* (n 169).

[185] *Reparation for Injuries* (n 169) p 182.

arises by necessary intendment out of the Charter.'[186] Nevertheless, as highlighted in the *Reparations Case*, powers conferred by necessary intendment must be seen to be more limited than general implied powers, because they must be 'essential' for the international organization to fulfil its functions.[187]

Ultra vires

The doctrine of autointerpretation helps us understand why a particular organ may be required to establish an interpretive position where none existed previously. However this doctrine does not evaluate the *consequences* of action based upon such an interpretation. The doctrine of ultra vires allows us to categorize an action as being not only interpretively incorrect, but also outside of the competence or power of the organization. Ultra vires means outside of legal competence; intra vires means within legal competence. When we say that something is ultra vires an organ, we mean that the organ cannot legally engage in such behaviour because it is outside of its powers. Ultra vires actions at the international level attract responsibility, meaning that the organization that has acted outside of its competence may be liable to compensate the injured party.

The doctrine of ultra vires will play an important role in cases where an international or regional organization has extensive and clearly-defined powers. But where an organization has very general competences it may not impose a significant restriction. In the case of the United Nations, for example, the early decisions of the International Court of Justice tended to side with the Organization on questions of competence. In the *Certain Expenses Case*, where the question arose as to whether expenses related to United Nations peacekeeping missions could be charged as normal expenses under the budget, the Court held that (1) there is a presumption that an action within the broad purposes of the UN Charter will not be ultra vires the Organization; and that (2) even if the action is ultra vires a particular organ of the UN (eg, the General Assembly), as long as it is within the powers of the Organization as a whole (ie could be done by another organ, such as the Security Council), then such an action will be intra vires the Organization as a whole.[188] This decision is particularly important for the legal implications of such acts for third states, which may not reasonably be expected to know the nuances of all of the competences and powers of particular organs.

[186] *Reparation for Injuries* (n 169) p 184.

[187] Of course the question of what is 'essential' is not without controversy. The powers recognized in the *Effects of Awards of Compensation Case* (to create a Compensation Tribunal where there existed no other mechanism to solve staff disputes) could be more easily acknowledged as being essential to the running of the United Nations than those recognized the *Reparation for Injuries Case* and the *Certain Expenses Case*. It could be queried, in the latter context, whether it was absolutely necessary for the UN to have the power to bring claims against non-Member States or for peacekeeping expenses to fall within the normal UN budget.

[188] *Certain Expenses of the United Nations (Article 17, Paragraph 2, of the Charter)* (Advisory Opinion) [1962] ICJ Rep 151, at p 168.

The concept of ultra vires is fundamentally linked to the idea of autointerpretation because each organ and the organization as a whole must decide precisely whether an action falls within its particular competence (is intra vires) the first time such an action is considered. It should be noted, however, that third parties may determine whether an action is ultra vires. These can include other international organizations (the UN Security Council, for example, may restrict the actions of regional organizations), appellate judicial institutions (whether at the international, regional, or national levels), organs with appellate competence, and special administrative bodies (such as Administrative Tribunals, Claims Commissions, etc).[189]

In sum, and as explored in the following chapters, these doctrines of international institutional law and the general rules of treaty interpretation are important to an understanding of the nature and functions of the constituent instruments of CARICOM and the OECS. In addition, the general historical, geographical, and economic background to the process of Caribbean integration, as seen in the context of the different modes of integration, is important to an understanding of both the current and future potentials of CARICOM and the OECS.

[189] See eg Crawford, *Brownlie's Principles of International Law* (n 154) 184–6; Philippe Sands QC and Pierre Klein, *Bowett's Law of International Institutions*, 6th edn (London: Thomson Reuters, 2009) 341–50.

PART II

THE INSTITUTIONAL AND TREATY STRUCTURES FOR CARIBBEAN REGIONAL INTEGRATION

Introduction

The present Part introduces the institutional structure of the two Caribbean regional integration movements being studied. Chapter 3 examines preliminary issues related to the constituent treaties of CARICOM and OECS, commencing with the status of the treaties and of the regional organizations. For the student of regional integration, it highlights challenges with the treaty texts and provides an overview of the purposes, functions and membership of the organizations. Chapter 4 engages in a detailed examination of the primary and secondary organs of both organizations, focusing on their competences and decision-making processes. Chapter 5 rounds up the analysis by examining the final provisions of the two treaties, looking at questions surrounding the international legal personality of the two organizations, their headquarters, and their privileges and immunities. It also provides an overview of the provisions dealing with the mechanics of entry into force of the two treaties, how they may be amended, whether reservations can be entered to them, and the possibility of accession.

3

Status, Objectives, and Membership

3.1 Current Status of the Treaties

3.1.1 CARICOM

The Caribbean Community has evolved considerably since the signature of the original 1973 Treaty Establishing the Caribbean Community and the Annex to the Treaty—The Caribbean Common Market. As highlighted in the previous chapter, nine new Protocols were drafted to amend the Treaty and in 2001 the RTC was opened for signature.[1] The RTC consolidated all of the amending Protocols into one document and instituted a few additional changes both to clarify and

[1] The nine Protocols which sought to amend the original CARICOM Treaty and Annex are: the Protocol Amending the Treaty Establishing the Caribbean Community Signed At Chaguaramas on 4 July 1973 (adopted 19 Feb 1997, not yet in force) (Protocol I), the Protocol Amending the Treaty Establishing the Caribbean Community (Protocol II: Establishment, Services, Capital) (adopted 1 Jul 1997, not yet in force) (Protocol II), the Protocol Amending the Treaty Establishing the Caribbean Community (Protocol III: Industrial Policy) (adopted 30 Jun 1998, not yet in force) (Protocol III), the Protocol Amending the Treaty Establishing the Caribbean Community (Protocol IV: Trade Policy) (adopted 4–7 Jul 1999, not yet in force) (Protocol IV), the Protocol Amending the Treaty Establishing the Caribbean Community (Protocol V: Agricultural Policy) (adopted 13 Jun 1998, not yet in force) (Protocol V), the Protocol Amending the Treaty Establishing the Caribbean Community (Protocol VI: Transport Policy) (adopted 4–7 Jul 1999, not yet in force) (Protocol VI), the Protocol Amending the Treaty Establishing the Caribbean Community (Protocol VII: Disadvantaged Countries, Regions and Sectors) (adopted 4–7 Jul 1999, not yet in force) (Protocol VII), the Protocol Amending the Treaty Establishing the Caribbean Community (Protocol VIII: Competition Policy, Consumer Protection, Dumping and Subsides) (adopted 13–14 Mar 2000, not yet in force) (Protocol VIII), and the Protocol Amending the Treaty Establishing the Caribbean Community (Protocol IX: Disputes Settlements) (adopted 13–14 Mar 2000, not yet in force) (Protocol IX). All nine protocols were being provisionally applied by those states which declared their intention to do so and are available at <http://www.caricom.org/jsp/secretariat/legal_instruments_index.jsp?menu=secretariat> (accessed 30 Sep 2011).

The Revised Treaty of Chaguaramas Establishing the Caribbean Community, Including the CARICOM Single Market and Economy (adopted 5 Jul 2001, in force 1 Jan 2006) 2259 UNTS 293 (RTC) is supported by the Protocol on the Provisional Application of the Revised Treaty of Chaguaramas (adopted and entered into force 4 Feb 2002) and the Protocol on the Revision of the Treaty of Chaguaramas (adopted 4 Feb 2002, in force 1 Jan 2006). The latter Protocol makes provision for the legal transition from the original Caribbean Community and common market to the new Caribbean Community including the CARICOM Single Market and Economy. This is necessary because the same Protocol terminates the former CARICOM Treaty (Art V) and dissolves the old organization (Art III(d)). Treaty information obtained from: CARICOM Secretariat, 'Matrix of Agreements', Last updated July 2012 (Georgetown, Guyana: CARICOM Secretariat, 2012).

streamline the Treaty.[2] The RTC was applied provisionally from 4 February 2002, until 1 January 2006.[3] It entered into force on the latter date through the operation of the 2005 Agreement to enable the Entry into Force of the Revised Treaty of Chaguaramas Establishing the Caribbean Community including the CARICOM Single Market and Economy.[4] This latter Agreement amended Article 234 of the RTC so as to allow it to enter into force with twelve, rather than fourteen, ratifications in the following terms:

> This Treaty shall enter into force on 1 January 2006 if Instruments of Ratification have been previously deposited by any twelve of the States mentioned in paragraph 1 of Article 3 and if not, then on such later date on which the twelfth such instrument has been deposited.[5]

The Agreement itself entered into force upon signature by the fourteen negotiating states of the RTC on 9 February 2006. Because twelve instruments of ratification had been deposited prior to the date of entry into force of the Agreement, however, the effect of the amended Article 234 was to bring the RTC into force retroactively, as of 1 January 2006.[6] As of September 2013, thirteen CARICOM member states are parties to the RTC, with the remaining two—The Bahamas

[2] For a comparison of the two treaty regimes, see David S Berry, 'The New Caribbean Community: An Introduction to the Institutional Changes in the *Revised Treaty of Chaguaramas*' (2002) 7(1) *Caribbean Law Bulletin* 1–58.

[3] Under the terms of Art 234 of the RTC all fourteen original CARICOM Members (ie, excluding Haiti) were required to ratify the RTC in order for it to come into force. Because it was anticipated that the ratification process might require some time, the Member States created a Protocol on the Provisional Application of the Revised Treaty on Chaguaramas. This Protocol allowed the Revised Treaty to be applied provisionally prior to its entry into force. See Art 25 of the Vienna Convention on the Law of Treaties (adopted 23 May 1969, in force 27 Jan 1980) 1155 UNTS 331 (VCLT). Provisional application arose from the date of entry into force of the Protocol, which was 4 February 2002, for the following Member States: Antigua & Barbuda, Barbados, Belize, Dominica, Grenada, Guyana, Jamaica, St Kitts & Nevis, St Lucia, St Vincent & the Grenadines, Suriname, and Trinidad & Tobago. Thus from February 2002 twelve CARICOM Member States were operating under the Revised Treaty regime, as provisionally applied. Neither The Bahamas nor Montserrat were parties to the Protocol and thus did not provisionally apply the Revised Treaty.

[4] (Adopted 21 December 2005, in force 9 Feb 2006).

[5] ibid.

[6] The general rule under Art 28 of the VCLT is one of non-retroactivity, subject to the intention of the parties. However the intention to bring the RTC into force retroactively may be inferred from the Preamble to the RTC and is confirmed by correspondence from the Office of the General Counsel of CARICOM. The Preamble to the RTC states in part: 'MINDFUL of the imperative necessity that the Revised Treaty enter into force for the definitive operation of the CARICOM Single Market and Economy prior to 1 January 2006' and 'DETERMINED to secure the entry into force of the Revised Treaty by 1 January 2006'. The (then) Assistant General Counsel to the CARICOM Secretariat, Ms Safiya Ali, provided the following clarification on the matter:

> In terms of such intention being 'otherwise established' pursuant to the VCLT, it should be noted that the entry into force of the Revised Treaty was linked to the proposed commencement of the Single Market, scheduled for 1 January 2006 by way of numerous Conference decisions and declarations as well as the timeframe set out in the Programme for the Removal of Restrictions which required all identified restrictions to be removed by 31 December 2005. In the specific contemplation of the proposed Agreement to Enable the Entry into force of the Revised Treaty, the Conference at its Eleventh Special Meeting in December 2005 recognised the need for entry into force by 1 January 2006.

Statement by Safiya Ali, (then) Assistant General Counsel, CARICOM Secretariat (Personal email correspondence 24 Aug 2010).

and Montserrat—retaining CARICOM membership under special bilateral agreements with CARICOM, without becoming parties to the RTC.[7] The RTC is accompanied by the Agreement Establishing the Caribbean Court of Justice.[8] All of the parties to the RTC, except Haiti, are also parties to the Agreement.[9]

3.1.2 Non-party members of CARICOM

The Bahamas and Montserrat have been unable to ratify the RTC for different reasons. Montserrat, as an Overseas Territory of the United Kingdom, cannot ratify the RTC without an Instrument of Entrustment from the United Kingdom. The Bahamas is capable but unwilling, perhaps due to its longstanding reluctance to become fully subject to CARICOM's trade and economic integration obligations. The bilateral Agreements concluded by Montserrat and The Bahamas, respectively, and CARICOM, maintain the 'status quo' with respect to CARICOM in light of their particular circumstances, stating in Article II, respectively, of each Agreement:

> Montserrat shall remain a Member of the Community in accordance with the terms and conditions existing immediately prior to the entry into force of the Revised Treaty notwithstanding that it has not deposited its Instrument of Ratification by the date of entry into force thereof and therefore that the Revised Treaty is not in force for Montserrat. Thereafter, upon receipt of the relevant Instrument of Entrustment and notwithstanding Article 238 of the Revised Treaty, Montserrat shall be entitled to sign and ratify or accede to the Revised Treaty, as the case may be, on the same terms and conditions as the original States Parties.

[7] Haiti acceded to the Revised Treaty on 8 February 2008, bringing the number of parties today up to thirteen Member States: See CARICOM Secretariat, *Matrix of Agreements*, Last updated July 2012 (Georgetown, Guyana: CARICOM Secretariat, 2012). The treaties governing the status of The Bahamas and Montserrat are the Agreement Between the Caribbean Community and the Government of Montserrat (adopted and entered into force 29 Jan 2006) and the Agreement Between the Caribbean Community and the Government of The Bahamas (adopted and entered into force 10 Feb 2006).

[8] (Adopted 14 Feb 2001, entered into force 23 Jul 2002) 2255 UNTS 319.

[9] The following states are parties to the RTC (dates of ratification in brackets): Antigua and Barbuda (17 Feb 2005); Barbados (22 Jul 2002); Belize (27 Nov 2002); Dominica (8 Apr 2003); Grenada (26 Jun 2003); Guyana (23 Jul 2002); Jamaica (9 Jun 2003); St Kitts and Nevis (14 Jan 2004); St. Lucia (5 Jul 2002); St Vincent (17 Mar 2003); Suriname (9 Jun 2003); Trinidad and Tobago (18 Oct 2002). See CARICOM Secretariat, *Matrix of Agreements*, last updated July 2012 (Georgetown, Guyana: CARICOM Secretariat, 2012). With respect to the question of whether the Court can exercise jurisdiction over non-parties to the Agreement Establishing the Caribbean Court of Justice (such as Haiti) on the basis of the RTC alone, Duke E Pollard, at p 41 of *The Caribbean Court of Justice: Closing the Circle of Independence* (Kingston, Jamaica: The Caribbean Law Publishing Company, 2004), has suggested that parties to the RTC are bound to accept the compulsory the jurisdiction of the CCJ even if not they are not parties to the Agreement. Although such a position is technically possible, it would be unlikely for it to be accepted by the CCJ because several important provisions of the Agreement are not reproduced in Chapter 9 of the RTC. These gaps could place unacceptable limitations upon the Court in relation to non-parties to the Agreement. Compare, for example, Art XXVI of the Agreement, mandating contracting parties to take all necessary steps including enactment of legislation so as to allow enforcement of judgments, orders, decrees, or sentences of the Court in their domestic jurisdictions, with the less precise and less far-reaching obligations imposed by Art 224 of the RTC, which stipulates that '[e]ach Member State undertakes to employ its best endeavours to complete the constitutional and legislative procedures required for its participation in the regime establishing the Court as soon as possible.'

The Bahamas shall remain a Member of the Community in accordance with the terms and conditions existing immediately prior to the entry into force of the Revised Treaty. Notwithstanding the foregoing, The Bahamas shall be entitled without more, to sign and ratify or accede to the Revised Treaty on these terms and conditions or any other terms and conditions that may be agreed pursuant to Articles 237 and 238 of the Revised Treaty.[10]

The Bahamas appended a Declaration to its Agreement, which spells out in some detail what it understands to be the meaning of the phrase 'the terms and conditions existing immediately prior to the entry into force of the Revised Treaty'.[11] This Declaration states that The Bahamas understands itself to be a member of the Caribbean Community, a party to Protocol I amending the 1973 Treaty and to nearly twenty regional Agreements on functional cooperation, but not a party to the RTC or Protocol on Provisional Application of the Revised Treaty.[12] The Bahamas also understands itself as participating and being entitled to participate 'as a full member in meetings of the Conference, and relevant Councils, and Bodies of the Community but not in the CSME arrangements', as being a contributor to the Community budget and Caribbean Court of Justice trust fund (as a third party), and as not being subject to either the original or appellate jurisdiction of the CCJ. Further, by its Declaration The Bahamas expressly preserves any reservations or concessions in relation to the CSME or any other part of the RTC or any protocols thereto which exist in any agreements, arrangements, or understandings, and states that it will be entitled to benefit from these understandings if and when it signs the RTC.[13] It is of interest to note, however, that historically The Bahamas attended meetings of the Common Market Council as an observer under the original Treaty of Chaguaramas and so did not fully confine itself to the institutional, non-economic aspects of CARICOM.[14] It is likely that such a pattern of behaviour will continue.[15]

The exact scope of obligations assumed by The Bahamas and Montserrat may need to be clarified in the future, given the substantial differences between the old

[10] Agreement Between the Caribbean Community and the Government of Montserrat (adopted and entered into force 29 Jan 2006), Agreement Between the Caribbean Community and the Government of The Bahamas (adopted and entered into force 10 Feb 2006). Interestingly, despite this limited bilateral arrangement, Montserrat appears to be participating in the free movement of skilled Community nationals regime. Interview with Safiya Ali, General Counsel, CARICOM Secretariat, Georgetown, Guyana (6 Aug 2012).

[11] Attached to the Agreement (n 10).

[12] Protocol amending the Treaty Establishing the Caribbean Community Signed At Chaguaramas on 4 July 1973 (adopted 19 Feb 1997, not yet in force), which amended or replaced CARICOM's organs, voting rules, and related procedures, was being provisionally applied prior to entry into force of the RTC.

[13] Protocol amending the Treaty Establishing the Caribbean Community (n 12).

[14] See Gladstone Mills et al, *Report on a Comprehensive Review of the Programmes, Institutions and Organisations of the Caribbean Community* (Georgetown, Guyana: Caribbean Community Secretariat, 1990) 36 [3.03] and 43. However at p 45 it is noted that The Bahamas was excluded from the Standing Committee of Ministers Responsible for Industry under the original Treaty of Chaguaramas.

[15] The General Counsel of CARICOM noted that although The Bahamas does not vote in decisions of CARICOM related to the CSME under the RTC, it is actively interested in CARICOM matters related to agriculture and trade in agriculture. Interview with Safiya Ali, General Counsel, CARICOM Secretariat, Georgetown, Guyana (6 Aug 2012).

and new treaty regimes and the potential of the CCJ to flesh out the normative values of the Community.[16] But some questions may be deemed to have been settled for both members as a result of the operation of the Protocol on the Revision of the Treaty of Chaguaramas, which terminated the original 1973 Treaty of Chaguaramas and consequently terminated the organs existing under that treaty. As a result, as also noted in the Declaration of The Bahamas, the names and functions of the relevant CARICOM organs, their voting procedures and competences will be the same for all fifteen CARICOM member states, namely, those existing under the RTC.

3.1.3 OECS

The OECS also recently updated its treaty arrangement. The original OECS treaty structure was made up of several parts, including the 1981 Treaty Establishing the Organisation of Eastern Caribbean States ('Treaty'), Annex A (establishing a Conciliation Commission), and the 1968 Annex I—The Agreement Establishing the Eastern Caribbean Common Market ('Annex I').[17] As with CARICOM, the OECS Treaty and Annex I combined two separate treaty regimes, with the Treaty providing the institutional structure and Annex I setting out the trade regime. But since the OECS instruments were created thirteen years apart the Treaty made provision in Article 9 to bring Annex I and its central organ, the Council of Ministers, directly into the OECS Treaty, 'to the extent that [the provisions of Annex I] are not incompatible with the provisions of this Treaty'.[18]

In 2004 the OECS Authority decided to authorize the creation of a new treaty to replace the original one, and mandated a special Technical Committee on Economic Union to proceed with the drafting processes.[19] The outcome was the RTB, which was opened for signature on 18 June 2010, and entered into force on 21 January 2011.[20] All of the independent states of the OECS are parties to the

[16] See eg the Court's elaboration of the legal requirements for consultations under Art 26 of the RTC in the case of *Trinidad Cement Ltd v Caribbean Community*, Judgment, [2009] CCJ 4 (OJ) 10 August 2009.

[17] Treaty Establishing the Organisation of Eastern Caribbean States (adopted 18 Jun 1981, in force 2 Jul 1981) 1338 UNTS 97. See generally PK Menon, 'Sub-Regional Integration in the Caribbean: the OECS Experience' (unpublished paper presented at the 1995 Latin American Studies Association meeting, 28–30 September 1995, on file at the University of the West Indies Faculty of Law Library, Cave Hill Campus).

[18] OECS Treaty, Art 9(4).

[19] OECS Secretariat, 'Communique on the 38th Meeting of the OECS Authority, Castries, 22–23 January 2004', as available through <http://www.oecs.org/doc-lib/communiques> (accessed 20 Sep 2011) at 7–8. See also Dr Len Ishmael, OECS Director General, 'Remarks at the Signing Ceremony of the Revised Treaty of Basseterre Establishing the OECS Economic Union' (18 Jun 2010) as available through <http://www.oecs.org/doc-lib/addresses/cat_view/94-addresses/188-signing-ceremony-for-the-revised-treaty-of-basseterre-establishing-the-oecs> (accessed 20 Sep 2011) 2.

[20] Revised Treaty of Basseterre Establishing the Organisation of Eastern Caribbean States Economic Union (adopted 18 Jun 2010, in force 21 Jan 2011). OECS Secretariat, 'Press Release: OECS Economic Union Launch' (Friday, 21 Jan 2011 14:30) as available at <http://www.oecs.org/regional-integration/press-releases/745-oecs-member-states-achieve-historic-milestone-ahead-of-52nd-authority-meeting-> (accessed 30 Sep 2011); see also the Message by Chairman of OECS, Dr

RTB and have enacted it in domestic law.[21] The Overseas Territories of Anguilla and the British Virgin Islands are participating in OECS meetings. Montserrat, having received the necessary entrustments from the United Kingdom in order to ratify the treaty, and having deposited its instruments of ratification and accession, is also a party to the RTB.[22]

The RTB combines three regimes linked by a single instrument: (1) the Revised Treaty of Basseterre Establishing the Organisation of Eastern Caribbean States Economic Union (2011), (2) the Annex on Settlement of Disputes, and (3) the Protocol of OECS Economic Union. All three documents are formally linked by Article 24.1 of the RTB, which states: 'The Dispute Settlement Annex and the Economic Union Protocol shall form an integral part of this Treaty.'

3.2 Reading the Treaties: Introductory Provisions, Definitions, and Caveats on Cross-References in the RTC

Both the RTC and RTB commence with preambular paragraphs which set out the context of the organization and the treaty. These paragraphs may properly be relied upon to help interpret the meaning of the respective treaties.[23] Both the RTB and RTC also commence with a definitional provision—Article 1—entitled 'Use of Terms', which defines the meanings of the terms set out in the article 'unless the context indicates otherwise'. For the most part the definitions are self-explanatory. However a couple of points should be made in relation to the defined terms in the RTC. Firstly, several of the terms which are central to the CARICOM Single Market and Economy are defined in Article 1, rather than later in the treaty (such as in the particular section where the rule is elaborated). This practice differs from that of many regional and international organizations, which do not include substantive, definitional sections in their constituent treaties.[24] The practical

the Hon Denzil Douglas, 'Operationalisation of OECS Economic Union' (2011-01-24) as available through <http://www.oecs.org/> (accessed 30 Sep 2011) p 1.

[21] OECS Secretariat, 'Communiqué: Fifty-Seventh Meeting of the OECS Authority', posted 5 Jun 2013, as available at <http://www.oecs.org/media-center/press-releases/secretariat/60-authority/751-communiqué-fifty-seventh-meeting-of-the-oecs-authority> (18 Jul 2013).

[22] See eg OECS Secretariat, 'Communiqué: Fifty-Seventh Meeting of the OECS Authority', posted 5 Jun 2013, as available at <http://www.oecs.org/media-center/press-releases/secretariat/60-authority/751-communiqué-fifty-seventh-meeting-of-the-oecs-authority> (18 Jul 2013); OECS Secretariat, 'Communiqué—Fifty-Sixth Meeting of the OECS Authority', Dominica, 22–23 Nov 2012 (issued 25 Nov 2012), as available at <http://www.oecs.org/news-a-events/9-secretariat/856-communique-fifty-sixth-meeting-of-the-oecs-authority> (9 Feb 2013); 'Remarks' by Dr Len Ishmael, Director General, at the Opening Ceremony of the Meeting of Leaders of the Opposition, at Gros Islet, St Lucia, on 4 May 2012 (Castries, St Lucia: OECS Secretariat, May 2012), p 2, as available through <http://www.oecs.org/doc-lib/addresses/cat_view/94-addresses/201-meeting-of-the-leaders-of-the-opposition> (3 Feb 2013).

[23] Art 31(2) of the 1969 VCLT expressly authorizes reference to the treaty 'text, including its preamble and annexes' to establish its context for the purposes of interpretation.

[24] See, for example, the constituent documents of the Organization of American States, the (pre-AU) Organization of African Unity, the European Union, and the United Nations: Charter of the Organization of American States (adopted 30 Apr 1948, in force 13 Dec 1951) 119 UNTS 46, OASTS No 1, as amended,

consequence is that the reader of the RTC must consistently refer back to Article 1 in order to interpret and apply the treaty.

Secondly, as demonstrated by the very first defined term of the RTC, in many cases the cross-referencing of articles in the RTC is incorrect. The definition of 'anti-competitive business conduct' in Article 1 refers to Article 173, which is clearly incorrect. Article 173 sets out the functions of the Competition Commission. The RTC contains numerous mis-linked cross-references of this kind. As a result, the reader must be alert to cross-referencing failures throughout the treaty and, until they have been corrected, must be prepared to engage in painstaking textual archaeology to ascertain which provision the cross-reference was meant to refer to. This archaeological exercise must involve: (1) an initial examination of any similar provisions in the original 1973 Treaty of Chaguaramas, (2) which should be followed by an examination of the relevant Protocol amending that 1973 Treaty, and (3) finally end with a comparison of the RTC articles most similar to those cross-referenced in the 1973 Treaty and subsequent Protocols. For example, the inaccurate cross-reference to Article 173 in the Article 1 definition of 'anti-competitive business conduct' can be corrected by tracing the same defined term to Protocol VIII, which refers to the article entitled 'Prohibition of Anti-Competitive Business Conduct' (Article 30(i)).[25] The provision in the RTC which most closely parallels the latter article is Article 177. Thus Article 177 should be substituted for Article 173 in the definition.

As one can imagine, this will require significant effort on the part of those interpreting and applying the RTC and thus it is hoped that such textual errors may be speedily rectified. However it is unlikely that such faulty cross-referencing will frustrate the operation of the RTC. No member state has yet (publicly) relied upon such errors to avoid obligations, and would most likely be barred from doing so as a result of the obligation to interpret treaties in good faith.[26] In addition, the Caribbean Court of Justice has demonstrated its willingness to 'correct' inadequacies in the RTC by employing the teleological form of interpretation.[27] In this book cross-referencing will be corrected only when necessary when discussing provisions of the RTC.

available at <http://www.oas.org/dil/treaties_ A-41_Charter_of_the_Organization_of_American_States.htm> (accessed 30 Sep 2011); Charter of Organization of African Unity (adopted 25 May 1963, in force 13 Sep 1963) 479 UNTS 39, as available at <http://www.au.int/en/content/oau-charter-addis-ababa-25-may-1963> (accessed 30 Sep 2011); Consolidated versions of the Treaty on European Union and the Treaty on the Functioning of the European Union (OJ C83, 30.3.2010) as available through <http://eur-lex.europa.eu/en/treaties/index.htm> (accessed 30 Sep 2011); Charter of the United Nations (adopted 26 Jun 1945, in force 24 Oct 1945) 1 UNTS xvi, 39 AJIL Supp 190.

Note that the African Union has followed a practice similar to that of CARICOM: Constitutive Act of the African Union (adopted 11 Jul 2000, in force 26 May 2001) as available at <http://www.au.int/en/content/constitutive-act-african-union> (accessed 30 Sep 2011).

[25] Protocol Amending the Treaty Establishing the Caribbean Community (Protocol VIII: Competition Policy, Consumer Protection, Dumping and Subsides) (adopted 13–14 Mar 2000, not yet in force) available at <http://www.caricom.org/jsp/secretariat/legal_instruments_index.jsp?menu=secretariat> (accessed 30 Sep 2011).

[26] See VCLT, Art 31(1).

[27] *Trinidad Cement Ltd and TCL Guyana Inc v Guyana*, Judgment (Jurisdiction) [2009] CCJ 1 (OJ) (2009) 74 WIR 302, 15 January 2009 [38].

3.3 Status of the Organizations: Creation or Continuation

CARICOM and the OECS have taken two different approaches in amending their constituent instruments. CARICOM has replaced the 1973 Treaty with the RTC and in the process has also replaced the organization itself. Article 2 of the RTC makes clear that the present Caribbean Community including the CARICOM Single Market and Economy is the *successor* to the original Caribbean Community and common market. This transition was accomplished by the Protocol on the Revision of the Treaty of Chaguaramas, which entered into force at the same time as the RTC.[28] The Protocol both terminated the original Treaty (Article V) and replaced the former Caribbean Community (Article I). Article I states: 'The Caribbean Community and Common Market shall be succeeded by the Caribbean Community including the CARICOM Single Market and Economy, which shall assume the rights and obligations of the Caribbean Community and Common Market.'[29] Article III of the Protocol requires states parties to enact legislation to give effect to Article I, including by vesting all existing property, rights privileges, and immunities in the new Community and by allowing legal proceedings related to the old Community to continue in relation to the new Community. Article III also requires states parties to enact legislation to dissolve the Caribbean Community and Common Market.

The OECS in contrast has not sought to extinguish its original treaty or organization. Instead it has preserved and continued the OECS and merely replaced the constituent treaty.[30] Even here, however, the replacement is not complete. Article 2.3 of the RTB contemplates the continued application of the original OECS Treaty in the following terms:

> 2.3 Upon the coming into force of this Treaty in respect of a Member State, the provisions of the Treaty of Basseterre 1981 shall cease to apply between that Member State and any other Member State which is a party to this Treaty, except to the extent that this Treaty provides for the continued application of the Treaty of Basseterre 1981.

Such a provision would prove troublesome if it allowed aspects of the original OECS Treaty to continue and potentially conflict with the RTB. However Article 2.3 of the RTB is unlikely to have such an effect and instead may prove relevant only in limited circumstances, such as where a dispute under the original Treaty continues after the entry into force of the RTB.[31]

[28] Protocol on the Revision of the Treaty of Chaguaramas (adopted 4 Feb 2002, in force 1 Jan 2006).
[29] Protocol on the Revision of the Treaty of Chaguaramas (n 28).
[30] RTB Arts 2.1 and 2.2.
[31] RTB Art 18.6 provides:

> 18.6 The provisions of this Article and the Dispute Settlement Annex do not apply to proceedings commenced before the coming into force of this Treaty. Such proceedings shall be governed solely by the provisions of the Treaty of Basseterre 1981, which shall continue to apply in full force until such proceedings are completed or discontinued by the complainant Member State under that Treaty.

See also para 4.6 of the Annex on Settlement of Disputes which continues the terms of office of conciliators.

3.4 Objectives, Purposes, and Functions

In addition to the preambular sections of the treaties establishing CARICOM and the OECS, two other opening articles provide some insight into the respective organization's scope, purposes, and functions: Article 6 of the RTC sets out the objectives of the Caribbean Community, and Article 4 of the RTB sets out the purposes and functions of the OECS. These articles demonstrate that the two organizations have similar purposes, including that of enhancing cooperation between members within and outside of the region in such areas as economic development and trade.

However clear differences exist between the two regional organizations. For example, even though both constituent documents speak to cooperation in the area of foreign policy, the vocabulary is strikingly different. Article 6(h) of the RTC seeks 'enhanced co-ordination of Member States' foreign and [foreign] economic policies' whereas Article 6.1(d) of the RTB encourages the OECS to seek 'the fullest possible harmonisation of foreign policy among the Member States, [and] to seek to adopt wherever possible, common positions on international issues, and to establish and maintain, wherever possible, arrangements for joint overseas representation and common services'. Such differences reveal the OECS' deeper conception of regional integration, one that includes the goal of establishing the OECS' 'Economic Union as a single economic and financial space'. The RTB also highlights the role of the OECS in helping members collectively to defend their 'sovereignty, territorial integrity and independence' and to assist them 'in the realisation of their obligations and responsibilities to the international community with due regard to the role of international law as a standard of conduct in their relationship'.[32] Article 4.2 of the RTB expressly lists a significant number of fields of human activity that the OECS is to take decisions in and in which member states are to 'endeavour to co-ordinate, harmonise and undertake joint actions and pursue joint policies'.[33] This extensive list—covering everything from mutual defence and security, to external transportation and communications, to scientific, technical and cultural cooperation—ends with an open ended section allowing member states to attribute further competences.[34] As discussed later, the need for such an extensive list is at least partly explained by the existence of a provision in the RTB which gives the organization exclusive or pre-emptive legislative competence in a number of fields.[35] In such a context, where the scope of sovereign powers of member states is being limited by the scope of competences of the organization, it would seem helpful to have a more detailed picture of the latter's nature and purpose.

Regardless of these differences, the articles describing the objects and purposes of CARICOM and the OECS will be equally important to the development of

[32] RTB Art 4.1(b)–(c). [33] RTB Art 4.2(a)–(x). [34] RTB Art 4.2(x).
[35] RTB Art 14. See Chapter 6.

both regional organizations. Such provisions, revealing the goals of each organization, will be significant aids for both textual and teleological forms of interpretation, since they flesh out both the context and purpose of the respective organization.

3.5 Membership and Other Forms of Participation

As summarized in Table 3.1, CARICOM has fifteen member states, of which thirteen are parties to the RTC; the OECS has seven member states, of which six are parties to the RTB. Territories which are members of both regional organizations are highlighted with shading.

3.5.1 CARICOM AND OECS membership and treaty status

Table 3.1 Membership and treaty status for CARICOM and OECS

CARICOM	OECS
Antigua and Barbuda	Antigua and Barbuda
The Bahamas (not a party to RTC)	
Barbados	
Belize	
Dominica	Dominica
Grenada	Grenada
Guyana	
Jamaica	
Haiti	
Montserrat (not a party to RTC)	Montserrat
St. Kitts and Nevis	St. Kitts and Nevis
Saint Lucia	Saint Lucia
St. Vincent and the Grenadines	St. Vincent and the Grenadines
Suriname	
Trinidad and Tobago	

3.5.2 CARICOM

There are two general categories of membership under the RTC, namely, those of being a member state and an associate member. Article 1 of the RTC defines 'Member State' as meaning 'a Member State of the Community excluding an Associate Member within the meaning of Article 231'.

Members

Article 3(1) of the RTC lists fourteen of the fifteen member states of the Community: Antigua and Barbuda, The Bahamas, Barbados, Belize, Dominica, Grenada, Guyana, Jamaica, Montserrat, St. Kitts and Nevis, Saint Lucia, St. Vincent and the Grenadines, Suriname, and Trinidad and Tobago. The fifteenth member, Haiti, secured provisional membership in CARICOM on 4 July 1998, became a full member on 3 July 2002, and acceded to the RTC on 8 February 2008.[36] As noted earlier, however, not all fifteen members are parties to the RTC: The Bahamas and Montserrat have maintained the 'status quo' of their membership in CARICOM by means of separate agreements, without becoming parties to the RTC.[37]

Article 3(2) also extends the possibility of future membership in the Community to 'any other State or Territory of the Caribbean Region that is, in the opinion of the Conference, able and willing to exercise the rights and assume the obligations of membership'. The term 'Caribbean Region' although capitalized, is not defined and thus presumably includes any state located in the Caribbean Sea Basin area.

The membership of CARICOM includes independent states and an Overseas Territory of the United Kingdom, Montserrat. The inclusion of a dependent territory as a full Member is unusual for regional organizations and, as noted in Chapter 2, has the effect of removing the RTC from the scope of the 1969 VCLT.

Associate Members

Article 231 of the RTC describes the category of associate membership in CARICOM, a status which is to be granted by the Conference 'on such terms and conditions as [the] Conference thinks fit'. At present CARICOM has five associate members; the British Virgin Islands and the Turks and Caicos joined in July 1991, Anguilla joined in July 1999, the Cayman Islands joined in May 2002, and Bermuda joined in July 2003.[38]

Generally associate membership in regional and international organizations does not entitle the holder to the complete set of rights and privileges available to full members. For example, voting rights do not automatically accrue to associate members.[39] However under Article 231 it is left to the Conference to

[36] CARICOM Secretariat, 'History of the Caribbean Community', as available at <http://www.caricom.org/jsp/community/history.jsp?menu=community> (accessed 3 Oct 2011). CARICOM Secretariat, *Matrix of Agreements*, last updated July 2012 (Georgetown, Guyana: CARICOM Secretariat, 2012). It is of interest to note that Haiti applied as early as 1974, albeit unsuccessfully, for membership in CARICOM: AR Carnegie, 'Commonwealth Caribbean Regionalism' (1979) 33 *Year Book of World Affairs* 180–200, at 189 (note 46).

[37] Agreement Between the Caribbean Community and the Government of Montserrat (adopted and entered into force 29 Jan 2006) and Agreement Between the Caribbean Community and the Government of The Bahamas (adopted and entered into force 10 Feb 2006).

[38] CARICOM Secretariat, 'History of the Caribbean Community', as available at <http://www.caricom.org/jsp/community/history.jsp?menu=community> (accessed 3 Oct 2011). The relationships of these Associate Members with CARICOM are governed by separate bilateral agreements: Agreement between The Caribbean Community and the Government of The British Virgin Islands (adopted and entered into force 2 Jul 1991), Agreement between CARICOM and the Government of the Turks and Caicos Islands (adopted and entered into force 2 Jul 1991), Agreement between the Caribbean Community and the Government of Anguilla (adopted and entered into force 4 Jul 1999), Agreement between the Caribbean Community and the Government of the Cayman Islands (adopted and entered into force 15 May 2002), Agreement between the Caribbean Community and the Government of Bermuda (adopted and entered into force 2 Jul 2003).

[39] Henry Schermers and Niels Blokker, for example, in *International Institutional Law*, 4th edn (Boston: Martinus Nijhoff Publishers, 2003) at p 124, explain that 'Associate membership usually

decide precisely the scope and meaning of such membership, and in doing so the Conference may choose to differentiate between individual associate members, or categories of associate membership. The pre-RTC bilateral Agreements between CARICOM and Anguilla, the Cayman Islands, and Bermuda all exclude the respective territory from voting and being counted for the purposes of voting and quorum in relation to CARICOM organs, and from participating in decisions of the Council for Foreign and Community Relations (COFCOR) and foreign policy generally. However these territories are allowed to attend meetings of organs and subsidiary bodies of the Community and to participate (without voting) in their deliberations.[40] They are also allowed to accede to the Protocol on Privileges and Immunities of the Caribbean Community and other relevant Community instruments, and are required to accept the CARICOM (*laissez-passer*) travel document and to make budgetary contributions.[41]

More developed and less developed countries

Articles 4–5 and Chapter 7 of the RTC establish, and elaborate upon, a distinction between more and less developed countries. Article 4 identifies six members as more developed countries for the purposes of the RTC—The Bahamas, Barbados, Guyana, Jamaica, Suriname, and Trinidad and Tobago. The remaining members are therefore less developed countries—Belize, Dominica, Grenada, Montserrat, St Kitts and Nevis, Saint Lucia, and St Vincent and the Grenadines. Article 5 indicates that the Conference may change this status by means of a simple majority vote.

The consequences of being characterized as a less developed country are elaborated in Chapter 7, which creates 'a special regime for the Less Developed Countries in order to enhance their prospects for successful competition within the Community, and redress, to the extent possible, any negative impact of the establishment of the

entails membership without the right to vote or hold office in the principal organs of the organization.' But see Art IV(2) of the Convention Establishing the Association of Caribbean States (adopted 24 Jul 1994, in force 4 Aug 1995) 1985 UNTS 3, which provides an example of automatic, albeit limited, voting rights to associate members in the following terms:

> Associate Membership shall be open to the States, Countries and Territories of the Caribbean listed in Annex II of this Convention. Associate Members shall have the right to intervene in discussions and vote at meetings of the Ministerial Council and Special Committees on matters which affect them directly, falling within their constitutional competence. The Council shall conclude relationship agreements with the respective State, Country or Territory which agreements shall set out the terms and conditions and the manner in which the Associate Member may participate in, and vote at meetings of the Ministerial Council and Special Committees.

[40] Such participation may even include participation in closed meetings of organs (in caucus), albeit without the right to vote: Interview with Safiya Ali, General Counsel, CARICOM Secretariat, Georgetown, Guyana (6 Aug 2012).

[41] See paragraphs i–vii of the Agreement between the Caribbean Community and the Government of Anguilla (adopted and entered into force 4 Jul 1999), Agreement between the Caribbean Community and the Government of the Cayman Islands (adopted and entered into force 15 May 2002), Agreement between the Caribbean Community and the Government of Bermuda (adopted and entered into force 2 Jul 2003).

CSME'.[42] This regime is part of the broader system of preferences and exemptions for disadvantaged countries, regions, or sectors set out in the chapter and in other provisions of the RTC.[43]

The charitable rationale underlying the more developed/less developed distinction and the regimes established in Chapter 7 is clear. However historically it has been less than successful.[44] It also creates challenges to the potential uniformity of Community law, by creating significant exceptions which allow countries, regions, and sectors to derogate from a number of the important obligations established by the RTC.[45]

Observers

The category of observers is specifically mentioned in the RTC in the context of the functions and powers of the Conference. Under Article 12(10) the Conference is empowered 'to admit at its deliberations as observers representatives of non-Member States of the Community and other entities'.[46] CARICOM maintains a list of accredited third states and their representatives, including countries from nearly every continent and a delegation from the European Union.[47] The other organs of CARICOM are not expressly authorized to admit observers but several have made provision for such in their rules of procedure. Such a practice is also supported historically, since all organs of CARICOM under the original Treaty of Chaguaramas did so.[48] Under Rule 10 COFAP 'may decide to admit to its deliberations as Observers, individuals, representatives of non-Member States, or other organisations'.[49] Likewise the Council for Human and Social Development (COHSOD), or the Chairman acting on behalf of COHSOD, may invite observers under Rule 13.[50] The Council for Trade and Economic Development (COTED), under

[42] RTC Art 142(1).

[43] In addition to the provisions set out in Chapter 7 of the RTC, see Arts 49, 59(4), 77, and 84.

[44] For a summary of criticisms of the similar regime under the original 1973 Treaty see Earl Huntley, 'The LDCs and CARICOM', in Kenneth O Hall (ed), *The Caribbean Community: Beyond Survival* (Kingston, Jamaica: Ian Randle Publishers, 2001) 35–8.

[45] See Chapter 6.

[46] For historical reasons, the University of the West Indies and the OECS Secretariat are invited as observers to Conference meetings: Interview with Safiya Ali, General Counsel, CARICOM Secretariat, Georgetown, Guyana (6 Aug 2012).

[47] As of 9 Nov 2012, the list at the website of the CARICOM Secretariat, 'Plenipotentiary Representatives of Third States Accredited to the Caribbean Community (CARICOM)', as available at <http://www.caricom.org/jsp/community/plenipotentiary_representatives.jsp?menu=community> (accessed 9 Feb 2013) includes the following states and organizations: Argentina, Australia, Austria, Botswana, Brazil, Canada, Chile, Colombia, Cuba, Delegation of the European Union, Finland, France, Germany, India, Italy, Japan, Mexico, Portugal, Singapore, Slovenia, Spain, South Africa, Turkey, United Kingdom, United States of America, and Venezuela.

[48] See Gladstone Mills et al, *Report on a Comprehensive Review of the Programmes, Institutions and Organisations of the Caribbean Community* (Georgetown, Guyana: Caribbean Community Secretariat, 1990) 39 [3.14].

[49] CARICOM Secretariat, 'Rules of Procedure for the Council for Finance and Planning (COFAP)' adopted at the 1st Meeting of COFAP Castries, Saint Lucia, 29 Jun 1998, as available at <http://www.caricom.org/jsp/community_organs/rules_cofap.jsp?menu=cob> (accessed 4 Oct 2011).

[50] CARICOM Secretariat, 'Rules of Procedure for the Council for Human and Social Development (COHSOD)' [no date], as available at <http://www.caricom.org/jsp/community_organs/rules_cohsod.jsp?menu=cob> (accessed 4 Oct 2011).

its Draft Rule 14, makes provision for the invitation of observers but only 'to attend meetings of the Council for specific agenda items'.[51] Such observers may participate in the meetings of the Council for Finance and Planning (COFAP), COHSOD, and COTED, but have no voting rights.[52] The Community Council has not made express provision for observers, but its Rules could be read to allow observers if so decided by the Council: 'All meetings of the Community Council shall be conducted in private unless the Community Council decides otherwise.'[53] Rules of procedure for COFCOR are not publicly available.

The question of observers received scrutiny by the Bureau of the Conference of Heads of Government during its Eleventh Meeting in Grenada in October 1998 and led to the request that the Ministerial Councils re-examine the basis for, and criteria regarding, the granting of observer status.[54] COHSOD reacted at its Second Meeting in November 1998 by deleting several observers from its list.[55]

3.5.3 OECS

Full members

Article 1 of the RTB distinguishes between 'full Members', as set out in Article 3, and 'Members', which term includes associate members. Article 3.1 continues the full membership of the seven entities possessing that status in the original OECS Treaty, namely, the states and territories of: Antigua and Barbuda, The Commonwealth of Dominica, Grenada, Montserrat, St Christopher and Nevis, Saint Lucia, and St Vincent and the Grenadines.

Article 3.3 allows a 'State or Territory in the Caribbean region not party to the Treaty of Basseterre 1981' to become either a full member state or associate member state, in accordance with Article 27. Article 27 allows the OECS Authority to decide questions of membership, and such membership is effective upon receipt of the relevant instrument of accession by the OECS Commission. Since the phrase 'Caribbean region' is not defined in the RTB, all of the states surrounding the Caribbean Sea Basin area potentially could become member states.

[51] Jamaica Information Service, 'CARICOM Member States: Observers at Meetings of the Ministerial Councils of the Caribbean Community', as available at <http://www.jis.gov.jm/special_sections/CARICOMNew/CaricomMemberStates.html> (accessed 5 Oct 2011). Note that in practice there are standing invitations to a number of civil society organizations to attend as observers: Statement by Milton Haughton, (then) Deputy Executive Director, CRFM Secretariat (Personal communication 8 Dec 2011).

[52] Jamaica Information Service, 'CARICOM Member States' (n 51).

[53] Rule 6(1) of the Rules of Procedure of the Community Council of Ministers, adopted at the Second Meeting of the Community Council of Ministers, Guyana, 15–16 May 1998, as available at <http://www.caricom.org/jsp/community_organs/rules_council.jsp?menu=cob&prnf=1> (accessed 4 Oct 2011).

[54] Jamaica Information Service, 'CARICOM Member States: Observers at Meetings of the Ministerial Councils of the Caribbean Community', as available at <http://www.jis.gov.jm/special_sections/CARICOMNew/CaricomMemberStates.html> (accessed 5 Oct 2011).

[55] Jamaica Information Service, 'CARICOM Member States' (n 51).

As with CARICOM, since the membership of the OECS includes an Overseas Territory of the United Kingdom, Montserrat, the RTB does not fall within the full scope of the 1969 VCLT.

Associate members

Article 3.2 of the RTB continues the associate membership status of Anguilla and the British Virgin Islands. Under Article 27 new states or territories can apply to the OECS Authority to become associate members and, if the Authority so decides, their membership is effective upon the receipt of their instrument of accession by the OECS Commission. Both Martinique and Guadeloupe have recently applied for associate membership status.[56] The rights and obligations of new associate members are to be determined by the OECS Authority.[57] Associate members can become parties to the RTB under Article 25.1, and as a result may also become parties to the Protocol, under Article 24.2.[58]

Observers

Observers are specified in Article 20.2 of the RTB, which states that '[t]he Organisation may decide, in accordance with its rules of procedure, to admit as observers at its deliberations representatives of non-Member States or other entities.' No other reference is made to observers in the RTB and its Protocol and thus, as with CARICOM, it is assumed that such matters will be dealt with under the forthcoming rules of procedure of particular organs.[59]

[56] 'Remarks' by Dr Len Ishmael, Director General, at the Opening Ceremony of the Meeting of Leaders of the Opposition, at Gros Islet, St Lucia, on 4 May 2012 (Castries, St Lucia: OECS Secretariat, May 2012) 2, as available through <http://www.oecs.org/doc-lib/addresses/cat_view/94-addresses/201-meeting-of-the-leaders-of-the-opposition> (3 Feb 2013); OECS Secretariat, 'Communiqué—Fifty-Sixth Meeting of the OECS Authority', Dominica, 22–23 Nov 2012 (issued 25 Nov 2012), as available at <http://www.oecs.org/news-a-events/9-secretariat/856-communique-fifty-sixth-meeting-of-the-oecs-authority> (9 Feb 2013).

[57] RTB, Art 3.3.

[58] To date Anguilla, the British Virgin Islands, and Montserrat do not appear to have been able to ratify the RTB, and thus could not be parties to the Protocol. As summarized by the OECS Director General Dr Len Ishmael in her 'Remarks' at the Opening Ceremony of the Meeting of Leaders of the Opposition, at Gros Islet, St Lucia, on 4 May 2012 (Castries, St Lucia: OECS Secretariat, May 2012) at 3–4:

> Montserrat has received [from the UK] the entrustments necessary and is working to secure a date for accession. To this end the Secretariat is engaged with the Premier's office, the Attorney General and the Commissioner designate to provide support to the work which is now required and to engage in a process of sustained public awareness. The same process is being planned for both the BVI and Anguilla.

[59] As indicated in the OECS Secretariat, 'Press Communiqué: Historic Signing by Antigua and Barbuda facilitates deeper OECS Economic Integration' (4 Jan 2011) as available at <http://www.oecs.org/regional-integration/press-releases/742-historic-signing-by-antigua-and-barbuda-facilitates-deeper-oecs-economic-integration> (5 Oct 2011) '[c]onsiderable technical work [has] gone into the implementation process, including the elaboration of the rules of procedure for the various organs of the Organization . . .'.

3.6 Summary

Both CARICOM and the OECS have replaced their original treaties. Although the members and associate members of the two organizations have not changed significantly, the relation of two members of CARICOM to the RTC has become more complex. Neither Montserrat nor The Bahamas has become a party to the RTC. Instead the relation of each to CARICOM is determined by the terms of its particular bilateral agreement with CARICOM, not the text of the RTC. As discussed, this has implications for the competence of both territories to vote in certain areas of CARICOM decision-making, and regarding the rights and obligations they can assume. It is likely that Montserrat will become a party to the RTC soon (given its recent accession to the RTB), but the anomaly caused by the status of The Bahamas may continue indefinitely and will require further legal clarification.

The texts of the two new treaties have been expanded, clarified, and deepened. In interpreting these texts their preambles and definitional sections will be important. However in the case of the RTC the reader must be alert to cross-referencing errors and, as a consequence, also be ready to interpret provisions of the RTC in light of the texts of the original 1973 CARICOM treaty and the relevant amending protocol. The objects and purposes of both organizations have been considerably expanded and deepened, particularly in the case of the OECS. Both treaties therefore support stronger and deeper regional integration movements.

In terms of transition to the new regime, CARICOM has undergone a process of succession under the Protocol on the Revision of the Treaty of Chaguaramas.[60] The Protocol effectively terminated the original treaty and organization and replaced them with the RTC and the new Caribbean Community including the CARICOM Single Market and Economy. The OECS, in contrast, preserved and continued its organizational identity and has instead simply replaced its treaties. Unlike the case of CARICOM, this means that the original OECS treaties continue to exist. They may even need to be relied upon in certain narrow cases.

Both regional organizations have continued to include members and associate members in their organizational structures. Each also retains the possibility of observer participation in most of its organs. CARICOM, however, maintains another sub-division in its membership, classifying some member states as more developed countries and others as less developed countries. The latter are granted special privileges and dispensations under the RTC, and an entire chapter of the treaty—Chapter 7—is dedicated to disadvantaged countries, regions, and sectors. The nature and implications of the exceptions created under this regime are analysed in Chapter 6. No similar permanent distinction is created in the OECS

[60] (Adopted 4 Feb 2002, in force 1 Jan 2006).

context, perhaps because all of the OECS member states would fall under the same category in CARICOM, namely, as being less developed countries. Such distinctions are beneficial to the Caribbean regional integration project, since they recognize and attempt to ameliorate economic and other disadvantages. However, by diminishing the uniformity of obligations in CARICOM, they may lessen the incentives for compliance by more developed countries.

4

Organs—Structure, Competences, and Decision-Making Processes

4.1 Introduction

Both CARICOM and the OECS have transformed their organizational structures with their respective new, revised treaties. They have simplified and substituted organs, clarified competences, and increased the efficiency of decision-making processes by allowing greater use of qualified majority voting procedures for binding decisions.

CARICOM has retained two principal organs, but has dramatically reduced the number of its secondary organs.[1] The Conference of Heads of Government ('Conference') is the principal organ under the RTC; the Community Council of Ministers ('Community Council') is the second highest organ. Below these are four Ministerial Councils. The Caribbean Court of Justice, an important entity connected with the RTC, is not an organ per se.[2] To contrast the earlier and later CARICOM treaty models, one could describe the original 1973 Treaty as following an organizational pattern similar to a national parliament, with numerous Standing Committees and other bodies fulfilling the roles of the various national ministries. The RTC, in contrast, allocates all responsibilities to four second-level organs: COFAP, COTED, COFCOR, and COHSOD.[3] Such changes have greatly streamlined the organization and have the potential to increase its efficiency.

[1] See generally David S Berry, 'The New Caribbean Community: An Introduction to the Institutional Changes in the *Revised Treaty of Chaguaramas*' (2002) 7(1) *Caribbean Law Bulletin* 1–58.

[2] The Caribbean Court of Justice is integral to the RTC, and many of the provisions related to its jurisdiction and competences are set out in Chapter 9 of the RTC. However the choice not to make the Court an organ of CARICOM was intentional. As noted by Duke E Pollard, in *The Caribbean Court of Justice: Closing the Circle of Independence* (Kingston, Jamaica: The Caribbean Law Publishing Company, 2004) at 177:

> [A]lthough the provisions on disputes settlement of the Revised Treaty identifies [sic] the Caribbean Court of Justice as the principal instrument for the judicial settlement of disputes, the Court has not been accorded the status of an organ of the Community. In fact, important political considerations argued persuasively at the material time, against making the Caribbean Court of Justice an organ of the Community [and] thereby subjecting it to the political direction and control of the Conference of Heads of Government, the supreme policy-making organ.

See also at p 183.

[3] See generally CARICOM Secretariat, 'Restructuring of the Organs and Institutions of the Caribbean Community' (Georgetown: CARICOM Secretariat, 26 Aug 1993) p 2.

Nevertheless a 'quasi-Cabinet' structure has re-emerged under the RTC regime at the member state level, with lead responsibility in certain areas having been assigned to specific member states.[4] These responsibilities have been re-defined and re-assigned as circumstances have changed, but at present are allocated as shown in Table 4.1:[5]

Table 4.1 Quasi-cabinet responsibilities of CARICOM member states

Portfolio	Country
Services	Antigua and Barbuda
Tourism (including Land, Cruise, ACP/EU Partnership Agreement provisions etc)	The Bahamas
Single Market and Economy (including Monetary Union)	Barbados
Justice and Governance	Belize
Labour (including intra-Community Movement of Skills)	Dominica
Science and Technology (including Information and Communications)	Grenada
Agriculture, Agricultural Diversification and Food Security (including the Regional Transformation Programme (RTP) and Bananas)	Guyana
External Trade Negotiations	Jamaica
Human Resource Development, Health, and HIV/AIDS	St Kitts and Nevis
Sustainable Development (including Environment and Disaster Management and Water)	Saint Lucia
Transport (Maritime and Aviation)	St Vincent and the Grenadines
Community Development and Cultural Cooperation (including Culture, Gender, Youth, and Sport)	Suriname
Energy	Trinidad and Tobago
Security (Drugs and Illicit Arms)	

The OECS has likewise retained two top-level organs, although the second highest organ differs under the RTB and its Protocol. The former is served by the Council of Ministers and the latter by the Economic Affairs Council. The OECS has also replaced the committee structure of its secondary organs with one more closely reflecting the different interests of the citizens (the OECS Assembly), their countries (the Council of Ministers and the Economic Affairs Council), and the regional organization itself (the OECS Commission). Such changes have the potential to increase the efficiency and representational capacity of the organization. Additionally, the OECS has limited the powers of all of its organs to those

4 CARICOM Secretariat, 'Regional Portfolios of CARICOM Heads of Government', as available at <http://www.caricom.org/jsp/community/regional_portfolios.jsp?menu=community> (accessed 10 Feb 2013).

5 Information as available from CARICOM Secretariat (n 4).

conferred upon them by the RTB.[6] Such a limitation is known as the principle of conferral or attributed powers in the law of the European Union, the ramifications of which will be discussed later.[7]

4.2 Primary Organs

4.2.1 CARICOM Conference of Heads of Government

Nature and competences

The Conference of Heads of Government is described in Article 12 as being the 'supreme Organ of the Community'. It is composed of the Heads of Government of the member states, or their alternates, and serves the role of determining and providing policy direction.[8] The Conference is the ultimate authority for all financial decisions and treaty obligations and is empowered to establish new 'Organs or Bodies'.[9] It may act as a dispute settlement body under Article 12(8), specifically to deal with disputes between member states. In addition, the Conference may consult with 'entities within the Caribbean Region or with other organisations' and may admit observers at its deliberations.[10] Article 230 gives the Conference the power to designate any organ or body to negotiate agreements on behalf of the Community, and it 'may delegate to the Secretary General the conclusion of agreements, particularly technical assistance agreements, on behalf of the Community'. Moreover, the Conference may be granted further powers, without the requirement for treaty amendment. Article 12(5) specifies that '[s]ubject to the relevant provisions of this Treaty, the Conference shall exercise such powers as may be conferred on it by or under any instrument elaborated by or under the auspices of the Community.'

[6] RTB Art 7.2 provides:

> 7.2 The Organs of the Organisation shall perform the functions and act within the limits of the powers conferred upon them by or under this Treaty and by the Dispute Settlement Annex and the Economic Union Protocol.

[7] See further the discussion in Chapter 8. Art 5.2 of the Treaty on European Union provides:

> 2. Under the principle of conferral, the Union shall act only within the limits of the competences conferred upon it by the Member States in the Treaties to attain the objectives set out therein. Competences not conferred upon the Union in the Treaties remain with the Member States.

Consolidated versions of the Treaty on European Union and the Treaty on the Functioning of the European Union (OJ C 83, 30.3.2010) as available through <http://eur-lex.europa.eu/en/treaties/index.htm> (accessed 30 Sep 2011).

[8] RTC Arts 11 and 12.

[9] RTC Art 12(3)–(4) and (6). Note that the latter power represents an increase over that provided by the original Treaty and Protocol I. Compare Art 12(6) of the Revised Treaty (Organs and Bodies) with Art 8(2) of the original Treaty (institutions) and Art 7(a)(6) of Protocol I (Organs).

[10] RTC Art 12(9)–(10).

Decision-making

Article 27 of the RTC sets out the common voting rules for all organs, and Article 28 sets out those specifically applicable to the Conference. Under these rules, subject to Article 27(2), each member state has one vote and a simple majority of member states constitutes a quorum.[11] For these purposes the membership of the Community must include all fifteen member states, not just the states parties to the RTC.[12] Article 27(2) sets out the exception to the 'one vote' rule, by excluding member states who fall into two years' arrears in their budget contributions. Such states shall not have the right to vote 'except on matters relating to the CSME', unless the Conference is satisfied that the budgetary failure is due to conditions beyond their control. If the latter is the case, they will be permitted to vote. In addition, Article 27(2) provides that even if a state is not entitled to vote it may 'otherwise participate in the deliberations of Community Organs and Bodies'.

The Conference may make two types of decisions—procedural and substantive—and both are binding.[13] Article 27(3) provides that procedural issues are to be decided by a simple majority. No guidance, however, is provided on which issues are to be considered procedural. In deciding such questions, it is submitted that the question of classification should be decided by a non-procedural voting majority under Article 28. In other words, if an issue is argued to be procedural, the question of its characterization should itself be treated as a substantive question requiring adherence to the voting rules set out in Article 28.

Under Article 28(1), unless otherwise provided, substantive decisions of the Conference require an affirmative vote of all of its members. Such a provision would appear to create a unanimous voting requirement. However other provisions modify this unanimity rule to such an extent that it would be preferable to call the Conference's substantive voting pattern a 'qualified unanimity' one. It is qualified by Article 28(2), which allows abstentions, and Article 28(3), which allows omissions, so long as three-quarters of the member states vote in favour of the decision. The effect of these latter two subsections is that a binding decision of the Conference can be taken by a three-quarters majority of the member states even if the remainder do not vote affirmatively. It must be noted, however, that if one member state casts a negative vote, or veto, the decision cannot pass. The Conference's unanimity voting requirement is qualified also by Article 28(4) which excludes parties to a dispute or against which sanctions are being considered from voting on that matter. This provision could be used to exclude more than one member state. Finally, the Conference may make substantive decisions in specific areas under other voting rules. Article 5, for example, allows the Conference by a

[11] RTC Art 27(1).

[12] The term 'Member State' is defined in Art 1 as meaning 'a Member State of the Community...'. The definition does not refer to states parties to the RTC. As a result the term 'Member State' can be deemed to include all fifteen members of the Caribbean Community, including those not parties to the RTC. See the discussion of the status of The Bahamas and Montserrat in Chapter 3. Neither territory is a party to the RTC but both remain members of the Caribbean Community.

[13] RTC Art 28(1).

majority decision to modify the status of a member state from more developed to less developed country, or vice versa.

These represent the formal decision-making rules for the Conference. But informal practices, such as consensus voting, tend to be frequently applied. These practices include what officers of the CARICOM Secretariat have termed the 'consensus procedure'.[14] Under this procedure when officials from member states encounter a particularly divisive problem or issue, they seek to resolve the matter informally and privately so as to arrive at a consensus. Such consensus-building is also used when votes are taken in the absence of the representative of a particular member state. In such a case information about the content of the proposed decision is sent to the state that was not present so as to obtain its feedback on the matter. This latter process could be termed a kind of 'paper consensus' and, as discussed later, is similar to the decision-making processes utilized by the OECS under the RTB.[15] Interestingly, consensus processes were not codified in the RTC and remain purely informal in nature. Perhaps a reason for their not being included was that their formalization would be viewed as politically unpalatable, since consensus processes limit the ability of each state to unreservedly register its vote for or against a decision at a meeting, and to have that matter thereby recorded and definitely determined.

Another aspect of Conference decision-making processes, one that has drawn some criticism, is the 'closed door' nature of the meetings. Although some public events are held, most Conference decisions appear to be made behind closed doors in caucus, by Heads of Government either alone or accompanied by a few officials.[16] This practice has been strongly criticized by Stoneman, Pollard, and Inniss in their 2012 Report for being both wasteful and inefficient.[17] They argue that closed door decision-making results in the exclusion of key officials of member states from decisions (since they are made in caucus) even though those same officials are required to be in attendance for the duration of Conference gatherings. In a region with limited human and financial resources such criticisms have bite.

The Conference may also make recommendations. Under Article 27(6) recommendations shall be made by a two-thirds majority and are not legally binding. Despite being non-binding, Article 27(6) imposes a duty on a member state that does not comply with the recommendation to inform the Secretariat in writing within six months stating the reasons for its non-compliance. Presumably this latter requirement is meant to prompt member states to provide reasonable justifications for their non-compliance, and embarrass those that can provide none.

14 Interview with Duke Pollard, Thelma Rodney-Edwards, and Michelle Walker at CARICOM Secretariat, Georgetown, Guyana (10 Dec 1998). See also Duke E Pollard, 'Approaches to Regional Governance in the Caribbean Community', in Richard Stoneman, Justice Duke Pollard, and Hugo Inniss, 'Turning Around CARICOM: Proposals to Restructure the Secretariat', Landell Mills Ltd/ Final Report/January 2012, as available at <http://www.caricom.org/jsp/communications/caricom_online_pubs/Restructuring%20the%20Secretariat%20-%20Landell%20Mills%20Final%20Report.pdf> (9 Feb 2013) at 121 (Appendix 3).

15 See eg Art 8.5 of the RTB.

16 See eg Stoneman, Pollard, and Inniss, 'Turning Around CARICOM' (n 14) pp 40–1.

17 Stoneman, Pollard, and Inniss, 'Turning Around CARICOM' (n 14) pp 40–1.

Interestingly, a consequence of the phrase 'shall inform' in Article 27(6), is that although there is no obligation to comply with the recommendation, there is a binding obligation to inform the Secretariat of the reason for non-compliance. In other words, non-compliance per se would not involve a breach of the RTC, but not providing a reason for such non-compliance would amount to a breach.

Under Article 12(7) the Conference also is empowered to 'issue policy directives of a general or special character to other Organs and Bodies of the Community concerning the policies to be pursued for the achievement of the objectives of the Community and effect shall be given to such directives'. The voting requirements for such policy directives are not specified in the treaty, nor does the RTC state definitively that they are binding in nature. However the use of the mandatory phrase 'effect shall be given' in Article 12(7) suggests that they are binding, at least as to result, upon other organs or bodies. This would follow if the voting procedure used is the same one that is used for substantive decisions under Article 28. If such were the case, then there would be no reason not to consider policy directives equivalent to a decision and therefore binding. If, however, a simple majority voting procedure was used to make a policy directive, a much stronger reliance would have to be placed upon the mandatory phrasing of Article 12(7) to justify any binding effect on the part of those directives. For such reasons if the Conference wishes to issue a binding policy directive, it should use the normal voting procedures for decisions set out in Article 28.

The Conference also is empowered under Article 27(4) to allow a member state to opt out of obligations arising from the decisions of competent organs 'provided that the fundamental objectives of the Community, as laid down in the Treaty, are not prejudiced thereby'. Such an 'opt out' is subject to the agreement of the Conference, although Article 27(4) does not elaborate upon the nature of the 'agreement'. Since an 'opt out' might involve a substantial derogation from a member state's obligations under the RTC framework, the agreement of the Conference should be reflected in a formal decision, taken under Article 28. If so, the derogation would have the approval, or at least acquiescence, of all member states.

One possible example of an agreed opt-out exists in relation to the 2009 decision of the Conference to expand the scope of CARICOM Skilled Nationals to include household domestics. In response to concerns by Antigua and Barbuda the Conference is reported to have agreed to a five-year derogation in the following terms:

> Also agreed in light of the above, that the Conference will grant Antigua and Barbuda a five-year derogation on the free movement of the new category—domestics—agreed upon during this Thirtieth Meeting of the Conference of Heads of Government in order for that Member State to make the necessary adjustments to its infrastructure and other imperatives to facilitate the fulfillment of its Treaty obligations with respect to free movement of skills[.][18]

18 As reported on the Official Website for the Government of Antigua and Barbuda, 'Antigua and Barbuda Received Five Year Derogation from Expansion of Free Movement of Persons' (posted 8 Jul 2009), as available at <http://www.ab.gov.ag/article_details.php?id=50&category=34> (17 Mar 2013). Interestingly, no mention is made of this derogation in the official Communique issued at

This derogation would have allowed Antigua and Barbuda to vote in favour of the Conference decision, without facing any obligations for a period of five years.

Another potential example of the exercise of an 'opt out' arose in *Shanique Myrie v Barbados*.[19] In that case the CCJ closely examined the wording of a 2007 decision of the Conference, which stated:

> THE CONFERENCE
>
> **AGREED** that all CARICOM nationals should be entitled to an automatic stay of six months upon arrival in order to enhance their sense that they belong to, and can move in the Caribbean Community, subject to the rights of Member States to refuse undesirable persons entry and to prevent persons from becoming a charge on public funds.
>
> **NOTED** the reservation entered by **Antigua and Barbuda** in this regard.[20]

The Court rejected arguments that the decision had not been validly made as a result of either its wording or the reservation of Antigua and Barbuda. The CCJ held that use of the word 'agreed' rather than 'decided' was of no consequence, that the Antiguan reservation was not intended to amount to a veto, and that subsequent practice of member states and organs of CARICOM treated the decision as valid and binding.[21] With respect to whether the reservation by Antigua and Barbuda constituted an opt out, the Court simply denied that such a question was relevant to the validity of the decision. The CCJ held that '[t]he position of Antigua and Barbuda is not at stake in this case and any possible difficulties as to the position of that particular State will have to be decided if and when those issues come before the Court.'[22]

This reliance upon judicial economy by the Court is far from helpful. It is not clear how a reservation can be applied to the entire content of a decision by an organ of a regional organization without constituting a negative vote. It is also not clear what effect a reservation has upon a decision, or the obligations of the reserving state and the other states.[23] If the Court had classified the position of Antigua and Barbuda as falling under the category of an opt out under Article 27(4), all aspects of the decision could have been located within the four corners of the RTC.

The 'opt out' established by Article 27(4) must be recognized as a significant innovation of the RTC related to decision-making. It allows states not to accept any obligations created by a decision of any organ of CARICOM which they do not favour. It will likely have two consequences. On the one hand it should allow

the end of the meeting: CARICOM Secretariat, 'Press release 270/2009 (4 Jul 2009): Communique Issued at the Conclusion of the Thirtieth Regular Meeting of the Conference of Heads of Government of the Caribbean Community, 2–5 July 2009, Georgetown, Guyana', as available at <http://www.caricom.org/jsp/pressreleases/pres270_09.jsp> (17 Mar 2013).

19 Judgment [2013] CCJ 3 (OJ).

20 *Shanique Myrie v Barbados* (n 19) [43] (emphasis in original).

21 *Shanique Myrie v Barbados* (n 19) [46]–[47].

22 *Shanique Myrie v Barbados* (n 19) [48].

23 Reliance upon the rules on reservations of the Vienna Convention on the Law of Treaties (adopted 23 May 1969, in force 27 Jan 1980) 1155 UNTS 331 (VCLT), by analogy, would not be particularly helpful here. In the case of the decision discussed in the *Myrie* case the reservation was to the *entire* decision, not to a particular provision of a treaty imposing a number of obligations. See eg VCLT, Arts 19–23.

Community organs to make a greater number of decisions, since member states will be able to opt out of, rather than veto, decisions to which they do not wish to be bound. On the other hand, extensive use of Article 27(4) would erode the uniformity of Caribbean Community obligations. By 'opting out', different member states would assume different obligations and such disparities would create a 'variable geometry' of Community obligations.[24] A variable geometry of obligations need not be harmful to the Caribbean Community, and different levels of commitment already are enshrined in such distinctions at those between less developed and more developed countries, described earlier.[25] Nevertheless, if the 'opt out' option is used frequently it will add significantly to the complexity of the Community and may have the effect of generally decreasing the will of all member states to accept obligations.

The Bureau

Under the RTC the Conference gained the assistance of a new Committee, called the Bureau. The Bureau, described in Article 12(11), is made up of 'the current Chairman and the immediately outgoing and incoming Chairmen of the Conference'. It plays the general role of assisting the Conference in its relations with member states and other organs of CARICOM, such as the Secretariat, and initiates proposals for development by the Ministerial Councils. Similar to the Troika of the Council of the European Union, the Bureau ensures consistency in decision-making by bringing past, present, and future Chairs together and by meeting with greater frequency than the principal organ.

The functions that may be delegated to the Bureau by the Conference include initiating proposals for development and approval by the Ministerial Councils, updating the consensus of the member states on issues, facilitating implementation of Community decisions, and providing guidance to the Secretariat on policy issues.[26] The first of these functions, initiating proposals, could serve as the basis for later legal acts by the Community and thus can be considered part of the general Community 'legislative' processes.

The Bureau was the compromise accepted by the drafters of the RTC when it became clear that CARICOM member states were unable to accept the recommendation of the West Indian Commission for the establishment of a

[24] The concept of a 'variable geometry' of legal obligations is one that has developed in EU law. Paul Craig and Gráinne de Búrca, in *EU Law: Text, Cases and Materials*, 5th edn (Oxford: Oxford University Press, 2011) at 16, note that the 'variable geometry' introduced by the Maastrict TEU 'was not a temporary feature of European integration', and that its advantages in the EU context outweigh its disadvantages:

> While the disadvantages of variable geometry may be a perceived lack of unity and increasing fragmentation (the dangers of '*á la carte*' integration) the advantages of providing a means for accommodating difference and reaching consensus in the face of strong divergence, for permitting progress in crucial areas such as EMU or foreign policy which might otherwise be deadlocked, are evidently considered sufficient to outweigh the former. [Citations omitted.]

[25] On the LDC/MDC distinction and its consequences for uniformity of Community obligations see, respectively, Chapters 3 and 6.

[26] See RTC Art 12(11)(a)–(d).

'CARICOM Commission', modelled on the European Commission.[27] Clearly the Bureau has more limited powers than the European Commission. Whether it will prove as integral to the Caribbean integration movement as perhaps a slightly more similar EU organ, the Committee of Permanent Representatives (COREPER), is uncertain.[28]

4.2.2 OECS Authority of Heads of Government

Nature and competences

The Authority of Heads of Government of the member states ('Authority') is the supreme policy-making organ, responsible for the overall guidance of the Organisation, final decisions on financial matters, and the conclusion of treaties and international agreements on the Organisation's behalf.[29] As part of its power over finances the Authority is responsible for the budget.[30] It comprises the Heads of Government of member states, or Ministers designated as alternates, led by a Chairman, who is rotated annually in accordance with the principle of alphabetical order of member states (except where otherwise agreed).[31] Participation in the deliberations of the Authority, however, is restricted. Article 8.3 states that '[o]nly Member States possessing the necessary competence in respect of matters under consideration from time to time shall take part in the deliberations of the OECS Authority.' This restriction is seen in relation to other organs of the OECS, and may in part have been necessitated by the foreign affairs limitations encumbering its non-independent member, Montserrat. The Authority meets at least twice a year, but may convene additional extraordinary sessions as necessary.[32] Under Article 7.2 of the RTB the Authority has been given the role of approving proposals of organs to establish new, subsidiary organs, and under Article 8.12 the Authority itself may establish such organs. The Authority is also limited by Article 7.2, which requires that the Authority and other organs of the OECS 'perform the functions and act within the limits of the powers conferred upon them by or under this Treaty and by the Dispute Settlement Annex and the Economic Union Protocol'. This latter limitation is similar to the principle of conferral under European Union law, and is discussed later.[33]

[27] Report of the West Indian Commission, *Time for Action* 2002 (Kingston, Jamaica: The Press—the University of the West Indies, 1993) ch 12. See also, Pollard, 'Approaches to Regional Governance in the Caribbean Community' (n 14) at 119 (Appendix 3).

[28] On the nature and role of the COREPER, see eg TC Hartley, *The Foundations of European Union Law*, 7th edn (Oxford: Oxford University Press, 2010) 24, Paul Craig and Gráinne de Búrca, in *EU Law: Text, Cases and Materials*, 5th edn (Oxford: Oxford University Press, 2011) 43–4.

[29] RTB Art 8.4, 8.13–8.14.

[30] RTB Art 17.

[31] RTB Art 8.1–8.2 and 8.15.

[32] RTB Art 8.15–8.16.

[33] See Chapter 8. See also TEU Art 5.2.

Decision-making

The Authority has the power to make decisions, recommendations, and directives and to enact Acts of the OECS.[34] Decisions of the OECS Authority are achieved under a 'qualified unanimity' system similar to that of CARICOM's Conference. As stipulated in Article 8.5, all substantive decisions, unless otherwise provided for in the RTB, require an affirmative vote of all full member states present and voting, 'provided that such decisions shall have no force and effect until the Heads of Government of those full Member States, if any, which were not present at that meeting, have within the consideration periods expressed either support for, or abstention in relation to, the decision'. The consideration period for those full member states not present is thirty days from the receipt of notice of the decision by the OECS Commission. The lack of a response to such notice by the relevant Head of Government within this time period is deemed to be an abstention and will not impair the decision.[35]

Decisions can be made, however, without requiring the participation of all full members in four cases. The first is a decision involving an area in which a member state does not possess the necessary competence to participate in the deliberations of the Authority, as specified in Article 8.3. Such a decision would exclude the relevant member state. The second is where the Authority is taking a decision in relation to the Economic Union Protocol, which decision only requires the affirmative votes of full member states which are parties to that Protocol.[36] The third is where a full member state is in arrears in the payment of its financial contributions to the Organisation in an amount equal to or exceeding that due from it for the preceding full year.[37] In such a case, unless a majority of the other member states of the OECS Authority permits the member state in arrears to vote, the full member state in arrears 'shall be deemed to be abstaining, and shall not be considered as present and voting, in all votes on matters falling for the OECS Authority's decision'.[38] The final category is that of decisions on procedural matters. Procedural decisions only require a simple majority of all full member states present and voting. The question of whether a decision is procedural in nature is determined by a normal qualified unanimity vote.[39] All decisions of the Authority are 'binding on all Member States and on all Organs of the Organisation and effect shall be given to any such decisions provided that it is within the sovereign competence of Member States to implement them'.[40] The latter phrase is notable and was no doubt meant to deal with the situation of Montserrat. Montserrat is eligible for full membership status under Article 3.1 of the RTB, but as an Overseas Territory does not possess full competence in relation to foreign affairs. However because Article 8.8 does not limit itself to Overseas Territories it would be possible for any member state to raise issues related to competence as a grounds for non-implementation of a decision. Whether any state would do so remains doubtful given the political ramifications of such a position.

[34] RTB Art 8.5, 8.10–8.11. [35] RTB Art 8.5. [36] RTB Art 8.9(a).
[37] RTB Art 8.9(b). [38] RTB Art 8.9(b). [39] RTB Art 8.6–8.7. [40] RTB Art 8.8.

The OECS Authority's powers in relation to recommendations and directives are set out in Article 8.11, which describes their scope and function as follows:

> 8.11 The OECS Authority may make such recommendations and give such directives as it deems necessary for the achievement of the purposes of the Organisation and for ensuring the smooth functioning of the Organs of the Organisation. In particular, the OECS Authority may give directives to and reverse any decision of another Organ or any officer of the Organisation, without prejudice to rights which may have accrued prior to giving such directives or reversing such decision.

This provision is silent on several features of the Authority's recommendations and directives, including the voting rules required for each and whether either is binding in nature. Neither is expressly stated to be binding. Recommendations need not be considered as binding unless such an intention is expressly or implicitly established in the text of the treaty. No such intention is manifest in relation to recommendations of the OECS Authority, the OECS Council of Ministers, or the OECS Commission and therefore these generally should not be considered binding.

Directives, however, may be deemed to have a binding quality when used by the Authority to reverse a decision of another Organ or officer of the Organisation. The term 'reverse' used in Article 8.11 must have the legal effect of quashing the relevant decision, since the Article goes on to make provision to protect any rights which may have existed prior to the Authority's directive. Whether directives made in relation to other matters will have a similar binding effect will depend upon the wording of the directive, the intention of the Authority, and the voting procedure used to make the directive.

The RTB also does not establish voting rules in relation to directives and therefore the Authority will have to decide upon such rules in its future practice or rules of procedure. If in creating a directive the Authority uses the same qualified unanimity vote required for a decision, then the directive should be seen to be equally binding. If, in contrast, a directive were created using a simple majority voting procedure, it should not be considered binding (unless it falls under Article 8.11). In relation to recommendations, the RTB does not set out the applicable voting rules for most of the organs of the OECS which it empowers to make recommendations, including the Authority, the Council of Ministers, and the Commission.[41] It does provide voting rules for recommendations for the Conciliation Commission, as described in the Dispute Settlement Annex (DSA), and for the Economic Affairs Council, under the Protocol of Eastern Caribbean Economic Union (Protocol), but even in such cases the practice is not uniform.[42] As with directives, the Authority and other organs of the OECS will need to establish the voting requirements for recommendations, either in their practice or rules of procedure. Also, as with directives, it is submitted that if the voting rule which is established for recommendations

[41] See RTB Arts 8.11, 9.2, 12.5(c), and 15.4.

[42] See the DSA [4.8], and Protocol Arts 11.6, 28.4, 30.3, and 32.3.

is the same qualified unanimity that is required for the Authority's decisions, recommendations should yield a binding result. In contrast, if a lesser voting majority is utilized, such as a simple majority, such recommendations should not be considered binding.

4.3 Secondary Organs

4.3.1 CARICOM Community Council of Ministers

The RTC replaced the original Treaty's secondary organ, the Common Market Council, with a combination of two new organs, the Community Council of Ministers and the Council for Trade and Economic Development.

Nature and competences

The Community Council of Ministers ('Community Council') is described in Article 10(1)(b) as being the 'second highest organ'. Its membership, as stated under Article 13(1), consists of 'Ministers responsible for Community Affairs *and* any other Minister designated by the Member States in their absolute discretion'.[43] Two things should be noted about the composition of this organ. Firstly, the use of the word 'and' rather than 'or' in Article 13(1) could be read to allow member states to send two representatives to meetings of the Community Council. Such a reading is not to be preferred since it would make Community Council meetings unwieldy.[44] The Rules of Procedure of the Community Council suggest that only one representative will be permitted to attend meetings, except for the member state whose representative is serving as the Chairman.[45] Secondly, Article 13(1) implies that member states should establish national Ministers or Ministries of Community Affairs. Such an approach would allow a national authority in each member state to become the specific focal point for CARICOM matters. When first conceived—in Article VI of Protocol I Amending the Treaty Establishing the Caribbean Community in 1997—this formulation was an advance upon the

[43] Emphasis added.

[44] The practice has been for states to send only one representative: Interview with Safiya Ali, General Counsel, CARICOM Secretariat, Georgetown, Guyana (6 Aug 2012).

[45] Rule 11(2) of the Rules of Procedure of the Community Council of Ministers, adopted at the Second Meeting of the Community Council of Ministers, Guyana, 15–16 May 1998, as available at <http://www.caricom.org/jsp/community_organs/rules_council.jsp?menu=cob> (accessed 6 Oct 2011) is phrased in the singular. For convenience, Rule 11 states:

1. Each Member State shall be represented at meetings of the Community Council by Ministers duly designated by that State save that where a Member State provides the Chairman or acting Chairman of the meeting, that Member State may nominate another member of the delegation to act as the designated representative.
2. If the Minister designated under paragraph 1 of this Rule is unable to attend a meeting of the Community Council, the Member State or the designated Minister, as the case may be, may nominate another member of the delegation to represent the Minister.

European Union position.[46] The function of a Minister of Community Affairs is to be generally responsible for promoting and helping to implement CARICOM matters within the domestic jurisdiction of the Minister's state, and to coordinate and present that state's position at CARICOM organs.[47] As of 2011 not all CARICOM member states appear to have created such Ministries, and this may reflect the human resource constraints and other challenges faced by small states.[48]

The Community Council, under the policy direction of the Conference, has 'primary responsibility for the development of Community strategic planning and co-ordination in the areas of economic integration, functional co-operation and external relations'.[49] To differentiate it from the Conference, the Community Council is responsible for the operational or functional aspects of CARICOM (its day-to-day running and resource prioritization), whereas the Conference is responsible for the Community's overall policy direction and overarching goals.[50]

In fulfilling its functions the Community Council acts as a supervisory body for the four Ministerial Councils. It is responsible for approving or amending existing proposals, or suggesting new proposals to be generated by the Ministerial Councils, subject to the limitation that it may only modify such proposals 'to the extent and in the manner agreed with the originating Organ'.[51] This latter restriction helps ensure inter-organ cooperation, an increasingly common goal in regional organizations.[52] It prevents the Community Council from dictating its views in place of those of the more specialized organ that has developed the proposal, and which should thereby have greater knowledge of all of the relevant factors that shaped it.

The several functions of the Community Council are listed in Article 13(4) and include mobilizing resources for the implementation of Community plans

[46] At that time EU states had not yet managed to unify EU responsibilities under one portfolio. See Ben Soetendorp and Kenneth Hanf, 'Small States and the Europeanisation of Public Policy' and 'Conclusion: The Nature of National Adaptation to European Integration', in *Adapting to European Integration: Small States and the European Union*, ed K Hanf and B Soetendorp (London: Longman, 1998) 1–13 and 186–94. One of the conclusions of these authors was that in Europe small states had not dramatically changed their governmental structure so as to unify EU responsibilities with, for example, EU Ministries.

[47] CARICOM Secretariat, 'Restructuring of the Organs and Institutions of the Caribbean Community' (26 Aug 1993), p 20.

[48] The following states are listed on the CARICOM Secretariat, 'Free Movement in the CARICOM Single Market and Economy (CSME)' as available at <http://www.caricom.org/jsp/single_market/skill.jsp?menu=csme> (accessed 6 Oct 2011) as having a 'Ministry responsible for Caribbean Community Affairs': Grenada, Guyana, St Lucia, and Trinidad and Tobago.

[49] RTC Art 13(2).

[50] Note, however, the harsh criticisms of Richard Stoneman, Justice Duke Pollard, and Hugo Inniss in their report, 'Turning Around CARICOM' (n 14) at 21–2. The authors blame the Community Council for not fulfilling its functions of strategic planning and coordination, and instead describe it as a mere filter for the Conference.

[51] RTC Arts 13(3) and 20(5).

[52] See eg Art 13(2) of the Treaty on European Union which provides that '[t]he institutions shall practice mutual sincere cooperation' and Art 294 Treaty on the Functioning of the European Union which sets out the ordinary legislative procedure, one which requires extensive inter-institutional cooperation. Consolidated versions of the Treaty on European Union and the Treaty on the Functioning of the European Union (OJ C83, 30.3.2010) as available through <http://eur-lex.europa.eu/en/treaties/index.htm> (accessed 30 Sep 2011).

and programmes and then monitoring those regional and national implementation processes. Such coordinating and supervisory functions are essential to the development of the Community and follow the recommendations of the 1990 Mills Report.[53] The Community Council also has been entrusted with the overall task of ensuring 'the efficient operation and orderly development of the CSME, particularly by seeking to resolve problems arising out of its functioning, taking into account the work and decisions of COTED'.[54]

Some of the powers and responsibilities set out in Article 13(4) would seem to overlap with those of the Conference or other organs. But the Community Council's role may be distinguished. For example, Article 13(4)(e) makes the Community Council into a 'preparatory body for meetings of the Conference'. This function might seem to overlap with that of the Bureau, which as we have seen also has preparatory functions. But the Community Council's role should be different from that of the Bureau, since it is a higher level organ and does not simply set the agenda for Conference meetings. In addition, Article 13(4)(g) provides a dispute settlement function to the Community Council. It is mandated to 'receive and consider allegations of breaches of obligations arising under this Treaty, including disputes between Organs of the Community'. This parallels the Conference's power to settle disputes between member states, including disputes over the RTC, and therefore means that there are at least two organs of the RTC to which member states may submit disputes regarding RTC breaches.[55] But the RTC differentiates between the roles of these two organs, since only the Community Council is given explicit powers to settle inter-organ disputes. Finally, the Community Council's power to issue directives under Article 13(4)(h) can be distinguished from the similar power of the conference in three ways. Firstly, this power is to be exercised 'on the instructions of the Conference' and thus is a subsidiary power. Secondly, the scope of the Community Council's directives is more limited. They are to be 'aimed at ensuring the timely implementation of Community Decisions' and are to be issued to organs and to the Secretariat. The Conference's directives, in contrast, are policy directives of a general or special character and can be issued to any other organs and bodies of the Community.[56] Thirdly, the directives of the Community Council, unlike those of the Conference, are not endowed with any mandatory quality.[57]

Decision-making

The Community Council is empowered to make directives, decisions, and recommendations. Most of its voting rules are the same as those applicable to the Conference,

[53] Gladstone Mills et al, *Report on a Comprehensive Review of the Institutions and Organisations of the Caribbean Community* (Georgetown, Guyana: CARICOM Secretariat, 1990) (*Mills Report*).

[54] RTC Art 13(4)(f).

[55] For the Conference's dispute settlement function see RTC Art 12(8).

[56] Compare RTC Art 12(7) and Art 13(4)(h).

[57] The Community Council's directives are usually arrived at by consensus, are addressed to Ministerial Councils, and are not generally binding: Interview with Safiya Ali, General Counsel, CARICOM Secretariat, Georgetown, Guyana (6 Aug 2012).

as set out in common Article 27, except for those on directives and decisions.[58] As with the Conference, the Community Council's power to make directives is not fully elaborated under the RTC. No mention is made of the relevant voting procedure for directives, or whether they are binding in nature. Unlike in the case of the Conference, however, the non-mandatory wording used to describe directives in Article 13(4)(h) makes them unlikely to be considered binding. However if the Community Council wished to employ the voting procedure used to make a binding decision, and labelled that decision a 'directive', then such a directive could be deemed to be binding in nature.

The substantive decisions of the Community Council and the four Ministerial Councils are governed by common rules established in Article 29.[59] These rules stipulate that decisions are to be made by a 'qualified majority vote' and are binding.[60] Article 29(2) defines a qualified majority vote as meaning 'an affirmative vote of the member states comprising no less than three-quarters of the membership of the Community'. As a result, binding decisions can be made by the Community Council and Ministerial Councils so long as three-quarters of the member states vote affirmatively, and such a vote is not subject to a veto. This is a substantial development for CARICOM and a great improvement over the rules of the original 1973 Treaty, which greatly restricted majority voting and the ability of subsidiary organs to make binding decisions.[61]

Nevertheless, Article 29, subsections (3)–(5) sets out a major exception to this qualified majority voting rule, namely, a situation where the issue to be decided is of 'critical importance to the national well-being of a Member State'. In such circumstances the decision must be reached by an affirmative vote of all member states, or by an affirmative vote of not less than three-quarters of the membership with the remainder abstaining.[62] This is similar to the Conference's decision-making procedure and would thus allow the exercise of veto powers.

Whether something is of 'critical importance to the national well-being of a Member State' cannot be unilaterally determined by the state concerned. Instead it requires a separate decision in favour of the issue's critical importance, reached by a two-thirds majority of the member states.[63] As a consequence, if a state wishes for

[58] See the description of the voting rules established by Art 27, including those related to quorum, restrictions based upon budgetary arrears, procedural decisions, recommendations, and opt-outs, earlier in the chapter.

[59] The rules set out in Art 29 of the RTC must be deemed to be applicable to the Community Council even though the subsections of the article refer to 'Ministerial Councils' without also referring to the Community Council. This would appear to be a drafting error, since the definition of 'Ministerial Councils' in Art 1 as meaning 'COFAP, COFCOR, COHSOD and COTED' does not include the Community Council. Nevertheless support for the inclusion of the Community Council under the article may be gleaned from its title—'Voting in the Community Council and Ministerial Councils'—and the practice of the Community Council in following such voting rules. See Rule 30 of the Rules of Procedure of the Community Council of Ministers, adopted at the Second Meeting of the Community Council of Ministers, Guyana, 15–16 May 1998, as available at <http://www.caricom.org/jsp/community_organs/rules_council.jsp?menu=cob&prnf=1> (accessed 4 Oct 2011).

[60] RTC Art 29(1).

[61] See Art 13 of the 1973 Treaty of Chaguaramas which required a kind of qualified unanimity vote for decisions of Institutions (the organs equivalent to Ministerial Councils) and did not specify that such decisions were binding.

[62] RTC Art 29(3) and (5).

[63] RTC Art 29(4).

a matter be considered one of critical importance, it must convince two-thirds of the member states that such is the case.[64] As of August 2012, no decision appears to have been made in an organ of CARICOM under the Article 29 critical importance procedure.[65]

4.3.2 CARICOM Ministerial Councils: COFAP, COTED, COFCOR, and COHSOD

Below the Community Council are four Ministerial Councils: COFAP, COTED, COFCOR, and COHSOD. Each Ministerial Council is composed of Ministers or alternates designated by each member state. Each Ministerial Council is also governed by the same voting rules as the Community Council and can make binding decisions.[66]

The Council for Finance and Planning (COFAP) is governed by Article 14 of the RTC and holds the primary responsibility for the economic policy coordination and financial and monetary integration of member states, including matters such as promoting the coordination and convergence of national macro-economic policies of member states and the execution of a harmonized policy on foreign investment, promoting and facilitating the adoption of measures for fiscal and monetary cooperation among member states, recommending measures to maintain fiscal discipline by the Governments of member states, recommending arrangements for reciprocal free conversion of currency, promoting the establishment and integration of capital markets in the Community, and undertaking additional functions as assigned by the Conference arising under the RTC. In addition, Article 14(2)(d) hints at the role of COFAP in assisting with the establishment of a CARICOM monetary union.[67] COFAP is to be assisted by the Committee of Central Bank Governors in performing its functions.

[64] In a strange passage in the case of *Hummingbird Rice Mills Limited v Suriname and the Caribbean Community*, Judgment [2012] CCJ 1 (OJ) at [48], the CCJ relies upon the challenges posed by the 'critical importance' voting requirements in order to excuse COTED's relative inaction in response to requests for enforcement of the Common External Tariff against Suriname:

> In the circumstances, it is not obviously unreasonable for the Council to have taken the calculated approach that the emotional sensitivity implicated in the assertion by Suriname that affordable pricing and availability of bread were critical to the social, economical [sic], and political stability in the country, could quite likely have led to a finding that the issue involved critical importance to national well-being. In that event Suriname would surely have vetoed any decision which required it to take precipitate action contrary to its perceived national interest and well-being; and similarly to block other COTED actions suggested by the Claimant such as invoking the modes of settlement specified in Article 188, including litigation in the Caribbean Court of Justice.

[65] Interview with Safiya Ali, General Counsel, CARICOM Secretariat, Georgetown, Guyana (6 Aug 2012).

[66] RTC Arts 14(1), 15(1), 16(1), 17(1), 27, and 29.

[67] Note that Richard Stoneman, Justice Duke Pollard, and Hugo Inniss, in their report 'Turning Around CARICOM' (n 14) at p 35, are deeply sceptical about the possibility of a single CARICOM currency by the original target date of 2015.

The Council for Trade and Economic Development (COTED) is governed by Article 15 and is responsible for the promotion of trade and economic development in the Community, including matters such as promoting the development and overseeing the operation of the CARICOM Single Market and Economy.[68] Such a role is complementary to that of the Community Council and therefore the two organs must work closely together. COTED is also mandated to promote the international competitiveness of industrial and agricultural commodities (including their structural diversification and sustainability), and to promote: the accelerated development and marketing of services, the transportation of people and goods, the sustainable development of energy and natural resources, the accelerated development of science and technology, the protection and preservation of the environment, sustainable development, and (in collaboration with COFCOR) the coordination and enhancement of external economic and trade relations of the Community. COTED is further empowered to undertake additional functions as assigned by the Conference, arising under the RTC.

The Council for Foreign and Community Relations (COFCOR) is governed by Article 16 and is responsible for determining the relations between the Community, international organizations, and third states. Given its foreign affairs mandate, the Ministerial representatives attending COFCOR are specified as being the 'Ministers Responsible for Foreign Affairs of Member States'.[69] COFCOR is mandated to promote friendly and mutually beneficial relations among member states, coordinate joint representation and common Community positions, and coordinate the positions of member states with respect to inter-governmental organizations. It is also mandated to collaborate with COTED in promoting and developing external economic and trade relations, and generally is responsible for coordinating Community policy on international issues. COFCOR can also be assigned additional functions by the Conference, arising under the RTC. However, Article 16(4) stipulates that only member states 'possessing the necessary competence with respect to the matters under consideration from time to time' may take part in COFCOR deliberations. This provision is unique for CARICOM organs, although as will be seen later, it is common in the OECS system. It is clearly designed to deal with the position of Montserrat which, as an Overseas Territory of the United Kingdom, has no competence over foreign affairs matters.[70] As a result, voting calculations in COFCOR have to be adjusted for the smaller number of eligible states if Article 16(4) is applicable.

The Council for Human and Social Development (COHSOD) is governed by Article 17 and is responsible for the promotion of human and social development in the Community. It is mandated to promote the improvement of health,

[68] RTC Art 15(2)(a).

[69] RTC Art 16(1).

[70] This was confirmed in an Interview with Safiya Ali, General Counsel, CARICOM Secretariat, Georgetown, Guyana (6 Aug 2012). For evidence of the exclusion of Montserrat from the previous CARICOM organ dealing with foreign affairs, the Standing Committee of Ministers Responsible for Foreign Affairs, see Gladstone Mills et al, *Report on a Comprehensive Review of the Programmes, Institutions and Organisations of the Caribbean Community* (n 53) p 44.

education, the living and working conditions of workers (including by developing harmonious labour and industrial relations), the development of youth and women, the development of culture and sports, and the 'maintenance of a healthy human environment in the Community'. COHSOD may also undertake additional functions as assigned by the Conference arising under the RTC. Under Article 17(3) COHSOD is mandated to 'promote co-operation among the Member States in the areas set out in the schedule hereto in furtherance of the objectives set out in Article 5'. Unfortunately this provision appears to be flawed. No relevant schedule has been appended to the RTC, nor to Protocol I, which first included this provision. Similarly, the reference to Article 5 is incorrect and must mean Article 6.[71] In such circumstances, the most that can be gleaned from Article 17(3) is that COHSOD is also mandated to promote cooperation in areas within its competence to further the objectives of the Community.

4.3.3 CARICOM Secretariat

Although the Secretariat is not labelled as an organ in Article 10 of the RTC, its description as the 'principal administrative organ of the Community' in Article 23(1) clearly accords it such status. Additionally, its functions are those of an organ of the Community.[72] The Secretariat includes the Secretary General and staff and is located in Georgetown, Guyana. It has a multi-level structure, headed by the Secretary General and his Office, assisted by a Deputy Secretary General and his Office, and four Directorates (Trade and Economic Integration, Foreign and Community Relations, CARIFORUM, and Human and Social Development) and the Office of the General Counsel. An Assistant Secretary General is in charge of each Directorate, with Advisers, Directors, or Executive Directors serving under them.[73]

In staffing the Secretariat, Article 23 of the RTC seeks to ensure the recruitment of the highest quality staff, while at the same time paying regard to geographical representation. It imposes strict obligations upon both the Secretariat staff and member states to respect their independence and exclusively international character. The Secretariat is governed by Staff Regulations (approved by the Conference), Financial Regulations (approved by the Community Council), and Staff Rules (established by the Secretary General).[74]

The Secretary General heads the Secretariat and is described under Article 23(3) as 'the Chief Executive Officer of the Community'. Since the quoted phrase is not a defined term under the RTC, it is likely that the capitalization of the Secretary General's title reflects the increased importance of the office under the RTC.

[71] The similar provision in Art VI of Protocol I cross-references Art 4 of the original 1973 Treaty, which sets out the 'Objectives of the Community'.

[72] See eg Hans J Geiser, Pamela Alleyne and Carroll Gajraj, *Legal Problems of Caribbean Integration: A study of legal aspects of CARICOM* (Leyden: Sijthoff, 1976) 37 and endnote 16.

[73] See CARICOM Secretariat, 'Organisational Structure' (chart, updated to 13 Feb 2009), as available at <http://www.caricom.org/jsp/secretariat/organigram_feb_09.pdf> (accessed 7 Oct 2011).

[74] RTC Art 23(6)–(8).

Under the original Treaty the Secretary General was described as the 'chief administrative officer' and the functions of the office were described in the same article as the Secretariat.[75] In the RTC, in contrast, the title has changed and an entire article is dedicated to describing the Secretary General's functions. Article 24 sets out an extensive list of functions of the Secretary General, including: representing the Community, developing Community decisions into implementable proposals, identifying and mobilizing external resources to implement decisions and undertake studies, implementing decisions at the regional level, implementing, with the consent of the member state concerned, decisions that do not require action by national authorities, monitoring and reporting on implementation of Community decisions, and initiating proposals for consideration by organs. This latter function gives the office of the Secretary General scope for independent initiative.[76] To these functions others can be added by the Conference or other competent organs. Under Article 26 of the RTC the Secretary General is also required to assist the Community Council to 'establish and maintain an efficient system of consultations at the national and regional levels'. This obligation was subject to judicial scrutiny by the CCJ in the case of *Trinidad Cement Ltd v Caribbean Community*.[77] In that case the Court held that the Secretary General's obligations under Article 26 were meaningful and that therefore he had a duty to ensure that the consultative process is properly followed.[78] Likewise, in the case of *Hummingbird Rice Mills Limited v Suriname and the Caribbean Community* the Court admonished the Secretary General for relying upon inadequate information provided by a member state and suggested that 'a much more proactive approach would be appropriate'.[79]

In addition, Article 230 allows the Conference to delegate to the Secretary General the authority to conclude agreements, particularly technical assistance agreements, on behalf of the Community. The term 'agreements' does not exclude international legal agreements. In sum, the Secretary General under the RTC can initiate Community decision-making processes, follow their progress, ensure that

[75] 1973 Treaty Art 15(2).

[76] Independent initiative has served as the basis for substantial development of the office of the Secretary General of the United Nations without requiring amendment of the Charter of the United Nations in such areas as mediation, conciliation, and peacekeeping. cf JG Merrills, *International Dispute Settlement*, 4th edn (Cambridge: Cambridge University Press, 2005) 244–50.

[77] Judgment [2009] CCJ 4 (OJ), (2009) 75 WIR 194, 10 August 2009.

[78] In *Trinidad Cement Ltd* (n 77) at [68] the Court held that '[g]iven his duty…to assist in maintaining an efficient system of consultation, the Secretary General has a residual responsibility not to look the other way if it comes to his attention that the consultative process has not been followed by a Competent Authority at the domestic level, or that it is at best doubtful whether it has been followed.' After assessing his actions, the Court made a declaration, at [81], that the Secretary General had failed to satisfactorily fulfil his consultation obligation:

> As the Court has previously indicated, the Secretary-General's authorisation of the suspension for Jamaica suffered from a procedural flaw, but for the reasons expressed above at [75] the Court is content to issue the following declaration: it was wrong for the Secretary-General to accept as a sufficient answer to his inquiry regarding a request for suspension by Jamaica, the response of Trinidad and Tobago that it had 'no objections' to Jamaica's request.

[79] *Hummingbird Rice Mills Limited v Suriname and the Caribbean Community*, Judgment [2012] CCJ 1 (OJ) [39].

they are carried out, and monitor their implementation. As a result the office of the Secretary General will be crucial for the legal and policy-making processes of the Community.

The Secretariat as a whole has been provided with extensive functions under Article 25, in addition to those which may be assigned by organs of the Community, including: servicing meetings and taking follow up actions, initiating studies, providing services to member states, collecting, storing, and disseminating information, assisting community organs in the development and implementation of proposals and programmes, coordinating the activities of donor agencies and international, regional, and national institutions for the fulfilment of Community objectives, preparing the draft budget, providing technical assistance, conducting fact finding assignments, and initiating or developing proposals for consideration and decision by competent organs. As part of its role in assisting with the development of proposals for decision, the Secretariat is also mandated under Article 27(5) to bring to the attention of each organ the financial implications of any decision, and any other matters which may be relevant, prior to that decision being made by an organ.[80] In addition, Article 227 specifies that the Secretariat is the entity through which notice is to be provided to other organs of the Community, where the treaty requires such notice. Similarly, Article 233 envisages the Secretariat as being the depository for instruments of ratification of the RTC and any amendments thereto.

The development of the roles and functions of the Secretariat and Secretary General under the RTC is in accordance with the suggestions of the Mills Report.[81] Mills et al highlighted a number of challenges in relation to CARICOM decision-making and implementation:

> One of the perennial complaints, expressed orally and in writing, about the functioning of CARICOM—and we heard similar comments in several States—concerns the long process involved both in taking and in implementing decisions. In respect of the former, important items continuously reappear on the agenda of meetings whether at the level of the Organs or the Institutions; decisions having been deferred because of the lack of political will on the part of the representatives of one or more Member States and/or reluctance to use the Unanimity Rule.
>
> Even after decisions have been taken, and Ministers have endorsed agreements on regional issues, there is no guarantee that implementation will follow in Member States. Where national legislation is required to bring the provisions of such agreements in force, most governments are dilatory in doing so; generally, local constituency or national interest pressures succeed in overriding the objectives and requirements of the wider regional interest. The protracted processes of decision-making and implementation are well illustrated in the areas of Industrial Programming, the Common External Tariff, the Rules of Origin

[80] Note, however, the statement in the report by Richard Stoneman, Justice Duke Pollard, and Hugo Inniss, 'Turning Around CARICOM' (n 14) at 21:

> The one constant however is that Article 27:5 of the Treaty of Chaguaramas, which stipulates that the financial implications of decisions should be drawn out before any decisions are made, is rarely, if ever, invoked.

[81] Gladstone Mills et al, *Report on a Comprehensive Review of the Programmes, Institutions and Organisations of the Caribbean Community* (n 53).

and the Harmonisation of Fiscal Incentives. Moreover, no effective institutional machinery exists for monitoring and evaluating implementation.[82]

The RTC attempts to overcome these challenges by providing the Secretary General and Secretariat with the functions of continuously reviewing implementation of Caribbean Community obligations. This may not be enough, since political challenges and the unwillingness of member states to surrender any elements of national sovereignty may continue to impair the effectiveness of CARICOM.[83] But at least the Secretary General and Secretariat have been expressly empowered to draw attention to implementation deficits.

One recommendation that is not directly pursued in Articles 23–25 is that of a 'good offices' role for the Secretary General. Such a 'good offices' role would allow the Secretary General to serve as a neutral third party to mediate or otherwise assist with dispute settlement. It is a common role for Secretary Generals in other organizations, and has been frequently and prominently employed by the Secretary General of the United Nations to help resolve difficult disputes.[84] It is only much later in the RTC, in Chapter Nine, that a good offices role is expressly provided to the Secretary General. Article 191(1) allows member states who are parties to a dispute to employ the good offices of a third party, 'including those of the Secretary-General, to settle the dispute'.

4.3.4 Other CARICOM Entities: Bodies, Institutions, Subsidiary Institutions, Committees

CARICOM also embraces further levels in its institutional structure. The RTC makes reference to Bodies, Institutions, and Subsidiary Institutions. CARICOM itself has labelled two additional entities as 'Treaty Entities'—the CARICOM Development Fund and the CARICOM Competition Commission—which were created under Articles 158 and 171 of the RTC, respectively.[85]

CARICOM Bodies are described in Article 18 as including the Legal Affairs Committee, the Budget Committee and Committee of Central Bank Governors. Additional bodies may be established by organs of the Community.[86] These bodies are made up of high-ranking national officials—Ministers responsible for Legal Affairs, 'senior officials of the Member States who shall perform their functions in a professional capacity' and Governors or Heads of Central Banks, respectively—and

[82] Gladstone Mills et al, *Report on a Comprehensive Review of the Programmes, Institutions and Organisations of the Caribbean Community* 32 [2.10]–[2.11].

[83] See eg Gladstone Mills et al, *Report on a Comprehensive Review of the Programmes, Institutions and Organisations of the Caribbean Community* 32 [2.12].

[84] See eg JG Merrills, *International Dispute Settlement*, 4th edn (Cambridge: Cambridge University Press, 2005) 244–50 and ch 2.

[85] CARICOM Secretariat, 'CARICOM System', as available at <http://www.caricomlaw.org/Resources/CARICOMSystem.aspx> (3 Nov 2011). See also Arts 172–174 of the RTC on the composition, functions, and powers of the Competition Commission. The Agreement Relating to the Operation of the CARICOM Development Fund (CDF) (adopted 4 Jul 2008, not yet in force), has been provisionally applied since 4 July 2008 by its signatories.

[86] RTC Art 18(3).

are tasked to help the Community with matters falling within their remit. The Legal Affairs Committee is tasked with providing advice on 'treaties, international legal issues, the harmonisation of laws of the Community and other legal matters'. The Budget Committee is mandated to examine and provide advice on the draft budget of the Community. The Committee of Central Bank Governors is to 'make recommendations to COFAP on matters relating to monetary co-operation, payments arrangements, free movement of capital, integration of capital markets, monetary union and any other related matters referred to it by the Organs of the Community'.[87] The bodies are governed by the same voting rules and procedures as the Community Council and Ministerial Councils.[88]

At a lower level Article 21 of the RTC recognizes the *Institutions* of the Community and Article 22 the Associate Institutions of the Community.[89] Institutions are entities which were established by or under the auspices of the Community, and include the following, as listed under Article 21: the Caribbean Disaster Emergency Response Agency, the Caribbean Meteorological Institute, the Caribbean Meteorological Organisation, the Caribbean Environmental Health Institute, the Caribbean Agricultural Research and Development Institute, the Caribbean Regional Centre for the Education and Training of Animal Health and Veterinary Public Health Assistants, the Assembly of Caribbean Community Parliamentarians, the Caribbean Centre For Developmental Administration, and the Caribbean Food and Nutrition Institute. Further entities may be designated as Institutions by the Conference under Article 21, and such subsequently designated Institutions include: the Caribbean Examinations Council, the Caribbean Disaster Emergency Management Agency, the Caribbean Aviation Safety and Security Oversight System, the CARICOM Implementation Agency for Crime and Security, and the Caribbean Agricultural Health and Food Safety Agency.[90] CARICOM also lists the following additional organizations which were established by the Community but which have not yet been designated as Institutions: the CARICOM Regional Organisation for Standards and Quality, the Caribbean Regional Fisheries Mechanism, and the Caribbean Community Climate Change Centre.[91]

Article 22 lists the *Associate Institutions* of the Community, which are entities 'with which the Community enjoys important functional relationships which contribute to the achievement of the objectives of the Community'. These include the Caribbean Development Bank, the University of Guyana, the University of the West Indies, the Caribbean Law Institute/Caribbean Law Institute Centre, and the Secretariat of the Organisation of Eastern Caribbean States.[92] The latter

[87] RTC Art 19(1)–(3). [88] RTC Art 19(4) makes reference to Arts 27 and 29.

[89] Note that this terminology may be confusing to those familiar with the previously-existing categories of CARICOM 'Institutions' and 'Associate Institutions', described in Arts 11 and 12 of the original 1973 Treaty of Chaguaramas. The 'Associate Institutions' described in the original treaty are nearly identical; but the 'Institutions' have been amalgamated and converted into what the RTC calls Ministerial Councils.

[90] CARICOM Secretariat, 'CARICOM System' (n 85).

[91] CARICOM Secretariat, 'CARICOM System' (n 85). [92] RTC Art 22.

presumably would now refer to the OECS Commission under the RTB. Other entities may be designated as Associate Institutions by the Conference.

The nature of the relationship of CARICOM and its Institutions was clarified by the Caribbean Court of Justice in an original jurisdiction case, that of *Doreen Johnson v Caribbean Centre for Development Administration (CARICAD).*[93] This case involved a suit by Ms Johnson against CARICAD for a number of alleged wrongs arising from the termination of her employment on grounds of redundancy—including abuse of power, wrongful dismissal, violation of labour laws, breach of contract, and breach of the Barbados constitution. She also alleged that she had been discriminated against on the basis of nationality, contrary to Article 7 of the RTC, on the ground that Barbadian employees of CARICAD such as herself were not afforded the pension rights conferred upon employees who were nationals of other countries.[94] The two questions that arose for consideration by the Court were (1) whether CARICAD could be sued under the Court's original jurisdiction, and (2) which, if any, of the complaints made were justiciable by the Court.[95]

Counsel for the applicant argued that the Court had jurisdiction because CARICAD was listed under Article 21 of the RTC as an 'Institution of the Community' and as such had legal personality and the capacity to be sued, as per Article 228 of the RTC, which provides for the legal capacity of the Community. In response the Court noted that while CARICAD was an Institution of the Community, it was not listed as one of the principal or other 'Organs of the Community' or even as one of its 'Bodies'.[96] The Court held that, in contrast to the language of the articles establishing those organs and bodies, which was 'positive and forthright', the language of Article 21 reveals that the Institutions were not intended to be an integral part of the Community.[97] The Court noted that Institutions and Associate Institutions were not mentioned in other, substantive sections of the RTC, and there was no reference to any role to be played by them in implementing the Treaty.[98] As a result, the CCJ held that, unlike CARICOM organs and bodies, which reflected the Community's will and have the power to bind and represent it, Institutions and Associate Institutions were 'merely entities that have some connection with the Community. [...] Their acts and omissions are not necessarily attributable to the Community as are the acts and omissions of the Organs and Bodies.'[99] According to the Court it was 'clear' that 'CARICAD, an Institution of the Community, cannot be sued in proceedings before this Court'.[100] The Court

[93] *Doreen Johnson v CARICAD*, Judgment (Jurisdiction) [2009] CCJ 3 (OJ) 2 March 2009.

[94] *Johnson v CARICAD* (n 93) [3].

[95] *Johnson v CARICAD* (n 93) [4].

[96] *Johnson v CARICAD* (n 93) [7]–[10].

[97] *Johnson v CARICAD* (n 93) [11].

[98] *Johnson v CARICAD* (n 93) [13]–[14].

[99] *Johnson v CARICAD* (n 93) [14].

[100] *Johnson v CARICAD* (n 93) [15]. Note that the Court has taken a more nuanced position recently in *Trinidad Cement Ltd v Competition Commission*, Judgment [2012] CCJ 4 (OJ), 12 November 2012. In that case the Court recognized the ability of the Competition Commission to sue and be sued in the original jurisdiction of the CCJ even though the Commission is not listed as an organ or body of CARICOM.

also established that CARICAD could not derive its legal personality from that conferred upon the Community by Article 228 of the RTC.[101]

In view of these determinations it was unnecessary for the Court to consider the justiciability of the applicant's claims. However in dismissing the special leave application, the Court noted in passing that the sole claim that it would have been competent to hear in its original jurisdiction was that invoking Article 7 of the RTC, which prohibits discrimination on grounds of nationality only.[102] Since the original jurisdiction involves the interpretation of the RTC, only a dispute involving a breach of that treaty would be justiciable—not ordinary domestic law disputes, such as breach of contract, labour law disputes, or violation of constitutional rights. In sum, *Johnson v CARICAD* establishes that Institutions and Associate Institutions are not so closely connected with CARICOM that they can be sued as part of the Community.

Assembly of Caribbean Community Parliamentarians

Even though clearly subsidiary in nature, one of the Institutions described in Article 21 should be examined in more detail. This is the Assembly of Caribbean Community Parliamentarians (ACCP), an Institution founded by the 1992 Agreement for the Establishment of an Assembly of Caribbean Community Parliamentarians ('ACCP Agreement').[103] The ACCP consists of representatives from member states and associate members elected or appointed by their Parliaments, in the manner decided by those Parliaments, and is chaired by a Speaker of the Assembly and serviced by a Clerk.[104] The term 'Parliament' includes the Legislature of a member or associate member state.[105] Member states are allowed to send up to four representatives or their alternates, and associate members up to two representatives or their alternates.[106]

When the idea for an Assembly of Caribbean Community Parliamentarians was first aired there was significant resistance to the idea of allowing members of the opposition to be state representatives at Assembly meetings. This reluctance was gradually overcome so that the ACCP Agreement leaves it up to each member or associate member to decide who to send. This contrasts with the OECS Assembly, discussed later, the membership of which must include members of the opposition.[107]

The ACCP functions as a deliberative and consultative body for the discussion of policies, programmes, and other matters falling within the scope of the Treaty, and is empowered to make recommendations to CARICOM organs, request information from the same organs, discuss and make recommendations on any matter within the scope of the objectives of the Community or that is expressly referred

[101] *Johnson v CARICAD* (n 93) [18].
[102] *Johnson v CARICAD* (n 93) [19]–[20].
[103] (Adopted 31 Jul 1992, in force 3 Aug 1994) as available through <http://www.caricomlaw.org/Details.aspx?EntryId=165&Command=Core_Download&Method=attachment> (accessed 20 Oct 2011).
[104] ACCP Agreement (n 103) Arts 3(1), 6(3), and 7(1).
[105] ACCP Agreement Art 1.
[106] ACCP Agreement Art 3(2)–(3).
[107] See p 91.

to it, and adopt resolutions on any issue or matter arising under the Treaty.[108] The objectives of the Assembly can be generally summarized as those of deepening Caribbean integration, allowing popular participation and involvement, and providing greater possibility for the monitoring and coordinating of Community policies.[109]

The powers of the Assembly are limited. It can deliberate, consult, discuss, recommend, question, and make non-binding resolutions. It has no binding authority. As a result, the strongest action it can take is to investigate, publicize, and criticize Community policies and decisions. In its workings the ACCP is to follow accepted parliamentary procedures and practices. It may establish committees, agencies, or other bodies, and admit observers to its proceedings.[110] As stipulated in Article 5(4), however, the ACCP is not competent to discuss or adopt any resolution on any matter which is exclusively within the domestic jurisdiction of a member state or associate member of the Community. Such questions of exclusive jurisdiction are decided by the Speaker. The ACCP is to meet once a year and the CARICOM Secretariat and the government of the host state in which the Assembly meeting is held are to assist with administrative matters related to the meeting.[111] Member states and associate members must meet their own costs for attending meetings of the ACCP.[112]

Representatives of member states have the right to one vote, representatives of associate members have the right to speak, but not to vote, and observers may be granted the right to speak with the permission of the ACCP.[113] Decisions of the ACCP, unless otherwise provided, are by simple majority of those present and voting, and a quorum is reached by the attendance of one-third of the representatives of member states.[114] Meetings of the ACCP are conducted in public.[115]

The inaugural meeting of the Assembly was held in Barbados on 27–29 May 1996, the second meeting in Grenada on 14–15 October 1999, and the third meeting in Belize on 17–20 November 2000.[116] Subsequent meetings have proved difficult, in part as a result of the cost of attending and hosting such meetings.[117] The Technical Sub Group on the Assembly of Caribbean Community Parliamentarians, established by the Conference's Prime Ministerial Expert Group in 2003, also raised the challenges related to the organization of meetings, including the preparation of Order Papers, a task which had fallen to the CARICOM

[108] ACCP Agreement Art 5(1)–(2). The reference to 'Treaty' is to the 1973 Treaty Establishing the Caribbean Community, without mention of the possibility of amendment or revision: Art 1. However it is likely that the ACCP Agreement would be construed to refer to the RTC, under a purposive interpretation, since otherwise it would be rendered ineffective.

[109] ACCP Agreement Art 4.

[110] ACCP Agreement Art 5(3).

[111] ACCP Agreement Art 6(1) and 7(2)–(3).

[112] ACCP Agreement Art 6(4).

[113] ACCP Agreement Art 6(5)–(7).

[114] ACCP Agreement Art 6(8)–(9).

[115] ACCP Agreement Art 6(10).

[116] CARICOM Secretariat, 'Assembly of Caribbean Community Parliamentarians (ACCP)', as available at <http://www.caricom.org/jsp/community/accp.jsp?menu=community> (accessed 31 Oct 2011).

[117] CARICOM Secretariat, *Report of the Technical Sub Group on the Assembly of Caribbean Community Parliamentarians (ACCP)* REP 96/1/48 ACCP, Oct 24, 2003, as available at <http://www.caricom.org/jsp/community/accp_technical_sub_group_report.jsp> (accessed 31 Oct 2011).

Secretariat as a result of inaction on the part of member states.[118] But there have been discussions about revising the nature of the Assembly to make it more effective (albeit still without binding decision-making powers), and so it may recommence meetings in the future.[119]

In outlining the potential role of the ACCP to the wider project of Caribbean integration, former Barbadian Prime Minister Erskine Sandiford placed great emphasis on its ability to help deepen democracy in CARICOM. Expressing optimism about the relatively modest powers of the Assembly, he stated:

> These powers should give the Assembly scope to bring the values, insights, aspirations and sensibilities of its members to bear on the issues affecting CARICOM. At the same time the existing powers should enable the Assembly to begin the process of holding the CARICOM executive, the Heads of Government, accountable to the people of CARICOM with respect to CARICOM matters.[120]

Thus Sandiford placed significant emphasis on the deliberative and publicizing roles of the ACCP. The ACCP must meet more frequently in order to be effective, but within its structure could lie the seeds for the deepening of Caribbean integration. The European Parliament, it should be recalled, was similar in nature at its conception.[121]

National Committees for the Charter of Civil Society

One further category of entity related to the CARICOM structure that requires mention is that of the National Committees for the Charter of Civil Society. The Charter of Civil Society for the Caribbean Community, adopted at the Eighth Inter-Sessional Meeting of the Conference of Heads of Government, on 19 February 1997, is a document 'intended to provide the normative principles underpinning the Community'.[122] The Charter has been invested with high hopes, with the West Indian Commission, for example, imbuing it with the potential to be the soul of the Community:

> We attach much importance to this proposal for a Charter of Civil Society. CARICOM needs normative moorings; we have found widespread yearning for giving the 'Community'

[118] See eg CARICOM Secretariat, 'Draft Agenda for the Twenty Third Meeting of the Bureau of the Conference of Heads of Government of the Caribbean Community' (16 Nov 2007), Agenda Item 5.1 The Future of the Assembly of Caribbean Community Parliamentarians (ACCP) [on file at CARICOM Secretariat].

[119] CARICOM Secretariat, *Report of the Technical Sub Group on the Assembly of Caribbean Community Parliamentarians (ACCP)* REP 96/1/48 ACCP, 24 Oct 2003, as available at <http://www.caricom.org/jsp/community/accp_technical_sub_group_report.jsp> (accessed 31 Oct 2011). See also the lucid suggestions of the West Indian Commission, in *Time for Action: Report of the West Indian Commission* (Black Rock, Barbados: The West Indian Commission, 1992) at 485–90.

[120] L Erskine Sandiford, 'The Assembly of Caribbean Community Parliamentarians', *CARICOM Perspective*, No 68, June 1998, p 74.

[121] See eg Desmond Dinan, *Ever Closer Union? An Introduction to the European Community* (Boulder, Colorado: Lynne Rienner, 1994) ch 9.

[122] CARICOM Secretariat, *Annual Report of the Secretary-General 1996* (Georgetown, Guyana: CARICOM Secretariat, 1997) p 57; Charter of Civil Society for the Caribbean Community,

a qualitative character—values beyond the routine of integration arrangements; indeed, standards by which these arrangements themselves can be judged and to which they can be made to conform. The Charter can become the soul of the Community, which needs a soul if it is to command the loyalty of the people of CARICOM.[123]

The Charter seeks to guarantee a variety of human rights, including civil, political, economic, social, and cultural rights. These rights include the rights to life, liberty, and security of the person (Article IV); the right to equality before the law (Article V); the right to non-discrimination (Article V(3)); the right to 'a fair and open democratic system through the holding of free elections at reasonable intervals, by secret ballot' (Article VI(1)); the right to form, join, participate in (including by being nominated for election to public office), and attend the meetings of political parties or other organizations, and to peacefully express political beliefs (Article VI(3)); the right to freedom of assembly, which includes the rights to peacefully demonstrate and to present petitions (Article VII); freedom of expression (Article VIII); freedom of religion (Article IX); cultural rights and freedoms, including the freedom to participate in the cultural life of one's choice (Article X); rights related to education (Article XV); and rights of the family (Article XVI). The Charter also requires respect for and the protection of the human dignity of the person (Article III) and offers some separate protection for indigenous peoples (Article XI), women (Article XII), children (Article XIII), and disabled persons (Article XIV). In addition to promoting and seeking to ensure good governance, such as by ensuring the rule of law and judicial independence (Article XVII), the Charter also seeks to guarantee social and economic rights, including rights related to participation in the economy (Article XVIII), workers' rights (Article XIX), rights related to health (Article XX) and basic necessities (Article XXI), and environmental rights (Article XXIII). Finally, the Charter recognizes special responsibilities on the part of the state to 'build awareness, engender support and establish programmes to foster sound values and positive attitudes and [to] enhance individual and institutional capacities' in order to secure the objectives of the Charter (Article XXIV).

Such a wide-ranging list of rights seeks to ensure that human rights remain a central aspect of Caribbean societies and cultures. However the status of the Charter, despite the strong mandatory language seen in many of its provisions, remains non-binding, and this impairs its overall effectiveness.[124] The non-binding

as available at <http://www.caricom.org/jsp/secretariat/legal_instruments/chartercivilsociety.jsp> (11 Jan 2011) and also reproduced in CARICOM Secretariat, *Charter of Civil Society* (Georgetown, Guyana, 1997).

[123] West Indian Commission, *Time for Action* (n 27) 496. See generally pp 490–7.

[124] eg Art 2(1) of the Charter provides that the 'States *shall* respect the fundamental human rights and freedoms of the individual....' (emphasis added). Interestingly, during the early stages of negotiation of the Charter there was some discussion about conceiving of the Charter as a binding treaty, or at least incorporating some of the enforcement mechanisms found in other international human rights agreements. See eg CARICOM Secretariat, 'First Meeting of the IGTF [Inter-Governmental Task Force]', 20–22 April 1993, Georgetown, Guyana, Agenda Item 8: The Draft Charter of Civil Society. The matter rose to a head in 1996, but was definitively resolved in favour of creating the Charter as a non-binding document: CARICOM Secretariat, 'Report of the Sixth Meeting of the

nature of the Charter is evident from its status as declaration of the Conference (rather than being, for example, a treaty), and also from its weak implementing provision: Article XXVI simply provides that the 'States declare to pay due regard to the provisions of this Charter.'

Nevertheless the Charter may have within it the seeds for developing stronger human rights frameworks, both at the national and Community levels. It can help germinate such frameworks in two ways. The first is as a result of the activities of, and awareness generated by, the National Committees established under the Charter; the second is through the use of the Charter as an interpretive lens to help understand the nature and content of provisions of the RTC. Let us examine each potential in turn.

The Charter requires states parties to set up special National Committees, which are to ensure its implementation.[125] These National Committees are made up of representatives of states, representatives of other social partners, and other persons of 'high moral character and recognised competence'.[126] The term 'Social Partners' is defined in Article I(a) as including the government of a state, associations of employers, workers organizations, and non-governmental organizations recognized by the state, and the term 'State', as defined in Article I(b) includes associate members of the Community. The role of these National Committees is to review the implementation of the Charter in their respective states and to receive reports on allegations of breaches or non-compliance with the Charter by the state or its social partners.[127] National Committees are to inform the state or social partner upon receipt of such allegations and request its comments.[128] The National Committee then reports to the Secretary General of the Caribbean Community regarding the allegations and related comments, and includes its own views on the matter. The Secretary General collects all of these National Committee reports and submits them to the Conference for its consideration. The Secretary General must inform states and social partners of the results of such Conference deliberations.[129]

Such a complaint and reporting process would allow National Committees, and through them, the CARICOM Secretary General, to draw attention to human rights breaches by states or their social partners. Since some of the rights found in the Charter are not already protected in all Commonwealth Caribbean constitutions, these National Committees can play a role in broadening respect for fundamental human rights in the Caribbean.

The second role of the Charter, discussed in more depth later under the topic of general principles of law in Chapter 8, is as an interpretive guide to the human rights which may be protected under the RTC. Granted, most of the rights provided for by the RTC are not human rights per se, but are rather economic ones, like the right of establishment, the right to provide services, and the right to move capital.

IGTF', 2–4 October 1996, Georgetown, Guyana, Agenda Item 4: Consideration of the Draft Charter of Civil Society. Both of the latter documents are restricted access, but are on file with the CARICOM Secretariat.

125 Charter Art XXV(4).
126 Charter Art XXV(4)(1).
127 Charter Art XXV(4)(2).
128 Charter Art XXV(4)(3).
129 Charter Art XXV(5)(1)–(2).

Nevertheless it may be possible for a court or other tribunal interpreting the RTC to read into its text particular human rights protections which are necessary to ensure its effectiveness. This is supported by a few textual references to human rights in the RTC. Although the RTC does not set out a list of human rights in its provisions, it does allude to them, and to the Charter of Civil Society, in the penultimate paragraph of its Preamble and also does so indirectly in later articles.[130] In such a context the CCJ could use both textual and teleological forms of treaty interpretation to support Community-level human rights protections. Such an interpretive approach has been used by the Inter-American Court of Human Rights.[131] A similar approach, one relying upon general principles, has been used by the European Court of Justice to find that human rights fall under EU law.[132]

4.3.5 OECS Council of Ministers

Nature and competences

Perhaps as a result of the trifurcated nature of the OECS treaty regime—composed of the RTB, the DSA, and the Protocol—the OECS has retained two second level organs. The Council of Ministers operates under the RTB and the Economic Affairs Council operates under the Protocol.

The Council of Ministers ('Council') comprises member states acting through Ministers of Government. More than one Minister may be appointed to sit on the Council, but each member state is only entitled to one vote.[133] The Council may determine its own procedure and is headed by a Chairman, who is rotated annually 'in accordance with the principle of alphabetical order of the Member States except where otherwise agreed'.[134] The Council is responsible to the OECS Authority and is empowered to take appropriate action on matters remitted to it by, and make recommendations to, the Authority.[135] It also has a strong role in the OECS legislative process, since it is responsible for considering and reporting to the Authority on OECS Commission recommendations related to Acts of the Organisation, and for considering and enacting into OECS law Regulations and other implementing instruments to give effect to Acts of the Organisation.[136] In discharging these latter functions, the Council is mandated to follow the directions of the Authority regarding consultation with the OECS Assembly, and may undertake such consultations of its own volition.[137] Under Article 7.2 of the RTB the Council may establish subsidiary organs with the approval of the OECS Authority. The same provision also sets out a substantial limit upon the competence of the Council and other organs of the OECS, namely, the requirement that they 'perform the functions and act within

[130] See eg RTC Arts 64(3) [speaking of the human rights of the farming community] and 186(1)(l) [consumer rights, which could be construed to include property rights].

[131] *Interpretation of the American Declaration of the Rights and Duties of Man Within the Framework of Article 64 of the American Convention on Human Rights*, Advisory Opinion OC-10/89, 14 July 1989, I-A Ct HR (Ser A) No 10 (1989).

[132] For the EU developments see the seminal cases of the European Court of Justice: Case C-29/69 *Stauder v Ulm* [1969] ECR 419 and Case 4/73 *Nold v Commission* [1974] ECR 491.

[133] RTB Art 9.1. [134] RTB Art 9.10(c). [135] RTB Art 9.2. [136] RTB Art 9.3.

[137] RTB Art 9.4.

the limits of the powers conferred upon them by or under this Treaty and by the Dispute Settlement Annex and the Economic Union Protocol'.

Decision-making

The Council is empowered to make Regulations, decisions, and recommendations. Regulations, as described under Article 9.5 of the RTB, are to possess the same binding force as the Acts of the Organisation which authorize them, and any question about whether the Council is authorized to make a Regulation is subject to judicial review. The RTB is silent about the voting rules governing the making of such Regulations, but given their potentially binding nature the voting rules applicable to decisions should be applied. Council decisions 'on all matters within its competence' are authorized under Article 9.6 and require fulfilment of a qualified unanimity voting rule (termed 'unanimous decisions' in the RTB). Decisions require 'the affirmative vote of all full Member States present and voting at the meeting of the Council of Ministers at which such decisions were taken, provided that such decisions shall have no force and effect until the Ministers of those full Member States, if any, which were not represented at that meeting, have within the consideration periods expressed either support for, or abstention in relation to, the decision'.[138] Abstentions do not impair the Council's vote and the consideration period is stated to be the period terminating thirty days after the Minister has received advice of the decision in question from the OECS Commission. The absence of a response from a member state during the consideration period is deemed to be an abstention and there is no maximum number for abstentions. As a result, although any member state can veto a decision of the Council of Ministers, and will have the opportunity to do so at a Council meeting or up to thirty days after receiving notice of the decision, if the member state does nothing the decision will carry. Decisions on procedural matters require a majority vote by all full member states present at the meeting. Both procedural and substantive decisions are binding upon all member states and organs of the Organisation except the Authority, and 'effect shall be given to any such decisions provided that it is within the sovereign competence of Member States to implement them.'[139]

These voting rules are subject to an exception in Article 9.9 which bars a member state from voting if it is in arrears in payment of its financial contributions in an amount equal to, or exceeding, its contributions due for the preceding full year. In such circumstances the member state is deemed to be abstaining and shall not be considered as present and voting on all matters. However Article 9.9 moderates this rule by allowing a majority of the other member states in the OECS Authority to permit the member state in arrears to vote.

[138] RTB Art 9.6.

[139] RTB Art 9.8. See the comments on the same phrase used in relation to the Authority, at p 77.

4.3.6 OECS Economic Affairs Council

Nature and competences

The Economic Affairs Council is governed by Article 11 of the RTB and Article 28 of the Protocol and is described in the latter as being the 'principal organ' of the Economic Union. It comprises member states acting through Ministers of Government. As with the Council, if a member state designates more than one Minister to sit on the Economic Affairs Council, it remains entitled to only one vote.[140] Participation in the Economic Affairs Council is restricted by Article 11.2, which only permits 'Member States possessing the necessary competence in respect of matters under consideration' to participate in its deliberations. Such wording would exclude a member state of the OECS from participating in an area under the Protocol with respect to which it had made a reservation.[141] Equally it could exclude a member state otherwise deemed incompetent to deal with a matter, such as Montserrat in the area of foreign affairs.

The functions of the Economic Affairs Council are set out in the Protocol, the provisions of which—to the extent that they are not incompatible—are deemed to be incorporated in and to form an integral part of the RTB.[142] Under Article 28.1 of the Protocol the Economic Affairs Council is responsible for exercising the powers and functions conferred on it by the Protocol, for supervising the application of the Protocol, and keeping it under review. The Economic Affairs Council is also responsible for considering whether further action should be taken to achieve the objectives of the Economic Union and to establish closer links with other countries, groups of countries, or international organizations. It is also vested with the 'powers of implementation of the Economic Union', acting under the direction of the OECS Authority, and is therefore tasked with the overall responsibility of ensuring the effective operation of the Economic Union.[143] The Economic Affairs Council also may delegate such powers to the OECS Commission, but again subject to the direction of the OECS Authority.[144]

Decision-making

In exercising these powers of implementation the Economic Affairs Council may, with the approval of the OECS Authority, make binding decisions and recommendations for all Protocol member states.[145] Article 28.3 of the Protocol does not specify whether its recommendations are binding. Under international institutional law recommendations are generally not binding in nature. But since recommendations of the Economic Affairs Council are subject to the same voting rules as decisions, there is no reason not to consider them as binding if the Protocol member states evidence an intention to make them so. The binding

[140] RTB Art 11.1.

[141] Art 24.3 of the RTB provides that '[e]xcept as provided in Article 24.2 [which allows reservations to the Protocol], a party to this Treaty is a party to the Economic Union Protocol.'

[142] RTB Art 11.3–11.4. [143] Protocol Art 28.2. [144] Protocol Art 28.2.

[145] Protocol Art 28.3.

nature of Economic Affairs Council decisions is established by Article 11.5 of the RTB, which accords them the same binding quality as the provisions that authorize them under the RTB and the Protocol. However, as with other organs, the authority of the Economic Affairs Council to make such decisions may be challenged by means of judicial review.[146]

Both decisions and recommendations of the Economic Affairs Council, unless otherwise provided in the Protocol, are made by the unanimous vote of Protocol member states.[147] 'Unanimous' decisions and recommendations are described in Article 28.4 of the Protocol as being such unless a Protocol member state casts a negative veto, and so long as they receive 'the affirmative votes of not less than two-thirds of all Protocol Member States who are full Member States'. As a result 'unanimity' here is similar to the qualified unanimity voting rules we have seen for other organs in the region. Nevertheless, some decisions, including procedural ones, those regarding establishment of new organs, and those made in relation to the Protocol's complaints procedure, may be made by means of a simple majority vote.[148]

4.3.7 OECS Assembly

The OECS Assembly comprises parliamentary or legislative representatives of member states, including both members of the government and the opposition. Under Article 10.2 each Parliament of an independent full member state shall be entitled to elect five of its members to the OECS Assembly, whereas each legislature of the other member states shall be entitled to elect three of its members to the Assembly. Article 10.3 ensures proportionate representation by prescribing, in the case of Members of Parliament, that the numbers of government and opposition representatives reflect their proportions in Parliament, subject to the requirement that there be at least one opposition member selected. For members of the Legislature at least two government representatives should be selected and one opposition member. Article 10.3 also provides that the Head of Government and Leader of the Opposition must be included in the members selected for the OECS Assembly and that, in the event that there is no elected opposition in a territory, the Head of State must appoint one person to represent the opposition parties. Article 10.4 provides that in the event of uncertainty about the proportion of members to be elected, the respective Parliament or legislature shall resolve the uncertainty by means of its ordinary procedures.

These provisions are notable since they attempt to cure one of the main deficiencies in representation in the regional organizations of the Caribbean by mandating the inclusion of members of the opposition from member states. This is not a requirement for the Assembly of Caribbean Community Parliamentarians, nor is it a requirement for representation on any other organs of the OECS or

[146] RTB Art 11.5. [147] Protocol Art 28.4.
[148] See eg Protocol Arts 28.5(a), 29.1, and 30.

CARICOM. On all other organs Government Ministers or their delegates represent members, and thus only government views are guaranteed to be included in discussions and decision-making processes. By requiring opposition representation the OECS Assembly opens up its decision-making processes to greater public scrutiny and accountability, and brings a much higher level of democracy to the OECS. Although not as accountable to the electorate as the European Parliament, the members of which are directly elected as MEPs, the OECS Assembly represents a great stride in favour of democracy in the Caribbean.

The tenure of members of the OECS Assembly is two years from the date of election to the Assembly or until the next general election of Parliament or the legislature, whichever period is shorter.[149] Provision is also made in Article 10 of the RTB for the election of a Speaker and Deputy Speaker to the OECS Assembly, their terms of office, and the filling of vacancies in those offices, and for the appointment by the Director General of a Clerk and other support staff.[150] The OECS Assembly is to determine its own procedure subject to the directions of the OECS Authority.[151]

The function of the OECS Assembly is to consider and report, within the time prescribed, to the Authority on any proposal to enact an Act of the Organisation under Article 8.10 and on any other matter referred to it by the Authority.[152] It is also to consider and report on any proposal to make a regulation which has been referred to it by the Council of Ministers under Article 9.4, again within the time period prescribed by the Authority. As a result of this role, the OECS Assembly has the potential to open up democratic debate over any Acts or Regulations of the Organisation, debate which will be especially important given the expanded legislative competence of the OECS over areas previously under national authority.[153]

4.3.8 OECS Commission

The OECS Commission is governed by Articles 12–13 of the RTB and Article 29 of the Protocol, and is the successor to the OECS Secretariat.[154] It is designated as the 'principal Organ responsible for the general administration of the Organisation' and the 'principal administrative organ of the Economic Union'.[155] The Commission comprises the Director General, who heads the Commission, and one Commissioner of Ambassadorial rank named by each member state.[156] The RTB does not set out a process for the removal of Commissioners, with such matters presumably being left to each member state. Each Commissioner is to

[149] RTB Art 10.5. [150] RTB Art 10.6–10.12. [151] RTB Art 10.14.
[152] RTB Art 10.13(a). [153] See RTB Art 14.
[154] See RTB Art 13.8–13.9 for the transitional provisions for the Director General and Secretariat staff from the 1981 Treaty of Basseterre. Note that the succession has not been seamless: OECS reports and documents made subsequent to the entry into force of the RTB are still labelled as having been authored by the Secretariat.
[155] RTB Art 12.1 and Protocol Art 29.1. [156] RTB Art 12.1–12.2.

represent the OECS Commission in the member state appointing him and the Commission takes decisions by a simple majority vote. There is no provision for a casting vote by the Director General.[157]

The functions of the Commission are primarily those of an administrative organ. It is to service meetings of organs of the Organisation, including the preparation of draft agendas for the meetings of the OECS Authority, and is to follow up and take action on decisions, recommendations, or directives approved at such meetings.[158] It plays an important role in overseeing OECS activities, being required under Article 12.5 to keep the functioning of the Organisation under continuous review, report the findings to the relevant organs, and monitor the implementation of Acts and Regulations of the Organisation. It also plays a key role in the OECS legislative process, since it is mandated to make recommendations to OECS organs 'on the making of Acts and Regulations of the Organisation and [to] provide drafts of such Acts and Regulations to be considered for enactment'.[159] The Commission is mandated to serve as a depository for the RTB, and presumably for the Protocol.[160] Additionally, the Commission is provided with a more general mandate to 'undertake such other work and studies and perform such other services relating to the functions of Organisation as may be required under this Treaty or by the OECS Authority or by any other Organ from time to time and also make proposals relating thereto as may assist in the efficient and harmonious functioning and development of the Organisation'.[161]

This latter mandate is phrased so broadly as to allow the Commission to exercise independent initiative for the purpose of the efficient and harmonious functioning and development of the Organisation. Such a mandate may prove crucial to the development of its functions under the RTB, since it could be used to authorize the Commission to act as a watchdog over the RTB and the general development of the OECS. The EU's Commission, which acts with a similar, albeit stronger mandate, has proved crucial to the development of the law of the European Union.[162]

Under the Protocol the Commission may be entrusted by the Economic Affairs Council with 'such functions as the Economic Affairs Council considers necessary to assist it in accomplishing its tasks'.[163] Such a provision could be used to significantly expand the Commission's functions.[164] Other functions are specifically set out in Article 29.2 of the Protocol, and include those of servicing and helping to coordinate the meetings of the Economic Affairs Council and any other organs established by it under the Protocol, and collecting, collating, analysing, and distributing 'all information pertinent to the workings of the Economic Union'. Importantly, the Commission has been assigned the role of reporting 'all difficulties as they arise in the administration of', and all 'breaches of', the Protocol to the

[157] RTB Art 12.3. [158] RTB Art 12.4 and 12.5(e). [159] RTB Art 12.5(c).
[160] RTB Art 25. [161] RTB Art 12.5(f).
[162] On the role of the European Commission see Art 17 of the TEU and Hartley, *The Foundations of European Union Law* (n 28) ch 1.
[163] Protocol Art 29.1.
[164] See also Protocol Art 29.2(e) which allows the Economic Affairs Council to assign other functions to the Commission.

Economic Affairs Council.[165] This latter role again highlights the potential of the Commission to be a watchdog over the OECS Economic Union, including the specific rules of the Protocol, and hints at its potential to be an enforcement mechanism of Union law. Thus although the *Commission* itself is not expressly empowered to raise a complaint under the consultation and complaints procedures established under Articles 30 and 31 of the Protocol, the Organisation, as represented by the Director General of the Commission, is one of the eligible parties under the RTB's procedure for resolution of disputes.[166] Since the wording in Article 18 does not restrict the Organisation to being a defendant in disputes, the OECS properly may bring complaints against member states involving the interpretation or application of the RTB, including the Protocol.[167] The Director General may submit such disputes to the procedures provided for in the DSA or to the Eastern Caribbean Court of Appeal.[168]

The Director General is specified to be the 'Chief Executive Officer of the Organisation', is in charge of its day-to-day operations, and represents the legal personality of the OECS.[169] The Director General is appointed by the OECS Authority for a four-year term, is eligible for re-appointment, and is responsible to the Authority, to the Commission, and through the Commission, to the Council of Ministers, Economic Affairs Council, and any other organ established by the Authority under Article 7.2. The Director General is responsible for preparing draft, balanced budgets for the Organisation (and presumably its special budgets).[170]

The Director General also plays a prominent role in coordinating and harmonizing the foreign policy of member states. Under Article 15.1 the OECS member states agree to establish and maintain joint overseas diplomatic or other representation, 'including, where appropriate, the accreditation of one representative to one or more States, international organisations or conferences'. The Director General is also important in cases where such joint representation is not possible, for example, where the rules of the international organization concerned do not permit it. In such circumstances, under Article 15.2 the Director General is authorized to take 'all appropriate steps... to ensure the optimum realisation of the benefits of their membership of such organisation or conference'. As the legal representative of the OECS, the Director General is entrusted with the responsibility of transmitting directives of the OECS Authority on joint foreign policy matters to heads of overseas joint diplomatic or other missions, and is accorded precedence in protocol over such heads of missions.[171] The Director General is also responsible for the staffing of OECS missions, with the exception of the heads of such missions who are appointed by member states.[172]

[165] Protocol Art 29.2(c) and (d). [166] RTB Arts 18.1, 18.5, and 21.3.

[167] RTB Art 24.1 provides that the 'Dispute Settlement Annex and the Economic Union Protocol shall form an integral part of this Treaty.'

[168] RTB Art 18.2–18.3. [169] RTB Arts 13.1 and 21.3.

[170] RTB Art 17. Under Art 17.8, providing for special budgets, no draft preparing authority is indicated. However it is assumed that the Director General and the Commission would be equally responsible for drafting them.

[171] RTB Art 15.3. [172] RTB Art 15.4 and 15.5.

This foreign affairs role of the Director General has been greatly expanded under the RTB. To contrast, under Article 7 of the original 1981 Treaty of Basseterre many of the Director General's functions would have fallen within the remit of the Foreign Affairs Committee, an organ of the OECS comprised of Ministers responsible for foreign affairs in their respective governments. With the transfer of these powers to the Director General and Commission the RTB regime appears to have strengthened the role of these organs and brought foreign affairs within the main administrative apparatus of the OECS. This is striking because foreign affairs matters tend to be considered amongst the most closely guarded functions of sovereignty. In the EU, for example, foreign affairs have only been gradually brought within the competence of organs of the European Union, and are still not entirely subsumed within the main EU *acquis communautaire*, the accumulated body of EU law.[173] But the OECS, perhaps out of necessity due to smallness of size and resources, has taken the bold step to form joint diplomatic and technical missions in Brussels, Geneva, Ottawa, and Puerto Rico.[174]

The rules and regulations governing the Director General and staff of the Commission are approved by the OECS Authority, and the Director General is entrusted with appointing all staff of the Commission other than Directors. Directors are to be appointed by the Director General with the prior approval of the Commission. Article 13.4 ensures the integrity and representativeness of the staff of the Commission by mandating that, with respect to appointments, 'due regard shall be paid, subject to the paramount consideration of securing the highest standards of efficiency, competence and integrity, to the desirability of maintaining an equitable distribution of appointments to such posts among citizens and belongers of the Member States'.[175] Subsections 5 and 6 of Article 13 reinforce the integrity of the Director General and staff of the Commission by imposing duties upon them and the member states of the OECS to ensure their independence and exclusively international character. These provisions do not expressly impose similar duties on the Commissioners themselves, who are appointed and subject to removal by their member states. This omission could pose challenges. If Articles 12 and 13 are not interpreted as requiring independence on the part of the Commissioners, this would impair the independence and integrity

[173] Only recently have general foreign affairs matters been dealt with by the organs of the European Union, and in the beginning they fell almost entirely within the competence of the European Council, rather than the Council. After the Treaty of Lisbon, however, many foreign affairs matters fall under the competence of both the European Council and Council, under Title V of the TEU and Part Five of the TFEU. On the evolution of treaty-making powers of the EU see eg Hartley, *The Foundations of European Union Law* (n 28) ch 6.

[174] OECS Secretariat, 'Units & Missions' as available at <http://www.oecs.org/about-the-oecs/units-a-missions> (accessed 20 Oct 2011).

[175] The term 'belonger' was once common in the context of Commonwealth Caribbean nationality laws. It refers to persons who have very close connections with, but not citizenship of, a state and who thereby derive rights to reside in and travel to and from that state. See eg the case of *Godfrey Frederick Seymour and Jermaine Seymour v Attorney-General, Director of Immigration, Honourable A. Loftus Roker (Minister of National Security) and the Board of Immigration*, Supreme Court of the Commonwealth of the Bahamas, Common Law Side No 1330 of 1986 (25 Jun 1987) [unreported] [discussing the availability of 'Belonger' status arising from pre-independence Bahamian legislation].

of the Commission more generally. One hopes that the rules and regulations governing the Commission staff will be applied more generally so as to also cover Commissioners.

Under the Office of the Director General fall a number of OECS Units, including the Administrative and General Services Unit, the Communications Unit, the Education and Human Resource Development Unit, the Environment & Sustainable Development Unit (formerly Natural Resources Management Unit), the Export Development Unit, the Agricultural Diversification Coordinating Unit, the Finance Unit, the Functional Cooperation and Programme Management Unit, the HIV/AIDS Project Unit, the Human Resource Unit, the Information Services Unit, the Information Technology Unit, the Internal Audit Unit, the Legal Unit, the Macro-Economic and Sector Policy Unit, the Pharmaceutical Procurement Service (PPS), the Regional e-Government Unit, the Regional Integration Unit, the Social Development Unit, and the Trade Policy Unit.[176]

In addition to administrative functions, under the DSA the Director General may provide 'good offices' to help resolve a dispute, and is to assist in bringing a dispute before the Conciliation Commission.[177] The Director General serves in a secretarial role for the Conciliation Commission and acts as a depositary for its report.[178] In addition, the Director General is to bring disputes before an Arbitral Tribunal under paragraph 5.7 of the DSA, and may be required to appoint the Chairman or other members of the Arbitral Tribunal. The Director General serves as the secretariat for the Arbitral Tribunal and depository for its report.[179] If, however, the Commission itself is a party to a dispute under Article 18.5 of the RTB, the role of the Director General in managing the dispute resolution process is to be filled by the Chief Justice of the Eastern Caribbean Supreme Court, through the Court's Chief Registrar.[180] The Director General, as the legal representative of the OECS, may also be subject to suit before the Eastern Caribbean Court of Appeal, and as mentioned earlier, may bring legal actions to the same Court, or to the bodies established under the DSA.[181]

4.3.9 OECS External Auditor

In addition to the organs of the Organisation, Article 16 makes provision for an External Auditor, who may be appointed or removed by the Authority. The Authority is responsible for the Regulations governing the terms and conditions of service of the External Auditor.

[176] OECS Secretariat, 'Units & Missions' (n 174).
[177] DSA [2] and [4.7]. Para 2 does not specifically mention the Director General, but does not exclude that person serving in a good offices role.
[178] DSA [4.11]–[4.12]. [179] DSA [5.10]–[5.11]. [180] DSA Art [5.12].
[181] RTB Art 21.3 and DSA [10(d)].

4.3.10 OECS institutions

Under Article 6 of the RTB three institutions of the Organisation are identified: the Eastern Caribbean Supreme Court, the Eastern Caribbean Central Bank, and the Eastern Caribbean Civil Aviation Authority. Article 6.2 provides that the OECS Authority may add to this list of Iinstitutions by unanimous decision. An additional institution, the Eastern Caribbean Telecommunications Authority, is also listed.[182]

4.4 Summary

The organizational structures of CARICOM and the OECS have become significantly more robust under their new treaties. The primary organs of each organization are supported by a limited number of secondary organs, each of which has competences in a number of different areas of human activity.

In CARICOM primary decision-making authority still resides with the Conference, even though the Community Council and Ministerial Councils have each been given binding authority. Given the similarity in terms of composition of primary and secondary organs in CARICOM (all being composed of Head of Government or ministerial level representatives, respectively), the organization retains a strong inter-governmental character. The creation of the Assembly of Caribbean Community Parliamentarians (ACCP) offers some hope of a deeper, more meaningful integration process, one involving a level of popular accountability. However the lack of recent meetings of the ACCP, and its entirely consultative character, are causes for concern. The CARICOM Secretariat and Secretary General have both been further empowered by the RTC, and thus provide the possibility of an independent, technocratic arm for the organization. But until the Secretariat and the political directorates of member states both embrace such a strong independent role, the Secretariat's functioning will remain constrained.

The voting rules for organs of CARICOM have been relaxed by the RTC and have moved slightly further away from formal unanimity. The Conference still retains what has been described as a qualified unanimity decision-making process, and thus remains subject to the possibility of a veto or the pressures of consensus-based decisions. But the Community Council and Ministerial Councils have moved to the qualified majority rule for most decisions. If the member states are able to accept the consequences of the latter rule in practice, the RTC should promote a much greater number of decisions being made by secondary organs. This would be tremendously beneficial to the development of CARICOM, since it would ensure that decisions are made by organs comprised of representatives who should possess detailed knowledge of the matters being considered, and who should be able to meet more frequently.

[182] OECS Secretariat, 'Units & Missions' (n 174).

The organizational structure of the OECS under the RTB is very different from that of CARICOM. Although the Authority retains its role under the RTB as the primary organ of the OECS, it is given new, more powerful competences, such as the ability to enact Acts of the Organisation. These Acts, as discussed in Chapter 6, are binding upon member states and must be directly effective in their laws. Likewise, the secondary organs of the OECS have stronger powers, such as the ability of the Council of Ministers (Council) to enact binding, and directly effective, Regulations. Nevertheless, the RTB is rendered less efficient by essentially duplicating its main secondary organ: it provides for a Council under the RTB and an Economic Affairs Council under the Protocol. Whether this double-organ structure could be overcome and made more efficient by holding simultaneous, or immediately consecutive, meetings of these organs remains to be seen. The RTB also falls slightly short by generally relying upon qualified unanimity decision-making processes. This may be a necessary evil considering the real powers that have been granted these organs. But perhaps the most significant structural change of the OECS is the introduction of a kind of quasi-legislative process, involving the drafting of Acts and Regulations by the Commission, which are considered and reported on by the Assembly prior to adoption by the Authority or Council, respectively. Such a process should ensure participation by all three categories of organs commonly found in international institutions: independent technocrats (the Commission), representatives of the people (the Assembly), and representatives of governments (the Authority, Council, and Economic Affairs Council). When one takes into account the delegation of exclusive competences by member states to the OECS, it is clear that the OECS is moving towards a potentially very strong regional integration model.

5

Final Provisions of the Treaties

This chapter concludes the examination of the main institutional structures of the Caribbean Community and the Organisation of Eastern Caribbean States. It looks at the interrelated topics of legal personality, privileges, and immunities, and the miscellaneous final provisions of the treaties related to the management of the respective treaty regimes. The latter include articles related to the entry into force of the treaties, depositaries, reservations, accession, amendments, and the right of withdrawal.

These provisions demonstrate the way in which the Caribbean regional treaties attempt to carefully balance the rights and duties of the two organizations with those of their member states. On the one hand, the separate legal personalities of CARICOM and the OECS are recognized under both national law and international law, with the latter providing the ability to enter into international relations with third states or other entities. In addition privileges and immunities, which exist almost entirely in the national jurisdictions of member states, bolster the independence of each organization by removing the potential for interference in its activities by member states. On the other hand, the needs of member states are protected by the restrictions inherent in such privileges and immunities, including the limitations imposed by the doctrine of functional necessity and the general inapplicability of immunities at the international level. The final provisions demonstrate the key roles of the member states in creating the organizations, in restricting their competences, changing them, or even rejecting them entirely.

5.1 Personality and Legal Capacity

An international organization can have legal personality as a matter of domestic and/or international law. In other words personality can exist under the national laws of its member states only. It also can have international legal personality, that is, the capacity to independently bear rights and obligations under international law.[1]

[1] Jan Klabbers, *An Introduction to International Institutional Law* (Cambridge: Cambridge University Press, 2002) 42. See generally ch 3; Philippe Sands QC and Pierre Klein, *Bowett's Law of International Institutions*, 6th edn (London: Thomson Reuters, 2009) ch 15; Henry Schermers and Niels Blokker, *International Institutional Law*, 4th rev'd edn (Boston: Martinus Nijhoff Publishers 2003) ch 11.

The nature of the international legal personality accorded to international and regional organizations, however, is not uniform. It varies from subject to subject. In this sense a conceptual distinction must be drawn between the question of the *existence* of international legal personality, and the *scope* of competences it includes.[2] The two are closely interlinked, since one cannot have international legal competences without international legal personality, and vice versa. In fact the determination of existence of international personality will in most cases depend upon proof of possession of attributes of such personhood.[3] As a result the question of the existence of international personality on the part of CARICOM and the OECS must be in a large measure answered through an analysis of the scope of the international legal competences the two organizations exercise.[4] Such an analysis reveals that both CARICOM and the OECS possess international legal personality, but with different scope in competences.

5.1.1 CARICOM

The Caribbean Community is provided with 'full juridical personality' under Article 228(1) of the RTC. This wording is identical to that found in Article 20 in the original 1973 Treaty of Chaguaramas, but differs from that found in Article 63 of the Annex to the Treaty—The Caribbean Common Market, which specified that the 'Common Market shall have international juridical personality'.[5]

Whether CARICOM under the RTC has been accorded international legal personality is determined by interpreting the ordinary meaning of the phrase 'full juridical personality' as used in Article 228(1), in the context of the other provisions of the treaty and in the light of its object and purpose. Such a question also requires an analysis of CARICOM's functions, and whether international legal personality has been recognized by other international legal actors.[6] Stated more

[2] See eg AS Muller, *International Organizations and their Host States: Aspects of their Legal Relationship* (The Hague: Kluwer Law International, 1995) 82–6.

[3] The tautological or even circular nature of this exercise has been extensively noted in the literature. See eg Roland Portmann, *Legal Personality in International Law* (Cambridge: Cambridge University Press, 2010) 10.

[4] Note that some authors attempt to define international legal personality with fixed objective criteria. Muller, for example, suggests that international legal personality will exist if an organization fulfils the definition of an international organization under public international law, namely, that it is '(1) an entity established, (2) by an agreement under public international law, with (3) separate, permanent organs, manifesting a will distinct from that of its members': AS Muller, *International Organizations and their Host States* (n 2) 77.

[5] Applying the inductive approach to the question of legal personality, Hans J Geiser, Pamela Alleyne, and Carroll Gajraj, in *Legal Problems of Caribbean Integration: A study of legal aspects of CARICOM* (Leyden: Sijthoff, 1976) at 83, weigh the effect of the differences in wording between the original Treaty and Annex. They conclude that the two phrases will have the same effect simply because international legal personality also requires recognition by third parties at the international level. In other words, they point out that regardless of terminology, the member states of CARICOM could not create an objectively existing international legal person by themselves, only at most a subjective one (ie, recognized as such by member states).

[6] For a discussion of the doctrine of recognition as one of the theoretical foundations of international legal personality, using the *Reparations for Injuries Case* as an example, see Roland Portmann, *Legal Personality in International Law* (Cambridge: Cambridge University Press, 2010) 99–110.

broadly, the question of whether an international or regional organization has international legal personality requires an assessment of its functions, powers, and competences, as set out in its constituent document and as exercised in practice in relation to its member states and third states and organizations.

In terms of context, Article 228(2) of the RTC specifies that the Community must be accorded in the territory of member states 'the most extensive legal capacity accorded to legal persons under its laws including the capacity to acquire and dispose of movable and immovable property and to sue and be sued in its own name'. This provision grants CARICOM full national legal personality. In addition, Article 228(3) empowers the Community to conclude agreements with 'States and International Organisations'.[7] This is an express treaty-making power and applies to member states, non-member states, and international organizations.[8] It is supported by Article 12(3) of the RTC, which mandates that the Conference be the 'final authority for the conclusion of treaties on behalf of the Community and for entering into relationships between the Community and international organisations and States'. Such a treaty-making power, it should be noted, can only be exercised by an entity possessing some form of international legal personality. For this reason the power to conclude treaties has been identified as a key indicator of such status.[9]

A treaty-making power may arise under general international law or, as in the case of CARICOM, may be granted by the organization's constituent document.[10] In the *Reparation for Injuries Case* the International Court of Justice highlighted the treaty-making power of the UN and its practice of entering into treaties as confirming its character as an international person.[11] The Court also noted the existence of the 1946 Convention on the Privileges and Immunities of the United Nations, and stated that '[i]t is difficult to see how such a convention could operate except upon the international plane and as between parties possessing international personality.'[12] In reaching the conclusion that the United Nations had international personality, the International Court of Justice held:

In the opinion of the Court, the Organization was intended to exercise and enjoy, and is in fact exercising and enjoying, functions and rights which can only be explained on the basis of the possession of a large measure of international personality and the capacity to operate on an

[7] See also RTC Arts 229–230.

[8] See Art 21(3) of the original 1973 Treaty which specified all three categories of actors.

[9] See eg Klabbers, *An Introduction to International Institutional Law* (n 1) at 44, who lists (1) the right to enter into international agreements, (2) the right to send and receive legations, and (3) the capacity to bring and receive international claims, as the three indicators of subjectivity at international law.

[10] Klabbers, at pp 45–6, argues that the power to enter into treaties may derive directly from public international law, rather than the constituent treaty, but that this power will be governed not only by the rules of international law but also the specific rules of the organization.

[11] *Reparation for Injuries Suffered in the Service of the United Nations* (Advisory Opinion) [1949] ICJ Rep 174, at p 179. The UN's power to enter into treaties is implicit in Arts 16, 75–77, 80–83, 85, 87 (trusteeship agreements) 43, 45 (standby forces agreements), and 63 (ECOSOC agreements) of the Charter of the United Nations (adopted 26 Jun 1945, in force 24 Oct 1945) 1 UNTS xvi, 39 AJIL Supp 190.

[12] *Reparation for Injuries* (n 11). Note that the United Nations itself is not a party to the Convention on the Privileges and Immunities of the United Nations (adopted 13 Feb 1946, in force 17 Sep 1946)

> international plane. It is at present the supreme type of international organization, and it could not carry out the intentions of its founders if it was devoid of international personality. It must be acknowledged that its Members, by entrusting certain functions to it, with the attendant duties and responsibilities, have clothed it with the competence required to enable those functions to be effectively discharged.
>
> Accordingly, the Court has come to the conclusion that the Organization is an international person. That is not the same thing as saying that it is a State, which it certainly is not, or that its legal personality and rights and duties are the same as those of a State. Still less is it the same thing as saying that it is 'a super-State', whatever that expression may mean. It does not even imply that all its rights and duties must be upon the international plane, any more than all the rights and duties of a State must be upon that plane. What it does mean is that it is a subject of international law and capable of possessing international rights and duties, and that it has capacity to maintain its rights by bringing international claims.[13]

In weighing the factors highlighted by the Court in the *Reparation for Injuries Case*, it should be noted that CARICOM's express treaty-making power is similarly complemented by the privileges and immunities it is granted under several treaties, including two headquarters agreements with Guyana, to which it is a party.[14] These latter conventions have been continued by Article 229 of the RTC. CARICOM also receives accredited representatives of third states and regional organizations (passive legation), and the legal personalities of both the Caribbean Community and its common market have been recognized by the United Kingdom and the European Union.[15] CARICOM is a permanent observer at the United Nations and provides official Caribbean Community Representation in Haiti (active legation).[16] It also has the capacity to bring and receive international legal claims in

1 UNTS 15 and 90 UNTS 327 (corrigendum to vol 1). It is, however, a party to numerous international treaties including the Agreement Between the United Nations and the United States Regarding the Headquarters of the United Nations (adopted 25 Jun 1947, approved by the UN General Assembly 31 Oct 1947) annexed to the Agreement Between the United Nations and the United States Regarding the Headquarters of the United Nations (1947) UNGA Res 169, Second Session (A/RES/169 (II)) as available at <http://daccess-dds-ny.un.org/doc/RESOLUTION/GEN/NR0/038/76/IMG/NR003876.pdf?OpenElement> (accessed 2 Nov 2011).

[13] *Reparation for Injuries* (n 11) at p 179.

[14] Under the original 1973 Treaty regime CARICOM and its common market were conceptually distinct and required separate treaty arrangements. See the Protocol on the Privileges and Immunities of the Caribbean Community (adopted 14 Jan 1985, in force 15 Jan 1990) 2324 UNTS 493; Protocol on the Privileges and Immunities of the Caribbean Common Market (adopted 14 Jan 1985, in force 15 Jan 1990); Agreement between the Government of Guyana and the Caribbean Community Relating to the Privileges and Immunities to be Granted in Connection with the Secretariat (adopted and entered into force 23 Jan 1976) 2398 UNTS 1; Agreement between the Government of Guyana and the Caribbean Common Market Relating to the Privileges and Immunities to be Granted in Connection with the Common Market (adopted and entered into force 23 Jan 1976) as available at <http://www.caricomlaw.org/Details.aspx?EntryId=155&Command=Core_Download&Method=attachment> (2 Nov 2011).

[15] See eg CARICOM Secretariat, 'Plenipotentiary Representatives of Third States Accredited to the Caribbean Community (CARICOM)', as available at <http://www.caricom.org/jsp/community/plenipotentiary_representatives.jsp?menu=community> (accessed 2 Nov 2011); Geiser, Alleyne, and Gajraj, *Legal Problems of Caribbean Integration* (n 5) 90–1 and 147–50; William G Demas, *West Indian Development and the Deepening and Widening of the Caribbean Community* (Kingston, Jamaica: Ian Randle Publishers/UWI ISER, 1997) 77–8.

[16] CARICOM is listed on the UN's website as one of the 'Intergovernmental organizations having received a standing invitation to participate as observers in the sessions and the work of the General

the original jurisdiction of the Caribbean Court of Justice, under Article 211(1)(b) of the RTC. Finally, numerous provisions of the RTC point to ways in which the Caribbean Community is required to engage in international relations.[17] As such, CARICOM must be recognized as possessing international legal personality, the scope of which includes the powers to conclude treaties, to send and receive representatives in relation to third states and international organizations, and to bring and receive international legal claims before the Caribbean Court of Justice.

The international legal personality of CARICOM is supported by the general undertaking provision, Article 9 of the RTC, which requires member states to take all appropriate measures to 'ensure the carrying out of obligations arising out of this Treaty or resulting from decisions taken by the Organs and Bodies of the Community' and to 'abstain from any measures which could jeopardise the attainment of the objectives of this Treaty'. The wording of this provision is flexible, applying to obligations 'arising out of' the RTC and 'resulting from' decisions of CARICOM organs and bodies. For this reason Article 9 can be read as applying to any additional international legal obligations that could be said to arise out of the RTC or from decisions taken thereunder.[18] In this way Article 9 underpins and protects CARICOM's international legal competence by including international acts under its terms. It requires member states to respect any international treaties entered into by CARICOM and restricts them from entering into agreements with third parties that would jeopardize the objectives of the RTC.

The international legal competence of CARICOM is limited in relation to its member states, however, by Article 240(1) of the RTC. This provision states that '[d]ecisions of competent Organs taken under this Treaty shall be subject to the relevant constitutional procedures of the Member States before creating legally binding rights and obligations for nationals of such States.' Article 240(1) only speaks to 'decisions' and thus would not seem to apply to international legal agreements entered into by the Community. However to the extent that an international legal agreement is mandated by a decision of a CARICOM organ, its enforceability in the domestic law of member states would appear to be expressly limited by

Assembly and maintaining permanent offices at Headquarters': <http://www.un.org/en/members/intergovorg.shtml> (accessed 3 Nov 2011). Its Representation in Haiti is formally recognized in the Agreement between the Government of Haiti and the Caribbean Community Relating to the Privileges and Immunities to be granted in Connection with the Caribbean Community in Haiti (adopted and in force in 2002) [exact date not specified]: CARICOM Secretariat, 'Agreement between The Government of Haiti and The Caribbean Community Relating to The Privileges and Immunities to be granted in Connection with The Caribbean Community in Haiti' as available through <http://www.caricomlaw.org/Details.aspx?EntryId=81> (accessed 3 Nov 2011).

[17] See eg RTC Arts 6(d), (g), and (h) [objectives], 12(3) and (9) [Conference], 15(2)(i) [COTED], 16(2)–(3) [COFCOR], 19(1) [Legal Affairs Committee], 24(2)(a) [Secretary General], 25(f) [Secretariat]. These powers were also noted in relation to the Secretariat under the original Treaty of Chaguaramas in Gladstone Mills et al, *Report on a Comprehensive Review of the Programmes, Institutions and Organisations of the Caribbean Community* (Georgetown, Guyana: Caribbean Community Secretariat, 1990) at 71, where it was stated that the Secretariat 'can assume international obligations'.

[18] For a similar extension of treaty making powers of CARICOM under its original Treaty and Annex, on the basis of functional necessity, see Geiser, Alleyne, and Gajraj, *Legal Problems of Caribbean Integration* (n 5) 138–9.

the Article 240 transformation requirement.[19] This transformation requirement, it should be noted, would in any event be required for international legal treaties in Commonwealth Caribbean states.[20]

5.1.2 OECS

The legal personality of the OECS is established in Article 21.1 of the RTB which states that the 'Organisation, as an international organization, shall enjoy legal personality'. This phrasing does not specify whether the OECS is to be accorded international legal personality. Such a question, as in the case of CARICOM, must be answered through an interpretation of the ordinary meaning of the words used, in the context of the other provisions of the treaty and in the light of its object and purpose and functions. International personality must also be weighed against whether such status has been recognized by other international legal actors.

Article 21.2 recognizes the OECS as possessing full national legal capacity. It specifies that the OECS is to be accorded in the territory of each member state the 'legal capacity required for the performance of its functions under this Treaty' and the 'power to acquire, hold or dispose of real or personal, moveable or immoveable property'. The possibility of the Organisation also possessing international legal personality is raised by the designation of the OECS as an 'international organisation' in Article 21.1, which expressly highlights its international character. This is supported by several of the express competences granted to the OECS and its organs under the RTB. Under Article 8.13 of the RTB, for example, the OECS Authority is mandated to be the final authority for the conclusion of treaties on behalf of the Organisation and for entering into relationships between the Organisation and other international organizations and third countries. This express treaty-making power provides strong evidence of international legal personality.[21] The OECS' treaty-making power is exercisable by the Director General, who under Article 21.3 is mandated to represent the Organisation in the exercise of its legal personality.

In addition, similar to CARICOM, the scope of the international personality of the OECS is strengthened by Article 5.1 of the RTB, which describes the nature of the binding commitment undertaken by member states as including the obligation to 'take all appropriate measures, whether general or particular, to ensure the carrying out of obligations arising out of this Treaty or resulting from decisions taken by the Institutions of the Organisation'. Since the entry of the OECS into a treaty obligation most likely would require a decision of a competent organ (Institution),

[19] But see the possibilities arising from the doctrine of direct effect, described in Chapter 8.

[20] For a discussion of the transformation requirement in relation to the original CARICOM Treaty and Annex see Geiser, Alleyne, and Gajraj, *Legal Problems of Caribbean Integration* (n 5) 145–7. For the common law position see eg *R v Lyons* [2003] 1 AC 976 (HL), *Higgs v Minister of National Security and Others* [2000] 2 AC 228 (PC Bah), *JH Rayner (Mincing Lane) Ltd v Department of Trade and Industry* (also called *Maclaine Watson & Co Ltd v International Tin Council*) [1990] 2 AC 418 (HL), *R v Secretary of State for the Home Department, ex parte Brind* [1991] 1 AC 696 (HL), *Salomon v Commissioners of Customs and Excise* [1967] 2 QB 116 (CA Eng).

[21] RTB Art 20.1, Protocol Art 33. See also the discussion of the Advisory Opinion on *Reparation for Injuries* (n 11).

all such treaties could be deemed to fall under the general undertaking provision. Article 5.2, which requires member states to 'take all steps to secure the enactment of such legislation as is necessary to give effect to this Treaty and decisions taken thereunder' also could be interpreted as embracing any implementing legislation for international treaties entered into as a result of a decision of the Organisation.

In addition to treaty-making competence, the OECS has been accorded the right of passive legation. It receives representatives from third states, other entities, and international organizations, including Puerto Rico, Mexico, Brazil, and Germany.[22] It is also expressly empowered to admit observers from third states and other organizations at its deliberations. With respect to active legation, the OECS has been recognized as having the competence to send representatives to the United Nations, where it has been granted observer status, and also has established OECS Missions in Brussels, Geneva, and Puerto Rico.[23] Further, the OECS Commission and senior officials of the Organisation are accorded privileges and immunities under Article 21.4 equivalent to those provided by the 1961 Vienna Convention on Diplomatic Relations, and such privileges and immunities were recognized by the International Court of Justice in the *Reparations for Injuries Case* as being relevant to questions of international personality.[24] The RTB also contemplates the OECS being a party to a dispute under the Dispute Settlement Annex (DSA), including a dispute before the Eastern Caribbean Court of Appeal.[25]

Several provisions of the RTB expressly contemplate foreign and international roles for, and functions of, the OECS. Article 1 defines 'third countries' or 'third states' for the purposes of the RTB, and Article 4.1(c) specifies that one of the purposes and functions of the Organisation is 'to assist the Member States in the realisation of their obligations and responsibilities to the international community'. Under Article 4.2 member states are required to undertake joint actions and pursue joint policies in the field of external relations, including overseas representation, and in the area of international trade agreements and other external economic relations.[26] One of the Organisation's exclusive areas of legislative competence is in relation to maritime boundaries, which would include international boundaries between OECS member states and third states.[27] Moreover the OECS is required, through the office of the Director General, to assist in the coordination and harmonization of the foreign policy of member states, through joint overseas or other diplomatic representation, and 'overseas diplomatic and other missions established by the Organisation'.[28] The OECS is mandated in Article 20.1

[22] See RTB Art 20.2 and OECS Secretariat, 'Milestones' as available at <http://www.oecs.org/about-the-oecs/oecs-milestones> (accessed 3 Nov 2011).

[23] The OECS is listed on the UN's website as one of the '[i]ntergovernmental organizations having received a standing invitation to participate as observers in the sessions and the work of the General Assembly and not maintaining permanent offices at Headquarters': <http://www.un.org/en/members/intergovorg.shtml> (accessed 3 Nov 2011). On its Missions, see OECS Secretariat, 'Units & Missions', as available at <http://www.oecs.org/about-the-oecs/units-a-missions> (accessed 3 Nov 2011).

[24] Vienna Convention on Diplomatic Relations (adopted 18 Apr 1961, in force 24 Apr 1964) 500 UNTS 95; *Reparation for Injuries* (n 11) at p 179.

[25] See RTB Art 18.2 and 18.5, and the DSA.

[26] RTB Art 4.2(c)–(d).

[27] RTB Art 14.1(d)

[28] RTB Art 15.3.

to 'seek to establish such relations with other international organisations and other countries as may facilitate the attainment of its purposes' including by concluding 'formal agreements' or establishing 'effective working relationships with such organizations and Governments of other countries'.[29] These provisions are notable since in the original OECS Treaty member states were expressly authorized to make reservations withholding their 'participation in respect of Foreign Affairs and/or Defence and Security matters of the Organisation'.[30] In contrast, reservations to the legislative competences of the Organisation are limited in Article 14.4 of the RTB to a party to the Treaty of Basseterre of 1981 which is (a) a full member state which is not independent and (b) an associate member state.[31]

In conclusion, the OECS must be recognized as possessing international legal personality in addition to personality in the national law of member states. Within the scope of its international legal personality the OECS is empowered to conclude treaties, to send and receive representatives in relation to third states and international organizations, and to bring and receive international legal claims before dispute settlement mechanisms including the Eastern Caribbean Court of Appeal.

5.2 Headquarters

The headquarters of CARICOM and the OECS are located in, respectively, Georgetown, Guyana, and Castries, St Lucia. The RTC specifically identifies the location of CARICOM's headquarters in Article 23(1), but the RTB does not do so.[32] Rather, Article 22 of the RTB simply provides that '[t]he location of the headquarters of the Organisation shall be determined by the OECS Authority.'[33] The latter wording would allow the OECS to relocate its headquarters easily. In contrast, the specific mention of Georgetown, Guyana, in the RTC might appear to restrict any similar movement of the CARICOM Secretariat. However such differences in wording should not pose significant additional challenges for CARICOM, which must be deemed to have the power to move its headquarters should the circumstances require it. Such a power to relocate may be implied either from the Conference's authority to enter into treaties (which would include a new headquarters agreement), or to be the 'final authority on questions arising in relation to the financial affairs of the Community' (which would include the financial affairs of the CARICOM Secretariat).[34] Nevertheless as a practical matter, it should be noted that both organizations would face significant challenges in moving their headquarters, considering their long establishment in their respective countries,

[29] This provision is also extended to the Economic Union by Art 33 of the Protocol.

[30] See Art 23 of the original Treaty of Basseterre of 1981.

[31] RTB Art 24.2 imposes identical conditions for reservations to the Economic Union Protocol.

[32] The relevant passages of Art 23(1) of the RTC and of Art 15(1) of the original 1973 Treaty specify respectively that '[t]he headquarters of the Community shall be located in Georgetown, Guyana' and '[t]he headquarters of the Secretariat shall be located in Georgetown, Guyana'.

[33] Art 18 of the original Treaty of Basseterre of 1981 used similar wording.

[34] RTC Art 12(3)–(4).

their long-standing commercial relations, and the requirement for the drafting of new headquarters agreements, amongst other documents.

5.3 Privileges and Immunities

5.3.1 CARICOM

CARICOM's privileges and immunities are reaffirmed in Article 229 of the RTC which provides for the continuity of the 'Headquarters Agreement concluded between the Caribbean Community and Common Market and the Government of Guyana on 23 January 1976' and the 'Protocol on Privileges and Immunities concluded by the Member States in connection with the Caribbean Community and Common Market'. The singular wording in this article is slightly misleading since under the original CARICOM regime the Treaty and Annex constituted two distinct arrangements, and as a result Article 21 of the 1973 Treaty and Article 64 of its Annex each provided for the establishment of a separate protocol on privileges and immunities and headquarters agreements. CARICOM under the RTC is therefore a successor to two Protocols on privileges and immunities and two headquarters agreements.[35] Nevertheless, since the same Secretariat provided services to both the Caribbean Community under the original Treaty of Chaguaramas and the common market under the Annex to the Treaty, the drafters of the agreements and protocols effectively merged the two regimes by means of a simple incorporation clause in both the Agreement and Protocol related to the common market. The sole article in the Agreement between the Government of Guyana and the Caribbean Common Market Relating to the Privileges and Immunities to be Granted in Connection with the Common Market states:

> The provisions of the Agreement relating to the Headquarters of the Community concluded in accordance with Paragraph 2 of Article 21 of the Treaty shall be deemed to be incorporated in this Agreement for the purpose of providing for the privileges and immunities to be recognised and granted in connection with the Common Market in accordance with paragraph 2 of Article 64 of the Annex to the Treaty.
>
> Accordingly those provisions shall be read and construed with such adaptations and modifications as may be necessary for their application to the Common Market.[36]

[35] Protocol on the Privileges and Immunities of the Caribbean Community (adopted 14 Jan 1985, in force 15 Jan 1990) 2324 UNTS 493; Protocol on the Privileges and Immunities of the Caribbean Common Market (adopted 14 Jan 1985, in force 15 Jan 1990); Agreement between the Government of Guyana and the Caribbean Community Relating to the Privileges and Immunities to be Granted in Connection with the Secretariat (adopted and entered into force 23 Jan 1976) 2398 UNTS 1; Agreement between the Government of Guyana and the Caribbean Common Market Relating to the Privileges and Immunities to be Granted in Connection with the Common Market (adopted and entered into force 23 Jan 1976) as available at <http://www.caricomlaw.org/Details.aspx?EntryId=155&Command=Core_Download&Method=attachment> (2 Nov 2011).

[36] (Adopted and entered into force 23 Jan 1976). The Protocol on the Privileges and Immunities of the Caribbean Common Market employs very similar wording, incorporating the privileges and immunities granted in the Protocol on the Privileges and Immunities of the Caribbean Community into its terms in the following language:

Consequently, the applicable rules are found in the Agreement and Protocol related to the Caribbean Community Secretariat.[37]

The parties bound by the Agreement between the Government of Guyana and the Caribbean Community Relating to the Privileges and Immunities to be Granted in Connection with the Secretariat [Headquarters Agreement] are Guyana and CARICOM.[38] As such, the Headquarters Agreement itself provides further evidence of the international legal personality of CARICOM. Only the original 12 CARICOM member states are listed as parties to the Protocol on the Privileges and Immunities of the Caribbean Community [Protocol], and this could give rise to issues related to the availability of privileges and immunities in relation to Suriname and Haiti.[39] Haiti is, however, party to a separate treaty governing privileges and immunities for the Caribbean Community Representation in Haiti. The Agreement between the Government of Haiti and the Caribbean Community Relating to the Privileges and Immunities to be granted in Connection with the Caribbean Community in Haiti [Haitian Agreement] offers similar protections to those existing under the Protocol.[40] Suriname is party to a Headquarters Agreement related to the CARICOM Competition Commission, but the privileges and immunities in the Agreement are restricted to staff and facilities associated with the latter body, and thus would only cover CARICOM personnel if they were, for example, performing missions with or visiting the seat of the Commission.[41]

The privileges and immunities accorded to CARICOM under the Headquarters Agreement, Protocol, and Haitian Agreement, include those related to: immunity of Community property, including archives, and assets;[42] inviolability of the

> The provisions of the Protocol relating to the privileges and immunities of the Caribbean Community concluded in accordance with paragraph 1 of Article 21 of the Treaty shall be deemed to be incorporated in this Protocol for the purpose of providing for the privileges and immunities to be recognised and granted by the Member States in connection with the Common Market in accordance with paragraph 1 of Article 64 of the Annex to the Treaty. Accordingly, those provisions shall be construed with such adaptations and modifications as may be necessary for their application to the Common Market.

[37] Protocol on the Privileges and Immunities of the Caribbean Community (adopted 14 Jan 1985, in force 15 Jan 1990) 2324 UNTS 493 [Protocol]; Agreement between the Government of Guyana and the Caribbean Community Relating to the Privileges and Immunities to be Granted in Connection with the Secretariat (adopted and in force 23 Jan 1976) 2398 UNTS 1 [Headquarters Agreement].

[38] On the privileges and immunities related to headquarters agreements see AS Muller, *International Organizations and their Host States* (n 2).

[39] The CARICOM Secretariat, *Matrix of Agreements*, last updated July 2012 (Georgetown, Guyana: CARICOM Secretariat, 2012), lists the following twelve parties (and their date of ratification): Antigua (15 May 1989); Bahamas (18 May 1988); Barbados (29 Feb 1988); Dominica (21 Jun 1988); Grenada (19 Apr 1988); Guyana (17 May 1988); Jamaica (4 May 1987); Montserrat (24 Jul 1987); St Lucia (21 Jul 1988); Trinidad and Tobago (15 Jan 1990); St Kitts and Nevis (30 Jan 1986); St Vincent and The Grenadines (16 Sep 2009). The UN Treaty Service website only lists ten parties, omitting St Kitts and Nevis and St Vincent and the Grenadines.

[40] (Adopted and in force 2002) [exact date not specified].

[41] Agreement Between the Government of the Republic of Suriname and the Caribbean Community Establishing the Seat and the Office of the Competition Commission (adopted and entered into force on 13 Feb 2007) Art 12. See also the Protocol on Privileges and Immunities of the Competition Commission (adopted and entered into force 12 Feb 2007).

[42] Protocol on the Privileges and Immunities of the Caribbean Community (adopted 14 January 1985, in force 15 Jan 1990) 2324 UNTS 493 Arts 2 and 4 [Protocol]; Agreement between the

Community's premises, including its Headquarters;[43] protection of the Community's premises, and its essential services;[44] freedom from financial controls, including the freedom to hold and transfer funds, gold, or currency of any kind;[45] immunities from direct taxation, customs duties, and restrictions upon imports and exports;[46] freedom of communication;[47] freedom of transit;[48] immunities for representatives of member states, including immunities from arrest and detention, and seizure of baggage, inviolability of documents, and immunity for official acts.[49] Community officials also obtain immunities, including under the Protocol, immunity for official acts, exemption from taxes on salaries, personal and family exemptions from immigration restrictions, currency and exchange privileges, repatriation facilities, and import and export privileges.[50] Under the Headquarters Agreement and Haitian Agreement, immunities are provided from arrest and detention and seizure of baggage, immunity for official acts, exemptions from taxes on salaries and foreign income, immunity from national service obligations, freedoms in relation to foreign currencies and accounts, repatriation facilities, and, for senior officials of the Community, exemptions from customs duties and other privileges and immunities similar to those enjoyed by diplomatic personnel.[51] Under the Protocol special privileges and immunities are also provided for the Secretary General and his family equivalent those possessed by heads of diplomatic missions under international law,[52] privileges and immunities for experts on missions on behalf of the Community or those invited to the premises of the Community for official business,[53] and *laissez-passer* privileges.[54] Disputes on the privileges and immunities provided by these treaties are subject to resolution by the Conference under the Protocol,[55] and to arbitration under the Headquarters Agreement and Haitian Agreement.[56] Finally, under the Headquarters Agreement the Government

Government of Guyana and the Caribbean Community Relating to the Privileges and Immunities to be Granted in Connection with the Secretariat (adopted and in force 23 Jan 1976) 2398 UNTS 1 Art 4 [Headquarters Agreement]; Agreement between the Government of Haiti and the Caribbean Community Relating to the Privileges and Immunities to be granted in Connection with the Caribbean Community in Haiti (adopted and in force 2002) [date not specified] Art 4 [Haitian Agreement].

43 Protocol Art 3, Headquarters Agreement Art 2(3), Haitian Agreement Art 2(3).

44 Headquarters Agreement Art 6, Haitian Agreement Art 6.

45 Protocol Art 5, Headquarters Agreement Art 5, Haitian Agreement Art 5.

46 Protocol Art 6, Headquarters Agreement Art 4(4), Haitian Agreement Art 4(4).

47 Protocol Art 7, Headquarters Agreement Art 3, Haitian Agreement Art 3.

48 Headquarters Agreement Art 7, Haitian Agreement Art 7.

49 Protocol Art 8.

50 Protocol Art 10.

51 Headquarters Agreement Art 8(1), Haitian Agreement Art 8(1).

52 Protocol Art 11.

53 Protocol Art 12, Headquarters Agreement Art 9, Haitian Agreement Art 9.

54 Protocol Art 13, Headquarters Agreement Art 10, Haitian Agreement Art 10. Note in relation to laissez-passer privileges that the definition of 'official of the Community' in the Protocol is to be amended by the Further Protocol to Amend the Protocol on the Privileges and Immunities of the Caribbean Community for the Purpose of Extending the Facility of the Use of the Laissez-Passer Issued to the Staff of the Caribbean Community Secretariat for Travel on Official Duty to Certain Officials of Other Regional Organisations (adopted 17 May 1994, not yet in force) to read: '"official of the Community" means the Secretary-General and staff of the Secretariat, and for the purposes of Article 13, includes an official of a regional organisation designated by the Secretary-General and ratified by the Conference.'

55 Protocol Art 16.

56 Headquarters Agreement Art 13, Haitian Agreement Art 12.

of Guyana is obligated to provide a permanent Headquarters premises for CARICOM.[57]

CARICOM's privileges and immunities are subject to four general limitations. The first is that they only apply in the national jurisdictions of member states. They do not apply to international legal proceedings, such as arbitration under Chapter IX of the RTC, or in the case of a dispute before the Caribbean Court of Justice acting in its original jurisdiction.[58] The second is that they do not apply to a person located in a territory who is either a national of, or permanently resident in, that territory, except to provide 'immunity from jurisdiction and inviolability in respect of official acts performed in the exercise of his functions'.[59] Such a restriction on immunities of nationals and permanent residents is common in general international law and is found, for example, in Article 38 of the Vienna Convention on Diplomatic Relations.[60] A third, albeit minor, limitation on privileges and immunities is the obligation of officials of the Community to cooperate with local authorities to facilitate the proper administration of justice, to ensure the observance of police regulations, and to prevent abuses of privileges and immunities.[61] A fourth, more general restriction is the ability of all such privileges and immunities to be waived. This is set out in Article 14 of the Protocol, which states:

> The privileges and immunities accorded by this Protocol are granted in the interest of the Community and not for the personal benefit of the individuals themselves. The Secretary-General may waive the immunity of any person entitled thereto in any case, where, in his opinion such immunity impedes or is likely to impede the course of justice and can be waived without prejudice to the interests of the Community. In the case of the Secretary-General, the Conference shall have the power to waive his immunity.[62]

Such a limitation draws attention to the particular nature of privileges and immunities accorded to international organizations, namely, their basis in functional necessity.[63] In contrast to the privileges and immunities provided to states and to

[57] Headquarters Agreement Art 11.

[58] A consequence is that international organizations will be responsible at international law for breaches of their international legal obligations. See eg the International Law Commission's 'Draft articles on the responsibility of international organizations, with commentaries' (2011) *Yearbook of the International Law Commission, 2011*, vol II, Part Two.

[59] Protocol Art 15. See also Headquarters Agreement Art 8(4), and Haitian Agreement Art 8(4).

[60] (Adopted 18 Apr 1961, in force 24 Apr 1964) 500 UNTS 95. In the International Law Commission's 'Draft Articles on Diplomatic Intercourse and Immunities with commentaries', an earlier draft of the Convention, as reproduced in the *Yearbook of the International Law Commission, 1958*, vol II, at p 102, the ILC noted in its Commentary to Article 37, paras (3)–(4) that it 'considered it essential for a diplomatic agent who is a national of the receiving state to enjoy at least a minimum of immunity to enable him to perform his duties satisfactorily' but that the 'privileges and immunities to be enjoyed beyond the stated minimum…will depend upon the decision of the receiving state'. See also Art 71 of the Vienna Convention on Consular Relations (adopted 24 Apr 1963, in force 19 Mar 1967) 596 UNTS 261.

[61] Headquarters Agreement Art 8(3)(b), Haitian Agreement Art 8(3)(b).

[62] See also Headquarters Agreement Art 8(3)(a) and Haitian Agreement Art 8(3)(a) for nearly identical provisions.

[63] See eg Klabbers, *An Introduction to International Institutional Law* (n 1) 147–53; Schermers and Blokker, *International Institutional Law* (n 1) 324–35; Muller, *International Organizations and their Host States* (n 2) 151–4.

diplomatic officials of states, which are established under customary international law and general international treaties, the privileges and immunities of regional organizations are subjective in nature, meaning that they are created by and govern the relations of states parties to their treaties. Moreover they generally only apply in national law and are limited to protecting the objects and purposes of those treaties.

As noted in the *Reparations for Injuries Case*, an international organization is not a state, let alone a 'super state'.[64] Rather it is a limited body, composed of an association of states, which is formed to achieve particular purposes. These purposes are not open ended, and if the organization ceases to fulfil them it will be abandoned or terminated. For this reason it is crucial that the executive officer of the organization, in CARICOM's case the Secretary General, be entitled to waive privileges and immunities where their use would not further the purposes of the organization or would otherwise impair its functions. In other words, if the assertion of an official's immunities from a state's jurisdiction is not necessary for the effective functioning of the organization, his immunities should be waived by the Secretary General.[65] Such a waiver should be express, in writing, and made in relation to the specific act.[66] It may extend to the suit only, or to the suit and execution proceedings, although the latter will in most cases require a second waiver of the same character.[67]

In addition, since regional organizations are almost entirely treaty-based, the extent of privileges and immunities recognized by non-member states will depend upon the latter's discretion. In other words, privileges and immunities of regional organizations are guaranteed solely in the territories of the member states. They will extend to third parties only to the extent that those third parties expressly grant them, or to the extent that such immunities arise in customary international law.[68]

[64] *Reparation for Injuries* (n 11) at p 179.

[65] See eg Schermers and Blokker, *International Institutional Law* (n 1) 536–7; AS Muller, *International Organizations and their Host States* (n 2) 162–71.

[66] cf Muller (n 2) 163.

[67] See eg Muller 165–71. Muller points out that an agreement to arbitrate will constitute a waiver of immunity for the arbitration proceedings, but may not amount to a waiver in relation to execution proceedings, which could arise before national courts. On the enforceability of arbitral awards see the case of *BCB Holdings Ltd and the Belize Bank Ltd v AG* [2013] CCJ 5 (AJ) (BZE).

[68] Privileges and immunities in third states are very limited in international law, even in the context of the immunities of diplomats. See eg Art 40 of the *Vienna Convention on Diplomatic Relations* (adopted 18 Apr 1961, in force 24 Apr 1964) 500 UNTS 95 which provides limited immunities to diplomatic representatives while in transit. See also Eileen Denza, *Diplomatic Law: Commentary on the Vienna Convention on Diplomatic Relations*, 3rd edn (Oxford: Oxford University Press, 2008) 451–9 (on the meaning and effect of Art 40). On the possibility of privileges and immunities arising in customary international law, see eg Muller (n 2) 47–54.

5.3.2 OECS

The privileges and immunities of the OECS, as briefly set out in Article 21.4 of the RTB, expressly parallel those provided by the Vienna Convention on Diplomatic Relations (VCDR) in relation to individuals and diplomatic missions:

> 21.4 The privileges and immunities to be granted to the members of the OECS Commission and to the senior officials of the Organisation at its headquarters and in the Member States shall be the same accorded to members of a diplomatic mission accredited at the headquarters of the Organisation and in the Member States under the provisions of the Vienna Convention on Diplomatic Relations of 18 April 1961. Similarly the privileges and immunities granted to the OECS Commission at the headquarters of the Organisation shall be the same as granted to diplomatic missions at the headquarters of the Organisation under the said Convention. Other privileges and immunities to be recognised and granted by the Member States in connection with the Organisation shall be determined by the OECS Authority.[69]

Such pithy phrasing accords members of the 'OECS Commission and senior officials of the Organisation' the same privileges and immunities as 'members of a diplomatic mission' under the provisions of the VCDR. These immunities only apply to the national laws of member states and would not prevent suit, or legal responsibility, at the international level, including suit before the Eastern Caribbean Court of Appeal under its Treaty Jurisdiction.[70]

The clarity of Article 21.4, however, is illusory. If one examines the text of the VCDR the general suitability of the regime of diplomatic immunities for a regional organization may be seriously questioned. To start, the VCDR does not define the phrase 'members of a diplomatic mission' which is employed in Article 21.4 of the RTB, but instead defines terms such as 'members of the mission' as including the 'head of the mission and members of the staff of the mission'.[71] The term 'members of the staff of the mission' is in turn defined as 'members of the diplomatic staff, of the administrative and technical staff and of the service staff of the mission'.[72] Each of the latter three categories of staff is accorded substantially different levels of privileges and immunities under the VCDR.[73] As a result, the wording of Article 21.4 of the RTB raises considerable ambiguity for the privileges and immunities regime of the OECS. It simply could be meant to provide the privileges and immunities of one category of personnel described under the VCDR—for example, the 'members of the diplomatic staff'—to the officials of the OECS; but equally it could be read to extend all of the different categories of personnel covered by the VCDR to OECS officials. If the latter is taken to be the case, then in a dispute about privileges and immunities it will be necessary to decide whether a particular OECS official would best be categorized as being similar to either (a) diplomatic staff, (b) administrative and technical staff, or (c) service staff of the

[69] This provision is nearly identical to Art 17(4) of the original Treaty of Basseterre.

[70] See RTB Art 18, the DSA, and Protocol Art 30. See also Chapter 14.

[71] Vienna Convention on Diplomatic Relations (adopted 18 Apr 1961, in force 24 Apr 1964) 500 UNTS 95 (VCDR) Art 1.

[72] VCDR (n 71).

[73] See VCDR Arts 29–38.

mission, by drawing comparisons with the meaning of those terms as employed in the VCDR.

As a result it is difficult to specify the exact privileges and immunities conferred by Article 21.4 of the RTB. In the event of conflict over privileges and immunities one would need to carefully study the official practices of both the OECS and St Lucia, the territory in which the headquarters is located. One would also need to keep in mind that privileges and immunities of international organizations are judged against a test of functional necessity.[74] For this reason, the extensive privileges and immunities granted to diplomats need not automatically be granted to officials of international or regional organizations.

However on the assumption that Article 21.4 means to grant privileges and immunities similar to those afforded diplomatic staff under the VCDR—the highest level of immunity provided by that treaty—it would seem to include the following in relation to 'members of the OECS Commission and to the senior officials of the Organisation': freedom of movement and travel;[75] inviolability of the person, including immunity from any form of arrest or detention, any attack on his person, freedom or dignity, and the requirement that he be treated with due respect;[76] immunity from criminal jurisdiction and, except in very limited cases, civil and administrative jurisdiction;[77] exemption from social security provisions;[78] exemption from most dues and taxes, personal or real, national, regional, or municipal;[79] exemption from all customs duties, taxes, and most related charges;[80] exemptions from personal or public service;[81] exemption of personal baggage from inspection;[82] freedom of transit rights;[83] and certain exit-related rights, in times of emergency.[84] The phrasing of Article 21.4, however, would appear to exclude family members of OECS staff, who are not classifiable as 'members of the OECS Commission' or 'senior officials of the Organisation'.[85]

Article 21.4 of the RTB also specifies that the headquarters of the OECS Commission is to be granted the same privileges and immunities as those provided to a diplomatic missions under the VCDR. It thus incorporates by reference the vast majority of privileges and immunities that would be protected in a formal headquarters agreement. Such mission-related privileges and immunities would likely include: inviolability of the headquarters, the requirement for protection of the premises, and immunity of the headquarters premises their furnishings and

[74] eg Klabbers, *An Introduction to International Institutional Law* (n 1) 147–53; Schermers and Blokker, *International Institutional Law* (n 1) 324–35; Muller, *International Organizations and their Host States* (n 2) 151–4.

[75] Vienna Convention on Diplomatic Relations (adopted 18 Apr 1961, in force 24 Apr 1964) 500 UNTS 95 (VCDR) Art 26.

[76] VCDR Art 29.

[77] See VCDR Art 31.

[78] VCDR Art 33.

[79] VCDR Art 34.

[80] VCDR Art 36.

[81] VCDR Art 35.

[82] VCDR Art 36(2).

[83] See VCDR Art 40. Such transit rights would be more limited in the context of a regional organization, the privileges and immunities of which are unlikely to be underpinned by a substantial body of customary international law, as is the case for diplomatic privileges and immunities.

[84] VCDR Art 44.

[85] But note the protections offered to family members in VCDR Art 37(1).

other property thereon and the means of transport of the mission from search, requisition, attachment, or execution;[86] immunity from taxes; [87] inviolability of documents and archives;[88] the requirement for provision of full facilities;[89] freedom of communication and inviolability of correspondence;[90] exemptions from dues and taxes on fees and charges;[91] and exemption from all customs duties, taxes, and most related charges.[92] It is doubtful whether the same privileges and immunities that are accorded to the private residence of a diplomatic agent under Article 30 of the VCDR, including inviolability, are to be granted to the private residence of an OECS official, since Article 21.4 of the RTB appears to only relate to the OECS headquarters and its property.

Some of the provisions of the VCDR may limit the privileges, immunities, and related powers of the OECS. However once again the differences between the regimes of privileges and immunities required for diplomatic staff of states, and those required for regional organizations, raise questions about the intent of Article 21.4 of the RTB. For example, under Article 8 of the VCDR the ability of a state to appoint nationals of the receiving state or a third state is limited by the requirement for consent of the receiving state. In other words the United Kingdom, for example, would require the consent of France if it wished to appoint a French national as the UK's Ambassador to France. In the context of the OECS the equivalent to the 'receiving state' would be St Lucia, the state in which the headquarters is based. However it is unlikely that Article 8 of the VCDR was intended to similarly apply in the context of the OECS, since the Organisation is not equivalent to a foreign state and such a restriction would diminish employment opportunities for the people of St Lucia, who would be ineligible for appointment without the (express) consent of St Lucia.

Provisions of the VCDR relating to 'receiving state' nationals and permanent residents, however, may be applicable to the OECS context.[93] These provisions restrict the immunities available to nationals or permanent residents of the state in which the diplomatic mission is located and are justified by the need for at least one of the two states concerned—the sending or receiving state—to ultimately have jurisdiction over a wrongful act committed by diplomatic official.[94] It might be questioned whether limiting privileges and immunities of nationals and permanent residents in the context of regional organizations would be similarly justified, since in such a case persons from numerous countries are employed and are accorded privileges and immunities in the territories of all member states. In such a case it would appear to be inequitable to exclude nationals or permanent residents of the headquarters state from the majority of such protections. However

[86] VCDR Art 22. [87] VCDR Art 23. [88] VCDR Art 24. [89] VCDR Art 25.
[90] VCDR Art 27. [91] VCDR Art 28. [92] VCDR Art 36. [93] See VCDR Art 38.
[94] Granting privileges and immunities to the nationals of a receiving state who work in a foreign mission could frustrate the application of the nationality and territoriality principles of state criminal jurisdiction, which would be the basis for prosecution of most ordinary crimes. On state criminal jurisdiction see eg James Crawford, *Brownlie's Principles of International Law*, 8th edn (Oxford: Oxford University Press, 2012) ch 21.

CARICOM has a provision similar to Article 8 of the VCDR and thus the OECS may wish to similarly exclude the majority of privileges and immunities of nationals or permanent residents of St Lucia.[95]

Other provisions of the VCDR also would likely restrict the privileges and immunities of the OECS. Article 41 of the VCDR, extended by analogy, requires the officials of the OECS to respect the laws and regulations of the state in which the headquarters is situated, and not to interfere in its internal affairs. In the headquarters territory they also may be prohibited from practising for personal profit any professional or commercial activity.[96] Similarly, the premises of the headquarters must not be used in any manner incompatible with its functions, or with other rules of general international law or with any special agreements in force between the OECS and state in which it is located.[97] Finally, as in the case of CARICOM, the general privileges and immunities accorded under the RTB will be subject to waiver by the OECS Director General.[98] This waiver should be express, in writing, and made in relation to the specific act, and a second waiver would likely be required for subsequent execution proceedings.[99]

5.4 Final Provisions

At the end of both the RTC and RTB are a number of articles governing how each treaty is to enter into force, how it may be amended, whether reservations can be entered with respect to it, and the possibility of accession. These articles, although common in most treaties establishing international organizations, reveal some ambiguities. The RTC also has one additional provision, an article entitled 'Saving', that will be crucial to the effect of the RTC and decisions taken thereunder in the domestic law of member states.[100]

5.4.1 CARICOM

The concluding provisions of the RTC specify the way in which it is to enter into force, namely, by signature, followed by ratification and deposit of all instruments of ratification by the states mentioned in Article 3(1) with the Secretariat.[101] Article 235 also specifies that the RTC is to be registered with the Secretariat of the United Nations, in accordance with Article 102 of the Charter of the United Nations.[102]

95 See CARICOM's Protocol Art 15, Headquarters Agreement Art 8(4), and Haitian Agreement Art 8(4).

96 VCDR Art 42.

97 VCDR Art 41(3).

98 See VCDR Art 32.

99 See Muller, *International Organizations and their Host States* (n 2) 163–71.

100 See the discussion of RTC Art 240 in Chapter 6.

101 RTC Arts 232–234. The RTC opened for signature on 5 Jul 2001.

102 Art 102 of the Charter of the United Nations (adopted 26 Jun 1945, in force 24 Oct 1945) 1 UNTS xvi, 9 AJIL Supp 190, requires UN member states to register their treaties with the UN Secretariat; it also prohibits the invocation of any unregistered treaty before any organ of the United

Unfortunately, however, Article 234 of the RTC was unable to operate as originally intended. As highlighted in Chapter 3, in order for the RTC to enter into force Article 234 required 'the deposit of the last instrument of ratification by the States mentioned in paragraph 1 of Article 3'. This meant that all of the fourteen states specified in Article 3 (all original CARICOM members, plus Suriname, but excluding Haiti), were required to ratify the RTC. This proved to be impossible. As a result a separate treaty was created to amend Article 234 so as to allow the RTC to enter into force with a lower threshold of ratifications, namely, the Agreement to enable the Entry into Force of the Revised Treaty of Chaguaramas Establishing the Caribbean Community including the CARICOM Single Market and Economy.[103] This Agreement substituted the requirement of twelve, rather than fourteen, ratifications for entry into force of the RTC, and retroactively brought the RTC into force as of 1 January 2006.[104]

Article 236 allows amendments to the RTC 'by the unanimous decision of the Parties'. Any such amendments are to enter into force one month after the date of the deposit of the last instrument of ratification with the Secretariat. Since the RTC has thirteen parties at present, amendments would not require a unanimous decision by all fifteen CARICOM member states.[105] Two amendments to the RTC have entered into force: the Agreement to enable the Entry into Force of the Revised Treaty of Chaguaramas Establishing the Caribbean Community including the CARICOM Single Market and Economy, and the Protocol to the Revised Treaty of Chaguaramas Establishing the Caribbean Community, including the Caribbean Single Market and Economy regarding the Relationship between provisions on the Original Jurisdiction of the Caribbean Court of Justice and the Constitutions of State Parties.[106] The Agreement already has been subject to

Nations (including the International Court of Justice). The RTC has been so registered: Registration Number I-40269 (26 May 2004).

[103] (Adopted 21 December 2005, in force 9 Feb 2006).

[104] The Agreement amended Art 234 so as to read: '[t]he Treaty shall enter into force on 1 January 2006 if Instruments of Ratification have been previously deposited by any twelve of the States mentioned in paragraph 1 of Article 3 and if not, then on such later date on which the twelfth such instrument has been deposited.'

[105] The current parties to the RTC are: Antigua and Barbuda, Barbados, Belize, Dominica, Grenada, Guyana, Haiti, Jamaica, St. Kitts and Nevis, St Lucia, St Vincent and the Grenadines, Suriname, and Trinidad and Tobago. The Bahamas and Montserrat are CARICOM Members, but are not parties to the RTC. See Chapter 3 for more on the distinction between parties to the RTC and Members of CARICOM.

[106] Agreement to enable the Entry into Force of the Revised Treaty of Chaguaramas Establishing the Caribbean Community including the CARICOM Single Market and Economy (adopted 21 Dec 2005, in force 9 Feb 2006); Protocol to the Revised Treaty of Chaguaramas Establishing the Caribbean Community, including the Caribbean Single Market and Economy regarding the Relationship between provisions on the Original Jurisdiction of the Caribbean Court of Justice and the Constitutions of State Parties (adopted 17 Feb 2005, in force 6 Mar 2006). The Protocol entered into force one month after the date of receipt of the last instrument of ratification of the parties to the RTC. Since the parties at that time did not include Haiti, which acceded to the RTC on 8 February 2008, the receipt of the instrument of ratification of Suriname on 6 February 2006 triggered the entry into force of the Protocol. In any event, Article II of the Agreement specifically applied its amended version of Article 234 (and notwithstanding Article 236) to the Protocol—enabling the latter to enter into force with only twelve parties.

comment. It should be noted in this context, however, that by allowing the RTC to enter into force with twelve ratifications the provisions of the Agreement had the novel effect of amending a treaty not yet in force, by an amending majority that would not be sufficient under the RTC itself. The Protocol added a new Article 222 (*bis*), which states that '[t]he provisions regarding the original jurisdiction set out in this Chapter shall not be construed to require a Contracting Party to enact legislation that is inconsistent with its constitutional structure or the nature of its legal system.' Further amendments to the RTC which are not yet in force include the Protocol to Amend Article 83 of the Revised Treaty of Chaguaramas[107] and the Protocol Amending the Revised Treaty of Chaguaramas to incorporate the Council for National Security and Law Enforcement (CONSLE) as an Organ of the Community and the CARICOM Implementation Agency for Crime and Security (IMPACS) as an Institution of the Community.[108]

Article 237 of the RTC allows reservations 'with the consent of the signatory States'. There is no time limit specified for the application of this provision, and so technically reservations could be entered at any time. This would differ from the understanding of reservations as set out in the Vienna Convention on the Law of Treaties, which provides for reservations to be made at specific times, namely, 'when signing, ratifying, accepting, approving or acceding to a treaty'.[109]

Article 238 of the RTC allows accession by a 'State or Territory of the Caribbean' if the Conference so determines, and on such terms and conditions as the Conference decides. Accession under Article 238 takes effect one month after the deposit of the instrument of accession with the Secretariat. Since the term 'Caribbean' is not defined in the RTC, accession could be open to any state or territory even remotely geographically proximate to the Caribbean.[110]

There is no provision specifying a right of withdrawal in relation to the RTC. Unlike in the case of the RTB, the RTC does not discuss matters such as the ability of a member state to terminate or withdraw from its treaty obligations, the necessity of satisfying financial and other commitments before doing so, and any rights on the part of the terminating state over the common assets of the Caribbean Community at the time of its departure.[111] Nevertheless the question of withdrawal is covered in the general law of treaties and the more specific customary rules of international institutional law. Under the Vienna Convention on the Law of Treaties (VCLT) a

[107] (Adopted 12 Mar 2010, not yet in force). Article II of this Protocol provides for is entry into force upon signature by twelve parties notwithstanding the provisions of Articles 233 and 236. To date it has received eleven signatures.

[108] (Adopted 13 Mar 2009, not yet in force). Article XI of the Protocol provides that it is to enter into force on the date of deposit of the twelfth instrument of ratification by a Member of the Community. However this is inconsistent with Article 236 of the RTC which requires a unanimous decision of the parties and deposit of all of their instruments of ratification. Since Haiti became a party on 8 February 2008, its ratification (the thirteenth) also should be required.

[109] See Vienna Convention on the Law of Treaties (adopted 23 May 1969, in force 27 Jan 1980) 1155 UNTS 331 (VCLT) Arts 2(1)(d) and 19.

[110] Suriname is a CARICOM member state even though the Atlantic Ocean, not the Caribbean Sea, washes its shores.

[111] See RTB Art 28.

state may terminate its status as a party to a treaty in conformity with the provisions of the treaty, or at any time with the consent of all of the parties to the treaty, or under the other rules of the VCLT or customary international law.[112] As a result, even though Article 56 of the VCLT states that denunciation and termination will not be allowed in cases where it cannot be established that the parties intended to admit the possibility of such a right, or where no such right may be implied by the nature of the treaty, nevertheless the rules of international institutional law establish that a state remains free to withdraw from an international organization unless it has expressly or impliedly surrendered that right.[113] Such a right to withdrawal may be implied, as seen in Article 56 of the VCLT, or may simply be acknowledged as a right flowing from state sovereignty. In either case it should generally be accompanied by a notification period, such as exists in the VCLT.[114] In addition, although these rules are difficult to satisfy, Articles 60–62 of the VCLT allow a state to invoke material breach, supervening impossibility, and fundamental change of circumstances to terminate its treaty obligations.[115] Finally, a state's membership in an organization necessarily will be terminated by the dissolution of that organization.[116]

Article 239 sets out an undertaking by member states to elaborate in a further Protocol the policies and rules related to: electronic commerce, government procurement, the treatment of goods produced in free zones and similar jurisdictions, the free circulation of goods in the CSME, and the rights contingent on establishment, provision of services, and movement of capital in the Community.

Article 240, termed the 'Saving' provision, governs the way in which decisions of organs of CARICOM are to become enforceable in the national laws of member states.[117] Article 240(1) provides that the '[d]ecisions of competent Organs taken under this Treaty shall be subject to the relevant constitutional procedures of the Member States before creating legally binding rights and obligations for nationals of such States.' Such language requires CARICOM decisions to be transformed into domestic law, a requirement already well-established in the common law, where international treaties can have no binding force in domestic law without transformation.[118] Article 240(1), however, only applies to 'decisions', not to other potential forms of legislative action by CARICOM organs. It also does not apply to the articles of the RTC.

[112] See VCLT Art 54.

[113] See eg Schermers and Blokker, *International Institutional Law* (n 1) 95–105; Sands and Klein, *Bowett's Law of International Institutions* (n 1) 552–3; Klabbers, *An Introduction to International Institutional Law* (n 1) 124–7. Note that in cases of treaties of limited duration (eg a treaty of five years' duration) it will be difficult to rebut the presumption that a right of withdrawal has been surrendered for the duration of that treaty.

[114] Art 56(2) VCLT. On the notification requirement and its reasons see eg Schermers and Blokker (n 1) 92–4.

[115] But see Schermers and Blokker (n 1) 104, who argue against the applicability of fundamental change of circumstances to the context of international organizations, noting that 'members are estopped from claiming such a right, since they are in a position, in their capacity as members of these organizations, to influence the operation of the organization'.

[116] Schermers and Blokker (n 1) 118 and ch 11(III).

[117] See also the discussion of Art 240 of the RTC in Chapter 6.

[118] See eg *R v Lyons* [2003] 1 AC 976 (HL); *Higgs v Minister of National Security and Others* [2000] 2 AC 228 (PC Bah); *JH Rayner (Mincing Lane) Ltd v Department of Trade and Industry* (also called

Article 240(2) requires member states 'to act expeditiously to give effect to decisions of competent Organs and Bodies in their municipal law' and Article 240(3) requires COTED to 'monitor and keep under review the implementation of the provisions of this Article'. Article 240(3) also requires COTED to 'convene a review conference of Member States within five years from the entry into force of this Treaty', a requirement not yet observed.

5.4.2 OECS

The final provisions of the RTB are not set out in a separate chapter as in the case of the RTC, but include Articles 23–30. Article 23 is a transitional provision which provides guidance to the Authority for its first meeting after the entry into force of the RTB. Article 24 clarifies the relationship of the RTB, its DSA, and the Protocol. Under Article 24.1 the DSA and Protocol are specified to be an 'integral part' of the RTB, and Article 24.3 stipulates that, subject to Article 24.2, a party to the RTB is also a party to the Protocol. Article 24.2 authorizes a non-independent full member state and an associate member state to make reservations to the Protocol at the time of ratifying or acceding to the RTB. Such reservations, unlike in the case of the RTC, are limited to the times of ratification or accession.

Article 25 deals with signature, ratification, and accession. Article 25.1 allows all of the countries specified in Articles 3.1 and 3.2 of the RTB to sign the treaty (the previous OECS full member states and associate member states, respectively). Article 25.2 specifies that the RTB is subject to ratification or accession in accordance with the relevant constitutional processes of signatories, and paragraphs 4 and 5 of Article 25 indicate that instruments of ratification and accession are to be deposited with the OECS Secretariat, and OECS Commission, respectively. This distinction is necessary because following the entry into force of the RTB the OECS Secretariat was replaced by the OECS Commission. The OECS Secretariat is named as the depository for the RTB under Article 25.3, a role presumably assumed by the Commission after its entry into force.[119]

Article 26 provides for entry into force of the RTB, which occurs immediately upon receipt by the OECS Secretariat of the fourth instrument of ratification from the independent countries specified in Article 3.1. Article 30 requires registration of the RTB with the Secretariat of the United Nations and with the Secretariat of the Caribbean Community. Such registration is required by Article 102 of the Charter of the United Nations.[120]

Maclaine Watson & Co Ltd v International Tin Council) [1990] 2 AC 418 (HL); *R v Secretary of State for the Home Department, ex parte Brind* [1991] 1 AC 696 (HL); *Salomon v Commissioners of Customs and Excise* [1967] 2 QB 116 (CA Eng).

[119] This role also should extend to the Protocol, which has no depository provision.

[120] Art 102 of the Charter of the United Nations (adopted 26 Jun 1945, in force 24 Oct 1945) 1 UNTS xvi, 9 AJIL Supp 190, requires UN member states to register their treaties with the UN Secretariat; it also prohibits the invocation of any unregistered treaty before any organ of the United Nations (including the International Court of Justice).

The RTB and its Protocol expressly provide for the right of withdrawal in Articles 28 and 34, respectively. As we have seen, such a right has not been specified in relation to CARICOM, but would arise in any event through the operation of the law of treaties or the general rules of international institutional law (including customary international legal rules). The advantages of expressly setting out such a right in the RTB include predictability and certainty. However if the right of withdrawal were to be used too frequently, it would be detrimental to the operation of the OECS.[121] The RTB is specified to be of unlimited duration in Article 28.1. Article 28.2 provides that '[a]ny Member State may withdraw from the Organisation upon giving written notice of such withdrawal to the Director-General who shall promptly notify the other Member States and the OECS Commission.'[122] Withdrawal is specified to be effective twelve months after receipt of such notice, and Article 28.3 imposes the requirements upon member states to satisfy their financial obligations to the Organisation and to respect any commitments assumed before the effective date of withdrawal. Article 28.4 deals with questions of the value of assets in the Organisation over which the withdrawing state may have rights. It stipulates that a member state which withdraws while the Organisation is still in operation 'has no claim to any part of the proceeds until the liquidation of the assets of the Organisation on the termination of this Treaty, at which time it shall be entitled to the value of its assets as at the date of withdrawal.'

Taken together these provisions have several consequences. Firstly, withdrawal must be deemed to have two effects: withdrawal of the respective state from membership in the Organisation, and withdrawal from the RTB (and thereby termination of the state's future treaty obligations). Secondly, withdrawal does not affect the obligations, financial and otherwise, assumed by the state prior to the date of effectiveness of that withdrawal. Thirdly, withdrawal does not give a state a right to its share of the assets of the Organisation until the Organisation itself has been wound up, following the termination of the RTB. Since the withdrawing state presumably has a claim on its share of the assets at the date of its withdrawal, however, it would be expedient of the OECS Commission to undertake and record a valuation of the assets of the Organisation whenever a state exercises its right to withdraw.

Article 34 of the Protocol provides two categories of rights of withdrawal. For a full member state of the Organisation, withdrawal from the Protocol is conditional upon withdrawal from the RTB in accordance with Article 28 of the RTB.[123]

[121] See eg Schermers and Blokker, *International Institutional Law* (n 1) 95 (noting the challenges produced by the exercise of such a right in the case of the League of Nations).

[122] This provision can be contrasted with Art 24(2) of the original Treaty of Basseterre, which provided: 'Any Member State, whether a Full Member or an Associate Member, may withdraw from the Organisation if it decides that extraordinary events, related to the subject-matter of this Treaty, have seriously endangered its supreme national interests. It shall give written notice of such withdrawal to the Director-General who shall promptly notify the other Member States and the Government of Saint Lucia. Such withdrawal shall take effect twelve (12) months after the notice is received by the Director-General.'

[123] RTB Art 34.2.

Although Article 28 of the RTB does not specify the consequences of withdrawal from that treaty for the Protocol, Article 34 of the Protocol suggests that withdrawal from the RTB entails withdrawal from the Protocol. In relation to Protocol member states which are not full member states of the Organisation, Article 34.1 of the Protocol allows them to 'withdraw from participation in this Protocol provided that the Government thereof gives twelve months notice in writing to the OECS Commission which shall notify the other Protocol Member States'. The use of the term 'participation' here gives rise to some uncertainty. This kind of language may have specific meaning in such a context. It was used by the United Nations, for example, to characterize the purported withdrawal of Indonesia from the UN in 1965–66 as merely being a period of 'cessation of cooperation' or 'non-participation', not withdrawal per se, hence leaving Indonesia's membership uninterrupted.[124] When read in the context of Article 24.3 of the RTB—which deems a party to the RTB to also be a party to the Protocol (subject to an Article 24.2 reservation)—the wording in Protocol Article 34.1 implies that a non-full member state does not actually withdraw from the Protocol, merely from participation in its arrangements.[125] As a result such a non-full member state could remain a party to the RTB and the Protocol, but be excluded from decision-making in Protocol areas and from future Protocol-related obligations.

Article 29.1 allows any member state party to the RTB, its DSA, or the Protocol to propose amendments. Amendments require a unanimous decision of the OECS Authority and come into force on either the date fixed by the Authority, or thirty days following its receipt by the OECS Secretariat or OECS Commission.[126] The text of any such amendment is distributed by the Director General to the OECS Commission, and the latter then transmits certified copies to all parties to the RTB and informs them of the date of the entry into force of the amendment. Amendments to the Protocol are also governed by Article 29 of the RTB.[127]

The requirement for unanimity in relation to the amendment of both the RTB and RTC is a sensible one and avoids a situation in which some states may be parties to the original treaty and others parties to the new (amended) treaty—with the obvious problems that such an arrangement would entail (such as different obligations, different organs, and different voting requirements for decisions). In this regard the use of the Agreement to enable the Entry into Force of the Revised Treaty of Chaguaramas Establishing the Caribbean Community including the CARICOM Single Market and Economy by CARICOM is unfortunate, even if it was necessary.

[124] See eg Schermers and Blokker, *International Institutional Law* (n 1) 100–1.

[125] RTB Art 24.3 provides: 'Except as provided in Article 24.2, a party to this Treaty is a party to the Economic Union Protocol.'

[126] The naming of both the Secretariat and Commission in Art 29.2 allowed amendments to be made prior to, or after, the date of entry into force of the RTB.

[127] Protocol Art 35.

5.5 Summary

The final provisions of the RTC and RTB flesh out and complete our understanding of the institutional structures of CARICOM and the OECS. They help us answer the question of whether each organization possesses international legal personality, and if so, what competences and limitations accompany that personality. By interpreting the RTC and RTB and applying international institutional law it is clear that both CARICOM and the OECS must be recognized as possessing international legal personality, the scope of which includes the powers to conclude treaties, to send and receive representatives in relation to third states and international organizations, and to bring and receive international legal claims before relevant regional tribunals. This international legal personality is important for an understanding of the nature of the organizations and also for their potential future powers. As discussed in relation to the two general undertaking clauses in the RTC and RTB (Articles 9 and 5, respectively), the obligations of member states include not only obligations 'arising out of' the treaty concerned, but also obligations 'resulting from decisions' of the treaty organs. The latter category would include obligations arising from treaties concluded between CARICOM or the OECS and third states and other international organizations.

In looking at the headquarters agreements of both regional organizations an interesting difference emerges in relation to the specification or non-specification of the headquarters location. In the RTC CARICOM's headquarters is stated to be in Georgetown, Guyana; in the RTB the location is not expressly named. Will any consequences flow from these differences? It is possible that the express naming of the host state in the RTC may give rise to greater political challenges if there is a desire to move the headquarters site. However the power to relocate headquarters can be implied from the text of the RTC, and also exists under international institutional law.

In terms of privileges and immunities, the CARICOM regime is clearer since it is governed by specific headquarters agreements and separate Protocols on privileges and immunities. The OECS regime adopts the privileges and immunities available under the Vienna Convention on Diplomatic Relations (VCDR). Although both regimes provide similar privileges and immunities, it is clear that the reliance of the OECS upon the VCDR will create serious interpretive challenges if a dispute arises in relation to privileges and immunities. This is because the privileges and immunities required for diplomats and other representatives of sovereign states are not the same as those required for representatives of international organizations. International organizations do not need the same level of privileges and immunities. Rather, to fulfil their purposes the privileges and immunities of international organizations must be strictly limited by the requirements of functional necessity.

Other challenges that emerge from the text of the RTC include the nearly impossible entry into force requirements. The original version of Article 234 of the RTC required fourteen ratifications. Such a number proved challenging. As a result the member states of CARICOM had to devise another treaty, an amending

Agreement, which effectively replaced Article 234 prior to entry into force of the RTC. This convoluted process demonstrates a serious commitment gap on the part of some of the original CARICOM member states, one that required resort to extraordinary measures—amending measures which would not be permissible under the RTC itself—to bring the RTC into force. The untidy result, as seen in Chapter 3, is that despite the fact that CARICOM has fifteen member states, the RTC only has thirteen parties.

The RTB, in contrast, was able to attract its requisite, smaller number of ratifications to enter into force. However the OECS faces its own treaty-derived challenges, including the availability of an express right to withdraw under Article 28 of the RTB and Article 34 of the Protocol. An express right to withdraw could diminish the level of commitment of member states. However this must be balanced against the fact that such a right already exists under general international institutional law and the law of treaties.

Finally, the formal entrenchment of the requirement for transformation of international obligations in Article 240 of the RTC may give rise to a number of consequences for CARICOM law. It is clear that decisions of organs must be transformed before they give rise to binding rights or obligations in national law. But does Article 240 require transformation before those same decisions can give rise to rights and obligations as a matter of international (or Community) law?[128] Also, does Article 240 exclude the possibility of direct effect arising from the RTC or from the decisions of CARICOM's organs? Although the latter question remains unresolved at present, a potential answer is suggested in Chapter 8.

[128] See the discussion in Chapter 6.

PART III

THE LEGAL SYSTEMS

6

The Creation, Implementation, and Enforcement of Legal Obligations

In order to understand the nature of the CARICOM and OECS legal systems it is important to be able to distinguish between the different phases in the creation, existence, and enforcement of a legal obligation, both as a matter of international law and national (domestic) law. Most of the actions of the organs of CARICOM and the OECS under the RTC and RTB are international legal actions. As such, they must be subject to the international and national legal rules on the creation of legal obligations in their respective fields. The former include the rules related to ratification; the latter include the rules related to transformation of international legal obligations. This chapter traces the progress of a legal obligation in both CARICOM and the OECS, from the moment of its conception. It looks at potential limitations on the implementation of the obligation, and at its possible enforcement by a member state or a regional or national tribunal.

6.1 Creation of Legal Obligations

In addition to the legal rules set out in the RTC and RTB, the decisions of the organs established under these treaties create law.[1] As seen in Chapter 4, the central organs of CARICOM and the OECS have been accorded extensive competences and decision-making powers and thus can create a wide range of legal obligations. The main six organs of CARICOM—the Conference, the Community Council, COTED, COFAP, COFCOR, and COHSOD—all have binding decision-making powers, under Articles 28 and 29 of the RTC. Similarly, in the OECS the Authority, Council of Ministers and Economic Affairs Council have

[1] For this reason in *Shanique Myrie v Barbados*, Judgment [2013] CCJ 3 (OJ) at [8] the CCJ defines Community law as including the RTC, the decisions of organs, and the judgments of the Court itself:

> The forms of secondary 'legislation' referred to here (i.e. the decisions and other determinations made by the relevant authorities *under the RTC*) are in principle part and parcel of Community law the content of which encompasses the provisions of the RTC, the decisions adopted by competent Organs and Bodies for its further development and implementation and the judgments of this Court pertaining to the interpretation and application of the Treaty.

binding decision-making powers, under Articles 8, 9, and 11 of the RTB and Article 28 of the Protocol. In addition, the OECS Authority and Council of Ministers are empowered to enact Acts, Regulations, and Orders of the Organisation, respectively, which under the RTB are to be directly effective in national legal systems.[2]

6.1.1 Procedural and substantive validity

In order for an international legal act to come into effect it must satisfy the rules regarding procedural and substantive validity. If the act is a decision of an organ of either CARICOM or the OECS, it is subject to a number of conditions for *procedural validity*. For example, a decision of CARICOM's Council of Trade and Economic Development (COTED), requires attendance by a quorum or greater of the membership of COTED (Article 27(1)), and the decision must be made by a favourable vote of either a qualified majority (in ordinary cases), or (qualified) unanimity in cases of critical importance under Article 29. Other procedural rules, such as those providing for the barring of voting in cases of budgetary arrears (Article 27(2)), the possibility of an opt out (Article 27(4)), and cooperation by Community organs (Article 20), may also affect the process of creation, and the subsequent nature, of a COTED decision.[3]

In addition to procedural rules, COTED decisions must also satisfy the conditions for *substantive validity*, namely, that the subject matter and scope of the decision must fall within the competence of the organ. Any decision of COTED must fall within the express or implied powers granted to it, either under Article 15 of the RTB or arising elsewhere in the treaty.

The same types of rules for procedural and substantive validity apply to decisions of all organs of CARICOM and the OECS. The decisions must be made in accordance with the proper procedure and fall within the scope of competences attributed to the particular organ, or the organization as a whole.

6.1.2 Ratification and acceptance

Further, as an international legal act, in order for a decision to have binding force it must be accepted by the state to which it is directed. In other words, there must be evidence of consent. For some international legal acts, such as treaties, such consent must be formally demonstrated, such as through ratification or related processes.[4] 'Ratification' describes the formal legal process by which a state accepts

[2] See RTB Arts 5, 8, 9, and 14.

[3] Note that there does not appear to be any significant restriction on the terminology used to make a decision. In *Shanique Myrie v Barbados* (n 1) at [45], the Court held that 'it is of no consequence that the 2007 Conference Decision used the word "agreed" and not "decided"'.

[4] See Vienna Convention on the Law of Treaties (adopted 23 May 1969, in force 27 Jan 1980) 1155 UNTS 331 (VCLT), Arts 11–17. Art 11 lists the following forms of consent: 'The consent of a State to be bound by a treaty may be expressed by signature, exchange of instruments constituting a treaty, ratification, acceptance, approval or accession, or by any other means if so agreed.'

an international legal obligation, and can be accomplished in a number of different ways—the most common being either to have the international agreement approved by the Executive of the State, or by Parliament after discussion.[5]

In relation to the CARICOM regime, some authors have suggested that decisions of organs must not only be validly made, but they also must be subject to subsequent formal acceptance by the member states by means of the submission of an instrument of ratification to the CARICOM Secretary General.[6] However, such a formal legal requirement would not appear to be necessary in the context of either CARICOM or the OECS, and does not appear to be supported by practice. Rather, member states appear to have at least implicitly accepted that a decision once validly made is binding as a matter of international (or Community) law. Consent is subsequently demonstrated when the state acts in accordance with the decision, either through legislative transformation or change in state practice.

Nevertheless, it may be useful to establish a more formal practice in relation to the making of legal acts by organs of Caribbean regional organizations which demonstrates acceptance by member states. Rather than instruments of ratification, however, which add another step to the norm-creating process, acceptance might be demonstrated through a formalization of the current decision-making practice. This could be done in two ways: firstly, by formally recording and publicizing votes, and secondly, by indicating formal consent to the final text of the decision. In other words, when the Conference meets to make a decision the CARICOM Secretariat could record and *publicize* the formal votes of member states. If the decision is by consensus, all member states should be listed as voting in favour of, or approving, the decision in its published text. This is the practice of the United Nations where individual votes in meetings of organs of the UN are recorded and published along with the decision. Such a practice would provide a clear and incontrovertible record of the position of each member state at the time of the making of the decision. The record of this practice could be used for a variety of purposes, including to support arguments of acquiescence or estoppel by other states, or even to generate customary international law.[7] For these reasons it would appear advisable to record votes for all CARICOM and OECS organs.

[5] Art 2(1)(b) of the VLCT defines 'ratification' as '"ratification", "acceptance", "approval" and "accession" mean in each case the international act so named whereby a State establishes on the international plane its consent to be bound by a treaty'. See eg Peter Malanczuk, *Akehurst's Modern Introduction to International Law*, 7th rev'd edn (London: Routledge, 1997) 65–8.

[6] eg Kathy-Ann Brown, 'The CARICOM—"Unity for Survival"', in N Lacasse and L Perret (eds), *Le libre-échange dans les Amériques (Une perspective continentale)/Free trade in the Americas (A hemispheric approach)* (Montreal: Wilson & Lafleur, 1994) 335–68, in note 31, argues that decisions are not binding until ratified *and* the Secretary General of CARICOM has been notified of the state's action.

[7] The International Court of Justice, for example, has taken account of the voting positions of parties to a dispute in resolutions of international organizations, both as evidence of the recognition by those states of a general legal obligation (*opinio juris*), and as evidence of acceptance of the applicability of that legal obligation to themselves. See eg *Military and Paramilitary Activities in and against Nicaragua (Nicaragua v USA)* (Merits) [1986] ICJ Rep 14, at pp 99–101 [188]–[190] and 107 [203]–[204]. In this context the Court noted at p 100 [188], that a vote in favour of a resolution represented

In addition, to generate greater certainty and transparency the text of decisions of organs might be finalized at the conclusion of the meeting concerned and, if possible, formally signed by a representative of each member state or by a representative of CARICOM. The usefulness of such a practice of formal agreement on the wording of the text of a legal act is apparent in the context of the OECS. Under Article 5.3 of the RTB Acts, Regulations, and Orders of the Authority and Council of Ministers are to be directly effective in national law, meaning that they are to give rise to legal rights and obligations in national law. Such Acts, Regulations, and Orders of OECS organs therefore will serve the same purpose as legislation. They will create legal rights and obligations and must be capable of legal interpretation and enforcement. In this context the agreed wording of the text will be important. The same applies for decisions of CARICOM organs, which may give rise to binding rights for persons that are enforceable before the Caribbean Court of Justice (CCJ), in its original jurisdiction.[8]

6.1.3 Binding nature

Once validly made, in accordance with the conditions for both procedural and substantive validity, the decisions of organs under both the RTC and RTB, and Acts, Regulations, and Orders under the RTB, will give rise to binding rights and obligations as a matter of international law. Their binding nature is underpinned by the most fundamental rule of the law of treaties, *pacta sunt servanda*.[9] This phrase, as summarized in Article 26 of the Vienna Convention on the Law of Treaties (VCLT), means that '[e]very treaty in force is binding upon the parties to it and must be performed by them in good faith'. As made clear in Article 26, not only are treaties (1) binding as a matter of international law and (2) must be performed; they must be (3) performed in good faith.[10] The good faith requirement, as we saw in Chapter 2, flows through the law of treaties generally, and applies to both the application and interpretation of treaties.[11] The Article 26 rule applies to the commitments set out in the text of the treaties, but also more generally to the commitments lawfully arising from the decisions made and actions taken

an indication of acceptance of the applicability of the resolution to the state itself: 'The effect of consent to the text of such resolutions cannot be understood as merely that of a "reiteration or elucidation" of the treaty commitment undertaken in the Charter. On the contrary, it may be understood as an acceptance of the validity of the rule or set of rules declared by the resolution by themselves.'

[8] In the case of *Shanique Myrie v Barbados* (n 1), the Court held that a 2007 Conference decision created binding legal obligations upon member states, obligations which could be enforced before the Court even if they had not been transformed into domestic law.

[9] See eg PK Menon, *An Introduction to the Law of Treaties* (Bridgetown, Barbados: UWI/USAID Caribbean Justice Improvement Project, 1992) 43–7; *Designation of the Workers' Delegate for the Netherlands at the Third Session of the International Labour Conference* (Advisory Opinion) [1922] PCIJ Rep, Series B, No 1, at p 19 (a treaty goes beyond 'a mere moral obligation' and rather imposes a binding one).

[10] The *pacta sunt servanda* rule may be argued to be binding both as a matter of customary and conventional international law. cf Malcolm Shaw, *International Law*, 5th edn (Cambridge: Cambridge University Press, 2003) 811–12.

[11] See eg Richard Gardiner, *Treaty Interpretation* (Oxford: Oxford University Press, 2008) 148–50.

under the treaties. This is reinforced by the general undertaking provisions of both the RTC and RTB.

6.1.4 The general undertaking in CARICOM law

Article 9 of the RTC clarifies and crystallizes the formal, binding obligation underpinning all of the commitments of the RTC. Its phrasing balances the discretion accorded to member states regarding how to achieve the RTC's obligations, on the one hand, with a binding obligation as to result, on the other. Article 9 states:

> Member States shall take all appropriate measures, whether general or particular, to ensure the carrying out of obligations arising out of this Treaty or resulting from decisions taken by the Organs and Bodies of the Community. They shall facilitate the achievement of the objectives of the Community. They shall abstain from any measures which could jeopardise the attainment of the objectives of this Treaty.

Article 9 imposes both positive and negative obligations. Member states have a positive duty to ensure the carrying out of obligations and to facilitate the achievement of the objectives of the Community. They have a negative duty not to take measures which could prejudice the objectives of the Treaty.

The positive duty requires states parties, where necessary, to enact domestic legislation to implement treaty obligations (subject to Article 240 RTC).[12] Most CARICOM member states have attempted to fulfil this obligation by enacting statutes that transform RTC obligations into domestic law.[13] The negative duty could be construed as barring states from enacting new law inconsistent with their RTC obligations. In this regard it should be noted that the word 'measures' is broad enough to cover a variety of state acts, including legislation, administrative practices, and even international legal acts, such as the ratification of a treaty.[14] The word 'ensure' carries with it an obligation as to result.[15]

[12] The European Court of Justice held that a positive duty to enact laws derived from the parallel provision of EU law in Case C-265/95 *Commission v France* [1997] ECR I-6959.

[13] The statutes of CARICOM member states which transform the RTC include, alphabetically by territory: Caribbean Community Act, Laws of Antigua and Barbuda, Act No 9 of 2004; Caribbean Community Act, Laws of Barbados, Act No 8 of 2003; Caribbean Community Act, Laws of Belize, Act No 17 of 2004; Caribbean Community Act 2005, Laws of Dominica, Act No 22 of 2005; Revised Treaty of Chaguaramas Act, Laws of Grenada, Act No 10 of 2006; Caribbean Community Act, Laws of Guyana, Act No 8 of 2006; Caribbean Community Act, Laws of Jamaica, Vol IIIA 2009, Act No 15 of 2004; Caribbean Community Act 2005, Laws of St Christopher and Nevis, Act No 27 of 2005; Caribbean Community Act, Laws of Saint Lucia, Revised Edition 2008, Cap 19.21; Caribbean Community Act, Laws of Saint Vincent and the Grenadines, Revised Edition 2009, Cap 184; Caribbean Community Act, Laws of Trinidad and Tobago, LRO 2009, Chap 81:11. Information regarding Haiti, Montserrat, and Suriname was not found.

[14] In the case of *Shanique Myrie v Barbados* (n 1), the CCJ appears to draw a distinction between the form, and application, of the law. The Court suggests that even where an obligation has not been transformed into domestic law (ie by statute), the state must ensure that *in its application* its law upholds the Community obligation. The CCJ states at [52]: '[i]t is the obligation of each State, having consented to the creation of a Community obligation, to ensure that its domestic law, at least in its application, reflects and supports Community law.'

[15] See eg the seminal judgment of the Inter-American Court of Human Rights in the *Case of Velásquez-Rodríguez v Honduras* (Merits), I-A Ct HR, Judgment of 29 July 1988, Series C, No 4, at

In addition, as made clear in Article 27 of the VCLT, the positive obligation under Article 9 of the RTC to ensure the carrying out of the obligations of the RTC, including obligations arising thereunder, is not subject to any limitations imposed upon the state by its own domestic law. Article 27 of the VCLT provides as follows: 'A party may not invoke the provisions of its internal law as justification for its failure to perform a treaty. This rule is without prejudice to article 46.'[16] Article 46 of the VCLT only allows the invocation of domestic legal limitations as a reason for invalidating a state's *consent* to a treaty on the grounds that that consent was unlawfully given, with the violation both being manifest and concerning a rule of internal law of fundamental importance.[17] Importantly, Article 46 does not allow a state to challenge the *performance of treaty obligations* on the basis of domestic limitations. It only allows a state to challenge the legality of its consent to be bound to the treaty.

The rule regarding non-applicability of domestic law limitations is one of both conventional and customary international law.[18] As noted by the International Court of Justice in its judgment in the *PLO Observer Mission Case*:

It would be sufficient to recall the fundamental principle of international law that international law prevails over domestic law. This principle was endorsed by judicial decision as

[166]–[167], where the Court interpreted the meaning of the word 'ensure' in Art 1 of the American Convention on Human Rights as requiring effective implementation of the protected rights:

> 166. The second obligation of the States Parties is to 'ensure' the free and full exercise of the rights recognized by the Convention to every person subject to its jurisdiction. This obligation implies the duty of States Parties to organize the governmental apparatus and, in general, all the structures through which public power is exercised, so that they are capable of juridically ensuring the free and full enjoyment of human rights. As a consequence of this obligation, the States must prevent, investigate and punish any violation of the rights recognized by the Convention and, moreover, if possible attempt to restore the right violated and provide compensation as warranted for damages resulting from the violation.
>
> 167. The obligation to ensure the free and full exercise of human rights is not fulfilled by the existence of a legal system designed to make it possible to comply with this obligation—it also requires the government to conduct itself so as to effectively ensure the free and full exercise of human rights.

[16] In Case 1/86 *Commission v Belgium* [1987] ECR 2797, at p 2805 [9], the ECJ applied this rule strictly, so that even though Belgium had started to implement the EU obligation, but proved unable to do so as a result of national legal challenges, it was not excused from the breach:

> It must be stated that the fact that the procedure for the adoption of implementing measures has been initiated in respect of the Walloon region and the Brussels region does not put an end to the failure to fulfil obligations. Furthermore, according to settled case-law, a Member State may not plead provisions, practices or circumstances existing in its internal legal system in order to justify a failure to comply with obligations resulting from Community directives.

[17] Art 46 of the VCLT, entitled 'Provisions of internal law regarding competence to conclude treaties', states:

> 1. A State may not invoke the fact that its consent to be bound by a treaty has been expressed in violation of a provision of its internal law regarding competence to conclude treaties as invalidating its consent unless that violation was manifest and concerned a rule of its internal law of fundamental importance.
> 2. A violation is manifest if it would be objectively evident to any State conducting itself in the matter in accordance with normal practice and in good faith.

[18] For a customary international law expression of the rule under VCLT Art 27 see eg the *Alabama Claims Arbitration (United States v Great Britain)*, Moore (1872) 1 Int Arb 495, at p 656.

long ago as the arbitral award of 14 September 1872 in the *Alabama* case between Great Britain and the United States, and has frequently been recalled since, for example in the case concerning the *Greco-Bulgarian 'Communities'* in which the Permanent Court of International Justice laid it down that

> 'it is a generally accepted principle of international law that in the relations between Powers who are contracting Parties to a treaty, the provisions of municipal law cannot prevail over those of the treaty' (P.C.I.J., Series B, No. 17, p. 32).[19]

As a result states have been held to be bound by international legal obligations even if, for example, they subsequently were unable to perform them as a result of constitutional limitations.[20] States also have been required to change their most basic laws, including their constitutions, if those laws proved incompatible with their treaty obligations.[21]

6.1.5 The general undertaking in OECS law

The general undertaking provision in Article 5 of the RTB is more detailed than that found in the RTC, primarily because of the potentially deeper nature of the integration regime of the OECS.[22] The RTB not only imposes binding treaty obligations, by means of Article 14 it authorizes the Organisation to legislate in areas previously under the sovereign competence of its members. As a result Article 5 requires OECS member states not only to ensure the carrying out of their RTB obligations; it also expressly requires them to enact laws that give effect to the RTB and decisions taken thereunder, including laws that delegate areas of competence to the Organisation and that ensure that Acts, Regulations, and Orders of

[19] Advisory Opinion [1988] ICJ Rep 12, at pp 34–5.

[20] See eg *Attorney-General for Canada v Attorney-General for Ontario* [1937] AC 326, where the Judicial Committee of the Privy Council held that although the federal government (executive) may have the power to enter into treaties, the provinces nevertheless retain the constitutional right refuse to perform them within their spheres of authority.

[21] eg Barbados was effectively required to repeal s 26 of its constitution—the 'savings law' clause—by the Inter-American Court of Human Rights in both the *Case of Boyce v Barbados* (Preliminary Objections, Merits, Reparations and Costs), I-A Ct HR, Judgment of 20 November 2007, Series C, No 169, and the *Case of DaCosta Cadogan v Barbados* (Preliminary Objections, Merits, Reparations and Costs), I-A Ct HR, Judgment of 24 September 2009, Series C, No 204.

[22] For legislation transforming the RTB (or original Treaty if the RTB information is unavailable) see, by territory: Revised Treaty of Basseterre Establishing the Organisation of Eastern Caribbean States Economic Union Act, 2011, Laws of Antigua and Barbuda, Act No 17 of 2011 [RTB]; Organisation of Eastern Caribbean States Act, Laws of Dominica, Revised Edition 1990, Chap 17:01 [original Treaty]; Revised Treaty of Basseterre Establishing the Organisation of Eastern Caribbean States Act, Laws of Grenada, Act No 4 of 2012 [RTB]; Revised Treaty of Basseterre Establishing the Organisation of Eastern Caribbean States Economic Union Act, 2013, Laws of Montserrat, Act No 6 of 2012 [RTB]; Organisation of Eastern Caribbean States Act, Laws of St Christopher and Nevis, Revised Edition 2002 [original Treaty]; Organisation of East Caribbean States Act, Laws of St. Lucia, Act No 17 of 2011 [RTB]; Revised Treaty of Basseterre Establishing the Organisation of Eastern Caribbean States Economic Union Act, Laws of Saint Vincent and the Grenadines, Act No 22 of 2011 [RTB].

the Organisation have direct effect in national law.[23] Article 5.3 sets out this latter obligation in the following terms:

> 5.3 Without prejudice to the generality of the foregoing –
> (a) a full Member State which is independent undertakes to enact the legislation necessary to –
> (i) delegate to the Organisation the said Member State's authority to legislate in the areas of competence of the Organisation outlined in Article 14; or
> (ii) receive Acts of the Organisation made by the OECS Authority, and Regulations and Orders made by the Council of Ministers, from the Organisation in the areas of competence of the Organisation outlined in Article 14;
>
> with the intention that the Acts, Regulations and Orders have direct effect in the laws of the Member State;
>
> (b) a Member State which is not an independent State undertakes to enact legislation to provide for the reception into its law of the legislation made under this Article. The legislation–
> (i) shall enable reception of Acts of the Organisation made by the OECS Authority, and Regulations and Orders made by the Council of Ministers, from the Organisation without the need for enactment by the Member State's Legislature either generally or on a case by case basis;
> (ii) may make the reception of the Acts, Regulations and Orders subject to the discretion of a competent authority in the Member State.

The phrase 'direct effect' as used in Article 5.3 is borrowed from the law of the European Union, which early on developed a judicial doctrine that allowed certain forms of EU law to become automatically part of the domestic law of member states, to the extent that they could be relied upon by individuals before national courts.

If interpreted in the same manner, direct effect in OECS law would allow individuals to sue OECS member states, and possibly other individuals, in order to enforce their RTB-derived rights. This would be revolutionary in the Caribbean context. It would bring into being an entirely distinct, *national* enforcement mechanism (through domestic courts) for OECS law, in addition to the enforcement tools existing under the RTB and its Protocol. Such a double level of enforcement—both at the national and regional level—would give rise to what is called 'dual vigilance' in EU law, with the vigilance of the Union organs being complemented by the vigilance of the individuals.[24] The full potential of direct effect, including direct effect in the OECS, is discussed in Chapter 8.

[23] RTB Arts 5.1–5.3.

[24] As stated by the ECJ in the famous decision in Case 26/62 *NV Algemene Transport-en Expeditie Onderneming van Gend en Loos v Nederlandse Administratie der Belastingen* [1963] ECR 1, at 13, when discussing the consequence of direct effect, 'the vigilance of individuals concerned to protect their rights amounts to an effective supervision *in addition to* the supervision entrusted by Articles 169 and 170 [now Arts 258 and 259 of the TFEU] to the diligence of the Commission and the Member States' (emphasis added).

Before we leave Article 5.3, it should be noted that its two subsections distinguish obligations based on the nature of the member state concerned. Independent member states are required either to delegate authority to the OECS to legislate in the areas covered by Article 14, or to receive legislative acts of the OECS under the same article, so as to enable OECS Acts, Regulations, and Orders to have direct effect in their national legal systems.[25] Non-independent member states, in contrast, although being required to enact legislation to provide for the reception into law of OECS legislation, may make that reception subject to the discretion of a competent authority.

This distinction could have important consequences for the uniformity of OECS law. Independent OECS member states are held to a higher standard. They must ensure that OECS law becomes part of their legal system immediately, without any requirement for national action. Non-independent member states are permitted to exercise discretion in relation to the reception of OECS law. Such discretion could bar the reception of an OECS Act, Regulation, or Order. This distinction was no doubt motivated by the division of powers which exists between Overseas Territories, such as Montserrat, and their metropolitan centres, which division could exclude competence in a particular area for the Overseas Territory. Nevertheless, understanding these limitations, it is unfortunate that no express constraint is imposed by the RTB on the exercise of discretion under Article 5.3. Nor does the RTB expressly contemplate any procedure under which an unfavourable discretionary decision could be challenged.

In any event, the implementation of Article 5.3 has already been hindered by subsequent legislative developments. In the case of Montserrat, Article 5.3 has been expressly precluded from having the force of law. Section 3(2) of the Revised Treaty of Basseterre Establishing the Organisation of Eastern Caribbean States Economic Union Act, 2013 provides:

> **Revised Treaty & Protocol to have force of law**
>
> 3. (1) Subject to subsection (2), the Revised Treaty and the Protocol shall have the force of law in Montserrat.
>
> (2) Article 5.3 of the Revised Treaty shall not have the force of law in Montserrat.[26]

[25] For examples of a statute expressly according direct effect to OECS law see: Organisation of East Caribbean States Act, Laws of St Lucia, Act No 17 of 2011, ss 4(1)–(2).

[26] Laws of Montserrat, Act No 6 of 2012. Montserrat's position can be contrasted with that of the UK in its relations with the EU. In relation to the latter, s 2(1) of the European Communities Act 1972 (UK), c 68, as amended by the European Union (Amendment) Act 2008 (c 7), ss 3, 8, Sch Pt 1, SI 2009/3143, provides:

> All such rights, powers, liabilities, obligations and restrictions from time to time created or arising by or under the Treaties, and all such remedies and procedures from time to time provided for by or under the Treaties, as in accordance with the Treaties are *without further enactment* to be given legal effect or used in the United Kingdom shall be recognised and available in law, and be enforced, allowed and followed accordingly; and the expression 'enforceable EU right' and similar expressions shall be read as referring to one to which this subsection applies. (emphasis added)

Section 2(2) allows the UK to enact statutes to implement EU law, but s 2(1) does not *require* enactment. As a result, the UK would be able to comply with directly applicable EU rules, such as Regulations, without enacting any domestic legislation.

The Act rejects the possibility of OECS Acts, Regulations and Orders being directly effective in the laws of Montserrat.

Montserrat's statute raises serious legal issues. By enacting a statute that directly contradicts Article 5.3, Montserrat would seem to be prima facie in breach of Article 5 of the RTB. The same can be said of St Vincent and the Grenadines and Antigua and Barbuda, both of which enacted legislation excluding Article 5.3.[27] All three territories appear to be in breach of the RTB. Unless the RTB is amended, the only way these three territories might be deemed *not* to be in breach of the RTB would be if they had entered a reservation to Article 5 when they signed, ratified, or acceded to the RTB. No such reservation appears to have been made.[28]

The RTB expressly allows reservations in only two cases. It allows for reservations to be made to the obligations in Article 14 and in the Protocol.[29] It does not contemplate, or allow, reservations to be made to Article 5. However reservations are permissible under the general law of treaties. The default position, as expressed in the VCLT, is to allow reservations if they are made when 'signing, ratifying, accepting, approving, or acceding to a treaty' so long as they do not fall within certain expressly prohibited categories of reservations. Article 19 of the VCLT provides:

> A State may, when signing, ratifying, accepting, approving or acceding to a treaty, formulate a reservation unless:
> (a) the reservation is prohibited by the treaty;
> (b) the treaty provides that only specified reservations, which do not include the reservation in question, may be made; or
> (c) in cases not falling under sub-paragraphs (a) and (b), the reservation is incompatible with the object and purpose of the treaty.

Article 19(a) of the VCLT is inapplicable. Questions could arise, however, as to whether a reservation to Article 5 of the RTB would fall under either of the categories set out in Article 19(b) or (c) of the VCLT. Given that the RTB does contain provisions authorizing reservations, and these do not include reservations to Article 5, a reservation to Article 5.3 might be caught under Article 19(b). In addition, if one considers the doctrine of direct effect to be part of the very core of the RTB, then any reservation to Article 5.3 could be deemed to be contrary to the object and purpose of the RTB and therefore impermissible under Article 19(c).[30]

[27] See Revised Treaty of Basseterre Establishing the Organisation of Eastern Caribbean States Economic Union Act, Laws of Saint Vincent and the Grenadines, Act No 22 of 2011, s 3(2); Revised Treaty of Basseterre Establishing the Organisation of Eastern Caribbean States Economic Union Act, 2011, Laws of Antigua and Barbuda, Act No 17 of 2011, s 3(2).

[28] Confirmed by the OECS Commission: Statement by Elma Gene Isaac, Head of the OECS Regional Integration Unit (Personal communication 24 Jul 2013).

[29] See RTB Arts 14.4 and 24.2.

[30] For an example of a case where a reservation was deemed to be contrary to the object and purpose of the treaty see UNCHR, Communication No 845/1999, *Rawle Kennedy v Trinidad and Tobago*, CCPR/C/67/D/845/1999 (31 Dec 1999) at p 10 [6.7].

In either case, the reservation itself—if not accepted by other member states—would not be lawful.[31]

In any event, domestic legislation and reservations aside, *all* states parties to the RTB, including Montserrat, St Vincent and the Grenadines, and Antigua and Barbuda, remain fully bound by the remaining provisions of the RTB and its Protocol, including the remainder of Article 5. Subsections (1) and (2) of Article 5 require member states to take measures to ensure the carrying out of obligations arising under the treaty and to enact legislation so as to give effect to the treaty and decisions taken thereunder, respectively. As a result, all states party to the RTB and its Protocol must comply with their obligations under both treaties in full, including their obligation to transform the treaties and decisions made thereunder. As a result, the non-implementation of Article 5.3 by these three states may only slow down, and make more onerous, their compliance with their RTB and Protocol obligations. It cannot frustrate them.

It should be noted that Article 5.4 potentially limits the effects of the RTB and its general undertaking provision by stating that '[n]othing in this Treaty requires a Member State to undertake amendments to its Constitution, and its obligations as to implementation are circumscribed accordingly.' Article 5.5 similarly excludes the possibility of the RTB requiring 'a Member State to act prejudicially to the requirements of public participation and discussion which flow from good governance in a democratic society'. These limitations may not be significant since they must be interpreted by member states in a manner compatible with the overarching requirements of the RTB. For this reason it is unlikely that either subsection could be used by member states to significantly hinder the development of OECS law. In addition, in relation to the suggested constitutional limitation in Article 5.4, it should be remembered that the United Kingdom—a state which, although it does not have a written constitution, shares most of the constitutional traditions of the Commonwealth Caribbean—has been able to embrace a similar level of integration, including the doctrine of direct effect, by joining the European Union.

In sum, because Article 9 of the RTC and Article 5 of the RTB formally identify the binding commitment assumed by states parties under each treaty, they will play a pivotal role in any enforcement process related to those treaty obligations, or obligations arising from the respective decisions of CARICOM's organs and bodies and decisions of the OECS Institutions. These general undertakings provisions may also have more far-reaching implications for Caribbean integration law, as illustrated by the way in which the parallel provision in EU law has been interpreted and applied by the European Court of Justice. The wording of Article 9 of the RTC and Article 5.1 of the RTB is nearly identical to that of Article 4(3) of the Treaty on European Union, which in its previous incarnations played a central role in the development of such concepts as direct applicability, direct effect, indirect effect, and state liability.[32]

[31] See Arts 20–23 of the VCLT.

[32] For a discussion of these concepts see Chapter 8. See also Chapter 11 for examples of the use of general undertaking provisions like Art 4(3) of the TFEU by the ECJ in developing the EU's legal regime related to anti-competitive conduct by states and public undertakings.

6.1.6 Legislative competences of the OECS

Article 14 of the RTB fundamentally distinguishes the OECS from CARICOM, by setting out areas of legislative competence for the OECS. Unlike in the case of the European Union treaties, however, Article 14 does not expressly use terms like 'exclusive' or 'shared' to describe that legislative competence.[33] As a result the nature of the competences listed in Article 14 must be interpreted in accordance with the ordinary meaning of the text and in light of the object and purposes of the RTB.[34] The first two subsections of Article 14 provide:

> 14.1 The Member States agree to accord to the Organisation under Article 5.3 and subject to Article 5.4 legislative competence in relation to –
> (a) common market including customs union;
> (b) monetary policy, the competence in this category to be exercised on the recommendation of the Monetary Council;
> (c) trade policy;
> (d) maritime jurisdiction and maritime boundaries; and
> (e) civil aviation, the competence in this category to be exercised on the recommendation of the Board of Directors of the Eastern Caribbean Civil Aviation Authority;
>
> provided that a Member State need not take steps to repeal its laws in relation to such matters (which laws are otherwise compatible with this Treaty) in advance of the enactment of any Act of the Organisation, but shall refrain with effect from the date of coming into force of this Treaty from enacting any new legislation in relation to such matters save with the approval of or under powers delegated by the OECS Authority.
>
> 14.2 The Member States agree to accord to the Organisation under Article 5.3 and subject to Article 5.4 legislative competence in relation to –
> (a) common commercial policy;
> (b) environmental policy; and
> (c) immigration policy;
>
> reserving their right to legislate in relation to those matters within aspects of such policy not pre-empted by or under the authority of any Act of the Organisation.

Article 14.1 may not seem to provide exclusive competence to the Organisation, since it neither uses the term 'exclusive' nor requires the immediate repeal of national legislation in the areas described. However the formal requirement imposed upon member states not to enact new legislation in the areas set out in Article 14.1 suggests a kind of semi-permanent transfer of competence in those areas to the OECS (subject to the Authority's ability to re-delegate). This is reinforced by Article 5.3(a) which requires independent full member states to enact legislation necessary to 'delegate to the Organisation the said Member State's authority to legislate in the areas of competence of the Organisation outlined in Article 14'. Delegation is not the same as a complete transfer of power.[35]

[33] See Arts 2–4 of the TFEU.
[34] See the discussion of Art 31 of the VCLT and the rules of treaty interpretation in Chapter 2.
[35] cf HRW Wade and CF Forsyth, *Administrative Law*, 8th edn (Oxford: Oxford University Press 2000) ch 11, for an overview of the administrative law regarding the retention of discretion.

Nevertheless—subject to the requirements for prior legislative action by the Organisation, the potential effect of a reservation made under Article 14.4, and the retained power of the Authority to re-delegate—Article 14.1 may best be described as setting out areas of potentially exclusive legislative competence for the OECS.

This is significant, both in terms of institutional development and because of the substantive areas covered by Article 14.1, all of which are fundamental to the operation of the Economic Union. The Organisation is given the competence to legislate over the common market, the customs union, monetary policy, trade policy, civil aviation, and maritime jurisdiction and boundaries. The latter three areas are important because they relate to the imperatives of transportation, sustenance, and tourism. Moreover, competence over maritime boundaries is one of the most closely guarded aspects of sovereignty under international law, and therefore the delegation of this authority reveals the high level of trust placed in the Organisation by its member states.

Article 14.2 sets out areas of shared or concurrent legislative competence, subject to a pre-emptive power on the part of the Organisation. The competences are shared because member states remain free to legislate in the listed areas prior to the Organisation legislating in those areas. Competences are pre-emptive because once the OECS legislates in an area (eg, by enacting an Act of the Organisation), the member states lose their competence to do so. Article 14.2 provides legislative competence to the OECS in the areas of common commercial policy, environmental policy, and immigration policy.

However, it must be noted that the legislative powers of the OECS are subject to reservation under Article 14.4, which allows associate members and 'a full Member State which is not an independent State' (ie, Montserrat) to make reservations to Article 14 at the time of ratifying or acceding to the RTB. There is no evidence that any associate member or non-independent member state entered such a reservation, and therefore the effect of Article 14.4 would appear to be limited.[36]

Article 14.3 allows the OECS to assume legislative competence in additional spheres, subject to what in EU law is termed the 'principle of subsidiarity'.[37] Article 14.3 provides:

> 14.3 In the areas of legislative competence of the Organisation which do not fall under Article 14.1, the Organisation shall enact Acts of the Organisation only

[36] The absence of any reservation to the RTB was confirmed by the Head of the OECS Regional Integration Unit: Statement by Elma Gene Isaac, Head of the OECS Regional Integration Unit (Personal communication 24 Jul 2013).

[37] On subsidiarity see eg TC Hartley, *The Foundations of European Union Law*, 7th edn (Oxford: Oxford University Press, 2010), pp 121–7. Art 5(3) of the TEU describes the concept as follows:

> 3. Under the principle of subsidiarity, in areas which do not fall within its exclusive competence, the Union shall act only if and in so far as the objectives of the proposed action cannot be sufficiently achieved by the Member States, either at central level or at regional and local level, but can rather, by reason of the scale or effects of the proposed action, be better achieved at Union level.

> if and in so far as the objectives of the proposed action cannot, in the opinion of the OECS Authority, be sufficiently achieved by the Member States and can therefore, by reason of the scale or effects of the proposed action, be better achieved by enacting an Act of the Organisation.

Article 14.3 does not limit those additional legislative areas to those listed in Article 14.2, and therefore implicitly allows the OECS to legislate in entirely new areas, in addition to those listed in Article 14.1–14.2. However such new OECS legislative competence is reserved to areas in which member states cannot sufficiently achieve, and the Organisation has a superior ability to achieve, the objectives of the proposed action, by reason of the scale or effects. In other words, Article 14.3 establishes a two-part test for new, non-exclusive OECS legislative competence: (1) legislative actions of *member states* must be deficient, and (2) legislative actions of the *OECS* must be superior, for the purpose of achieving the objective.

Taken collectively, these provisions demonstrate the way that the RTB establishes a comprehensive framework for regulating the competences of the Organisation. The RTB grants significant exclusive and shared competences. But it also circumscribes them in two ways. Firstly, through provisions such as Articles 14.1, 14.2, and 7.2, the RTB establishes clear limits on the competences of the OECS. Secondly, through Article 14.3 the RTB not only *limits* those competences, but also may circumscribe their *use*. In other words, Article 14.3 can be used to exclude the possibility of certain forms of legislative action by the Organisation. It also can provide a subsequent check on actions already undertaken. A similar situation obtains in EU law, where the limits of Union competence are set by the principle of conferral, and the use of Union competences is governed by the principles of subsidiarity and proportionality.[38]

The principle of conferral is established in OECS law by Article 7.2 of the RTB, which expressly mandates that the OECS organs 'perform the functions and act within the limits of the powers conferred upon them by or under this Treaty and by the Dispute Settlement Annex and the Economic Union Protocol'. In other words, OECS organs must act within the limits established by the OECS treaties; actions not falling under the treaties will be unauthorized (ultra vires). However the phrase used in Article 7.2 is 'by or under' the treaties. Such wording allows actions to be authorized by the text of the treaties (as interpreted by the organs) and by the decisions and legislative actions of the organs.

Article 14.3, in setting out a version of the principle of subsidiarity, does not specify the consequence for OECS legislative action which is not compliant with the

[38] See eg Hartley, *The Foundations of European Union Law* (n 37) 121–7. Art 5.1–5.2 of the TEU sets out the relations, and descriptions, of these terms as follows:

1. The limits of Union competences are governed by the principle of conferral. The use of Union competences is governed by the principles of subsidiarity and proportionality.
2. Under the principle of conferral, the Union shall act only within the limits of the competences conferred upon it by the Member States in the Treaties to attain the objectives set out therein. Competences not conferred upon the Union in the Treaties remain with the Member States.

principle. But since such legislation would fall outside the areas of competence of the Organisation, it should be considered ultra vires and subject to legal challenge on that ground. In the EU, in comparison, recent amendments to the EU treaties and the addition of a new protocol on subsidiarity, Protocol (No 2) on the Application of the Principles of Subsidiarity and Proportionality, make clear that non-compliance with the principle of subsidiarity can give rise to legal challenge before the ECJ.[39] Moreover, Protocol No 2 goes to great lengths to ensure that the issue of subsidiarity is carefully evaluated by EU organs and member states. Protocol No 2 requires all draft EU legislation to contain a detailed statement regarding its compliance with the principle, and this must be transmitted with the draft legislation to all national Parliaments of member states.[40] These national Parliaments are empowered under the Protocol in certain situations to require the draft legislation to be reviewed for non-compliance with the principle of subsidiarity, and may, along with their member states, initiate actions before the ECJ challenging such non-compliance.[41]

A similar system arguably has been established by the RTB, since the OECS Assembly considers draft legislation of the Organisation and may notify the Authority or Council of Ministers of any legislation that it believes breaches Article 14.3.[42] Moreover the Commission may interpret Article 12.5(f) of the RTB as providing it with a mandate to deal with breaches of the principle of subsidiarity by, for example, making reports to other OECS organs or to taking independent actions to correct such breaches. Article 12.5(f) mandates the Commission to 'undertake such other work and studies and perform such other services relating to the functions of Organisation as may be required under this Treaty'. The phrase 'as may be required under this Treaty' is broad in nature. It would include work, studies, or services expressly provided for in the text of the treaty. It also could be deemed to include work, studies, or services not found in the RTB text, but which are necessary to uphold the object and purpose of the treaty. A breach of the subsidiarity requirement by one organ of the OECS may frustrate the object and purpose of the treaty. As a result the Commission may be warranted in drawing the attention of other organs to this breach, or even bringing the matter before the Eastern Caribbean Court of Appeal or the dispute settlement procedures established by the DSA (as provided under Article 18 of the RTB).

[39] See the Protocol (No 2) on the Application of the Principles of Subsidiarity and Proportionality, attached to the Consolidated versions of the Treaty on European Union and the Treaty on the Functioning of the European Union (OJ C83, 30.3.2010) as available through <http://eur-lex.europa.eu/en/treaties/index.htm> (accessed 30 Sep 2011). Article 8 of the Protocol provides, in part:

> The Court of Justice of the European Union shall have jurisdiction in actions on grounds of infringement of the principle of subsidiarity by a legislative act, brought in accordance with the rules laid down in Article 263 of the Treaty on the Functioning of the European Union by Member States, or notified by them in accordance with their legal order on behalf of their national Parliament or a chamber thereof.

[40] Protocol (n 39) Arts 5–6.

[41] Protocol Art 7. But see TC Hartley, *The Foundations of European Union Law* (n 37) 123–7, on the issue of whether Parliaments themselves have separate locus standi before the ECJ, or whether they are to be represented by member states.

[42] See RTB Art 10.13.

In addition to the requirement for respect for subsidiarity, the legislative competence of the OECS will be limited by the source of its authority under the RTB. Thus whether the OECS legislative act is authorized, or enacted, under Article 14.1, Article 14.2, or Article 14.3 could have legal implications. In all three cases an Act of the Organisation will supersede national laws, but under Article 14.3 that Act must be justifiable under the principle of subsidiarity. In addition, although Article 14.1 has the effect of removing areas from the sphere of national legislation, Article 14.2 and 14.3 leave legislative areas within the national sphere of authority until that legislative competence is pre-empted by OECS legislation. As a result, the legal basis of an Act may determine whether national legislation enacted after the entry into force of the RTB is merely superseded by subsequent OECS legislation (Article 14.2–14.3) or whether it is ultra vires and therefore invalid (Article 14.1). In this context it should be noted that the legal basis of an act is of fundamental importance in EU law where, for example, measures adopted under the wrong EU treaty article, or adopted in the absence of conferred competence, are subject to annulment.[43]

6.2 Potential Limitations: Overarching Exceptions to Obligations

Although the RTC and RTB create binding obligations for CARICOM and OECS member states, respectively, through their general undertaking provisions, the *texts* of these treaties reveal a number of exceptions to the specific obligations contained therein. Several articles of the treaties, for example, expressly authorize ad hoc exceptions to obligations for circumstances such as economic hardship.[44] In addition, the RTC and RTB also establish general categories of exceptions, two of which are discussed here. The first is found in the RTC, which releases the four categories of less developed countries, disadvantaged countries, disadvantaged regions, and disadvantaged sectors from numerous obligations. The second is found in both the RTC and RTB, in the nature of broad security and general exception clauses. It is likely that these general categories of exceptions will be relied upon by defendant states when they are challenged before dispute settlement mechanisms, including the Caribbean Court of Justice.

6.2.1 Less developed countries, disadvantaged countries, regions, and sectors in CARICOM

Under both the original 1973 Treaty and the RTC, CARICOM expressly distinguishes between member states that are more and less developed. Such a distinction

[43] See eg Alina Kaczorowska, *European Union Law*, 2nd edn (London: Routledge, 2011) chs 4 and 16, TC Hartley, *The Foundations of European Union Law* (n 37) chs 4 and 15.

[44] See eg RTC Arts 43, 47, 48, 92, 118; RTB Protocol Art 32.

seeks to mitigate the disparities in wealth and resources between CARICOM members, and does so by providing exceptions to the otherwise general Community obligations.[45] It may be argued to be necessary in the context of CARICOM. Unlike in the EU context, where at least at some point in the past sufficient wealth was available to provide programmes and resources to promote the development of the EU's poorer members, CARICOM's membership is composed entirely of developing countries. Moreover the CARICOM Secretariat itself has no independent resources to distribute to its members. Even some of the states classified as 'more developed' face substantial economic challenges. Such factors help us to understand the rationale and structure of the RTC, even though we may also note the additional complexity and ambiguity created by such categories of treaty-founded exceptionalism.[46]

Article 4 of CARICOM's RTC designates six countries as having more developed country status: (1) The Bahamas, (2) Barbados, (3) Guyana, (4) Jamaica, (5) Suriname, and (6) Trinidad and Tobago. All of the rest of the members of the Caribbean Community are considered less developed countries. This designation remains in effect until the Conference otherwise determines by a majority decision.[47] As in the original 1973 CARICOM Treaty, there are no criteria set out in the RTC regarding what makes a state fall under either of these categories.[48]

Chapter 7 of the RTC creates 'a special regime for the less developed countries in order to enhance their prospects for successful competition within the Community, and redress, to the extent possible, any negative impact of the establishment of the CSME'.[49] This regime is part of the broader system of preferences and exemptions for disadvantaged countries, regions, or sectors set out in the chapter and in other provisions of the RTC, and constitutes one of the major exceptions to the uniformity of Community obligations.[50] The exceptions affect both categories of countries: less developed and more developed. More developed countries assume greater obligations; less developed countries assume lesser obligations or are granted exemptions. For example, when setting out the Community rules of origin, Article 84 of the RTC allows goods which have been consigned from one member state to another for repair, renovation, or improvement to be treated for the purposes of re-importation as goods of Community origin provided that, inter alia, the value of non-Community material used in the process of repair, renovation or improvement

[45] See the economic and human development data in Chapter 2, which demonstrates the wide gaps existing between some CARICOM member states.

[46] The 'more and less developed' distinction also hinders the potential uniformity of CARICOM law and increases what could be called the 'variable geometry' of the Community's architecture. For a commentary on the variable geometry of the EU see eg John A Usher 'Variable Geometry or Concentric Circles: Patterns for the European Union' (1997) 46 ICLQ 243–73, Neil Walker, 'Sovereignty and Differentiated Integration in the European Union' (1998) 4 *European Law Journal* 355–88.

[47] RTC Art 5.

[48] Hans J Geiser, Pamela Alleyne, and Carroll Gajraj, *Legal Problems of Caribbean Integration: A study of legal aspects of CARICOM* (Leyden: Sijthoff, 1976) 36.

[49] RTC Art 142(1).

[50] In addition to the provisions set out in Chapter 7 of the RTC, see Arts 49, 59(4), 77, and 84.

does not exceed: (a) in the case of a more developed country, 65 per cent of the cost, and (b) in the case of a less developed country, 80 per cent of the cost.[51] Such a provision benefits companies in less developed countries since they will be able to source and use a higher percentage of foreign, presumably cheaper, materials to service products.

A less developed country is automatically a 'disadvantaged country', which term also can embrace, upon designation by the Conference, developed countries that require special support measures of a transitional or temporary nature by reason of things such as: natural disasters, the impact of the CSME upon their economies, temporary low levels of economic development, or classification as a 'Highly-Indebted Poor Country... [by a] competent inter-governmental organisation'.[52]

The preliminary provisions dealing with 'disadvantaged countries, regions and sectors', set out in Chapter 7, Part One of the RTC, explain the objectives of the regimes of the RTC, which seek to help disadvantaged countries, regions, and sectors to move 'towards becoming economically viable and competitive by appropriate interventions of a transitional or temporary nature'.[53] These interventions, which fall under the purview of COTED and COFAP, include special measures, technical and financial assistance, transitional or temporary arrangements, other forms of assistance, and the establishment of monitoring and assistance mechanisms.[54] The Community Council is empowered to review the effectiveness of these measures, subject to the ultimate authority of the Conference, and to 'make adequate arrangements to extend to disadvantaged countries, regions, and sectors such technical and financial assistance as may be required to allow them to participate effectively in the CSME and to administer international trade agreements'.[55] The RTC also establishes a Development Fund 'for the purpose of providing financial or technical assistance to disadvantaged countries, regions and sectors', and makes clear that the benefits of Chapter 7 are additional to, rather than replacements for, those available from any other technical assistance programme.[56]

The specific regime for *disadvantaged countries, regions, and sectors* is set out in Part Two of Chapter 7. Under this regime COTED is empowered to adopt temporary measures to address economic dislocation, and these measures can derogate from rights and obligations set out in the RTC.[57] COTED can allow derogations from national treatment in relation to the provision of services and right of establishment, can authorize the limitation of imports for three or more years, can allow suspension

[51] See RTC Art 84(2).

[52] See RTC Arts 142(2) and 1(b)(iv), the latter defining 'disadvantaged countries'. See also Art 156, which authorizes COTED to apply the special regime to Highly Indebted Poor Countries.

[53] RTC Art 143(1).

[54] RTC Art 143(2) and 144.

[55] RTC Arts 145, 144, and 157.

[56] RTC Arts 158 and 159. See also the Agreement Relating to the Operation of the CARICOM Development Fund (CDF) (adopted 4 Jul 2008, not yet in force). This Agreement has been provisionally applied since 4 Jul 2008 by its signatories.

[57] RTC Art 146.

of Community treatment for sensitive industries, and can authorize protection of domestic production by public undertakings.[58] In addition to a broad competence to stimulate development, COTED is mandated to assist member states in providing access to technological and research facilities by nationals of disadvantaged countries through encouraging closer collaboration between research institutions and facilities.[59] Similarly, COFAP is empowered to promote investment in disadvantaged countries, and special provision is made to allow Guyana to continue to benefit from wheat imports.[60]

The *less developed country regime*, set out in Part Three of Chapter 7, provides concessions, exemptions and special treatment to less developed countries in relation to import duties (Article 160), the rules of Community origin, including opportunities for suspension (Articles 161 and 164), incentive regimes (Article 162), the Common External Tariff (Article 163), and the rules related to public undertakings (Article 165).[61] More developed countries also have *additional* obligations imposed upon them, such as the obligation under Article 166 'to provide opportunities for the use of their technological and research facilities by the less developed countries'.

6.2.2 Articles 225–226 of the RTC

The RTC contains two additional overarching provisions which allow for derogation from its obligations. The first provision, Article 225, exempts actions by member states that are necessary to protect their essential security interests. Subsection (a) of Article 225 exempts security-related information from disclosure under the RTC, and subsection (b) allows a member state to take action necessary to protect its essential security interests, including the supply of military related services and action 'in time of war or other emergency in international relations'. Article 225(c) exempts actions done in pursuance of obligations for the maintenance of international peace and security. There is no definition of 'other emergency' in the RTC. As a result Article 225(b) either could be narrowly construed, so as to cover only military-related emergencies, or could be interpreted as applying to a broader category of emergencies, including natural disasters, severe economic crises, or any other seriously challenging situation. Given the nature of Article 225 as an exception to the obligations of the RTC, however, and taking into account the broader coverage of Article 226, it is preferable to interpret Article 225(b) in a narrow manner. Moreover, the Article 225 list is exhaustive.

Article 226 sets out general exceptions to the obligations of the RTC. It is much broader in scope and will likely be relied upon by states in cases where their behaviour cannot be justified under a more specific exception contained in another provision of the RTC. The opening phrase of Article 226 contains a textual error, since it provides that nothing 'in this Chapter' shall prevent the

[58] RTC Arts 148–151. [59] RTC Arts 153–154. [60] RTC Arts 147 and 155.

[61] Note that Belize was given special exemptions in relation to beer and cigarettes, but this expired on 31 December 2000: Art 167 RTC.

measures set out in the article. Article 226 is the second article in Chapter Ten of the RTC, which sets out general and final provisions, including provisions regarding the legal capacity of the Community, its privileges and immunities, how the RTC is to enter into force, and on amendments and reservations. Construed literally, the phrase 'nothing in this Chapter' would render Article 226 virtually meaningless, since the obligations for which it clearly seeks to excuse performance are those of the Community's CSME, set out in the earlier Chapters of the RTC.

The interpretation of the word 'Chapter' in Article 226 as being a textual error is supported by the drafting history of the RTC. Article 23 of the original 1973 Treaty, provided a similar, albeit shorter and more limited, list of general exceptions. It specified that those exceptions were only to two articles of the Treaty, Articles 21–22, which prohibited quantitative restrictions on imports and exports. Subsequently, under Protocol II the function of Article 23 of the original Treaty was assumed by Article 38(b)(*bis*). This article exempted a similar, but again brief, list of measures from the obligations in 'this Chapter'. The term 'Chapter' in this case, however, referred to Chapter V, which set out some of the most fundamental Community rights, namely, those related to establishment, provision of services and movement of capital. In other words, both of the earlier drafts applied to a broader category of obligations than is contained in Chapter Ten of the RTC. Given this history and the scope of exceptions set out in Article 226, it is clear that it cannot be interpreted as being confined to Chapter Ten. Rather, it should be interpreted as referring to the RTC as a whole, as is the case with Article 225.

Article 226 exempts a wide range of measures from the obligations set out in the RTC. Given its likely importance to the interpretation and application of the RTC it is useful to reproduce the full text of Article 226:

1. Nothing in this Chapter [Treaty] shall be construed as preventing the adoption or enforcement by any Member State of measures:
   (a) to protect public morals or to maintain public order and safety;
   (b) to protect human, animal or plant life or health;
   (c) necessary to secure compliance with laws or regulations relating to customs enforcement, or to the classification, grading or marketing of goods, or to the operation of monopolies by means of state enterprises or enterprises given exclusive or special privileges;
   (d) necessary to protect intellectual property or to prevent deceptive practices;
   (e) relating to gold or silver;
   (f) relating to the products of prison labour;
   (g) relating to child labour;
   (h) imposed for the protection of national treasures of artistic, historic or archaeological value;
   (i) necessary to prevent or relieve critical food shortages in any exporting Member State;
   (j) relating to the conservation of natural resources or the preservation of the environment;

(k) to secure compliance with laws or regulations which are not inconsistent with the provisions of this Treaty including those relating to:
  (i) the prevention of deceptive and fraudulent practices, and the effects of a default on contracts;
  (ii) the protection of the privacy of individuals in relation to the processing and dissemination of personal data and the protection of confidentiality of individual records and accounts; and

(l) to give effect to international obligations including treaties on the avoidance of double taxation,

but only if such measures do not constitute arbitrary or unjustifiable discrimination between Member States where like conditions prevail, or a disguised restriction on trade within the Community.

2. Measures taken by the Member States pursuant to paragraph 1 shall be notified to COTED.
3. The Community Council shall take appropriate measures to co-ordinate applicable legislation, regulations and administrative practices established in accordance with Article 44.

Article 226(1) sets out a very long list of grounds justifying non-compliance with provisions of the RTC, thus potentially giving the article enormous scope.

However it must be noted that Article 226(1) only allows such measures as long as they 'do not constitute arbitrary or unjustifiable discrimination between Member States where like conditions prevail, or a disguised restriction on trade within the Community'. Further, Article 226(2) mandates that such measures be notified to COTED, and Article 226(3) requires the Community Council 'take appropriate measures to co-ordinate applicable legislation, regulations and administrative practices established in accordance with Article 44'. Article 44 of the RTC requires two other organs, COTED and COFAP, to adopt measures to facilitate rights related to establishment, provision of services and movement of capital.

Taken as a whole Article 226 sets out a broad list of areas over which member states may exercise authority outside of RTC obligations, but subject to two important conditions: (a) that any such measures do not constitute arbitrary or unjustifiable discrimination between member states or a disguised restriction on trade, and (b) that such measures must be notified to COTED. These two conditions do not appear to be mere formalities. The measures must be communicated to COTED, and therefore that organ will be provided with formal notice of derogations by member states from their RTC obligations. Since COTED is entrusted with general responsibility for the development and operation of the CSME, and any derogation could negatively affect the CSME, COTED will no doubt require a reasoned justification of the derogation by the member state concerned. Such a justification should include an explanation as to why the measure should not be considered an arbitrary or unjustifiable discrimination or disguised restriction on trade.[62] COTED may also wish to suggest time limits or other conditions for the derogation.

[62] On COTED's responsibilities in relation to the CSME see RTC Art 15(2)(a).

In addition, the lack of notification to COTED by a member state may be considered a ground for diminishing the weight to be accorded to, or as a basis for rejecting entirely, an Article 226 justification. Article 226(2) is phrased in mandatory language and thus non-compliance with its notification requirement would breach of the RTC. There is no indication as to what consequence should follow from such a breach. Two views could be held. Since no consequence, or even time limit, is specified, it might be argued that the reporting obligation in Article 226(2) should be considered a mere formality. However, when one considers the object and purpose of the RTC, including its aim to create a customs union and Single Market and Economy, the negative consequences of allowing any significant derogation from RTC obligations should be apparent. Such derogations would diminish the uniformity and effectiveness of the RTC regime and could, if fundamental, frustrate its essential aims. As a result Article 226(2) must be recognized as providing a vital mechanism through which such derogations can be monitored, scrutinized, and checked. By mandating transparency, Article 226(2) helps COTED fulfil its function of ensuring the successful operation of the CSME.

For these reasons, all aspects of Article 226 should be strictly interpreted, and it should be read to impose a formal requirement for notification. Such an approach finds some support in diverse areas of international and regional law. In EU law, the international law of human rights and the international law regarding use of force, a state's failure to communicate with a relevant organ in some circumstances has not been considered a mere formality. Instead non-communication has been deemed to provide a ground for annulling a legal act and for barring the use of the relevant exception to the rule.[63] Finally, the Article 226 list is exhaustive and, since the provision sets out exceptions to the obligations of the RTC, it must, like Article 225, be interpreted narrowly.[64]

The most similar provision to Article 226 in EU law is Article 36 of the TFEU. This article is more narrowly focused since it merely allows exceptions to the prohibition of quantitative restrictions found in Articles 34–35 of the TFEU. However

[63] In EU law, for example, the requirement that the Council consult with the European Parliament is a formal one, and failure to consult will be a ground for annulment of a legal act: Case 138/79 *Roquette Frères v Council* [1980] ECR 3333. In Inter-American human rights law, as established in the *Case of Zambrano-Vélez et al v Ecuador* (Merits, Reparations and Costs) I-A Ct HR, Judgment of 4 July 2007, Series C, No 166, at [69]–[70], the lack of *timely* notification by a state of the existence of a state of emergency will amount to a breach of Art 27(3) of the American Convention on Human Rights; the lack of *any notification* may diminish the weight to be accorded to a national state of emergency, as seen in the *Case of Cantoral-Benavides v Peru* (Merits) I-A Ct HR, Judgment of 18 August 2000, Series C, No 69, at [33]. In general public international law the failure of a state to formally report to the UN Security Council its reliance upon an exception to the general prohibition on the use of force—the doctrine of self-defence—may call into question the bona fides of such action. As stated by the International Court of Justice in *Military and Paramilitary Activities in and against Nicaragua (Nicaragua v USA)* (Merits) [1986] ICJ Rep 14, p 105 [200]: 'the absence of a report [to the Security Council] may be one of the factors indicating whether the State in question was itself convinced that it was acting in self-defence.'

[64] In *Shanique Myrie v Barbados* (n 1) at [65]–[66] the CCJ indicates that exceptions to, or restrictions of, Community rights, including those set out in RTC Arts 225 and 226, must be interpreted narrowly and strictly, and that the burden of proof rests on the member state seeking to restrict the right.

the drafting history of the RTC, as highlighted earlier, demonstrates that Article 226 originated as an exception to quantitative restrictions, and thus the EU jurisprudence remains relevant. Like Article 226 of the RTC, Article 36 of the TFEU sets out an exhaustive list of exceptions, each of which has been interpreted strictly and narrowly by the ECJ. For example, in the UK's *Poultry Case* the ECJ held that laws banning import of poultry products because of fears of the infectious 'Newcastle disease' amounted to a disguised restriction on intra-Community trade; they constituted measures having an equivalent effect to quantitative restrictions and were not justifiable under the equivalent of Article 36 of the TFEU.[65] The Court came to this conclusion after examining all of the circumstances surrounding the enactment of the legislation, including its timing (to cover the Christmas holiday season), the competing French market in turkeys, the public demands of British poultry producers for a block of French imports, and the lack of scientific studies supporting the UK measures. The ECJ held that even if such measures could be justified in some cases, such a restriction was not justified in the present context and the UK measures constituted a disguised restriction on imports of poultry products from other member states.[66] The ECJ has taken a similarly strict approach with respect to justifications based on grounds of public morality, public policy, and protection of health and life of humans, animals, or plants.[67] The ECJ has been more sympathetic to claims of public security, but even in such cases the justifications of member states will be carefully examined.[68] Moreover the burden of proof that the measure constitutes an Article 36 exception rests with the member state.[69]

In sum, although Article 226 appears to set out an extensive list of areas in which CARICOM member states may exclude the applicability of the RTC and its obligations, several features of Article 226 must be seen as limiting its potential to disrupt the enforceability and uniformity of the obligations imposed by the RTC. These include the nature of Article 226 as a provision setting out exceptions to more specific rules, its exhaustive character, its exclusion of measures that constitute an arbitrary or unjustifiable discrimination between member states or a disguised restriction on trade, and the formal requirement it imposes for notification of COTED, which itself must entail the need for the member state to justify and prove the necessity (and perhaps proportionality) of its measures.[70]

[65] Case 40/82 *Commission v UK* [1982] ECR 2793.

[66] Case 40/82 *Commission v UK* (n 65) [40]. Further, the Court noted that there were less stringent measures that the UK could have used to attain the same result, thus applying the principle of proportionality. *Commission v UK* [40]–[41]. On the general principle of proportionality see Chapter 8.

[67] See eg Case 121/85 *Conegate Ltd v Commissioner of Customs and Excise* [1986] ECR 1007 [public morality], Case 231/83 *Cullet v Centre Leclerc* [1985] ECR 305 [public policy], and Case 40/82 *Commission v UK* (n 65), Case 124/81 *Commission v UK* [1983] ECR 203, Case 272/80 *Frans-Nederlandse Maatschappij voor Biologische Producten* [1981] ECR 3277 [protection of health and life of humans, animals or plants]. On the Art 36 exceptions and related jurisprudence see eg Catherine Barnard, *The Substantive Law of the EU: The Four Freedoms*, 3rd edn (Oxford: Oxford University Press, 2010) ch 6, Kaczorowska, *European Union Law* (n 43) ch 21, Paul Craig and Gráinne De Búrca, *EU Law, Text, Cases and Materials*, 5th edn (Oxford: Oxford University Press, 2011) ch 19.9.

[68] Case 72/83 *Campus Oil Ltd v Minister for Industry and Energy* [1984] ECR 2727.

[69] Case 227/82 *Leendert van Bennekom* [1983] ECR 3883.

[70] The principle of proportionality was applied in this manner in the case of *Shanique Myrie v Barbados* (n 1) at [70].

6.2.3 Article 32 of the Protocol to the RTB

Article 32 of the RTB establishes a more limited scheme of derogations in OECS law. It stipulates that if a Protocol member state experiences an appreciable rise in unemployment in a particular sector of industry or region as a result of a substantial decrease in internal demand for a domestic product, and if this decrease in demand is due to an increase in imports consigned from other Protocol member states as a result of the progressive reduction or the elimination of duties, charges, and quantitative restrictions, then it may limit those imports by quantitative restrictions for a period of up to eighteen months, or take other measures as authorized by the Economic Affairs Council.[71] The level of quantitative restrictions is limited to a rate not less than the rate of such imports during any period during the year before the restrictions enter into force.[72] The period of application of the quantitative restrictions may be extended by the Economic Affairs Council, by majority vote, if it so decides.[73] Further, in applying such quantitative restrictions the Protocol member state must give like treatment to imports consigned from all Protocol member states, and must notify the Economic Affairs Council of the restrictions, if possible before they come into force.[74] The Economic Affairs Council is vested with authority to consider such restrictions and may, by majority vote, 'make recommendations designed to moderate any damaging effect of those restrictions or to assist the Protocol member state concerned to overcome its difficulties'.[75] Article 32.4 also provides that Article 32 only has effect to the extent that the Council of Ministers of the former East Caribbean Common Market before 30 April 1973 extended the provisions of the preceding paragraphs of the Article. This wording is unusual but is included in the RTB because the provision allowing imposition of quantitative restrictions in the original Agreement Establishing the East Caribbean Common Market was fixed to expire by 30 April 1973, unless extended by the Council of Ministers.[76] As a result the RTB provision only allows historically recognized categories of exceptions.

The exception provided by Article 32 to the RTB's Protocol regime therefore is significantly more limited than the similar provisions in CARICOM's RTC. This highlights another difference between the two regimes which may be attributable to the deeper level of integration sought by the OECS. Any consistent derogation from the obligation not to impose quantitative restrictions would threaten the generality and uniformity of the RTB and thereby threaten its overall effectiveness. For such reasons derogations should be strictly limited and monitored, as the OECS regime seeks to do.

[71] RTB Art 32.1. [72] RTB Art 32.1. [73] RTB Art 32.1.
[74] RTB Art 32.2–32.3. [75] RTB Art 32.3.
[76] *Agreement Establishing the East Caribbean Common Market* (adopted 11 Jun 1968, in force 1 Jul 1968) 1338 UNTS 55, Art 22(4)–(5).

6.3 Implementation and Enforcement of Binding Obligations in Domestic Law[77]

Once decisions of organs of regional organizations have been validly made, and have not been excluded or substantially restricted by the exceptions and limitations available under both the RTC and RTB, they generally must be implemented in domestic law in order to have effect there. In most cases for Commonwealth Caribbean states this means that in order for the decisions to give rise to rights and obligations in domestic law, they must be transformed by legislation. In civil law systems, such as those of Suriname and Haiti, international and regional obligations may not require transformation.[78] The question of effective transformation of treaty obligations has raised a number of challenges in the two regional integration movements.[79]

The historical problems involved in implementing CARICOM decisions in the national sphere have been highlighted in a number of reports including the 1992 Report of the West Indian Commission, *Time for Action*.[80] Member states have long been less than diligent in completely and effectively implementing their Community obligations in domestic law. Several patterns of behaviour were evidenced in relation to the original Treaty. Firstly, some states did not enact the necessary legislation at all. Secondly, some states only partially enacted it. Thirdly, some states incorrectly transformed their obligations, such as by imposing

[77] For overviews of the relationship between international law and municipal law and the several schools of thought on the topic see eg James Crawford, *Brownlie's Principles of International Law*, 8th edn (Oxford: Oxford University Press, 2012) 48–111; Sir Robert Jennings and Sir Arthur Watts, *Oppenheim's International Law*, 9th edn (London: Longman, 1996) 52–86; Malcolm Shaw, *International Law*, 4th edn (Cambridge: Cambridge University Press, 1997) 99–136; Peter Malanczuk, *Akehurst's Modern Introduction to International Law* (n 3) 63–74; Pierre-Marie Dupuy, 'International Law and Domestic (Municipal) Law', in R Wolfrum (ed), *The Max Planck Encyclopedia of Public International Law* (Oxford: Oxford University Press, 2008), online edition, as available through <http://www.mpepil.com> (17 Jul 2013). For a Caribbean analysis see Winston Anderson, 'Treaty Implementation in Caribbean Law and Practice' (1988) 8 Carib LR 185.

[78] For a useful overview of the approach of civil legal systems to both customary and conventional international law see Crawford, *Brownlie's Principles of International Law* (n 77) 88–111.

[79] See eg the stinging criticisms of Duke E Pollard, in *The Caribbean Court of Justice: Closing the Circle of Independence* (Kingston, Jamaica: The Caribbean Law Publishing Company, 2004) at 245–6. At the latter page he states:

> There appears to be no culture in the Caribbean Community impelling compliance with international obligations. Consequently, many a treaty is ratified without being enacted into domestic law, and even when enacted into domestic law, there is no assurance that the enabling legislation will adequately address the obligations of the enacting States.

Pollard, however, predicts that such attitudes will change as a result of cases filed under the compulsory and binding original jurisdiction of the CCJ.

[80] West Indian Commission, *Time for Action: Report of the West Indian Commission* (Black Rock, Barbados: The West Indian Commission, 1992) 462–3. This Report also devised a legislative mechanism to overcome the implementation gap, namely, the creation of 'Instruments of Implementation' by the (then proposed) CARICOM Commission in consultation with national Governments: at pp 478–80. These Instruments, although not binding, would provide guidance to national legislators and could be implemented by means of Regulations under the respective national CARICOM Acts. This aspect of the Report was not adopted.

limitations or conditions not found in the international legal obligation. These patterns of behaviour, unfortunately, have continued under the RTC regime despite the clear obligations imposed by Articles 9 and 240. They also arise under the RTB despite the requirements of Article 5.

6.3.1 Article 240 of the RTC and the transformation requirement under the common law

Article 240, innocuously titled 'Saving', provides as follows:

1. Decisions of competent Organs taken under this Treaty shall be subject to the relevant constitutional procedures of the Member States before creating legally binding rights and obligations for nationals of such States.
2. The Member States undertake to act expeditiously to give effect to decisions of competent Organs and Bodies in their municipal law.
3. COTED shall monitor and keep under review the implementation of the provisions of this Article and shall convene a review conference of Member States within five years from the entry into force of this Treaty.[81]

Article 240(1) imposes, at least for Commonwealth Caribbean states, the obligation to transform decisions of CARICOM organs before those decisions can create legally binding rights and obligations for nationals in domestic law. Article 240(2) requires member states to undertake such transformation 'expeditiously'.[82] Article 240(3) requires COTED to keep Article 240 under review.[83]

There is no similar provision to Article 240 in the RTB. But the general common law rules discussed in what follows are equally applicable to the OECS in cases of legal obligations which are not meant to be directly effective. Directly effective obligations under Article 5 of the RTB, however, would not require subsequent transforming legislation.

Several observations should be made about the wording of Article 240(1). Firstly, it only speaks to decisions of *organs*, not to the legal effect of the RTC itself. It is silent about the latter. As a result, Article 240(1) does not itself impose a requirement to transform the RTC into domestic law before the RTC can create legally binding rights and obligations for nationals. Other rules, such as the

[81] The previous version of this provision made distinctions between those states that were members of the common market and those that were not (The Bahamas) as well as restricted the ability of member states to participate in decisions only with respect to subjects of which they possessed 'the necessary competence' (thus potentially excluding a non-sovereign territory such as Montserrat from certain foreign relations decisions). The first distinction has been removed in the RTC because at present there is no separation of the Caribbean Community from its related economic arrangement (previously the common market and now the CSME). As we have seen, the distinction on the basis of possession of 'necessary competence' is retained in Art 16(4) of the RTC, and so the omission of a reference in Art 240 will be of no consequence.

[82] Compare Art 31(3) of the original Treaty, which states: '*Where necessary*, Member States undertake to take steps as expeditiously *as possible* to give full effect in law to all decisions of the organs and institutions of the Community which are binding on them' (emphasis added).

[83] According to the General Counsel of CARICOM no plans exist at present with respect to convening the review conference contemplated by Art 240(3) of the RTC. Interview with Safiya Ali, General Counsel, CARICOM Secretariat, Georgetown, Guyana (6 Aug 2012).

common law rules related to the requirement for transformation of treaties, may produce a similar result, as discussed later. But this limitation on the scope of application of Article 240(1) is important because, as seen in Chapter 8, it means that no provision in the RTC expressly precludes the potential for the RTC to be directly effective. The second thing to notice about Article 240(1) is that it imposes a blanket transformation requirement. It applies to *all* decisions of competent organs. This may be contrasted with the wording of Article 31(2) of the original Treaty, which only requires transformation of decisions 'requiring such action [transformation]'.[84] This difference between the two treaties may have been necessary because of the final words of Article 240(1), which specify the consequences of transformation, namely, that it would allow the decisions to create 'legally binding rights and obligations for nationals'. As a result it is at least arguable that a decision of a CARICOM organ that is not intended to, nor capable of, creating rights and obligations for nationals should not require transformation. A third challenge arising from the text, one highlighted in written and oral submissions of parties in the case of *Shanique Myrie v Barbados*, concerns the effect of the word 'creating' in Article 240(1), or more accurately, to which legal sphere the word applies—the national sphere or the regional sphere or both. In other words, when Article 240(1) requires transformation before a decision of an organ can create rights, does this mean that without transformation no rights exist at *domestic law* (the common law position), or that no rights exist *at all* (ie, as a matter of CARICOM law and national law)?

In order to ensure the uniformity of CARICOM law the former interpretation must be preferred. The word 'creating' must be construed to apply to the domestic law of the member state concerned. As clearly established in the case of *Shanique Myrie v Barbados*, decisions of organs create rights and obligations as a matter of Community law from the moment they have been validly made.[85] They will not be effective in the domestic law of member states until they have been transformed (if necessary), in accordance with Article 240(1).[86] But by creating rights and obligations as a matter of *Community law* from inception, they ensure its 'uniformity, certaintly and predictability'.[87] The immediate, right-creating authority of decisions also could provide the basis for a claim in the original

[84] Art 31(2) of the original Treaty provides: 'Decisions taken under this Treaty requiring such action shall be subject to the relevant constitutional procedures of the respective Member States.'

[85] *Shanique Myrie v Barbados* (n 1) [55].

[86] The CCJ held in the case of *Shanique Myrie v Barbados* (n 1) at [52]:

> Article 240 RTC is not concerned with the *creation* of rights and obligations *at the Community level*. The Article speaks to giving effect to such rights and obligations *in domestic law*. This is clearly reflected in its second paragraph which requires Member States to give effect to decisions of competent Organs and Bodies in their *municipal law* so as to enable Community nationals to enforce their rights at the national level and in the municipal courts. If binding regional decisions can be invalidated at the Community level by the failure on the part of a particular State to incorporate those decisions locally the efficacy of the entire CARICOM regime is jeopardized and effectively the States would not have progressed beyond the pre-2001 voluntary system that was in force (emphasis in original).

[87] *Shanique Myrie v Barbados* (n 1) [53].

jurisdiction of the Caribbean Court of Justice prior to transformation. Such a claim may be necessary if, for example, a state subsequently enacted domestic legislation contrary to the CARICOM decision. Such action would give rise to a claim for the violation of Articles 9 and 240(2) of the RTC. On the same legal basis a claim could be made against a state which significantly *delayed* enacting the legislation necessary to give effect to the CARICOM decision.[88]

Such an interpretation of Article 240(1) is also congruent with the requirements of the common law. Under the common law it is well established that international legal obligations under a treaty must be 'transformed' or 'incorporated' into municipal law before they can create rights and obligations in that domestic legal system.[89] As established in the *International Tin Council Case*:

> A treaty is a contract between the governments of two or more sovereign states. International law regulates the relations between sovereign states and determines the validity, the interpretation and the enforcement of treaties. A treaty to which Her Majesty's Government is a party does not alter the laws of the United Kingdom. A treaty may be incorporated into and alter the laws of the United Kingdom by means of legislation. Except to the extent that a treaty becomes incorporated into the laws of the United Kingdom by statute, the courts of the United Kingdom have no power to enforce treaty rights and obligations at the behest of a sovereign government or at the behest of a private individual.[90]

In other words, under the common law, treaties generally do not give rise to enforceable rights in domestic law until they have been incorporated or transformed into that domestic law. The phrases 'transformation' and 'incorporation' are interchangeably used to describe the act of converting an international treaty obligation into a domestic one. Transformation is usually accomplished by means of a municipal statute or other legal measure.[91]

States can transform treaties in several ways. They can enact the text of the treaty by specifying that the entire treaty is, or sections of the treaty are, to have the force of law in the domestic legal system and attach the relevant treaty text as a schedule to the act.[92] They can also transform a treaty more directly, by drafting a statute for

[88] See the suggestion in *Shanique Myrie v Barbados* at [55] that Community decisions should stipulate a time limit for their implementation, which should be expeditious.

[89] See generally Crawford, *Brownlie's Principles of International Law* (n 77) ch 3; Sir Jennings and Watts, *Oppenheim's International Law* (n 77) 52–86. For an assessment of the application of these rules by the Judicial Committee of the Privy Council and the Caribbean Court of Justice, see David S Berry, 'The Use of International Law by Domestic Tribunals in the Caribbean in Death Penalty Cases', in DS Berry and T Robinson (eds), *Transitions in Caribbean Law: Lawmaking Constitutionalism and the Confluence of National and International Law* (Kingston, Jamaica: Ian Randle Publishers, 2013) 102–27.

[90] *JH Rayner (Mincing Lane) Ltd v Department of Trade and Industry* (also called *Maclaine Watson & Co Ltd v International Tin Council*) [1990] 2 AC 418 (HL) at pp 476–7 (per Lord Templeman).

[91] Two helpful articles that discuss the requirements for transformation of treaty law obligations into municipal law in the specific context of the Commonwealth Caribbean are Winston Anderson, 'Treaty Implementation in Caribbean Law and Practice' (1998) 8 Carib LR 185–211, and Winston Anderson, 'Treaty Making in Caribbean Law and Practice: The Question of Parliamentary Participation' (1998) 8 Carib LR 75–115.

[92] See eg FAR Bennion, *Bennion on Statutory Interpretation: A Code*, 5th edn (London: Lexisnexis Reed Elsevier (UK), 2008) 684.

the specific purpose of incorporating the international legal obligations within the precise language of domestic statutory provisions.[93] This latter approach would seem preferable because it allows the international legal obligations to be tailored to the specific statutory language of domestic legislation. It has the drawback, however, of potentially decreasing the uniformity of application of the treaty throughout the region, if different states enact the treaty using different words. Perhaps for such reasons the RTC has been attached as a schedule to the domestic legislation which transforms it in most CARICOM member states.[94]

Transformation fulfils a basic constitutional requirement because it ensures that parliament, not the executive, remains the branch of government that makes law. By transforming a treaty, parliament ensures that it remains the body that creates legal rights and duties in domestic law, not the executive or judiciary.[95] Transformation also has the effect of making international law into domestic law: a treaty, once enacted by statute, completely changes its legal nature and ceases to be international law. As will be seen in what follows, this has important consequences for the interpretation of domestic statutes which transform treaty obligations. It also means that a domestic court can never actually interpret or apply international treaty law; rather, it must interpret or apply the domestic legislation which contains rights and obligations that mirror those contained in the treaty.[96]

The rule requiring transformation does not necessarily apply to customary international law.[97] It also does not challenge the *existence* of the international

[93] See eg Bennion, *Bennion on Statutory Interpretation* (n 92) 683.

[94] All of the following statutes of CARICOM member states transform the RTC by means of a Schedule: Caribbean Community Act, Laws of Antigua and Barbuda, Act No 9 of 2004; Caribbean Community Act, Laws of Barbados, Act No 8 of 2003; Caribbean Community Act, Laws of Belize, Act No 17 of 2004; Caribbean Community Act 2005, Laws of Dominica, Act No 22 of 2005; Revised Treaty of Chaguaramas Act, Laws of Grenada, Act No 10 of 2006; Caribbean Community Act, Laws of Guyana, Act No 8 of 2006; Caribbean Community Act, Laws of Jamaica, Vol IIIA 2009, Act No 15 of 2004; Caribbean Community Act 2005, Laws of St Christopher and Nevis, Act No 27 of 2005; Caribbean Community Act, Laws of Saint Lucia, Revised Edition 2008, Cap 19.21; Caribbean Community Act, Laws of Saint Vincent and the Grenadines, Revised Edition 2009, Cap 184; Caribbean Community Act, Laws of Trinidad and Tobago, LRO 2009, Chap 81:11. Information regarding Haiti, Montserrat, and Suriname was not found.

[95] For this reason the Court's suggestion in the case of *Shanique Myrie v Barbados* (n 1), at [54], that executive or judicial transformation would be acceptable must be greeted with caution. The Court stated in its analysis of Art 240(1) of the RTC:

> If these constitutional procedures require domestic legislation, then the State's legislature must be involved in order to give municipal courts the authority to adjudicate those rights and obligations at the municipal level. But in lieu of enacting new or amending old legislation this objective may in some cases also be accomplished administratively or even judicially in cases where the Constitution or the existing domestic legislation leaves room for so doing. In such cases domestic effect to the State's treaty obligations can and, given the duties imposed on Member States by Articles 9 and 240(2) RTC, *must*, if possible, be given by the executive or judicial branches of that State.

[96] This is highlighted by Lord Hoffman in *R v Lyons* [2003] 1 AC 976 (HL) at p 992 [27]:

> Parliament may pass a law which mirrors the terms of the treaty and in that sense incorporates the treaty into English law. But even then, the metaphor of incorporation may be misleading. It is not the treaty but the statute which forms part of English law.

[97] As succinctly summarized by Crawford, in *Brownlie's Principles of International Law* (n 77) at p 67, 'customary rules are to be considered "part of the law of the land" provided that they are not

legal obligation prior to transformation, as implicitly acknowledged in the ambiguity rule as discussed in what follows.

The result of the combination of these rules and Article 240(1) of the RTC is that even if the Conference makes a binding decision requiring a state to behave in a certain manner, and the state is on record as consenting, nevertheless the decision remains *non-binding as a matter of municipal law* until the same state brings it into force in its own legal system, by transformation. This can create a difficult 'conflict' of legal obligations at the national and international levels.[98] At the international level a Caribbean Community member state may be legally bound to implement a Conference decision, as a matter of international law. But at the municipal level, as a matter of municipal law, the Conference decision can have no binding effect before national bodies until it is adopted or transformed by municipal law.

As a consequence, when a member state does not transform an international legal obligation into its municipal law, at the *municipal level* the actors in that state's legal system, such as courts and the police, remain bound to follow the existing municipal law—even if that municipal law breaches the RTC. As a matter of municipal law this makes good sense. Until Parliament has passed a law specifying that a new form of conduct is required, police officers, courts, and all other national officials must continue to apply existing law. Nonetheless, since the state remains legally bound at the international level, it will be responsible for any actions of its legal authorities—including judicial authorities—that cause it to breach its binding CARICOM commitment.

inconsistent with Acts of Parliament'. See also Jennings and Watts, *Oppenheim's International Law* (n 77) 56–7. The automatic incorporation of customary international law must be qualified as follows. Firstly, the existence of the customary rule relied upon must be strictly proved. See eg *West Rand Central Gold Mining Company Ltd v R* [1905] 2 KB 391, p 407 (Div Ct Eng). Secondly, the customary rule must be either universally recognized by states around the globe or accepted as a binding customary rule by the state concerned. See eg Jennings and Watts (n 77) 56–7 and *West Rand* at p 407. Thirdly, the applicability of rules of customary international law in the domestic legal order is subject to the overriding effect of statute law and, with one exception, that of binding judicial precedent. The exception is regarding domestic judicial precedent that relies upon a superseded rule of customary international law. In such a situation, the doctrine of *stare decisis* does not prevent a national court from applying the current, existing rule of international law: *Trendtex Trading Corporation v Central Bank of Nigeria* [1977] QB 529 (CA Eng). In sum, if an existing, unambiguous statute or binding judicial precedent is applicable, then the domestic court must uphold that domestic law, regardless of whether it is compatible with the state's international legal obligations. See eg *R v Lyons* [2003] 1 AC 976 (HL); *Higgs v Minister of National Security and Others* [2000] 2 AC 228 (PC Bah); *JH Rayner (Mincing Lane) Ltd v Department of Trade and Industry* (also called *Maclaine Watson & Co Ltd v International Tin Council*) [1990] 2 AC 418 (HL); *R v Secretary of State for the Home Department, ex parte Brind* [1991] 1 AC 696 (HL); *Salomon v Commissioners of Customs and Excise* [1967] 2 QB 116 (CA Eng).

[98] Note that there can be no conflict of law, strictly speaking. The treaty imposes clear obligations under international law. The state's legal system imposes clear obligations as a matter of domestic law. The obligations simply point in different directions. For a view of international law and domestic law as being two different fields of law, which can never conflict, see Sir Gerald Fitzmaurice, 'The General Principles of International Law Considered from the Standpoint of the Rule of Law' (1957-II) 92 *Recueil des Cours de l'Académie de Droit International* 5.

The ambiguity exception

There is one limited exception to the rule requiring transformation for treaties to have legal effect in domestic law. This is the common law rule related to ambiguity. Under this rule it is well established that if domestic legislation is unclear or ambiguous—in other words, to use the phrase of Lord Bridge, that 'it is capable of a meaning which either conforms to or conflicts with the Convention'—then a domestic court can look to an unincorporated treaty to interpret the legislation.[99] As summarized by Lord Diplock in the case of *Salomon v Commissioners of Customs and Excise*, unambiguous rules must be enforced, regardless of consequence, but ambiguous rules allow a court to refer to an unincorporated treaty:

> If the terms of the legislation are clear and unambiguous, they must be given effect to whether or not they carry out Her Majesty's treaty obligations, for the sovereign power of the Queen in Parliament extends to breaking treaties (see *Ellerman Lines Ltd v Murray*), and any remedy for such a breach of an international obligation lies in a forum other than Her Majesty's own courts. If the terms of the legislation are not clear, however, but are reasonably capable of more than one meaning, the treaty itself becomes relevant, for there is a prima facie presumption that Parliament does not intend to act in breach of international law, including therein specific treaty obligations; and if one of the meanings which can reasonably be ascribed to the legislation is consonant with the treaty obligations and another or others are not, the meaning which is consonant is to be preferred. Thus, in case of lack of clarity in the words used in the legislation, the terms of the treaty are relevant to enable the court to make its choice between the possible meanings of these words by applying this presumption.[100]

The presumption referred to by Lord Diplock is rebuttable, meaning that it is subject to any available counter presumptions.[101] Also, it will not even arise unless the court has failed to determine the meaning of the legislation through the application of ordinary principles of statutory interpretation: if the law is clear, the domestic courts must apply it regardless of the consequences. However if the presumption applies, its effect is startling. The domestic court must, under the terms of the presumption, uphold the interpretation of the domestic provision that complies with the international obligation.[102]

[99] The full statement of Lord Bridge is set out in *R v Secretary of State for the Home Department, Ex Parte Brind* [1991] 1 AC 696 (HL) at pp 747–8, as follows:

> It is accepted . . . that, like any other treaty obligations which have not been embodied in the law by statute, the Convention is not part of the domestic law, that the courts accordingly have no power to enforce Convention rights directly and that, if domestic legislation conflicts with the Convention, the courts must nevertheless enforce it. But it is already well settled that, in construing any provision in domestic legislation which is ambiguous in the sense that it is capable of a meaning which either conforms to or conflicts with the Convention, the courts will presume that Parliament intended to legislate in conformity with the Convention, not in conflict with it.

[100] [1966] 3 All ER 871 (CA) at pp 874–5.

[101] See eg *Mortensen v Peters* (1906) 8 F(J) 93, 14 SLT 227 (HC Justiciary Scot) at p 233 (per Lord Kyllachy).

[102] The presumption is so strong that it may even be applicable 'retroactively,' allowing a court to interpret a statute created long before the state became a party to the treaty, with the text of the later

As can be imagined, this entire process of ratification and transformation greatly increases the potential for delay in effectively implementing Community decisions. As a result it would have been preferable for CARICOM member states to enact legislation that would allow decisions by Community organs to automatically have immediate, or nearly immediate, effect. The United Kingdom achieved this kind of automatic transformation when it passed a special statute to allow EU law to have immediate effect in the UK, the European Communities Act 1972.[103] The OECS seeks to achieve this objective through Article 5.3 of the RTB.

6.3.2 Problems of improper transformation

Several Caribbean cases illustrate the types of problems which may arise from not transforming, partially transforming, or incorrectly transforming either the original Treaty or RTC.

Non-transformation

The problems posed by the complete non-transformation of a treaty are illustrated in the case of *J Astaphan & Co (1970) Ltd v AG Dominica.*[104] In this case the appellant successfully challenged an order of the Minister refusing to grant it a licence to import flour on the grounds that the Minister had improperly relied upon the original CARICOM and OECS treaties and the decisions of an organ of CARICOM. Evidence suggested that the Minister had refused to issue the licence on the grounds that flour should be sourced from the OECS sub-region, as required by the CARICOM and OECS treaties and the resolutions of the CARICOM Council of Ministers. In finding the order of the Minister to be ultra vires, Redhead JA held that since none of the CARICOM resolutions, the original CARICOM Treaty or the OECS Treaty had been incorporated into the law of Dominica, the Minister was not entitled to consider them. They amounted to irrelevant considerations for the purposes of exercising Ministerial discretion. As

treaty. As stated by Lord Hoffman in *Boyce v R* [2004] UKPC 32, [2005] 1 AC 400 (Bdos) at p 416 [26]:

> This principle is obviously at its strongest when it appears that the domestic law was passed to give effect to an international obligation or may otherwise be assumed to have been drafted with the treaty in mind. Its application to laws which existed before the treaty is more difficult to justify as an exercise in construction but their Lordships are willing to proceed on the hypothesis that the principle requires one to construe the Constitution and other contemporary legislation in the light of treaties which the government afterwards concluded.

[103] European Communities Act 1972 (UK), c 68, as amended by the European Union (Amendment) Act 2008 (c 7), ss 3, 8, Sch Pt 1, SI 2009/3143. Section 2 of the Act creates a special rule that allows incorporation of a whole category of treaties and rules *in advance* and operates for an indeterminate duration. For a brief analysis see Hartley, *The Foundations of European Community Law* (n 37) 250–6.

[104] *J Astaphan & Co (1970) Ltd v AG Dominica*, Commonwealth of Dominica, Court of Appeal, Civil Appeal No 5 of 1997, CARILAW # DM 1997 CA 1 (Redhead JA), 29 Sep 1997 (unreported, no pagination).

a result, the complete lack of transformation of the original CARICOM Treaty and OECS Treaty resulted in the nullification of the orders of a Minister which attempted to comply with Dominica's regional obligations. Such transformation challenges have continued under the RTC regime. One recent case, for example, denied the ability of national actors to rely upon unincorporated treaties.[105]

Partial transformation

A case involving partial transformation is that of *DS Maharaj Furniture and Appliances Ltd v Comptroller of Customs and Excise*.[106] In this case the incomplete transformation of the original CARICOM Treaty and Annex by Trinidad and Tobago frustrated the applicant's challenge to a customs duty allegedly imposed contrary to the Community's rules of origin. Maharaj Furniture argued that the Trinidadian Comptroller's actions in imposing customs duties on refrigerators imported from Grenada breached the requirements of the Treaty and Annex, and relied upon a Grenadian Certificate of Origin issued by the Grenada customs authorities.[107] In dismissing the application Judge Lucky noted that only portions of the CARICOM Treaty and Annex had been transformed into the domestic law of Trinidad and Tobago, and these portions did not include all of the Community rules of origin.[108] Since treaty obligations must be transformed in order to be effective at domestic law, Judge Lucky held that the Comptroller of Customs rightly applied the Trinidadian regulations only.[109] The Trinidadian regulations allowed exemptions for goods 'wholly produced' within CARICOM and specifically excluded products merely assembled in a CARICOM state, including the applicant's refrigerators.[110] Moreover Judge Lucky held that the Comptroller's treatment of the Certificate of Origin of Grenada was correct. The Certificate was subject to, and could only be accorded the weight allowed under, the Trinidadian regulations.[111] In concluding, Judge Lucky held that the Comptroller of Trinidad and Tobago had not erred and dismissed the application with costs.[112] The result was that a good potentially included under the Community origin rules was subjected

[105] See the case of *Chandresh, Sharma*, Trinidad and Tobago, High Court of Justice, Suit HCA No Civ 1537 of 2003, CARILAW # TT 2003 HC 104 (Jamadar J) 30 Sep 2003 (unreported), where the ability of the Chief Justice of Trinidad and Tobago to exercise powers under the Agreement Establishing the Caribbean Court of Justice was challenged. The Court dismissed the claim after finding that there was no evidence that the Chief Justice sought to exercise, or exercised, powers under the CCJ Agreement, which had not been transformed into the laws of Trinidad and Tobago.

[106] *DS Maharaj Furniture and Appliances Ltd v Comptroller of Customs and Excise*, Trinidad and Tobago, High Court of Justice, Case Number S-1499/93, CARILAW # TT 1994 HC 147 (Lucky J), 13 Dec 1994 (unreported).

[107] *DS Maharaj Furniture* (n 106) pp 1–4.

[108] *DS Maharaj Furniture* (n 106) p 8.

[109] *DS Maharaj Furniture* (n 106) pp 8–9.

[110] *DS Maharaj Furniture* (n 106) p 10. Article 14 of the Annex to the original Treaty, in contrast, allowed Community origin status for goods produced in part from materials outside of the Community.

[111] *DS Maharaj Furniture* p (n 106) 10.

[112] *DS Maharaj Furniture* (n 106) p 10. Note that this decision was overturned upon appeal on other grounds, including procedural unfairness and unreasonableness: *DS Maharaj Furniture and Appliances Limited v The Comptroller of Customs and Excise*, Trinidad and Tobago, Court of Appeal,

to customs duties because the relevant provisions of the Treaty and Annex had not been transformed into domestic law.

Incorrect transformation

An example of a recent incorrect transformation of regional obligations is found, ironically, in the CARICOM model legislation specifically drafted to guide member states in implementing Article 46 of the RTC—the Caribbean Community Skilled Nationals Act.[113] This model legislation included a requirement for reciprocity not found in the RTC, and thereby imposes an additional condition for the granting of CARICOM Skilled National status.[114]

Another recent case, that of *Linton v Attorney General*, one arising in Antigua and Barbuda and involving exercise of CARICOM Skilled National rights by a media worker, raises a number of issues related to the enforcement of treaty obligations in domestic law.[115] It appears to simultaneously raise problems that could be classified as falling under the categories of non-transformation, partial transformation, and/or incorrect transformation. In this case Mr Linton, a national of Dominica, entered Antigua and Barbuda for the purposes of seeking employment and, prior to the end of his authorized period of stay, applied for, and was granted, six months to remain in the country on the basis of his CARICOM Skilled National Certificate.[116] However, prior to the end of his authorized six-month period, Mr Linton was expelled from the country because Antiguan Immigration officers allegedly 'suspected that he was working'.[117] No such ground for expulsion is contemplated in Article 46 of the RTC and the action appears to be contrary to the purpose of the provision.

Before moving to the substance of the case, Judge Blenman examined the preliminary question of whether the matter should be referred to the Caribbean Court of Justice under its referral jurisdiction, as set out in Article 214 of the RTC.[118] Taking a 'preliminary view' that the matter might require the interpretation or application of the RTC, and acknowledging that Article 214 of the RTC might bind the Court to refer the case to the CCJ, Judge Blenman asked whether a binding obligation to refer arose in the case.[119] She held that it did not, for the

Suit No HCA No S-1149 of 1993, Civil Appeal No 6 of 1995, CARILAW # TT 2002 CA 11 (de la Bastide CJ) 6 Feb 2002 (unreported). Judge Lucky's findings on the status of the CARICOM Treaty, however, were not challenged.

[113] As available at <http://www.caricom.org/jsp/secretariat/legal_instruments/model_legislation_skilled_nationals_act.pdf> (21 Jul 2013).

[114] Caribbean Community Skilled Nationals Act. Section 14 incorrectly imposes a condition of reciprocity for exercise of privileges under the Act. This error, unfortunately, has been reproduced in national legislation. See eg Immigration Act, Laws of Barbados, LRO 1997, Cap 190 (2 Feb 1976), s 17E; Caribbean Community Skilled Nationals Act, Laws of Antigua and Barbuda, Act No 3 of 1997 (11 Mar 1997), s 14.

[115] *Linton v Attorney General*, Antigua and Barbuda, High Court of Justice, CARILAW # AG 2009 HC 23 (Blenman J), 29 Jun 2009 (unreported).

[116] *Linton v Attorney General* (n 115) [69].

[117] *Linton v Attorney General* (n 115) [70].

[118] *Linton v Attorney General* (n 115) [71]. For analysis of the CCJ's referral jurisdiction see Chapter 14.

[119] *Linton v Attorney General* (n 115) [71]–[75].

simple reason that the legislation meant to transform the RTC had not entered into force. Section 1 of the Caribbean Community Act 2004 stipulated that the Act 'shall come into operation on such date as the Minister may, by notice published in the *Gazette,* appoint.'[120] The Act had been passed by the House and Senate, had received the Governor-General's assent, and had been published in the *Gazette*. But the required *notice* from the Minister had not been published in the *Gazette*. As a result, the Court held that because the RTC was not part of the domestic law of Antigua no referral obligation could arise.[121]

This portion of the case demonstrates a significant consequence of non-transformation of the RTC, namely, that no rights or obligations under the RTC, including the referral obligation in relation to the CCJ, can arise as a matter of domestic law until the RTC has been transformed.[122] This is a deeply problematic result. By not transforming the RTC Antigua and Barbuda frustrated the ability of a judge to refer questions related to the RTC to the CCJ, as intended by Article 214. Such non-transformation also potentially breached the RTC, since no referral was made in a case which appeared to require one.[123]

In turning to the substance of the claim, Judge Blenman applied the Antiguan CARICOM Skilled Nationals Act, which brought into force some aspects of the

[120] Caribbean Community Act, Laws of Antigua and Barbuda, Act No 9 of 2004 (emphasis in original).

[121] *Linton v Attorney General* (n 115) [75]–[81]. At the latter paragraph Judge Blenman states: 'In view of all of the above, the court is left to conclude, as urged by the learned Deputy Solicitor General, that the RTC is not part of the local law of Antigua and Barbuda and therefore the referral obligation does not arise as a matter of statutory provision.' The Court does not discuss another possible basis, through the operation of the Caribbean Court of Justice Act, 2004, Laws of Antigua and Barbuda, Act No 10 of 2004. The latter Act gives the Agreement Establishing the Caribbean Court of Justice—including Article XIV, the referral provision—the force of law in Antigua and Barbuda. The Act, however, has the same kind of entry into force provision as the Caribbean Community Act 2004. It is thus possible that the Agreement's obligations likewise may not have been transformed by the time of the Court's judgment.

[122] Note in this regard that Judge Blenman also canvasses the possibility that a referral obligation might arise under the common law doctrine of legitimate expectation. She decides in paragraph [85], however, in agreement with (then) Professor Winston Anderson, that legitimate expectation cannot found a right to referral:

> In concluding on this question of referral, the court also finds very instructive the view of Professor Anderson in the Article referenced above ['The Caribbean Court of Justice in its Original Jurisdiction: Ensuring the Integrity of CARICOM Law and the Stability of the Caribbean Community'], that in the circumstances of non-incorporation of the RTC, an applicant may be able to invoke the doctrine of legitimate expectation. However such invocation could only be in relation to rights claimed by the applicant under the RTC and not as regards provisions regarding the referral obligation. In the Professor's words: 'that even if a court was to accept that legitimate expectation was applicable in the circumstances of non-incorporation, this could be only in relation to rights claimed by the applicant under the Treaty and not in relation to the referral provisions of the RTC'. The Court respectfully accepts this approach and finds, accordingly, that in the case at bar there is no basis on which it can conclude that a question of referral to the CCJ arises.

[123] Judge Blenman is clearly aware of this problem, stating at [86]: 'The Court cannot leave this matter without emphasizing that it has been compelled to undertake its own interpretation of a statute which is clearly intended to implement aspects of the CSME regime, without the benefit of a reference to the CCJ. This state of affairs is occasioned by the fact that the statute to implement the RTC has not been brought into force, as alluded to earlier.'

Article 46 regime for Antigua and Barbuda.[124] A preliminary question was whether Mr Linton was required to present his CARICOM Skilled National Certificate at the moment of *entry* into Antigua, as stated in Section 5(2)(b) of the Act. In interpreting the Act Judge Blenman rejected the literal form of interpretation as producing an absurd result and instead looked at both the mischief the Act was aimed to correct and the intention of the legislature.[125] The Court concluded that a CARICOM Skilled National Certificate could be produced after a person has entered the country. Notably, the Court did not examine the RTC, the basis of the obligations the legislation was meant to implement. Article 46 of the RTC does not impose any requirement for production of a certificate at the time of entry.

Applying the Act to the facts of the case, Judge Blenman held that Antigua and Barbuda had provided no grounds for revocation of Mr Linton's permission to stay. After deciding that the Government's decision was subject to judicial review on grounds of illegality and irrationality, the Court held that he had been unlawfully arrested, taken into custody, and removed from the country.[126] Judge Blenman dismissed arguments based upon legitimate expectation, both on the basis that legal rights preclude the application of the doctrine, and on the basis that the RTC had no legal force or effect in Antigua.[127] The Court awarded damages for breach of Mr Linton's rights under the Act, for his wrongful arrest and expulsion.[128]

In sum, the case of *Linton v Attorney General* provides a good overview of challenges involved in enforcing RTC obligations in the national sphere. Non-transformation of the RTC by Antigua and Barbuda posed a number of difficulties for Mr Linton and for the judge trying the case. The partial and/or incorrect transformation of Article 46 of the RTC by Antigua and Barbuda hindered recognition of Mr Linton's CARICOM Skilled National status and frustrated the exercise of his rights. Both deficiencies could give rise to international legal responsibility on the part of Antigua and Barbuda for breaches of Articles 9 and 240(2) of the RTC. The state did not take all appropriate measures, whether general or particular, to ensure the carrying out of obligations arising out of the RTC, nor did it transform its RTC treaty obligations expeditiously.

[124] Laws of Antigua and Barbuda, Cap No 3 of 1997.

[125] *Linton v Attorney General* (n 115) [90]–[92]. The Court held at [93]:

> I have no doubt that the legislature intended to facilitate the free movement of certain skilled Caricom nationals, within the countries that are signatories to the RTC, and not to fetter their right to do so. By way of emphasis, it is pellucid that there can be no harm in allowing a Caricom visitor, who is properly qualified, from seeking to change his status provided that all of the other prerequisites are met. Once the requisite Certificate is provided it seems to me that it is of little, if any, moment whether it was presented on entry into Antigua and Barbuda or while the visitor is in Antigua and Barbuda. This in no way negates the fact that ordinarily it should be presented on entry into Antigua and Barbuda.

[126] *Linton v Attorney General* (n 115) [99], [106], [111]–[112], [114], and [116]–[119].

[127] *Linton v Attorney General* (n 115) [120], [127]. Note that the latter position is unlikely to be correct since legitimate expectation does not require a legal foundation, strictly speaking, and can arise in the context of unincorporated treaties. See eg *AG v Joseph* [2006] CCJ 3 (AJ), (2006) 69 WIR 104 (Bdos).

[128] *Linton v Attorney General* (n 115) [135]–[137].

7

The Concept of General Principles of Law

CARICOM and the OECS are bound by legal obligations arising from a number of different sources, including their constituent treaties, treaties entered into with third parties, customary international law, regional customary rules, judicial precedent, and general principles of law.[1]

General principles of law deserve special mention because of their potential to shape the nature of Caribbean integration law. The present chapter discusses the meaning and possible forms of general principles of law and analyses their bases, or potential bases, in the RTC and RTB. It starts with an overview of the origin and meaning of the concept in both public international law and EU law and concludes with a brief analysis of the legal philosophy on the topic. Chapter 8 analyses specific general principles which are either established by, or that may potentially be established by, Caribbean treaties or jurisprudence. It also examines legal concepts which may arise *through* general principles, as a source of law, even though those concepts may not properly be classified as principles of law per se.[2]

The meaning of the term 'general principles of law' differs slightly in international law and EU law, as explored more fully later. With respect to EU law, Tridimas defines general principles as the 'fundamental propositions of law which underlie a legal system and from which concrete rules or outcomes may be derived'.[3] In international law the term is used to refer to a source of law at the international level, derived from principles of domestic law, natural law, and legal systems more broadly. For present purposes, it will be useful to distinguish two different aspects of the term. On the one hand, 'general principles of law' can be used to describe the origin or *source* of a legal concept, one different from, for example, a treaty-based or customary legal source. On the other hand, 'general principles of law' can be used to describe the *function* of the legal concept, as a principle rather than a rule. Both of these aspects have important legal consequences.

[1] See generally Chapters 2 and 6.

[2] The phrase 'other foundational legal concepts' in the title of the Chapter 8 alerts the reader to the idea that the concepts discussed therein may not all be general principles in terms of either their origin or nature. Some may arise in Caribbean regional integration law, for example, through other legal mechanisms, including through processes of treaty interpretation. However because all of these concepts could be founded upon general principles, as a *source of law*, they can conveniently be dealt with together.

[3] Takis Tridimas, *The General Principles of EU Law* 2nd edn (Oxford: Oxford University Press, 2006) at 1.

Any legal concept that originates as a general principle of law brings with it an inherent flexibility and adaptability. Such a concept may be changed or adapted to suit present needs because its fundamental source—for example, a general principle of national legal systems—may itself change and adapt over time. In other words, a general principle of regional integration law may grow in parallel with its national legal source. It may also change and develop to suit the needs of the regional legal system if, for example, it was derived from the general principles necessary for the effective functioning of that legal system.

By functioning as a legal principle, rather than a rule, a general principle of law can fulfil a variety of important needs in its legal system. As will be fleshed out more fully, principles complete and give meaning to legal systems. They provide reasons or justifications for both rules and decisions, and can help fill gaps in the law. Perhaps most importantly, they make the legal system more consistent and coherent, and bring key values into the law.

7.1 In International Law[4]

In international law the phrase 'general principles of law' refers to a source of law at the international level, derived from principles of domestic law, natural law, and legal systems more broadly. It became prominent in international legal writing following its inclusion in Article 38 of the Statute for the Permanent Court of International Justice (PCIJ Statute), the article listing the sources of law the Permanent Court is authorized to apply.[5] Article 38(3) mandates the Court to apply 'the general principles of law recognized by civilized nations', in addition to treaties and custom.[6] This source is also identified in Article 38(1)(c) of the Statute of the International Court of Justice.[7]

In including such a provision, the drafters of these treaties sought to empower their respective international tribunals to refer to principles of natural law and justice as part of the international judicial repertory.[8] This natural law potential

[4] See generally Antonio Cassese, *International Law in a Divided World* (Oxford: Clarendon Press, 1986) 170–4; Malcolm Shaw, *International Law*, 5th edn (Cambridge: Cambridge University Press, 2003) 92–103; James Crawford, *Brownlie's Principles of Public International Law*, 8th edn (Oxford: Oxford University Press, 2012) 34–7; Bin Cheng, *General Principles of Law as Applied by International Courts and Tribunals* (London: Stevens and Son Ltd, 1953); Sir Humphrey Waldock, 'General Course on Public International Law' (1962-II) 106 *Hague Recueil des Cours* 54–69.

[5] (1921) 6 LNTS 389–413 (PCIJ Statute).

[6] PCIJ Statute. Note that the term 'civilized nations' is now considered antiquated, if not offensive, and simply is read to mean 'independent states'. See eg Waldock, 'General Course on Public International Law' (n 4) 65; Giorgio Gaja, 'General Principles of Law' in R Wolfrum (ed), *The Max Planck Encyclopedia of Public International Law* (Oxford University Press, 2008–), online edition, [<http://www.mpepil.com>] (accessed 23 Feb 2013).

[7] Annex to the Charter of the United Nations, 26 June 1945, 1 UNTS xvi, UKTS 67 (1946) (ICJ Statute).

[8] See generally, Cassese, *International Law in a Divided World* (n 4) 170–4; Michel Virally, 'The Sources of International Law' in Max Sørensen, ed, *Manual of Public International Law* (London: Macmillan, 1968) 147–8.

of general principles caused the most controversy. It is highlighted in the phrase first proposed by the Chairman of the Advisory Committee of Jurists entrusted to draft the PCIJ Statute, Baron Descamps, who suggested that the Court should be able to refer to 'the rules of law as recognized by the legal *conscience* of civilized nations'.[9] Descamps' formulation was rejected in favour of 'general principles of law'. But the more restrained terminology that was finally adopted does not diminish the potential of general principles to be used to incorporate broader moral and natural law viewpoints.[10] As noted by Judge Tanaka in the *South West Africa Cases*, 'it is undeniable that in Article 38, paragraph 1(c), some natural law elements are inherent.'[11]

As a result, the idea of general principles in international law has a revolutionary potential. General principles allow a court to bring to bear a source of law that is not entirely based upon the consent of states. Rather, general principles can be based upon immutable truths (if interpreted in a natural law manner), or upon the fundamental principles of law that are implicit in all legal systems.[12] Nevertheless it must be noted that the members of the Advisory Committee of Jurists who drafted the PCIJ Statute were in agreement that judges should not legislate and that general principles merely brought to the fore latent principles already existing in the legal system.[13]

In international legal practice general principles tend to be derived by analogy from principles existing in the domestic legal systems of the world and from the principles of legal logic or general jurisprudence.[14] They can be identified by judges in part because common legal traditions underpin or are shared by most legal systems in the world.[15] Some general principles also arise simply because they are part of the fundamental requirements of *any* legal system, being necessary for the operation of the law. In addition, general principles can be 'inferred by way of induction and generalization from conventional and customary rules of international law' or can be identified in those principles established by states 'for the

[9] As cited in Cassese, *International Law in a Divided World* (n 4) 170 (emphasis added). For an analysis of the different views of the Statute drafters, and on the distinctions between the French and English meanings of the word 'conscience' in this context, see Bin Cheng, *General Principles of Law as Applied by International Courts and Tribunals* (n 4) 7–10.

[10] Cassese *International Law in a Divided World* (n 4) 170–4.

[11] *South West Africa Cases (Ethiopia v South Africa, Liberia v South Africa)* (Second Phase) [1966] ICJ Rep 3, p 298 (Dissenting Opinion Judge Tanaka).

[12] Cassese, *International Law in a Divided World* (n 4) 170–1. See also *South West Africa Cases* (n 11) p 297 (Dissenting Opinion Judge Tanaka).

[13] Bin Cheng, in *General Principles of Law as Applied by International Courts and Tribunals* (n 4) at 19, summarizes the position of the Advisory Committee of Jurists who drafted the PCIJ Statute as follows: 'Actuated by the belief that existing international law consisted in more than the sum total of positive rules, in adopting the formula "the general principles of law recognized by civilised nations," they were only giving a name to that part of existing international law which is not covered by conventions and custom *sensu stricto*. It was said that the application of these principles had hitherto been a constant practice of international tribunals and although it might be said that the latter, in applying them, brought *latent* rules to light, they did not *create* new rules; for the members of the Committee were in agreement that a judge should not legislate' (emphasis in original and citations omitted).

[14] Cassese, *International Law in a Divided World* (n 4) 172–3.

[15] eg Waldock, 'General Course on Public International Law' (n 4) 66.

purpose of setting out the fundamental standards of behaviour of the international community'.[16] Both of these latter types of general principles are derived from international law itself.[17]

In terms of the identification of general principles, international tribunals have not considered it necessary to look into every known legal system in order to determine whether a municipal law principle is 'general' enough to serve as the foundation for a general principle of international law.[18] Rather, the International Court of Justice has tended to gauge generality by testing the acceptance of the proposed principle amongst members of the bench.[19] As pointed out by Virally, the judges of the Court themselves come from the majority of the legal systems of the world, and thus provide a solid testing ground for whether a principle is general in nature.[20]

Moreover in assessing generality it is important to understand that international courts and tribunals refer to municipal law principles by analogy. In this way general principles must be seen as not coming so much from the different national systems per se, as from 'the general concept of law underlying them'.[21] This idea is born out in the Separate Opinion of Judge McNair in the *International Status of South West Africa*, where he notes that Article 38(1)(c) authorizes the Court to 'recruit many of its rules and institutions from private systems of law', but in doing so 'international law borrows from this source... not by means of importing private law institutions "lock, stock and barrel", ready-made and fully equipped with a set of rules.'[22] Rather, 'the duty of international tribunals in this matter is to regard any features or terminology which are reminiscent of the rules and institutions of private law as an indication of policy and principles rather than as directly importing these rules and institutions.'[23]

Regarding their importance in relation to other sources of international law, there is disagreement amongst international lawyers about whether general principles are subsidiary to custom and treaties. Akehurst, for example, argues that general principles were only included in the PCIJ Statute for the purpose of filling gaps in treaties and customary law, and that 'they can therefore be applied only in the absence of rules (or at least specific rules) of treaty law or customary law.'[24]

16 Cassese, *International Law in a Divided World* (n 4) 174. See eg Declaration on Principles of International Law Concerning Friendly Relations and Cooperation Among States in Accordance With the Charter of the United Nations (1970), UNGA Res 2625, GAOR, 25th Sess, Supp No 28, UN Doc A/8028 (24 Oct 1970).

17 James Crawford, *Brownlie's Principles of Public International Law* (n 4) at 37, lists the following as examples of general principles based upon international legal rules and concepts: 'the principles of consent, reciprocity, equality of states, finality of awards and settlements, the legal validity of agreements, good faith, domestic jurisdiction, and the freedom of the seas.' See also Giorgio Gaja, 'General Principles of Law' (n 6).

18 Cassese, *International Law in a Divided World* (n 4) 173.

19 See eg Waldock, 'General Course on Public International Law' (n 4) 66–7.

20 Michel Virally, 'The Sources of International Law' (n 8) 146.

21 Waldock, 'General Course on Public International Law' (n 4) 65.

22 *International Status of South-West Africa* (Advisory Opinion) [1950] ICJ Rep 128, p 148.

23 *International Status of South-West Africa* (n 22).

24 Michael Akehurst, 'Notes: The Hierarchy of the Sources of International Law' (1974–75) 47 *British Yearbookk of International Law* 273–85, 279.

He also argues that treaties and custom will override general principles in the event of conflict.[25]

Perhaps this states the position in too stark terms. As discussed more fully later, general principles can play a variety of roles in every legal system. A more helpful view may be to understand general principles of international law as being guiding standards rather than binding rules, and therefore as being less likely to conflict directly with treaties or custom. This is borne out by the fact that three general principles are themselves frequently relied upon in the international sphere to help decide between competing rules of international law, namely, the principles of *lex superior derogat inferiori, lex posterior derogat priori*, and *lex specialis derogat generali*.[26] Understood in this way, it does not make sense to see general principles as being distinct and subsidiary.[27] Rather, they must be seen as an integral part of the legal system as a whole. In any event, as pointed out by Jennings and Watts, Article 38(1)(c) of the Statute of the International Court of Justice treats general principles in the same manner as custom and treaties, and does not categorize them under the subsidiary means listed in Article 38(1)(d).[28] Thus on a formal, textual level no hierarchy exists.

There are three main uses to which general principles may be put in international law. Firstly, as highlighted earlier, they provide a means of bringing natural law ideas or ideals into the law, including natural law assumptions about justice and fairness. In his dissenting opinion in the *South West Africa Cases*, for example, Judge Tanaka argued that a court's power to look at general principles of law allows it to look at the 'underlying or guiding "principles"' in various fields of domestic and international law, to 'the fundamental concepts of each branch of law as well as to law in general'.[29] These fundamental concepts, according to Judge Tanaka, include human rights which, *as a general principle of law* are binding upon *all* states.[30]

The second use of general principles of law is to fill any gaps or lacunae in international law. Some technical areas of international law remain underdeveloped and general principles have been used by the international courts and tribunals to fill in gaps and flesh out areas of law. The International Court of Justice and its predecessor, under the rubric of general principles of law, have employed domestic rules and principles by analogy to decide questions related to the administration of justice (eg, questions of procedure, evidence, jurisdiction),[31] circumstantial

[25] Akehurst, 'Notes: The Hierarchy of the Sources of International Law' (n 24).

[26] These phrases can be roughly translated as: 'superior rules prevail over inferior ones', 'later rules prevail over earlier ones' and 'particular rules prevail over general ones'. See eg Akehurst, 'Notes: The Hierarchy of the Sources of International Law' at p 273.

[27] See eg Giorgio Gaja, 'General Principles of Law' (n 6).

[28] Sir Robert Jennings and Sir Arthur Watts (eds), *Oppenheim's International Law*, 9th edn, Vol 1 (Harlow, Essex: Longman Group UK, 1992) 40.

[29] *South West Africa Cases (Ethiopia v South Africa, Liberia v South Africa)* (Second Phase) [1966] ICJ Rep 3, p 295 (Dissenting Opinion Judge Tanaka).

[30] In his Dissenting Opinion in the *South West Africa Cases* at p 298, Judge Tanaka states: '[a]s an interpretation of Article 38, paragraph 1 (*c*), we consider that the concept of human rights and of their protection is included in the general principles of law mentioned in that article.'

[31] eg Waldock, 'General Course on Public International Law' (n 4) 59.

evidence,[32] the questions of ownership and identity of corporations at the international level,[33] the relation of treaties and custom,[34] state responsibility,[35] abuse of rights,[36] good faith,[37] estoppel,[38] acquiescence,[39] *res judicata*,[40] *ex injuria jus non oritur*,[41] whether one can be judge in one's own suit,[42] and respect for vested rights.[43]

General principles have also grounded judicial use of the concept of equity. In *The Diversion of Water from the Meuse Case*, Judge Hudson held that 'under Article 38 of the Statute, if not independently of that Article, the Court has some freedom to consider principles of equity as part of the international law which it must apply.'[44] In the *Tunisia/Libya Continental Shelf Case*, the International Court of Justice held:

71. Equity as a legal concept is a direct emanation of the idea of justice. The Court whose task is by definition to administer justice is bound to apply it. In the course of the history of legal systems the term 'equity' has been used to define various legal concepts. It was often contrasted with the rigid rules of positive law, the severity of which had to be mitigated in

[32] *Corfu Channel Case (UK v Albania)*, Judgment of 9 April 1949 [1949] ICJ Rep 4, p 18.

[33] *Barcelona Traction, Light and Power Company, Limited (Belgium v Spain)* (Second Phase) [1970] ICJ Rep 3, pp 38–9 (lifting the corporate 'veil') and 42–3 (nationality of companies).

[34] eg *lex superior derogat inferiori, lex posterior derogat priori*, and *lex specialis derogat generali.*

[35] The Court held in the *Case Concerning the Factory at Chorzów (Germany v Poland)* (Merits) [1928] PCIJ, Series A, No 17, at p 29, that 'it is a principle of international law, and even a general conception of law, that any breach of an engagement involves an obligation to make reparation.'

[36] *Free Zones of Upper Savoy and the District of Gex* (Second Phase) [1930] PCIJ, Series A, No 12, p 12.

[37] In the *Nuclear Tests Case (Australia v France)* [1974] ICJ Rep 253, at p 268, the Court stated: 'One of the basic principles governing the creation and performance of legal obligations, whatever their source, is the principle of good faith.'

[38] eg *Temple of Preah Vihear (Cambodia v Thailand)* (Merits) [1962] ICJ Rep 6, p 32; *Sovereignty over Pedra Branca/Pulau Batu Puteh, Middle Rocks and South Ledge (Malaysia/Singapore)* (Merits) [2008] ICJ Rep 12, p 81.

[39] eg *Island of Palmas Case (Netherlands v USA)* [1928] 2 RIAA 829, p 869; *Temple of Preah Vihear (Cambodia v Thailand)* (Merits) [1962] ICJ Rep 6, p 23.

[40] The Court in the *Corfu Channel Case (UK v Albania)*, Judgment of 15 December 1949 [1949] ICJ Rep 244, at p 248, stated that its previous decision in the case was 'final and without appeal, and that therefore the matter is *res judicata*'.

[41] In the case concerning the *Gabčíkovo-Nagymaros Project (Hungary/Slovakia)* [1997] ICJ Rep 7, at p 76, the Court noted that the treaty regime was not affected by facts flowing from wrongful conduct: 'This does not mean that facts—in this case facts which flow from wrongful conduct—determine the law. The principle *ex injuria jus non oritur* is sustained by the Court's finding that the legal relationship created by the 1977 Treaty is preserved and cannot in this case be treated as voided by unlawful conduct.'

[42] The Court held in the *Interpretation of Article 3, Paragraph 2, of the Treaty of Lausanne* (Advisory Opinion) [1925] PCIJ, Series B, No 12, at p 32, that '[t]he well-known rule that no one can be judge in his own suit holds good.'

[43] The Permanent Court stated in the *Case Concerning Certain German Interests in Polish Upper Silesia* [1926] PCIJ, Series A, No 7, at p 22, that the expropriation allowed under the treaty in question 'is a derogation from the rules generally applied in regard to the treatment of foreigners and the principle of respect for vested rights'.

[44] *Diversion of Water from the Meuse Case (Netherlands v Belgium)* [1937] PCIJ, Series A/B, No 70, at p 77 (Ind Opinion Judge Hudson). See also the *Case Concerning the Frontier Dispute (Burkina Faso/Republic of Mali)* [1986] ICJ Rep 4, at [27]–[28] and [149]–[150]. On equity more generally, see Vaughan Lowe, 'The Role of Equity in International Law' 12 *Australian Yearbook of International Law* 54–81.

order to do justice. In general, this contrast has no parallel in the development of international law; the legal concept of equity is a general principle directly applicable as law.[45]

In this way general principles of law have been used by tribunals to fill in gaps in the law or, in the case of equity, moderate the harshness of a legal rule.

The third way in which general principles can be used is to prevent a *non liquet*. A *non liquet* is a situation when, for want of legal rules, a court is unable to give a decision based upon law.[46] General principles of law, by allowing reference to a reservoir of national principles and rules which can be employed by analogy, preclude the possibility of a *non liquet* arising.[47]

In sum, the role of general principles in international law is to add 'a flexible element which enables the Court to give greater completeness to customary law and in some limited degree to extend it'.[48] General principles of law have therefore significantly expanded the judicial repertoire in international law.

7.2 In EU Law

General principles in EU law have been derived by the ECJ from the legal systems of the member states and other sources, independently of an express EU treaty basis. According to Tridimas, general principles have played a very important role in EU law precisely because at its inception the Community was a new legal order, representing a new development in the law of international organizations, one without historical or contemporary equivalent.[49] They have proved helpful in interpreting the texts of the EU treaties, which often use general language that needs to be fleshed out and applied to concrete circumstances. General principles also help EU law to remain dynamic and evolutive in nature.[50]

In their application in EU law, general principles have been unconstrained by their particular sources or origins. As pointed out by Tridimas, the nature, content, and scope of what originally may have been *domestic* legal principles can change when those principles are transformed into principles of EU law: 'the general principles of law are children of national law but, as brought up by the Court, they become *enfants terribles*: they are extended, narrowed, restated, transformed by the creative and eclectic judicial process.'[51]

[45] *Case Concerning the Continental Shelf (Tunisia/Libyan Arab Jamahiriya)* [1982] ICJ Rep 18, at p 60 [71].

[46] See eg the definition of *non liquet* in Georg Schwarzenberger and ED Brown, *A Manual of International Law*, 6th edn (Milton, UK: Professional Books Ltd, 1976) 562.

[47] See eg Cassese, *International Law in a Divided World* (n 4) 171. Note that a strict positivist would argue 'general principles' are not required for this third purpose; a *non liquet* should never occur in international law since anything not prohibited is, by reason of the state sovereignty, expressly allowed. Thus if there is 'no law' on an issue, this means that in fact such behaviour is legal: at p 171.

[48] Waldock, 'General Course on Public International Law' (n 4) 64.

[49] Tridimas, *The General Principles of EU Law* (n 3) at 18.

[50] See eg Tridimas, *The General Principles of EU Law* 11 and 18.

[51] Tridimas, *The General Principles of EU Law* 6.

In addition to domestic sources, general principles in EU law have been derived from specific EU treaty provisions. When this has occurred, it is notable that these general principles have tended to be applied beyond their original treaty-based scope and context. This process is described by Hartley as follows:

> [T]he Court declares that a specific provision in one of the Treaties is an application of some more general principle which is not itself laid down in the Treaty. This then is applied in its own right as a general principle of law. An example of this is Article 18 TFEU [12/6 EC], which prohibits all discrimination based on nationality between EU citizens as regards matters within the scope of the Treaty. This, together with other texts, has been used by the Court as the foundation for a general doctrine of equality which forbids arbitrary discrimination on any grounds. . . .[52]

A classic ECJ decision illustrating this approach, one highlighted by Hartley, is the decision in Case 9/56 *Meroni v High Authority of the European Coal and Steel Community*.[53] In this case Meroni challenged a levy issued by the High Authority. The Court upheld the challenge, but in doing so relied upon Article 36 of the ECSC Treaty.[54] The text of the latter provision allowed appeals against fines and penalties, but not levies per se. The Court extended the text, at least implicitly, to include a levy. In justifying its decision the Court held that

> Article 36 should not be regarded as a special rule, applicable only in the case of pecuniary sanctions and periodic penalty payments, but as the application of a general principle, applied by Article 36 to the particular case of an action in which the Court has unlimited jurisdiction.[55]

In other words, the ECJ held that Article 36 of the ECSC Treaty was merely a particular manifestation of the more general principle, one that could be applied to various measures, and which the Court relied upon to decide the case.

General principles of EU law have not only developed and expanded beyond their original sources, they also have become so firmly entrenched in EU law that they are now considered part of its legal foundations. This is clearly demonstrated in the decision of the ECJ in Joined Cases C-402/05 P and C-415/05 P *Kadi and Al Barakaat International Foundation v Council and Commission*.[56] In this case the appellants challenged the freezing of their funds by the EU under a regulation made to implement the United Nations Security Council's sanctions regime for persons linked to Al-Qaeda and other terrorist organizations. The Court of First Instance dismissed their challenge on the basis of the superior nature of UN Security Council resolutions made under Chapter VII of the UN Charter.[57] These

[52] TC Hartley, *The Foundations of European Union Law*, 7th edn (Oxford: Oxford University Press, 2010) 142.

[53] [1958] ECR 133.

[54] Treaty Instituting the European Coal and Steel Community (adopted 18 Apr 1951, in force 23 Jul 1952, expired 23 Jul 2002) 261 UNTS 140 (ECSC Treaty).

[55] Case 9/56 *Meroni v High Authority of the European Coal and Steel Community* [1958] ECR 133, at p 140.

[56] [2008] ECR I-06351.

[57] Charter of the United Nations (adopted 26 Jun 1945, in force 24 Oct 1945) 1 UNTS xvi, 39 AJIL Supp 190 (UN Charter).

resolutions impose binding obligations upon EU member states, which under Article 103 of the UN Charter must take precedence over all other treaty obligations, including EU treaty obligations.[58] Therefore, according to the Court of First Instance, the internal lawfulness of the contested EU regulation could not generally be subject to judicial review under EU law.[59]

The ECJ reversed and upheld the supremacy of EU law, including general principles of EU law, within the EU legal system. The Court held that the EU is based upon the rule of law, which entails judicial review under a complete system of legal remedies and procedures, one that is autonomous and cannot be affected by an international agreement.[60] The Court also held that 'fundamental rights form an integral part of the general principles of law whose observance the Court ensures', the respect for which is a condition of legality under EU law.[61] Moreover such principles could not be displaced through the operation of Article 351 TFEU—the provision of the EU treaties dealing with the rights and obligations under non-EU treaties concluded before 1958—nor could they be superseded by EU acts meant to give effect to non-EU obligations, even Security Council obligations. Using striking phrasing, the Court held:

> 304. Article 307 EC [now Article 351 *TFEU*] may in no circumstances permit any challenge *to the principles that form part of the very foundations of the Community legal order*, one of which is the protection of fundamental rights, including the review by the Community judicature of the lawfulness of Community measures as regards their consistency with those fundamental rights.
>
> 305. Nor can an immunity from jurisdiction for the contested regulation with regard to the review of its compatibility with fundamental rights, arising from the alleged absolute primacy of the resolutions of the Security Council to which that measure is designed to give effect, find any basis in the place that obligations under the Charter of the United Nations would occupy in the hierarchy of norms within the Community legal order if those obligations were to be classified in that hierarchy.[62]

With these words the Court clearly emphasizes the independent nature of the legal order created by the EU, an order in which the general principles of EU law, including the principle of fundamental rights, are recognized as foundational. In concluding, the Court reaffirms its obligation 'in accordance with the powers conferred on it by the EC Treaty, [to] ensure the review, in principle the full review, of the lawfulness of all Community acts in the light of the fundamental rights forming an integral part of the general principles of Community law, including review of Community measures which, like the contested regulation, are designed to give effect to the resolutions adopted by the Security Council under Chapter VII

[58] Art 103 of the UN Charter provides: 'In the event of a conflict between the obligations of the Members of the United Nations under the present Charter and their obligations under any other international agreement, their obligations under the present Charter shall prevail.' Member states of the EU are also UN member states.

[59] See Joined Cases C-402/05 P and C-415/05 P *Kadi and Al Barakaat International Foundation v Council and Commission* [2008] ECR I-06351, at [280].

[60] *Kadi and Al Barakaat* (n 59) [281]–[282].

[61] *Kadi and Al Barakaat* (n 59) [283]–[284].

[62] *Kadi and Al Barakaat* (n 59) [304]–[305] (emphasis added).

of the Charter of the United Nations'.[63] In exercising this power of review, the Court held that the contested regulation was not compatible with the right of defence and the principle of effective judicial protection, and constituted an unjustified restriction on the right to property.[64]

The *Kadi and Al Barakaat* case demonstrates the substantial power of general principles of law for the EU. The case involved a serious potential conflict of obligations between the legal systems governing the EU and the UN. All EU member states are bound to comply with their UN Charter obligations, and Article 103 of the Charter makes clear that in the event of a conflict with any other treaty, the Charter must prevail. However under EU law the respect for general principles of law, including fundamental rights, is a condition for legality of EU legal acts. The Court's decision carefully balances the competing interests at stake, but requires the EU to live up to its own standards, including those imposed by general principles, when complying with its international legal obligations. These principles are foundational in nature.

A number of different general principles have been recognized in the jurisprudence of the ECJ, including the principles of equality and non-discrimination, proportionality, legal certainty, protection of legitimate expectations, fundamental rights, effectiveness, confidentiality/legal privilege, non-retroactivity, unjustified enrichment, the right to judicial review, and the rights of defence.[65]

Regarding their use, Tridimas suggests that general principles have performed three functions in EU law: they have operated as an aid to interpretation, as grounds of review, and as rules of law breach of which may give rise to tortious liability.[66] In relation to the first, Tridimas summarizes that '[a]ccording to a general rule of interpretation which derives from the principle of hierarchy of norms, where a Community measure falls to be interpreted, preference must be given as far as possible to the interpretation which renders it compatible with the Treaty and the general principles of law.'[67] This approach applies not only to EU law, but also to national legal rules, under the principle of conform interpretation (or indirect effect).[68] General principles have operated as grounds of review in cases under Articles 263 and 267 of the TFEU, which allow the Court to scrutinize the legality of legislative acts of the EU institutions, and to provide preliminary rulings to

[63] *Kadi and Al Barakaat* (n 59) [326].

[64] *Kadi and Al Barakaat* (n 59) [352] and [370]. The Court therefore decided that the regulation must be annulled. See at [372]. However, in recognition of the possibility that the regulation's measures might be justified in the case of the appellants, the Court allowed the EU authorities a three-month grace period before the annulment became effective, so as to allow them to remedy the infringements found. See at [374]–[376].

[65] See generally Tridimas, *The General Principles of EU Law* (n 3). See also Anthony Arnull, *The European Union and its Court of Justice* (Oxford: Oxford University Press, 1999) ch 6; Alina Kaczorowska, *European Union Law*, 2nd edn (London: Routledge, 2011) 205–12; Nigel Foster, *Foster on EU Law*, 3rd edn (Oxford: Oxford University Press, 2011) 120–30.

[66] Tridimas, *The General Principles of EU Law* (n 3) 29–35.

[67] Tridimas, *The General Principles of EU Law* (n 3) 29 (citations omitted).

[68] Cf Tridimas, *The General Principles of EU Law* (n 3) 31. On the general principle of indirect effect see Chapter 8.

national courts, respectively.[69] In their third function, the breach of general principles may give rise to tortious liability as against the institutions of the EU, and at least potentially, as against member states.[70]

7.3 In Legal Theory[71]

To understand the foundational role of general principles of law it is useful to examine some of the philosophical justifications for their derivation and use. Such an understanding is particularly important in the context of Caribbean integration, where traditional views about state sovereignty may not encourage states and tribunals to rely upon sources of law not formally based upon state consent.

7.3.1 Role of principles

Legal principles, including general principles of law, exist in every legal system and generally take the form of guiding standards or norms. They may be derived from legal sources such as constitutions, statutes, and judicial decisions, and may be replaced by the same legal sources.[72] They also may be derived from non-legal sources, including moral or ethical sources, or even from the set of standards necessary for the creation and maintenance of a legal system.[73]

Principles are necessary because no legal order has a specific rule to cover every particular factual circumstance. In a situation where no express rule exists, as noted by Shaw, a decision maker will need to 'deduce a rule that will be relevant, by analogy from already existing rules, or directly from the general principles that guide the legal system, whether they be referred to as emanating from justice, equity or considerations of public policy'.[74] In this way, at the simplest level, general principles of law can help adjudicators decide which legal rule applies to a factual situation and, if there are two potentially applicable rules, which is best suited to achieve the goals inherent in the legal system.

[69] These acts can include international legal acts of institutions, such as treaties. See eg Tridimas, *The General Principles of EU Law* (n 3) 51.

[70] Tridimas, *The General Principles of EU Law* (n 3) 35.

[71] See generally Ronald Dworkin, *Taking Rights Seriously* (Guildford: Duckworth, 1977), Ronald Dworkin, 'Is Law a System of Rules?', in Ronald M Dworkin (ed), *The Philosophy of Law* (Oxford: Oxford University, 1977) 37–65; Ronald Dworkin, *Law's Empire* (Cambridge, MA: Belknap Press of Harvard University, 1986); Neil MacCormick, *Legal Reasoning and Legal Theory* (Oxford: Clarendon Press, 1978); Robert Alexy, *A Theory of Constitutional Rights*, Julian Rivers (tr) (Oxford: Oxford University Press, 2002).

[72] cf MacCormick, *Legal Reasoning and Legal Theory* (n 71) 154–5, Alexy, *A Theory of Constitutional Rights* (n 71) 80–2. Alexy also emphasizes the 'double aspect' of constitutional provisions, noting that whenever 'a constitutional rights provision makes some sort of decision relative to the requirements of competing principles, then it has not merely enacted a *principle*, it has also enacted a *rule*': at 83–4 (emphasis in original).

[73] cf HLA Hart, *The Concept of Law* (Oxford: Clarendon Press, 1961) ch V (on the nature of secondary rules).

[74] Shaw, *International Law* (n 4) 93.

In addition, principles support and interact with rules in numerous ways. As noted by MacCormick, principles 'underpin [rules], hedge them in, qualify them, justify the enunciation of new rulings as tested out by consequentialist arguments, and so on'.[75] More broadly, principles can substantiate the framework for, and make coherent and rationalize, the rules of a legal system.[76] They can complete a legal system by providing standards which may be applied when there are gaps in the legal rules, or where the legal rules are no longer appropriate and must be replaced.[77] They provide the adjudicator with a rational justification for the legal solution to the problem, or for replacing the rule.

At a more theoretical level, principles also serve the fundamental role of providing an underlying set of *values* for each legal system, upon which rules themselves are based. As pointed out by Dworkin, rules are not self-applying and instead must be considered in light of the principles that underlie them, give them meaning, and make them binding.[78] In this way principles have been argued to help make a legal system coherent by guiding a decision maker towards that system's overarching purpose.[79] In Dworkin's conception, for example, principles enable a vision of law as 'integrity', one in which decision makers must 'assume, so far as this is possible, that the law is structured by a coherent set of principles about justice and fairness and procedural due process, and...enforce these in the fresh cases that come before them, so that each person's situation is fair and just according to the same standards'.[80] Principles thus both underpin rules and provide the rational context for the development and change of those same rules. In Dworkin's view they ensure high order consistency and continuity in legal practice—by requiring consistency in *principle* with the purpose of the legal system.[81]

According to MacCormick, who both refines and challenges Dworkin's theory, principles authorize and justify decisions. However MacCormick argues that they do not provide a complete or sufficient justification. Rather, any decision must

[75] MacCormick, *Legal Reasoning and Legal Theory* (n 71) 244.

[76] See eg MacCormick, *Legal Reasoning and Legal Theory* (n 71) chs 7 and 9.

[77] See eg Dworkin, *Taking Rights Seriously* (n 71) 37.

[78] Dworkin, 'Is Law a System of Rules?' (n 71) 37–65; Dworkin, *Law's Empire* (n 71) 96, 152, and 244. For a brief explanation and application of Dworkin's theory of interpretation see eg David S Berry, 'Interpreting Rights and Culture: Extending *Law's Empire*' (1998) 4(1) *Res Publica* 3–28.

[79] Dworkin identifies the 'purpose' of law as being either the task of 'making government more coherent in principle', or the broader pursuit of 'justice', or 'to establish a justifying connection between past political decisions and present coercion': Ronald Dworkin, 'Law, Philosophy and Interpretation' (1994) 80 *Archiv für Rechts-und Sozialphilosophie* 463–75, 471 and 474; and Dworkin, *Law's Empire* (n 71) 98, respectively. Each of these purposes reveals the close links between law, politics, and morality, as acknowledged when Dworkin states that '[law] is an interpretive, self-reflective attitude addressed to politics in the broadest sense': Dworkin, *Law's Empire* 413. Note however that Dworkin is *not* saying that law is identical to politics, merely fitting his theory within the broader political context. This means that in order to interpret principles in the light of purpose judges are sometimes required to look beyond 'law' (narrowly conceived) to substantive political morality: at 248–9.

[80] Dworkin, *Law's Empire* (n 71) 243; see generally chs 6 and 7.

[81] Dworkin, *Law's Empire* 167. As pointed out by Stephen Guest, in *Ronald Dworkin* (Edinburgh: Edinburgh University Press, 1992) at 40, 'integrity' requires more than simple consistency because the law must be able to correct itself rather than blindly follow past mistakes: 'Bare consistency...is an impossible requirement because we all accept, as properly characteristic of legal argument, that some previous decisions are mistaken.'

be tested by consequentialist arguments and arguments intended to ensure the coherence of the legal system:

Principles of law certainly authorize decisions: if there is no relevant principle or analogy to support a decision, that decision lacks legal justification; and if there is a relevant principle or analogy the decision supported thereby is a justifiable decision—but the adduction of the principle or analogy although necessary to is not sufficient for a complete justification of the decision. The ruling which directly governs the case must be tested by consequentialist argument as well as by the argument from 'coherence' involved in the appeal to principle and analogy. And just as the absence of any supporting principle or analogy renders a decision impermissible, so the test for consistency must be applied: it must be shown that the ruling in question does not controvert any established rule of law, given a 'proper' interpretation or explanation of such a rule in the light of principle and policy.[82]

As a result, under the models of both Dworkin and MacCormick, principles play complex roles in both justifying and completing a legal system. But for MacCormick they remain necessary and not sufficient, and always must be employed in the context of governing rules. To justify a decision they must both be compatible with existing rules and support the overall coherence and purpose of the legal system.

7.3.2 Relation to rules

Several views exist regarding the relation of principles to rules. Dworkin argues that rules can be distinguished because they 'are applicable in an all-or-nothing fashion… [i]f the facts a rule stipulates are given, then either the rule is valid, in which case the answer it supplies must be accepted, or it is not, in which case it contributes nothing to the decision.'[83] In other words, generally speaking rules can be observed, overturned, or broken (in which case there will be a legal consequence). Rules are either applicable to a particular factual situation or not; they may be valid or not.[84] In contrast, a principle, according to Dworkin, 'states a reason that argues in one direction, but does not necessitate a particular decision'.[85] Principles may guide, but will not determine, a decision: they 'incline a decision one way, though not conclusively, and they survive intact when they do not prevail'.[86] Several competing legal principles or policies may be assessed as part of a decision-making process and if so, they will need to be weighed against one another in order to determine which is to take priority.[87]

[82] MacCormick, *Legal Reasoning and Legal Theory* (n 71) 250.

[83] Dworkin, *Taking Rights Seriously* (n 71) 24.

[84] Note however that MacCormick alludes to the possible application of a rule by analogy, in which case 'a rule can contribute to a decision on facts to which it is not directly applicable': *Legal Reasoning and Legal Theory* (n 71) 155.

[85] Dworkin, *Taking Rights Seriously* (n 71) 26.

[86] Dworkin, *Taking Rights Seriously* (n 71) 35.

[87] See MacCormick, *Legal Reasoning and Legal Theory* (n 71) ch 7. Dworkin, in *Taking Rights Seriously* (n 71) at p 22, distinguishes between policies and principles by stating that the former are oriented towards particular goals whereas the latter are not related to specific goals, but are more concerned with ensuring the requirements of justice, fairness, or some other dimension of morality.

For this reason MacCormick suggests that when a judge is confronted by a case involving competing principles, 'although appeal to one or the other principle is a necessary, it cannot be a sufficient or conclusive justification of the decision actually given.'[88] Arguments based upon principle only show the 'permissibility of proposed decisions' and do not make them obligatory.[89] The 'principle determines the legitimate range of justifying considerations... it does not, and cannot, be represented as yielding a conclusive answer.'[90]

Alexy pushes our understanding of the relation between rules and principles further. He understands principles and rules as both being norms and reasons, but as qualitatively distinguishable.[91] Principles, according to Alexy, are optimization requirements, meaning that they are 'norms which require that something be realized to the greatest extent possible given the legal and factual possibilities'.[92] Principles are not definitive, or absolute, but are only prima facie reasons.[93] They can be satisfied to varying degrees, and the degree of satisfaction depends upon both what is factually and legally possible, with the 'scope of what is legally possible [being] determined by opposing principles and rules'.[94] Further, although principles 'represent reasons which can be displaced by other reasons... [they] lack the resources to determine their own extent in the light of competing principles and what is factually possible.'[95] According to Alexy principles are limited by the requirement of 'norm consistency', meaning that they must be valid within the particular legal system, and are circumscribed by the requirements of proportionality, which is inherent in the nature of principles as optimization requirements.[96]

Alexy argues that rules, in contrast, are norms that either apply or do not apply and are either valid or invalid; they constitute '*fixed points* in the field of the factually

[88] MacCormick, *Legal Reasoning and Legal Theory* (n 71) 169.

[89] MacCormick, *Legal Reasoning and Legal Theory* (n 71) 188–9.

[90] MacCormick, *Legal Reasoning and Legal Theory* (n 71) 177. Even well-established principles are not conclusive because they must always be evaluated in the light of countervailing considerations: at p 180.

[91] Alexy, *A Theory of Constitutional Rights* (n 71) 45 (norms) and 59 (reasons).

[92] Alexy, *A Theory of Constitutional Rights* (n 71) 47. Alexy, at p 51 (note 37), notes that 'principles on their own or in isolation, that is, independently from their relationship with other principles, are maximization requirements.' However such a characterization does not 'express the constitutive relation that principles have with other principles' or help describe the process of resolution of conflicts between principles. For this reason Alexy prefers the general definition of principles as *optimization* requirements.

[93] Alexy, *A Theory of Constitutional Rights* (n 71) 57, 59, and 64. On the latter page Alexy clarifies that principles which may seem to be absolute, such as the principle of 'human dignity' in the German constitution, are not. Rather, 'the impression of absoluteness arises from the fact that there are two human dignity norms, a human dignity rule and a human dignity principle', and only the former could be absolute. But see also at pp 84–5 (implied limitations read into absolute constitutional rights).

[94] Alexy, *A Theory of Constitutional Rights* (n 71) 48.

[95] Alexy, *A Theory of Constitutional Rights* (n 71) 57.

[96] Alexy, *A Theory of Constitutional Rights* (n 71) 62. Alexy provides the principle of racial segregation as an example of an invalid principle. This principle may have been formally 'valid' in particular legal systems in the past, but is excluded under German constitutional law: at p 61. See also pp 66–9, 397. Alexy further subdivides the principle of proportionality into the three sub-principles of suitability, necessity, and 'proportionality in the narrow sense', which he defines as being equivalent to the Law of Balancing ('the greater the degree of non-satisfaction of, or detriment to, one principle, the greater must be the importance of satisfying the other'): eg at pp 397–401.

and legally possible', 'they contain a decision about what is to happen within the realm of the legally and factually possible.'[97] If there is a conflict between rules then either an exception must be read into one, or at least one of the rules declared invalid.[98] However the possibility of *exceptions* requires Alexy to depart from Dworkin's 'simplistic' all-or-nothing model of rules.[99] When an exception is incorporated into a rule, perhaps on the basis of a principle, the rule loses its definitive character for the case.[100] For this reason Alexy qualifies his understanding of rules by explaining that they 'are *definitive reasons*, so long as no exception is to be read into them'.[101] Nevertheless Alexy maintains that rules and principles, although in this sense both having a prima facie character, remain qualitatively different. Unlike a principle, which will be trumped by another principle of greater weight, a rule will not automatically be trumped by a principle having greater weight than the principle underpinning the rule on the facts of the case.[102] This is because rules are always underpinned by more than one principle; they are supported by '*formal* principles', such as *stare decisis* and the principle that 'rules passed by an authority acting within its jurisdiction are to be followed.'[103] Alexy further distinguishes principles and rules in terms of their practical effects. Unlike rules, principles can never in and of themselves be definitive reasons:

> If a rule is a reason for making a concrete ought-judgment, which is the case when it is valid, applicable and without relevant exception, then it is a *definitive reason*. If the content of the concrete ought-judgment is that an individual has a certain right, then that right is a *definitive right*. By contrast, principles can only ever be *prima facie reasons*. In and of themselves they can only create prima facie rights.... We can therefore say that whenever a principle turns out to be the dominant reason for a concrete ought-judgment, then that principle is a reason for a rule, which in turn is the definitive reason for the judgment. Principles in themselves are never definitive reasons.[104]

Further, as *reasons for rules*, principles will help determine conflicts between rules. As Alexy points out, conflicts between rules are not self-resolving, and must be decided and justified by either referring to 'maxims' or by evaluating the substantive importance of the two competing rules.[105]

7.3.3 Relation to other principles

Conflicts between principles, in contrast, require a determination of precedence. Like Dworkin, Alexy argues that principles carry different weights and in cases

[97] Alexy, *A Theory of Constitutional Rights* (n 71) 48 (emphasis in original), and 57.
[98] Alexy, *A Theory of Constitutional Rights* (n 71) 49.
[99] Alexy, *A Theory of Constitutional Rights* (n 71) 57.
[100] Alexy, *A Theory of Constitutional Rights* (n 71) 58.
[101] Alexy, *A Theory of Constitutional Rights* (n 71) 59 (emphasis in original).
[102] Alexy, *A Theory of Constitutional Rights* (n 71) 58.
[103] Alexy, *A Theory of Constitutional Rights* (n 71) 58 (emphasis in original).
[104] Alexy, *A Theory of Constitutional Rights* (n 71) 60. Note that Alexy also differs from Dworkin in arguing that principles provide reasons for collective interests, and therefore collective rights, not just individual rights: at pp 65–6.
[105] Alexy, *A Theory of Constitutional Rights* (n 71) 49.

of competition one principle will have to be 'outweighed' by the other on the facts of the particular case: '[c]onflicts of rules are played out at the level of validity; since only valid principles can compete, competitions between principles are played out in the dimension of weight instead.'[106] But precedence for principles is not fixed, and thus Alexy founds what he calls the 'law of competing principles' upon a 'conditional relation of precedence between the principles in the light of the circumstances of the case'.[107] In other words, two principles which may be considered equal in the abstract, will assume a relation of precedence in the context of the factual circumstances of a particular case. Further, although this precedence of principles may be characterized in terms of 'soft orderings'—through either 'prima facie preferences' or 'through a network of concrete preference decisions' (ie, past judicial decisions)—it is impossible to formally rank them, in either a cardinal or ordinal sense.[108] In this sense principles can only have 'relative' weight.[109]

Moreover, in coming to a concrete decision Alexy argues that competing principles must not only be weighed or balanced, they must also be justified.[110] Justification entails a particular type of balancing of principles, which he names the 'Law of Balancing'. In the context of competing principles, this 'Law' requires that '[t]he greater the degree of non-satisfaction of, or detriment to, one principle, the greater must be the importance or satisfying the other.'[111] Although Alexy concedes that his law of balancing will not produce 'an intersubjectively binding calculation of the result' in a particular conflict of principles, it identifies the essential components of a justification of a decision to give precedence to one principle over another.[112]

7.4 Conclusions

General principles of law fulfil a number of crucial needs in any legal system. As seen in international law and EU law, they help decision makers to fill lacunae in the law, choose between applicable rules, and provide justifications for both legal decisions and the rules of the legal system. They provide guiding standards or norms and make the legal system more consistent, coherent, and meaningful. In

[106] Alexy, *A Theory of Constitutional Rights* (n 71) 50.

[107] Alexy, *A Theory of Constitutional Rights* (n 71) 52–4. At the latter page Alexy defines the 'Law of Competing Principles' as follows: 'The circumstances under which one principle takes precedence over another constitute the conditions of a rule which has the same legal consequences as the principle taking precedence.' In other words, a particular factual circumstance will generate a concrete legal result (rule) for a competition between two principles.

[108] Alexy, *A Theory of Constitutional Rights* (n 71) 96–100.

[109] Alexy, *A Theory of Constitutional Rights* (n 71) 102.

[110] Alexy, *A Theory of Constitutional Rights* (n 71) 100–2.

[111] Alexy, *A Theory of Constitutional Rights* (n 71) 102.

[112] Alexy, *A Theory of Constitutional Rights* (n 71) 102–5. See also the Postscript where Alexy further explores and clarifies the Law of Balancing in the context of dealing with the problems of discretion and arbitrariness in relation to constitutional norms.

this latter sense, which has been partly developed in EU law, principles can be said to provide a *foundation* for the legal system as a whole.

Principles must be understood in this broader legal-philosophical context in Caribbean integration law. Rather than simply being gap fillers, general principles of law can bring coherence and purpose to CARICOM and OECS law, allowing those legal systems to develop beyond the textually-based rules and exceptions found in the RTC and RTB. In fact, by adding flesh to the skeletal frame created by their constituent treaties, general principles can allow CARICOM and the OECS to develop unique, legal, internally-coherent identities. As seen in the long list of potential general principles set out in the next chapter, if CARICOM, the OECS, and their respective tribunals were to seriously embrace general principles of law, the nature of each organization would be fundamentally changed.

8

General Principles of Law and Other Foundational Legal Concepts Potentially Arising in CARICOM and the OECS

Chapter 7 demonstrated the importance of general principles of law and their basis in legal theory, international law, and regional law. This chapter examines several general principles and other foundational legal concepts which are either expressly or implicitly included, or which may in the future be included, in the legal frameworks of CARICOM and the OECS. None are identified at present as general principles per se in the texts of the RTC or RTB. However those that can be conceptualized as general principles of Caribbean Community and OECS Economic Union law should be so classified, since this characterization would fit them within the most logical source of law and also give them the greatest potential scope.[1] Even if they cannot properly be classified as principles per se, and instead may more appropriately be described as legal concepts, they may nevertheless be derived from general principles of law, as a source of law.[2]

As illustrated in what follows, specific general principles of law already have been accepted by the CCJ in its early original jurisdiction decisions. The Court is clearly aware of their potential. In *Trinidad Cement Ltd v Caribbean Community*,

[1] Some of the legal concepts discussed later in the chapter may arise through a generous textual interpretation of the RTC or RTB, for example, through the doctrine of implied powers or necessary intendment. See Chapter 2 for more on implied powers and treaty interpretation. However, because an interpretive foundation may limit the development and scope of these concepts, being too closely tied to the texts of the treaties, it is not explored in depth here. Rather, this chapter focuses on the potential of general principles of law as the base for the legal concepts discussed herein, since this foundation will be more easily adaptable to changing circumstances and needs, and should be capable of greater development, application, and scope.

[2] As highlighted in Chapter 7, principles of law can only guide, not determine a legal decision. Principles provide a reason for ruling in a particular way but do not mandate one specific result in each case. Rules, in contrast, are either applicable or inapplicable. If they are applicable, rules can only be observed or breached. Several of the legal concepts discussed later, such as direct applicability and direct effect, are more similar to rules than principles. For example, it could be said that either something *is* directly effective, or *is not*; one would not say that something is *more* directly effective. For this reason terms that would not easily fall under the category of principles are labelled legal concepts.

when discussing the types of law that may be examined by the CCJ in its original jurisdiction, the Court noted:

> The search in the application and interpretation of the Revised Treaty is to discover Community law. In this quest the Court has to apply such rules of international law as may be applicable [Article 217(1) of the Revised Treaty]. Part of that law is the emerging customary international law on, for example, the concept of *ultra vires* acts of organs of international organizations. The Court may also consider 'the general principles of law recognized by civilized nations'. If one applies Article 217 of the Revised Treaty the principles of law common to the principal legal systems of the Community are a source of law for this Court, as it is for the International Court of Justice: see Article 38(1)(c) of the Statute of the International Court of Justice. This Court may take into account the principles and concepts common to the laws of Member States. The search is for general principles of law common to Member States. It is not necessary for the principle to be expressed identically in all Member States. It is sufficient if the general principle is widely accepted: see the opinion of Advocate General Sir Gordon Slynn in *AM & S Europe Ltd v Commission* and of the ECJ. If the general principle is widely accepted throughout the Community and relevant it may become part of Community law. These are tests that will have to be applied if this Court is asked to strike down the decisions authorizing suspension of the CET on grounds that derive from the domestic law applicable to judicial review in common law jurisdictions.[3]

This understanding of the wide-ranging scope of sources of law available to the Court bodes well for the development and implementation of general principles of law in its jurisprudence.

Let us examine the various general principles and legal concepts that may arise, or have arisen, in CARICOM and OECS law.

8.1 Conferral (Attributed Competence)

As noted by Schermers and Blokker, it is a basic principle of international institutional law that 'the powers of international organisations are limited to those attributed to them by states (attributed competence, *compétence d'attribution*).'[4] This principle of attributed competence, which in EU law is termed the principle of conferral, may be said to be implicit in the textual form of treaty interpretation, which is frequently employed to limit an organization to exercising only those powers expressly conferred upon it by the text of the treaty. The principle also may be said to arise from the very nature of international organizations. Unlike states, international organizations are not sovereign and independent, and do not possess a general competence.[5] As summarized by the International Court of Justice in its Advisory Opinion on the *Legality of the Use by a State of Nuclear Weapons in Armed*

[3] Judgment [2009] CCJ 2 (OJ), (2009) 74 WIR 319, 5 February 2009 [41] (citations omitted).

[4] Henry G Schermers and Niels M Blokker, *International Institutional Law*, 4th edn (Boston: Martinus Nijhoff, 2003) 155 (§209). The terms 'principle of conferral' and 'principle of attributed competence' are used synonymously here.

[5] Schermers and Blokker, *International Institutional Law* (n 4) 155–6 (§209).

Conflict, requested by the World Health Organization, international organizations only have the competence conferred upon them by their member states:

> 25. The Court need hardly point out that international organizations are subjects of international law which do not, unlike States, possess a general competence. International organizations are governed by the 'principle of speciality', that is to say, they are invested by the States which create them with powers, the limits of which are a function of the common interests whose promotion those States entrust to them. The Permanent Court of International Justice referred to this basic principle in the following terms:
>
> > 'As the European Commission is not a State, but an international institution with a special purpose, it only has the functions bestowed upon it by the Definitive Statute with a view to the fulfilment of that purpose, but it has power to exercise these functions to their full extent, in so far as the Statute does not impose restrictions upon it.' (*Jurisdiction of the European Commission of the Danube, Advisory Opinion, P.C.I.J., Series B, No. 14,* p. 64.)[6]

The principle of conferral draws attention to the fact that an international organization is created and empowered only to fulfil *specific* purposes and thereby has limited competences.

In the context of CARICOM, a form of the principle of conferral is applied to the Conference under Articles 12(5) of the RTC, in the following words:

> 5. Subject to the relevant provisions of this Treaty, the Conference shall exercise such powers as may be conferred on it by or under any instrument elaborated by or under the auspices of the Community.

It should be noted that Article 12(5) does not limit the powers of the Conference to those conferred by the RTC alone; other instruments created by the Community may also confer powers to the Conference. Such phrasing allows the Conference to derive powers from further Community legal acts, such as international legal agreements with third parties. Article 12(5) also could be interpreted more broadly, as allowing conferral to arise from subsidiary legal acts, such as decisions of the Conference itself. It is submitted that the latter interpretation would not be advisable, since its application could defeat the intention of CARICOM member states to accord primacy to the RTC itself.

The principle of conferral is also alluded to in relation to the powers of the CARICOM Secretary General under Article 23(3) of the RTC, which provides:

> 3. The Secretary-General shall, in addition to the powers conferred by or under the Treaty, be the Chief Executive Officer of the Community and shall act in that capacity at all meetings of Community Organs and Bodies. He shall make an annual report to the Conference on the work of the Community.[7]

[6] *Legality of the Use by a State of Nuclear Weapons in Armed Conflict* (Advisory Opinion) [1996] ICJ Rep 66, pp 78–9 [25].

[7] Note as well that Art 222(a) of the RTC, in describing the requirements for locus standi for persons in original jurisdiction proceedings before the CCJ, uses the phrase 'a right or benefit conferred by or under this Treaty'. It remains to be seen whether this phrasing will bring into play the limitations inherent in the principle of conferral, such as the requirement for a clear textual basis for such rights or benefits.

This provision is closer to the normal sense of the principle of conferral, since the second clause of the first sentence merely elaborates upon one of the powers set out in the RTC itself.

In the context of the OECS, the principle of conferral is expressly set out in Article 7.2 of the RTB. This provision states:

> 7.2 The Organs of the Organisation shall perform the functions and act within the limits of the powers conferred upon them by or under this Treaty and by the Dispute Settlement Annex and the Economic Union Protocol.

Similarly, Article 28.1(a) of the Protocol of Eastern Caribbean Economic Union restricts the OECS Economic Affairs Council to exercising 'such powers and functions as are conferred upon it by this Protocol'. These two provisions set out the principle in very clear terms and restrict its application to the constituent treaties. It would be useful for CARICOM to emulate such phrasing.

In comparison, in Europe, the principle of conferral forms a fundamental component of the architecture of EU law. It is now codified in Article 5(1)–(2) of the TEU, as follows:

> 1. The limits of Union competences are governed by the principle of conferral. The use of Union competences is governed by the principles of subsidiarity and proportionality.
> 2. Under the principle of conferral, the Union shall act only within the limits of the competences conferred upon it by the Member States in the Treaties to attain the objectives set out therein. Competences not conferred upon the Union in the Treaties remain with the Member States.[8]

This statement of the principle of conferral is helpful because it makes explicit the division of competences between the regional organization and its member states. It establishes two things: firstly, that the EU can only act within the limits of the competences conferred upon it by its constituent treaty and, secondly, that any competences not conferred upon the EU remain with its member states. As a consequence, the EU cannot confer powers on itself, and has no inherent powers.[9]

In terms of scope, the principle of conferral in the EU requires adherence not only to the text of the EU treaties, but also to their objects and purposes. This is expressly stated in paragraph (2) of Article 5 of the TEU. It is also highlighted in the quoted section of the Advisory Opinion on *Jurisdiction of the European Commission of the Danube*, where the Court highlighted the need for the European Commission to exercise its powers in a functional manner, so as to fulfil its purpose. Such a strict interpretation of the principle limits the scope of competences of the organization to those expressly set out in its constituent document(s) and their use to the confines of the objects and purposes of the organization.

[8] Consolidated versions of the Treaty on European Union and the Treaty on the Functioning of the European Union (OJ C83, 30.3.2010) as available through <http://eur-lex.europa.eu/en/treaties/index.htm> (accessed 30 Sep 2011). See also TEU Art 4(1).

[9] See TC Hartley, *The Foundations of European Union Law*, 7th edn (Oxford: Oxford University Press, 2010) 110.

Nevertheless it must be recognized that the principle of conferral is not absolute. Like any principle is can be outweighed by other principles or rules. For example, an organization's competences may in some cases be expanded through the doctrine of implied powers.[10] Attributed competence may also be modified by open-ended provisions in the text of the constituent treaty of the organization. In the case of the EU, for example, Article 352(1) of the TFEU allows the institutions of the European Union to adopt appropriate measures, when necessary, and 'within the framework of the policies defined in the Treaties, to attain one of the objectives set out in the Treaties, [where] the Treaties have not provided the necessary powers…'.[11] This provision is very broad in its scope, but not unlimited. Article 352 has been interpreted in light of the restrictions inherent in the principle of conferral and in the text of the article itself.[12] For this reason the ECJ reads general competence provisions narrowly, restricting their use to situations in which they are absolutely necessary. Such a reading can be said to be a natural consequence of the principle of conferral itself, which encourages the foundation of legal actions upon specific textual authority.

This line of ECJ jurisprudence is relevant to the Caribbean region, since several provisions of the RTC and RTB which could be read to extend the competences of organs may need to be read narrowly. An example of the ECJ preferring a specific legal base for legislative action over a more general base is found in Case 45/86 *Commission v Council*.[13] This case involved a challenge by the Commission to two Regulations adopted by the Council. The Regulations applied generalized tariff preferences to certain products originating in developing countries. The Commission refused to accept Article 235 of the Treaty Establishing the European Economic Community (EEC Treaty) (now Article 352 of the TFEU), as a suitable base for legislative action.[14] The Commission challenged the Regulations because they did not state the reasons upon which they were based, as required under what was then Article 190 of the EEC Treaty (now under Article 296 of the TFEU), and therefore did not provide clear evidence of their legal basis. The Council itself

[10] See generally, *Reparation for Injuries Suffered in the Service of the United Nations* (Advisory Opinion) [1949] ICJ Rep 174. For the EU context see Hartley (n 9) 110–11.

[11] Consolidated versions of the Treaty on European Union and the Treaty on the Functioning of the European Union (OJ C83, 30.3.2010) as available through <http://eur-lex.europa.eu/en/treaties/index.htm> (accessed 30 Sep 2011). For convenience, the full text of Art 352(1) of the TFEU reads:

> 1. If action by the Union should prove necessary, within the framework of the policies defined in the Treaties, to attain one of the objectives set out in the Treaties, and the Treaties have not provided the necessary powers, the Council, acting unanimously on a proposal from the Commission and after obtaining the consent of the European Parliament, shall adopt the appropriate measures. Where the measures in question are adopted by the Council in accordance with a special legislative procedure, it shall also act unanimously on a proposal from the Commission and after obtaining the consent of the European Parliament.

[12] See Hartley, *The Foundations of European Union Law* (n 9) 111–16.

[13] Case 45/86 *Commission v Council* [1987] ECR 1493.

[14] Treaty Establishing the European Economic Community (adopted 25 Mar 1957, in force 1 Jan 1958) (1958) 294 UNTS 17 (French original), (1958) 298 UNTS 11 (English translation) (EEC Treaty).

admitted that the wording was designed to leave the legal basis of the Regulations vague, as a result of differences of opinion.[15] However the Council submitted that the Regulations were in fact based upon two articles of the EEC Treaty: Articles 113 and 235.[16] The Court responded by noting that the need to determine the correct legal basis was not a formality, since the two articles raised by the Council entailed different decision-making rules and could thus affect the content of the contested Regulations.[17] It also noted that the Council had voted unanimously in adopting these Regulations, as required under Article 235 of the EEC Treaty. When analysing the latter article, which was the predecessor to the first paragraph of Article 352 of the TFEU, the Court held that it could be relied upon as a legal basis only when strictly necessary:

> It follows from the very wording of Article 235 that its use as the legal basis for a measure is justified only where no other provision of the Treaty gives the Community institutions the necessary power to adopt the measure in question.[18]

In other words, the use of a broad, empowering provision (a more general legislative basis) would only be justified if no other provision of the EU treaties (a more specific legislative basis) would allow the adoption of the measure. Given this conclusion, the Court then looked at the text of the alternative provision suggested by the Council, Article 113 of the EEC Treaty, and held that the Regulations could have been adopted under that more specific provision. Since the Regulations could have been adopted under Article 113, the ECJ held that the Council had both failed to specify the precise legal basis of the Regulations and was not justified in taking Article 235 as a basis. As a result, the Court declared the Regulations void.[19]

The ECJ has consistently rejected similar attempts by institutions of the EU to use more general legislative bases in place of specific ones. This practice has led Weatherill to comment that the 'Court has never deviated from this view'.[20] For example, in answering the controversial question of whether it would be compatible with the EU Treaty for the Community to accede to the European Convention

[15] Case 45/86 *Commission v Council* [1987] ECR 1493 [8].

[16] Case 45/86 *Commission v Council* (n 15) [10].

[17] Case 45/86 *Commission v Council* (n 15) [12].

[18] Case 45/86 *Commission v Council* (n 15) [13].

[19] Case 45/86 *Commission v Council* (n 15) [21]–[22].

[20] Stephen Weatherill, *Cases & Materials on EU Law*, 9th edn (Oxford: Oxford University Press, 2010) p 36. For cases dealing with a similar general legislative provision—the harmonization provision found in what is now Art 114 of the TFEU—see eg Case C-376/98 *Germany v European Parliament and Council of the European Union* [2000] ECR I-8419, and Case C-491/01 *R v Secretary of State for Health, ex parte British American Tobacco (Investments) Ltd and Imperial Tobacco Ltd* [2002] ECR I-11453. Both cases involved attempts by the EU to regulate tobacco products by means of the harmonization provision, which allowed adoption of measures for the approximation (harmonization) of laws with the objective of improving the internal market. In the first case the Court rejected directives relying on the harmonization provision because they did not genuinely aim to improve the conditions for the establishment and functioning of the internal market. In the second case, the directive did satisfy the requirement that it have as its object the improvement of the internal market, even if health considerations strongly influenced the choices involved in the harmonizing measures. Taken together, and as affirmed in later decisions of the ECJ, these cases show that the Court will interpret a general legislative basis strictly, requiring any legislative act to clearly, and genuinely, fall within its terms. See further Weatherill 37–47.

for the Protection of on Human Rights and Fundamental Freedoms, the ECJ noted that the 'principle of conferred powers must be respected in both the internal action and the international action of the Community'.[21] Finding no express or implied powers that would enable the Community to join the Convention,[22] the Court examined whether this would be permissible under Article 235 of the EU Treaty (now Article 352 TFEU). The ECJ emphasized that Article 235 served a limited role:

> [29] Article 235 is designed to fill the gap where no specific provisions of the Treaty confer on the Community institutions express or implied powers to act, if such powers appear none the less to be necessary to enable the Community to carry out its functions with a view to attaining one of the objectives laid down by the Treaty.
>
> [30] That provision, being an integral part of an institutional system based on the principle of conferred powers, cannot serve as a basis for widening the scope of Community powers beyond the general framework created by the provisions of the Treaty as a whole and, in particular, by those that define the tasks and the activities of the Community. On any view, Article 235 cannot be used as a basis for the adoption of provisions whose effect would, in substance, be to amend the Treaty without following the procedure which it provides for that purpose.[23]

In concluding, the Court held that acceding to the Convention would be of constitutional significance, going beyond the scope of Article 235 and the Community's competence, and instead requiring amendment of the EU Treaty.[24]

This line of jurisprudence related to the choice of specific over general legislative provisions is not only helpful, but may be necessary to give proper effect to the principle of conferral in the Caribbean region. Both CARICOM and the OECS would be wise to follow a similar legislative pattern, basing legislative action on the narrowest and most appropriate provision of their respective treaties, rather than turning immediately to broader, general provisions. In doing so, the actions of organs of CARICOM and the OECS would be more likely to survive legal challenges before their respective regional tribunals on the grounds of exceeding their competences, and the legal basis for decision making would be both transparent and certain.

8.2 Direct Applicability

Direct applicability is a legal concept that may be said to be implicit in the treaty regimes of CARICOM and the OECS and may be further substantiated as a general principle of law. More familiar to readers for its use in the EU legal system, it is likely to have a narrower, but important impact upon Caribbean regional

[21] *Accession by the Community to the European Convention for the Protection of Human Rights and Fundamental Freedoms (Opinion 2/94)* [1996] ECR I-01759, at [24].
[22] *Accession by the Community to the European Convention* (n 21) [28].
[23] *Accession by the Community to the European Convention* (n 21) [29]–[30].
[24] *Accession by the Community to the European Convention* (n 21) [35]–[36].

organizations. It may be best described as a legal norm or concept, rather than principle, since direct applicability acts in a manner more similar to a rule than a principle. It is either applicable, and therefore creates necessary consequences, or inapplicable, and does not.

In the Caribbean direct applicability simply describes the manner in which the two regional integration treaties impose obligations as a matter of international law on their member states and their organs: regional integration law applies directly to the member states of CARICOM and OECS and creates binding rights and obligations for them *within that regional system*. In other words, by describing a provision of the RTC as being 'directly applicable', we highlight (1) its binding nature (upon the state and, indirectly, upon organs) as a matter of international and regional law, which (2) is directly enforceable under the legal system established by the RTC, including the CCJ. This is not exactly the same meaning ascribed to the concept in EU law, and thus it is helpful to examine the origins and meaning of the direct applicability, and to contrast it with a related concept, namely, direct effect.

Direct applicability is grounded in international law, where it is well accepted that states must not act contrary to their treaty obligations. Likewise, under international law states must ensure that their international legal obligations are satisfactorily upheld, even if this requires changes to their domestic legal systems.[25] Direct applicability may therefore be said to be implicit in the rule of *pacta sunt servanda*, namely, that treaties are binding and must be observed in good faith. It is expressed in regional treaties in Article 9 of the RTC and Article 5 of the RTB. These provisions both require member states to 'ensure the carrying out of obligations' under the respective treaty regimes. Such a requirement, it should be noted, is one of effect.

Nevertheless, direct applicability in the Caribbean does not at present go as far as it does in the EU. It does not automatically entail enforceability of regional law at the *domestic level*, as occurs in some cases in the EU. It is limited by the rules related to the effect of international treaties in domestic law, and by the other provisions of the RTC and RTB.

8.2.1 Potential objections

The idea of direct applicability existing at all in the Caribbean may be considered controversial for a variety of reasons.

Direct applicability v direct effect

Firstly, direct applicability is sometimes confused with direct effect, a term used in Article 5.3 of the RTB but not found in CARICOM law. Several authors have

[25] Cf Arts 26–27 of the Vienna Convention on the Law of Treaties (adopted 23 May 1969, in force 27 Jan 1980) 1155 UNTS 331 (VCLT).

sought to draw a clear distinction between the two concepts.[26] Kaczorowska, for example, argues that the principle of *direct applicability* merely refers to the way in which Community law is considered automatically part of national law, but does not necessarily entail *enforceability* in that legal order. In her view, direct applicability is the doctrine that requires rules of EU law to be 'fully and uniformly applied in all Member States from the date of their entry into force and for so long as they continue to be in force', without the need for transformation by Act of Parliament or other legislative device.[27] However the principle itself does not necessarily entail enforceability in the domestic legal system. It ensures that treaty-based obligations become an integral part of national law which, *in the EU legal system*, national judges are bound to apply as EU law, not as national law.[28] In other words, in the EU, the concept of direct applicability brings regional law directly into the national legal sphere while at the same time preserving its status as Union law.[29] *Direct effect*, in contrast, goes further. Direct effect refers to the way in which regional law is not only part of national law, but also is *actionable before national courts* by private actors.

The distinction between direct effect, which entails enforceability, and direct applicability, which may not, is brought out in the ECJ cases on the obligation not to enact new laws contrary to treaty obligations (sometimes referred to as a 'standstill' obligation). The Court's jurisprudence on directives, for example, establishes that member states must not only enact appropriate legislation within the time period allowed by the directive, but they must also *refrain* from enacting legislation incompatible with the directive, even prior to the conclusion of the time period provided for its implementation.[30] The 'standstill' obligation, it should be noted, arises *before* the directive itself is enforceable or directly effective. Logically, therefore, the standstill obligation must be derived from the direct applicability of the directive, which is distinct from its direct effectiveness, since the latter can only arise after the time period for implementation has expired.[31] Similarly, the ECJ has held that in some cases individuals can rely upon directives prior to the expiry of the transposition period to challenge national rules which conflict with the directive.[32] For example, the ECJ established in the case of *Velasco Narvarro v Fogasa* that from the date of notification of the directive a national court is obliged

[26] See the discussion in Alina Kaczorowska, *European Union Law*, 2nd edn (London: Routledge, 2011) ch 11.

[27] Kaczorowska, *European Union Law* (n 26) 296.

[28] Kaczorowska, *European Union Law* (n 26) 298–9.

[29] For this reason the European Court of Justice has held that some EU obligations cannot be transformed by domestic legislation—because transformation would impermissibly change the nature of the EU obligation into a domestic one and obstruct its direct applicability. See eg Case 34/73 *Variola v Amministrazione delle Finanze* [1973] ECR 981. Hartley, however, in *The Foundations of European Union Law* (n 9) 216, reminds us that some regulations may in fact require implementing legislation.

[30] Case C-129/96 *Inter-Environnement Wallonie ASBL v Région Wallone* [1997] ECR I-7411; Case C-422/05 *Commission v Belgium* [2007] ECR I-4749. See generally, Kaczorowska, *European Union Law* (n 26) 300–3.

[31] The Court in Case C-246/06 *Velasco Navarro v Fogasa* [2008] ECR I-105, at [25] notes that 'it is settled case-law that a directive can have direct effect only after the expiry of the time-limit laid down for its transposition into national law' (citations omitted). See also Kaczorowska (n 26) 302.

[32] eg Case C-422/05 *Commission v Belgium* (n 30).

to interpret national law which is within the scope of the directive in compliance with 'the general principles and fundamental rights recognised in the Community legal order'.[33] This interpretive obligation does not require compliance with the actual rules of the directive prior to its transposition into national law, but rather with general EU norms within the area covered by the directive.[34] This distinction again can be used to demonstrate the difference between direct applicability and direct effect: the former relates to the binding nature of the obligations on the state and its organs, the latter deals with its enforceability before national courts.[35]

Such a distinction is helpful in analysing Caribbean regional integration regimes. Note that direct applicability must exist in a more limited form in CARICOM and the OECS than it does in the EU. In the EU certain acts that are directly applicable can be enforced through national law.

Relation to dualism

A second concern may arise because the concept of direct applicability appears antithetical to the well-established rules of dualism that are entrenched in Caribbean common law legal systems. These rules require treaties to be transformed before they can have any binding force in domestic law.[36] Of course in Commonwealth Caribbean states one form of international law—*customary* international law—may become part of domestic law without transformation. But even in this case the applicability of rules of customary international law in the domestic legal order remains subject to the overriding effect of statute law and, with one exception,[37] that of binding judicial precedent.[38]

In the Commonwealth Caribbean other international acts, including treaties, which have not been transformed into domestic law can have no binding force or effect in domestic law. The only commonly accepted role for unincorporated treaties is as an interpretive one. However even here the House of Lords has suggested that this role is limited to situations in which one is confronted with real ambiguity in the domestic law.[39]

[33] Case C-246/06 *Velasco Navarro v Fogasa* [2008] ECR I-105.

[34] See eg *Velasco Navarro v Fogasa* (n 33) [25]–[30].

[35] Cf Kaczorowska, *European Union Law* (n 26) 298.

[36] See eg *R v Lyons* [2003] 1 AC 976 (HL), *Higgs v Minister of National Security and Others* [2000] 2 AC 228 (PC Bah); *JH Rayner (Mincing Lane) Ltd v Department of Trade and Industry* (also called *Maclaine Watson & Co Ltd v International Tin Council*) [1990] 2 AC 418 (HL); *R v Secretary of State for the Home Department, ex parte Brind* [1991] 1 AC 696 (HL); *Salomon v Commissioners of Customs and Excise* [1967] 2 QB 116 (CA Eng). See generally David S Berry, 'The Use of International Law by Domestic Tribunals in the Caribbean in Death Penalty Cases' in DS Berry and T Robinson (eds), *Transitions in Caribbean Law: Lawmaking Constitutionalism and the Confluence of National and International Law* (Kingston, Jamaica: Ian Randle, 2013) 103–27.

[37] *Trendtex Trading Corporation v Central Bank of Nigeria* [1977] QB 529 (CA Eng).

[38] See James Crawford, *Brownlie's Principles of International Law*, 8th edn (Oxford: Oxford University Press, 2012) 67–71, and Sir R Jennings and Sir A Watts, *Oppenheim's International Law*, 9th edn (London: Longman, 1996) at 56–7.

[39] See eg *Salomon v Commissioners of Customs and Excise* [1967] 2 QB 116 (CA Eng) at pp 143–4 (per Lord Diplock); *R v Secretary of State for the Home Department, ex parte Brind* [1991] 1 AC 696 (HL) at pp 747–8 (per Lord Bridge).

Not all member states of CARICOM follow common law traditions. Suriname and Haiti, being civil law states, follow more of a monist approach and so the principle of direct applicability may resonate strongly in their legal systems. In addition, in the Commonwealth Caribbean, jurisprudence can be found which gives a more prominent role to international law in dualist states. Several cases provide examples of notable derogations from the strict dualist doctrine, in the jurisprudence of both the Judicial Committee of the Privy Council[40] and the Caribbean Court of Justice.[41]

However, even if such exceptions did not exist, the conflict between direct applicability and dualism would appear to be overstated in the Caribbean region for two basic reasons. Firstly, the strong version of direct applicability, one that has powerful and enforceable legal consequences in domestic law, represents a particular EU law manifestation of the idea. In CARICOM and the OECS the concept has not developed, and is unlikely to develop, in exactly the same form. Direct applicability exists in the constituent treaties of CARICOM and the OECS only in terms of regional or international legal obligations, ones which may not be enforced at the domestic level.

8.2.2 Nature and scope of the principle in CARICOM and OECS law

As highlighted earlier, neither of the texts of the RTC nor RTB per se gives rise to a full-fledged, EU-style version of the principle of direct applicability. Neither treaty, for example, includes a legislative device similar to the regulation in EU law.[42] However both treaties create the kinds of binding obligations that underpin the concept of direct applicability. Under Article 9 of the RTC, the provision establishing a general undertaking on implementation, member states are required to:

> take all appropriate measures, whether general or particular, to ensure the carrying out of obligations arising out of this Treaty or resulting from decisions taken by the Organs and Bodies of the Community. They shall facilitate the achievement of the objectives of the Community. They shall abstain from any measures which could jeopardise the attainment of the objectives of this Treaty.

[40] On the right to conclude the international petition processes founded on unincorporated treaties see eg *Thomas v Baptiste* [2000] 2 AC 1 (PC T&T) and *Lewis v AG* [2001] 2 AC 50 (PC Ja).

[41] The CCJ relied upon the doctrine of legitimate expectation in *AG v Joseph* [2006] CCJ 3 (AJ) (2006) 69 WIR 104 (BDS), to found a right not to be executed prior to the consideration by the local mercy committee (the Privy Council) of the conclusions of the organs of the Inter-American system of human rights related to an individual petition. The relevant Inter-American treaties were not incorporated into Barbadian law. See generally, David S Berry, 'The Use of International Law' (n 36) 103–27.

[42] In TFEU Art 288 a regulation is described as follows: 'A regulation shall have general application. It shall be binding in its entirety and directly applicable in all Member States.'

This provision imposes binding legal obligations upon member states at the international or regional levels. Similarly, Articles 5.1 and 5.2 of the RTB impose nearly identical obligations for OECS member states:

> 5.1 Member States shall take all appropriate measures, whether general or particular, to ensure the carrying out of obligations arising out of this Treaty or resulting from decisions taken by the Institutions of the Organisation. They shall facilitate the achievement of the purposes of the Organisation.
>
> 5.2 In particular and without prejudice to the generality of the preceding paragraph, each Member State shall take all steps to secure the enactment of such legislation as is necessary to give effect to this Treaty and decisions taken thereunder.

These articles create legally binding obligations at the international level and may be said to be directly applicable in the sense of binding member states to their obligations under the RTC and RTB as a matter of international and regional law. The obligations apply to the member states themselves but also, under the general international legal rules of state responsibility, apply indirectly to all of their organs: under the law of state responsibility each state is responsible for the acts of its organs, including acts that breach that state's treaty obligations.[43]

In addition, the texts of Article 9 of the RTC and Article 5.1 of the RTB must be understood to have broad meaning. Both provisions require member states to *ensure* the carrying out of obligations. Article 9 of the RTC goes further in requiring member states to 'abstain from any measures which could jeopardise the attainment of the objectives of this Treaty'. Both of these phrases limit potential actions by state *organs* at the domestic level since in ensuring that obligations are carried out, or in abstaining from undesirable actions, each member state must rely upon its appropriate organs and institutions.

Moreover, since the obligation imposed by both Article 9 and Article 5 is one of *result*, member states are required both to change their laws so as to comply with the requirements of the RTC and to abstain from enacting new laws which are contrary to the RTC. Although Article 5 of the RTB does not contain phrasing similar to the final sentence of Article 9 of the RTC, the requirement to abstain from measures which would jeopardize the attainment of the objectives of the treaty may be implied from the overarching obligation to ensure the carrying out of treaty obligations.[44] Thus no formal distinction should be drawn between the two treaties in this regard.

[43] See eg International Law Commission, 'Draft Articles on Responsibility of States for Internationally Wrongful Acts with commentaries 2001' (2001) *Yearbook of the International Law Commission, 2001,* Vol II, Part Two, Commentary to Art 4, at 84–92; Crawford, *Brownlie's Principles of International Law* (n 38) Part IX—The Law of Responsibility. For convenience, Draft Art 4 provides:

1. The conduct of any State organ shall be considered an act of that State under international law, whether the organ exercises legislative, executive, judicial or any other functions, whatever position it holds in the organization of the State, and whatever its character as an organ of the central government or of a territorial unit of the State.
2. An organ includes any person or entity which has that status in accordance with the internal law of the State.

[44] This is supported by the good faith requirement for performance of binding treaty obligations: *pacta sunt servanda*. See Art 26 of the VCLT.

The impact of Article 9 of the RTC and the potential of direct applicability have been given additional force following the special leave decision of the Caribbean Court of Justice in the case of *Trinidad Cement Ltd and TCL Guyana Inc v Guyana*.[45] In this decision the Court interpreted the RTC as not only creating rights and obligations for states, but as creating correlative rights for nationals. This case involved the applicants Trinidad Cement Ltd ('TCL') and TCL Guyana Inc ('TGI'), limited liability companies incorporated in Trinidad and Tobago and Guyana, respectively, whose main business was the production, packaging, sale, and distribution of cement in the common market established by the RTC. The applicants brought a claim against Guyana alleging breach of Article 82 of the RTC for the latter's suspension of the Common External Tariff (CET) on cement imported from third states. The applicants alleged that the suspension caused them prejudice and damages (by lessening demand for their own cement products). In response, Guyana fully admitted that it had suspended the CET, and that this suspension had not been authorized by the competent CARICOM organ, COTED.[46]

Nevertheless in its defence Guyana contended that the applicants did not have locus standi to institute proceedings before the CCJ under Article 222 of the Revised Treaty.[47] Article 222, entitled 'Locus Standi of Private Entities', sets out a long, cumulative test for the Court to assert its original jurisdiction over claims brought by nationals. The first two parts of the test require an applicant to establish that RTC intended that a right or benefit conferred by or under the RTC on a contracting party shall enure to the benefit of the applicant directly, and that the applicant has been prejudiced in respect of the enjoyment of that right or benefit. As a result, under Article 222 it became crucial for the two applicants to establish that the CET regime gives rise to rights which have enured to them directly. On a literal reading, the CET provisions appeared to grant rights and obligations to member states only. However the Court held that the RTC, although not always expressly conferring such rights or benefits to persons, nonetheless allows their derivation from correlative obligations imposed upon parties: 'Where an obligation is [imposed on Member States (or a class of Member States) collectively], it is capable of yielding a correlative right that enures directly to the benefit of private entities throughout the entire Community.'[48] This 'correlative right' doctrine is a significant judicial development, one that makes the Revised Treaty potentially relevant for persons in any case where a concrete duty is imposed upon a member state. Correlative rights were also crucial to the applicants' case, since without them the first part of the Article 222 test could not have been satisfied and the case would have been dismissed.

What is significant about the 'correlative rights' doctrine from the present perspective is that the Court at least implicitly limited the availability of such rights to judicial proceedings under the Court's original jurisdiction. There is no suggestion

[45] Judgment [2009] CCJ 1 (OJ), (2009) 74 WIR 302, 15 January 2009.

[46] *Trinidad Cement Ltd v Guyana* (n 45) [3].

[47] *Trinidad Cement Ltd v Guyana* (n 45) [3].

[48] *Trinidad Cement Ltd v Guyana* (n 45) [32].

that a correlative right could be actionable before a domestic court. Rather, correlative rights appear to be enforceable before, and by, the CCJ itself.

Conceptualized in this manner, the CCJ's correlative rights doctrine reinforces the concept of direct applicability in CARICOM. Through this correlative rights doctrine the CCJ emphasized the binding nature of RTC obligations on all member states and also extended the category of right-holders under the RTC. The Court provided an avenue for enforcement of RTC rights and obligations by *persons* against member states at the regional level before the CCJ in its original jurisdiction. Whether the Court's referral jurisdiction under Articles 211(1)(c) and 214 could add to the strength of the RTC in another sphere, in the domestic legal order, remains to be seen.[49]

In sum, although the RTC and RTB are formally binding on member states as a matter of international law at the international level, the *obligations* imposed by the two treaties have important consequences for state action at the national level. The obligations under the RTC also create enforceable rights for persons at the regional level. In this way the RTC and RTB can be seen to be directly applicable, in the sense that they apply directly to the member states of CARICOM and OECS, respectively, and create binding rights and obligations for those states and their organs which are enforceable within that regional system. In contrast to the EU, however, direct applicability in CARICOM and the OECS is not enforceable in domestic law.

8.3 Direct Effect

The concept of direct effect, as currently understood, can be said to have originated in the judicial activity of the ECJ when interpreting the nature and effect of the EU treaties.[50] As noted earlier, however, direct effect is also a treaty-created concept for the OECS, having been expressly included in Article 5.3 of the RTB. In order to flesh out the potential meaning of the term for the OECS regime, and to think about whether it could be applicable to CARICOM, it will be useful to briefly review its development and meaning in EU law.

8.3.1 In EU law

The seminal case in this area in EU law is Case 26/62 *Van Gend en Loos v Nederlandse Administratie der Belastingen*.[51] This case involved a challenge by Van Gend en Loos to a customs duty which was alleged to have been imposed in violation of

[49] For a discussion of the CCJ's referral jurisdiction see Chapter 14.

[50] See generally, Kaczorowska, *European Union Law* (n 26) ch 12; Hartley, *The Foundations of European Union Law* (n 9) ch 7; Paul Craig and Gráinne De Búrca, *EU Law, Text, Cases and Materials*, 5th edn (Oxford: Oxford University Press, 2011) ch 7; Stephen Weatherill, *Cases and Materials on EU Law* (n 20) chs 4–5. Takis Tridimas, in *The General Principles of EU Law*, 2nd edn (Oxford: Oxford University Press, 2006) at 3, identifies the principle of direct effect as a general principle of EU law.

[51] [1963] ECR 1.

Article 12 of the Treaty Establishing the European Economic Community (EEC Treaty). The Dutch court referred to the ECJ the question of 'whether Article 12 of the EEC Treaty has direct application within the territory of a member state, in other words, whether nationals of such a state can, on the basis of the Article in question, lay claim to individual rights which the [national] courts must protect.'[52] In answering this question the ECJ considered the spirit, the general scheme, and the wording of the provisions of the EEC Treaty. The Court determined that the 'objective of the EEC Treaty, which is to establish a common market, the functioning of which is of direct concern to interested parties in the Community, implies that this Treaty is more than an agreement which merely creates mutual obligations between the contracting states.'[53] The Court noted that the preamble to the Treaty referred not only to governments but to 'peoples', the Treaty itself established 'institutions endowed with sovereign rights, the exercise of which affects member states and also their citizens', and the preliminary reference procedure provided by Article 177 (now Article 267 TFEU) confirmed that 'the states have acknowledged that Community law has an authority which can be invoked by their nationals before those [national] courts and tribunals.'[54] As a result of such features of the European system, the ECJ held:

> The conclusion to be drawn from this is that the Community constitutes a new legal order of international law for the benefit of which the states have limited their sovereign rights, albeit within limited fields, and the subjects of which comprise not only member states but also their nationals. Independently of the legislation of Member States, Community law therefore not only imposes obligations on individuals but is also intended to confer upon them rights which become part of their legal heritage. These rights arise not only where they are expressly granted by the treaty, but also by reason of obligations which the Treaty imposes in a clearly defined way upon individuals as well as upon the Member States and upon the institutions of the Community.[55]

In other words, the Court considered that the parties to the EEC Treaty agreed not only to achieve particular treaty-mandated results, but also to create a new legal order, one conferring rights upon individuals that could be *enforced before national courts and tribunals*.[56] The Court held that 'according to the spirit, the general scheme and the wording of the Treaty, Article 12 must be interpreted as producing direct effects and creating individual rights which national courts must protect.'[57] As a factual matter, it does not appear that such a possibility was intended by the original drafters of the EU treaties. It was also vigorously resisted by states and the Advocate General during the *Van Gend en Loos* hearing.[58]

[52] *Van Gend en Loos* (n 51) 3. [53] *Van Gend en Loos* (n 51)12. [54] *Van Gend en Loos* (n 51)12.

[55] *Van Gend en Loos* (n 51) 12. In the CARICOM context, compare the statements of the Caribbean Court of Justice in the cases of *Trinidad Cement Ltd and TCL Guyana Inc v Guyana*, Judgment [2009] CCJ 1 (OJ), (2009) 74 WIR 302, 15 January 2009, at [18] and *Trinidad Cement Ltd v Caribbean Community*, Judgment [2009] CCJ 2 (OJ), (2009) 74 WIR 319, 5 February 2009, at [32], respectively. See further the discussion of these decisions starting at p cdlxxxviii.

[56] Cf Hartley, *The Foundations of European Union Law* (n 9) 205.

[57] *Van Gend en Loos* (n 51) at p 13.

[58] See Anthony Arnull, *The European Union and its Court of Justice* (Oxford: Oxford University Press, 1999) 77–86.

Nevertheless the Court's decision effectively created a system of dual vigilance in EU law. As stated by the ECJ: 'the vigilance of individuals concerned to protect their rights amounts to an effective supervision *in addition to* the supervision entrusted by Articles 169 and 170 [now Articles 258 and 259 of the TFEU] to the diligence of the Commission and the Member States.'[59] In other words, at the first, regional level of vigilance, member states and the Commission are capable of bringing claims for enforcement of Community law before the ECJ; at the second, national level of vigilance, individuals are empowered to bring claims for enforcement of Community law in national courts.

In hindsight, the concept of direct effect may be seen as a necessary corrective to ensure the uniformity of EU law. Without something akin to direct effect, EU law, being treaty-based, could have been rendered effective only in accordance with the constitutional rules of the national legal systems of its Member States. In those states which had monist legal systems, EU rules automatically would be made part of national law and thereby could be effective and enforceable. But in those dualist systems that required transformation of treaty obligations, the legal effect of a treaty provision would be entirely dependent upon whether the state in question had accurately transformed the obligation into its domestic law by statutory enactment. Such a two-tier system, with persons having different rights in monist and dualist states, would allow for serious variations in the levels of obligations accepted by different states. As noted by Anthony Arnull, such a lack of uniformity of obligation would cause difficulties for all international treaties, but simply would be incompatible with the nature of a common market:

> It is the very essence of a common market that the rules governing its operation should have the same meaning and effect wherever they fall to be applied: an economic regime such as that created by the EC Treaty could not function if an importer in Belgium, France, or the Netherlands could rely in the national courts on the Treaty prohibitions against quantitative restrictions on imports, but an importer in England could not.[60]

In order for EU law to be effective, it requires relatively uniform legal obligations. Differences between national legal systems regarding implementation and enforceability of treaties would frustrate that uniformity.

In addition, the ability of persons to enforce EU law in the *domestic* legal systems of member states through direct effect makes sense, both practically and legally. Individuals should be able to bring claims on their own behalf before national courts, rather than being required (in the pre-*Van gend en Loos* EEC context) to rely solely upon representation by regional organs and member states. After all, the goals of the two types of legal challenges are fundamentally different. A claim by an individual under EU law will be to protect individual rights in a specific case. A claim by a member state will be to protect its own interests. A claim by the Commission will be to ensure the general and uniform observance of EU law.[61]

[59] *Van Gend en Loos* (n 51) p 13 (emphasis added).

[60] Arnull, *The European Union and its Court of Justice* (n 58) 75–6.

[61] See eg the discussion of Case 28/67 *Molkerei-Zentrale Westfalen v Hauptzollamt Paderborn* [1968] ECR 143, in Arnull 88–9.

Moreover, an individual may wish to bring a claim at the national level rather than ask the Commission to espouse a complaint for several practical reasons. For example, the individual could be concerned that the Commission might decide not to espouse the claim, or even if it did so, might not pursue it vigorously. In addition, the particular form of compensation or other remedy sought by the individual might not be available before the ECJ. Further, an individual claimant may also wish to challenge other private actors, which is not possible before the ECJ under Article 258 TFEU proceedings. For such reasons direct effect has become a welcome addition to EU law.

In deciding that Article 12 of the EEC Treaty was directly effective the ECJ in the *Van Gend en Loos* case emphasized that it imposed a clear and unconditional prohibition which did not require positive enactment by member states.[62] The test for direct effectiveness has been formulated recently by Kaczorowska as requiring: (1) a clear and precise provision, (2) which is unconditional, meaning that there is no need for the adoption of further implementing measures, either at the national or the EU level, and (3) which is capable of creating rights for individuals.[63] The jurisprudence of the ECJ has adapted this test for different legislative mechanisms, including directives, and has recognized that direct effect can be both vertical (allowing an individual to challenge a state) and horizontal (allowing an individual to challenge another individual) in nature.[64] Treaty provisions, Regulations, directives, decisions, international agreements, and acts of institutions established by international agreements all have been held to be directly effective by the ECJ.[65] It should be noted, however, that not all treaty provisions will be directly effective. Those that are insufficiently precise, or that require implementing legislation or that allow discretion will not be directly effective.[66]

In sum, to contrast direct applicability and direct effectiveness, the former may be said to arise automatically as a consequence of the creation of a treaty regime which is considered to be an integral part of the national law of member states. Direct applicability requires that the rules of the treaty regime be fully and uniformly applied in all member states from the date of their entry into force and for so long as they continue to be in force (and, in monist states, without the need for transformation by legislative device), and is enforceable at the regional level. Direct

[62] *Van Gend en Loos* (n 51) p 13.

[63] Kaczorowska, *European Union Law* (n 26) 338. Note that some scholars, such as Hartley in *The Foundations of European Union Law* (n 9) at 210, leave out the third prong of the test, no doubt on the assumption that a provision must be capable of creating rights for individuals to be directly effective. For further clarification of the first two prongs, see eg Hartley 210–14.

[64] On the jurisprudence regarding vertical and horizontal direct effect, including the seminal decisions in Case 36/74 *Walrave v Union Cycliste Internationale* [1974] ECR 1405 and Case 43/75 *Defrenne v SABENA* [1976] ECR 455, see eg Arnull, *The European Union and its Court of Justice* (n 58) 89–91, and Hartley, *The Foundations of European Union Law* (n 9) 224–31.

[65] See eg Hartley ch 7. Hartley points out that the ECJ appears to have approved the idea of general principles of law being directly effective in Case C-144/04 *Mangold* [2005] ECR I-9981. But he refrains from offering a definitive opinion on this development as a result of the 'defective reasoning' in that case: at pp 239–40.

[66] eg Arnull, *The European Union and its Court of Justice* (n 58) 91–5.

effect in EU law, in contrast, is a judicially-created doctrine that allows treaty and other legal obligations to be *enforced* before domestic courts, as regional obligations, if they satisfy at minimum a test requiring clarity and precision, unconditionality, and the ability to create rights for individuals. Direct effect is the mechanism created by the ECJ to ensure the effectiveness and uniformity of EU obligations at the national level, and enlists the aid of national courts as enforcers of EU law. It creates a system of dual vigilance in which the vigilance of the individual at the national level complements the vigilance of the member states and organs of the EU at the regional level.

8.3.2 Meaning of direct effect in OECS law

The concept of direct effect has been expressly included in Article 5.3 of the RTB. However no definition of the term is found in the RTB, or any further elaboration of its meaning. Article 5.3 simply indicates that member states must enact legislation that will allow Acts, Regulations, and Orders of the organs of the OECS in the areas of competence set out in Article 14 to be directly effective. Due to its importance, a full quotation of Article 5.3 is necessary:

> 5.3 Without prejudice to the generality of the foregoing –
> (a) a full Member State which is independent undertakes to enact the legislation necessary to –
> (i) delegate to the Organisation the said Member State's authority to legislate in the areas of competence of the Organisation outlined in Article 14; or
> (ii) receive Acts of the Organisation made by the OECS Authority, and Regulations and Orders made by the Council of Ministers, from the Organisation in the areas of competence of the Organisation outlined in Article 14;
> with the intention that the Acts, Regulations and Orders have direct effect in the laws of the Member State;
> (b) a Member State which is not an independent State undertakes to enact legislation to provide for the reception into its law of the legislation made under this Article. The legislation –
> (i) shall enable reception of Acts of the Organisation made by the OECS Authority, and Regulations and Orders made by the Council of Ministers, from the Organisation without the need for enactment by the Member State's Legislature either generally or on a case by case basis;
> (ii) may make the reception of the Acts, Regulations and Orders subject to the discretion of a competent authority in the Member State.

Several things should be noted about this important provision. Firstly, direct effect is only to be accorded to Acts, Regulations and Orders authorized under the competences set out in Article 14 of the RTB. Article 14 allows the Organisation competence in such areas as the common market (including the customs union), monetary policy, trade policy, maritime jurisdiction and maritime boundaries, civil aviation, common commercial policy, environmental policy, and immigration policy. This list is not exhaustive, but any additional areas of competence are subject to the subsidiarity requirement imposed by Article 14.3.

Secondly, direct effect under the RTB itself first requires legislative implementation. It is not automatic. Both independent and non-independent member states must first enact legislation which allows for the reception of Acts, Regulations, and Orders into domestic law. Such a legislative requirement is not novel, and in fact is required by the dualist system shared by Commonwealth Caribbean states. The UK enacted such legislation when it joined the European Community. Section 2(1) of the European Communities Act 1972 provides:

> All such rights, powers, liabilities, obligations and restrictions from time to time created or arising by or under the Treaties, and all such remedies and procedures from time to time provided for by or under the Treaties, as in accordance with the Treaties are without further enactment to be given legal effect or used in the United Kingdom shall be recognised and available in law, and be enforced, allowed and followed accordingly; and the expression 'enforceable EU right' and similar expressions shall be read as referring to one to which this subsection applies.[67]

Thirdly, the level of reception required by Article 5.3 of the RTB differs between the two categories of OECS Membership. For *independent* full member states, this legislation is to 'have direct effect in the laws of the Member State'. For *non-independent* member states, in contrast, the legislation must simply provide for the reception of OECS laws 'without the need for enactment by the Member State's Legislature either generally or on a case by case basis', but with such reception being subject to the 'discretion of a competent authority'. Given the latter element of discretion, it would appear that non-independent member states are not subject to the full requirement for direct effect.

Fourthly, there is no express indication that Article 5.3 enables directly effective OECS laws to be *enforced* in national courts. This should be the case if the OECS follows the EU model, as discussed earlier, since the distinguishing feature of direct effect is enforceability before national courts. Such an interpretation is also supported by the lack of other effective enforcement options in the OECS. Persons, for example, are unable to access the OECS dispute settlement mechanisms established under Article 18 of the RTB, since Article 18.5 limits the 'eligible parties for the purpose of Article 18.1' to 'full Member States, the Associate Member States and the Organisation'. For such reasons enforceability may naturally arise through the interpretation of the domestic legislation required under Article 5.3. The purpose of this legislation, after all, is to allow for the reception of Acts, Regulations, and Orders into domestic law, thereby making them *part of domestic law*. As part of domestic law, any binding legal obligations or rights arising under OECS laws should be enforceable before domestic courts.

This gives rise to a final issue, namely, the question of the precise nature of the legal obligation created by the RTB and the related domestic legislation enabling the reception of OECS law. Since Article 5.3 expressly requires national legislation to make Acts, Regulations, and Orders directly effective, one might assume that

[67] European Communities Act 1972, c 68, as amended by the European Union (Amendment) Act 2008 (c 7), ss 3, 8, Sch Pt 1; SI 2009/3143, s 2.

such legislation would *transform* the OECS obligation into domestic law. If so, the OECS obligation would be enforceable in domestic law *as domestic law*. The regional obligation would thereby be fundamentally changed through the transformation process: from being an act of a regional organization (international legal act), to being an act of Parliament or the legislature (domestic legal act).

A number of consequences would flow from the re-characterization of the OECS obligation as being one of domestic law, some of which would be problematic. If an OECS Act literally were to become part of domestic law, for example, then *as such* it would be capable of being superseded by subsequent domestic legislation. Also, as part of domestic law, the meaning of the Act presumably would become subject to the restrictive rules of statutory interpretation, rather than the more liberal rules of treaty interpretation. Similarly, its enforcement would depend entirely upon national law, including the remedial procedures available in different legal systems. This could give rise to the potential for differences between the remedies available for the same OECS Act in different national legal systems. Such differences would impair the uniformity of the application of the OECS legal obligation.

For these reasons it would be preferable not to view the OECS obligation as literally becoming part of domestic law. Rather, the regional obligation should be conceptualized as permanently retaining its regional legal (Union) character, even subsequent to its transformation. For clarity, such a viewpoint should be reflected in the transformation legislation required by Article 5.3 of the RTB. But in the absence of legislative clarity, the nature of the OECS obligation equally could be established by the jurisprudence of the Eastern Caribbean Court of Appeal.

In the EU the approach of viewing EU acts as continuing to retain their EU character has gained some traction. In Case 34/73 *Variola v Amministrazione delle Finanze*, for example, the ECJ held that one type of EU legislation, Regulations, must be directly applicable in the laws of the member states, meaning that they must have immediate effect and cannot depend upon legislative enactment by member states.[68] Member states are under a duty not to obstruct the direct applicability of Regulations, including by enacting domestic legislative provisions which potentially conceal the EU nature of the legal rule.[69] Such provisions would compromise the essential character of the Regulations as Union rules per se and also challenge the supremacy of EU law. As summarized by the ECJ in paragraph 15 of its judgment:

> A legislative provision of internal law could not be set up against the direct effect, in the legal order of Member States, of Regulations of the Community and other provisions of Community law, [...] without compromising the essential character of Community rules as such and the fundamental principle that the Community legal system is supreme.[70]

[68] [1973] ECR 981.

[69] *Variola v Amministrazione delle Finanze* (n 68) at p 991 [11].

[70] *Variola v Amministrazione delle Finanze* (n 68) p 992. At p 994 (operative para 4), the Court holds: '4. A legislative measure under national law which reproduces the text of a directly applicable rule of Community law cannot in any way affect such direct applicability, or the Court's jurisdiction under the Treaty.'

Although there is no parallel to the EU's regulation in OECS Economic Union law, the principle that transformation should not challenge the essential Union nature of the OECS obligation should be equally applicable. This principle is recognized in other areas of EU law, such as in the area of remedies. Although the ECJ in its early jurisprudence recognized the suitability of national procedures for remedying directly effective EU rights, it held that such procedures are governed by EU requirements, including the principles of equivalence (equivalent to the procedure applicable to a similar domestic right) and effectiveness.[71] The Court also made clear that national legislation and procedures could not displace the EU right, which continued to exist even after transformation. In Case C-62/00 *Marks and Spencer plc v Commissioners of Customs and Excise*, for example, the Court held that the legal force of a directly effective directive was not spent following transformation, but continued:

> [T]he adoption of national measures correctly implementing a directive does not exhaust the effects of the directive. Member States remain bound actually to ensure full application of the directive even after the adoption of those measures. Individuals are therefore entitled to rely before national courts, against the State, on the provisions of a directive which appear, so far as their subject-matter is concerned, to be unconditional and sufficiently precise whenever the full application of the directive is not in fact secured, that is to say, not only where the directive has not been implemented or has been implemented incorrectly, but also where the national measures correctly implementing the directive are not being applied in such a way as to achieve the result sought by it.[72]

In other words, the obligation imposed by the EU legal act, the directive, remains in full force even after transformation.

In sum, although the meaning and effect of Article 5.3 of the RTB has not been subject to judicial scrutiny or elaborated by state practice, the most meaningful interpretation of the provision would be one in which the direct effect of OECS Acts, Regulations, and Orders is enforceable by persons before national courts and retains its OECS character following transformation.

8.3.3 Direct effect in CARICOM law

Direct effect is expressly incorporated into OECS law by Article 5.3 of the RTB. In contrast, there is no mention of the concept in CARICOM's RTC. Moreover, there are several features of the RTC which would suggest that direct effect is neither necessary, nor possible under the RTC. In contrast to the EU, for example, a kind of dual vigilance already exists under the RTC, which allows for direct challenges to be brought to the CCJ by persons.[73] It therefore could be argued that there is no

[71] See eg Case 45/76 *Comet BV v Produktschap voor Siergewassen* (preliminary ruling requested by the College van Beroep voor het Bedrijfsleven) [1976] ECR 2043.

[72] [2002] ECR I-06325, pp 6358–9 [27].

[73] RTC Arts 211(1)(d) and 222 allow persons to bring claims directly to the CCJ. These provisions have already been used extensively. In fact, all of the original jurisdiction judgments and orders made by the CCJ to date have been under Art 222 cases.

need for direct effect under CARICOM's regime. Moreover, CARICOM does not have a legislative mechanism similar to the EU's regulation and so there is no parallel in CARICOM of a Community-based legal act which is automatically part of the domestic law of member states. It may also be argued that other obstacles, such as Article 240 of the RTC, would greatly hinder, if not prohibit outright, the development of the principle of direct effect.[74]

However several, if not all, of the juridical building blocks which were relied upon by the ECJ in its jurisprudence to create and substantiate direct effect also exist in CARICOM and are worth highlighting. The objectives of the RTC, for example, emphasize the fact that Caribbean integration is for the benefit of the peoples of the region.[75] The RTC creates rights and obligations for persons in addition to states, under the CCJ's correlative rights doctrine.[76] Similarly, the referral procedure established in Article 214 of the RTC necessarily implies some ability of the RTC to produce legal effects in domestic law. The referral procedure, as discussed later, allows a national tribunal which is 'seised of an issue whose resolution involves a question concerning the interpretation or application of this Treaty', and regarding which a decision is 'necessary to enable it to deliver judgment', to refer the issue to the CCJ for its determination.[77] By its very nature this referral procedure assumes that, and only makes sense if, treaty-related issues can have effects at the national level. In addition, CARICOM shares the need for effectiveness and uniformity of Community law, one of the fundamental motivations for the development of the doctrine of direct effect in the EU.

Further, there are two limitations to the CCJ's jurisdiction over applications by persons which support the introduction of direct effect in CARICOM. Firstly, under Article 222 a person, whether natural or juridical, must satisfy a four-part cumulative test in order to meet the Court's jurisdictional requirements, one portion of which requires a finding 'that the interest of justice requires that the persons be allowed to espouse the claim'.[78] This Article 222 test, although generously interpreted by the CCJ in its early original jurisdiction cases, is more restrictive than the requirements for direct effect—that the provision be clear and precise, unconditional, and capable of creating rights for individuals.

Secondly, the jurisdiction of the CCJ over applications by persons is necessarily limited by the very nature and institutional structure of the Court. There are significant differences in capacity between a system of direct effect, which allows individuals to enforce regional rights in their various national legal systems, and a system of individual applications before a single regional court. If direct effect obtained in the territories of CARICOM, individual claims could be decided by the national courts of at least the thirteen parties to the RTC.[79] But if only one

[74] See the discussion of RTC Art 240 in Chapters 5 and 6.

[75] See the Preamble and Art 6 of the RTC.

[76] See the earlier discussion of the case of *Trinidad Cement Ltd and TCL Guyana Inc v Guyana* [2009] CCJ 1 (OJ), (2009) 74 WIR 302, 15 January 2009.

[77] RTC Art 214. See also the discussion of the referral procedure in Chapter 14.

[78] RTC Art 222(d). See further the discussion of Art 222 in Chapter 14.

[79] It is uncertain whether the non-parties to the RTC—The Bahamas and Montserrat—would wish to adopt direct effect.

court, the CCJ, is entrusted with the responsibility to adjudicate all individual claims arising under the RTC, it will either need to implement severe jurisdictional restrictions or expand the number of persons sitting on the Court. Although the CCJ has yet to face a deluge of individual applications, if its jurisprudence continues to yield decisions attractive to persons and companies throughout the region it may reasonably be predicted that its caseload will increase. In fact it may increase substantially. To offer a comparison from the EU system, the caseload of the ECJ is staggering, even though it does not decide the individual claims which are resolved by the application of the doctrine of direct effect. In 2011, for example, over 1,400 new cases were opened before the Court of Justice and General Court, with nearly another 2,100 cases pending.[80] Given such statistics, one may wonder how the seven judges presently sitting on the CCJ could decide all such RTC individual applications, in addition to their appellate caseload. For such reasons the CCJ may be forced to consider implementing some kind of national level judicial enforcement mechanism, like the doctrine of direct effect, simply to help deal with an ever-increasing caseload.

Direct effect also has significant benefits which support its adoption. It would allow CARICOM and the CCJ to rely upon national courts to help ensure the effectiveness and uniformity of Community law. Such uniformity is very difficult to achieve if matters are left entirely to the national legal systems of member states without the kind of coordination potentially provided by a concept like direct effect. Legislative transformation of treaty obligations always has the potential to create different obligations in each national system. This would be so even if the statutes incorporating the RTC were all identically worded, since different words may have different meanings in individual national legal systems. In addition, the processes and procedures by which national laws are enforced may also differ substantially between member states. To give an example, even if two states protect exactly the same right—say a right not to have duties imposed upon a CARICOM origin good—their legal systems may generate different results if a case is brought before their domestic courts to protect that right: one state may empower national courts to void inconsistent law, another state may require them to disapply it, a third may require the national court to enforce the national law even if doing so breaches the treaty obligation. There also may be differences in national laws between the levels of compensation that may be provided in such cases, including caps or other limitations.[81]

[80] Statistics for 2011 for the Court of Justice and General Court of the EU reveal that, in the case of the Court of Justice, 688 new cases were brought, 638 cases were completed, and 849 cases were pending, and in the case of the General Court, 722 new cases were brought, 714 cases were completed, and 1,308 cases were pending: Court of Justice of the European Union, *Annual Report 2011: Synopsis of the work of the Court of Justice, the General Court and the Civil Service Tribunal* (Luxembourg: Court of Justice, 2012), as available through <http://curia.europa.eu/jcms/jcms/Jo2_7000/> (accessed 17 Feb 2013) at 95 and 193, respectively.

[81] The ECJ has struggled with how to strike the balance between respecting *national* priorities in relation to legal remedies, on the one hand, with the *regional* need for uniformity of EU obligations on the other. For a review of the ECJ cases regarding remedies in national courts see eg Craig and de Búrca, *EU Law, Text, Cases and Materials* (n 50) ch 8.

Finally, the fundamental premise underpinning the decision in *Van Gend en Loos* was the idea that European states had created a new legal order, under which they had limited their sovereign rights, and which included both states and individuals as subjects, and which conferred upon them obligations and rights. These developments are already recognized as having occurred in the context of the Caribbean Community, in the first original jurisdiction decisions of the Caribbean Court of Justice. In its special leave decision in the case of *Trinidad Cement Limited and TCL Guyana Inc v Guyana*, the CCJ examined the context, object, and purpose of the RTC and held that CARICOM was created to ensure the sustainable economic and social development of its peoples and that the CSME, the appropriate framework for this end, was 'intended to be private sector driven'.[82] The Court also expressly recognized that the RTC provides rights to private entities:

> Given the important role envisaged for private economic entities in achieving the objectives of the CSME, the Contracting Parties clearly intended that such entities should be important actors in the regime created by the *RTC*; that they should have conferred upon them and be entitled to enjoy rights capable of being enforced directly on the international plane.[83]

As noted earlier, the Court further established that these individual rights may be derived, as correlative rights, from the obligations imposed upon states by the RTC.[84] In addition, in the case of *Trinidad Cement Limited v CARICOM*, the CCJ indicated clearly that the member states had created a new regime with the RTC, one established under the rule of law and one which creates legal accountability:

> By signing and ratifying the Revised Treaty and thereby conferring on this Court *ipso facto* a compulsory and exclusive jurisdiction to hear and determine disputes concerning the interpretation and application of the Revised Treaty, the Member States transformed the erstwhile voluntary arrangements in CARICOM into a rule-based system, thus creating and accepting a regional system under the rule of law. A challenge by a private party to decisions of the Community is therefore not only not precluded, but is a manifestation of such a system. Therefore it is not correct to say that by such challenge the functioning of the Community will be greatly hindered or that the exercise of state sovereignty by Member States parties to the Revised Treaty would be unduly constrained. The rule of law brings with it legal certainty and protection of rights of states and individuals alike, but at the same time of necessity it creates legal accountability. Even if such accountability imposes some constraint upon the exercise of sovereign rights of states, the very acceptance of such a constraint in a treaty is in itself an act of sovereignty.[85]

As a result of all of these developments, it would be fair to say that most, if not all, of the building blocks for the doctrine of direct effect already have been assembled in Caribbean Community law.

[82] *Trinidad Cement Ltd and TCL Guyana Inc v Guyana*, Judgment [2009] CCJ 1 (OJ) (2009) 74 WIR 302, 15 January 2009 [*TCL & TCI v Guyana* (Special Leave)], at [13].

[83] *Trinidad Cement Ltd v Guyana* (n 82) [18].

[84] *Trinidad Cement Ltd v Guyana* (n 82) [32].

[85] *Trinidad Cement Ltd v Caribbean Community*, Judgment [2009] CCJ 2 (OJ) (2009) 74 WIR 319, 5 February 2009 [*TCL v CARICOM* (Special Leave)], at [32].

Whether the CCJ proceeds in this direction will depend upon its view of the necessity of direct effect for the successful operation of CARICOM law. As in the case of *Van Gend en Loos*, it is likely that the Court will wait until the question is raised in the context of its referral jurisdiction, since any question referred by a domestic tribunal to the Court will require the Court to pronounce on the legal meaning of the RTC, and its effect, in domestic law.

8.4 Indirect Effect

A related general principle that has developed in EU law is that of indirect effect, sometimes called the principle of 'conform interpretation'. Under this principle the ECJ has held that national courts must interpret national law so as to conform to EU obligations. More specifically, indirect effect requires the national courts of the member state to interpret local law so as not to violate EU law (where the obligation exists for the member state at the EU level), even in cases where the obligation is not directly applicable (regulation) or directly effective. In EU law indirect effect is limited by general principles of the EU,[86] but it applies to all legislation, enacted before or after the EU obligation.[87]

The ECJ developed the doctrine of indirect effect in the case of *Von Colson and Kamann v Land Nordrhein-Westfalen*.[88] In this case the two female plaintiffs were refused employment in an all-male prison for reasons related to their sex. Yet under German law, which purported to implement the EU's Equal Treatment Directive 76/207, they were limited to nominal damages for discrimination. In coming to the conclusion that national compensation must be effective, the Court held that by accepting a duty under Article 5 of the TEC (now Article 4(3) of the TEU) to

[86] See eg Case 80/86 *Officier van Justitie v Kolpinghuis Nijmegan* [1987] ECR 3969. At p 3986 [13] of this case the ECJ held that the 'obligation on the national court to refer to the content of the directive when interpreting the relevant rules of its national law [the principle of indirect effect] is limited by the general principles of law which form part of Community law and in particular the principles of legal certainty and non-retroactivity.'

[87] See eg Case C-91/92 *Paola Faccini Dor v Recreb Srl* [1994] ECR I-3325, in which the ECJ held at p I-3357 [26]:

> It must also be borne in mind that, as the Court has consistently held since its judgment in Case 14/83 *Von Colson and Kamann v Land Nordrhein-Westfalen* [1984] ECR 1891, paragraph 26, the Member States' obligation arising from a directive to achieve the result envisaged by the directive and their duty under Article 5 [now Article 4(3) of the TEU] of the Treaty to take all appropriate measures, whether general or particular, is binding on all the authorities of Member States, including, for matters within their jurisdiction, the courts. The judgments of the Court in Case C-106/89 *Marleasing v La Comercial Internacional de Alimentación* [1990] ECR 1-4135, paragraph 8, and Case C-334/92 *Wagner Miret v Fondo de Garantía Salarial* [1993] ECR 1-6911, paragraph 20, make it clear that, when applying national law, *whether adopted before or after the directive*, the national court that has to interpret that law must do so, as far as possible, in the light of the wording and the purpose of the directive so as to achieve the result it has in view and thereby comply with the third paragraph of Article 189 [now Article 288 TFEU] of the Treaty (emphasis added).

[88] Case 14/83 *Von Colson and Kamann v Land Nordrhein-Westfalen* [1984] ECR 1891.

take all appropriate measures whether general or particular to ensure the fulfilment of Community obligations, the state had created a binding obligation for itself and its organs, including its national courts.[89] The ECJ held that:

the Member States' obligation arising from a directive to achieve the result envisaged by the directive and their duty under Article 5 [now Article 4(3) *TEU*] of the Treaty to take all appropriate measures, whether general or particular, to ensure the fulfilment of that obligation, is binding on all the authorities of Member States including, for matters within their jurisdiction, the courts. It follows that, in applying the national law and in particular the provisions of a national law specifically introduced in order to implement Directive No 76/207, national courts are required to interpret their national law in the light of the wording and the purpose of the directive in order to achieve the result referred to in the third paragraph of Article 189 [now Article 288 TFEU].[90]

In other words, the binding obligation in the treaty extended to national courts, and required them to interpret national legislation in order to achieve the result required by directives under EU law. This is a very strong statement about the interpretive obligations of member state courts with respect to EU directives. However the Court dilutes its decision somewhat by re-phrasing the obligation in paragraph 28 as being 'for the national court to interpret and apply the legislation adopted for the implementation of the directive in conformity with the requirements of Community law, *in so far as it is given discretion to do so under national law*'.[91] This latter limitation brings the obligation of conform interpretation into closer alignment with the interpretive position potentially available to courts in the Commonwealth Caribbean.

The justification for imposing such a duty upon national courts has been explained by the ECJ as being due to the fact that directives impose obligations upon the entire member state, including its judicial organs. This would be easy to understand if the local court was examining domestic legislation that was meant to implement a directive, as in the *Von Colson* case. But the ECJ has not limited the scope of indirect effect to such cases. The Court held in the later Joined Cases of C-397/01 to C-403/01 *Bernhard Pfeiffer v Deutsches Rotes Kreuz* that domestic courts have a duty to interpret 'national law as a whole' in order to ensure

[89] Article 4(3) of the TEU provides:

3. ...The Member States shall take any appropriate measure, general or particular, to ensure fulfilment of the obligations arising out of the Treaties or resulting from the acts of the institutions of the Union.The Member States shall facilitate the achievement of the Union's tasks and refrain from any measure which could jeopardise the attainment of the Union's objectives.

[90] Case 14/83 *Von Colson and Kamann v Land Nordrhein-Westfalen* [1984] ECR 1891, at p 1909 [26]. In subsequent cases, however, the ECJ has made clear that national courts neither have the duty to interpret the law *contra legem*, nor beyond the range of legitimate interpretation, nor to interpret it in such a way as to ignore the general principles of EU law, in particular the principles of legal certainty and non-retroactivity in criminal matters. See, respectively, Case C-105/03 *Pupino* [2005] ECR I-5285, at pp I-5323 [24], I-5328 [44], and I-5329 [47]; Case C-334/92 *Wagner Miret v Fondo de Garantía Salarial* [1993] ECR I-6911, at p I-6932 [22]; and Case C-80/86 *Kolpinghuis Nijmegen* [1987] ECR 3969, at p 3986 [13].

[91] *Von Colson and Kamann* (n 90) at p 1909 [28] (emphasis added).

conformity with EU law.[92] Moreover, in the same decision the Court held that the doctrine of direct effect 'is inherent in the system of the Treaty'.[93] The latter statement entrenches the doctrine of indirect effect at a deeper level in EU law, and also potentially allows its application to be extended to all forms of EU law.[94]

In monist legal systems the principle of conform interpretation may not cause significant challenges, since in such systems international obligations may be considered as being either superior to, or part of, national law. But in a dualist system of law, such as obtains in most CARICOM member states, such a principle poses challenges. For common law states the international legal obligations derived from treaties must be expressly incorporated into domestic law before they can have any binding force or effect.[95] Treaties and the jurisprudence of international courts and tribunals may legitimately be referred to by national judges as examples of applications of principles or rules of law. But common law judges cannot ascribe any binding power or force to such international materials. In fact, the only generally accepted exception that would allow an international treaty to have force in national law arises when a national court is permitted to use an unincorporated treaty to interpret ambiguous domestic law.[96] This is a rare and limited situation, however. The doctrine of indirect effect has no such interpretive limitation. It therefore would not fit squarely under this branch of common law jurisprudence.

National courts, including the CCJ in its appellate jurisdiction, might nevertheless decide to adopt the principle of indirect effect as part of their general interpretive powers. The Court came close to doing so in its judgment in the case of *Shanique Myrie v Barbados*, when it held that 'that the domestic courts of Barbados, including this Court in its appellate jurisdiction, are constrained to interpret domestic laws so as, if possible, to render them consistent with international treaties such as the RTC'.[97] The key phrase in this passage, however, is 'if possible', the meaning of which the Court does not explain in its decision. If the phrase refers to the restrictions imposed upon domestic courts by the common law

[92] Joined Cases C-397/01 to C-403/01 *Bernhard Pfeiffer v Deutsches Rotes Kreuz* [2004] ECR I-8835, at p I-8918 [15].

[93] *Bernhard Pfeiffer v Deutsches Rotes* Kreuz (n 92) at p I-8918 [114].

[94] Stephen Weatherill, for example, in *Cases and Materials on EU Law* (n 20) at 151, notes that indirect effect has been applied to Regulations and other sources of EU law, such as Framework Decisions (citing: Case C-60/02 *Rolex* [2004] ECR I-651 and Case C-105/03 *Criminal proceedings against Maria Pupino* [2005] ECR I-5285).

[95] See eg *R v Lyons* [2003] 1 AC 976 (HL); *Higgs v Minister of National Security and Others* [2000] 2 AC 228 (PC Bah); *JH Rayner (Mincing Lane) Ltd v Department of Trade and Industry* (also called *Maclaine Watson & Co Ltd v International Tin Council*) [1990] 2 AC 418 (HL); *R v Secretary of State for the Home Department, ex parte Brind* [1991] 1 AC 696 (HL); *Salomon v Commissioners of Customs and Excise* [1967] 2 QB 116 (CA Eng).

[96] See eg *Salomon* (n 95) pp 143–4 (Lord Diplock) and *Brind* (n 95) pp 747–8 (Lord Bridge). Note that the ambiguity rule applies to statutes enacted prior or subsequent to the assumption of the treaty obligation: *Boyce v R* [2004] UKPC 32, [2005] 1 AC 400 (BDS), p 416 [26].

[97] Judgment [2013] CCJ 3 (OJ) [80]. The CCJ, at [81], further indicates in relation to the potentially inconsistent Barbadian legislation cited in the case, that '[t]he Court expects that so far as these provisions apply to Community nationals, the Barbados domestic courts will, where possible, apply them liberally so as to harmonise them with Community law' (citations omitted).

rules regarding unincorporated treaties highlighted earlier, then the CCJ's decision appears to simply re-state the traditional position.

If the CCJ decides to consider further the principle of indirect effect, whether under its appellate or original jurisdiction, it will need to balance its understanding of its exclusive authority to apply the RTC, on the one hand, with the utility of enlisting the assistance of national courts in ensuring uniform implementation Caribbean Community obligations, on the other.

8.5 Supremacy

The principle of supremacy, in its most limited form, could be taken to refer to the idea that the rules of a regional organization are supreme in that organization's own sphere.[98] In other words, regional legal acts cannot be challenged with domestic law before regional organs or tribunals. Such a concept merely re-states the fundamental rule of international law of *pacta sunt servanda*, literally translated as 'treaties must be observed'.[99] *Pacta sunt servanda* expresses the idea that agreements are binding and must be implemented in good faith. It, and one of its consequences, are codified in Articles 26 and 27 of the Vienna Convention on the Law of Treaties, which state: '[e]very treaty in force is binding upon the parties to it and must be performed by them in good faith' and '[a] party may not invoke the provisions of its internal law as justification for its failure to perform a treaty', respectively.[100]

But the principle of supremacy also has deeper, more far-reaching meaning in EU law, namely, that potentially all EU law, whether directly effective or not must prevail over the domestic law of member states.[101] As summarized by Hartley, the rule of supremacy 'which is not found in any of the Treaties but has been proclaimed with great emphasis by the Court, applies irrespective of the nature of the Union provision (constitutive Treaty, Union act, or agreement with a non-member State) or that of the national provision (constitution, statute, or subordinate legislation); it also applies irrespective of whether the Union provision came before, or after, the national provision: in all cases the national provision

[98] Note that some authors refer to supremacy as a 'rule': see eg Hartley, *The Foundations of European Union Law* (n 9) 243. Other authors refer to it as a 'principle': see eg the opinion of the Council Legal Service, 'Primacy of EC Law', 22 June 2007, 11197/07 (JUR 260). The latter term will be used here since, given the lack of express textual support for supremacy in either of the treaties of CARICOM or the OECS, its introduction would most likely come in the form of a general principle of law.

[99] See eg Michel Virally, 'The Sources of International Law' in Max Sørenson (ed), *Manual of Public International Law* (London: Macmillan, 1968) 116–74 at 127.

[100] Vienna Convention on the Law of Treaties (adopted 23 May 1969, in force 27 Jan 1980) 1155 UNTS 331. See also the decision of the International Court of Justice in the *PLO Observer Mission Case* (Advisory Opinion) [1988] ICJ Rep 12, at pp 34–5.

[101] See generally Craig and de Búrca, *EU Law: Text, Cases and Materials* (n 50) ch 9; Weatherill, *Cases and Materials on EU Law* (n 20) ch 3. Note that Craig and de Búrca, in p 260, suggest that supremacy could exist even in relation to EU norms that are not directly effective. Takis Tridimas, in *The General Principles of EU Law* (n 50) at 3, identifies the principle of primacy as a general principle of EU law.

must give way to Union law.'[102] As a consequence the principle of supremacy removes, for example, the ability of states to pass new legislation contradicting EU rules. It can also create an obligation to repeal existing legislation, even if not applied.[103] Moreover, supremacy applies to all domestic laws, including the constitution.[104] The principle of supremacy requires national courts and tribunals to disapply conflicting national law; it does not require them to invalidate or render non-existent the national legal provision.[105] Although there is no provision in the EU treaties expressly stating the principle, the direct applicability of Regulations under Article 288 of the TFEU has been argued by Hartley to assume a 'certain degree of supremacy'.[106]

One of the earliest applications of the principle by the ECJ arose in Case 6/64 *Costa v* ENEL.[107] This case concerned a request for a preliminary ruling arising out of litigation concerning Italian legislation which nationalized the production and distribution of electricity and created a new National Electricity Board (Ente Nazionale Energia Elettrica, or ENEL). The Italian Government challenged the ability of the matter to be heard by the ECJ under the preliminary reference procedure on a variety of grounds, including that the Italian court was bound to apply national law and therefore did not have the competence to ask for a preliminary ruling under what is now Article 267 of the TFEU. In response the ECJ outlined the nature of the legal system established by the EU treaties and grounded the concept of supremacy in several of their provisions. Because the applicability of

[102] Hartley, *The Foundations of European Union Law* (n 9) 243 (citing the opinion of Advocate General Reischl in Case 106/77 *Simmenthal* [1978] ECR 629, at pp 651–2, for a succinct survey of the relevant case-law).

[103] See eg Hartley, *The Foundations of European Union Law* 244–5.

[104] In Case 11/70 *Internationale Handelsgesellschaft mbH v Einfuhr- und Vorratsstelle für Getreide und Futtermittel* [1970] ECR 1125, at p 1134 [3], the ECJ held:

> 3 Recourse to the legal rules or concepts of national law in order to judge the validity of measures adopted by the institutions of the Community would have an adverse effect on the uniformity and efficacy of Community law. The validity of such measures can only be judged in the light of Community law. In fact, the law stemming from the Treaty, an independent source of law, cannot because of its very nature be overridden by rules of national law, however framed, without being deprived of its character as Community law and without the legal basis of the Community itself being called in question. *Therefore the validity of a Community measure or its effect within a Member State cannot be affected by allegations that it runs counter to either fundamental rights as formulated by the constitution of that State or the principles of a national constitutional structure* (emphasis added).

[105] For example, in Cases C-10-22/97 *Ministero delle Finanze v IN.CO.GE.'90 Srl* [1998] ECR I-6307, the ECJ held:

> 21 It cannot therefore, contrary to the Commission's contention, be inferred from the judgment in *Simmenthal* that the incompatibility with Community law of a subsequently adopted rule of national law has the effect of rendering that rule of national law non-existent. Faced with such a situation, the national court is, however, obliged to disapply that rule, provided always that this obligation does not restrict the power of the competent national courts to apply, from among the various procedures available under national law, those which are appropriate for protecting the individual rights conferred by Community law (see Case 34/67 *Lück v Hauptzollamt Köln-Rheinau* [1968] ECR 245).

[106] Hartley, *The Foundations of European Union Law* (n 9) 206–7.

[107] [1964] ECR 585.

the concept of supremacy in CARICOM and OECS law is likely to be contested, it is useful to quote a longer passage from the judgment in *Costa v ENEL*, in which the Court responded to the challenge of the Italian Government. The ECJ held:

> By contrast with ordinary international treaties, the EEC Treaty has created its own legal system which, on the entry into force of the Treaty, became an integral part of the legal systems of the Member States and which their courts are bound to apply.
>
> By creating a Community of unlimited duration, having its own institutions, its own personality, its own legal capacity and capacity of representation on the international plane and, more particularly, real powers stemming from a limitation of sovereignty or a transfer of powers from the States to the Community, the Member States have limited their sovereign rights, albeit within limited fields, and have thus created a body of law which binds both their nationals and themselves.
>
> The integration into the laws of each Member State of provisions which derive from the Community, and more generally the terms and the spirit of the Treaty, make it impossible for the States, as a corollary, to accord precedence to a unilateral and subsequent measure over a legal system accepted by them on a basis of reciprocity. Such a measure cannot therefore be inconsistent with that legal system. The executive force of Community law cannot vary from one State to another in deference to subsequent domestic laws, without jeopardizing the attainment of the objectives of the Treaty set out in Article 5(2) [Article 4(3) TEU] and giving rise to the discrimination prohibited by Article 7 [Article 18 TFEU].
>
> The obligations undertaken under the Treaty establishing the Community would not be unconditional, but merely contingent, if they could be called in question by subsequent legislative acts of the signatories. [. . .]
>
> The precedence of Community law is confirmed by Article 189 [Article 288 TFEU], whereby a regulation 'shall be binding' and 'directly applicable in all Member States'. This provision, which is subject to no reservation, would be quite meaningless if a State could unilaterally nullify its effects by means of a legislative measure which could prevail over Community law.
>
> It follows from all these observations that the law stemming from the Treaty, an independent source of law, could not, because of its special and original nature, be overridden by domestic legal provisions, however framed, without being deprived of its character as Community law and without the legal basis of the Community itself being called into question.
>
> The transfer by the States from their domestic legal system to the Community legal system of the rights and obligations arising under the Treaty carries with it a permanent limitation of their sovereign rights, against which a subsequent unilateral act incompatible with the concept of the Community cannot prevail. Consequently Article 177 [Article 267 TFEU] is to be applied regardless of any domestic law, whenever questions relating to the interpretation of the Treaty arise.[108]

In this passage the Court founds the concept of supremacy ('the precedence of Community law') on a number of bases, including the distinct nature of the EU legal system (which includes directly applicable obligations); the requirements of effectiveness, uniformity, and non-discrimination; and the binding obligations assumed by member states (the general undertaking). It should be noted that all of

[108] *Costa v ENEL* (n 107) 593–4.

these bases, with the exception of a textually-supported form of direct applicability, exist in CARICOM at present.

The ECJ reinforced the rule of supremacy and spelled out some of its implications in a subsequent decision, Case 106/77 *Amministrazione delle Finanze v Simmenthal.*[109] This case involved a challenge by Simmenthal S.p.A. to Italian veterinary and public health inspections of beef imported from France, and their associated fees, as being obstacles to the free movement of goods. Following the ruling of the ECJ in its first hearing of the case, the Italian magistrate (*Pretore*) held that the fees were incompatible with the provisions of EU law and ordered the Italian Finance Administration to repay the fees unlawfully charged, together with interest.[110] The Italian Finance Administration appealed, challenging the *Pretore's* decision on the basis that under Italian law the question of whether a law is unconstitutional can only be decided by the Constitutional Court. The *Pretore*, faced with two incompatible obligations, requested a second preliminary ruling from the ECJ. The Court held that the supremacy of EU law had the consequence of rendering inapplicable both prior and subsequent inconsistent national law:

> [I]n accordance with the principle of the precedence of Community law, the relationship between provisions of the Treaty and directly applicable measures of the institutions on the one hand and the national law of the Member States on the other is such that those provisions and measures not only by their entry into force render automatically inapplicable any conflicting provision of current national law but—in so far as they are an integral part of, and take precedence in, the legal order applicable in the territory of each of the Member States—also preclude the valid adoption of new national legislative measures to the extent to which they would be incompatible with Community provisions.[111]

In the view of the Court, any recognition of the legal effect of incompatible national legislative measures 'would amount to a corresponding denial of the effectiveness of obligations undertaken unconditionally and irrevocably by Member States pursuant to the Treaty and would thus imperil the very foundations of the Community'.[112] In supporting this position the Court referred to the preliminary reference procedure itself, commenting that 'the effectiveness of [what is now Article 267 TFEU] would be impaired if the national court were prevented from forthwith applying Community law in accordance with the decision or the case-law of the Court.'[113] As a result the ECJ held that each national court was required to give full effect to EU law, if necessary by refusing to apply the national law, without waiting for the legislature or other body to set it aside ('by legislative or other constitutional means').[114] In this way the *Simmenthal* case adds another juridical basis for the principle of supremacy—the preliminary reference procedure—as well as clearly sets out its consequences, namely, the immediate non-applicability of national law by the Court deciding the matter. Again, it should be noted that

[109] [1978] ECR 629, at [17]–[18].

[110] *Simmenthal* (n 109) 631 and 641 [3]. The previous decision of the ECJ was in Case 35/76 *Simmenthal SpA v Italian Minister of Finance* [1976] ECR 1871.

[111] [1978] ECR 629, at p 643 [17].

[112] *Simmenthal* (n 109) 643 [18].

[113] *Simmenthal* (n 109) 644 [20].

[114] *Simmenthal* (n 109) 644 [24].

CARICOM's RTC includes a procedure nearly identical to the ECJ's preliminary reference procedure: the CCJ's referral jurisdiction.[115]

Whether the courts of CARICOM member states, including the CCJ, will adopt the concept of supremacy in its most far-reaching form remains to be seen. In the case of *Shanique Myrie v Barbados* the Court raised, but then deftly avoided answering, the question when it stated:

> Implementation of the very idea and concept of a Community of States necessarily entails as an exercise of sovereignty the creation of a new legal order and certain self-imposed, albeit perhaps relatively modest, limits to particular areas of State sovereignty. Community law and the limits it imposes on the Member States must take precedence over national legislation, in any event at the Community level.[116]

Although leaving the door open ('in any event'), the Court appears to adopt the more traditional form of supremacy, namely, supremacy at the *Community*, not national, level. This position may change. As already highlighted, most of the ingredients from which the ECJ created the concept already exist in CARICOM law. Nevertheless, because the RTC does not expressly support the concepts of direct applicability or direct effect, and in fact contains provisions that appear to preserve a dualist system of law, the adoption of an EU-styled doctrine of supremacy in CARICOM cannot be assumed.[117]

The RTB, in contrast, expressly requires direct effectiveness of OECS Acts, Regulations, and Orders and therefore may provide a more substantial basis for supremacy.[118] The RTB also requires national legislation to implement the direct effectiveness of these OECS legislative acts, and such legislation would likely be necessary to ground supremacy.

It should be highlighted in this regard that even in the EU, at least according to national legal systems, supremacy depends upon national legal recognition.[119] Although monist member states of the EU would be better equipped to accept the concept of supremacy, such acceptance nevertheless formally relies upon their national constitutional structures and *legal systems*. In other words, the principle of supremacy applies in national law *because of an express rule of national law*. For dualist EU member states specially-created national legislation has been used to ground the principle of supremacy of EU law in their national legal systems.[120]

[115] See RTC Art 214. [116] Judgment [2013] CCJ 3 (OJ) [69].

[117] See RTC Art 240. See also the earlier discussion on direct effect, both in the OECS and potentially in CARICOM.

[118] RTB Art 5.3.

[119] See eg Hartley, *The Foundations of European Union Law* (n 9) 203–8. For a brief survey of national approaches see Craig and de Búrca, in *EU Law: Text, Cases and Materials* (n 50) 268–96. For the ECJ, in contrast, the supremacy of EU law is absolute and cannot be dependent upon national recognition. However it is subject to some limitations including those imposed by the principle of conferral, the general principles of EU law, and international agreements entered into by a member state prior to its accession to the EU (see eg Art 351 of the TFEU).

[120] For an example of transformation legislation in a dualist country see the UK's European Communities Act 1972, s 2(1), reproduced at p cdlxxvi. Note in this context that Lord Bridge, in *Factortame Ltd v Secretary of State for Transport (No 2)* [1991] 1 AC 603, at p 658, highlighted the fact that supremacy was well established in EU law long before the UK joined the EU, and

In either case the rule of supremacy, which is a rule of EU law, requires adoption and acceptance as part of the national law of each member state before it also becomes part of national law. Understood in this way, the principle of supremacy is less of a threat to the sovereignty of member states of CARICOM and the OECS, since it ultimately must be founded on national legal acceptance.

8.6 Pre-emption

The principle of pre-emption is closely related to supremacy, and could be argued to be a consequence of it. The term 'pre-emption' is used because under the principle once a regional organization assumes competence over an area, the organization's competence displaces, or pre-empts, the competence of member states. In EU law pre-emption goes further and in many cases entails the assumption of exclusive competence over an area of previously shared competence. When this occurs, the competence of the regional organization pre-empts domestic competence and member states lose the power to act independently in the field.[121] In the words of the ECJ in Case 22/70 *Commission v Council* 'each time the Community, with a view to implementing a common policy envisaged by the Treaty, adopts provisions laying down common rules, whatever form these may take, the Member States no longer have the right, acting individually or even collectively, to undertake obligations with third countries which affect those rules.'[122] This competence of the EU, according to the Court, may also exclude concurrent powers on the part of member states.[123]

The principle of pre-emption is inexorably tied to supremacy in EU law since without the latter concept, concurrent powers and competences would be justifiable in most cases. In the context of Caribbean regional organizations the principle of pre-emption may be more readily adopted in the OECS than in CARICOM. In the RTC there is no evidence of the delegation of exclusive powers to CARICOM and therefore both member states and the regional organization retain full competences in relation to the creation of legal obligations. In fact, certain decisions of CARICOM organs require express transformation under Article 240 of the RTC. More generally CARICOM practice reveals a strong reliance upon the relatively loosely coordinated actions and legislative initiatives of member states. Such practice does not exclude the possibility of pre-emption. If member states or the CCJ decided that it would be useful for CARICOM to have exclusive competence over

therefore 'whatever limitation of its sovereignty Parliament accepted when it enacted the European Communities Act 1972 was entirely voluntary.'

[121] Note, however, that pre-emption may be limited by (1) the prior need for actual exercise of competence, (2) the scope or extent of that exercise of power, and (3) the possibility that the regional organization will cease to exercise, or abandon, competence with the result that competence over the area will revert to member states. See Craig and de Búrca, in *EU Law: Text, Cases and Materials* (n 50) 84–5.

[122] [1971] ECR 263, at p 274 [17].

[123] Case 22/70 *Commission v Council* (n 122) 276 [31].

certain activities, for example, by reason of their regional nature, then the principle could be applied and developed incrementally and organically.

In contrast, the principle of pre-emption is likely to flourish in the OECS context. This is because Article 14 of the RTB creates both areas of exclusive competence for the Organisation, and expressly enshrines the principle of pre-emption in relation to shared competences.[124] Whether the principle of pre-emption will develop in OECS law in a manner similar to that of EU law, including the exclusion of concurrent powers and the extension of pre-emption to areas not expressly delegated (a kind of creeping competence), remains to be seen.[125]

8.7 State Liability

The Caribbean Court of Justice already has formally adopted one general principle found in EU law, that of state liability. In the case of *Trinidad Cement Limited and TCL Guyana Inc v. Guyana*, the CCJ for the first time considered the issue of whether a state could be sanctioned for breaching the RTC.[126] After noting that '*RTC* contains no specific provisions dealing with sanctions for breaching its provisions', the Court discussed the approach taken by the ECJ when faced with a similar silence under the European treaty regime.[127] Citing the ECJ cases of *Francovich v Italy* and *Brasserie du Pêcheur SA v Germany* and *R v Secretary of State for Transport, ex parte Factortame*, the CCJ held that the doctrine of state liability had developed in the ECJ jurisprudence on the basis of 'two grounds: the principle of effectiveness and Article 5 EC (equivalent to Article 9 of the *RTC*)'.[128] With respect to the latter, the CCJ noted that Article 5 EC (now Article 4(3) of the TEU) and Article 9 RTC were 'almost identical' and that although the first ECJ case had applied the provision to support a directive, the joined *Brasserie* and *Factortame* cases had applied it to help enforce an article of the EU treaties. Such factors led the CCJ to hold in paragraph 27 of its judgment that the principle of state liability also applies to the RTC regime:

> [27] This Court holds that a similar principle applies under the *RTC* and that the new Single Market based on the rule of law implies the remedy of compensation where rights

[124] See RTB Art 14.1 and 14.2. Compare Arts 2–3 TFEU, describing pre-emption and the exclusive competences of the EU. Note the text of Protocol (No 25) on the exercise of shared competence, in Consolidated versions of the Treaty on European Union and the Treaty on the Functioning of the European Union (OJ C83, 30.3.2010) as available through <http://eur-lex.europa.eu/en/treaties/index.htm> (accessed 30 Sep 2011), at 307, which states:

> With reference to Article 2(2) of the Treaty on the Functioning of the European Union on shared competence, when the Union has taken action in a certain area, the scope of this exercise of competence only covers those elements governed by the Union act in question and therefore does not cover the whole area.

[125] On the role of pre-emption in the EU's international relations see Hartley, *The Foundations of European Union Law* (n 9) ch 6.

[126] Judgment, [2009] CCJ 5 (OJ) 20 August 2009.

[127] *Trinidad Cement v Guyana* (n 126) [24].

[128] *Trinidad Cement v Guyana* (n 126) [24]. See Cases C-6/90 and C-9/90 *Francovich and Others v Italian State* [1991] ECR I-5357 and Joined Cases C-46/93 and C-48/93 *Brasserie du Pêcheur SA v*

which enure to individuals and private entities under the Treaty are infringed by a Member State. But State liability in damages is not automatic. A party will have to demonstrate that the provision alleged to be breached was intended to benefit that person, that such breach is serious, that there is substantial loss and that there is a causal link between the breach by the State and the loss or damage to that person.

In this way the Court acknowledged the existence of the principle of state liability as a principle of CARICOM law.

This passage of the CCJ's judgment is very significant for the development of CARICOM law in two ways. Firstly, it demonstrates an understanding by the Court of the potential of both the general undertaking in Article 9 of the RTC and the concept of general principles of law. The general undertaking enshrines and makes express the principle of *pacta sunt servanda*, or the rule that promises must be kept in good faith, in the RTC.[129] Secondly, it shows an awareness of, and readiness to use as a persuasive authority the jurisprudence of the ECJ. This should not be surprising, given the extensive and sophisticated nature of ECJ jurisprudence and the strong textual parallels between the RTC and the TEU and TFEU.

It must be noted in this context that the second ECJ authority referred to by the CCJ, Joined Cases C-46/93 and C-48/93 *Brasserie du Pêcheur SA v Germany* and *R v Secretary of State for Transport, ex parte Factortame Ltd and Others*, described the principle of state liability as being 'inherent in the system of the [EU] Treaty'.[130] The ECJ also held that state liability was founded on the general principles regarding non-contractual liability common to the laws of member states.[131] Later EU cases have also made clear that states are liable for the acts of all of their organs, including judicial ones.[132]

The two findings just highlighted in Joined Cases C-46/93 and C-48/93 have far-reaching consequences that will likely require further examination in the CARICOM and OECS contexts. The first statement of the ECJ is striking because it suggests that the general principle of state liability could arise independent of any clear textual support from the treaties, simply by being inherent in the system. If the CCJ follows this approach then it may derive general principles of CARICOM law without any textual support from the RTC. As seen in Chapter 7, general principles may legitimately be derived from sources outside the constituent treaty. For example, they may be derived from norms common to the domestic legal systems of member states, or even from the fundamental norms or principles that are necessary for the effective functioning of a regional legal system. The second statement, suggesting that the source of the general principle of state liability

Germany and *R v Secretary of State for Transport, ex parte Factortame Ltd and Others* [*Factortame III*] [1996] ECR I-1029.

[129] Art 26 of the Vienna Convention on the Law of Treaties (adopted 23 May 1969, in force 27 Jan 1980) 1155 UNTS 331, expresses the principle as follows: 'Every treaty in force is binding upon the parties to it and must be performed by them in good faith.'

[130] [1996] ECR I-1029, at p I-1144 [31].

[131] *Brasserie du Pêcheur* (n 130) at p I-1144 [27]–[29].

[132] See eg Case C-224/01 *Gerhard Köbler v Republik Österreich* [2003] ECR I-10239.

lies in the principles regarding non-contractual liability common to the laws of member states, is notable for two reasons. Firstly, this source is independent of EU law. Secondly, it is derived from the common principles of the legal systems of EU member states. Framed in this way, state liability logically arises from the national legal orders of member states. This is strong foundation for general principles, one that could serve equally well in the development of CARICOM and OECS law. A general principle at least partly derived from the common principles of national legal systems should achieve greater support from national authorities and national courts.

However the CCJ's enunciation of the burden of proof necessary to establish state liability in individual cases may substantially limit the effectiveness of the general principle. In *Trinidad Cement Limited and TCL Guyana Inc v Guyana* the Court held that the threshold for proof of damages was a high one and therefore a person seeking to make a state liable must establish that the breach was sufficiently serious to warrant the award of damages.[133] The Court also held that a claimant must prove a strong causal connection between the precise breach and the losses suffered, or in other words, that the 'losses were incurred in circumstances that rendered them sufficiently proximate to the precise breach in question'.[134]

The threshold of seriousness was satisfied in the case before the Court, but the requirement for proof of losses sufficiently proximate to the breach was not. As a result no damages were awarded to the victorious claimants. Of course the inability of the Court to award damages in the case may have been due to the particular facts in dispute. But it should be noticed that the Court's burden of proof has prevented the award of damages in almost *every* original jurisdiction case that has come before the Court to date.[135] Such a pattern may discourage future claimants, who would no doubt notice the Court's unwillingness to award damages even in cases involving the most flagrant breaches of the RTC.

In the context of the OECS no similar jurisprudence exists at present. However it is likely that a parallel principle of state liability will arise. This is because the same two principles highlighted by the CCJ in finding that state liability arises under the RTC also apply in the OECS context: the principle of effectiveness and the principle of *pacta sunt servanda* (that undertakings must be kept). In fact Article 5.1 of the RTB uses substantially the same wording as Article 9 of the RTC. Thus it is likely that the Eastern Caribbean Court of Appeal will develop a similar line of jurisprudence when it is confronted with the same question.

133 *Trinidad Cement Ltd and TCL Guyana Inc v Guyana*, Judgment, [2009] CCJ 5 (OJ) 20 August 2009, at [28].

134 *Trinidad Cement v Guyana* (n 133) [33]. This wording may be contrasted with that employed by the ECJ in Cases C-6/90 and C-9/90 *Francovich and Others v Italian State* [1991] ECR I-5357, at p I-5415 [40] when setting out the final condition for state liability: 'the third condition is the existence of a causal link between the breach of the State's obligation and the loss and damage suffered by the injured parties.'

135 See eg *Trinidad Cement Ltd and TCL Guyana Inc v Guyana*, Judgment, [2009] CCJ 5 (OJ) 20 August 2009, at [34] and [40] (denial of damages and exemplary damages), and *Hummingbird Rice Mills Limited v Suriname and the Caribbean Community*, Judgment [2012] CCJ 1 (OJ) at [65] (failure to prove loss for damages). Exceptionally, the CCJ, in the case of *Shanique Myrie v Barbados* (n 97), awarded non-pecuniary damages. See Chapter 14.

However in further developing and implementing the principle of state liability in CARICOM and the OECS it may be useful for the regional courts to take note of some of the practical hurdles with respect to implementing the principle that have arisen in the jurisprudence of the ECJ. In CARICOM the challenge at present appears to be the burden of proof. This burden, having been imposed by the CCJ in its original jurisdiction, will be the same for all CARICOM member states. In the EU, in contrast, challenges have arisen in the context of enforcing state liability in the various domestic legal systems of member states. Because legal rules made at the EU level do not contain exhaustive standards related to enforcement, the ECJ has relied at least in part upon the laws and procedures of member states to deal with such issues as timeliness (ie, when a claim might be barred), possible damage caps, and rules regarding access to interest on damages. On the one hand such a move by the ECJ to delegate enforcement to national courts is prudent. Co-opting national courts and legal systems to aid in the enforcement of EU law lessens the workload of the ECJ, makes enforcement more effective, and encourages national authorities to become champions of EU law. On the other hand, however, the danger posed by reliance upon national rules and procedures is one of the decreased uniformity of EU law because of the differences between national legal systems. For example, an EU treaty provision may give rise to the same substantive EU-based right in France and England, but the amount of damages that a citizen may be able to claim for breach of that right might vary dramatically between the two states as a result of national rules and procedures.

In reaction to this challenge, the ECJ has attempted to balance what can be argued to be the two essential competing interests involved, namely, the desire of national states to maintain sovereign control over their legal systems (as echoed in the principle of subsidiarity), and the desire of the Union to ensure the equal, uniform application of EU law. In its jurisprudence, which has developed incrementally and in an ad hoc manner, the ECJ can be described as having followed a kind of pendulum movement. The earlier cases could be characterized as paying greater deference to national remedial systems, with the substance of EU rights being seen to be an EU matter, but the remedies for breaches of these rights being governed by national bodies and national rules and procedures.[136] Later cases appear to have pushed more in the opposite direction, requiring remedies to be provided in greater conformity with principles of EU law, including the principle of equivalence (national procedures must be no less favourable than those available for similar domestic claims) and the principle of effectiveness.[137] In Joined Cases C-46/93 and C-48/93 *Brasserie du Pêcheur SA v Germany* and *R v Secretary of State for Transport, ex parte Factortame Ltd and Others* for example, the Court made clear that the question of the existence and extent of state liability is a matter of EU law.[138]

[136] See eg Roberto Caranta, 'Government Liability after Francovich' (1993) 52 *Cambridge Law Journal* 272.

[137] See eg Case 45/76 *Comet BV v Produktschap voor Siergewassen* (preliminary ruling requested by the College van Beroep voor het Bedrijfsleven) [1976] ECR 2043, at p 2053 [12]–[19]; Cases C-6/90 and C-9/90 *Francovich and Others v Italian State* [1991] ECR I-5357, at pp I-5415–16 [42]–[43].

[138] [1996] ECR I-1029.

The ECJ noted that 'the State must make reparation for the consequences of the loss and damage caused in accordance with the domestic rules on liability, provided that the conditions for reparation of loss and damage laid down by national law must not be less favourable than those relating to similar domestic claims and must not be such as in practice to make it impossible or excessively difficult to obtain reparation (see also Case 199/82 *Amministrazione delle Finanze dello Stato San Giorgio* [1983] ECR 3595).'[139]

It is likely that the jurisprudence of the CCJ will follow a similar, although perhaps truncated pattern. Even though the CCJ may seek to jealously guard the exclusive nature of its original, treaty-interpreting jurisdiction, the Court must ultimately use national remedial procedures to enforce its decisions. Under Article 215 of the RTC and Article XV of the Agreement Establishing the Caribbean Court of Justice, Member States, Organs and Bodies of the Community, and persons are required to comply with the judgments of the Court ('promptly' in the case of Article 215).[140] Article XXVI of the CCJ Agreement provides for legal acts of the Court to be enforced in the same manner as legal acts of national superior courts.[141] As a result, parties in original jurisdiction cases will be required to comply with judgments of the Court and at least some aspects of those judgments must be enforceable in national law. To the extent that national legal procedures can produce different remedial results, the CCJ will have to directly address the question of uniformity of CARICOM law. In contrast, the Eastern Caribbean Court of Appeal will not face this particular challenge of differing national remedial procedures, since all of the full and associate members of the OECS are governed by the same Court.

8.8 Non-discrimination (Equality)

The obligation not to discriminate on grounds of nationality is fundamental to the RTC and is set out clearly in Article 7 in the following words:

1. Within the scope of application of this Treaty and without prejudice to any special provisions contained therein, any discrimination on grounds of nationality only shall be prohibited.
2. The Community Council shall, after consultation with the competent Organs, establish rules to prohibit any such discrimination.

139 *Brasserie du Pêcheur* (n 138) at p I-1153 [67].

140 (Adopted 14 February 2001, entered into force 23 July 2002) 2255 UNTS 319 (CCJ Agreement).

141 CCJ Agreement Art XXVI(a) states:

The Contracting Parties agree to take all the necessary steps, including the enactment of legislation to ensure that:

(a) all authorities of a Contracting Party act in aid of the Court and that any judgment, decree, order or sentence of the Court given in exercise of its jurisdiction shall be enforced by all courts and authorities in any territory of the Contracting Parties as if it were a judgment, decree, order or sentence of a superior court of that Contracting Party....

The question that arises regards the legal effect of this provision. Article 7(1) sets out a clear and express prohibition and thus could be relied upon by persons, member states and the Community in enforcement proceedings under Chapter 9 of the RTC.[142] However three things should be noted about this provision. Firstly, Article 7(1) is expressly limited. It begins with the phrase '[w]ithin the scope of application of this Treaty'. This phrase highlights the fact that the right of non-discrimination only applies to matters falling within the scope of the RTC. As a result, before there can be any determination of whether there has been an act of discrimination under Article 7, one must first identify a right existing under the RTC the exercise of which is being impaired. In other words, the right of non-discrimination is not free standing or open ended. Secondly, Article 7(1) must be read in conjunction with Article 7(2), which places a duty upon the Community Council to create rules prohibiting discrimination. No such rules have been made as of the date of writing. Does the lack of such rules render Article 7(1) ineffective? Or in other words, is the right of non-discrimination in Article 7(1) conditional upon the rules established in Article 7(2)? Such a view could be held. However given the clear and express nature of the prohibition in Article 7(1), the better view must be that the obligation already exists, and that future rules created by the Community Council will merely help flesh out its scope and meaning.

Thirdly, Article 7(1) contains the word 'only' in the phrase 'discrimination on grounds of nationality only'. This is an unusual phrase and is not paralleled in the text of treaties of other regional organizations. The first paragraph of Article 18 of the Treaty on the Functioning of the European Union (TFEU), for example, provides:

> Within the scope of application of the Treaties, and without prejudice to any special provisions contained therein, any discrimination on grounds of nationality shall be prohibited.[143]

Article 18 of the TFEU prohibits 'discrimination on grounds of nationality'. Article 7 of the RTC prohibits 'discrimination on grounds of nationality *only*'. What is the effect of this difference of terminology? It could be argued that the use of the word 'only' in Article 7 of the RTC prohibits discrimination solely on the basis of nationality and excludes discrimination on any other ground. But does Article 7 also exclude discrimination on multiple bases? A literal reading of the text could yield such a result. A case involving discrimination on the basis of nationality *and* on some other basis, such as sex, for example, arguably could be excluded. However the better reading is not the strict literal reading. It would be offensive to read Article 7 as catching discrimination on grounds of nationality, but not catching a case of multifaceted discrimination, where a person is targeted on

[142] As established by the CCJ in the case of *Shanique Myrie v Barbados* (n 97), at [85], '[t]he right contained in Article 7 is granted to Member States and enures to the nationals of those States.'

[143] Consolidated versions of the Treaty on European Union and the Treaty on the Functioning of the European Union (OJ C83, 30.3.2010) as available through <http://eur-lex.europa.eu/en/treaties/index.htm>.

the basis of both nationality and some other attribute. The purpose of the provision is to catch discrimination on grounds of nationality. The world 'only' should be read to exclude entirely different categories of cases, not involving any form of discrimination on grounds of nationality, and only involving some other form of discrimination.

It will be interesting to see how far member states, the Community, and the CCJ will read meaning into Article 7. In the case of *Shanique Myrie v Barbados* the Court outlined the basic meaning of Article 7 when it held that '[d]iscrimination in the context of Caribbean Community law occurs where, within the scope of application of the Treaty, the facts of the case disclose treatment that is worse or less favourable than is accorded to a person whose circumstances are similar to those of the complainant except for their and the complainant's nationality, with no objective and reasonable justification for the difference in treatment.'[144] The Court held that evidence of discrimination could include statistical evidence or a proven pattern of conduct and, that if such evidence was strong and a prima facie case were to be made out, the burden would then shift to the defendant state.[145]

In future cases it may be possible for the CCJ to develop this principle further. For example, Article 7 could be considered to set out merely one aspect of a more general principle of non-discrimination, one that could apply more broadly in the CARICOM system. Similar provisions have been used robustly in other legal systems. In the EU, for example, the principle of non-discrimination has been used to strengthen rights related to the free movement of persons.[146] The ECJ has also referred to the non-discrimination provision as supporting the uniformity of EU law and ultimately, the supremacy of EU law.[147]

In fact, the jurisprudence of the ECJ related to what is now Article 18 of the TFEU highlights the great potential of such a principle. The ECJ has expressly held that the several articles of the EU treaties that refer to equality and non-discrimination are merely specific enunciations of the general principle of equality. In Cases 117/76 and 16/77 *Ruckdeschel v Hauptzollamt Hamburg-St Annen*, the Court held that 'the prohibition of discrimination laid down in the aforesaid provision is merely a specific enunciation of the general principle of equality which is one of the fundamental principles of Community law.'[148]

Thus Article 18 of the TFEU, and perhaps Article 7 of the RTC, can be described as specific examples of a more general principle. Other examples may arise under the text of the RTC and the principle of equality may be broadly applied. In EU law, for example, the principle of non-discrimination has founded extensive lines

[144] *Shanique Myrie v Barbados* (n 97) [84].

[145] In *Shanique Myrie v Barbados* [84]. At [91], the CCJ determined that the statistical evidence presented by Jamaica was 'incapable of raising a *prima facie* case' and dismissed the claim for breach of Art 7 of the RTC.

[146] See eg Catherine Barnard, *The Substantive Law of the EU: The Four Freedoms*, 3rd edn (Oxford: Oxford University Press, 2010) 237–41.

[147] See eg Case 6/64 *Costa v ENEL* [1964] ECR 585, at p 593.

[148] [1977] ECR 1753, at [7]. See generally Craig and de Búrca, *EU Law: Text Cases and Materials* (n 50) 538–41.

of jurisprudence, albeit on the basis of different treaty provisions, regarding cases of discrimination on grounds of sexual orientation.[149]

In the OECS a right of non-discrimination is not expressly set out in the text of the RTB in the same manner as in the RTC. But it may be possible to imply the principle of non-discrimination, or even the broader principle of equality, from the several provisions of the RTB and Protocol that promote equality or equitable distribution.[150] This possibility could arise if the Eastern Caribbean Court of Appeal follows an approach similar to that of the ECJ, where such references are seen to be merely specific enunciations of the general principle of equality and non-discrimination. The strongest example of non-discrimination is set out in the context of freedom of movement of persons under Article 12.2 of the RTB in the following terms:

> 12.1 Freedom of movement for citizens of Protocol Member States shall be secured within the Economic Union Area.
> 12.2 Such freedom of movement shall entail the abolition of any discrimination based on nationality between citizens of the Protocol Member States as regards employment, remuneration and other conditions of work and employment.

Article 12.2 mandates the abolition of a category of discriminatory measures related to freedom of movement of citizens. The duty to abolish such discriminatory measures falls upon individual member states. But it is foreseeable that a correlative right of non-discrimination may arise in favour of persons, since the article expressly links the obligation to citizens.

8.9 Most Favoured Nation Treatment

Article 8 of the RTC enshrines the most favoured nation (MFN) principle in Caribbean Community law in the following terms:

> Subject to the provisions of this Treaty, each Member State shall, with respect to any rights covered by this Treaty, accord to another Member State treatment no less favourable than that accorded to:
> (a) a third Member State; or
> (b) third States.

In EU law there is no identical provision. However several treaty provisions require equal treatment, and as seen earlier, a general principle of non-discrimination exists under EU law.[151]

[149] See eg Craig and de Búrca (n 50) 540.
[150] See eg RTB Art 13.4, and OECS Protocol Arts 2(e), 4.3, 4.4(a), 22.2, and 23.1
[151] See eg TEU Arts 4(2) (Union to respect equality of member states) and 9 (Union to observe principle of equality of citizens); TFEU Arts 8 (Union to promote equality between men and women), 55 (equal treatment of nationals re capital), and 199 (equal treatment to overseas countries and territories). But cf TFEU Art 52 (special treatment of foreign nationals).

In the OECS system, there is no single provision in the RTB setting out the MFN principle. However some articles of the Protocol require MFN treatment in particular areas.[152] Article 5.3 of the Protocol, for example, applies a kind of MFN standard to the provision of Economic Union Area tariff treatment to imports from Protocol member states:

> 5.3 Nothing in this Protocol shall prevent a Protocol Member State from accepting as eligible for Economic Union Area tariff treatment any imports consigned from another Protocol Member State, provided that the like imports consigned from any other Protocol Member State are accorded the same treatment.

Such a clause is conditional and is limited to Protocol member states. Whether a broader MFN principle will arise in OECS law will depend upon the views of the member states, the Commission, and the Eastern Caribbean Court of Appeal. It may be derived as a general principle of OECS law. As a practical matter, the MFN principle will in any event apply to the majority of the member states of the OECS through Article 8 of the RTC, since all of the OECS member states except Montserrat are also parties to the RTC.

The MFN principle contained in Article 8 of the RTC is expressed as applying to relations between states. It parallels the formulation of the MFN principle in international trade law, a principle that has been described as 'a cornerstone of the GATT and…one of the pillars of the WTO trading system'.[153] It imposes a relative minimum standard of protection: State A must treat State B no less favourably than it treats State C (either another CARICOM member state or a non-CARICOM member state). Its effect is to require as a minimum standard, the highest standard of treatment applied by one CARICOM member state to another CARICOM member state or a third state. It prevents, for example, one CARICOM member state from imposing higher food safety standards on goods coming from another CARICOM member state than those imposed upon goods imported from a third member state, or a non-CARICOM state.

Article 8 could give rise to correlative rights for nationals in addition to the rights it provides to states.[154] This is because a state's obligation to accord MFN treatment should extend equally to treatment of things and persons. Imposing a quantitative restriction on goods from all Trinidadian companies, for example, would amount to unfavourable treatment of both Trinidadian goods *and* the Trinidadian companies (persons) concerned. In such circumstances, recourse should be available to both the state and its persons. As highlighted by the CCJ in

[152] See also OECS Protocol Art 27.2 (restrictions on provision of economic services by nationals of another Protocol member state).

[153] WTO, *Canada: Certain Measures Affecting the Automotive Industry*—Appellate Body Report, (31 May 2000, adopted Jun 19, 2000) WT/DS139/AB/R, WT/DS142/AB/R, at 23 [69].

[154] On correlative rights, see *Trinidad Cement Ltd and TCL Guyana Inc v Guyana*, Judgment [2009] CCJ 1 (OJ), (2009) 74 WIR 302, 15 January 2009, at [32].

the case of *Shanique Myrie v Barbados*, MFN treatment is based upon the principle of non-discrimination:

The right to Most Favoured Nation (MFN) treatment set out in Article 8 RTC applies to all rights conferred by or under the RTC. It is a right that enures to Member States and, so far as applicable, to their nationals. The right to MFN treatment guarantees to Community nationals treatment by the defendant State that is no less favourable than is extended by that State to nationals of other States (whether CARICOM States or otherwise). It is significant to note that subject to the provisions of the RTC, MFN treatment does not necessarily require a State to treat nationals of other CARICOM States as favourably as it treats its own nationals. The right to MFN treatment may be regarded as a particular, albeit limited, manifestation of the principle of non-discrimination, although it is broader to the extent that it also allows for a comparison with treatment extended to third non-CARICOM States.[155]

The crucial requirement for Article 8, as illustrated in international trade law, will be the requirement for 'likeness'. For example, the rights under the RTC must apply to a particular product which is to be treated as favourably as the same kind of product from a third member state or a non-member state. As a result, member states, the Community, and the CCJ will have to decide upon the applicable standards or tests to determine the 'likeness' of products, no doubt borrowing from international trade law in doing so.[156] Whether Article 8 will extend to both de jure and de facto discrimination has yet to be determined, but there is nothing in principle to prevent it from applying to origin neutral measures.[157]

It also should be noted that the wording of Article 8 is broad and unconditional. It does not require the third state to grant like treatment. Therefore, for example, the exports of a third state (a non-CARICOM member state), could benefit from lower food safety standards in relation to a CARICOM state, without adopting those same standards for its own imports. As a consequence, an unconditional MFN clause such as that found in Article 8 has the potential to allow 'free-riders'—states whose exports benefit from MFN treatment without themselves extending similar favourable treatment.[158]

The MFN principle provides two benefits in international trade law. Firstly, it automatically converts to multilateral form any trade concessions made with another state in the trading system. If State A enters into a trade concession with

[155] Judgment [2013] CCJ 3 (OJ) [92]. At [92] the Court also dismissed the claim for breach of RTC Art 8 for lack of evidence.

[156] See eg Robert E Hudec, '"Like Products": The Differences in Meaning in GATT Articles I and III,' in Thomas Cottier and Petros Mavroidis (eds), *Regulatory Barriers and the Principle of Non-Discrimination* (Ann Arbor, Michigan: University of Michigan Press, 2000) 101–24.

[157] See eg WTO, *Canada: Certain Measures Affecting the Automotive Industry*—Appellate Body Report, (31 May 2000, adopted 19 Jun 2000) WT/DS139/AB/R, WT/DS142/AB/R, at 25–6 [78]–[81].

[158] See eg William Davey and Joost Pauwelyn, 'MFN Unconditionality: A legal analysis of the concept in view of its evolution in the GATT/WTO Jurisprudence with particular reference to "like product"' in Thomas Cottier & Petros Mavroidis (eds), *Regulatory Barriers and the Principle of Non-Discrimination* (Ann Arbor, Michigan: University of Michigan Press, 2000) 13–50.

State B, it must automatically extend it to State C if States A and C are part of the same trade regime. This is particularly helpful to smaller countries which may not have the clout to negotiate such concessions on their own. Article 8 of the RTC would multilateralize concessions made in any area falling within the scope of the RTC for all member states. Secondly, the MFN principle provides a benefit in prohibiting discrimination between like imports from different trading partners. If State A imposes a tariff of 5 per cent on a product from State B, it cannot impose a higher tariff on the same product from State C if States A and C are part of the same trade regime. As summarized by the Appellate Body in relation to the MFN provision in GATT, '[t]he object and purpose of Article I:1... is to prohibit discrimination among like products originating in or destined for different countries' and it 'serves as an incentive for concessions, negotiated reciprocally, to be extended to all other Members on an MFN basis'.[159] In this sense the MFN principle can be argued to strongly support the principle of non-discrimination.

The wording of Article 8 of the RTC makes clear, however, that the protections it offers must be directly linked to the rights and obligations existing under the RTC. Article 8 requires MFN treatment for 'any rights covered by this Treaty'; it does not create an autonomous or free standing right to MFN treatment, independent of the RTC. This limitation also exists under international trade rules, under the *ejusdem generis* principle. It has been described as follows:

The MFN clause is governed by the *Ejusdem Generis* principle, in that it may only apply to issues belonging to the same subject matter or the same category of subjects to which the clause relates.... This principle circumscribes the application of the MFN treatment clause to those subject matters regulated by the basic treaty. For instance, the MFN treatment clause of a commercial treaty between States A and B could not apply to or attract a benefit conferred by State A to State C (for the benefit of State B) related to diplomatic immunity or to aviation or to taxation benefits.[160]

The restricted scope of the MFN principle is also highlighted in draft Article 4 of the International Law Commission's Draft Articles on Most-Favoured-Nation Clauses, 1978. Draft Article 4 states: '[a] most-favoured-nation clause is a treaty provision whereby a State undertakes an obligation towards another State to accord most-favoured-nation treatment in an agreed sphere of relations.'[161] The Commentaries to draft Article 4 elaborate the meaning of the latter phrase:

(14) Article 4 states that the grant of most-favoured nation treatment to another State by a most-favoured nation clause shall be in 'an agreed sphere of relations'. Most-favoured-nation clauses have been customarily categorized as 'general' or 'special' clauses. A 'general' clause means a clause which promises most-favoured nation treatment in all relations between

[159] WTO, *Canada: Certain Measures Affecting the Automotive Industry*—Appellate Body Report, (31 May 2000, adopted Jun 19, 2000) WT/DS139/AB/R, WT/DS142/AB/R, at 27 [84].

[160] UNCTAD, *Most Favoured Nation Treatment* (New York: United Nations, 2010) at 24 [citations omitted].

[161] International Law Commission, 'Draft Articles on most-favoured-nation clause with commentaries 1978' (1978) *Yearbook of the International Law Commission, 1978*, vol II, Part Two, p 18.

the parties concerned, whereas a 'special' one refers to relations in certain limited areas. Although States are free to agree to grant to each other most-favoured-nation treatment in all fields which are susceptible to such agreements, this is rather an exception today.[162]

Therefore Article 8 should be interpreted as requiring member states to provide MFN treatment only to rights covered by the RTC. No other rights are subject to the MFN requirement. In the CARICOM framework it is unlikely that a general principle of Most Favoured Nation treatment that applies more broadly, for example, to other treaties or other spheres of relations, will arise.

8.10 Cooperation and Consultation by Community Organs

Two other legal concepts contained in CARICOM and OECS law which could be fleshed out as general principles of regional integration law are the duties of cooperation and consultation. Although each concept is set out expressly in various places in the treaties of one or both of the regional organizations in specific contexts, it is likely that they will be read to extend more broadly. Given the organizational frameworks of the RTC and RTB, and the strong need for coordination of the relations of organs and member states, it is likely that the principles of cooperation and consultation will emerge as general principles of regional law.

8.10.1 Cooperation

In the context of cooperation in CARICOM, Article 20(1) of the RTC expressly states that 'Community Organs shall co-operate with each other for the achievement of Community objectives.'[163] The remainder of Article 20 describes some of the requirements of cooperation. Article 20(2) indicates that the Bureau and the Community Council may initiate proposals for development by the Ministerial Councils within their respective areas of competence. Article 20(3) requires each Community organ which 'proposes to develop a proposal which is likely to impact importantly on activities within the sphere of competence of another Community Organ', to transmit the proposal to other interested Community organs 'for their consideration and reaction before reaching a final decision on the proposal'. This latter provision requires consultation between Community organs when acting in areas which may impact upon other organs. Article 20(3) is strengthened by

[162] International Law Commission, 'Draft Articles' (n 161) p 20. See also Draft articles 9 and 10 and the associated commentary at pp 27–33.

[163] Similarly, Art 15(2)(i) of the RTC mandates cooperation between COFAP and COFCOR and Art 16(3)(d) requires cooperation between COFCOR and COTED. Art 74(1) places a duty of inter-organ cooperation upon the Legal Affairs Committee and Art 173(2)(e) requires the CARICOM Competition Commission to cooperate with competent authorities in member states. Other provisions of the RTC also highlight the need for cooperation, including Arts 6(i), 13(2), 17(3), 19(3), 52(6)(e), 52(8)(c), 57(1)(m), 64, 65(4), 95, 116(8), 132, 133(5), 134(2)(c), 136(1), 138, 140, and 141.

Article 20(5), which only allows the Community Council to modify proposals by lower organs with their agreement:

5. Proposals approved by the Ministerial Councils and transmitted to the Community Council for prioritisation and resource allocation for implementation may be returned by the Community Council to the originating Organ for modification. The Community Council may modify the proposal to the extent and in the manner agreed with the originating Organ.[164]

Article 20(5) converts the requirement for consultation into one of cooperation, if the proposal is to be modified. Finally, under Article 20(6) the Secretariat is tasked with the role of monitoring the development and implementation of proposals and keeping the Community Council informed of such matters. This role allows the Secretariat to facilitate the CARICOM cooperative processes.

This duty of cooperation between organs in CARICOM has clear implications for the efficient development of Community law. Organs are required to consult and cooperate with one another in overlapping spheres of competence or interest, and higher organs (the Community Council) cannot change proposals from lower organs—which presumably will have greater expertise in the relevant legislative area—without their consent.[165] Similar duties of cooperation can be read into other areas of Community law, including the duties placed upon the Competition Commission, the CCJ, and member states.[166]

In the OECS there is no similar express duty to cooperate placed upon organs of the Economic Union. Rather, the RTB speaks to cooperation between member states and cooperation between organs and member states.[167] In fact, in the context of the decision-making process of the RTB, the Authority is empowered to reverse decisions of other organs of the OECS. In Article 8.11 the Authority is empowered to 'give directives to and reverse any decision of another Organ or any officer of the Organisation, without prejudice to rights which may have accrued prior to giving such directives or reversing such decision'. Such a unilateral power of reversal would not seem to encourage cooperation.[168]

164 See also RTC Art 13(3)(b).

165 Contrast RTC Art 20 with Arts 17–18 of the original 1973 Treaty. The duty to cooperate was only mandated for member states under Art 18 of the original Treaty, and functional cooperation and coordination was limited to foreign policies in Art 17 of the original Treaty.

166 eg RTC Art 17(3)(a) and (c) impose obligations upon national competition authorities to cooperate with the Competition Commission and other national competition authorities. Article 214, the referral provision, implies a mutual obligation to cooperate for both the CCJ and national courts and tribunals. Article 9, the general undertaking provision, may be read to impose an obligation upon member states to cooperate with one another and with CARICOM to ensure the carrying out of obligations arising under the RTC. cf Case C-137/91 *Commission v Greece* [1992] ECR I-4023, at p I-4032 [6], where the ECJ held that the 'failure [by the Hellenic Republic] to answer the Commission's questions within a reasonable period made it more difficult for the Commission to carry out its tasks and therefore constitutes an infringement of the obligation to cooperate under Article 5 of the Treaty [now Art 4(3) of the TEU]'. Article 4(3) of the TEU describes the obligation as being one of 'sincere cooperation': 'Pursuant to the principle of sincere cooperation, the Union and the Member States shall, in full mutual respect, assist each other in carrying out tasks which flow from the Treaties.'

167 See eg the Preamble to the RTB, and Arts 4.1(a) and 4.2(m) of the RTB; see also Protocol Arts 3(g) and 27(3).

168 Compare Art 12(7) of the RTC, describing the Conference's ability to issue policy directives. This provision is silent on whether such directives can reverse decisions of lower organs.

Nevertheless, as part of its overall responsibility, the Commission under Article 12.5(f) of the RTB is required to 'make proposals relating [to work, studies, and services] as may assist in the efficient and harmonious functioning and development of the Organisation'. This latter responsibility could be used by the Commission to increase cooperation between Union organs.[169]

A general principle of cooperation could be derived from the organizational needs of both CARICOM and the OECS, as a principle required for the fulfilment of each organization's purposes. It could be applied to limit unilateral actions of particular organs and to promote greater harmonization of activities between organs.

8.10.2 Consultation

CARICOM imposes an express requirement for consultation upon the Community Council and Secretariat by way of Article 26 of the RTC.[170] This requirement is aimed at consultation between the organs and member states, rather than consultation between organs. Article 26 states:

> 1. In order to enhance the decision-making process in the Community, the Community Council, assisted by the Secretary-General, shall, in collaboration with competent authorities of the Member States, establish and maintain an efficient system of consultations at the national and regional levels.
> 2. The system of consultations shall be structured to ensure that determinations of Community Organs and the Legal Affairs Committee are adequately informed by relevant information inputs and are reinforced by consultations undertaken at successively lower levels of the decision-making process.

Article 26(2) may be read as imposing a consultation requirement for each CARICOM organ with lower organs and other actors in the decision-making process. Article 26(1) also requires at least a minimum level of consultation between the Community Council and the Secretariat. Further, the requirement for consultation can be read into the treaty provisions requiring cooperation, since cooperation must be predicated upon the exchange of information. Therefore the duty to consult could be deemed to be a general principle of CARICOM law.

The CCJ has emphasized the importance of this duty of consultation in the case of *Trinidad Cement Limited v CARICOM*.[171] In that case the claimant argued that the decisions of COTED and the Secretary General to allow for waiver of the Common External Tariff (CET) on cement were '*ultra vires*, irrational and/or illegal and/or unreasonable, null and void and of no effect and should be quashed or revoked by the Court'.[172] In coming to its decision the CCJ made a substantial statement about the nature of the obligation to consult under the RTC. In its judgment the Court described the system established by Article 26 and noted that

[169] See also the Director General's powers of coordination under Art 13.2 of the RTB.

[170] See also RTC Art 13(4)(c).

[171] [2009] CCJ 4 (OJ), (2009) 75 WIR 194, 10 August 2009.

[172] *Trinidad Cement v CARICOM* (n 171) [10].

the obligation to consult rests with the Community Council and the Secretary General, that it is continual in nature and that, in the context of the Secretary General, it requires investigations and follow up actions if it appears not to have been fulfilled:

[68]...The duty to maintain an efficient system of consultation would include a duty to monitor the operation of that system once it has been established, as well as a duty to try and correct any weaknesses that emerge in the system and to ensure as far as possible scrupulous adherence to that system. These are duties which rest primarily on the Community Council but in the performance of which that Council is entitled to the assistance of the Secretary-General. There are of course limits on both the competence and the capacity of the Secretary-General to insert himself into the domestic plane. Member States therefore have a duty to provide the Secretary-General and COTED with accurate, relevant and timely information. The Secretary-General is ordinarily entitled to assume where a Competent Authority supplies information that ought to have been obtained as a result of consultation, that the necessary consultation has in fact taken place. Given his duty, however, to assist in maintaining an efficient system of consultation, the Secretary-General has a residual responsibility not to look the other way if it comes to his attention that the consultative process has not been followed by a Competent Authority at the domestic level, or that it is at best doubtful whether it has been followed. He must do what he reasonably can in order to ascertain from the Competent Authority whether the appropriate consultation has been held and if it has not, to encourage it to remedy that omission. It is not without significance that Article 26 makes it explicit that the system of consultations shall be structured to ensure that Community Organs are adequately informed by relevant information inputs.[173]

The duty of consultation is a strong one in the eyes of the CCJ. This is seen in the way that in the same judgment the Court went on to indicate what steps should have been taken by the Secretary General before exercising his discretion to grant a waiver.[174] At paragraph 74 of its judgment the Court expressly criticizes the Secretary General for his failure to properly consult:

[74] The practice by the Secretary-General of accepting as a sufficient answer to his inquiry as to a Member State's ability to supply the needs of another Member State which is seeking permission to suspend CET, the response that the first Member State has 'no objections' is wrong and must cease. It is a practice born out of the peculiar provisions of the original treaty as to unanimity but it does not comport with the terms of the *RTC*. Before the Secretary-General may exercise his discretion to authorise a suspension, the treaty provisions require that he must be satisfied as to the relationship between demand and supply with respect to the commodity concerned and not with whether a Member State objects or does not object to a request for suspension.

Despite such strong language, however, the Court ultimately characterized the Secretary General's failure to properly consult as being merely a 'procedural flaw' and, after weighing the serious challenges arising from an annulment of his decision,

[173] *Trinidad Cement v CARICOM* (n 171) [68].
[174] See *Trinidad Cement v CARICOM* (n 171) [69]–[71] and [74]–[77].

decided simply to issue a declaration indicating the wrongfulness of his actions.[175] Nevertheless the decision in *Trinidad Cement Limited v CARICOM* should serve as a clear warning to CARICOM organs and member states. Although the Court arguably let the Secretary General off lightly, the judgment as a whole provides notice that improper consultation may result in sanctions by the Court, potentially including the annulment of a contested decision.

The RTB formally requires consultation between organs in several articles. Under Article 8.10 the OECS Authority is required to refer proposals regarding Acts to the OECS Assembly for its report. This report is expressly stated to be non-binding. The OECS Assembly is likewise mandated to report to the Authority in Article 10.13. The Council of Ministers, under Article 9.4 of the RTB is required to follow the directions of the Authority regarding consultation with the OECS Assembly, and is also empowered to initiate such consultations on its own volition. The OECS Assembly is mandated to report to the Council on any proposals referred by it under Article 10.13, and the Commission is required to make recommendations to the Authority and the Council on Acts and Regulations and to provide drafts of both under Article 12.5(c).

It is likely that these requirements for consultation will be read strictly, in the sense that even if the Authority, for example, is not required to comply with a report by the Assembly, an omission to ask for that report (to consult) could lead to the annulment of the Act concerned. This consequence arose in EU law when under an earlier version of the treaties the Council was merely required to consult with Parliament. The ECJ held in the case of Case 138/79 *Roquette Frères v Council* that such consultation is an essential procedural requirement that must be observed:

> 33 The consultation provided for in the third subparagraph of Article 43 (2), as in other similar provisions of the Treaty, is the means which allows the Parliament to play an actual part in the legislative process of the Community. Such power represents an essential factor in the institutional balance intended by the Treaty. Although limited, it reflects at Community level the fundamental democratic principle that the peoples should take part in the exercise of power through the intermediary of a representative assembly. Due consultation of the Parliament in the cases provided for by the Treaty therefore constitutes an essential formality disregard of which means that the measure concerned is void.
>
> 34 In that respect it is pertinent to point out that observance of that requirement implies that the Parliament has expressed its opinion. It is impossible to take the view that the requirement is satisfied by the Council's simply asking for the opinion. The Council is, therefore, wrong to include in the references in the preamble to Regulation No 1293/79 a statement to the effect that the Parliament has been consulted.[176]

In this passage the ECJ imposes a real requirement for consultation. Not only must the measure be referred to Parliament, Parliament must express its opinion.

[175] *Trinidad Cement v CARICOM* (n 171) [75] and [81]. The declaration, in the latter paragraph, succinctly states: 'it was wrong for the Secretary-General to accept as a sufficient answer to his inquiry regarding a request for suspension by Jamaica, the response of Trinidad and Tobago that it had "no objections" to Jamaica's request.'

[176] [1980] ECR 3333, at pp 3360–1 [33]–[34].

Further, if no meaningful consultation is held, the EU legislative act in question is voidable, as in fact occurred in the *Roquette Frères* case.[177]

Subsequent ECJ case-law has clarified that this duty of consultation is not unlimited. In the Case C-65/93 *European Parliament v Council*, for example, the ECJ held that even though 'due consultation...constitutes an essential procedural requirement, disregard of which renders the measure concerned void' that nevertheless if the Parliament is at fault in not providing its opinion, the Council may be able to adopt a measure without receiving the opinion of the Parliament.[178] On the facts of the case, the Court held that the 'essential procedural requirement of Parliamentary consultation was not complied with because of the Parliament's failure to discharge its obligation to cooperate sincerely with the Council'.[179] Under such circumstances, Parliament's challenge to the legislative act was dismissed.[180]

In the OECS context, it is likely that a similar fault on the part of the OECS Assembly would defeat an attempt by the Assembly to void a legislative act on grounds of not fulfilling the consultation requirement. In any event, Article 10.13 of the RTB specifically empowers the Authority to prescribe time periods within which the Assembly must consider and report to it on Acts, Regulations, and other matters. Presumably a failure by the Assembly to report within that time period would terminate the Authority's requirement to consult, so long as the time period prescribed was reasonable.

The duties regarding consultation in both the RTC and RTB could give rise to a general principle of consultation in the same manner as suggested for a general principle of cooperation. Both general principles may be deemed necessary to support the organizational structures of the organizations and to enable both to fulfil their objects and purposes. As seen in the example of the EU, failure to observe a requirement for consultation could lead to the voiding of a particular legal act. But as a general principle the principle of consultation could be applied more broadly, to help resolve questions about the proper relations of organs, and the relations of organs and member states. As hinted at in Case 138/79 *Roquette Frères v Council*, principles such as consultation and cooperation may be seen to be part of the fundamental architecture of regional organizations. They may be viewed as essential for safeguarding the institutional balance of the organization and for maintaining the appropriate separation of competences between organs, and between organs and member states.

177 *Roquette Frères v Council* (n 176) at p 3361 [37].
178 [1995] ECR I-643, at pp I-668 [21] and I-669 [28].
179 *European Parliament v Council* (n 178) at p I-669 [28].
180 *European Parliament v Council* (n 178) p I-670 [30].

8.11 Human Rights

A general principle that may arise under Caribbean Community law, and which was raised in litigation before the CCJ, is that of human rights.[181] This general principle was established in EU law by the ECJ prior to the eventual inclusion of provisions related to human rights in the EU treaties.[182] Its development in EU law, in the absence of any significant reference to human rights in the texts of the treaties, is of interest to the Caribbean.[183]

The first EU case to raise the possibility of a principle of fundamental rights was Case 29/69 *Stauder v Ulm*.[184] In *Stauder* the applicant challenged the condition imposed by a Commission Decision that the sale of butter at reduced prices to beneficiaries under certain social welfare schemes required the divulging to retailers of the name of the beneficiaries, on the grounds of incompatibility with the general principles of Community law in force. The Court agreed that the Decision should not be read in such a way, holding 'that the provision in question must be interpreted as not requiring…the identification of beneficiaries by name'.[185] However the most important part of the judgment is a sentence that the Court

[181] The claimant and the intervener argued that a number of human rights had been violated in the case of *Shanique Myrie v Barbados* (n 97), citing in support the Universal Declaration of Human Rights, the International Covenant on Civil and Political Rights and the American Convention on Human Rights. The CCJ abruptly dismissed these arguments at [10], holding that the 'Court has no jurisdiction to adjudicate violations of international human rights treaties and conventions'. Nevertheless the Court did not fully close the door. The CCJ concluded the same paragraph by stating that 'in the resolution of a claim properly brought to its original jurisdiction, the Court can and must take into account principles of international human rights law when seeking to shape and develop relevant Community law'.

[182] At present there are several TEU articles expressly referring to fundamental human rights and these rights are also protected by the Charter of Fundamental Rights of the European Union, in Consolidated versions of the Treaty on European Union and the Treaty on the Functioning of the European Union (OJ C83, 30.3.2010) at 389–403. See eg TEU Arts 6, 7, 9, and 11 and the Charter of Fundamental Rights of the European Union. In Art 6(1) of the TEU the 'Union recognises the rights, freedoms and principles set out in the Charter of Fundamental Rights of the European Union…which shall have the same legal value as the Treaties.' Under Art 6(3) the EU is required to accede to the *European Convention for the* Protection of Human Rights and Fundamental Freedoms and Art 6(4) stipulates that the '[f]undamental rights, as guaranteed by the European Convention for the Protection of Human Rights and Fundamental Freedoms and as they result from the constitutional traditions common to the Member States, shall constitute general principles of the Union's law.' As a result human rights are part of EU law through three different sources, namely, (1) general principles of EU law, (2) the Charter of Fundamental Rights of the European Union, and once the EU becomes a party, (3) the European Convention for the Protection of Human Rights and Fundamental Freedoms. On the relation of these three sources see eg Hartley, *The Foundations of European Union Law* (n 9) 154–6.

[183] Note that the development of the general principle of human rights in the EU was linked to a particular threat to the legitimacy of the ECJ itself, and is in this sense tied to a political-legal struggle between the ECJ and national courts. This threat arose from challenges by national courts, in particular German courts, to the supremacy of EU law over the human rights provisions in national constitutions. German legal scholars argued that EU law could not be applied in Germany if it was inconsistent with the human rights provisions in the German constitution (*Grundgesetz*). The ECJ, in an attempt to head off this challenge, adopted an EU system of human rights. See eg Hartley 143–4.

[184] [1969] ECR 419.

[185] *Stauder v Ulm* (n 184) at p 425 [6].

adds, almost in passing, which simply states that '[i]nterpreted in this way the provision at issue contains nothing capable of prejudicing the fundamental human rights enshrined in the general principles of Community law and protected by the Court.'[186] Nowhere in the judgment does the Court indicate what these 'fundamental human rights' may be, because the Commission Decision in question does not prejudice them.

A second decision of the Court, Case 11/70 *Internationale Handelsgesellschaft*, firmly rooted fundamental human rights as a principle of EU law, one that could not be challenged in or by national law, but that could be inspired by the common constitutional traditions of member states.[187] The plaintiff in the case challenged a system of export licences and deposits existing under the EEC Treaty regime as being contrary to, amongst other things, the principle of proportionality.[188] In coming to the conclusion that the EEC regime did not violate the plaintiff's rights, the Court first firmly upheld the principle of supremacy of EU law over national law, including over human rights protected under national constitutions.[189] Secondly, the Court described, and then applied, the fundamental human rights *protected by the EU* to the facts of the case. In paragraph 4 of its judgment the Court held:

> 4 However, an examination should be made as to whether or not any analogous guarantee inherent in Community law has been disregarded. In fact, respect for fundamental rights forms an integral part of the general principles of law protected by the Court of Justice. The protection of such rights, whilst inspired by the constitutional traditions common to the Member States, must be ensured within the framework of the structure and objectives of the Community. It must therefore be ascertained, in the light of the doubts expressed by the Verwaltungsgericht, whether the system of deposits has infringed rights of a fundamental nature, respect for which must be ensured in the Community legal system.[190]

The Court upheld the system of licenses and deposits as not violating any of the EU's fundamental rights, implicitly including a right to proportionality.[191] In doing so, the Court further entrenched fundamental human rights as a principle of EU law. The ECJ also opened the door slightly to the influence (inspiration) of national human rights regimes and the 'constitutional traditions common to the Member States'.

A third case, Case 4/73 *Nold v Commission* went much further in developing the principle of fundamental rights.[192] In *Nold* a coal supplier was authorized by a Commission Decision to subject its dealers, including Nold, to onerous conditions before supplying them with coal. Nold could not meet these conditions and so challenged the Decision.[193] Nold challenged it, inter alia, on the basis that it

[186] *Stauder v Ulm* p 425 [7].

[187] Case 11/70 *Internationale Handelsgesellschaft mbH v Einfuhr- und Vorratsstelle für Getreide und Futtermittel* [1970] ECR 1125.

[188] *Futtermittel* (n 187) at p 1133 [2]–[3].

[189] *Futtermittel* (n 187) p 1134 [3], quoted in footnote 104.

[190] *Futtermittel* (n 187) p 1134 [4].

[191] *Futtermittel* (n 187) p 1139.

[192] [1974] ECR 491.

[193] *Nold v Commission* (n 192) at p 503 [1].

violated Nold's fundamental rights—arguing that it infringed property rights and the right to free pursuit of business activities.[194] Nold argued that these rights were protected in the constitutions of the various member states and in international human rights treaties, and must also be protected in EU law. In response, the Court held:

> As the Court has already stated, fundamental rights form an integral part of the general principles of law, the observance of which it ensures.
>
> In safeguarding these rights, the Court is bound to draw inspiration from constitutional traditions common to the Member States, and it cannot therefore uphold measures which are incompatible with fundamental rights recognized and protected by the Constitutions of those States.
>
> Similarly, international treaties for the protection of human rights on which the Member States have collaborated or of which they are signatories, can supply guidelines which should be followed within the framework of Community law.[195]

This is a very strong statement regarding the role of fundamental human rights, their potential effect and the sources from which they may be derived. Nevertheless the Court was unable to uphold Nold's claim because the fundamental human rights alleged to be violated are subject to public interest limitations, both in national laws and in EU law. In addition the Court held that mere commercial interests or opportunities could not be protected. It also suggested that Nold had not been prejudiced so much by the Decision as by the general economic changes in the coal market, which it should have adjusted and adapted itself to as part of its normal business practices.[196]

These statements by the ECJ reveal a power to strike down EU measures which are incompatible with the general principle of fundamental human rights. In the *Nold* case the Court sets out a broad interpretation of the principle of fundamental rights but, as in the *Stauder* case, does not find any violation of such rights on the facts. Later ECJ cases further entrench the general principle of fundamental rights, by linking the protected rights to those upheld in the regional human rights treaty—the European Convention on Human Rights—and the case-law of the European Court of Human Rights.[197] The ECJ also arrogates to itself the role of safeguarding EU human rights, but at the same time allows national courts, through the preliminary reference procedure, to participate in their enforcement.[198]

These cases demonstrate the way in which the ECJ has gradually developed the general principle of fundamental rights, relying upon the constitutions and treaty obligations of EU member states, without originally having a clear textual basis in the treaties.[199] It may be possible to establish a similar general principle in

[194] *Nold v Commission* (n 192) p 507 [12].

[195] *Nold v Commission* (n 192) p 507 [13].

[196] *Nold v Commission* (n 192) p 508 [14]–[15].

[197] See eg Case C-94/00 *Roquette Frères SA v Directeur général de la concurrence, de la consommation et de la répression des fraudes, and Commission of the European Communities* [2002] ECR I-9011, at [25].

[198] *Roquette Frères* (n 197) at [25].

[199] This textual basis now exists. See footnote 182.

CARICOM, since the countries of the Caribbean region share very similar human rights norms, perhaps more similar than those shared by EU countries at the time of adoption of the general principle by the ECJ. All CARICOM member states are also parties to the Charter of the Organization of American States, and are thus governed by the human rights protections available under that treaty, as interpreted by the American Declaration of the Rights and Duties of Man.[200] In addition, human rights are expressly referred to in the preamble of the RTC in relation to the CARICOM Charter of Civil Society.[201] As a result of these shared constitutional and international treaty-based human rights values, it would be possible to derive as a general principle of CARICOM law the principle of fundamental rights.

If such a general principle of human rights were to be recognized by the CCJ its scope would require definition. Two different positions could be adopted. The first, stronger position, would be to develop the general principle broadly so as to encompass all of the fundamental human rights shared in the constitutions and treaty commitments of CARICOM member states. Such a general principle would not be limited to the rights or obligations arising under the RTC. The second position would be to limit the category of fundamental human rights protected by the general principle to those reasonably connected to the rights, obligations and purposes of the RTC. This more conservative position is preferable since it would tie the general principle more closely to the text of the RTC, which is the best expression of the intent of the member states of CARICOM.

In the alternative, if a general principle of human rights were deemed to be unacceptable to member states or the CCJ, human rights could be read into the RTC through a process of treaty interpretation. Following the Inter-American human rights model, it could be possible to interpret the references to human rights in the RTC, under the general rules of interpretation in the law of treaties, in light of the protections offered in CARICOM's non-binding human rights declaration, the Charter of Civil Society.[202] In Advisory Opinion 10 of 1989 the Inter-American Court of Human Rights recognized the American Declaration as an authoritative guide to the interpretation of the meaning of the phrase 'fundamental rights of the individual' found in Articles 3(l) and 17 of the OAS Charter.[203] The Inter-American Court explained that although the American Declaration is not a treaty, the OAS

[200] Charter of the Organization of American States (1948) 119 UNTS 4 (amended 721 UNTS 324), as amended (OAS Charter). The American Declaration of Rights and Duties of Man (1948), as available at <http://www.oas.org/en/iachr/mandate/basic_documents.asp> (6 Jan 2013) (American Declaration).

[201] Interestingly, human rights are also mentioned in relation to the farming community in Art 64(3) of the RTC: '3. In particular, COTED shall promote and encourage research and development, and the adaptation, diffusion and transfer of appropriate technologies in order to achieve increased agricultural production and productivity, bearing in mind the need to protect the independence and human rights of the farming community.'

[202] Charter of Civil Society for the Caribbean Community, as reproduced in Caribbean Community Secretariat, *Charter of Civil Society* (Georgetown, Guyana, 1997). On the role of the Charter and its National Committees see Chapter 5.

[203] *Interpretation of the American Declaration of the Rights and Duties of Man Within the Framework of Article 64 of the American Convention on Human Rights* (Advisory Opinion OC-10/89) I-A Ct HR, Judgment of 14 July 1989, Series A, No 10.

Charter is, and the latter protects human rights.[204] According to the Court the Inter-American Commission was established under the OAS Charter to protect human rights and these 'rights are none other than those enunciated and defined in the American Declaration', as recognized in the Commission's Statute and by the General Assembly of the Organization.[205] As a result, the Court explained that '[f]or the member states of the Organization, the Declaration is the text that defines the human rights referred to in the Charter.'[206] If a similar interpretive route were to be taken in relation to the RTC and the Charter of Civil Society, the Charter could be given an important interpretive role in relation to a binding treaty, the RTC. Such a role could allow the CCJ to read human rights protections into the RTC as part of the interpretive process.

By means of a similar process of deduction a principle of human rights could arise in the OECS context. The preamble to the RTB mentions human rights. Links are made between human rights and education in Article 22.2, and between human rights and human and social development in Article 23, of the Protocol. Human rights might also be argued to be a necessary precondition for the achievement of other goals of the OECS, such as human development, under Article 13 of the Protocol. Although the OECS does not have an equivalent of the Charter of Civil Society applicable solely to the sub-region, all OECS member states are covered by the terms of the Charter through their membership in CARICOM. As a result the general principle of human rights could equally be derived from OECS law.

8.12 Need for Reasons

Another general principle that may arise in the context of CARICOM and the OECS is the requirement for reasons, or justifications.[207] A requirement for reasoning seems crucial to the effective functioning of any regional integration system, and is demonstrated by the experience of the EU. The need to state reasons is set out expressly in the TFEU and applies to all legal acts.[208] It mandates EU organs to set out reasons supporting a proposed measure. These reasons must include reference to both the facts and the law upon which the proposed measure is based, its objectives, and the rationale for attaining these objectives.[209]

[204] Advisory Opinion OC-10/89 (n 203) [33]–[34] and [39]–[40], respectively.

[205] Advisory Opinion OC-10/89 [41]. See also [42]–[47].

[206] Advisory Opinion OC-10/89 [45].

[207] Note that this is distinct from the requirement for reasonableness, which exists in many fields of international law: Olivier Corten, 'Reasonableness in International Law', in R Wolfrum (ed), *The Max Planck Encyclopedia of Public International Law* (Oxford University Press, 2008–) online edition, [<www.mpepil.com>] (accessed 23 Feb 2013).

[208] See eg the second paragraph of Art 296 of the TFEU, which states: 'Legal acts shall state the reasons on which they are based and shall refer to any proposals, initiatives, recommendations, requests or opinions required by the Treaties.' Under previous versions of the EU treaties it applied to a more limited category of legal acts.

[209] See Hartley, *The Foundations of European Union Law* (n 9) 135. See generally pp 134–9.

The requirement for reasons is important because it forces an organ to justify, and articulate in writing a justification for, any proposed measure. Reasons provided by an organ during the legislative process allow member states and other organs to make relevant representations to the originating organ to change a proposed measure prior to its adoption. Reasons also assist member states and other organs in deciding whether to challenge an adopted measure. Reasons are necessary for a court or tribunal to assess whether a measure falls within the competence of the originating organ or whether it has been adopted following the appropriate procedure. Third parties also find reasons helpful because they assist them in better assessing how a measure will be applied in practice.

In Case 45/86 *Commission v Council* the ECJ raised the requirement for reasoning in the context of a challenge to a Council Regulation dealing with external trade policy by the Commission.[210] The Council's Regulation contained no explicit statement of the law (treaty provision) upon which it was based. In assessing whether the Regulation complied with EU legal norms, the Court held that 'Community measures must include a statement of the facts and law which led the institution in question to adopt them, so as to make possible review by the Court and so that the Member States and nationals concerned may have knowledge of the conditions under which the Community institutions have applied the Treaty.'[211] The Court further noted:

> [F]ailure to refer to a precise provision of the Treaty need not necessarily constitute an infringement of essential procedural requirements when the legal basis for the measure may be determined from other parts of the measure. However, such explicit reference is indispensable where, in its absence, the parties concerned and the Court are left uncertain as to the precise legal basis.[212]

Applying this analysis to the facts, the Court held that the Council's Regulations were void for failing to satisfy the requirement for statement of reasons and because they were not adopted on the correct legal basis.[213] In other words, non-compliance with the principle of reasoning provided the grounds to void a measure.

The requirement for reasoning, although not set out in the decision-making provisions of the RTC, is expressed in wording in other articles which require reasons or justifications. Such a need for reasons is imposed upon member states and organs of CARICOM.[214] A similar kind of requirement for reasoning is found in the OECS context in several provisions of the RTB and its Protocol.[215] Although these treaty provisions are not general in their application and therefore cannot be said to give rise to a universal need for reasoning applicable to all organs of CARICOM and the OECS, it may be possible to read a need for reasoning into the frameworks of the RTC and RTB as a general principle of law. Such a

[210] [1987] ECR 1493. [211] Case 45/86 *Commission v Council* (n 210) at p 1519 [5].
[212] Case 45/86 *Commission v Council* (n 210) pp 1519–20 [9].
[213] Case 45/86 *Commission v Council* (n 210) p 1522 [21]–[22].
[214] See eg RTC Arts 27(6), Art 48(2), 89(3), 114(2), 193(4), and Art 207(5).
[215] See eg RTB Arts 11.7, 14.3, 15.2, and Protocol Art 30.5.

principle could have a tremendous impact upon the decision-making processes of CARICOM and the OECS which, as noted in the Introduction to this book, are far from transparent and in fact are conducted under what has been argued to be a 'culture of confidentiality'.[216]

8.13 Proportionality

The general principle of proportionality was judicially developed in EU law by the ECJ, originally finding no express basis in the treaties.[217] It is now reflected in Article 5(4) of the TEU, which provides:

> 4 Under the principle of proportionality, the content and form of Union action shall not exceed what is necessary to achieve the objectives of the Treaties.
>
> The institutions of the Union shall apply the principle of proportionality as laid down in the Protocol on the application of the principles of subsidiarity and proportionality.

The principle limits the legislative competence of EU institutions and imposes upon them, under Protocol (No 2), the obligation to justify draft legislative acts as complying with it.[218]

The meaning of the principle was fleshed out by the ECJ in Case 181/84 *R v Intervention Board, ex parte Man (Sugar) Ltd*.[219] This case involved a British sugar trader, E D & F Man (Sugar) Ltd ('Man Sugar'), submitting a tender for export of sugar outside of the EU. This tender required deposit of the substantial sum of nearly £1,700,000. The trader was unable to apply for its export licence in time (missing the deadline by four hours), and the British regulatory agency, the Intervention Board for Agricultural Produce (the 'Board'), kept the entire deposit. Man Sugar alleged that this penalty was disproportionate. The matter was referred

[216] Richard Stoneman, Justice Duke Pollard, and Hugo Inniss, 'Turning Around CARICOM: Proposals to Restructure the Secretariat', Landell Mills Ltd/ Final Report/ January 2012, as available at <http://www.caricom.org/jsp/communications/caricom_online_pubs/Restructuring%20the%20Secretariat%20-%20Landell%20Mills%20Final%20Report.pdf> (9 Feb 2013), 67.

[217] See eg Hartley, *The Foundations of European Union Law* (n 9) 165.

[218] Protocol (No 2) on the Application of the Principles of Subsidiarity and Proportionality, in Consolidated versions of the Treaty on European Union and the Treaty on the Functioning of the European Union (OJ C83, 30.3.2010) as available through <http://eur-lex.europa.eu/en/treaties/index.htm> (accessed 30 Sep 2011) 206. Art 5 of Protocol (No 2) at p 207 states:

> Draft legislative acts shall be justified with regard to the principles of subsidiarity and proportionality. Any draft legislative act should contain a detailed statement making it possible to appraise compliance with the principles of subsidiarity and proportionality. This statement should contain some assessment of the proposal's financial impact and, in the case of a directive, of its implications for the rules to be put in place by Member States, including, where necessary, the regional legislation. The reasons for concluding that a Union objective can be better achieved at Union level shall be substantiated by qualitative and, wherever possible, quantitative indicators. Draft legislative acts shall take account of the need for any burden, whether financial or administrative, falling upon the Union, national governments, regional or local authorities, economic operators and citizens, to be minimised and commensurate with the objective to be achieved.

[219] [1985] ECR 2889.

to the ECJ by means of the preliminary reference procedure. The Court agreed with Man Sugar. The test, according to the ECJ, is 'whether the means which [the provision of EU law] employs are appropriate and necessary to attain the objective sought'.[220] In applying this test to the facts, the Court drew a distinction between primary and secondary obligations imposed by EU law, the latter of which are of an administrative nature. The Court held that these two types of obligations could not be penalized at the same level without offending the principle of proportionality.[221] Since the primary obligation in this case was to export sugar, the Court held that automatic forfeiture of the entire security for failure to comply with a secondary obligation—the obligation to obtain export licences within a limited period of time—was 'too drastic a penalty in relation to the export licence's function of ensuring the sound management of the market in question'.[222] The Court therefore invalidated the relevant article of the Regulation.[223]

The principle of proportionality is not directly expressed in the same manner in either the RTC or RTB. However the RTC does expressly refer to the concept of proportionality in various articles,[224] and Article 14.3 of the RTB, in imposing a subsidiarity requirement, places a similar means/ends restriction on legislative action of the OECS.[225] The CCJ has alluded to the application of proportionality as a criterion to be used in judicial review of decisions of organs of CARICOM. In the case of *Trinidad Cement Ltd v Caribbean Community*, when assessing COTED's suspension of the Common External Tariff in relation to cement, the Court expressly relied upon the principle of proportionality and indicated that it 'must at all times be adhered to by COTED'.[226] This is a strong statement and could foreshadow a robust application of the principle by the Court's position in future cases.[227] In addition, as highlighted by Trevor Hartley, the principle is 'to some extent analogous to the English concept of reasonableness'.[228] As such, it

[220] *Ex parte Man (Sugar)* (n 219) at p 2903 [20].
[221] *Ex parte Man (Sugar)* (n 219) p 2903 [20].
[222] *Ex parte Man (Sugar)* (n 219) p 2905 [29].
[223] *Ex parte Man (Sugar)* (n 219) p 2906 [31].
[224] See eg RTC Arts 92(3) (difficulties occasioned by particular imports), 97(2)(a)(iii) (types of subsidies and specificity), and 111(1)(d)(iv) (types of subsidies causing serious adverse effects).
[225] Art 14.3 of the RTB provides:

> 14.3 In the areas of legislative competence of the Organisation which do not fall under Article 14.1, the Organisation shall enact Acts of the Organisation only if and in so far as the objectives of the proposed action cannot, in the opinion of the OECS Authority, be sufficiently achieved by the Member States and can therefore, by reason of the scale or effects of the proposed action, be better achieved by enacting an Act of the Organisation.

[226] Judgment [2009] CCJ 4 (OJ), (2009) 75 WIR 194, 10 August 2009. The Court noted at [78]:

> The amount of cement in respect of which the suspensions were given and the fact that the suspensions were only for a one year duration, although suspension for two years was sought, indicates an observance of the principle of proportionality which must at all times be adhered to by COTED. As previously indicated, in reviewing COTED's discretion this Court is not entitled to substitute its own judgment for that of COTED. If COTED's decision is so wholly disproportionate as to be unconnected with the facts, the decision might be set aside and the application for the suspension remitted to COTED for fresh consideration.

[227] See also the CCJ's reliance upon the principle of proportionality in *Shanique Myrie v Barbados* (n 97) at [70].
[228] Hartley, *The Foundations of European Union Law* (n 9) 166.

would be suitable for adoption in both CARICOM and OECS law, as a general principle of law. Proportionality is also a concept common to most, if not all, CARICOM member states, and thus could be derived as a general principle common to the legal systems of its membership. A general principle of proportionality would be of great utility to the CCJ and the Eastern Caribbean Court of Appeal in their roles as regional integration tribunals. It could be used to limit both the types, and consequences, of decisions made by the organs of CARICOM and the OECS, respectively, as well as to check retaliatory actions undertaken by member states under the RTC and RTB regimes.

8.14 Conclusions

As seen in the previous chapter, general principles of law fulfil a number of crucial needs in any legal system. Perhaps most importantly, they add flesh to the skeletal frame of a regional legal system by bringing key values into the law. This is clearly illustrated by the list of potential general principles, or concepts founded on general principles, covered in the present chapter: conferral, direct applicability, direct effect, indirect effect, supremacy, pre-emption, state liability, non-discrimination, Most Favoured Nation treatment, cooperation, consultation, human rights, reasoning, and proportionality.[229] If some or all of these principles and concepts are accepted in CARICOM and OECS law, the regional integration movement will be substantially deepened and made more meaningful.

[229] Note that additional general principles already existing in EU law also might arise in the Caribbean region, including the principles associated with legal certainty (such as non-retroactivity, vested rights, and legitimate expectations), the right to a fair hearing, and principles related to legal-professional privilege. See Hartley, *The Foundations of European Union Law* (n 9) 160–5 and 168–71.

PART IV

SUBSTANTIVE RULES AND POLICIES

Context

The legal rules of the CARICOM Single Market and Economy (CSME) and of the OECS Economic Union are set out at length in several chapters of the RTC and the RTB and its Protocol. A comprehensive analysis of all of these rules is outside of the scope of the present work. The modest purpose of Part IV is to introduce the general categories of substantive rules and policies and to highlight, where possible, important or unusual features of the two regional integration systems, starting with CARICOM and concluding with the OECS. Comparative reference is also made to the rules of the EU and WTO, upon which the regional systems appear to have been largely based, in order to reveal possible ways of interpreting and developing our regional rules.

In assessing the overall progress of CARICOM in the areas covered in the present Part, a study by the CARICOM Secretariat suggests that the Community is operating at a level of approximately 64 per cent compliance with respect to the five core regimes established by the CSME.[1] The compliance level of each of the five core regimes, as of January 2012, is was as follows:

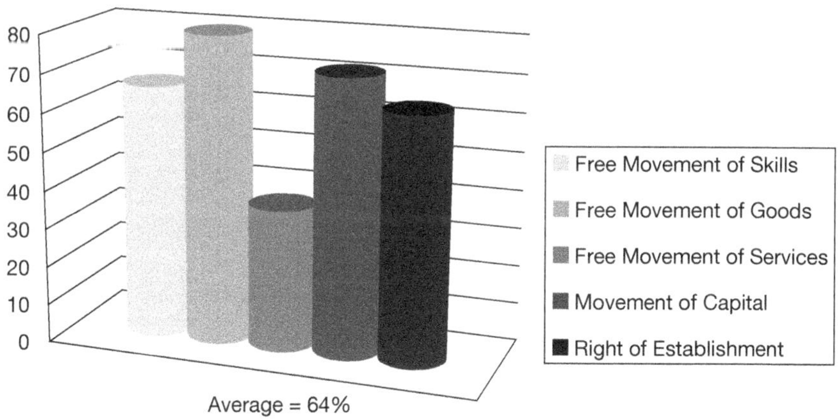

Figure 9.1 Compliance level in five core areas of CSME

[1] CARICOM Secretariat, 'Press Release: CARICOM Studies show the CSME operating at about 64% level of compliance', No 22/20122 (23 January 2012) (Turkeyen, Guyana: CARICOM Secretariat, 2012).

As illustrated by the chart in Figure 9.1, compliance levels are lowest in those areas which may require movement of natural and juridical persons. This should not be surprising. Issues of freedom of movement have challenged regional integration in the Caribbean since the time of the West Indies Federation.[2]

This slow progress is also attributable to a number of factors, including lack of capacity in all member states to implement the necessary legislative, administrative, and technical changes.[3] Such capacity problems are more pronounced for LDCs. Other challenges include the inability of existing institutions to implement the CSME, the limited absorptive capacity (real or perceived) of national markets, the at times negative attitudes to regional integration expressed at the political and popular levels, and parochial and nationalistic social and cultural attitudes.[4] Nevertheless, the CARICOM Secretariat does not appear to be unduly concerned with the present levels of non-compliance. It reports:

> On the basis of what Member States have actually done, the charge generally heard in the Community that Member States act more in the breach rather than in compliance, is not generally factually correct. Even where this is factually correct the charge rarely takes account of what Member states have committed to under the Treaty and the situations which they face including the capacity and economic issues...[5]

Moreover, in the same study the CARICOM Secretariat indicates that there is overall acceptance of the CSME regime as a whole, with there being no 'condemnation of the CSM [CARICOM Single Market] as a whole or any of its core components.'[6]

Popular comprehension and acceptance will be crucial to the effective operation of the CSME. However rule-based enforcement mechanisms will be equally important. As illustrated in the examples from the jurisprudence of the ECJ throughout this Part, a regional integration movement will significantly benefit from strong, creative, and purposive interpretation of its constituent instruments.

[2] In Gladstone Mills et al, *Report on a Comprehensive Review of the Programmes, Institutions and Organisations of the Carribean Community* (Georgetown, Guyana: Carribean Community Secretariat, 1990) at 32, the authors comment that '[d]isagreement over the question of freedom of movement was one of the rocks upon which the defunct West Indies Federation foundered.'

[3] See eg CARICOM Secretariat, *Summary Draft Report on the Appraisal of the State of Implementation of the CARICOM Single Market* (September 2009) (Georgetown, Guyana: CARICOM Secretariat, 2009) [hereafter '*Summary Draft Report*'], 36–8.

[4] CARICOM Secretariat, *Summary Draft Report* (n 2) 38–42.

[5] CARICOM Secretariat, *Summary Draft Report* (n 2) 41.

[6] CARICOM Secretariat, *Summary Draft Report* (n 2) 3.

9

Right of Establishment and Free Movement of Services, Capital, and Persons

This chapter explores aspects of integration not directly related to the free movement of goods, including the right of establishment, free movement of persons, services, and capital. Rules related to the free movement of goods will be explored in Chapter 10. Some of the topics in the present chapter have proved controversial because they raise questions related to the free movement of persons. Historically, fears of mass migration shaped the regional integration movement, presenting challenges to the West Indies Federation. Migration continues to influence the current Caribbean integration movements and its effects may make it an important force for regional integration.[7] It is in this context that we must examine the right of establishment and the movement of persons and services.

9.1 Right of Establishment[8]

9.1.1 CARICOM

The right of establishment, provided in Chapter 3 of the RTC, allows for the creation of, and staffing at the management and technical levels of, companies in other CARICOM jurisdictions.[9] It only applies to 'nationals of other Member States' and means the right to '(a) engage in any non-wage-earning activities [defined as 'activities of a self-employed person'] of a commercial, industrial, agricultural, professional or artisanal nature', and to '(b) create and manage

[7] It should be noted, however, that migration has been a powerful integrative force and continues to play this important role today. See eg Jessica Byron, 'Migration, National Identity and Regionalism in the Caribbean: A Leeward Islands Case Study' in Kenneth Hall and Dennis Benn (eds), *Contending With Destiny: The Caribbean in the 21st Century* (Kingston, Jamaica: Ian Randle Publishers, 2000), 80–90.

[8] For more on the EU regime on freedom of establishment see eg Catherine Barnard, *The Substantive Law of the EU: The Four Freedoms*, 3rd edn (Oxford: Oxford University Press, 2010) ch 10.

[9] The right of establishment should preclude the need for work permits for managerial, technical, and supervisory persons for the newly established companies. As a result, in the case of those member states which have not implemented the necessary national legislative changes, work permits that would otherwise be required are now waived. See eg CARICOM Secretariat, *Summary Draft Report* 21 and 23.

economic enterprises'.[10] The term 'economic enterprises' is defined in Article 32(5)(b) as including 'any type of organisation for the production of or trade in goods or the provision of services (other than a non-profit organization) owned or controlled by' a national of another member state. Article 32(5)(a) defines the term 'national' for the purposes of Chapter 3 as follows:

> 5. For the purposes of this Chapter:
>   (a) a person shall be regarded as a national of a Member State if such person –
>   (i) is a citizen of that State;
>   (ii) has a connection with that State of a kind which entitles him to be regarded as belonging to or, if it be so expressed, as being a native or resident of the State for the purposes of the laws thereof relating to immigration; or
>   (iii) is a company or other legal entity constituted in the Member State in conformity with the laws thereof and which that State regards as belonging to it, provided that such company or other legal entity has been formed for gainful purposes and has its registered office and central administration, and carries on substantial activity, within the Community and which is substantially owned and effectively controlled by persons mentioned in sub-paragraphs (i) and (ii) of this paragraph...

Article 32(5(a)(ii) describes a status known as 'Belonger' in the law of the Commonwealth Caribbean, which entitles persons who have established close connections to a territory (traditionally prior to its independence), to enter, leave and reside in the territory, even though they may not have acquired citizenship.[11] Article 32(5)(a)(iii) seems to extend the notion of Belonger to a company, but at the same time greatly restricts the kinds of companies that can exercise the right of establishment. As a result, to exercise a right of establishment a juridical person must have been (a) incorporated in a member state, (b) formed for gainful purposes, (c) have a registered office and central administration in a member state, (d) carry on substantial activity within the Community, (e) be substantially owned, and (f) effectively controlled by persons who are either citizens or Belongers of member states.

The term 'company' is defined in Article 32(5)(c) as follows:

> (c) a company or other legal entity is:
>   (i) substantially owned if more than 50% of the equity interest therein is beneficially owned by nationals mentioned in subparagraph (a) (i) or (ii) of this paragraph;
>   (ii) effectively controlled if nationals mentioned in sub-paragraph (a) of this paragraph have the power to name a majority of its directors or otherwise legally to direct its actions.

[10] RTC Art 32(1) and (3).

[11] See eg the pre-independence Bahamian legislation discussed in the context of the case of *Godfrey Frederick Seymour and Jermaine Seymour v Attorney-General, Director of Immigration, Honourable A. Loftus Roker (Minister of National Security), and the Board of Immigration*, Supreme Court of the Commonwealth of the Bahamas, Common Law Side No 1330 of 1986 (25 June 1987) [unreported]; see also *Nielsen v Barker and Another* (1982) 32 WIR 254 (Court of Appeal of Guyana).

This very restrictive test was considered, but not applied, by the CCJ in deciding what kinds of entities could seek special leave to bring a claim under the Court's original jurisdiction, in the case of *Trinidad Cement Ltd and TCL Guyana Inc. v Guyana*.[12] It was there argued by Guyana that the two claimant companies had to satisfy the test for nationality set out in Article 32 in order to espouse a claim under Article 222 of the RTC and Article XXIV of the Agreement Establishing the Caribbean Court of Justice (CCJ Agreement).[13] The latter provision used the term 'national', whereas Article 222 of the RTC used the term 'person', in relation to the potential locus standi of legal entities. Guyana argued that Article 222 must be read in light of Article 32.

This argument was rejected by the Court on the basis that the test for special leave must be that set out in the RTC rather than that established under the CCJ Agreement, since the Court is called upon to interpret and apply the RTC; the Court also noted that because the RTC is a later treaty it must, under the law of treaties, be deemed to supersede the prior treaty.[14] This is an important juridical step, since in these passages it can be argued that the Court began to establish a hierarchy of CARICOM treaties, with the RTC taking precedence.

The Court also held in relation to the test for nationality under Article 32 that the restrictions imposed by the article are for a particular purpose, namely, to protect the core rights established under Chapter 3 of the RTC. The Court therefore emphasized:

> These [Chapter 3 rights] are fundamental core rights given by the *RTC* and must be seen in the context of the resolve of the Contracting Parties "to establish conditions which would facilitate access by their nationals to the collective resources of the Region on a non-discriminatory basis". These core rights are not to be available to non-Community nationals merely doing business in the Community or to companies which, though incorporated in a Contracting Party, are not substantially owned or effectively controlled by Community nationals. These rights are available only to Community nationals in the restricted sense of that term as defined in Article 32(5) and are intended to ensure that strategic economic advantages remain with persons belonging to or having a close connection with the Community.[15]

It is likely that as a result of this jurisprudence Article 32 will be robustly applied by member states and the CCJ, especially in cases of legal, not natural, nationals, so as to limit access to Chapter 3 rights to Community nationals and companies substantially owned or controlled by Community nationals. Article 32 therefore will play a strong role in relation to all of the core rights of Chapter 3.

The right of establishment must be recognized as an important right under the RTC.[16] It is a right that may be enlarged by the Community Council and one for

[12] Judgment [2009] CCJ 1 (OJ), (2009) 74 WIR 302, 15 January 2009.

[13] *Trinidad Cement v Guyana* (n 12) [23]–[28].

[14] *Trinidad Cement v Guyana* (n 12) [25] and [27].

[15] *Trinidad Cement v Guyana* (n 12) [26] (citations omitted).

[16] For information on exercising the right of establishment, see CARICOM Secretariat, 'Entry Procedures for CARICOM Nationals Exercising the Right of Establishment', as available through <http://caricom.org/jsp/single_market/single_market_index.jsp?menu=csme> (accessed 16 Mar 2013).

which any existing restrictions must be notified to COTED, and eventually be removed.[17] The right of establishment is supported by provisions allowing for the common acceptance of evidence of the qualifications of nationals, and would be assisted by a number of other complementary measures, including those allowing transfer of benefits and limiting double taxation.[18] Pursuant to a decision of the Conference at its Thirteenth Inter-Sessional Meeting, the right is to be facilitated by Registrars of Companies across the region to ensure the 'minimising [of] costs including the time involved in multiple registration'.[19]

The scope of the right of establishment is restricted, however, by several other articles in Chapter 3. The first article of the Chapter, Article 30, purports to exclude from its scope any 'activities involving the exercise of governmental authority'. Article 30(3) defines the phrase 'activities involving the exercise of governmental authority' as meaning 'activities conducted neither on a commercial basis nor in competition with one or more economic enterprises', and as including (a) activities conducted by a public entity in pursuit of monetary or exchange rate policies, (b) activities for statutory social security or public retirement systems, (c) activities for a system of national security or public order, and (d) other activities conducted by a public entity for the account of or with the guarantee or using financial resources of the government. The latter area of exclusion could be interpreted broadly, but nevertheless must be seen to be limited by the prohibition in Article 30(3) that such activities must be neither commercial nor in competition with economic enterprises. Although Article 30 could be read in two different ways, as discussed in what follows, it must at least potentially remove from the scope of Chapter 3 rights any activities involving the exercise of governmental authority as defined in subsection (3).[20]

[17] RTC Arts 32(4) and (2), and 33, respectively. See also Art 34. Under Art 33(3) COTED, with the 'approval of the Conference, [and] in consultation with COHSOD and COFAP, shall, within one year from the entry into force of this Treaty, establish a programme providing for the removal of restrictions on the right of establishment of nationals of a Member State in the territory of another Member State'. This programme was established in 2002: CARICOM Secretariat, 'Communique Issued at the Conclusion of the 13th Inter-Sessional Meeting of the Conference of Heads of Government of the Caribbean Community, Belize City, 3–5 February 2002', as available at <http://www.caricom.org/jsp/communications/communiques/13inthgc_2002_communique.jsp> (4 Mar 2013). For an assessment of the progress made in implementing the programme see eg CARICOM Secretariat, *Summary Draft Report* 20–3. See also RTC Art 44.

[18] RTC Art 35. For the latter, see eg CARICOM Agreement on Social Security (adopted 1 Mar 1996, entered into force 1 Apr 1997), Protocol Amending the CARICOM Agreement on Social Security (adopted 8 Oct 2009, not yet in force), Agreement Among the Governments of the Member States of the Caribbean Community for the Avoidance of Double Taxation and the Prevention of Fiscal Evasion with Respect to Taxes on Income, Profits or Gains and Capital Gains and for the Encouragement of Regional Trade and Investment (adopted 6 Jul 1994, in force 30 Nov 1994) 2259 UNTS 251. For concerns about the effectiveness of the double taxation regime at present, see eg CARICOM Secretariat, *Summary Draft Report* 8.

[19] This was one of the facilitating measures to support the Programmes for the Removal of Restrictions, adopted at the 13th Inter-Sessional Meeting of the Conference of Heads of Government of the Caribbean Community, Belize City, 3–5 February 2002, as quoted in CARICOM Secretariat, *Summary Draft Report* 20.

[20] See section 9.5, at pp 264–265.

The right of establishment is also restricted in Article 31(1), which stipulates that 'Member States may determine that the public interest requires the exclusion or restriction of the right of establishment in any industry or in a particular sector of an industry.' Article 31(2) then goes on to specify that if a public or private monopoly is thereby maintained the rules of non-discrimination and competition, and national treatment, respectively, are applied to its operations.

Moreover the right of establishment is limited in practice by the actions of national officials tasked with implementing the right. As pointed out in a 2009 CARICOM report some national authorities remain convinced that citizens should have the first opportunity for employment, and have insisted that non-nationals demonstrate possession of sufficient capital to start new businesses.[21] Local officials have also expressed concerns about the issuance of contracts to foreign managerial, technical, and supervisory personnel under the right of establishment.[22] Although CCJ's judgment in the case of *Shanique Myrie v Barbados* may remove many of the hindrances experienced by CARICOM nationals seeking entry to another CARICOM member state, since the Court upheld the right of 'every Community national to enter any Member State and to stay there for up to six months', the restrictive practices and concerns of national officials need to be addressed in order to allow for a full implementation of the right.[23]

9.1.2 OECS

The RTB provides a stronger right of establishment than the RTC. In Article 3(c) of the Protocol to the RTB one of the fundamental principles through which the Economic Union is to achieve its objectives is stated to be 'the abolition, as between Protocol Member States, of the obstacles to the free movement of persons, services and capital'. Article 12 goes on to set out the free movement of persons and provides, in paragraph 2, that '[s]uch freedom of movement shall entail the abolition of any discrimination based on nationality between citizens of the Protocol Member States as regards employment, remuneration and other conditions of work and employment.' Such wording would allow citizens to enjoy not only the right of establishment, but also the right to seek employment in Protocol member states. Article 27 outlines the meaning of the right of establishment under the Protocol in the following terms:

> 27.1 No Protocol Member State may impose or maintain restrictions on the freedom of establishment of nationals of a Protocol Member State in the territory of another Protocol Member State, and in particular, no restrictions other than restrictions which apply to the nationals of the Protocol Member State may be imposed or maintained on –
> (a) the establishment of agencies, branches or subsidiaries by nationals of another Protocol Member State;
> (b) the right to take up and pursue activities as self-employed persons; or
> (c) the right to set up and manage undertakings.

[21] CARICOM Secretariat, *Summary Draft Report* (n 19) 43.
[22] CARICOM Secretariat, *Summary Draft Report* (n 19) 43.
[23] Judgment [2013] CCJ 3 (OJ) [62].

This right is broader than that set out in Article 32 of the RTC since it does not limit the categories of non-wage earning activities to which it applies. When combined with freedom of movement more generally under Article 12 (which applies to 'citizens'), the OECS framework provides greater rights to natural persons.[24] Although it does not expressly contemplate the right of establishment of a juridical person, this could be implied by the use of the term 'subsidiaries' in Article 27.1(a).

9.2 Movement of Services[25]

9.2.1 CARICOM

Article 36 of the RTC prohibits the introduction of 'any new restrictions on the provision of services in the Community by nationals of other Member States'. The term 'services' is defined in Article 36(4) as:

> 4. For the purposes of this Chapter, 'services' means services provided against remuneration other than wages in an approved sector and 'the provision of services' means the supply of services:
> (a) from the territory of one Member State into the territory of another Member State;
> (b) in the territory of one Member State to a service consumer of another Member State;
> (c) by a service supplier of one Member State through commercial presence in the territory of another Member State; and
> (d) by a service supplier of one Member State through the presence of natural persons of a Member State in the territory of another Member State...[26]

This definition allows cross-border provision of services, as well as provision of services within the territory of a member state by legal and natural persons of another member state.

In addition, discriminatory restrictions on the provision of services must be abolished, as specified in Article 37(1), but only 'within the Community in respect of Community nationals'.[27] Restrictions on banking, insurance, and other financial services must likewise be removed.[28] COTED is mandated to establish a programme to remove restrictions on the provision of services, as guided by the priorities set out in Article 37.[29] COTED is also required to promote the removal

[24] There is no definition of 'citizen' under the Protocol, but the term is specified to include 'belonger' in the context of the OECS Assembly in Art 10.11 of the RTB. However it is possible that the term 'national' under Art 27.1 of the Protocol will be read to exclude belongers, thereby limiting the right of establishment slightly.

[25] For more on the EU regime on freedom to provide and receive services see eg Barnard, *The Substantive Law of the EU* (n 1) ch 11.

[26] See also the identical wording in the definition of 'services' in RTC Art 1.

[27] Note that Art 37(1) must be read in light of the definition of 'national' in Art 1 of the RTC as meaning 'a national within the meaning of paragraph 5(a) of Article 32'.

[28] RTC Art 38.

[29] This programme was established in 2002: CARICOM Secretariat, 'Communique Issued at the Conclusion of the 13th Inter-Sessional Meeting of the Conference of Heads of Government of the

of obstacles to the provision of transport services by nationals of member states under Article 135(1)(f).

The right to provide services under the RTC also includes the right to 'temporarily engage in approved activities in the Member State where the services are to be provided under the same conditions enjoyed by nationals of that Member State'.[30] Since services can be provided by juridical or natural persons, this means that a national of one member state could engage in the provision of services in the territory of another member state.[31] Although this right is stated to be *temporary*, and therefore is more limited than the right of establishment, it could immediately open the doors to a wider range of economic activities by 'natural persons of a Member State' in the territory of another member state. It would appear that this temporary right to provide services in another state's territory must extend to a period of at least six months, given the recognition by the CCJ of the right of every Community national to enter any member state and to stay there for up to six months in the case of *Shanique Myrie v Barbados*.[32] The phrase 'natural persons of a Member State' used in RTC 36(4)(d), it should be noted, is not identical to the term 'national' as used in Article 32.[33] Further analysis of the implications of the provision of services by temporary service providers, especially in light of the need to protect consumers and the requirements of national tax laws, also will have to be undertaken.[34]

Caribbean Community, Belize City, 3–5 February 2002', as available at <http://www.caricom.org/jsp/communications/communiques/13inthgc_2002_communique.jsp> (4 Mar 2013). The programme recently was deemed a success by the CARICOM Secretariat, in its *Summary Draft Report*, at p 23 (reporting that '[l]iberalisation of services under Chapter Three of the Revised Treaty has succeeded').

30 RTC Art 36(2).

31 For information on exercising the right to provide services, see CARICOM Secretariat, 'Entry Procedures for CARICOM Nationals Exercising the Right to Provide Services Through Temporary Movement of Natural Persons', as available through <http://caricom.org/jsp/single_market/single_market_index.jsp?menu=csme> (accessed 16 Mar 2013).

32 *Shanique Myrie v Barbados* (n 18) [62]. The CCJ expressly refers to the right to provide services in the context of elaborating the scope of freedom of movment under the RTC, stating at [61]:

> In accordance with Article 36(4) RTC, 'services' in this context means 'services provided against remuneration other than wages in any approved sector' and 'the provision of services' means the supply of services not only 'from the territory of one Member State into the territory of another Member State' but also 'in the territory of one Member State to the service consumer of another Member State.' It is clear, therefore, that in certain approved sectors, nationals of a Member State who supply these services must in principle have the right freely to enter any other Member State in order to ply their trade; but, logically following from Article 36(4)(b), also nationals of a Member State desirous of receiving such services in another Member State must be allowed to enter the latter State in order to receive that service without being obstructed by unreasonable restrictions. Without doubt, one of the service sectors capable of triggering these rights is tourism as tourists can reasonably be considered recipients of services. [Citing: [6] Joined Cases 286/82 and 26/83 *Luisi and Carbone v Ministero del Tesoro*.]

33 Note, however, that Art 36(4)(d) would also have to be read in light of Art 36(1), which uses the term 'nationals'.

34 eg the CARICOM Secretariat, in its *Summary Draft Report*, at pp 43–4, expresses concerns about the enforcement of specific performance and liability in a context where temporary services providers have either left voluntarily or fled the jurisdiction. Blacklisting is suggested as one potential solution. The question of location-based taxation for provision of services will also have to be addressed: at p 45.

The right to provide services also will ultimately include rights related to spouses and immediate dependant family members and rights of 'access to land, buildings and other property situated in the territory of another Member State for purposes directly related to the provision of services'.[35]

9.2.2 OECS

Article 27.2 of the OECS Protocol provides an immediate right to provide services in the Economic Union in the following terms:

> 27.2 No Protocol Member State may impose or maintain restrictions on the provision of economic services by nationals of another Protocol Member State to persons in any other Protocol Member State which exceed restrictions on the provision of those services which apply to limit the provision of those services by the nationals of the Protocol Member State imposing the restrictions.

Although the wording of Article 27.2 is simpler than that found in the similar provisions of the RTC, it covers the same possible modalities of provision of services: cross border, with or without local presence, and by nationals of another Protocol member state. Since Article 27.2 includes the word 'maintain' it also requires the removal of existing restrictions. Unlike Article 37(1) of the RTC, this requirement for removal is not limited to 'discriminatory restrictions'. Rather, the test in Article 27.2 is whether the restrictions imposed upon nationals of other Protocol member states exceed the restrictions imposed upon local nationals. Article 27.3 also requires the Economic Affairs Council to draw to the attention of Protocol member states any restrictions prohibited under the Article and to 'co-operate with those Protocol member states in seeing to the removal of those restrictions'. Presumably if there was no cooperation, then a Protocol member state could refer the matter to the Economic Affairs Council for action under Articles 30 and 31 of the Protocol.

In addition to the obligations imposed upon Protocol member states not to impose any new restrictions and to remove existing restrictions upon the provision of services, Article 26.1 of the Protocol requires all Protocol member states to 'work towards the progressive harmonisation of policies on the services sector'. Article 26.1 goes on to indicate that such progressive harmonization 'shall involve where advisable the adoption of a common policy towards development and regulation of the services sector'. Article 26.2 describes the 'ultimate objective' of this common policy as 'the creation of a facilitative environment for balanced growth and development of services in the Economic Union Area, as well as the establishment of appropriate regulatory frameworks to ensure optimal social outcomes in areas where monopolies or near-monopolies exist'. These provisions go much further than the equivalent sections of the RTC and demonstrate another way in

[35] RTC Art 37(3)(c) and (d). The latter rights are to be provided under the programme to be established by COTED.

which the OECS Economic Union seeks to enable stronger and closer regional integration.

9.3 Movement of Capital[36]

9.3.1 CARICOM

Article 39 of the RTC prohibits member states from introducing 'any *new restrictions* on the movement of capital and payments connected with such movement and on current payments and transfers'; it also prevents them from making 'more restrictive existing regulations except as provided in Article 43 and Article [47]'.[37] The latter two articles allow the maintenance of restrictions to safeguard balance of payments, and to resolve difficulties or hardships arising from the exercise of rights, respectively.[38] Article 40 requires member states to *remove* among themselves restrictions on the movement of capital payments and restrictions on all current payments including payments for goods and services and other current transfers.[39] These provisions, however, must be read in light of Article 41, which retains the potential requirement for authorization to move capital, and includes a requirement for prior notification in relation to loans 'intended for State purposes'.[40] Given the exceptions carved out in Articles 43 and 47 (described earlier), the right of movement of capital remains limited and subject to extensive state control. In practice, there appears to have been greater movement on abolishing exchange controls than on abolishing restrictions related to the convertibility of currencies.[41]

Nevertheless, under Article 40(2) COFAP, in collaboration with the Committee of Central Bank Governors, is given responsibility for establishing a programme for the removal of such restrictions.[42] Under Article 42 member states are also

[36] For the EU's regime on free movement of capital see eg Barnard, *The Substantive Law of the EU* (n 1) ch 15.

[37] Emphasis added. The text of Art 39 of the RTC incorrectly cross-references Art 46, which deals with CARICOM skilled nationals. As seen in the earlier version of the text of Art 39—Art 37 of the Protocol Amending the Treaty Establishing the Caribbean Community (Protocol II: Establishment, Services, Capital) (adopted 1 Jul 1997, not yet in force)—the cross-reference is meant to refer to the article dealing with 'Restrictions to Resolve Difficulties or Hardships Arising from the Exercise of Rights', now set out in Art 47 of the RTC.

[38] Art 43(1) of the RTC provides: 'In the event of serious balance-of-payments and external financial difficulties or threat thereof, a Member State may, consistently with its international obligations and subject to paragraph 5 of this Article, adopt or maintain restrictions to address such difficulties.'

[39] RTC Art 40(3) defines 'capital and related payments and transfers' to include: '(a) equity and portfolio investments; (b) short-term bank and credit transactions; (c) payment of interest on loans and amortization; (d) dividends and other income on investments after taxes; (e) repatriation of proceeds from the sale of assets; and (f) other transfers and payments relating to investment flows.'

[40] There is no definition of the phrase 'State purposes' in the RTC.

[41] See eg CARICOM Secretariat, *Summary Draft Report* 24, indicating that the abolition of exchange controls has been successful for all member states except Barbados and Belize, for which '[s]ignificant policy considerations impact on [their] rate of progress'. Convertibility of currencies, however, has only succeeded in the case of the OECS dollar.

[42] The programme for removal of restrictions on the movement of capital was established in 2002: CARICOM Secretariat, 'Communique Issued at the Conclusion of the 13th

mandated to 'take such measures as are necessary to coordinate their foreign exchange policies in respect of the movement of capital between them and third States' and to keep one another informed of 'significant unusual movements of capital within their knowledge to and from third States'.

9.3.2 OECS

Under Article 3.1(c) of the OECS Protocol the Protocol member states are required to abolish as between themselves the obstacles to the free movement of capital. However there is no provision paralleling those found in the RTC prohibiting the imposition of new restrictions upon the movement of capital, or requiring the removal of existing restrictions on movement of capital. These gaps may be explained by the fact that all of the current OECS Protocol member states use a common currency, the Eastern Caribbean dollar, and because they also rely upon the Eastern Caribbean Central Bank.[43] Article 14 of the OECS Protocol mandates, for example, that the 'monetary policy of the Economic Union... be executed by the Monetary Council through the Eastern Caribbean Central Bank under the terms and conditions of the Eastern Caribbean Central Bank Agreement'. In addition, as one of the development policies set out in Article 13 of the Protocol, the member states agree to coordinate policies towards: 'the development, integration and regulation of money and capital markets within the Economic Union to optimise the mobilisation of savings and their most efficient allocation to the sectors, industries and firms which will facilitate the growth and development of the Economic Union'.[44] The second term, 'integration', reveals the more ambitious goal of the OECS Economic Union, namely, to 'establish the Economic Union as a single economic and financial space'.[45]

9.4 Movement of Persons[46]

9.4.1 CARICOM

Articles 45–46 of the RTC allow limited freedom of movement of persons. Article 45 commits member states to the 'goal of free movement of their nationals

Inter-Sessional Meeting of the Conference of Heads of Government of the Caribbean Community, Belize City, 3–5 February 2002', as available at <http://www.caricom.org/jsp/communications/communiques/13inthgc_2002_communique.jsp> (4 Mar 2013). See also, CARICOM Secretariat, *Summary Draft Report* 5–6.

[43] One associate member of the RTB, the British Virgin Islands, uses another currency, the US dollar. Although associate members may become parties to the RTB, and thereby, through Art 24.3, also become parties to the Protocol, Anguilla and the British Virgin Islands have not been able to ratify the RTB to date, and thus cannot be parties to the Protocol. See OECS Director General Dr Len Ishmael in her 'Remarks' at the Opening Ceremony of the Meeting of Leaders of the Opposition, at Gros Islet, St Lucia, on 4 May 2012 (Castries, St Lucia: OECS Secretariat, May 2012) at 3–4.

[44] Protocol Art 13.4(d).

[45] RTB Art 4.1(e). See also Protocol Art 2(a).

[46] For more on the EU regimes for free movement of workers and free movement of persons see eg Barnard, *The Substantive Law of the EU* (n 1) chs 8–9 and 12.

within the Community'. Article 45 has been supplemented by the decision of the Conference of Heads of Government at their Twenty Eighth Meeting, 1–4 July 2007. At that meeting the Conference

> **AGREED** that all CARICOM nationals should be entitled to an automatic stay of six months upon arrival in order to enhance their sense that they belong to, and can move in the Caribbean Community, subject to the rights of Member States to refuse undesirable persons entry and to prevent persons from becoming a charge on public funds.
> **NOTED** the reservation entered by **Antigua and Barbuda** in this regard.[47]

The meaning and effect of this Conference decision were interpreted by the Caribbean Court of Justice in the case of *Shanique Myrie v Barbados*.[48] The Court held that by means of this decision the Conference granted to every Community national the right to enter any member state and stay there for up to six months.[49] The right is one of automatic stay or definite entry for a period of six months upon arrival, and must be accorded 'without harassment or the imposition of impediments'.[50] The Court indicated that the right may be curtailed or restricted under Arts 225 and 226 of the RTC, and is subject to the requirements of desirability and financial means. However the Court also indicated clearly that such exceptions to, or restrictions on, the right of entry must be narrowly and strictly construed, and the burden rests with the state seeking to invoke a ground for refusing entry.[51]

According to the Court the exception on grounds of 'undesirability' must be 'construed against the background of Article 226(1)(a) and (b) RTC'.[52] Therefore any restrictions imposed by states must be 'concerned with such matters as the

[47] Quoted in *Shanique Myrie v Barbados* (n 18) at [43] (emphasis in original). See also CARICOM Secretariat, *Draft Report for the Twenty-Eighth Meeting of the Conference of Heads of Government of the Caribbean Community*, HGC/2007/28/DR, 1–4 July 2007, 8. This decision has been reiterated and reaffirmed on a number of subsequent occasions. See eg CARICOM Secretariat, 'Summary of Recommendations and Conclusions of the Thirty-Second Meeting of the Council for Trade and Economic Development (COTED)', 19–20 May 2011 (Item 6.2.1, 'Free Movement of Community Nationals and Contingent Rights'), CARICOM Secretariat, 'Working Document for the Thirty-Second Meeting of the Council for Trade and Economic Development (COTED)', 16–20 May 2011 (Item 2.4). Note that these documents, with the exception of the CCJ's judgment, are restricted but are on file with CARICOM Secretariat and with the Registry of the Caribbean Court of Justice.

[48] *Shanique Myrie v Barbados* (n 18).

[49] *Shanique Myrie v Barbados* (n 18) [62].

[50] *Shanique Myrie v Barbados* (n 18) [62]–[63]. The latter phrasing would likely catch any attempt by a member state to impose additional administrative requirements upon a visitor, such as the obligation to renew an entry permit.

[51] In *Shanique Myrie v Barbados* (n 18), at [67], the Court held:

> The refusal of a Member State to let Community nationals from other Member States enter its territory on the ground that they are either undesirable persons or because it is evident that they will become a charge on public funds, must be seen as an exception to, or a restriction on, the right of entry. The effect of that characterization is two-fold. Firstly, being an exception to a fundamental principle of free movement, the scope of the refusal and, in particular, the grounds on which it is based must be interpreted narrowly and strictly in order to avoid an unjustified watering down of the importance of the right it seeks to limit. Secondly, being an exception to this fundamental principle, the burden of proof must rest on the Member State that seeks to invoke either ground for refusing entry.

[52] *Shanique Myrie v Barbados* (n 18) [68].

protection of public morals, the maintenance of public order and safety and the protection of life and health'.[53] Restrictions to the right are also limited by the principle of proportionality and the requirement that the national actually poses or can reasonably be expected to pose 'a genuine, present and sufficiently serious threat affecting one of the fundamental interests of society'.[54] This threat must be to do something actually prohibited by national law, and for which nationals in the receiving state are routinely prosecuted or otherwise subject to legal sanction.[55] The Court expressly rejects as a ground for refusal of entry the suspicion that a person seeking entry might not be a bona fide visitor, or might intend to stay with someone 'not of good repute'.[56]

The exception on the ground that a person might become a 'charge on public funds' is even more restrictively interpreted by the CCJ. Immigration officials are only allowed to assess sufficiency of funds for the duration of the *intended stay*, not for the potential six-month period. As expressed by the Court: '[i]t would not be reasonable to require a visiting Community national to show sufficiency of funds for a period of six months if the national does not intend to stay that long.'[57] Factors that may be taken into consideration in this context by immigration officials include whether the person possesses a credit card and whether the intended stay is with a friend or relative, or in commercial accommodation.[58] Evidence of a return ticket may also be required.[59] Although other factors not mentioned by the Court might be relevant (such as the existence of a serious pre-existing medical condition requiring immediate treatment), the CCJ's restrictive analysis of this exception will likely prevent its use only in rare cases.

The Court also elaborated the procedural and substantive requirements for a lawful refusal. If a person is to be refused entry, reasons for that refusal must be given promptly, and in writing.[60] The refused Community national also must be informed of his or her right to challenge the decision and to contact a family member, attorney, or consular official.[61] Member states must provide for accessible appeal procedures, potentially including an immediate review by a higher placed official, and ultimately judicial review.[62]

[53] *Shanique Myrie v Barbados* (n 18) [68].

[54] *Shanique Myrie v Barbados* (n 18) [70].

[55] *Shanique Myrie v Barbados* (n 18)[71].

[56] *Shanique Myrie v Barbados* (n 18) [72]. In the context of the specific allegations against Ms Myrie, the Court held at [73] that Barbados had not established her untruthfulness.

[57] *Shanique Myrie v Barbados* (n 18) [76].

[58] *Shanique Myrie v Barbados* (n 18) [75].

[59] *Shanique Myrie v Barbados* (n 18) [76].

[60] *Shanique Myrie v Barbados* (n 18)[77]. The Court notes, however, that the requirement for reasons in writing may be subject to the security requirements of RTC Art 225(a). Even in such a case, however, the exception provided by Art 225(a) must be strictly and narrowly interpreted.

[61] *Shanique Myrie v Barbados* (n 18) [83].

[62] *Shanique Myrie v Barbados* (n 18) [78]. The Court notes, at [79], that existing Barbadian legislation provided for judicial oversight, but not in cases of refusal of entry. The CCJ suggests, however, at [80], that such inconsistencies might be resolved in practice if Barbadian courts 'are constrained to interpret domestic laws so as, if possible, to render them consistent with international treaties such as the RTC'. Such an approach echoes the principle of indirect effect, or conform interpretation, discussed in Chapter 8.

Prior to the decision in the *Myrie* case, the 2007 Conference decision was implemented in practice by many CARICOM member states, albeit administratively in some cases.[63] In order to enable 'hassle free travel' in the region by CARICOM nationals, most member states have created CARICOM lines at immigration areas at airports.[64] However given the scope of the decision in the *Myrie* case, it is likely that the majority of CARICOM states will be required to review and revise their immigration rules and procedures.

Article 46(1) creates free movement rights for the category of 'skilled Community nationals' in the following terms:

> 1. Without prejudice to the rights recognised and agreed to be accorded by Member States in Articles 32, 33, 37, 38 and 40 among themselves and to Community nationals, Member States have agreed, and undertake as a first step towards achieving the goal set out in Article 45, to accord to the following categories of Community nationals the right to seek employment in their jurisdictions:
>   (a) University graduates;
>   (b) media workers;
>   (c) sportspersons;
>   (d) artistes; and
>   (e) musicians,
>
>   recognised as such by the competent authorities of the receiving Member States.[65]

Article 46(2) sets out the legislative, administrative, and procedural arrangements required by member states to provide for movement of Community nationals into and within their jurisdictions without harassment or the imposition of impediments including: 'the elimination of the requirement for passports for Community nationals', 'the elimination of the requirement for work permits for Community nationals seeking approved employment', the 'establishment of mechanisms for certifying and establishing equivalency of degrees and for accrediting institutions', and the 'harmonisation and transferability of social security benefits'.[66] To help

[63] CARICOM Secretariat, 'Status of implementation of Six months entry Permit as Reported at April 2011 Joint Free Movement and Contingent Rights Meeting' [restricted access but on file with CARICOM Secretariat and with the Registry of the Caribbean Court of Justice]. See also CARICOM Secretariat, *Summary Draft Report* 19–20.

[64] See eg CARICOM Secretariat, *Summary Draft Report* 46 (hassle-free travel). Some criticisms have been made about the speed of these 'CARICOM-only' queues at airports. See eg at p 47.

[65] CARICOM Secretariat, in 'Free Movement in the CARICOM Single Market and Economy (CSME)', as available at <http://www.caricom.org/jsp/single_market/skill.jsp?menu=csme> (6 Feb 2013), defines the categories of free movement skills as follows:

> **Graduates** are persons who have obtained at least a Bachelor's Degree from a recognised university. **Media Persons** are persons whose primary source of income is drawn from media and media-related work or persons who are qualified to enter this field. **Artists** are persons who are active in or qualified to enter a particular field of art with the specific purpose to earn a living. **Musicians** are persons who are active in or qualified to enter a particular field of music with the specific purpose to earn a living. **Sportspersons** are persons who are active in or qualified to enter a particular field of sports with the specific purpose to earn a living as a professional or semi-professional (emphasis in original).

[66] RTC Art 46(2)(b)(i)–(iv).

implement the latter obligations CARICOM member states have created two new treaties, an Agreement and Protocol on social security.[67]

Skilled nationals are issued a Certificate of Recognition of CARICOM Skills Qualification by the designated Ministry of the country of origin of the national (the sending member state).[68] Upon presentation of this certificate the skilled national should be granted a definite right of entry of six months, followed by an indefinite entry after the national's qualifications have been verified by the receiving member state.[69] Spouses and dependents of the skilled national are provided with similar freedom of movement rights.[70]

Although there have been complaints about the time required to obtain skilled national certification, and to have it recognized in another member state, the regime appears to be generally working.[71] Some future problems, however, could arise as a result of improper transformation of Article 46 in the domestic laws of member states and as a result of judicial interpretation of those domestic laws.[72] Also some states may not have fully transformed the RTC provisions in their domestic law.[73] Nevertheless, according to the CARICOM Secretariat approximately 9,000 skilled national certificates had been issued up to 2010.[74]

Article 46(4) requires the Conference to monitor and secure compliance with the article, as well as to 'enlarge, as appropriate, the classes of persons entitled to

[67] CARICOM Agreement on Social Security (adopted 1 Mar 1996, entered into force 1 Apr 1997) and the Protocol Amending the CARICOM Agreement on Social Security (adopted 8 Oct 2009, not yet in force). See also, CARICOM Secretariat, *Social Security in CARICOM* (Bridgetown, Barbados: CARICOM Secretariat, 2010). Note, however, that the CARICOM Secretariat in the *Summary Draft Report*, at p 7, highlights the challenges involved in transferring social security benefits from Suriname and the continuing need to harmonize qualifying conditions in the area.

[68] CARICOM Secretariat, 'Free Movement in the CARICOM Single Market and Economy (CSME)', as available at <http://www.caricom.org/jsp/single_market/skill.jsp?menu=csme> (6 Feb 2013). See also, CARICOM Secretariat, 'Administrative Arrangements and Procedures for the Free Movement of Skills Based on Successive Decisions of the Conference of Heads of Government and Relevant Councils', as available through <http://caricom.org/jsp/single_market/single_market_index.jsp?menu=csme> (accessed 16 Mar 2013).

[69] See footnote 68.

[70] See eg the CARICOM Secretariat, 'Model Legislation on Free Movement of Skilled Nationals', entitled the 'Caribbean Community Skilled Nationals Act', s 11, as available at <http://www.caricom.org/jsp/secretariat/legal_instruments/model_legislation_skilled_nationals_act.pdf> (6 Feb 2013).

[71] For complaints that the skilled certification regime creates the same delays as the previous work permit regime, see eg CARICOM Secretariat, *Summary Draft Report* 50–1.

[72] Section 14 of the model law drafted by the CARICOM Secretariat to implement Art 46 of the RTC, the Caribbean Community Skilled Nationals Act, as available at <http://www.caricom.org/jsp/secretariat/legal_instruments/model_legislation_skilled_nationals_act.pdf> (21 Jul 2013), incorrectly imposes a condition of reciprocity for exercise of privileges under the Act. This error, unfortunately, has been reproduced in some national legislation. See eg Immigration Act, Laws of Barbados, LRO 1997, Cap 190 (2 Feb 1976), s 17E. The latter subsection is noted without comment in the case of *Sparman v Greaves et al*, Barbados, High Court of Justice, Suit No 529 of 2003, CARILAW # BB 2004 HC 21 (Kentish J) 15 Oct 2004, at p 20 [62]. This case also illustrates other challenges in implementing RTC obligations, since Judge Kentish refused to find that the Barbados Act conferred any special 'status' upon CARICOM skilled nationals: at pp 21–2 [67]–[69].

[73] See the discussion of the case of *Linton v Attorney General*, Antigua and Barbuda, High Court of Justice, CARILAW # AG 2009 HC 23 (Blenman J), 29 Jun 2009 (unreported), in Chapter 6.

[74] CARICOM Secretariat, 'News Feature: Five Years On—The CARICOM Single Market and Economy' Press release NF01/2011 (28 Jan 2011), as available at <http://www.caricom.org/jsp/pressreleases/presnf01_11.jsp?null&prnf=1> (6 Feb 2013).

move and work freely in the Community'. These categories have been expanded to include: nurses, teachers, artisans, persons who are holders of Associate Degrees or equivalent, and household domestics who are holders of Caribbean Vocational Qualifications.[75] According to the CARICOM Secretariat, all five of the original categories in Article 46 have been implemented in full in the domestic legislation of member states but less success has been experienced in relation to the others.[76]

9.4.2 OECS

The right of free movement of persons appears to be more developed in OECS Economic Union law. It is posited as one of the fundamental principles to achieve the objectives of the OECS Economic Union. Article 3(c) of the Protocol specifies the principle of abolition, as between Protocol member states, of the obstacles to the free movement of persons.

In addition, Article 12 of the OECS Protocol expressly provides for freedom of movement in the following terms:

> 12.1 Freedom of movement for citizens of Protocol Member States shall be secured within the Economic Union Area.
> 12.2 Such freedom of movement shall entail the abolition of any discrimination based on nationality between citizens of the Protocol Member States as regards employment, remuneration and other conditions of work and employment.
> 12.3 Citizens of Protocol Member States shall enjoy in the Economic Union Area the rights contingent to the right of freedom of movement that are agreed by Protocol Member States.

Article 12.4 also requires the OECS Authority and OECS Commission to regularly monitor the implementation of the article.

As a result, Article 12 recognizes freedom of movement for, amongst other things, the purposes of employment, as seen in Article 12.2. It also contemplates the recognition of contingent rights by Protocol member states, a point repeated in Protocol Article 23.1(f), which provides:

> To this end Protocol Member States agree to –
> (f) provide the enabling legislative, policy and administrative environment needed to support social relations and cohesion for children, youth, men and women in the Economic Union Area, with particular attention to the consequences and impact

[75] CARICOM Secretariat, 'News Feature: Five Years On' (n 74). See also CARICOM Secretariat, *Summary Draft Report* 14–18. Note that Antigua and Barbuda has been allowed derogations with respect to teachers, nurses and household domestics: CARICOM Secretariat, 'News release 147/2006 (6 Jul 2006): Communique Issued at the Conclusion of the Twenty-Seventh Meeting of the Conference of Heads of Government of the Caribbean Community (CARICOM)', 3–6 July 2006, as available at <http://www.caricom.org/jsp/communications/communiques/27hgc_2006_communique.jsp> (17 Mar 2013), Official Website for the Government of Antigua and Barbuda, 'Antigua and Barbuda Received Five Year Derogation from Expansion of Free Movement of Persons' (posted 8 Jul 2009), as available at <http://www.ab.gov.ag/article_details.php?id=50&category=34> (17 Mar 2013).

[76] CARICOM Secretariat, *Summary Draft Report* 16.

of the free movement of peoples on shared family responsibilities and economic stability...

Nevertheless Article 12.5 allows a Protocol member state, subject to the approval of the OECS Authority, to regulate the movement of citizens. How broadly this latter exception will be interpreted remains to be seen.

In understanding the freedom of movement regime under the OECS system more generally, it is important to note that a key constraint upon movement of persons—immigration policy—falls under the domain of the Organisation itself. Article 14.2(c) of the RTB grants the OECS shared, but pre-emptive, legislative competence in relation to immigration policy.[77] This most likely will mean that once the OECS acts in the area of immigration policy, member states will lose competence over that area.[78]

9.5 Exceptions to Chapter 3 of the Revised Treaty of Chaguaramas

The scope of the rights set out in Chapter 3—including the right of establishment, the right to provide services, and the right to move capital in the Community—is restricted by several provisions. As highlighted briefly earlier, the first article of the Chapter, Article 30, excludes from its scope any 'activities involving the exercise of governmental authority'. Article 30(3) defines the phrase 'activities involving the exercise of governmental authority' as meaning 'activities conducted neither on a commercial basis nor in competition with one or more economic enterprises', and as including (a) activities conducted by a public entity in pursuit of monetary or exchange rate policies, (b) activities for statutory social security or public retirement systems, (c) activities for a system of national security or public order, and (d) other activities conducted by a public entity for the account of or with the guarantee or using financial resources of the government. The latter area of exclusion could be interpreted broadly, but nevertheless must be seen to be limited by the prohibition in Article 30(3) that such activities must be neither commercial nor in competition with economic enterprises.

Article 30 therefore removes from the scope of rights in Chapter 3 activities involving the exercise of governmental authority as defined in subsection (3). A question arises, however, as to how far Article 30(2) is to be read. Read literally, it excludes activities involving governmental authority from *all* obligations under the Chapter, including the obligations found in Articles 30–50. Read in this way, Article 30 could apply to Articles 45–46 on freedom of movement. However read more restrictively, Article 30 could be interpreted merely to limit the availability of particular Chapter 3 rights to non-nationals where the exercise of those

[77] On the types of legislative competences of the OECS, see Chapter 6.

[78] See the discussion of the meaning and implications of the general principle of pre-emption in Chapter 8.

rights involves governmental authority. For example, under the latter reading a state could limit the availability of the right of establishment in a particular area of national security, such as in policing.[79] This reading, which was endorsed by the CCJ in the case of *Shanique Myrie v Barbados*, is closer to that governing Article 51 of the TFEU.[80]

Other potential limitations to the rights set out in Chapter 3 include the express permission granted to member states under Article 43 to safeguard balance-of-payments. The right to adopt or maintain restrictions under Article 43 is predicated upon 'serious balance-of-payments and external financial difficulties or threat thereof'; in addition, the restrictions must be consistent with the member state's international obligations and are subject to COFAP's power to make recommendations for their removal under Article 43(5).[81] The range of available restrictions includes quantitative restrictions on imports, restrictions on the right of establishment, restrictions on the right to provide services, restrictions on the right to move capital or on payments and transfers for connected transactions.[82] However, as mandated under Article 43(2)(a)–(d), these restrictions must be: non-discriminatory (between member states or in favour of third states), limited in nature (so as to 'minimise damage to the commercial, economic or financial interests of any other Member State'), proportionate, and temporary (no longer than eighteen months). A member state imposing such restrictions must also notify COFAP and COTED within three working days of doing so and is obliged to immediately consult with the competent organ if requested.[83] COFAP itself is mandated to establish procedures for periodic consultations, as described in Article 43(5)–(8).

An additional right to apply restrictions is found in Article 47, in cases where 'the exercise of rights granted under this Chapter creates serious difficulties in any sector of the economy of a Member State or occasions economic hardships in a region of the Community'. These restrictions can be applied unilaterally by CARICOM member states, but must be notified to the competent organ and be accompanied

[79] See CARICOM Secretariat, 'Report of the Eighth Meeting of the Inter-Governmental Task Force', REP. 97/8/23 IG/TF, held in St John's, Antigua and Barbuda, 24–26 February 1997, para 32 [classified, on file with CARICOM Secretariat].

[80] The Court held in *Shanique Myrie v Barbados* (n 18) at [57]:

> The purpose of Article 30 [of the RTC] is to allow Member States as part of the exercise of their sovereignty to reserve certain public service positions strictly for their own nationals. The justification for this exception/derogation is that these positions presume 'a special relationship of allegiance to the State' and 'reciprocity of rights and duties which form the foundation of the bond of nationality' [5]. Article 30(2) could therefore be applied to limit the right to seek employment in another Member State's armed forces, the police force, immigration, customs, the judiciary, etc. It is, however, not intended to limit the right to free movement as such nor can it be invoked to prevent the Court from subjecting to judicial scrutiny the actions of functionaries in those areas in the exercise of their duties in the context of the RTC. [Citing: [5] See ECJ, Case 149/79 *Commission v Belgium* Judgment of the Court of 17 December 1980 [10].]

For analysis of Art 51 TFEU see eg Paul Craig and Gráinne de Búrca, *EU Law, Text, Cases and Materials*, 5th edn (Oxford: Oxford University Press, 2011) 769; Barnard, *The Substantive Law of the EU* (n 1) 500–4.

[81] RTC Art 43(1). [82] RTC Art 43(2). [83] RTC Art 43(4).

by a plan or programme to resolve the difficulties or alleviate the hardships. The restrictions must be limited to those necessary to resolve the particular difficulties or hardships, must minimize the damage caused, must be non-discriminatory, and must be maintained only to the extent that the relevant conditions remain, and be relaxed as conditions improve.[84]

Member states may also apply under Article 48 of the RTC for a waiver of the requirement to grant the right of establishment, the right to provide services, and the right to move capital in the Community in respect of any industry sector or enterprise. Such applications for waiver must be made in a timely manner, must be justified, and are limited to a five-year duration.[85] Waivers also create a situation of estoppel, with the state granting the waiver being expressly denied the possibility of bringing a claim on behalf of a national in relation to the particular right.[86]

Finally, Chapter 3 recognizes the special needs and circumstances of less developed countries, and the competent CARICOM organs are required to take these into account when removing restrictions on the restrictions on the right of establishment, the right to provide services, and the right to move capital within the Community.[87]

These limitations and exclusions must be kept in mind when considering the rights of establishment, provision of services, and movement of capital within the Community. The security exceptions and general exceptions in Articles 225 and 226 also must be recalled.[88]

9.5.1 Obligations of COTED and COFAP under Chapter 3 of the RTC

Perhaps to mitigate the effect of the several exceptions to the rights provided in Chapter 3, COTED and COFAP have been given strong roles in adopting measures to facilitate their exercise. As set out in Article 44 of the RTC, COTED and COFAP are mandated, subject to the approval of the Conference, to adopt measures to: establish market intelligence and information systems; harmonize the legal and administrative requirements for the operation of partnerships, companies, or other entities; abolish exchange controls in the Community, and promote free convertibility of member state currencies; establish an integrated capital market in the Community; promote the convergence of macro-economic performance and policies through the coordination or harmonization of monetary and fiscal policies; establish economical and efficient land, sea, and air transport services throughout the Community; and establish efficient communication services.[89] COTED and COFAP are also mandated under Article 44(2) to establish comprehensive rules in these areas for the approval of the Conference.[90]

[84] RTC Art 47. [85] RTC Art 48(2) and (4). [86] RTC Art 48(5)(a).
[87] RTC Art 49. [88] See further Chapter 6.
[89] RTC Art 44(1)(a)–(g) [paraphrased].
[90] The Conference itself established a Programme for the Removal of Restrictions during its Thirteenth Inter-Sessional Meeting in 2002. See CARICOM Secretariat, *Summary Draft Report* 5–6, CARICOM Secretariat, 'Communique Issued at the Conclusion of the 13th Inter-Sessional Meeting

In addition, Article 50 specifically preserves the ability of member states to undertake accelerated implementation of their obligations, including by removing restrictions on the right of establishment, the right to provide services, or the right to move capital within the Community earlier than required under the articles of Chapter 3.

9.6 Exceptions Under the OECS Protocol

A different kind of exclusion is provided through Article 11 of the OECS Protocol, namely, one applicable to obligations derived from pre-Protocol treaties. Article 11.1 provides that the 'provisions of this Protocol shall subject to the following paragraphs not affect the rights and obligations under any agreements entered into by any Protocol Member State prior to the coming into force of this Protocol'. This kind of exemption assists OECS member states, which are already subject to a number of obligations under the CARICOM and WTO regimes. However Article 11 does not provide a blanket exemption. Article 11.2 requires exempted Protocol member states to 'take any steps at their disposal which are necessary to reconcile the provisions of any such agreements with the basic objectives of this Protocol'.[91] Under Article 11.6 the Economic Affairs Council must review the situation annually and, if necessary, make recommendations.

Moreover, in the event that the exemption provided under Article 11 prejudices another Protocol member state, Article 11.3–11.4 provides a dispute resolution procedure under the aegis of the Economic Affairs Council, which may include an examining committee under Article 31. Under this procedure the Economic Affairs Council may authorize 'any Protocol Member State to suspend, as regards the exempted Protocol Member State, the application of such obligation under this Protocol' as it considers fit.[92]

In sum, both the RTC and OECS Protocol provide the foundations for the exercise of the right of establishment and the freedoms of movement of services, persons, and capital. However some limitations exist in relation to the rights themselves and a number of exceptions are created in both treaty regimes. To the extent that CARICOM and OECS member states are able to cooperate in implementing the rights and freedoms, and resist self-interested policies of exceptionalism, these areas will greatly increase the strengths of the two regional integration movements.

of the Conference of Heads of Government of the Caribbean Community, Belize City, 3–5 February 2002', as available at <http://www.caricom.org/jsp/communications/communiques/13inthgc_2002_communique.jsp> (4 Mar 2013).

[91] See also the definitions of 'exempted Protocol Member State' and 'agreement' in Art 11.7 of the Protocol.

[92] Protocol Art 11.4.

10

Trade Policy—Free Movement of Goods, Subsidies, and Dumping

10.1 Introduction

10.1.1 CARICOM

Chapter 5 of the RTC, entitled 'Trade Policy' is divided into five parts dealing with preliminary issues, trade liberalization, subsidies, agricultural subsidies, and dumping. The first two parts will be examined here under the general rubric of movement of goods, with the remainder dealt with later in the chapter.

Issues related to movement of goods, as with the other topics covered in Chapter 5 of the RTC, must be analysed in light of the objectives of CARICOM's trade policy. Article 78 sets out the general goal of community trade policy, which is the 'sustained growth of intra-Community and international trade and mutually beneficial exchange of goods and services among the Member States and between the Community and third States'.[1] In order to fulfil this goal Article 78(2) lists a number of objectives that the Community must pursue, including 'full integration of the national markets of all Member States of the Community into a single unified and open market area', the widening of the Community market area, the active promotion of export of internationally competitive Community goods and services, and the securing of the most favourable terms of trade for Community goods and services exported to third states and groups of states.[2] The first objective is perhaps the most revealing about the natures of both Community trade policy and CARICOM's CSME in general. The objective of integration of national markets into a single unified and open market area is a very powerful and far-reaching one.[3] It envisages trade between member states as akin to trade between entities within a single member state. When examining the rules

[1] RTC Art 78(1).

[2] RTC Art 85 guides COTED on the measures which it is mandated to implement to promote exports.

[3] For similar wording see Art 26 of the Treaty on the Functioning of the European Union which describes the EU's internal market as 'an area without internal frontiers': Consolidated versions of the Treaty on European Union and the Treaty on the Functioning of the European Union (OJ C83, 30.3.2010), as available through <http://eur-lex.europa.eu/en/treaties/index.htm> (accessed 30 Sep 2011) [the respective portions of the Consolidated Versions are hereafter referred to as either 'TEU' or 'TFEU'].

related to duties, taxes, and quantitative restrictions, later in the chapter, it will be important to keep in mind this objective. Under this vision, for example, an impermissible duty between member states would be analogous to a duty imposed upon a good that is moved from one city to another in the same state (eg, from Chaguaramas to Port of Spain in Trinidad and Tobago).

Article 78(3) mandates the achievement of these objectives by imposing obligations on the Community, including those of the establishment of common instruments and common services and the establishment of joint regulation, operation, and efficient administration of the internal and external commerce of the CSME.[4] The same provision also requires the Community to employ common negotiating strategies in relation to trade agreements with third states and groups of states, to participate and engage in joint representation as appropriate in international and regional organizations related to trade, and to prohibit new restrictions by member states on imports and exports of products of Community origin.[5] Similarly, it imposes the obligation upon member states to eliminate existing restrictions on imports and exports of goods of Community origin, unless authorized by this treaty.[6]

Article 79 requires member states to establish and maintain a regime for free movement of goods and services within the CSME, and therefore prohibits them from introducing new restrictions on imports or exports of Community origin. Related obligations are found in Articles 86 and 95 which, respectively, require member states to grant freedom of transit within the Community to goods and vessels and other vehicles transporting those goods, and to cooperate in customs administration.[7] Perhaps most striking about Article 79 is the way in which its second subsection imposes a clear obligation on member states not to frustrate the trade regime of the CSME:

> Each Member State shall refrain from trade policies and practices, the object or effect of which is to distort competition, frustrate free movement of goods and services, or otherwise nullify or impair benefits to which other Member States are entitled under this Treaty.

[4] As this provision highlights, free movement of goods and services will depend to a large extent upon common standards. For this reason the CARICOM Regional Organization for Standards and Quality (CROSQ) was created. See the Agreement Establishing the CARICOM Regional Organisation for Standards and Quality (CROSQ) (adopted 4 Feb 2002, provisionally applied since 5 Feb 2002, not yet in force) 2324 UNTS 413, and Protocol on the Provisional Application of the Agreement Establishing the CARICOM Regional Organisation for Standards and Quality (CROSQ) (adopted and entered into force 5 Feb 2002) 2326 UNTS 359. Implementation of the CROSQ Agreement, however, has not been strong enough to guarantee its success to date. See eg CARICOM Secretariat, *Summary Draft Report on the Appraisal of the State of Implementation of the CARICOM Single Market* (September 2009) (Georgetown, Guyana: CARICOM Secretariat, 2009) [hereafter '*Summary Draft Report*'], at 8 [commenting that only five member states had enacted the Agreement into domestic law].

[5] Summary of RTC Art 78(3).

[6] RTC Art 78(4).

[7] Transit under RTC Art 86(2) essentially contemplates passage through a member state with the journey beginning and terminating beyond its borders. Freedom of transit entails the related rights not to be subject to delays, restrictions, or charges not for services rendered, and is subject to the requirements of non-discrimination and MFN treatment: Art 86(3).

This is a very broad and potentially far-reaching provision and, because it is phrased in mandatory language, could form the basis of a legal challenge to incompatible state conduct. It prohibits anti-competitive conduct, which is further regulated in Chapter 8 of the RTC. In prohibiting the frustration by member states of the free movement of goods and services with such open-ended phrasing, it would potentially allow challenge to *any* form of trade policy or practice that so frustrates that free movement. The final phrase, prohibiting states from otherwise nullifying or impairing 'benefits to which other Member States are entitled under this Treaty' is similarly far-reaching. If a benefit is accorded under the RTC, then any impairment of that benefit by a member state by trade policies or practices would be subject to challenge.

In relation to external relations, Article 80 imposes duties on member states to coordinate their trade policies with third states or groups of states, and the Community itself is obligated to 'pursue the negotiation of external trade and economic agreements on a joint basis in accordance with principles and mechanisms established by the Conference'. This latter obligation anticipates the establishment of a negotiation framework by the Conference, under which the Community is to jointly operate with the member states. Although member states remain free to enter into bilateral agreements, Article 80(3) makes clear that such agreements are without prejudice to their obligations under the RTC and must be certified by CARICOM as not prejudicing or placing at a disadvantage other member states in relation to the RTC.[8] Likewise, tariff concession negotiations require the prior approval of COTED, and all member state agreements related to trade or aid must be deposited with the CARICOM Secretariat.[9]

10.1.2 OECS

The objectives of the OECS with respect to trade and the Economic Union are stronger than those of CARICOM and similarly must be considered when interpreting the trade regime established by the RTB and its Protocol. Article 4.1(e) of the RTB, for example, sets out as a major purpose of the OECS, 'to establish the Economic Union as a single economic and financial space'. Under Article 4.2(q) of the RTB OECS member states are required to undertake joint actions and pursue joint policies towards the 'economic integration of the Member States through the provisions of the Economic Union Protocol'. The OECS therefore embraces the idea of the creation of a single economic and financial space, and at least potentially speaks to the broader notion of economic *integration* per se.

[8] RTC Art 80(5) grants specific rights and obligations to Belize in this context:

> Nothing in this Treaty shall preclude Belize from concluding arrangements with neighbouring economic groupings provided that treatment not less favourable than that accorded to third States within such groupings shall be accorded to the Member States of the Community, and that the arrangements make adequate provision to guard against the deflection of trade into the rest of CARICOM from the countries of such groupings through Belize.

[9] RTC Arts 80(4) and 81.

This is supported by the allocation of specific powers to the Organisation by OECS member states. Through Article 14.1 of the RTB, member states have given the Organisation exclusive legislative competence in relation to the common market, including the customs union, monetary policy and trade policy. Under Article 14.2 of the RTB member states accord the Organisation concurrent legislative competence over the common commercial policy. Through Acts of the OECS Authority these legislative competences can produce directly effective decisions.[10]

For the Protocol member states, economic integration is to be more firmly entrenched. The Preamble to the Protocol expresses the resolution of member states 'to ensure by common action the economic and social development of their countries by eliminating the barriers which divide them'. These barriers would include all of the topics covered in the present chapter. Moreover Article 2(a) of the Protocol expresses as one of the objectives of the Economic Union 'the creation of a single financial and economic space comprising Protocol Member States'. Article 2(d) implicitly identifies inter-Economic Union trade, when it identifies as central the 'continuous economic growth and expansion through the optimal utilisation of domestic and Economic-Union-wide resources'. At the policy level, Article 2(h) sets as an objective the 'economic growth, development and international competitiveness by the convergence and coordination of the economic policies of Protocol Member States'.

Article 3, which sets out the principles governing the Protocol, is quite explicit in relation to several Economic Union goals. Its first three subsections, for example, provide:

> 3. To achieve the objectives set out in Article 2, the activities of the Protocol Member States shall include under the conditions and timing set out in this Protocol –
> (a) the prohibition, as between Protocol Member States, of customs duties and of quantitative restrictions on the importation and exportation of goods, as well as of all other measures with equivalent effect;
> (b) subject to Article 32, the establishment of common customs tariffs and common commercial policies towards countries and territories not parties to this Protocol;
> (c) the abolition, as between Protocol Member States, of the obstacles to the free movement of persons, services and capital....

This provision, although not likely to be viewed as creating binding obligations per se, may prove crucial for the interpretation of other provisions of the Protocol, since it sets out at a broad level some of the core requirements of a free movement of goods regime.

In sum, both the RTC and RTB and its Protocol establish clear visions in relation to the CSME and Economic Union. Both regional organizations mandate the creation of a single economic space, one which must allow, amongst other things, the free movement of goods. It is in this context that we must analyse the ways in which both regimes create common external/customs tariffs and prohibit import duties,

[10] See RTB Art 5. For further analysis of the implications of Arts 5 and 14 of the RTB see Chapter 6.

export duties, discriminatory internal charges, unlawful quantitative restrictions, and impermissible subsidies and dumping.

10.2 Common External Tariff

10.2.1 CARICOM

Central to the free movement of goods in CARICOM is the successful implementation of a common external tariff (hereafter 'CET').[11] A necessary component of any customs union, the CET erects a kind of fiscal border around CARICOM member states. It allows tariff free trade among CARICOM member states (free circulation in the Community), but requires the imposition of tariffs on any goods imported from a non-CARICOM country.[12] The CET is supported by three legal elements. Firstly, it requires a legal framework to distinguish between CARICOM and non-CARICOM goods. This is established by the RTC provisions establishing Community rules of origin and providing for Community origin treatment.[13] Secondly, it requires a detailed and efficient goods classification system and related rules which ensure non-Community tariff treatment of non-CARICOM goods by all member states.[14] These are established by the provisions of Chapter 5, Schedule I to the RTC, the 'List of Conditions to be Complied with as Provided under Article 84 of the Treaty and the Rules Regarding Community Origin', and the determinations of COTED.[15] Thirdly, it requires a system which both allows waivers of the CET in exceptional circumstances and which sanctions member states for breaches of the CET. This system is set out in Part Two and is supported by the dispute settlement mechanisms in Chapter 2 (organs) and Chapter 9 of the RTC.

Article 82 sets out the framework for the CET by mandating that 'Member States shall establish and maintain a common external tariff in respect of all goods which do not qualify for Community treatment in accordance with plans and schedules set out in relevant determinations of COTED.' This provision creates a binding

[11] The similar term in EU law is the 'common customs tariff'. See eg Art 28 of the TFEU.

[12] Note that free circulation has not yet been fully implemented in the CSME. It has been included in the built in agenda in RTC Art 239(d).

[13] These two terms are defined in RTC Art 1 as:

> 'Community origin' means origin which complies with the Rules of Origin set out in Article 78 [84];
> 'Community treatment' means the access accorded to goods which are of Community origin to the markets of Member States without the application of import duties or quantitative restrictions;

The reference to RTC Art 78 is incorrect. The definition of the same term in Protocol IV cross-referenced Article VIII, which is comparable to Art 84 in the RTC. See Protocol Amending the Treaty Establishing the Caribbean Community (Protocol IV: Trade Policy) (adopted 4–7 Jul 1999, not yet in force) [hereafter 'Protocol IV'].

[14] Note that member states need not apply identical tariffs to a non-CARICOM origin product. Departures from the agreed rate are possible via Lists A, C, and D and the List of Conditional Duty Exemptions. I thank Dr Ononaiwu for clarifying this point.

[15] Schedule I is an integral part of the Commmunity rules of origin and supplements RTC Art 84. Schedule I is kept under continuous review by COTED: RTC Art 84(10).

obligation which is capable of being legally enforced. In administering the CET each member state is required to appoint a competent authority, which must be notified to COTED.[16] COTED itself is required to keep the CET regime under continuous review 'to assess its impact on production and trade, as well as to secure its uniform implementation throughout the Community, in particular, by reducing the need for discretionary application in the day to day administration of the Tariff'.[17]

The Community rules of origin are elaborated by Article 84 and Schedule I to the RTC. Under Article 84(1) goods may be classified as of Community origin if they have been consigned from one member state to a consignee in another member state and

(a) have been wholly produced within the Community; or
(b) have been produced within the Community wholly or partly from materials imported from outside the Community or from materials of undetermined origin by a process which effects a substantial transformation characterised:
  (i) by the goods being classified in a tariff heading different from that in which any of those materials is classified; or
  (ii) in the case of the goods set out in the List in Schedule I to this Treaty [...], only by satisfying the conditions therefor specified.

The expression 'wholly produced' is defined in Rule 2 of Schedule I. This Rule describes a variety of goods produced within the Community including mineral products, vegetable products, live animals, products from live animals, products obtained from hunting and fishing, 'marine products taken from the sea by a vessel of a Member State', and goods produced exclusively from some of the previous products or which contain no materials from outside of the Community.[18] Goods wholly produced within the Community also include, under Rule 2, 'used articles fit only for the recovery of materials provided that they have been collected from users within the Community and... scrap and waste resulting from manufacturing operations within the Community'. Goods which use small quantities of preservatives or other similar additives sources from outside the Community may still be classified as being wholly produced within the Community.[19] In addition, goods consigned from another member state may be treated as Community origin goods as a result of special trading arrangements, if the importing member state provides like imports from other member states the same treatment.[20]

Goods which may be classified as Community origin goods as a result of having undergone a process of substantial transformation, as specified in Article 84(1), are further described and clarified in the Rules. The term 'materials' is defined in Rule 1 of Schedule I as including 'raw materials, intermediate products, parts and components used in the process of production, repair, renovation or improvement

[16] RTC Art 83(4). [17] RTC Art 83(5).

[18] Interestingly the phrase in quotation marks could be read so as to allow marine products caught anywhere on the planet by member state vessels to be considered Community origin goods.

[19] Rule 2(2) in Schedule I to the RTC.

[20] RTC Art 84(9). Under this provision member states are required to advise COTED of such trading arrangements and COTED may recommend the adoption of alternative trading arrangements.

of the goods'. The meaning of substantial transformation is further clarified by Rule 3, and categories of actions not constituting substantial transformation are described in Rule 1. Rule 1(5), for example, excludes goods from this category if they merely have been subjected to, inter alia, operations to ensure their preservation, simple operations related to cleaning or classifying, changes of packaging, marking, simple mixing of materials, and fastening or assembling operations.

Substantial transformation must satisfy one of two conditions under Article 84. After transformation the goods must either be: (1) classified in a tariff heading different from that of the non-CARICOM materials or (2) those identified on the List set out in Schedule I and which have complied with the conditions imposed in that List for MDCs and LDCs.[21] Article 84(2) further specifies the Community treatment rules applicable upon re-entry for goods that have been sent to another CARICOM territory for repair, renovation, or improvement. Such goods are to be treated as Community origin goods for the purposes of re-importation only as long as they are reconsigned directly to that member state from which they were exported and the value of materials imported from non-Community sources does not exceed 65 per cent, in the case of MDCs, or 80 per cent, in the case of LDCs, of the cost of the repair, renovation, or improvement.[22] The different ratios of non-Community goods in this provision clearly benefits businesses in less developed countries and is further supported by Article 161, in Chapter 7, which provides special exemptions and preferences for disadvantaged countries, regions, and sectors.[23]

Article 84(3) provides a process whereby a manufacturer which uses regional materials but is unable to source those materials can inform the competent authority in the manufacturer's territory of the situation. The competent authority must investigate and, if it determines that the manufacturer is justified, submit an application to the Secretary General for a certificate authorizing the use of like materials from outside of the Community, subject to such conditions as the Secretary General may impose.[24] The competent authority, however, must at the time of its investigations inform the other member states of the shortfall in materials experienced by the manufacturer, including details of the quantities and specifications of the materials sought.[25] The Secretary General has a parallel duty to request information from competent authorities of other member states; the competent authorities have a duty to respond regarding their ability to provide the materials sought when making their own investigations prior to issuing the certificate.[26]

[21] The List set out in Schedule I to the RTC is lengthy—over 120 pages long—and hence cannot be subject to analysis in the present work.

[22] RTC Art 84(2).

[23] RTC Art 161 provides: 'The Member States agree that in the determination and operation of the criterion of substantial transformation pursuant to Article 84, the special needs of the less developed countries shall be taken into account.'

[24] RTC Art 84(4) and (7).

[25] RTC Art 84(4).

[26] RTC Art 84(5)–(6). It is likely that the Secretary General will be required to exercise a high degree of diligence in this investigation, given the requirements imposed by the CCJ on the Secretary General in *Trinidad Cement Ltd v Caribbean Community*, Judgment [2009] CCJ 4 (OJ), (2009) 75 WIR 194, 10 August 2009, at [68], in relation to similar investigations regarding applications for the waiver of the CET.

This process balances the need to protect manufacturers who experience shortfalls of Community materials from being subject to the CET with the need to allow other Community suppliers to meet regional demand if the material is available. The Secretary General's certificate, which must be notified to all member states and COTED at its next meeting, deems the goods manufactured from like materials Community origin goods.[27]

Goods which cannot be classified as Community origin goods must be subject to the CET. Article 89 includes within this category goods which have benefitted from an export drawback. An export drawback is defined in Article 89(6)(a) as 'any arrangement for the refund or remission, wholly or in part, of import duties applicable to imported materials: provided that the arrangement, expressly or in effect, allows refund or remission if certain goods or materials are exported, but not if they are retained for home use'.[28] Under Article 89, a good which has benefitted from an export drawback is not to be treated as a Community origin good or otherwise to be exempt from the CET. In treating such goods as non-Community origin goods, member states are required to accord the same treatment to goods from all CARICOM member states.[29] Member states wishing to allow an export drawback in relation to goods being exported from their jurisdiction must notify COTED and, in doing so, 'set out the circumstances which justify the need to apply an export drawback, the products which will benefit therefrom, the nature and proposed duration of the measures, and such other information as COTED may prescribe from time to time'.[30] Under Article 89(4) COTED is required to consider each notification, determine the appropriateness of the drawback, and is empowered to recommend modification of the drawback programme. COTED is also required to review annually all export drawback programmes.[31]

Article 83(2) sets out three circumstances in which COTED may authorize member states to alter or suspend the CET, namely, where '(a) a product is not being produced in the Community, (b) the quantity of the product being produced in the Community does not satisfy the demand of the Community, or (c) the quality of the product being produced in the Community is below the Community standard or a standard the use of which is authorised by COTED'.[32] To this list may be

[27] RTC Art 84(8) and (11).

[28] See also the related definitions of 'remission', 'duties', and 'materials' in RTC Art 89(6)(b)–(d).

[29] RTC Art 89(1). [30] RTC Art 89(3). [31] RTC Art 89(5).

[32] Suspension is available in cases of temporary interruption of supply, alteration when the interruption is of a more permanent nature: *Trinidad Cement Ltd v Caribbean Community*, Judgment [2009] CCJ 4 (OJ), (2009) 75 WIR 194, 10 August 2009, at [54]. Art 83 should also be read in conjunction with two official documents related to the CET that pre-date the RTC, but are still used to help decide issues including waivers. As summarized by the CCJ at [44]:

> The CET was originally provided for in an Annex to the 1973 Treaty of Chaguaramas ('the original Treaty') but agreement was never concluded on implementation of the measure until almost two decades later. There are two official published documents on the CET. The document titled 'Administrative Arrangements Relating to the Alteration or Suspension of Rates under the Common External Tariff' was published in January 1992 ('the 1992 document'). The other document—'Common External Tariff of the Caribbean Common Market – An Explanation of its Scope, Structure and Other Features'—was published in March 1993 ('the 1993 document'). These publications to this day remain the only existing

added a fourth ground for alteration or suspension, namely, where the quantity cannot be produced in a timely manner to satisfy the demand of the Community. This fourth ground was established in the judgment of the Caribbean Court of Justice in the case of *Trinidad Cement Ltd v Caribbean Community*, where the Court held that Article 83 allows COTED to suspend 'not only where the quantity of the product being produced in the Community does not satisfy the demand of the Community as a whole but also where the ongoing demand of a particular Member State will not be met either on a timely basis or at all by the regional producers of the commodity'.[33] COTED may authorize reduction or suspension of the CET in these four cases, subject to such terms and conditions as it may decide, and also subject to the requirement of Article 83(2) that 'in no case shall the product imported from third States be accorded more favourable treatment than similar products produced in the Member States'. In the periods between meetings the CARICOM Secretary General is delegated the authority of COTED to suspend the CET, but not to reduce or alter it, and is required to report any such exercise to COTED at its next meeting.[34]

In the future Article 83 may be amended by the Protocol to Amend Article 83 of the Revised Treaty of Chaguaramas so as to read:

1. Any alteration or suspension of the Common External Tariff on any item shall be decided by COTED.
2. Pursuant to paragraph 1, a suspension of the Common External Tariff shall be subject to such terms and conditions as COTED may decide provided that the decision to suspend takes into account any of the following:
   (a) the product is not being produced in the Community;
   (b) the quantity of the product being produced in the Community does not satisfy the demand of the Community;
   (c) the quality of the product being produced in the Community is below the Community standard or a standard the use of which is authorized by COTED;
   (d) support for the development of internationally competitive production in the CSME;
   (e) the need to encourage efficient production;
   (f) critical government revenue needs; or
   (g) cost of living issues.

authoritative documents on the CET emanating from official circles. As such, they suffer from the serious deficiency that each was published before the entry into force of the RTC the relevant provisions of which are different from the corresponding provisions of the original Treaty. [...] Moreover, the testimonies of both the Secretary-General and Ms Field-Ridley in these proceedings confirm that the 1992 and 1993 documents are still currently in use as official guides for the Community and its organs and the general public. The Court therefore holds that the two publications reflect the policies of COTED and that, until disavowed by the Community or disapproved by this Court, the guidelines and prescriptions contained in them should be taken as being still in force so far as they are consistent with the relevant provisions of the RTC.

33 *Trinidad Cement v Caribbean Community* (n 32) [56].

34 RTC Art 83(3). See also *Trinidad Cement Ltd v Caribbean Community* (n 32) [54].

3. In no case shall the product imported from third States, for which a suspension of the Common External Tariff has been authorized, be accorded more favourable treatment than similar products produced in Member States.
4. Notwithstanding paragraph 1, during any period between the meetings of COTED, the Secretary-General may suspend the Common External Tariff on behalf of COTED. When exercising the authority to suspend, the Secretary-General shall consider only the factors set out in subparagraphs (a), (b) or (c) of paragraph 2. Any exercise of such authority by the Secretary-General shall be reported to the next meeting of COTED.
5. Each Member State shall, for the purpose of administering the Common External Tariff, appoint a competent authority which shall be notified to COTED.
6. COTED shall continuously review the Common External Tariff, in whole or in part, to assess its impact on production and trade, as well as to secure its uniform implementation throughout the Community, in particular, by reducing the need for discretionary application in the day to day administration of the Tariff.[35]

This amendment responds to the decisions of the 25th Meeting of the Community Council and 29th Meeting of COTED to amend Article 83 so as to affirm COTED's discretionary authority with regard to alteration of suspension of the CET. It also is meant to respond to some of the requirements for suspension of the Common External Tariff which are set out in the judgment of the Caribbean Court of Justice in the case of *Trinidad Cement Ltd v Caribbean Community*.[36] However the lengthy list of justifications in the proposed Article 83(2) may end up frustrating the CET regime by allowing far too many waivers.[37] The 'cost of living issues' justification in subsection (2)(g), for example, is particularly likely to be subject to abuse. Issues related to cost of living were raised by the defendant states in both of the cases of *Trinidad Cement Ltd and TCL Guyana Inc v Guyana* and *Hummingbird Rice Mills Limited v Suriname and the Caribbean Community*.[38]

[35] Protocol to Amend Article 83 of the Revised Treaty of Chaguaramas (adopted 12 Mar 2010, not yet in force) Art I. Article II of this Protocol provides for is entry into force upon signature by twelve parties notwithstanding the provisions of Arts 233 and 236. To date it has received eleven signatures.

[36] See Protocol to Amend Article 83 (n 35) Preamble (4th para), and *Trinidad Cement Ltd v Caribbean Community* (n 32).

[37] Note that, perhaps for such reasons, CARICOM is currently engaged in discussions to amend Art 83 in a manner different from that contemplated by the Protocol discussed earlier.

[38] The several decisions in these cases are set out in, respectively: [2008] CCJ 1 (OJ), [2009] CCJ 1 (OJ), [2009] CCJ 5 (OJ), [2009] CCJ 6 (OJ), [2010] CCJ 1 (OJ); and [2011] CCJ 1 (OJ), [2012] CCJ 1 (OJ), [2012] CCJ 2 (OJ). In the case of *Hummingbird Rice Mills Limited v Suriname and the Caribbean Community*, Judgment [2012] CCJ 1 (OJ), the Protocol to Amend Article 83 of the Revised Treaty of Chaguaramas was relied upon by Suriname in its defence. However the Court rejected these arguments at [21] in the following terms:

> The Court readily and fully appreciates the sensitivity and societal importance involved in pricing and ensuring access to bread but would point out that Suriname had a four-year period prior to the definitive entry into force of the Revised Treaty to ensure the appropriate preparations to meet its treaty obligations. It might have been possible for Suriname to have entered a reservation to the CET on flour given the critical importance of affordable bread to the national well-being of the Surinamese society: Article 237. What could not have been done, consistent with its treaty obligations, was for Suriname to have taken the unilateral decision not to comply with Article 82, less so given the protestations of at least one Member State of the Community and the urging of COTED. The Draft Protocol can be of no assistance to Suriname as it has not received the required signatures for entry into force and there is no suggestion that it now represents State practice such as to form a rule of regional customary law. [Citations omitted.]

Likewise it must be mentioned that the issue of non-application of CET rules has been, and remains, a very serious challenge in CARICOM.[39] Out of the six original jurisdiction cases that have been considered by the Caribbean Court of Justice since its inception, three of them have involved complaints about breaches of CET obligations by member states or the Community.[40] As discussed in Chapter 14, these cases demonstrate a wilful disregard by CARICOM member states of the requirement to either apply the CET to goods or to apply for a waiver from COTED. They also reveal dissatisfaction on the part of businesses in the region with the processes by which CARICOM either decides waiver applications or acts in relation to continuing breaches of the CET obligation. However the public litigation of these matters before the Court may have the effect of encouraging member states to be more aware of the consequences of non-compliance, and CARICOM to be more vigilant when considering waiver applications. These cases may also have raised awareness in the business sector across the region of the potential of the CCJ to provide remedies for breaches of CET obligations.

10.2.2 OECS

The Protocol of Eastern Caribbean Economic Union sets up two regimes paralleling CARICOM's regimes on the Community rules of origin and the CET. The OECS Protocol establishes an Economic Union Tariff Treatment (EUTT) regime paralleling CARICOM's Community rules of origin regime, and a Common Customs Tariff regime paralleling the CET.[41]

With respect to Economic Union rules of origin, Article 4.1 of the Protocol establishes a customs union 'which shall cover all trade in goods eligible for Economic Union Tariff Treatment in accordance with Article 5'. Article 5.1 describes EUTT as follows:

> 5.1 For the purposes of Article 4 goods shall be accepted as eligible for Economic Union Area tariff treatment if they are consigned from a Protocol Member State to a

[39] For a historical perspective see eg Kathy-Ann Brown, 'The CARICOM—"Unity for Survival"', in N Lacasse and L Perret (eds) *Le libre-échange dans les Amériques (Une perspective continentale)/Free trade in the Americas (A hemispheric approach)* (Montreal: Wilson & Lafleur, 1994) 335–68. For a more current view, see CARICOM Secretariat, *Summary Draft Report* 11–12.

[40] See the various phases of the cases of *Trinidad Cement Ltd and TCL Guyana Inc v Guyana, Trinidad Cement Ltd v Caribbean Community*, and *Hummingbird Rice Mills Limited v Suriname and the Caribbean Community*: [2008] CCJ 1 (OJ), [2009] CCJ 1 (OJ), [2009] CCJ 5 (OJ), [2009] CCJ 6 (OJ), [2010] CCJ 1 (OJ); [2009] CCJ 2 (OJ), [2009] CCJ 4 (OJ); and [2011] CCJ 1 (OJ), [2012] CCJ 1 (OJ), [2012] CCJ 2 (OJ), respectively. Perhaps because of controversies regarding waivers of the CET, the CCJ was formally asked in the case of *Trinidad Cement Ltd v Caribbean Community*, Judgment [2009] CCJ 4 (OJ) (2009) 75 WIR 194, 10 August 2009, to establish criteria for waivers of the CET. The Court notes at para [12]:

> Counsel for TCL also indicated that, quite apart from the relief TCL was claiming, the company had instituted these proceedings in order to have the Court establish definitive criteria for the suspension of the CET. The business community needed to know with certainty what the proper procedures were for suspension of the tariff and what was the scope and extent of the powers of the Secretary-General and COTED in that regard.

[41] The EU also uses the term 'common customs tariff'. See eg Art 28 of the TFEU.

> consignee in the importing Protocol Member State and if they meet the requirements of rules of origin under the Revised Treaty of Chaguaramas.

Article 5.2 provides that the rules of origin under the RTC are to be applied *mutatis mutandis* (with the necessary changes being made) to the OECS Economic Union. Article 5.3 allows a Protocol member state to extend Economic Union Tariff Treatment to imports from another Protocol member state, so long as 'the like imports consigned from any other Protocol Member State are accorded the same treatment'.

Economic Union Tariff Treatment is supplemented by the requirement for free circulation of goods in Article 10. Article 10.1 allows goods which have been imported from outside of the Economic Union Area to generally enjoy the same privileges as Economic Union Area goods. To be eligible for free circulation in the Area, however, these goods must have complied with the applicable customs duties or charges of equivalent effect and not have benefitted from a total or partial export drawback.[42]

Article 6 provides for the establishment of a Common Customs Tariff by an Act of the OECS in the following terms:

> 6. The Common Customs Tariff will be set by or under the authority of an Act of the Organisation under Article 14.1(a) of this Treaty, provided that for any period when this tariff is not set the Common External Tariff under the Revised Treaty of Chaguaramas shall be the Common Customs Tariff. Protocol Member States may not impose higher tariffs than the Common Customs Tariff.

Although the Common Customs Tariff is set in the first instance at a rate paralleling the CET, it need not remain fixed at that rate. This is because OECS countries are accorded exemptions under the RTC, particularly in Chapter 7, which allow less developed countries (which would include all of the OECS) to modify their obligations under the RTC, including the obligations related to the CET.[43] Given the pattern of disputes which have come before the Caribbean Court of Justice related to the CET, it is likely that OECS member states would seek to set their Common Customs Tariffs at a level below that of CARICOM's CET, so as to allow cheaper access to foreign products in areas of domestic need.[44] Although it is theoretically possible for OECS Protocol member states to impose the Common

[42] Art 10.2 Protocol.

[43] See eg Art 163 of the RTC, entitled 'The Common External Tariff', which provides: 'The Member States agree that in the implementation of the Common External Tariff provided for in Article 82, the special needs of the less developed countries shall be taken into account.' See also Art 161 which contains similar wording in relation to Community origin treatment, and Art 160, allowing for the imposition of import duties on goods eligible for Community treatment.

[44] See the several decisions in the trilogy of original jurisdiction cases involving the CET: *Trinidad Cement Ltd and TCL Guyana Inc v Guyana* [2008] CCJ 1, [2009] CCJ 1, [2009] CCJ 5, [2009] CCJ 6, [2010] CCJ 1; *Trinidad Cement Ltd v Caribbean Community* [2009] CCJ 2, [2009] CCJ 4; *Hummingbird Rice Mills Limited v Suriname and the Caribbean Community* [2011] CCJ 1, [2012] CCJ 1, [2012] CCJ 2. In all three of these cases the facts involved countries which unlawfully either waived or dis-applied the CET so as to allow foreign imports to enter the country without customs duties.

Customs Tariff on CARICOM member states in addition to extra-regional states, such an action would require a specific exemption under the RTC itself, to which all OECS member states are also parties.[45]

Article 8 of the Protocol creates a similar regime for the OECS in relation to export drawbacks, in the following terms:

> Each Protocol Member State may refuse to accept as eligible for Economic Union Area tariff treatment goods which benefit from export drawback allowed by Protocol Member States in which the goods have undergone the processes of production which forms the basis of the claim to Economic Union Area origin. In applying this paragraph, each Protocol Member State shall accord the same treatment to imports consigned from all other Protocol Member States.

The term 'export drawback' is defined as meaning 'any arrangement for the refund or remission, wholly or in part, of import duties applicable to imported materials . . . [p]rovided that the arrangement, expressly or in effect, allows refund or remission if certain goods or materials are exported, but not if they are retained for home use'.[46]

10.3 Import and Export Duties[47]

10.3.1 CARICOM

The regime of freedom of movement of goods under the CSME necessarily entails the prohibition of import and export duties on goods of Community origin. Articles 87 and 88, respectively, prohibit import and export duties and 'any duties or charges with equivalent effect'.[48] The latter phrasing is important because it would catch a charge not specifically identified as an import or export duty.

[45] Art 3(b) of the OECS Protocol, for example, mandates the following action to achieve the objectives of the Protocol: '(b) . . . the establishment of common customs tariffs and common commercial policies towards countries and territories *not parties to this Protocol*' (emphasis added). The latter phrase, as with the phrase 'third countries' in Art 4.1, would include CARICOM member states.

[46] 'Remission' is defined in Art 8 as including 'exemption for materials brought into free ports and other places which have similar customs privileges'. 'Duties' is defined there as meaning: '(i) all charges on or in connection with importation, except fiscal charges to which Article 7 applies; and (ii) any protective element in such fiscal charges'. See also the definitions, in Art 8, of 'materials' and 'process of production'.

[47] For analysis of the EU's parallel regime on customs duties and internal taxation see eg Catherine Barnard, *The Substantive Law of the EU: The Four Freedoms*, 3rd edn (Oxford: Oxford University Press, 2010) ch 3.

[48] The definition of 'import duties' in RTC Art 1 is 'any tax or surtax of customs and any other charges of equivalent effect whether fiscal, monetary or exchange, which are levied on imports except those notified under Article 85 [90] and other charges which fall within that Article and the definition of export duty in Art 88(3).' The cross-reference to RTC Art 85 is incorrect. The definition of the same term Art XII of Protocol IV referred to Art XV, which is comparable to Art 90 in the RTC. The definition of 'export duties', found in RTC Art 88(3), is 'any duties or charges with equivalent effect imposed on or in connection with the exportation of goods'.

'Equivalent effect' has been interpreted very broadly in EU law.[49] It is likely that a similar approach would be taken in the Caribbean. For example, in Case 7/68 *Commission v Italy* the European Court of Justice held that the equivalent EU provision regarding export duties

prohibits the collection in dealings between Member States of any customs duty on exports and of any charge having an equivalent effect, that is to say, *any charge which, by altering the price of an article exported, has the same restrictive effect on the free circulation of that article as a customs duty.* This provision makes no distinction based on the purpose of the duties and charges the abolition of which it requires.[50]

In a subsequent case involving the same defendant, Case 24/68 *Commission v Italy*, the ECJ defined a charge having equivalent effect as including

any pecuniary charge, however small and whatever its designation and mode of application, which is imposed unilaterally on domestic or foreign goods by reason of the fact that they cross a frontier, and which is not a customs duty in the strict sense,...even if it is not imposed for the benefit of the State, is not discriminatory or protective in effect and if the product on which the charge is imposed is not in competition with any domestic product.[51]

The Court also noted that any such charge 'however small...constitutes an obstacle to the movement of such goods'.[52] As a result, Articles 87–88 of the RTC could be read as prohibiting any pecuniary charge, however small and whatever its designation and mode of application, which is imposed unilaterally on a domestic or foreign good by reason of its crossing a frontier.

Articles 87–88, however, include exceptions related to lawful internal charges, charges commensurate with services rendered, and measures necessary to prevent evasion of export duties.[53] The exception related to charges commensurate with services rendered has been interpreted very restrictively by the ECJ. For example, in Case 87/75 *Bresciani v Amministrazione Italiana delle Finanze*, the ECJ held that a charge for compulsory veterinary and public health inspections on the importation of raw cowhide was impermissible because it did not constitute a service rendered to the importer.[54] Rather, it represented a benefit to the general public. The Court held:

Nor, in determining the effects of the duty on the free movement of goods, is it of any importance that a duty of the type at issue is proportionate to the costs of a compulsory public health inspection carried out on entry of the goods. The activity of the administration of the State intended to maintain a public health inspection system imposed in the general interest cannot be regarded as a service rendered to the importer such as to justify the imposition of a pecuniary charge. If, accordingly, public health inspections are still justified at the end of the transitional period, the costs which they occasion must be met by the general public which, as a whole, benefits from the free movement of Community goods.[55]

[49] The provision comparable to Arts 87–88 of the RTC is Art 30 of the TFEU.
[50] Case 7/68 *Commission v Italy* [1968] ECR 423, at p 429 (emphasis added).
[51] Case 24/68 *Commission v Italy* [1969] ECR 193, at p 201 [9].
[52] Case 24/68 *Commission v Italy* (n 51) p 200 [7].
[53] See RTC Arts 87(2)–(3) and 88(2).
[54] [1976] ECR 129.
[55] *Bresciani v Amministrazione Italiana delle Finanze* (n 54) at pp 138–9 [10].

Article 87(3) of the RTC could be interpreted equally restrictively so as to prohibit charges for services rendered unless those services actually benefit the importer.[56]

10.3.2 OECS

The RTB and its Protocol set out ambitions for the OECS similar to those established in the RTC. Article 2(a) of the Protocol to the RTB, for example, sets out as one of the objectives of the Economic Union 'the creation of a single financial and economic space comprising Protocol Member States'. This provision is complemented by Article 3(a), which includes as one of the fundamental principles of the Protocol, 'the prohibition, as between Protocol Member States, of customs duties and of quantitative restrictions on the importation and exportation of goods, as well as of all other measures with equivalent effect'. However subsequent articles do not carry through with the full promise of these provisions, and it will be interesting to see whether the more restrictive later articles are read broadly in light of Articles 2–3 of the Protocol.

For example, Article 4.1 applies the principle in Article 3(a) by prohibiting import duties between Protocol member states. 'Import duties' are defined for the purposes of this provision in Article 4.2 as meaning 'any tax or surtax of customs and any other charges of equivalent effect—whether fiscal, monetary or exchange—which are levied on imports, except duties notified under Article 7 and other charges which fall within that Article'. Article 4.3 makes clear that import duties are also prohibited on products which the importing Protocol member state does not produce, or for which it produces a competitive substitute. Fees and similar charges for services rendered, however, are excluded from coverage by Article 4.3, as are non-discriminatory internal charges.[57]

This definition of import duties is similar to that obtaining under the RTC and covers the important category of charges of equivalent effect to an import duty, the scope of which has been noted in relation to EU law. However it must be highlighted that there is no parallel provision prohibiting export duties in Protocol Article 4. Such an omission is regrettable since it could frustrate the achievement of the single economic space envisaged by the Protocol. Whether Article 4 will be extended to exports through a teleological reading of the Protocol, as supported by Article 3(a), remains to be seen.

[56] It should be noted that the ECJ has applied a strict approach even in cases where the charge was for services required by EU law. See eg the multi-part test applied in Case 18/87 *Commission v Germany* [1988] ECR 5438, at p 5441 [8] for a fee charged in connection with inspections carried out pursuant to an EU provision.

[57] Protocol Art 4.4(a)–(b) defines 'non-discriminatory' as meaning 'non-discriminatory as between goods eligible for Economic Union Area tariff treatment as aforesaid and goods not so eligible' and clarifies that 'a charge shall not be deemed other than internal by reason only that it is collected at the time and place of importation.'

10.4 Internal Taxes[58]

10.4.1 CARICOM

Article 90 of the RTC supplements the prohibitions on import and export duties and charges of equivalent effect by imposing a ban on discriminatory internal taxation. It does so in order to ensure the free movement of goods in CARICOM. In the words of the European Court of Justice when discussing the parallel provision of EU law, the aim of a provision like Article 90 of the RTC is

> to ensure free movement of goods between the Member States in normal conditions of competition by the elimination of all forms of protection which result from the application of internal taxation which discriminates against products from other Member States. As the Commission has correctly stated, Article 95 [Article 110 TFEU] must guarantee the complete neutrality of internal taxation as regards competition between domestic products and imported products.[59]

Article 90(1)(a)–(b) of the RTC applies this prohibition to discriminatory taxation on like goods and competitive substitutes in the following terms:

> 1. Save as otherwise provided in this Treaty, Member States shall not:
>   (a) apply directly or indirectly to imported goods of Community origin any fiscal charges in excess of those applied directly or indirectly to *like domestic goods*, or otherwise apply such charges so as to protect like domestic goods; or
>   (b) apply fiscal charges to imported goods of Community origin of a kind which they do not produce, or which they do not produce in substantial quantities, in such a way as to protect the domestic production of *substitutes* which enter into direct competition with them and which do not bear, directly or indirectly, in the country of importation, fiscal charges of equivalent incidence.[60]

The term 'fiscal charges' is defined in Article 90(3) as meaning 'internal taxes and other internal charges with equivalent effect on goods'. Article 90(1)(a)–(b) addresses both direct and indirect forms of fiscal charges.

This structure catches discriminatory or protective internal taxation on goods that are both similar (like) and dissimilar.[61] Interestingly, however, Article 90(1)(b) only attempts to catch internal taxes on goods which are in 'direct competition'. This wording contrasts with the position adopted in EU law, where goods that are in 'partial, indirect or potential' competition are also caught.[62] As a result, under the RTC it would be possible to argue that goods that are neither in direct competition nor like goods would not be caught under Article 90, even in cases

[58] For analysis of the EU's parallel regime on customs duties and internal taxation see eg Barnard, *The Substantive Law of the EU* (n 47) ch 3.
[59] Case 168/78 *Commission v France* [1980] ECR 347, at [4].
[60] Emphasis added.
[61] For analysis of the EU position, see Case 168/78 *Commission v France* (n 59) [5]–[6].
[62] Case 168/78 *Commission v France* (n 59) [6] (emphasis added).

of discriminatory internal taxation. This would create a significant loophole, one which should be closed through formal amendment, creative judicial interpretation, or application of other provisions of the RTC.

Article 90(1)(a)–(b) will likely be read as being mutually exclusive.[63] Either a good must be classified as being (1) a *like* domestic good, or (2) a *substitute* which enters into direct competition with a domestic good.[64] In both cases in order for the fiscal charge to contravene Article 90 it must protect the domestic good. A member state is required to notify COTED of any fiscal charge which, although not identical for imported and like domestic goods, is considered by that state to be consistent with Article 90(1). Such a member state also has an obligation to supply information to other member states, upon request, about the compatibility of the charge with Article 90(1).[65]

The equivalent provision in EU law, Article 110 of the TFEU, has generated considerable jurisprudence that is helpful in predicting the likely interpretation of Article 90 of the RTC.[66] Article 110 TFEU has been interpreted so as to

[63] This is the position in EU law. In Case 168/78 *Commission v France* (n 59) at pp 359–60 [5]–[6], the Court distinguished between the roles of the first and second paragraphs of what is now Art 110 TFEU as follows:

> 5 The first paragraph of Article 95 [now *TFEU* Art 110], which is based on a comparison of the tax burdens imposed on domestic products and on imported products which may be classified as 'similar', is the basic rule in this respect. This provision, as the Court has had occasion to emphasize in its judgment of 10 October 1978 in Case 148/77, *H. Hansen jun. & O. C. Balle GmbH & Co. v Hauptzollamt Flensburg* [1978] ECR 1787, must be interpreted widely so as to cover all taxation procedures which conflict with the principle of the equality of treatment of domestic products and imported products; it is therefore necessary to interpret the concept of 'similar products' with sufficient flexibility. The Court specified in the judgment of 17 February 1976 in the *REWE* case (Case 45/75 [1976] ECR 181) that it is necessary to consider as similar products which 'have similar characteristics and meet the same needs from the point of view of consumers'. It is therefore necessary to determine the scope of the first paragraph of Article 95 on the basis not of the criterion of the strictly identical nature of the products but on that of their similar and comparable use.
>
> 6 The function of the second paragraph of Article 95 is to cover, in addition, all forms of indirect tax protection in the case of products which, without being similar within the meaning of the first paragraph, are nevertheless in competition, even partial, indirect or potential, with certain products of the importing country. The Court has already emphasized certain aspects of that provision in its judgment of 4 April 1978 in Case 27/77, *Firma Fink-Frucht GmbH v Hauptzollamt München-Landsbergerstrasse* [1978] ECR 223, in which it stated that for the purposes of the application of the first paragraph of Article 95 it is sufficient for the imported product to be in competition with the protected domestic production by reason of one or several economic uses to which it may be put, even though the condition of similarity for the purposes of the first paragraph of Article 95 is not fulfilled.

[64] For an example of dissimilar goods which entered into competition see the famous case involving a challenge to differential taxes on wine and beer in the UK: Case 170/78 *Commission v UK* [1983] ECR 2263. The ECJ held that beer and cheap, low alcohol types of wine could be viewed as being in competition, in terms of such factors as use, alcohol level, and price.

[65] RTC Art 90(2).

[66] Art 110 TFEU provides:

> No Member State shall impose, directly or indirectly, on the products of other Member States any internal taxation of any kind in excess of that imposed directly or indirectly on similar domestic products.
>
> Furthermore, no Member State shall impose on the products of other Member States any internal taxation of such a nature as to afford indirect protection to other products.

catch origin neutral internal taxes, in other words, taxes which on their face apply equally to local and foreign goods.[67] Article 110 TFEU has also been interpreted to catch instances of indirect discrimination, where the tax is imposed on the basis of objective criteria equally to domestic and imported goods, but is arranged in such a manner as to impose a greater burden on imported goods. For example, in Case 112/84 *Humblot v Directeur des Services Fiscaux* one level of annual automobile taxes was imposed upon cars with engines rated at a 16 CV (fiscal horsepower) power rating or less, and another level, a special tax, on those above a 16 CV power rating.[68] Such a tax scheme was origin neutral and not directly discriminatory. However, since all French cars fell below the 16 CV power rating, and the vast majority of imported vehicles fell above it, the result was that disproportionate taxes were imposed on foreign cars. The Court found the taxation scheme to be indirectly discriminatory:

> Although the system embodies no formal distinction based on the origin of products it manifestly exhibits discriminatory or protective features contrary to [Article 110], since the power rating determining liability to the special tax has been fixed at a level such that only imported cars, in particular from other Member States, are subject to the special tax whereas all cars of domestic manufacture are liable to the distinctly more advantageous differential tax.[69]

The problem highlighted in the *Humblot Case* was the discriminatory effect of the tax in relation to foreign goods.

In contrast, other cases demonstrate that it is possible for a tax regime to remain lawful even if it results in the imposition of taxes which indirectly affect foreign goods more severely than domestic goods if an objective justification can be provided which is not dependent upon nationality. For example, in Case 140/79 *Chemial Farmaceutici v DAF*, the Court considered whether a special duty imposed by Italy upon synthetic ethyl alcohol, which was far greater than that imposed upon ethyl alcohol produced by fermentation, could be justified on the basis of objective criteria such as the conditions of production and the raw materials used.[70] In deciding that such a tax could be compatible with what is now Article 110 TFEU the Court noted that although there was very limited synthetic ethyl alcohol production in Italy, nevertheless the two parts of the tax regime were applied equally to foreign and domestic produced synthetic and non-synthetic ethyl alcohol and that the Italian justification for the differentiation—preservation of petroleum derivatives for other economic use—was compatible with Community law. The Court held that:

> in its present stage of development Community law does not restrict the freedom of each Member State to lay down tax arrangements which differentiate between certain products on the basis of objective criteria, such as the nature of the raw materials used or the production processes employed. Such differentiation is compatible with Community law if it

[67] Case 20/76 *Schottle v Finanzamt Freudenstadt* [1977] ECR 247.

[68] [1985] ECR 1367.

[69] *Humblot v Directeur des Services Fiscaux* (n 68) [14].

[70] [1981] ECR 1.

pursues economic policy objectives which are themselves compatible with the requirements of the Treaty and its secondary law and if the detailed rules are such as to avoid any form of discrimination, direct or indirect, in regard to imports from other Member States or any form of protection of competing domestic products.[71]

The Court held that the legislation in question was not discriminatory since imports from other member states, on the one hand, and domestically produced ethyl alcohol, on the other hand, both qualified for the same treatment under Italian law. Importers and domestic manufacturers of ethyl alcohol produced by *fermentation* benefitted equally; importers and domestic manufactures of *synthetic* ethyl alcohol were equally disadvantaged by the tax.[72] As a result, to apply by analogy this ECJ jurisprudence to Article 90 of the RTC, internal taxes may be permitted even if they indirectly affect foreign goods more severely than domestic goods, so long as the taxes are not discriminatory, can be objectively justified without reference to nationality, and fulfil economic policy objectives which are themselves compatible with the requirements of the RTC.

10.4.2 OECS

Article 7 of the OECS Protocol imposes an internal tax regime very similar to that existing under the RTC and therefore would equally benefit from a comparative analysis of the similar regime in EU law, discussed earlier. Article 7.1, in nearly identical wording to Article 90(1) of the RTC, specifies that a Protocol member state shall not:

(a) apply directly or indirectly to imported goods any fiscal charges in excess of those applied directly or indirectly to like domestic goods, nor otherwise apply such charges so as to afford effective protection to like domestic goods; or
(b) apply fiscal charges to imported goods of a kind which they do not produce, or which they do not produce in substantial quantities, in such a way as to afford effective protection to the domestic production of goods of a different kind which are substitutable for the imported goods, which enter into direct competition with them and which do not bear, directly or indirectly, in the country of importation, fiscal charges of equivalent incidence.[73]

'Fiscal charges' is defined in Article 7.3 as meaning 'customs duties and other similar charges applied primarily for the purpose of raising revenue', 'internal taxes and other internal charges on goods'.[74] Interestingly, the phrase 'charges with equivalent effect' is not included in this definition, as it is in the CARICOM and EU regimes. This would be a regrettable omission if not for the use of the phrase 'other similar charges' in the definition of 'revenue duties' in Article 7.3, which could be

[71] *Chemial Farmaceutici v DAF* (n 70) [14].
[72] *Chemial Farmaceutici v DAF* [16].
[73] Note that Art 7.1(b) of the Protocol uses the same phrase 'direct competition' that is used in Art 90(1)(b) of the RTC. For the same reasons advanced earlier it is hoped that this phrase can be interpreted generously.
[74] This text provides a consolidated definition of both 'fiscal charges' and 'revenue duties' from Protocol Art 7.3.

interpreted to similar effect. Article 7.2 of the Protocol imposes the obligation on Protocol member states to notify the Economic Affairs Council of all fiscal charges that would appear incompatible with Article 7.1(a), but are considered compatible by the Protocol member state concerned, and to supply information about those charges at the request of any other Protocol member state.

10.5 Quantitative Restrictions[75]

10.5.1 CARICOM

The prohibition of quantitative restrictions is another crucial component in the CARICOM machinery to ensure free movement of goods in the Community. It complements and completes the RTC prohibitions on import duties, export duties, charges of equivalent effect, and discriminatory internal taxes by catching any non-fiscal measure that impedes free movement of goods across borders. As a result, all restrictions on the free movement of goods within CARICOM should be classifiable as falling under one of the following categories: an import or export duty, a charge of equivalent effect, an internal tax, a quantitative restriction, or a measure equivalent to a quantitative restriction.

To contrast the three main categories of trade-distorting conduct, import and export duties and charges of equivalent effect tend to be identifiable because they involve a fiscal charge imposed by reason of a good crossing a frontier. Internal taxes may involve fiscal charges imposed systematically in accordance with objective criteria—such as nature, quality, or function—regardless of the origin of the good. In other words, internal charges are origin neutral: they not depend upon the crossing of a frontier. Quantitative restrictions and measures equivalent to quantitative restrictions, on the other hand, are hindrances to the free movement of goods that do not involve a fiscal component.[76]

Subject to certain listed exceptions, Article 91 of the RTC prohibits quantitative restrictions on imports and exports.[77] 'Quantitative restrictions' are defined in

[75] For analysis of the EU's parallel regime on quantitative restrictions see eg Barnard, *The Substantive Law of the EU* (n 47) chs 4–5.

[76] For a more detailed attempt to distinguish between duties, charges of equivalent effect, internal taxes and quantitative restrictions in the context of EU law see Alina Kaczorowska, *European Union Law*, 2nd edn (London: Routledge, 2011) at 528–30.

[77] RTC Art 91(1)–(2) are subject to the provisions on public undertakings, general exceptions, security exceptions, and the Schedules to the RTC dealing with marketing arrangements for unrefined cane sugar, the development of the oils and fats sub-sector, and the protection of Guyanese petroleum products. The cross-references in RTC Art 91(1)–(2) are incorrect. Art XVI of the Protocol IV, the parallel provision to Art 91 of the RTC, cross-references Arts XIX, XX, and XXI of the Protocol. These latter provisions parallel Arts 94, 226, and 225 of the RTC. As a result Art 91(1)–(2) of the RTC should read as follows:

1. Save as otherwise provided in this Treaty, and in particular Articles [94], [226] and [225], and in Schedules II, III and IV, a Member State shall not apply any quantitative restrictions on the importation of goods which are of Community origin.
2. Except as otherwise provided in this Treaty, and particularly in Articles [226] and [225], and in Schedule III, a Member State shall not apply any quantitative restrictions on exports to any other Member State.

Article 91(4) as meaning 'prohibitions or restrictions on imports into, or exports from, any other Member State, as the case may be, whether made effective through quotas, import licences or other measures with equivalent effect, including administrative measures and requirements restricting imports or exports'.[78] The key phrase in this definition is 'or other measures with equivalent effect'. This phrase expands the scope of the article to cover any measure which has the same effect as a quantitative restriction, howsoever classified or characterized.[79] As a result such things as standards, technical regulations, and sanitary and phyto-sanitary measures could all fall under the rubric of quantitative restrictions.[80]

Article 91(3) nevertheless permits a member state to take 'such measures as are necessary to prevent evasion of any prohibitions or restrictions which it applies to imports from or exports to third States provided that less favourable treatment is not granted to Member States than to countries outside the Community'. In other words, quantitative restrictions may be available as a tool to prevent or restrict imports from and exports to non-CARICOM member states which are not in conformity with the RTC. Even in such cases, however, the quantitative restrictions are subject to the requirements of most favoured nation (MFN) treatment. Similarly, Article 92 allows for the imposition of restrictions on the importation of any product in certain limited cases.

The prohibition on quantitative restrictions in Article 91 will likely prove to be of considerable importance in maintaining CARICOM's free movement of goods regime. Defined in Article 91(4) as including measures equivalent to quantitative restrictions, it will prove especially helpful in catching sophisticated attempts by member states to discriminate against CARICOM origin goods in favour of their own domestic goods.

The jurisprudence of the ECJ is helpful in predicting potential interpretations of Article 91 of the RTC because it illustrates both (1) the wide range of state behaviour that has been caught by the provisions on quantitative restrictions under EU law, and (2) the breadth and depth of coverage extended to the relevant provisions of EU law.[81] For example, in the seminal case of Case 8/74 *Procureur du*

[78] Note that by including imports and exports in the same provision the RTC differs from the TFEU, which contains distinct articles on imports and exports. Whether CARICOM law will therefore take a unified approach to quantitative restrictions for both imports and exports remains to be seen. For the distinct positions in EU law for these two categories see eg Paul Craig and Gráinne de Búrca, in *EU Law, Text, Cases and Materials*, 5th edn (Oxford: Oxford University Press, 2011) 650–1.

[79] The ECJ has defined the term 'quantitative restrictions' as used in Arts 34 and 35 of the TFEU as: 'measures which amount to a total or partial restraint of, according to the circumstances, imports, exports or goods in transit': Case 2/73 *Geddo v Ente* [1973] ECR 865, at p 879 [7]. 'Measures having equivalent effect' have also been described by the Court as 'not only [taking] the form of restraint described; whatever the description or technique employed, they can also consist of encumbrances having the same effect'. At [7].

[80] See the critical discussion by CARICOM of the existing challenges to the free movement of goods arising from lack of Community standards in particular areas, the application of national standards, and the application of sanitary and phyto-sanitary measures in CARICOM Secretariat, *Summary Draft Report* 12–13.

[81] The Commission's Directive 70/50, [1970] OJ L13/29, which is no longer applicable to EU law, nevertheless provides an idea of the scope of matters which can be considered to be measures

Roi v Dassonville, the ECJ established a very broad scope of application for the EU's rules regarding quantitative restrictions when it held that '[a]ll trading rules enacted by Member States which are *capable of hindering, directly or indirectly, actually or potentially*, intra-Community trade are to be considered as measures having an effect equivalent to quantitative restrictions.'[82] In the absence of harmonization such measures may not be caught by Article 34 if they are reasonable and do not act as a hindrance to trade.[83] But the potential scope of Article 34 nevertheless remains very broad and it has been used to catch import and export licences, domestic product promotion campaigns, origin-marking requirements, public procurement conditions, administrative practices, price fixing regulations, and conditions which make it more difficult for a good to enter the market (such as roadworthiness tests for automobiles).[84]

Measures equivalent to a quantitative restriction included in the *Dassonville* case the requirement for a certificate of origin. Under Belgian law importers of products bearing a designation of origin, including Scotch whisky, were required to provide a certificate of origin, in this case from the UK. However since such certificates were not needed to import Scotch whisky into *other EU* member states such a requirement could constitute an impediment to trade. This was demonstrated in the facts of the case. The Belgian trader who imported Scotch whisky from France (where the goods were in free circulation) into Belgium could not easily provide a UK certificate of origin and was subject to charge under Belgian law. In deciding that the measure was equivalent to a quantitative restriction the Court held that 'the requirement by a Member State of a certificate of authenticity which is less easily obtainable by importers of an authentic product which has been put into free circulation in a regular manner in another Member State than by importers of the same product coming directly from the country of origin constitutes a measure having an effect equivalent to a quantitative restriction as prohibited by the Treaty'.[85] As a result *Dassonville* demonstrates that effect is more important

equivalent to a quantitative restrictions (MEQRs). As summarized by Craig and de Búrca, in *EU Law, Text, Cases and Materials* (n 78) at 639:

> The list of matters which can constitute an MEQR are specified in Article 2 [of the Directive] and include: minimum or maximum prices for imported products; less favourable prices for imported products; lowering the value of the imported product by reducing its intrinsic value or increasing its costs; payment conditions for imported products which differ from those for domestic products; conditions in respect of packaging, composition, identification, size, weight, etc, which apply only to imported goods or which are different and more difficulty to satisfy than in the case of domestic goods; the giving of a preference to the purchase of domestic goods as opposed to imports, or otherwise hindering the purchase of imports; limiting publicity in respect of imported goods as compared with domestic products; prescribing stocking requirements which are different from and more difficult to satisfy than those which apply to domestic goods; and making it mandatory for importers of goods to have an agent in the territory of the importing state.

[82] [1974] ECR 837, at p 852 [5] (emphasis added).

[83] *Procureur du Roi v Dassonville* (n 82) [6].

[84] See eg the cases discussed both later in the chapter, and in Craig and de Búrca, in *EU Law, Text, Cases and Materials* (n 78) 640–6.

[85] *Procureur du Roi v Dassonville* (n 82) [9].

than intent, and that mere formalities can constitute arbitrary discrimination or a disguised restriction in trade.[86]

EU jurisprudence has also extended the scope of quantitative restrictions to cover administrative practices in addition to formal legislative provisions. This line of authority would be relevant in the context of CARICOM since Article 91(4) of the RTC includes 'administrative measures and requirements' under the definition of quantitative restrictions. For example, in Case 21/84 *Commission v France* the ECJ examined a situation in which French legislative provisions related to approval of postal franking machines had been amended to comply with EU law, but French administrative practices remained protectionist and discriminatory.[87] The Court indicated that formal legislative compliance was not sufficient. The practice in implementing the rule also must be assessed to ensure that it did not create a form of quantitative restriction. For example, the Court highlighted that

> [u]nder the cloak of a general provision permitting the approval of machines imported from other Member States, the administration might very well adopt a systematically unfavourable attitude towards imported machines, either by allowing considerable delay in replying to applications for approval or in carrying out the examination procedure, or by refusing approval on the grounds of various alleged technical faults for which no detailed explanations are given or which prove to be inaccurate.[88]

However in order for administrative practices to be identified as quantitative restrictions, the Court required proof of 'a certain degree of consistency and generality'.[89] Such consistency and generality was found to exist on the facts of the case.

Other ECJ cases have held that state inaction in the context of disruption of free movement of goods by private citizens could constitute a measure equivalent to a quantitative restriction.[90] In Case C-265/95 *Commission v France*, for example, the blatant failure of French authorities to take all necessary measures to suppress violent agricultural protests by French farmers over a period of more than a decade was held to violate the rules against measures equivalent to quantitative restrictions.[91] The protests by the French farmers impaired the free movement of

[86] For another decision in which a mere formality nevertheless was found to be a quantitative restriction see Cases 51–54/71 *International Fruit Company v Produktschap voor Groenten en Fruit (No 2)* [1971] ECR 1107. This decision found legislative provisions of the Netherlands which prohibited imports and exports without a licence but which in fact are not applied because exemptions are granted from the prohibition and, where this is not so, because the licence is always issued on request, to be measures equivalent to a quantitative restriction. The Court held that the provisions of the EU treaties 'preclude the application to intra-Community trade of a national provision which requires, even purely as a formality, import or export licences or any other similar procedure'. See at p 1116 [9].

[87] [1985] ECR 1355.

[88] Case 21/84 *Commission v France* (n 87) p 1364 [11].

[89] Case 21/84 *Commission v France* pp 1364–5 [13]. The Court continued: 'That generality must be assessed differently according to whether the market concerned is one on which there are numerous traders or whether it is a market, such as that in postal franking machines, on which only a few undertakings are active. In the latter case, a national administration's treatment of a single undertaking may constitute a measure incompatible with Article 30 [now Art 34 of the TFEU].' At [13].

[90] Note that TFEU Art 34 catches state action or state inaction. Action by private citizens, strictly speaking, would have to be addressed by competition law. See eg Craig and de Búrca, in *EU Law, Text, Cases and Materials* (n 78) 646.

[91] [1997] ECR I-6959.

goods by threatening and harming those entities that dealt with foreign produce, including the lorry drivers who transported and supermarkets which attempted to sell such produce. The Court held that the obligation to prevent quantitative restrictions applied to both actions and inactions of the state:

As an indispensable instrument for the realization of a market without internal frontiers, Article 30 [now Article 34 of the TFEU] therefore does not prohibit solely measures emanating from the State which, in themselves, create restrictions on trade between Member States. It also applies where a Member State abstains from adopting the measures required in order to deal with obstacles to the free movement of goods which are not caused by the State.[92]

The Court acknowledged the exclusive competence of member states to maintain public order and safeguard internal security, and the margin of discretion they enjoyed in determining the appropriate measures by which to do so.[93] Nevertheless the ECJ indicated that it must verify, in cases coming before it and taking due account of that discretion, whether a member state has adopted appropriate measures for ensuring the free movement of goods.[94] The Court noted in this context that '[i]t is for the Member State concerned, unless it can show that action on its part would have consequences for public order with which it could not cope by using the means at its disposal, to adopt all appropriate measures to guarantee the full scope and effect of Community law so as to ensure its proper implementation in the interests of all economic operators.'[95] France was unable to justify its inaction on public order grounds and the Court therefore concluded that it had failed to fulfil its obligations under the provision on quantitative restrictions.[96]

The ECJ has also identified measures equivalent to a quantitative restriction as arising from product promotion campaigns, if those campaigns were capable of influencing the conduct of traders or consumers and discriminated on grounds of national origin. In the *Buy Irish Case*, for example, the ECJ held that a body promoting the sale and purchase of Irish products in Ireland, the Irish Goods Council, was a government body that could attract liability under EU law, and that the 'Buy Irish' campaign it promoted amounted to an attempt by the government to substitute domestic products for imports, and thereby to check the flow of imports.[97] Such government measures, even if they do not have binding effect, are subject to the prohibitions related to quantitative restrictions. As explained by the Court, '[e]ven measures adopted by the government of a Member State which do

[92] Case C-265/95 *Commission v France* (n 91) pp I-6998–9 [30].
[93] Case C-265/95 *Commission v France* (n 91) p I-6999 [33].
[94] Case C-265/95 *Commission v France* (n 91) p I-6999 [35].
[95] Case C-265/95 *Commission v France* (n 91) p I-7003 [56].
[96] In coming to the conclusion that the French response was 'manifestly inadequate' the Court highlighted the duration of the protests, the lack of action by French police (even where warned in advance of the protests, or where present in larger numbers than the protesters), and the lack of prosecution (even in cases where the protests were filmed and identities could easily be ascertained): Case C-265/95 *Commission v France* p I-7002 [52]. See also at p I-7005 [65]–[66]. It should be noted that the Court found France in violation of its obligations under both what is now Art 34 of the TFEU and Art 4 of the TEU. The latter imposes a general undertaking similar to Art 9 of the RTC.
[97] Case 249/81 *Commission v Ireland* [1982] ECR 4005, at pp 4020 [15] and 4022 [23].

not have binding effect may be capable of influencing the conduct of traders and consumers in that State and thus of frustrating the aims of the Community.'[98] As a result Ireland was found to be in breach of the treaty. Subsequent cases have, however, clarified issues related to the ability of states to promote national products under EU law. In Case 222/82 *Apple and Pear Development Council v Lewis*, for example, the ECJ drew the distinction between campaigns that, on the one hand, 'discourage the purchase of products of other states', 'disparage those products in the eyes of consumers', or discriminate on grounds of national origin, and on the other hand, those that promote the specific qualities or properties of a national product.[99] The first type of campaign would violate the prohibition on measures equivalent to a quantitative restriction; the second need not do so.[100] This line of authority will likely become important in the Caribbean region, where campaigns promoting products on the basis of national origin exist in several states.

10.5.2 OECS

Article 9.2 of the Protocol to the RTB deals with quantitative restrictions in the following terms:

> 9.2 Any products which have been exported from one Protocol Member State to a consignee in another Protocol Member State and have not undergone any manufacturing process since exportation shall, when reimported into the first Protocol Member State, be admitted free of quantitative restrictions and measures with equivalent effect. They shall also be admitted free of customs duties and charges with equivalent effect, except that any allowance by way of drawback relief from duty or otherwise, given by reason of the exportation from the first Protocol Member State, may be recovered.

This provision is brief and limited in comparison to Article 91 of the RTC. It only applies to imports in a particular context of consignment. It does not apply generally to other imports from Protocol member states or to exports. The omission in relation to exports is particularly striking, since it parallels an identical omission to prohibit export duties, as already seen. Perhaps, as suggested earlier, Article 9.2 of the Protocol could be interpreted expansively in light of the requirement in Article 3(a), under which Protocol member states must prohibit, amongst other things, 'quantitative restrictions on the importation and exportation of goods, as well as of all other measures with equivalent effect'. If not, OECS Protocol member states would appear to be free to impose quantitative restrictions and export duties on goods intended for other Protocol member states.

[98] Case 249/81 *Commission v Ireland* (n 97) p 4023 [28].
[99] [1983] ECR 4083, at p 4120 [18]–[19].
[100] See eg *Apple and Pear Development Council v Lewis* (n 99) [21].

10.5.3 Exceptions to the rules related to quantitative restrictions

Examples from the EU: Exclusions from or justifications for infringements of treaty obligations

Because of the potentially far-reaching scope of the provisions on quantitative restrictions in EU law the ECJ has developed what may be characterized as two general lines of jurisprudence that provide, respectively, exclusions from, or exceptions to, the ambit of Article 34 of the TFEU. It will be useful to analyse this jurisprudence because of its potential to strongly influence interpretations of the RTC and OECS Protocol.

Justifications

Certain actions which may prima facie amount to quantitative restrictions or measures equivalent to quantitative restrictions may nevertheless be justified under general principles of EU law or under Article 36 of the TFEU. The first form of justification arose in Case C-112/00 *Eugen Schmidberger, Internationale Transporte und Planzüge v Austria*, where the disruption of transport caused by a closure of a highway to allow public demonstrations would have amounted to a measure equivalent to a quantitative restriction, but was objectively justifiable on the facts of the case.[101] In *Schmidberger* the closure of the highway for approximately thirty hours for environmental protests was for the purpose of allowing the exercise of freedom of expression and freedom of assembly rights. Such fundamental rights, as noted by the Court, form an integral part of the general principles of Community law which must be respected by both the Community and its member states.[102] Under such circumstances, the Court held that 'the protection of those rights is a legitimate interest which, in principle, justifies a restriction of the obligations imposed by Community law, even under a fundamental freedom guaranteed by the Treaty such as the free movement of goods.'[103] As a result the Court suggested that the two sets of competing interests—that in favour of freedom of movement of goods and that of respect for fundamental rights—must be weighed.[104] Taking into account that the legitimate aim of the demonstration could not be accomplished by means of measures less restrictive of intra-Community trade, the Court held that the actions of the Austrian authorities were compatible with the requirements of EU law.[105]

The second group of justifications is established by Article 36 of the TFEU, which provides an exhaustive list of acceptable prohibitions or restrictions.[106] Such restrictions, however, must be justified and cannot constitute a means of arbitrary discrimination or a disguised restriction on trade between member states. ECJ jurisprudence has also made clear that the means used to protect the interest

[101] [2003] ECR I-5659, at p I-5715 [64].

[102] *Eugen Schmidberger* (n 101) pp I-5717–18 [69], [71]–[74].

[103] *Eugen Schmidberger* (n 101) p I-5718 [74].

[104] cf *Eugen Schmidberger* (n 101) p I-5720 [81].

[105] *Eugen Schmidberger* (n 101) p I-5723 [93]–[94].

[106] Art 36 TFEU provides:

enumerated under Article 36 must be the least restrictive means available and must be proportionate to the end.[107]

The means must also be necessary to achieve the end, as illustrated in the *Cassis de Dijon Case*.[108] In that case the ECJ found German rules which were indistinctly applicable (ie, equally applicable to domestic and imported goods) to be to be incompatible with what is now Article 34 of the TFEU as a measure equivalent to a quantitative restriction. The German rules fixed a minimum alcoholic strength for various categories of alcoholic products and thereby excluded Cassis de Dijon from the German market.[109] Germany sought to justify the rules on grounds of public health and consumer protection. The Court squarely rejected both arguments, although it left the door open to reasonable measures in other cases (under the 'rule of reason').[110] Health concerns did not justify the measure and consumer concerns could be satisfied with less restrictive means, such as through labelling.[111] In balancing German and Community interests, the Court held that 'the requirements relating to the minimum alcohol content of alcoholic beverages do not serve a purpose which is in the general interest and such as to take precedence over the requirements of the free movement of goods, which constitutes one of the fundamental rules of the Community.'[112] The German rules constituted an obstacle to trade, even though they were indistinctly applicable and covered an area not yet subject to common Community rules.[113]

> The provisions of Articles 34 and 35 shall not preclude prohibitions or restrictions on imports, exports or goods in transit justified on grounds of public morality, public policy or public security; the protection of health and life of humans, animals or plants; the protection of national treasures possessing artistic, historic or archaeological value; or the protection of industrial and commercial property. Such prohibitions or restrictions shall not, however, constitute a means of arbitrary discrimination or a disguised restriction on trade between Member States.

[107] See eg Case 40/82 *Commission v UK* [1982] ECR 2793, where UK laws restricting poultry imports on grounds of protecting the public from the Newcastle disease constituted disguised restrictions on imports from other member states and were not the least restrictive measures that could have been adopted. At p 2826–8 [40]–[45].

[108] Case 120/78 *Rewe-Zentral AG v Bundesmonopolverwaltung für Branntwein* [1979] ECR 649 (the *Cassis de Dijon Case*).

[109] The alcohol strength of Cassis de Dijon was between 15–20 per cent but the minimum strength allowed under German law for similar products was 32 per cent.

[110] In *Cassis de Dijon* (n 108) at p 662 [8] the Court left open the possibility of reasonable measures which might not be caught by Art 34, introducing what Craig and de Búrca call the 'rule of reason'. The Court held:

> Obstacles to movement within the Community resulting from disparities between the national laws relating to the marketing of the products in question must be accepted in so far as those provisions may be recognized as being necessary in order to satisfy mandatory requirements relating in particular to the effectiveness of fiscal supervision, the protection of public health, the fairness of commercial transactions and the defence of the consumer.

See Craig and de Búrca, in *EU Law, Text, Cases and Materials* (n 78) 649.

[111] *Cassis de Dijon* (n 108) pp 663 [11] and 664 [13].

[112] *Cassis de Dijon* (n 108) p 664 [14].

[113] cf *Cassis de Dijon* (n 108) pp 662 [8] and 664 [14]. Note that Craig and de Búrca, in *EU Law, Text, Cases and Materials* (n 78) at 638, cite the *Cassis de Dijon* case as an attempt by the Court to protect free movement of goods even when the other organs of the EU were unable to act, calling the decision 'an alternative means for ensuring the free flow of goods even in the absence of EU harmonizing legislation'.

In reaching this conclusion the Court supported the principle of mutual recognition, whereby goods lawfully being marketed in one member state should be imported into another member state without restriction, unless otherwise caught by EU rules. The German rules in the *Cassis* case had the effect of preventing a good in free circulation in France from being imported into Germany, without reasonable justification and without being saved by Article 36.[114]

In sum, this jurisprudence shows that the ECJ will very carefully scrutinize any attempt to justify a quantitative restriction or measure equivalent to a quantitative restriction under the rule of reason, general principles of EU law, or Article 36 of the TFEU, and will reject such a measure if it amounts to a form of arbitrary discrimination or a disguised restriction on trade between member states. National measures must also be necessary, least restrictive, and proportionate to the end.

Article 226 of the Revised Treaty of Chaguaramas

A similar provision in the RTC is Article 226 and the jurisprudence of the ECJ will provide a useful interpretive analogy. The list in Article 226 equally could be interpreted to be exhaustive, and is subject to the same conditions that the measures justifiable under it must not 'constitute arbitrary or unjustifiable discrimination between Member States where like conditions prevail, or a disguised restriction on trade within the Community'.[115] It is likely that the requirements of least restrictive means and proportionality of the measure to the end sought to be achieved may be similarly imposed on the exceptions set out in Article 226(1). However it will be interesting to see whether the requirement of necessity is also established, since some of the exceptions in Article 226(1) expressly impose a necessity requirement (Article 226(1)(c)(d) and (i)), but others do not. In addition, Article 226(2) imposes a requirement for notification of COTED. This notification requirement could be interpreted weakly, so as not to preclude a state from raising an Article 226 justification (perhaps merely creating a separate, actionable breach regarding failure to notify). However the better view, adopted in other fields of international law, would be to deem the notification requirement to be a pre-requisite for the availability of Article 226(1) justifications. This approach is supported by both the scope of Article 226 which, unlike Article 36 of the TFEU, most likely applies to all of the obligations under the RTC.[116] It is also supported

[114] Note that Craig and de Búrca, at 649, suggest that the exceptions to Art 34 permitted under the rule of reason are separate from those available under Art 36: 'The mandatory requirements that constitute the rule of reason are taken into account within the fabric of article 34, and are separate from what is now Article 36.'

[115] Art 226(1).

[116] The word 'Chapter' in the opening phrase 'Nothing in this Chapter shall be construed as preventing the adoption or enforcement by any Member State of measures' in RTC Art 226(1) cannot be correct. Literally interpreted, it would limit the scope of Art 226 to the obligations contained in Chapter Ten of the RTC. The previous version of RTC Art 226, Art XX of Protocol IV, commences with the phrase 'Nothing in Article XVI of this Protocol shall prevent the adoption or enforcement by any Member State of measures.' Art XVI of Protocol IV parallels Art 91 of the RTC, and therefore the Protocol IV provision very closely parallels Art 36 of the TFEU by expressly linking the exceptions

by the overarching goals of the RTC, which include that of 'full integration of the national markets of all Member States of the Community into a single unified and open market area' under Article 78(2)(a). Such comprehensive integration not only requires the full compliance by member states of their obligations under the RTC, it also requires any derogations to be subject to scrutiny and to require full justification. If Article 226(2) is interpreted as imposing a serious obligation, it will force member states to openly raise potential breaches of the RTC and their suggested justifications, if they wish to rely upon the latter. This would further enhance CARICOM as a system under the rule of law, a system bringing with it legal certainty and which protects the rights of both states and persons.[117]

Exclusion: Selling arrangements in the EU

In a more recent series of cases, starting with the Joined Cases C-267 and 268/91 *Criminal proceedings against Keck and Mithouard*, the ECJ has drawn a line between potential quantitative-type restrictions which relate to the characteristics of a good, on the one hand, and those dealing with the conditions under which goods are sold, on the other.[118] The latter concern selling arrangements, which according to *Keck* may fall outside the scope of Article 34 of the TFEU. The *Keck* case involved a prosecution of traders for reselling goods at a loss, contrary to French law. In assessing the factual matrix, the ECJ distinguished the French rules, which regulated selling arrangements and which were 'not designed to regulate trade in goods between Member States', from those specifying requirements for the production of goods.[119] Because the distinction is important, it is worth reproducing paragraphs [15]–[17] of the judgment in full, in which the Court held:

> [15] It is established by the case-law beginning with 'Cassis de Dijon' (Case 120/78 *Rewe-Zentral v Bundesmonopolverwaltung für Branntwein* [1979] ECR 649) that, in the absence of harmonization of legislation, obstacles to free movement of goods which are the consequence of applying, to goods coming from other Member States where they are

to the article dealing quantitative restrictions. It is therefore clear that Art 226 was at least meant to apply to Art 91. But given its placement at the end of the RTC, next to Art 225, a provision allowing derogation from *all* RTC obligations on the basis of security concerns, it is more likely that Art 226 was meant to have the same scope. As a result it is submitted that Art 226(1) should be interpreted as extending to all RTC obligations, and the word 'Chapter' should be interpreted as indicating 'Treaty'.

[117] In the case of *Trinidad Cement Ltd v Caribbean Community*, Judgment [2009] CCJ 2 (OJ), (2009) 74 WIR 319, 5 February 2009 at [32], the CCJ held that CARICOM operates under the rule of law:

> [32] By signing and ratifying the Revised Treaty and thereby conferring on this Court *ipso facto* a compulsory and exclusive jurisdiction to hear and determine disputes concerning the interpretation and application of the Revised Treaty, the Member States transformed the erstwhile voluntary arrangements in CARICOM into a rule-based system, thus creating and accepting a regional system under the rule of law. [...] The rule of law brings with it legal certainty and protection of rights of states and individuals alike, but at the same time of necessity it creates legal accountability. Even if such accountability imposes some constraint upon the exercise of sovereign rights of states, the very acceptance of such a constraint in a treaty is in itself an act of sovereignty.

For a similar pronouncement in relation to the CSME and state liability see *Trinidad Cement Ltd and TCL Guyana Inc v Guyana*, Judgment [2009] CCJ 5 (OJ), 20 August 2009 [27].

[118] [1993] ECR I-6097.

[119] *Keck and Mithouard* (n 118) p I-6130 [12]

lawfully manufactured and marketed, rules that lay down requirements to be met by such goods (such as those relating to designation, form, size, weight, composition, presentation, labelling, packaging) constitute measures of equivalent effect prohibited by Article 30 [now Article 34 of the TFEU]. This is so even if those rules apply without distinction to all products unless their application can be justified by a public-interest objective taking precedence over the free movement of goods.

[16] By contrast, contrary to what has previously been decided, the application to products from other Member States of national provisions restricting or prohibiting certain selling arrangements is not such as to hinder directly or indirectly, actually or potentially, trade between Member States within the meaning of the *Dassonville* judgment (Case 8/74 [1974] ECR 837), so long as those provisions apply to all relevant traders operating within the national territory and so long as they affect in the same manner, in law and in fact, the marketing of domestic products and of those from other Member States.

[17] Provided that those conditions are fulfilled, the application of such rules to the sale of products from another Member State meeting the requirements laid down by that State is not by nature such as to prevent their access to the market or to impede access any more than it impedes the access of domestic products. Such rules therefore fall outside the scope of Article 30 of the Treaty.[120]

The Court here clearly draws a distinction between arrangements affecting the production of goods and arrangements affecting the sale of goods. The latter are deemed to be excluded from coverage under Article 34. However in paragraph [16] the Court expressly warns that even selling arrangements will be caught if they do not apply to all relevant traders operating within the national territory, or do not affect in the same manner, in law and in fact, the marketing of domestic products and of those from other member states.

Following the *Keck* decision the Court has excluded from the category of selling arrangements rules related to packaging or the content of a product, as affecting the product itself.[121] The Court has also caught selling arrangements that have a differential impact, in law or in fact, for domestic traders and importers. Cases under the latter category have included ones involving prohibitions or restrictions upon advertising that have impeded the ability of the product from another member state to gain market access more than they have impeded access by domestic products.[122] Other cases have extended this principle to catch instances in which a selling arrangement impeded, rather than prevented, a product from gaining market access.[123] Finally, selling arrangements that impose limitations on the use

[120] *Keck and Mithouard* (n 118) p I-6131 [15]–[17].

[121] See eg Case C-12/00 *Commission v Spain* [2003] ECR I-459, at p I-505 [76], where the Court held that 'the need to alter the packaging or the labelling of imported products prevents such requirements from being selling arrangements within the meaning of the judgment in *Keck and Mithouard* (Case C-33/97 *Colim* [1999] ECR I-3175, paragraph 37).' For selling requirements that would alter the content of a product, see eg Case C-368/95 *Vereinigte Familiapress Zeitungsverlags-und vertriebs GmbH v Heinrich Bauer Verlag* [1997] ECR I-3689, at p I-3714 [11]–[12].

[122] See eg Cases C-34–36/95 *Konsumentombudsmannen (KO) v De Agostini (Svenska) Förlag AB and TV-Shop i Sverige AB* [1997] ECR I-3843 (ban on television advertising) and Case C-405/98 *Konsumentombudsmannen (KO) v Gourmet International Products AB (GIP)* [2001] ECR I-1795 (ban on magazine advertising).

[123] See eg Case C-254/98 *Schutzverband gegen unlauteren Wettbewerb v TK-Heimdienst Sass GmbH* [2000] ECR I-151 (selling based upon permanent establishment in a district or adjacent municipality).

of a product have also been considered measures equivalent to a quantitative restriction if, for example, they influence the behaviour of consumers and thereby affect market access.[124]

As can be seen, the *Keck* decision has increased the complexity of EU law in this area. Several authors, including Craig and de Búrca, have suggested that the *Keck* approach can be rationalized under a view that sees market access as the overarching principle in these cases.[125] In any event, although there is disagreement about the value of the approach in *Keck*, it is clearly one that will have to be weighed in considering how to interpret Article 91 of the RTC.

10.5.4 Exceptions in the OECS Protocol

Article 32 of the Protocol to the RTB provides similar, if more limited, exceptions for cases in which states experience difficulties in particular sectors. Article 32.1 sets out the conditions for and limitations regarding the imposition of quantitative restrictions. Quantitative restrictions can be imposed if a Protocol member state experiences an appreciable rise in unemployment caused by a substantial decrease in demand for a domestic product.[126] The decrease must be caused by an increase in imports from other Protocol member states as a result of the progressive reduction or the elimination of duties, charges, and quantitative restrictions.[127] If these two conditions are met the Protocol member state may limit those imports by quantitative restrictions, set at specified rates, for no longer than eighteen months unless authorized by the Economic Affairs Council.[128] The Protocol member state may also take such other measures as authorized by the Economic Affairs Council.[129] In applying these quantitative restrictions or other measures, a Protocol member state is required to give like treatment to imports consigned from all Protocol member states and to notify the Economic Affairs Council, if possible before the measures come into force.[130] The Economic Affairs Council also retains the power to consider the measures, make recommendations, or otherwise assist Protocol member states.[131]

Such a regime provides the tools for OECS Protocol member states to protect domestic sectors under a degree of supervision from the Economic Affairs Council. But its anticipated duration is limited. Article 32.4 expressly provides that Article 32 'shall only have effect after 30th April, 1973 to any extent that the Council of Ministers of the former East Caribbean Common Market may before that date have extended the provisions of the preceding paragraphs of the Article'. Given the inclusion of this provision in the RTB and Protocol in 2010, it was clearly contemplated that some of the provisions of Article 32 would be extended. However when one considers the clear objective of the Economic Union to be a 'single economic

[124] See eg Case C-142/05 *Åklagaren v Percy Mickelsson and Joakim Roos* [2009] ECR I-4273 (restrictions on use of personal watercraft).

[125] Craig and de Búrca, *EU Law, Text, Cases and Materials* (n 78) 661–8.

[126] Protocol Art 32.1(a).

[127] Protocol Art 32.1(b).

[128] Protocol Art 32.1(i).

[129] Protocol Art 32.1(ii).

[130] Protocol Art 32.2–32.3.

[131] Protocol Art 32.3.

and financial space', the continued imposition of quantitative restrictions and similar measures cannot be justified indefinitely.[132]

10.6 Subsidies

10.6.1 CARICOM

The regime on subsidies created by the RTC must be interpreted in light of the similar rules of the World Trade Organization, which clearly represented an influential model for CARICOM.[133] It must also be interpreted in light of the general objectives of CARICOM trade policy.[134] As we have seen, these include the goal of 'sustained growth of intra-Community and international trade and mutually beneficial exchange of goods and services among the Member States and between the Community and third States' and the objective of 'full integration of the national markets of all Member States of the Community into a single unified and open market area'.[135] Article 79(1)–(2) also requires member states to 'establish and maintain a regime for the free movement of goods and services within the CSME' and mandates that '[e]ach Member State shall refrain from trade policies and practices, the object or effect of which is to distort competition, frustrate free movement of goods and services, or otherwise nullify or impair benefits to which other Member States are entitled under this Treaty.' Such objectives and goals

[132] See RTB Art 4.1(e) and Protocol Art 2(a).

[133] See the Marrakesh Agreement Establishing the World Trade Organisation (with Final Act, Annexes and Protocol) (adopted 15 Apr 1994, in force 1 Jan 1995) 1867 UNTS 3 [hereafter 'WTO Agreement 1994'], including the Agreement on Subsidies and Countervailing Measures (adopted 15 Apr 1994, in force 1 Jan 1995) 1869 UNTS 14 and the Agreement on Agriculture (adopted 15 Apr 1994, in force 1 Jan 1995) 1869 UNTS 410. The following CARICOM member states are bound by the WTO Agreement 1994 (date of accession, definitive signature, ratification or acceptance in brackets): Antigua and Barbuda (01/01/95), Barbados (01/01/95), Belize (01/01/95), Dominica (01/01/95), Grenada (22/02/96), Guyana (01/01/95), Haiti (30/01/96), Jamaica (09/03/95), St Kitts and Nevis (21/02/96), St Lucia (01/01/95), St Vincent and the Grenadines (01/01/95), Suriname (01/01/95), Trinidad and Tobago (01/03/95). The Bahamas has not become a party but is in the process of acceding to the WTO: WTO, 'Accessions—The Bahamas', as available at <http://www.wto.org/english/thewto_e/acc_e/a1_bahamas_e.htm> (26 May 2013). The UK ratified the WTO Agreement 1994 on 1 January 1995 without territorial exclusions. Treaty statistics are as available from the UN Treaty Collection database through <http://treaties.un.org> (26 May 2013). CARICOM itself has observer status on the WTO Committee on Trade and Development: WTO, 'International intergovernmental organizations granted observer status to WTO bodies', as available at <http://www.wto.org/english/thewto_e/igo_obs_e.htm> (26 May 2013). For more on the GATT and WTO regimes see eg Michael Trebilcock, Robert Howse, and Antonia Eliason, *The Regulation of International Trade*, 4th edn (London: Routledge, 2013) [hereafter 'Trebilcock, Howse and Eliason, *Regulation of International Trade*'] chs 10 and 12, and World Trade Organization, 'WTO Analytical Index: Subsidies and Countervailing Measures' and 'WTO Analytical Index: Agreement on Agriculture', as available through <http://www.wto.org/english/res_e/booksp_e/analytic_index_e/analytic_index_e.htm> (6 June 2013).

[134] CARICOM has expressed concerns about the implementation of the requirements of Art XXIV of GATT in relation to subsidies, anti-dumping measures and safeguards. Art XXIV allows for the creation of preferential trade agreements, such as customs unions. See CARICOM Secretariat, *Summary Draft Report* 13–14.

[135] RTC Art 78(1) and (2)(a).

must be kept in mind when reviewing the RTC rules on subsidies and dumping. They collectively describe a robust vision of the CARICOM Single Market and Economy, one in which goods and services should flow freely between member states in the same way that they could move within, for example, districts of a single national territory (a single unified and open market area). The CSME also contemplates strong and meaningful competition, which requires the maintenance of market conditions that allow goods and services to be produced under similar conditions, not benefitting from or being hampered by incentives from particular member states.

It is in such a context that CARICOM focuses on eliminating several kinds of state subsidies to businesses and other productive sector actors. Part Three of Chapter 5 of the RTC sets out the general regime related to subsidies; Part Four sets out the subsidy regime for agriculture.

The term 'subsidy' is defined in Article 1 of the RTC as including 'the subsidies set out in Schedule V and shall apply only in relation to goods'.[136] Schedule V sets out a number of different examples of state assistance, including: direct subsidies contingent upon export; bonuses upon export; provision of products or services on more favourable terms for exported goods; remission, deferral, exemption, or deduction of taxes and other charges for exports; import drawbacks; export guarantee or insurance programmes; export credits; and '[a]ny other charge on the public account constituting an export subsidy in the sense of Article XVI of GATT 1994'.[137] Subsidies are further specified in Article 96, entitled 'Determination of a Subsidy', in the following words:

> For the purpose of this Part, a subsidy shall be deemed to exist if there is a financial contribution[138] by a Government or any public body within the territory of a Member State (hereinafter referred to as 'government') where:
> (a) a government practice involves direct transfer of funds (e.g., grants, loans and equity infusion) or potential direct transfer of funds or liabilities (e.g., loan guarantees);
> (b) government revenue that is otherwise due is foregone or not collected (e.g., fiscal incentives, such as tax credits);
> (c) a government purchases goods or provides goods or services other than general infrastructure;

[136] RTC Art 1 also defines 'goods' as: 'all kinds of property other than real property, money, securities or choses in action'. 'Services' is defined as: 'services provided against remuneration other than wages in an approved sector and "the provision of services" means the supply of services: (a) from the territory of one Member State into the territory of another Member State; (b) in the territory of one Member State to a service consumer of another Member State; (c) by a service supplier of one Member State through commercial presence in the territory of another Member State; and (d) by a service supplier of one Member State through the presence of natural persons of a Member State in the territory of another Member State'.

[137] Paraphrasing of Schedule V to the RTC.

[138] Note that the phrase 'financial contribution' in the Agreement on Subsidies and Countervailing Measures (adopted 15 Apr 1994, in force 1 Jan 1995) 1869 UNTS 14 [hereafter 'Agreement on Subsidies and Countervailing Measures'], has been interpreted to include both direct and indirect contributions by any level or type of government in a country, even a contribution routed through a private entity. See eg Trebilcock, Howse, and Eliason, *Regulation of International Trade* (n 133) 370.

(d) a government makes payments to a funding mechanism, or directs or entrusts to a private body the conduct of activities mentioned in subparagraphs (a), (b) and (c) which are normally conducted by governments;
(e) there is any form of income or price support,
and a benefit is thereby conferred.

Article 96 of the RTC is almost identical to Article 1.1 of the WTO Agreement on Subsidies and Countervailing Measures and its interpretation will likely be heavily influenced by it.[139] Two things may be noted about Article 96. Firstly, the forms of subsidies restricted by Article 1 of the RTC are those related to *goods*. Secondly, the goods must be *exported*. As a consequence a member state would appear to be free to subsidize a particular local good for non-export, or a service for export, without being caught under Parts Three or Four of Chapter 5.

Even though a subsidy to a service strictly speaking might not fall under Part Three of Chapter 5, such a subsidy might be caught under other provisions of the RTC.[140] This is because any form of major unilateral subsidy, whether to a good

[139] (Adopted 15 Apr 1994, in force 1 Jan 1995) 1869 UNTS 14.

[140] On a strict textual interpretation subsidies to services would be excluded. The WTO jurisprudence regarding Art 1 of the Agreement on Subsidies and Countervailing Measures also may discourage such a possibility for the RTC. In the case of *US: Large Civil Aircraft (2nd Complaint)*—Panel Report (31 Mar 2011) WT/DS353/R, at [7.969], for example—a case involving a challenge by the EU to funding of the Boeing aircraft company through US National Aeronautics and Space Administration (NASA) procurement contracts and US Department of Defence (USDOD) assistance instruments—the Panel held that a government purchase of services was excluded from the category of subsidies described in Art 1.1(a)(1)(iii) of the Agreement on Subsidies and Countervailing Measures.

However it may be possible to catch subsidies under Part Three of Chapter 5 of the RTC as a result of combination of textual and teleological forms of interpretation. Under the general principle of *lex specialis derogat generali*, Art 96 (which describes subsidies in detail for the purposes of Part Three, and neither expressly limits subsidies to goods nor excludes services subsidies from its coverage), could be preferred over the more general definition in Art 1. Under a teleological interpretation, the exclusion of subsidies of services from Chapter 5 may be argued to frustrate the free movement of goods and services under the RTC, since subsidies to exported services could significantly distort the market in favour of service providers from particular countries. As argued by the European Union in the case of *US: Large Civil Aircraft (2nd Complaint)* at [7.949], 'excluding purchases of services from the scope of Article 1.1(a)(1) [the definition of a subsidy] would create an enormous loophole in the coverage of and run counter to the overall object and purpose of the [Agreement on Subsidies and Countervailing Measures]'.

The Appellate Body decision in the same WTO case, applied by analogy, suggests a way of reading subsidies to services into Art 96 of the RTC. In its decision the Appellate Body chose to avoid entirely the question of whether the Agreement on Subsidies and Countervailing Measures covered subsidies to services per se. Instead it decided the matter by re-classifying the factual matrix as one involving financial contributions under Art 1.1(a)(1)(i) of the Agreement: WTO, *US: Large Civil Aircraft (2nd Complaint)*—Appellate Body Report (12 Mar 2012) WT/DS353/AB/R, [611]–[625]. It dismissed the question of whether Art 1 governed subsidies to purchases of services, holding that the earlier Panel's decision in this respect was 'moot' and of no legal effect: Appellate Body Report [590] and [620]. Rather, in its view the important question was one of properly characterizing the particular activities in the dispute. Instead of being services arrangements, the Appellate Body decided that the NASA procurement contracts and USDOD assistance instruments concluded with Boeing more closely resembled joint ventures and thereby constituted financial contributions within the meaning of Art 1.1(a)(1) of the Agreement. The result was that *the same facts*—which were characterized as services by the earlier Panel—were simply classified as a financial contribution, similar to a direct transfer of funds, by the Appellate Body.

or service, would likely conflict with the objective expressed in Articles 78–79 of creating a single, unified, and open market area, one in which goods and services are to move freely. For example, Article 93(1)(b), in regulating government assistance, prohibits member states from maintaining or introducing 'any other forms of assistance, the main purpose or effect of which is to frustrate the benefits expected from such removal or absence of duties and quantitative restrictions as is required by this Treaty'. Such a prohibition could be argued to cover subsidies to both goods and services if the phrase 'benefits expected from the removal or absence of duties and quantitative restrictions' is extended by analogy to the benefits expected from removal of restrictions on services.[141] In addition, a subsidy to a particular national service provider, depending upon the factual matrix, might be deemed to be both discriminatory and in violation of the MFN treatment principle under Articles 7 and 8 of the RTC, respectively.

The remainder of Part Three divides unlawful subsidies into three general categories: (1) prohibited subsidies, (2) subsidies which cause injury to a domestic industry, or result in nullification or impairment of benefits accruing directly or indirectly to any member state, or seriously prejudice the interests of any member state [hereafter 'subsidies causing injury, nullification, impairment, or serious prejudice'], and (3) subsidies causing 'serious adverse effects to a domestic industry of any Member State such as to cause damage which would be difficult to repair'.[142] This tripartite structure can be compared with the regime of the WTO Agreement on Subsidies and Countervailing Measures, which divides subsidies into prohibited, actionable, and non-actionable subsidies. Both regimes also contemplate unilateral and multilateral responses to subsidies.[143] Under the RTC, all three categories of subsidies must be 'specific to an enterprise or industry or group of enterprises or industries within the jurisdiction of the granting Member State'.[144] The conditions for determining specificity are set out in Article 97(2)(a)–(d) and generally describe situations where the subsidy is provided only to certain enterprises.[145]

To place this WTO case in the context of Part Three of Chapter 5 of the RTC, one could argue that a decision maker could simply characterize a factual matrix involving a subsidy as falling under one of the categories addressed in Art 96 of the RTC and thereby bring it under Part Three. If such an approach were to be adopted the further question of whether the facts involve a subsidy to a good or service would not arise. Whether this approach or the more strict textual approach is followed remains to be seen.

[141] For example, if the expected benefits in relation to goods are the availability of a wider variety of, and cheaper, goods, then the same benefits could be said to arise in relation to services (a wider variety of, and cheaper, services).

[142] RTC Art 97(1)(a)–(c).

[143] On the WTO regimes on subsidies see eg Trebilcock, Howse. and Eliason, *Regulation of International Trade* (n 133) ch 10. Note that non-actionable subsidies have not been applied under the WTO Agreement on Subsidies and Countervailing Measures since 1999.

[144] RTC Art 97(1). The term 'enterprise' is defined in Art 1 as meaning 'any person or type of organisation, other than a non-profit organisation, involved in the production of or the trade in goods, or the provision of services'. See Art 1.2 of the Agreement on Subsidies and Countervailing Measure for a similar specificity requirement. Specificity under the Agreement can be either *de jure* or *de facto*. See eg Trebilcock, Howse, and Eliason (n 133) 375.

[145] Compare Art 2 of the Agreement on Subsidies and Countervailing Measures.

Prohibited subsidies

Prohibited subsidies are described in Article 99 of the RTC as subsidies contingent in law or in fact upon export performance and upon the use of domestic over imported goods, but excluding Community origin agricultural commodities.[146] Articles 100–103 set out the processes for dealing with prohibited subsidies, commencing with a preliminary investigation by or on behalf of a domestic industry, followed by consultations between member states, followed by a referral of the matter to COTED for investigation.[147] Following sixty days from the commencement of COTED's investigations an aggrieved member state is entitled to implement provisional countermeasures 'to forestall injury or to prevent further injury to its domestic industry'.[148] If after its investigation COTED determines that the subsidy is a prohibited one and the concerned member states cannot reach an agreed solution, COTED must require the offending party, subject to Article 104, to remove the subsidy within a specified time frame.[149] If the offending party does not comply, COTED must authorize the aggrieved member state to take countermeasures on products benefitting from the subsidy.[150]

Subsidies causing injury, nullification, impairment, or serious prejudice

The second category of subsidy—subsidies causing injury, nullification, impairment, or serious prejudice—is described in Article 105.[151] Article 105 does not apply to agricultural subsidies.[152] A member state is authorized under this provision to take action against any other member state if, on the basis of an investigation, it can be established that the effect of a subsidy by the subsidizing state has been injury to

[146] Parallel phrasing is found in Art 3 of the Agreement on Subsidies and Countervailing Measures.

[147] The meaning of 'domestic industry' is defined in Annex I to the RTC. Requests for consultations under Art 101 should follow the procedures set out in Annex II, as provided in Art 98(3). Consultations are also required under Art 4 of the Agreement on Subsidies and Countervailing Measures. However a failure of consultations in the latter case would either result in the dispute being referred to the dispute settlement body or arbitration.

[148] RTC Art 102(2). Note that under Art 104(2) such provisional countermeasures may be subject to compensation if the alleged subsidy is determined not to be a prohibited one. Provisional countermeasures are also subject to the rules in Art 116.

[149] RTC Art 103(3). Art 104 allows the continuation of prohibited subsidies contingent on export performance by member states with a per capital GNP of less than $1,000 USD, and temporary continuation (until 1 Jan 2003) of other prohibited subsidies.

[150] RTC Art 103(3).

[151] Compare this regime to that of actionable subsidies under Art 5 of the Agreement on Subsidies and Countervailing Measures.

[152] RTC Art 105(4) incorrectly states that the provisions of the article 'shall not apply to Part Three'. Art 105 itself falls within Part Three. Rather, the cross-reference should exclude Part Four, Subsidies to Agriculture. For the previous drafts of these provisions see Protocol Amending the Treaty Establishing the Caribbean Community (Protocol VIII: Competition Policy, Consumer Protection, Dumping and Subsides) (adopted 13–14 Mar 2000, not yet in force) (Protocol VIII). Art 30(t) of Protocol VIII refers to 'Part V' of the Protocol, which is the Part dealing with Subsidies to Agriculture. Art 105(4) RTC finds a parallel in Art 5 of the Agreement on Subsidies and Countervailing Measures.

a domestic industry, nullification or impairment of benefits expected under the RTC, or serious prejudice to the aggrieved state's interests. Serious prejudice is described in Article 105(2) as including situations where: the total subsidization of a product exceeds 5 per cent of its value (ad valorem), subsidies cover the operating losses of an industry, subsidies cover recurrent operating losses by an enterprise, or subsidies provide forgiveness of government-held debt or government grants to cover debt repayment. Serious prejudice will not be deemed to occur under Article 105(3), however, where the member state granting the subsidy can demonstrate that its effect has not been to: displace or impede imports of like products to the subsidizing member state, displace or impede exports of like products from the aggrieved state to third member states; produce significant price undercutting, suppression, or depression by the subsidized product in comparison to like products; create losses of sales of another member state in the same market; increase its own market share within the CSME.[153] 'Like products' are defined in Article 106(6) as meaning 'a product which is identical, i.e., alike in all respects to the product under consideration, or in the absence of such a product, another product, which, although not alike in all respects, has characteristics closely resembling those of the product under consideration'.

The remainder of the provisions dealing with subsidies causing injury, nullification, impairment, or serious prejudice mirror those regarding prohibited subsidies.[154] Article 106 describes procedures for a preliminary investigation of an alleged unlawful subsidy. Article 107 provides for consultations between an aggrieved member state and a member state providing a subsidy. Articles 108–109 allow COTED to investigate the subsidy. Under Article 110 COTED is mandated to require the subsidizing state to remedy the effects of the subsidy within six months, and failing that, to authorize an aggrieved member state to impose countervailing duties.

Some differences exist, however, between the two sets of procedures. For example, because the complainant in cases involving subsidies causing injury, nullification, impairment, or serious prejudice may be an entire domestic industry in an aggrieved member state, rather than a single enterprise, Article 106(3) imposes a threshold for a request for an investigation as requiring the support of domestic producers who account for 25 per cent or more of the total production of the like product produced by the domestic industry.[155] With respect to the report of the investigation by COTED, Article 109(1)(b) only requires that this report be made available to 'the concerned Member States', rather than 'all Member States'

[153] Compare RTC Art 105 to Art 6 of the Agreement on Subsidies and Countervailing Measures. Note that Art 6.1 of the Agreement expired in 2000, as contemplated in Art 31.

[154] They also parallel the remedies available under Art 7 of the Agreement on Subsidies and Countervailing Measures, with the replacement of COTED under the RTC with the dispute settlement body or arbitration under the Agreement.

[155] The term 'domestic industry' is defined in Annex I to the RTC. The text of Art 106(3) imposes a double test involving a 25 per cent and 50 per cent threshold, but the above describes the minimum. Compare Art 11.4 of the Agreement on Subsidies and Countervailing Measures.

as specified in Article 103(2). In addition, in Article 110, the time frame to remedy the unlawful subsidy is stipulated to be six months from the date of the issue of the report by COTED, in contrast to the more flexible time period stipulated in Article 103(3), which merely refers to withdrawal within 'a specified time frame'.

Subsidies causing serious adverse effects

The final general category of unlawful subsidies is that of subsidies causing serious adverse effects.[156] The latter phrase is not expressly defined in the RTC but Article 97(1)(c) describes subsidies causing serious adverse effects to a domestic industry as causing 'damage which would be difficult to repair'.[157] Article 111 sets out a number of types of subsidies which may cause serious adverse effects. They include: subsidies that are not specific, subsidies that are specific but fall under allowable research activities, subsidies that are not specific but are granted to assist disadvantaged regions within the territory of a member state and that are given pursuant to a general framework of regional development, subsidies to assist entities in adapting to new environmental requirements, and non-specific subsidies granted to assist enterprises in training or retraining of employees and the upgrading of existing facilities to facilitate transition to competitive status within the Community.[158] Interestingly, as expressly provided in Article 111, such subsidies are ordinarily to be excluded from countervailing duties and countermeasures, although they must be notified to COTED and are subject to annual review.

Subsidies causing serious adverse effects are subject to the same investigative and consultative processes as the other subsidies described in Part Three. They are subject to preliminary investigation under Article 112, to requests for consultation under Article 113, to investigation by COTED under Article 114, and to corrective recommendations and measures by COTED under Articles 114–115. Despite the indication in Article 111(1) that subsidies causing serious adverse effects are ordinarily to be excluded from countervailing duties and countermeasures, Article 114(1) allows member states to take provisional countermeasures prior to a determination by COTED, and under Article 115(1) COTED can authorize the aggrieved member state to 'impose appropriate countervailing duties commensurate with the nature and degree of serious adverse effects determined to exist'.[159] Article 115(2) requires refund of any provisionally imposed duties and compensation for harm if the subsidy has not been deemed to cause serious adverse effects.

[156] Compare the provisions governing non-actionable subsidies in Art 8 of the Agreement on Subsidies and Countervailing Measures. Note that this article expired in 2000—see Art 31.

[157] See also RTC Art 113(1).

[158] Summary of RTC Art 111.

[159] Provisional countermeasures are subject to the rules in RTC Art 116.

Provisional measures and definitive actions

Article 98 generally entitles member states to take action against these three classes of unlawful subsidies.[160] These actions, however, cannot be definitive until the aggrieved member state has promulgated appropriate legislation, consulted with the subsidizing member state (as stipulated in Annex II), notified COTED regarding the preliminary investigations and the failure of consultations, and received authorization from COTED to introduce countervailing duties or countermeasures.[161]

Similarly, Article 116 sets out rules that must be complied with prior to introducing provisional measures against a state alleged to be implementing any one of the three categories of unlawful subsidies described earlier.[162] These rules require a preliminary investigation which is subject to public notice, an affirmative preliminary determination, a prior request for consultations, notification to COTED, and a determination by the authorities concerned that the provisional measures are necessary to prevent injury being caused during the investigation.[163] Provisional measures are limited to the form of countervailing duties, which must be guaranteed by cash deposits or bonds equal to the amount of the subsidization calculated on a provisional basis.[164] They cannot be applied prior to sixty days from the date of initiation of the COTED investigation, and can be applied only for 'as short a period as possible, not exceeding 120 days' or until a definitive determination is made by COTED.[165] Article 116(3) also allows a member state providing an allegedly unlawful subsidy to undertake to withdraw or limit the subsidy, or to require its domestic exporters to raise prices so as to eliminate the injurious effect of the subsidy. When such processes have been initiated the aggrieved member state is required to suspend proceedings and its provisional measures.[166] Following a determination by COTED that the subsidies are unlawful, Article 116(5) also allows the imposition of retroactive countervailing duties for the entire period during which provisional measures have been in force. These retroactive countervailing duties must, however, take into account the definitively assessed countervailing duties and the amount guaranteed by cash deposit or bond.[167] Article 116(6) also makes clear that only COTED can authorize definitive countervailing duties, and such duties must be 'governed by the relevant provisions of the WTO Agreement on Subsidies and Countervailing Measures'. COTED is also mandated to keep under review all countermeasures imposed by member states.[168]

[160] Note that the cross-references in RTC Art 98(1) are incorrect: Art 98(1)(b) should refer to Art 105 (Subsidies Causing Injury, Nullification, Impairment or Serious Prejudice) and Art 98(1)(c) should refer to Art 111 (Types of Subsidies Causing Serious Adverse Effects). For the previous drafts of these provisions see Protocol VIII, Art 30(p)(ter), referring to Arts 30(t) and 30(z).

[161] RTC Art 98(2)–(3). On remedies under the Agreement on Subsidies and Countervailing Measures see eg Trebilcock, Howse, and Eliason, *Regulation of International Trade* (n 133) 384–7.

[162] Compare Art 17 of the Agreement on Subsidies and Countervailing Measures.

[163] RTC Art 116(1)(a). [164] RTC Art 116(1)(b). [165] RTC Art 116(1)(c)–(d) and (2).

[166] RTC Art 116(4). [167] RTC Art 116(5). [168] RTC Art 116(7).

Agricultural subsidies

Issues related to trade in agriculture, including agricultural subsidies, are an important concern for developing countries including CARICOM member states, in some of which agriculture has played or continues to play a very important role. According to Trebilcock et al, at the global level agriculture accounts on average for 70 per cent of employment and 24 per cent of GDP in low-income countries, accounts for 25 per cent of employment in middle-income developing countries, and acts as a major foreign exchange earner for developing countries.[169] However developing countries are challenged in competing with developed countries in the trade of agricultural products because of the continued high levels of subsidies granted by the latter. In this context the playing field is far from level. Moreover the WTO rules on agriculture have not acted as an effective brake on subsidization of agriculture. The EU and the USA together spend approximately US $150 billion on agricultural subsidies while developing countries, in contrast, continue to liberalize.[170]

It is in such a global context that we must consider the CARICOM provisions on agricultural subsidies. In the RTC agricultural subsidies are governed by a separate regime in Part Four of Chapter 5 and, unlike other subsidies, are generally viewed as acceptable. Article 118 expressly affirms the right of CARICOM member states to use agricultural subsidies in order to meet the objectives of encouraging agricultural and rural development, promoting investments in agriculture generally, and assisting low-income or resource-poor producers, so long as they act consistently with their obligations under international agreements and Part Four.[171] One of those obligations is to notify COTED of existing and new agricultural subsidies, and COTED is mandated to keep the implementation of these provisions under review.[172]

Agricultural subsidies are defined in Article 117(1) of the RTC as 'any form of domestic support, financial or otherwise, including revenue foregone, provided by government or any public agency in favour of the producers of a specific agricultural product or to the agricultural sector as a whole'.[173] Agricultural products are listed in Annex IV, which is stated to be identical to the product coverage of the WTO Agreement on Agriculture.[174] Agricultural subsidies include: assistance provided by government or any public agency to foster agricultural and rural development

[169] Trebilcock, Howse, and Eliason, *Regulation of International Trade* (n 133) 467.

[170] Trebilcock, Howse, and Eliason, *Regulation of International Trade* (n 133) 467.

[171] Note Art 15 of the Agreement on Agriculture (adopted 15 Apr 1994, in force 1 Jan 1995) 1869 UNTS 410 [hereafter 'Agreement on Agriculture'], provides for special and differential treatment to developing countries, and this is supported by Art 9.4 of the Agreement, under which '[d]uring the implementation period, developing country Members shall not be required to undertake commitments in respect of the export subsidies listed in subparagraphs (d) and (e) of paragraph 1 above, provided that these are not applied in a manner that would circumvent reduction commitments.'

[172] RTC Arts 123–124.

[173] See Annex 2 to the Agreement on Agriculture for the WTO's criteria for domestic support in this area.

[174] See footnote 1 to Annex IV. See the Agreement on Agriculture, p 424 (Annex I).

or to assist low-income producers or producers with deficient resources; financial concessions to offset the costs of agricultural input or to encourage agricultural investments; any other financial concession which has the effect of providing price or income support to producers of agricultural products, administered through direct or indirect payments; and payments in kind to agricultural producers.[175]

Even though member states have a right to provide agricultural subsidies, Article 119 seeks to ensure that those subsidies are not used to distort production of, and intra-regional trade in, the subsidized products. Therefore subsidies in the form of transfers from consumers or direct payments to producers or processors that would amount to price support are not authorized.[176] Instead, subsidies should be made available through publicly funded programmes which benefit the agricultural sector generally, and any direct payments must be done in such a way as to ensure minimal production and trade distortion and so as not to constitute price support to producers.[177] Under Article 120, any subsidy not satisfying these conditions, and which exceeds 10 per cent of the total value of a member state's annual production of the relevant tradable agricultural product in any one year, shall be considered as a subsidy causing injury, nullification, impairment, or serious prejudice; it thereby becomes subject to the provisions of Articles 106–110, already described.[178] Article 121(4) provides guidance on what will constitute a threat or injury in the context of agricultural subsidies, and Article 122 requires due restraint on the part of aggrieved states in initiating any retaliatory actions.[179]

In sum, the general subsidies regime in Part Three of Chapter 5 closely parallels the regime governed by the World Trade Organization's Agreement on Subsidies and Countervailing Measures. The RTC's agricultural subsidies regime, in contrast, draws inspiration from, but does not closely parallel, the WTO Agreement on Agriculture. Nevertheless, in interpreting and applying both RTC regimes inspiration may be derived from, and analogies made to, the WTO provisions and jurisprudence.

In terms of practical implementation of the subsidies regime in the Community, however, more work remains to be done. The CARICOM Secretariat has commented on both the lack of a sufficient legal infrastructure to implement the subsidies and anti-dumping regimes, and the need for common application of such rules against third parties.[180]

[175] Compare Art 6 of the Agreement on Agriculture.

[176] RTC Art 119(2).

[177] RTC Art 119(3)–(4).

[178] RTC Arts 120–121(2). Note that WTO jurisprudence follows a similar pattern of applying the more general rules related to subsidies to agricultural subsidies. For example, in the case of WTO, *US: Upland Cotton (Article 21.5 – Brazil)*—Panel Report (18 Dec 2007) WT/DS267/RW, at para 14.45, the Panel held that in order to interpret the term 'export subsidy' under Art 10.1 of the Agreement on Agriculture the relevant provisions of the Agreement on Subsidies and Countervailing Measures could be relied upon. Similarly, the Appellate Body in the same case held, at paras 544–5, that compliance with Art 6.3 of the Agreement on Agriculture does not insulate the subsidy from the prohibition in Art 3.1(b) of the Agreement on Subsidies and Countervailing Measures; at para 584, the Appellate Body found payments to exporters to be export contingent payments under both Agreements: WTO, *US: Upland Cotton*—Appellate Body Report (3 Mar 2005) WT/DS267/AB/R.

[179] Compare Art 13 of the Agreement on Agriculture.

[180] CARICOM Secretariat, *Summary Draft Report* 13–14.

10.6.2 OECS: Subsidies and dumping

The OECS Protocol contains a single provision that deals with subsidies and dumping together, Article 9. Article 9.1 preserves the general right of member states to take action against dumped or subsidized imports from outside of the Economic Union Area consistent with their international obligations. Article 9.3 goes even further. It allows a Protocol member state to take action when dumped or subsidized imports in another member state affect it:

> 9.3 If any industry in any Protocol Member State is suffering or is threatened with material injury as the result of the importation of dumped or subsidised products into another Protocol Member State, the latter Protocol Member State shall, at the request of the former Protocol Member State, examine the possibility of taking, consistent with any international obligations to which it is subject, action to remedy the injury or prevent the threatened injury.

This provision is especially beneficial to OECS member states, which generally fall under CARICOM's category of less developed states, since it allows for a kind of collective action against subsidized or dumped imports. Article 9.4, in contrast, specifically allows Protocol member states to maintain subsidies related to agriculture in conformity with their international obligations. Again, given the importance of agriculture in some OECS countries, this provision would appear helpful.

10.7 Dumping

10.7.1 CARICOM

Part V of Chapter 5 of the RTC regulates dumping, another form of conduct involving unfair pricing of exports. Dumping differs from subsidization because the former generally involves a pricing policy by a private firm whereas the latter involves a distorting practice of governments.[181] The general definition of dumping is set out in Article 126(1) of the RTC which states

> For the purpose of this Part, a product is to be considered to be a dumped import where it is introduced into the commerce of another country at less than its normal value if the export price of the product exported from one Member state to another Member State is less than the comparable price, in the ordinary course of trade, for the like product when destined for consumption in the exporting Member State.

This definition is clarified by the remaining subsections of Article 126. 'Like product' is defined in Article 126(6) as 'a product which is identical, i.e., alike in all respects to the product under consideration, or in the absence of such a product, another product, which, although not alike in all respects, has characteristics closely resembling those of the product under consideration'. Article 126(2)–(3) and (5), respectively, deal with situations in which (a) there are no sales of the like

[181] See eg Trebilcock, Howse, and Eliason, *Regulation of International Trade* (n 133) 365.

product in the ordinary course of trade or where such sales do not permit a proper comparison, (b) there is no export price or the export price is unreliable, and (c) products are not imported directly from the country of origin but rather from an intermediate country. Article 126(4) provides guidance on what constitutes a fair comparison between the export price and normal value.

Article 125 allows member states to 'take action against dumped imports if such imports cause injury or pose a serious threat of injury to a domestic industry'.[182] Article 127(1) provides that for the purposes of Part V 'injury shall, unless otherwise specified, be taken to mean material injury to a domestic industry, threat of material injury to a domestic industry or material retardation of the establishment of such an industry.' In determining *injury*, Article 127(2) requires positive evidence and an objective examination of the volume of dumped imports, their effect on domestic prices, and their impact on domestic producers. To determine the existence of a *threat* of material injury, Article 127(3) requires competent authorities to consider, inter alia, a significant rate of increase of dumped imports into the domestic market, the capacity of the exporter and the availability of other export markets, whether imports are having a significant depressing or suppressing effect on domestic prices which would likely increase import demand, and the inventories of the product being investigated.

Allegations related to dumping are subject to similar investigative procedures as those applied to subsidies causing injury, nullification, impairment, or serious prejudice under Article 106, described earlier. Under Article 129(1)–(2) a domestic industry can initiate an investigation with the competent authority in its territory if the application has the support of domestic producers whose collective output makes up a sufficient percentage of the total production of the like product. The competent authority, when determining whether an investigation is justified, must issue a public notice and request the concerned member state, other interested member states, and the interested parties to provide the required information and comments.[183] Under Article 129(4), if the competent authority proceeds with the preliminary investigation the results must be made available by public notice. Where that investigation provides sufficient evidence that dumped imports have entered into the commerce of the member state and such imports seriously

[182] RTC Art 128 defines 'domestic industry' as having the meaning defined in Annex I to the RTC. Para 1 of Annex I essentially defines 'domestic industry' as either being (1) the domestic producers as a whole of the like products or (2) those of the domestic producers whose collective output of the products constitutes a major proportion of the total domestic production of those products. Para 2 allows in exceptional circumstances the division of the territory of a member state into two or more competitive markets so as to allow the producers in each market to be regarded as a separate industry. See generally, Annex I.

[183] RTC Art 129(3). The term 'interested parties is defined in Art 129(8) as including:

(a) an exporter or foreign producer or the importer of a product subject to investigation, or a trade or business association, a majority of the members of which are producers, exporters or importers of such product;
(b) the government of the exporting Member State; and
(c) a producer of the like product in the importing Member State or a trade and business association, a majority of the members of which produce the like product in the territory of the importing Member State.

threaten or have injured a domestic industry, the member state may submit a request for consultations to the competent authority of the exporting member state and that request must be notified to COTED.[184] If the consultations fail, under Article 129(9) the aggrieved member state may impose on a provisional basis anti-dumping measures and may request an investigation by COTED. Provisional measures must satisfy the conditions of Article 130 and may take the form of (1) a provisional duty, (2) a security—by cash deposit or bond—equal to the amount of the anti-dumping duty provisionally estimated, being not greater than the provisionally estimated margin of dumping, or (3) a withholding of appraisement.[185] Provisional measures may not be imposed sooner than sixty days from the date of initiation of investigation by the competent authority and must be of limited duration.[186] Provisional measures may be withdrawn if the exporter provides a voluntary price guarantee.[187] If provisional measures are found not to have been justified, they must be withdrawn and compensation may be required.[188]

Article 131 sets out the requirements for a COTED investigation, including satisfaction of a minimum threshold (*de minimis*) requirement in relation to the margin and volume of dumping and an eighteen-month time limit for completion of the investigation.[189] Requirements for cooperation with COTED and protection of confidentiality are also imposed.[190] Article 131(5)–(6) also provide that the competent authority for investigating is COTED itself if the CSME faces a threat or has suffered a serious injury from dumped imports by third states, and preserves member state rights in relation to previously signed international treaties.

If COTED is satisfied following its investigations that an injury or threat of injury exists in relation to dumped imports, and the party alleged to be responsible for the dumped import refuses to cooperate within the stipulated time period, COTED may authorize an aggrieved member state to take anti-dumping action.[191] COTED must set the date, duration, and conditions for the imposition of the anti-dumping measures, including anti-dumping duties, which may be imposed retroactively.[192] Anti-dumping duties can potentially be authorized for all affected member states, but are subject to conditions of non-discrimination and may be subject to a request by the exporter for a review by the competent authority, or COTED.[193] Anti-dumping measures must be kept under review by COTED and member states undertake to establish harmonized anti-dumping legislation.[194]

In sum, the anti-dumping regime has the potential to address cases of dumping, both by CARICOM member states and third states. However to date it has not been used to any significant extent. The CARICOM Secretariat has commented on both the lack of a sufficient legal infrastructure to implement the subsidies and anti-dumping regimes, and the need for common application of such rules against third parties.[195]

[184] RTC Art 129(5). [185] See RTC Art 130(2). [186] RTC Art 130(3)–(4).
[187] RTC Art 133(3)(h). [188] RTC Art 133(3)(f). [189] RTC Art 131(1)–(2).
[190] RTC Art 131(3)–(4). See also the further requirements for cooperation and publicity of the conclusions of investigations in Art 132.
[191] RTC Art 133(1). [192] RTC Art 133(2)–(3). [193] RTC Art 133(3).
[194] RTC Art 133(4)–(5). [195] CARICOM Secretariat, *Summary Draft Report* 13–14.

11

Competition Law and Consumer Protection

11.1 CARICOM Competition Law[1]

11.1.1 Goals, objectives, and responsibilities

Part One of Chapter 8 establishes the rules of competition and the Competition Commission (designated simply as the 'Commission' throughout the RTC).[2] With the exception of specifically identified areas, these competition rules create obligations for member states, CARICOM organs, and private actors.[3] It is important to highlight the latter—competition law is applicable to private actors, or enterprises. Other areas of the RTC create direct rights and obligations for member states and for the Community, and the CCJ has extended treaty rights to persons through its 'correlative rights' doctrine.[4] But Chapter 8 is unique in imposing clear obligations to persons, ones capable of enforcement by CARICOM organs and national

[1] For more on CARICOM competition law see Alina Kaczorowska-Ireland, *CSME Competition Law* (London: Routledge (forthcoming)). The OECS has no similar provisions on competition law or policy. RTB Art 4.2(k) speaks to harmonizing and pursuing joint policies in relation to 'regulatory and competition authorities'. OECS Protocol Art 3(l) provides as follows: 'To achieve the objectives set out in Article 2, the activities of the Protocol Member States shall include under the conditions and timing set out in this Protocol—[...] (l) a common competition policy.' As a result the focus in this section is entirely upon CARICOM competition law.

[2] The term 'Competition Commission' is formally abbreviated to 'Commission' in RTC Art 171. 'Commission' is defined in Art 1 as meaning 'the Competition Commission established by Article 167'. The latter reference should be corrected to refer to Art 171. The term 'rules of competition' is also defined in Art 1 as including 'the rules set out in sub-paragraph (a)(i) of paragraph 1 of Article 166 and Articles 176, 177, 178 and 179'. The first cross-reference is incorrect. Art 1 of Protocol VIII cross-references Arts 30(h), 30(i), and 30(k) of the Protocol and any other rules made pursuant to Art 30(b)(1)(a)(i). As a result the cross-references in Art 1 of the RTC should be to Arts 170(1)(a)(i), 176, 177, 178, and 179. See Arts I and II of Protocol Amending the Treaty Establishing the Caribbean Community (Protocol VIII: Competition Policy, Consumer Protection, Dumping and Subsidies) (adopted 13–14 Mar 2000, not yet in force) [hereafter 'Protocol VIII'].

[3] RTC Art 168 lists a number of areas excluded from coverage under Part One, including labour union and collective bargaining activities, and 'activities of professional associations designed to develop or enforce professional standards of competence reasonably necessary for the protection of the public and approved by the Commission'. Also excluded from the Part are duly notified business conduct within the meaning of Art 177(4), and negative clearance rulings or exemptions under Arts 180 or 181–182, respectively. Monopolies, however, are not exempted under Art 31.

[4] The correlative rights doctrine, established in para [32] of the case of *Trinidad Cement Ltd and TCL Guyana Inc v Guyana*, Judgment [2009] CCJ 1 (OJ), (2009) 74 WIR 302, 15 January 2009, allows correlative rights for persons to be derived from obligations imposed upon member states by the RTC.

authorities as a result of complaints made by, amongst other actors, natural and juridical persons.

The goal and objectives of the Community competition policy are set out in Article 169. The general goal, specified in subsection (1), is 'to ensure that the benefits expected from the establishment of the CSME are not frustrated by anti-competitive business conduct'. This goal expressly links competition rules to the CSME. It supports an application of competition law towards strengthening the single market, the RTC's vision for which includes full integration of national markets of all member states of the Community into a single unified and open market area.[5] To fulfil this goal the Community is required to pursue the objectives of promoting and maintaining competition, prohibiting anti-competitive business conduct, and promoting consumer welfare and the protection of consumer interests.[6] These objectives also support a reading of competition rules so as to enhance efficiency and to aid in consumer protection.

Both the Community and the member states have specific obligations in relation to these objectives. Under Article 170(1)(a)(i)–(ii) the Community is required to 'establish appropriate norms and institutional arrangements to prohibit and penalize anti-competitive business conduct' and to 'establish and maintain information systems to enable enterprises and consumers to be kept informed about the operation of markets within the CSME'.[7] Member states are required to legislate to ensure consistency and compliance with the rules of competition, to provide penalties for anti-competitive business conduct, and to provide information to facilitate consumer choice. They must also establish and maintain appropriate institutional arrangements to enforce competition law—arrangements which must allow access by nationals of other member states 'on an equitable, transparent and non-discriminatory basis'.[8]

As part of their institutional structure member states are required to establish national competition authorities which must cooperate with the Commission, including by investigating any allegations of anti-competitive business conduct referred to them by the Commission or another member state. Such national authorities also must cooperate with other national competition authorities in the detection, prevention, and exchange of information related to anti-competitive business conduct.[9] By 2009 nine CARICOM member states had established national competition authorities.[10]

[5] See RTC Art 78(2)(a). [6] Summary of RTC Art 169(2).

[7] The term 'enterprise' is defined in Art 1 of the RTC as meaning 'any person or type of organisation, other than a non-profit organisation, involved in the production of or the trade in goods, or the provision of services'.

[8] Summary of RTC Art 170(1)(b). Under Art 74(2)(f) member states are also required to harmonize their laws and administrative practices in respect of competition policy.

[9] Summary of RTC Art 170(3).

[10] CARICOM Secretariat, *Summary Draft Report on the Appraisal of the State of Implementation of the CARICOM Single Market* (September 2009) (Georgetown, Guyana: CARICOM Secretariat, 2009) [hereafter '*Summary Draft Report*'], 26. Note that Trinidad and Tobago transformed its obligations in relation to the Competition Commission (including referral obligations) by means of the Fair Trading Act, Laws of Trinidad and Tobago, LRO 2009, Chap 81:13 (26 Apr 2007). See likewise the

Exceptions to these requirements are permitted under Article 170(4), however. Confidential information 'which would be prejudicial to the public interest or to the legitimate commercial interests of enterprises, public or private' need not be disclosed. Member states are also required to notify COTED of existing laws and practices which would be inconsistent with Chapter 8, and COTED is required to establish a programme for the repeal or terminate such laws and practices.[11] Under Article 182 COTED is also tasked with developing and establishing appropriate policies and rules of competition within the Community, including special rules for particular sectors.

11.1.2 The Competition Commission

Articles 171–174 establish the Commission and describe its composition, functions, and powers. The Commission, which was formally established in 2008, is composed of seven members.[12] Commissioners are appointed for a term of five years by the Regional Judicial and Legal Services Commission, one of whom is also appointed Chairman.[13] As stipulated in Article 172(2), the members of the Commission are required collectively to possess 'expertise or experience in commerce, finance, economics, law, competition policy and practice, international trade and such other areas of expertise or experience as may be necessary'. Commissioners are required to take the Oath of Office set out in the Annex to the RTC.[14] They are subject to disciplinary procedures of the Regional Judicial and Legal Services Commission and may only be removed from office on grounds of inability to perform the functions of office or for misbehaviour by means of a vote of three-quarters or more of the membership of the Regional Judicial and Legal Services Commission.[15] A Commissioner may also resign.[16]

Article 173, in setting out the functions of the Commission, helps delineate the different roles of the Commission and the national competition authorities described in Article 170(3). The Commission, under Article 173(1)(a) is required to 'apply the rules of competition in respect of anti-competitive *cross-border* business conduct'.[17] National authorities, on the other hand, can address anti-competitive conduct without cross-border effect. In this sense CARICOM law creates a two-tier

Competition and Fair Trading Act, Laws of Guyana, Act No 11 of 2006; Fair Competition Act, Laws of Barbados, LRO 2007, Cap 326C (3 Jan 2003 – Parts I–VIII and X) (10 Mar 2008 – Part IX). Note that the Jamaican statute pre-dates the Commission and therefore does not make reference to it: Fair Competition Act, Laws of Jamaica, Vol IX 2009, Acts 9 of 1993, 22 of 2001 (9 Mar 1993).

[11] RTC Art 170(5).

[12] RTC Art 171(1). See also CARICOM Secretariat, Summary Draft Report 26.

[13] RTC Art 171(1) and (3). The term of appointment is renewable once. Art 172(8), allowing the Conference to act in place of the Regional Judicial and Legal Services Commission, has been rendered obsolete as a result of widespread ratification of the Agreement Establishing the Caribbean Court of Justice (adopted 14 Feb 2001, entered into force 23 Jul 2002) 2255 UNTS 319.

[14] See Annex V to the RTC, which is incorrectly labelled 'Oath of Offices of Judges of the Court'.

[15] RTC Art 172(4)–(5) and (7).

[16] RTC Art 172(6).

[17] Emphasis added. See also RTC Art 174(1) which allows the Commission to enforce competition law with respect to 'cross-border transactions or transactions with cross-border effects'.

system involving the Commission and national competition authorities. National authorities have exclusive competence to deal with anti-competitive conduct without cross-border effect. The Commission has exclusive competence to deal with anti-competitive cross-border business conduct.[18]

It is unlikely that a significant number of cases of anti-competitive conduct will arise that will be confined to a single member state or to a part of it. The jurisprudence of the European Court of Justice suggests that such cases will be limited.[19] Although the CCJ has warned that ECJ jurisprudence in relation to competition law, particularly that related to procedural aspects, must be used with caution, it remains useful for comparative and illustrative purposes.[20] Although CARICOM competition law may diverge substantially from EU competition law in the future, at this early stage of the former's development it remains helpful to examine the conceptual developments and strategic choices taken by the ECJ in the European system.

The *Consten and Grundig Case*, for example, helps us to see the potential scope of cross-border effect. The ECJ in that case defined 'trade between Member States' very broadly so as to catch a wide variety of agreements. The Court found that even agreements between unequal non-competitors, such as a sole distribution agreement which provided absolute territorial protection, might be caught under what is now Article 101 of the TFEU because it would restrict competition between one party to the agreement and third parties.[21] Such agreements may distort cross-border competition by restoring national divisions in trade between member states.[22] The Court went on to explain the reason for the Commission's limitation

[18] Subject to RTC Art 176.

[19] The ECJ has held that agreements between national undertakings limited to national territory nevertheless could be caught under Art 101 of the TFEU. See eg Case 61/80 *Coöperatieve Stremsel- en Kleurselfabriek v Commission* [1981] ECR 851, at pp 867–8 [14]–[15], where the ECJ held that a cooperative agreement between Dutch dairy producers hindered trade by reinforcing the partitioning of markets on a national basis.

[20] In *Trinidad Cement Ltd v Competition Commission*, Judgment [2012] CCJ 4 (OJ), 12 November 2012, at [27], the CCJ warned the parties that 'care must be taken in the use of precedents from the ECJ owing to the variance between the procedures of the European and CARICOM Competition regimes. As between the two, there are considerable dis-similarities that flow from the significant differences in the wording, nature and effect of the underlying legal instruments and the overarching governing system of law.'

[21] Cases 56 and 58/64 *Établissements Consten S.à.R.L. and Grundig-Verkaufs-GmbH v Commission* [1966] ECR 299, at p 339 [hereafter '*Consten and Grundig*']. Note that open exclusive licensing arrangements that do not provide absolute territorial protection and which instead can be justified on the basis of promoting other market goods, such as technological development, may be compatible with TFEU Art 101. See Case 258/78 *LC Nungesser KG and Kurt Eisele v Commission* [1982] ECR 2015, at pp 2068–9 [53], [57]–[58].

[22] *Consten and Grundig* (n 21), at p 340. For an extension of this rule to concerted practices see Case 48/69 *Imperial Chemical Industries Ltd v Commission* [1972] ECR 619, p 661 [120]–[124]. Note that the *Consten and Grundig Case* reveals a key distinction between EU competition law and other competition regimes, such as that of the US. See eg the decision of the US Supreme Court in *Continental TV v Sylvania* 433 US 36 (1977). In the *Consten and Grundig Case* the Court is concerned with the overall goal of EU market integration and thus penalizes market segregation even though the agreement per se might not have hindered competition (since consumers could switch to another brand if Grundig products were priced too high). Perhaps in reaction to concerns about such an approach, the EU has relaxed its posture on vertical agreements by means of the Commission's Regulation 330/2010. See the

to anti-competitive conduct that may affect 'trade between Member States' and set out a very broad test for determining whether a factual situation may be characterized as falling within that phrase:

> The concept of an agreement 'which may affect trade between Member States' is intended to define, in the law governing cartels, the boundary between the areas respectively covered by Community law and national law. It is only to the extent to which the agreement may affect trade between Member States that the deterioration in competition caused by the agreement falls under the prohibition of Community law contained in Article 85 [now TFEU Article 101]; otherwise it escapes the prohibition.
>
> In this connexion, what is particularly important is *whether the agreement is capable of constituting a threat, either direct or indirect, actual or potential, to freedom of trade between Member States* in a manner which might harm the attainment of the objectives of a single market between States.[23]

This passage explains the reason for the restriction of the Commission to trade between member states, namely, a division of competence between the Commission and national competition authorities. The test established by the Court, which uses language strongly reminiscent of that used in the *Dassonville Case*, also reveals how broadly the phrase 'trade between Member States' may be interpreted.[24] As noted by Craig and de Búrca, '[t]he focus on potential or indirect effects on trade means that it will be very rare for the EU to lack jurisdiction.'[25]

The CARICOM Competition Commission is also required to promote and protect competition in the Community, coordinate the implementation of the Community Competition Policy, and to perform any other function conferred on it by any competent body of the Community.[26] These functions can be delegated to one or more of the members of the Commission, in writing.[27]

In fulfilling these functions the Commission has a wide range of duties. It must 'monitor anti-competitive practices of enterprises operating in the CSME, and investigate and arbitrate cross-border disputes'.[28] The latter phrasing is interesting because no arbitral jurisdiction is specified for the Commission elsewhere in Chapter 8, and the Commission's dispute settlement and enforcement powers under Articles 174 and 175, including its ability to hold an enquiry, are more closely analogous to a standing quasi-judicial body. As a result perhaps the term 'arbitrate' is intended to have a non-technical meaning, referring to a dispute resolution role more akin to mediation.

Under Article 173(2)(b) the Commission's duties also include continually reviewing the Community Competition Policy and making appropriate recommendations to COTED. It must review the progress of member states in the area of competition,

discussion of the *Consten and Grundig Case* and the relevant regulations in Stephen Weatherill, *Cases & Materials on EU Law*, 10th edn (Oxford: Oxford University Press, 2012) at 455 and 477.

[23] *Consten and Grundig* (n 21) p 341 (emphasis added).

[24] See the test established in Case 8/74 *Procureur du Roi v Dassonville* [1974] ECR 837, at p 852 [5], discussed earlier in Chapter 10.

[25] Paul Craig and Gráinne de Búrca, *EU Law: Text, Cases and Materials*, 5th edn (Oxford: Oxford University Press, 2011) at 983.

[26] RTC Art 173(1)(b)–(c). [27] RTC Art 173(3). [28] RTC Art 173(2)(a).

and cooperate with them, exchange expertise, provide support with respect to consumer protection, and develop and disseminate information on competition and consumer protection policy.[29] The Commission must also promote the institutions and harmonized competition laws and practices so as to achieve uniformity in the administration of competition rules.[30]

The powers of the Commission, as set out in Article 174, facilitate the Commission both in its investigative and enforcement functions. Subject to the rules regarding determination of anti-competitive conduct, the Commission is empowered under Article 174(1) to 'in respect of cross-border transactions or transactions with cross-border effects, monitor, investigate, detect, make determinations or take action to inhibit and penalise enterprises whose business conduct prejudices trade or prevents, restricts or distorts competition within the CSME.' The Commission is also empowered to establish its own rules of procedure under Article 174(4), and did so in 2011.[31]

To ensure the effectiveness of its powers the Commission is entitled to compel the attendance of persons to give evidence, require the production of documents and take such other action as may be necessary for its investigations.[32] It is empowered to make binding legal determinations in relation to anti-competitive business conduct.[33] It also may impose sanctions under Article 174(4):

> 4. The Commission shall, to the extent required to remedy or penalise anti-competitive business conduct referred to in Article 177:
> [a] order the termination or nullification as the case may require, of agreements, conduct, activities or decisions prohibited by Article [177];
> [b] direct the enterprise to cease and desist from anti-competitive business conduct and to take such steps as are necessary to overcome the effects of abuse of its dominant position in the market, or any other business conduct inconsistent with the principles of fair competition set out in this Chapter;
> [c] order payment of compensation to persons affected; and
> [d] impose fines for breaches of the rules of competition.[34]

[29] RTC Art 173(2)(d)–(h). [30] RTC Art 173(2)(c).

[31] See CARICOM Competition Commission, 'Rules of Procedure 2011', as available at <http://www.caricomcompetitioncommission.com/images/registry/CCC-Rules-of-Procedure-2011.pdf> (31 Aug 2013). Note that it is likely that these Rules will be substantially amended as a result of the decision of the CCJ in *Trinidad Cement Ltd v Competition Commission*, Judgment [2012] CCJ 4 (OJ), 12 November 2012. In that case, following a discussion of problems likely to arise from the wording of several of the Rules, the Court stated at [48]: 'In all the circumstances, the Court would encourage the Commission to review its Rules so as to ensure that the same are in concert with the Revised Treaty and reflect the appropriate standards of fairness.'

[32] RTC Art 174(2). Note that such investigative powers may be restricted by the general principle of human rights under CARICOM law described in Chapter 8. Such has been the experience of the EU. See eg Case C-94/00 *Roquette Frères SA v Directeur général de la concurrence, de la consommation et de la répression des fraudes, and Commission of the European Communities* [2002] ECR I-9011.

[33] RTC Art 174(3) provides: 'The Commission may, on the basis of its investigations, make determinations regarding the compatibility of business conduct with the rules of competition and other related provisions of the Treaty.' Art 174(6) requires member states to enact legislation to ensure that determinations of the Commission are enforced in their jurisdictions.

[34] The mis-numbering of the subsections of RTC Art 174(4) has been corrected. The cross-reference in the first subsection also has been corrected. For the original version of Art 174 see Art II, inserting

These sanctions are potentially very powerful and, if effectively implemented by national authorities, will enable to Commission to function effectively.[35]

Interestingly, they are only mandatory under Article 174(4) 'to the extent required'. As a result the Commission appears to have been granted some flexibility with respect to the sanctioning of enterprises. It may be possible for the Commission to use such wording to justify not ordering fines in cases where enterprises otherwise subject to competition rules actively assist the Commission in its investigations. This kind of practice occurs in the EU, where 'leniency notices' are published in relation to situations where undertakings have been provided with immunities or reductions in fines.[36]

In order to determine whether anti-competitive conduct has taken place the Commission may, following consultations, commence an investigation upon receiving a request by a member state, or COTED, or on its own initiative (*proprio motu*).[37] Requests for an investigation by a member state or COTED under Article 175 must be in writing and contain sufficient information for the Commission to make a preliminary assessment.[38]

Upon receipt of a request for an investigation the Commission must determine, following consultations with interested parties, both whether it has jurisdiction and whether the investigation is 'justified in all the circumstances of the case'.[39] The latter phrasing would appear to provide the Commission with a level of discretion in deciding whether to investigate an allegation.

The CCJ examined the requirements for a request under Article 175 by COTED in the case of *Trinidad Cement Ltd v Competition Commission*.[40] In this case Trinidad Cement Ltd challenged the decision of the Commission to initiate an investigation of anti-competitive business conduct with respect to the TCL Group of Companies. Trinidad Cement Ltd alleged the decision to investigate, and the decision of the Commission to hold an Enquiry following the investigation, were both void.[41] As summarized by the Court, Trinidad Cement Ltd 'alleged that the Commission acted wrongly in initiating and conducting the investigation in two main regards: (a) there had been no proper request for the investigation; and (b) the Commission had failed to respect the rights of TCL as "an interested

a new Art 30(f), of the Protocol Amending the Treaty Establishing the Caribbean Community (Protocol VIII: Competition Policy, Consumer Protection, Dumping and Subsides) (adopted 13–14 Mar 2000, not yet in force). This latter article cross-references Art 30(i), which is equivalent to Art 177 of the RTC.

[35] For an overview of the strong enforcement powers of the European Commission and national authorities in the same field see Council, 'Council Regulation (EC) No 1/2003 of 16 December 2002 on the implementation of the rules on competition laid down in Articles 81 and 82 of the Treaty (Text with EEA relevance)' [2003] OJ L/1/1, 4.1.2003, as available at <http://eur-lex.europa.eu/LexUriServ/LexUriServ.do?uri=OJ:L:2003:001:0001:0025:EN:PDF> (26 Jun 2013).

[36] See eg European Commission, 'Commission Notice on Immunity from fines and reduction of fines in cartel cases (Text with EEA relevance)' [2006] OJ C298/17 (8/12/2006), as available at <http://eur-lex.europa.eu/LexUriServ/LexUriServ.do?uri=OJ:C:2006:298:0017:0022:EN:PDF> (26 Jun 2013).

[37] RTC Arts 175–176.

[38] RTC Art 175(3).

[39] RTC Art 175(4).

[40] Judgment [2012] CCJ 4 (OJ), 12 November 2012.

[41] *Trinidad Cement v Competition Commission* (n 40) [2].

party" within the meaning of Article 175 of the Revised Treaty'.[42] Regarding the first issue—whether the COTED request for the investigation was valid—the Court examined the original decision of COTED, the correspondence between the Secretary General and the Commission, and the reaffirmation of its position in relation to the matter by COTED.[43] Although there were clearly some irregularities in this process, the Court nevertheless held that the request had been properly made:

> The Court is satisfied from the evidence that from the inception, the substantive intention of COTED was to request that the Commission investigate TCL. The conclusion of technical error in the drafting of the Conference resolution emanating from the Twenty-Sixth Meeting is irresistible. At the first meeting of COTED after the nature of the defect in its resolution was brought to its attention, COTED ratified the investigation that had been initiated by the Commission on the request formulated in the letter addressed by the Secretary-General. This ratification validated the request made by the Secretary-General. In sum, without prejudice to the position stated before (at [17] above) that TCL should have addressed its concerns about the propriety of COTED's request to the Enquiry Panel, the Court considers that the Commission was authorized to function in accordance with Article 175.[44]

As made clear in this passage the Court will seek to look at the intent of COTED when determining whether a request for an investigation has been properly made. Regarding the second issue, the Court determined that Trinidad Cement Ltd could not be deemed to be an 'interested party' under Article 175 and, after assessing several of the arguments on the merits of the application, dismissed it.[45] This conclusion makes sense because in some cases the Commission may wish to commence an investigation without alerting the business concerned in order to prevent, for example, the destruction of evidence.

Consultations, which must be concluded within thirty days of receipt of the request for investigation, need not include the enterprise potentially

42 *Trinidad Cement v Competition Commission* (n 40) [3].

43 See *Trinidad Cement v Competition Commission* (n 40) [29]–[36].

44 *Trinidad Cement v Competition Commission* (n 40) [37].

45 *Trinidad Cement v Competition Commission* (n 40) [49]. At [26], the CCJ squarely rejected Trinidad Cement Limited's claim to be an interested party:

> No legitimate interest of TCL has been identified which could have been impacted at the preliminary stage where the Commission was engaged in deciding whether the potential investigation was within its jurisdiction and was justified in all the circumstances of the case. Equally, there is no legitimate interest which would require a targeted company to be notified of the commencement of the investigation. It is true that at the investigation stage the Commission is entitled to exercise certain investigative powers and measures as set out in Article 174(2). These are potentially quite extensive and intrusive powers but they are to be exercised not at the international plane but instead 'in accordance with applicable national laws' where the targeted enterprise has the possibility of recourse to domestic courts for vindication of its rights. Finally, Article 175(8) does speak of the Commission notifying 'the interested parties' of the determination of the Enquiry and this requirement is consistent with an interpretation that suggests that 'the interested parties', unlike the party complained of, are not involved in the Enquiry. In principle, therefore, the Court finds that a party complained of does not fall within the expression 'an interested party' as that expression is used in the Revised Treaty. [Citations omitted.]

subject to investigation. Following a decision to commence an investigation, the Commission must notify the interested parties and COTED.[46] The investigation should be completed within 120 days.[47] The conclusion of the investigation should take the form of a report and the CCJ, in the case of *Trinidad Cement Ltd v Competition Commission*, has elaborated on some of the information which should be included in that report.[48] If the results of the investigation justify it, the Commission may decide to hold an enquiry at which the party complained of may defend its interests.[49] Following the conclusion of the enquiry the Commission is required to notify the interested parties of its determination and, where an enterprise has been found to have engaged in anti-competitive conduct, the Commission must require it to take the action necessary, within a thirty-day time period, to remove the effects of its conduct.[50] If the enterprise does not comply, the Commission may apply to the Caribbean Court of Justice for an order. Interestingly, this provision allows the Commission to refer matters involving enterprises to the Court, but does not also expressly grant a similar power with respect to matters involving breaches by Member States. In contrast, Article 175(12) also allows a 'party' which has been sanctioned under Article 174(4), which presumably includes enterprises and member states, to apply to the Court for a review of the Commission's determination.[51] Such a review

[46] RTC Art 175(6). [47] RTC Art 175(6).

[48] In *Trinidad Cement Ltd v Competition Commission*, Judgment [2012] CCJ 4 (OJ), 12 November 2012, at [46], the CCJ stated:

> The Court notes that the Commission's Rules of Procedure do not replicate what is required by Article 175(3), (4), (5) and (8) of the Revised Treaty. Such replication is, of course, not strictly necessary, but it would seem to be useful nevertheless if only to remind the Investigating Panel of the steps it is required to take. The absence of any such reminder may perhaps serve to explain some flaws in the report of the Investigating Panel. One would expect such a report to state, for example, when the Commission received the request, which 'interested parties' the Commission consulted, when these consultations were concluded, when the Commission decided to conduct the investigation, who was notified of that decision and in what manner, when the investigation was completed, whether the time period for completion was extended and if so, why and when, and whether the 'interested parties' were notified of that extension and if so, when. Given the importance of separating the investigating from the adjudicating function of the Commission, it would also seem logical and prudent to indicate in the report which of the Commissioners did in fact investigate the matter reported by them. In the circumstances of this particular case, none of these omissions would appear to cause the decision to commence an Enquiry to be void, but nevertheless, inclusion of such details is an obvious way in which the report could be improved.

[49] RTC Art 175(7).

[50] RTC Art 175(8)–(9). The thirty-day time period for compliance may be extended: Art 175(10).

[51] Note that the CCJ has yet to hear a matter under these provisions. In the case of *Trinidad Cement Ltd and TCL Guyana Inc v Guyana*, Judgment [2009] CCJ 5 (OJ), 20 August 2009, at [17], the Court expressly excluded from consideration the competition law issues pled by the claimant on the following grounds:

> On the first morning of the oral hearing the Court acceded to an application by the Claimants to strike out those paragraphs of the submissions of Guyana that alleged predatory pricing and abuse by the Claimants of their dominant position in the regional cement market. In so far as predatory pricing was concerned it was a new allegation made for the first time in Guyana's submissions in reply. More significantly however, the Court noted

can include review of the procedural steps taken by the Commission during the investigation stage.[52]

The Commission may commence an investigation on its own initiative under Article 176 if it has reason to believe that business conduct by an enterprise in the CSME prejudices trade and prevents, restricts, or distorts competition within the CSME and has cross-border effects. In such a case the Commission must first request the relevant national competition authority to undertake a preliminary examination of the business conduct of the enterprise within the time frame stipulated by the Commission.[53] If the Commission is not satisfied with the response of the national competition authority, the Commission may initiate its own preliminary examination.[54] If the finding from either of these preliminary examinations merits it, the Commission and the relevant member state must consult to determine who has jurisdiction to investigate.[55] If the Commission has jurisdiction to investigate it shall follow the procedure set out in Article 175, described earlier. If, however, the Commission and the relevant member state disagree about the need for an investigation or about the appropriate authority to investigate, all examinations must cease and the matter must be referred to COTED for its decision.[56] The member state also may refer the matter to the Caribbean Court of Justice at any time.[57]

11.1.3 Anti-competitive business conduct

The definition of anti-competitive business conduct is set out in Article 177. This provision describes the general forms of anti-competitive business conduct in its first subsection, provides examples in subsection (2), sets out the consequences in subsection (3), and lists exceptions in subsection (4).[58] The three

> that such issues would be more appropriately and effectively investigated by a national Fair Trading Board or the regional Competition Commission. The allegations as to abuse of dominant position were irrelevant to the issues in this case as, even if proved, they were incapable of excusing a breach of the obligation undertaken by Guyana under the RTC or of relieving Guyana of any liability it may have incurred as a result of such a breach. At an early stage of the oral hearing therefore allegations of anti-competitive conduct ceased to form part of these proceedings.

[52] In *Trinidad Cement Ltd v Competition Commission* (n 40) [17], however, the CCJ noted that court challenges to investigations should normally await the conclusion of the Enquiry phase:

> Where no Enquiry of the Commission has as yet been held, this Court will not ordinarily take cognizance of allegations that certain procedural steps taken by the Commission during the investigation stage are unlawful or void.

[53] RTC Art 176(1)–(2). The CCJ, in *Trinidad Cement Ltd v Competition Commission* (n 40) [35], suggested that without a request to national authorities to undertake a preliminary examination, an investigation *proprio motu* by the Commission would be inappropriate.

[54] RTC Art 176(3). [55] RTC Art 176(4). [56] RTC Art 176(5).

[57] RTC Art 176(6).

[58] The definition of 'anti-competitive business conduct' in RTC Art 1 defines the term in relation to Art 173. This is an incorrect cross-reference and should refer to Art 177. The definition of the same term in Art 1 of Protocol VIII cross-references Art 30(i) of the Protocol, which is the earlier draft of Art 177.

general forms of anti-competitive business conduct set out in Article 177(1) are as follows:

(a) agreements between enterprises, decisions by associations of enterprises, and concerted practices by enterprises which have as their object or effect the prevention, restriction or distortion of competition within the Community;
(b) actions by which an enterprise abuses its dominant position within the Community; or
(c) any other like conduct by enterprises whose object or effect is to frustrate the benefits expected from the establishment of the CSME.

The first form involves anti-competitive behaviour between two or more enterprises, whether by means of an agreement or a concerted practice. In addition it would cover decisions of associations of enterprises. As demonstrated by EU jurisprudence, these three terms can cover a wide range of conduct. The term 'agreement' in EU law has been held to embrace informal, gentlemen's agreements.[59] Concerted practices extend to situations where without any formal agreement parties knowingly substitute practical cooperation for the risks of competition.[60] Concerted practices may be proved by parallel conduct which cannot be justified on the basis of normal market forces.[61] The second form involves abuse of a dominant position, which involves either one enterprise or two or more enterprises.[62] The third paragraph provides a catch-all phrase that would allow one to catch anti-competitive conduct that does not fall under either of these two categories the object or effect of which is to frustrate the benefits of the CSME.

A similar arrangement for comprehensive coverage of anti-competitive conduct is found in EU law, although under provisions which clearly distinguish anti-competitive conduct between undertakings (agreements, decisions, or concerted practices) from abuse of a dominant position.[63] An interesting issue that

[59] See eg Case 41/69 *ACF Chemiefarma NV v Commission* [1970] ECR 661, at pp 693–5 [110]–[124]. Even the act of participating in a meeting where an anti-competitive agreement is concluded without opposing it may reverse the burden of proof in relation to the agreement: Case C-199/92 *Hüls AG v Commission* [1999] ECR I-4287, at p I-4385 [155].

[60] See Case 48/69 *Imperial Chemical Industries Ltd. v Commission* [1972] ECR 619, pp 655 [64] and 660 [119].

[61] See generally *ICI v Commission* (n 60). Note, however, that in Joined Cases C-89/85, C-104/85, C-114/85, C-116/85, C-117/85, and C-125/85 to C-129/85 *A Ahlström Osakeyhtiö and others v Commission* [1993] ECR I-1307, at p I-1613 [126], the Court imposed a high threshold in rejecting an argument in favour of concerted practices by holding that 'concertation [was] not the only plausible explanation for the parallel conduct' in a market with oligopolistic tendencies. In Case C-199/92 *Hüls AG v Commission* [1999] ECR I-4287, at p I-4387 [163], in contrast, the ECJ held that concerted practices are prohibited regardless of their effect when they have an anti-competitive object: 'a concerted practice as defined above is caught by Article 81(1) EC [now Art 101(1) of the TFEU], even in the absence of anti-competitive effects on the market.'

[62] RTC Art 178(b) appears to adopt the doctrine of a single economic unit. It provides that 'any two enterprises shall be treated as interconnected enterprises if one of them is a subsidiary of the other or both of them are subsidiaries of the same parent enterprise'. As a result abuse of a dominant position could also include a situation of collective abuse of a dominant position by several enterprises.

[63] See Arts 101 and 102 of the TFEU. These two provisions have been read together to establish a complementary regime of effective competition. In Case 6/72 *Europemballage Corporation and Continental Can Company Inc. v Commission* [1973] ECR 215, at p 244 [25] the Court held that

will arise in relation to Article 177(1) of the RTC is whether it provides a *broader* scope for coverage of anti-competitive conduct than Articles 101 and 102 of the TFEU. This is because Articles 101 and 102 do not provide complete coverage of all forms of anti-competitive conduct. The ECJ, for example, has excluded unilateral practices by a firm not in a dominant position from coverage under the EU treaty regime.[64]

The specific types of conduct that will be deemed anti-competitive are set out in Article 177(2) and include: direct or indirect price fixing; limitation or control of production, markets, investment, or technical development; the artificial dividing up of markets or supply sources; the application of unequal conditions to equivalent transactions; subjecting contracts to additional obligations unrelated to the subject matter of the contract; unauthorized denial of access to networks or essential infrastructure; predatory pricing; price discrimination; loyalty discounts or concessions; exclusionary vertical restrictions; and bid-rigging.[65] This list embraces a wide range of behaviour and is not exhaustive.

Article 177(3) sets out the consequences of an agreement found to be anti-competitive. Subject to Article 168, it requires each member state to ensure that all such 'agreements and decisions…shall be null and void within its jurisdiction'. It is interesting to compare this provision with the parallel provision in EU law, which *automatically* renders void such agreements and decisions.[66] Whether Article 177(3) will be interpreted as likewise automatically voiding agreements and decisions remains to be seen. But in either case the legal effect of the voiding of such agreements and decisions will likely engender jurisprudence at both the regional and national levels, as it has in the EU.[67]

'Articles 85 and 86 [now TFEU Arts 101 and 102] seek to achieve the same aim on different levels, *viz.* the maintenance of effective competition within the Common Market.'

[64] See Case C-73/95 *Viho Europe BV v. Commission* [1996] ECR I 5457, at pp I-5495–6 [16]–[17], where an undertaking and its subsidiaries were identified as a single economic unit, with the result that their actions could not be covered by what is now Art 101 of the TFEU. Since the undertaking also did not demonstrate market dominance, it could not be caught under Art 102. See also Cases 56 and 58/64 *Établissements Consten S.à.R.L. and Grundig-Verkaufs-GmbH v Commission* [1966] ECR 299, at p 340.

[65] For a 2004 survey of anti-competitive conduct in CARICOM, which provides examples of price fixing by trade associations, collusion by import and export cartels, exclusionary distribution contracts, and abuses of dominant positions (in relation to cement, beer and steel), see Taimoon Stewart, 'The Role of Competition Policy in Regional Integration: The Case of the Caribbean Community', paper presented at *The CARICOM Single Market and Economy: Legal, Political, Economic and Social Dimensions*, SALISES, UWI, St Augustine, Trinidad and Tobago, 2004, as available at <http://sta.uwi.edu/salises/workshop/papers/tstewart.pdf> (3 Jul 2013).

[66] Art 101(2) of the TFEU reads: 'Any agreements or decisions prohibited pursuant to this Article shall be automatically void.' See also Case C-126/97 *Eco Swiss China Time Ltd v Benetton International NV* [1999] ECR I-3055, p I-3092 [36].

[67] See eg Case C-453/99 *Courage Ltd v Bernard Crehan* [2001] ECR I-6297, at p I-6322 [22], where the Court held:

> 22 That principle of automatic nullity [in Art 101(2) of the TFEU] can be relied on by anyone, and the courts are bound by it once the conditions for the application of Article 85(1) [now Art 101(1) TFEU] are met and so long as the agreement concerned does not justify the grant of an exemption under Article 85(3) [now Art 101(3) TFEU] of the Treaty (on the latter point, see *inter alia* Case 10/69 *Portelange* [1969] ECR 309, paragraph 10).

Article 177(4) sets out three exceptions that will render conduct lawful that would ordinarily be deemed anti-competitive. The enterprise will not be found to be in violation of Article 177 if it can establish that its activity

(a) contributes to:
  (i) the improvement of production or distribution of goods and services; or
  (ii) the promotion of technical or economic progress,

  while allowing consumers a fair share of the resulting benefit;
(b) imposes on the enterprises affected only such restrictions as are indispensable to the attainment of the objectives mentioned in subparagraph (a); *or*
(c) does not afford the enterprise engaged in the activity the possibility of eliminating competition in respect of a substantial part of the market for goods or services concerned.[68]

This provision likely contains a drafting error in the inclusion of the word 'or' at the end of paragraph (b). This is because under a strict textual interpretation it would appear to set out three distinct exceptions, not a cumulative list of requirements for a single exception.[69] Such a reading is problematic and could result in absurdity. Article 177(4)(b), for example, if read as a stand-alone exception, would require only a demonstration of the necessary restrictions it refers to, without any proof that the activity *actually contributes to the objectives* mentioned in sub-paragraph (a). In contrast, the parallel provision in EU law is found in Article 101(3) of the TFEU, which reads:

3. The provisions of paragraph 1 may, however, be declared inapplicable in the case of:
   — any agreement or category of agreements between undertakings,
   — any decision or category of decisions by associations of undertakings,
   — any concerted practice or category of concerted practices,

   which contributes to improving the production or distribution of goods or to promoting technical or economic progress, while allowing consumers a fair share of the resulting benefit, *and* which does not:
   (a) impose on the undertakings concerned restrictions which are not indispensable to the attainment of these objectives;
   (b) afford such undertakings the possibility of eliminating competition in respect of a substantial part of the products in question.[70]

> Since the nullity referred to in Article 85(2) is absolute, an agreement which is null and void by virtue of this provision has no effect as between the contracting parties and cannot be set up against third parties (see the judgment in Case 22/71 *Béguelin* [1971] ECR 949, paragraph 29). Moreover, it is capable of having a bearing on all the effects, either past or future, of the agreement or decision concerned (see the judgment in Case 48/72 *Brasserie de Haecht II* [1973] ECR 77, paragraph 26).

As a result the Court held that any individual is entitled to rely on Art 101(1) TFEU and the nullity set out in Art 101(2) TFEU in proceedings before a national court even if that individual is a party to a prohibited agreement. *Courage v Crehan* pp I-6323–4 [26]–[28].

[68] Emphasis added. Note that Art 177(a) of the RTC actually includes two conditions: (1) improvement or promotion, and (2) allowing consumers a fair share in the benefit. I thank Professor Kaczorowska-Ireland for drawing this point to my attention.

[69] Art 30(i)(4) of Protocol VIII is identically worded.

[70] Emphasis added.

Article 101(3) of the TFEU is cumulative and therefore requires satisfaction of all three requirements specified in Article 177(4) of the RTC. Given the nearly identical wording of these two provisions, Article 177(4) should be interpreted to establish a single, cumulative test for exclusion of otherwise anti-competitive conduct.[71] This would require the challenged activity: to contribute to an economic good (ie, efficiency gains), while allowing consumers to share in the benefit; to only impose the necessary restrictions (in terms of the agreement and in terms of restrictions of competition); and not to eliminate competition from the market or a substantial part of the market.[72]

It should be emphasized here that the exceptions to competition rules, such as those provided in Article 177(4) and elsewhere in the RTC, should not be considered incongruous given the nature of competition law in general. The aim of competition rules in regional trade arrangements cannot be to ensure perfect competition, which is impossible given current economic conditions. Rather, as seen in the EU context in Case 26/76 *Metro SB-Großmärkte GmbH & Co. KG v Commission*, the presumption is for a market with '*workable competition*, that is to say the degree of competition necessary to ensure the observance of the basic requirements and attainment of the objectives of the Treaty, in particular the creation of a single market achieving conditions similar to those of a domestic market'.[73] Workable competition means that at times anti-competitive conduct may be acceptable, such as when it produces levels of specialization and efficiency that benefit consumers.[74]

Two additional exceptions to Article 177(1) will exist in cases where the anti-competitive business conduct has minimal impact, or where a member state is

[71] For an analysis of the cumulative nature of TFEU Art 101(3) and an illustration of its successful application see Commission Decision 73/323, *Prym-Beka* [1973] OJ L296/24 (8 Oct 1973).

[72] On the application of TFEU Art 101(3) see European Commission, 'Communication from the Commission—Notice—Guidelines on the application of Article 81(3) of the Treaty', Official Journal C101, 27.04.2004, pp 97–118, also available at <http://eur-lex.europa.eu/LexUriServ/LexUriServ.do?uri=CELEX:52004XC0427(07):EN:NOT> (23 Jun 2013), and Paul Craig and Gráinne de Búrca, *EU Law: Text, Cases and Materials*, 5th edn (Oxford: Oxford University Press, 2011) 984–7. It should be noted that in EU law the existence of Art 101(3) has been used to exclude a prior, 'rule of reason' exception to Art 101(1) (as developed, for example, in the jurisprudence related to quantitative restrictions). See eg Case T-112/99 *Métropole télévision (M6), Suez-Lyonnaise des eaux, France Télécom and Télévision française 1 SA (TF1) v Commission* [2001] ECR II-2459, pp II-2488–9 [74]–[77]. In para [74] of the judgment the Court held that 'Article 85(3) of the Treaty [now TFEU Art 101(3)] would lose much of its effectiveness if such an examination [weighing the pro and anti-competitive aspects of a restriction] had to be carried out already under Article 85(1) of the Treaty.' After reviewing its jurisprudence, the Court also noted in para [76] that its previous judgments 'cannot, however, be interpreted as establishing the existence of a rule of reason in Community competition law.'

[73] Case 26/76 *Metro SB-Großmärkte GmbH & Co. KG v Commission* [1977] ECR 1875, p 1904 [20] (emphasis added).

[74] An example of anti-competitive conduct deemed permissible under EU law is found in Case C-309/99 *Wouters, JW Savelbergh, Price Waterhouse Belastingadviseurs BV v Algemene Raad van de Nederlandse Orde van Advocaten* [2002] ECR I-1577, where Dutch Bar Regulations that were restrictive of competition were nevertheless justifiable and did not go beyond what was necessary to ensure the proper practice of the legal profession. See also Case C-67/96 *Albany International BV v Stichting Bedrijfspensioenfonds Textielindustrie* [1999] ECR I-05751, which allowed collective employer-employee agreements to escape Art 101(1).

able to obtain a negative clearance ruling from the Commission.[75] The latter such rulings are described in Article 180. Under Article 180(1) a member state can apply to the Commission for an advance ruling on whether business conduct is anti-competitive. If the Commission determines that the conduct is not prohibited, it will issue a negative clearance ruling to that effect. Such rulings are conclusive for any judicial proceedings in CARICOM except for a case in which the Commission applies to the Caribbean Court of Justice for review of a decision of the Commission which was induced by deceit or improper means.[76]

A final set of exemptions in relation to Article 177 is set out in Article 183. Under the latter provision COTED may suspend the application of Article 177 to specific sectors of the Community, which are to be governed by special rules, pending the adoption of those rules.[77] COTED is also entrusted with a general power, upon application by a member state or of its own volition, to exclude or suspend the application of Article 177 to any sector or any enterprise or group of enterprises in the public interest.[78]

Abuse of a dominant position

One form of anti-competitive conduct under Article 177 is further clarified in Articles 178–179, namely, abuse of a dominant position. Article 178(a) provides guidance on what constitutes a dominant position, stating that 'an enterprise holds a dominant position in a market if by itself or together with an interconnected enterprise, it occupies such a position of economic strength as will enable it to operate in the market without effective constraints from its competitors or potential competitors.'[79] This phrase is important because it shows that the test requires unilateral and effectively unchecked capacity to act in the market. The term 'interconnected enterprise' is defined in Article 178(b), which provides that 'any two enterprises shall be treated as interconnected enterprises if one of them is a subsidiary of the other or both of them are subsidiaries of the same parent enterprise.'

[75] See RTC Art 181 which sets out the *de minimis* rule. For guidance on the EU approach to the *de minimis* exception to Art 101(1) of the TFEU, see European Commission, 'Commission Notice on agreements of minor importance which do not appreciably restrict competition under Article 81(1) of the Treaty establishing the European Community (de minimis) (Text with EEA relevance)' OJ C368, 22.12.2001, pp 13–15, as available at <http://eur-lex.europa.eu/LexUriServ/LexUriServ.do?uri=OJ:C:2001:368:0013:0015:EN:PDF> (23 Jun 2013). This Notice is being re-drafted as a result of the decision in Case C-226/11 *Expedia Inc. v Autorité de la concurrence and Others* [not yet published], as available at <http://curia.europa.eu/juris/liste.jsf?language=en&jur=C,T,F&num=226/11&td=ALL> (15 Nov 2013).

[76] RTC Art 180(3). [77] RTC Art 183(1). See also Art 182. [78] RTC Art 183(2).

[79] The ECJ uses similar phrasing in Case 27/76 *United Brands Company and United Brands Continentaal BV v Commission* [1978] ECR 207, at p 277 [65], when it states that '[t]he dominant position referred to in this article [TFEU Art 102] relates to a position of economic strength enjoyed by an undertaking which enables it to prevent effective competition being maintained on the relevant market by giving it the power to behave to an appreciable extent independently of its competitors, customers and ultimately of its consumers.' See also Case 85/76 *Hoffmann-La Roche & Co. AG v Commission* [1979] ECR 461, at p 520 [38].

Being in a dominant position, however, is not prohibited under the RTC. Only abuse of such a position is prohibited. Article 179(1) describes the kinds of activities that would constitute abuse of a dominant position by preventing, restricting, or distorting competition in the market. The non-exhaustive list includes the following activities which must have the effect of frustrating the benefits expected from the CSME: restricting the entry of enterprises into the market; preventing or deterring enterprises from engaging in competition; eliminating or removing any enterprise from the market; directly or indirectly imposing unfair prices or other restrictive practices; limiting the production of goods or services to the prejudice of consumers; making the conclusion of an agreement subject to supplementary obligations unconnected with the agreement; and engaging in any business conduct that results in the exploitation of customers or suppliers. The latter is a catch-all provision which ties competition law to consumer protection.

It should be noted that the focus in Articles 178–179 is not expressly upon *trade between CARICOM member states*. This is to be contrasted with Article 102 of the TFEU which makes a determination of abuse of a dominant position conditional upon affecting trade between member states.[80] The lack of such express wording in the RTC could give CARICOM's competition law even greater scope than that of the EU, since it would also catch an abuse of a dominant position that does not affect trade between states.

Article 179(2) sets out the factors to take into consideration when determining whether an enterprise has abused its dominant position. These factors include:

(a) the relevant market defined in terms of the product and the geographic context;
(b) the concentration level before and after the relevant activity of the enterprise measured in terms of annual sales volume, the value of assets and the value of the transaction;
(c) the level of competition among the participants in terms of number of competitors, production capacity and product demand;
(d) the barriers to entry of competitors; and
(e) the history of competition and rivalry between participants in the sector of activity.

Satisfaction of these requirements will be crucial to proving abuse of a dominant position and may require the accumulation of significant economic and statistical data about the relevant market conditions.

Determination of the relevant market is a necessary first step since it provides the framework within which to assess the anti-competitive conduct. In the words of the European Commission:

> Market definition is a tool to identify and define the boundaries of competition between firms. It serves to establish the framework within which competition policy is applied by the Commission. The main purpose of market definition is to identify in a systematic way the competitive constraints that the undertakings involved face. The objective of defining

[80] Note, however, that the jurisprudence of the ECJ has interpreted 'trade between states' very broadly by looking at the effect of anti-competitive conduct. See eg Case 61/80 *Coöperatieve Stremsel- en Kleurselfabriek v Commission* [1981] ECR 851.

a market in both its product and geographic dimension is to identify those actual competitors of the undertakings involved that are capable of constraining those undertakings' behaviour and preventing them from behaving independently of effective competition pressure. It is from this perspective that the market definition makes it possible *inter alia* to calculate market shares that would convey meaningful information regarding market power for the purposes of assessing dominance or for the purposes of applying Article 85 [now TFEU Article 101].[81]

Defining the relevant market requires assessment of demand substitution (whether alternative products will be viewed as substitutes by the consumer), supply substitution (the ability of suppliers to switch production to supply the desired products in the short term, without incurring significant costs and risks), and potential competition.[82]

The very wide-ranging factors and evidence that may need to be assessed by a court are revealed in the seminal judgment of the ECJ in the *Chiquita Bananas Case*.[83] This case involved an appeal against a decision by the European Commission that a global banana producer, the United Brands Company (UBC), abused its dominant position. It is worth examining briefly here because of its multi-stage, comprehensive analysis of the questions related to abuse of a dominant position.

In its analysis the Court was required to determine the relevant market.[84] In doing so it first had to assess whether the *product market* for bananas in the EU was the broader fresh fruit market, or a narrower market consisting solely of bananas. In coming to the conclusion that the banana market was sufficiently distinct from the other fresh fruit markets so as to fall under the latter category, the Court examined factors including: the small fluctuation in purchasing patterns as a result of availability of other seasonal fruits; the specific qualities of bananas which allow them to satisfy the constant needs of an important section of the population, including the very young, the old, and the sick; the year-long availability of bananas; and the fact that banana production exceeds demand.[85] In assessing the *geographic scope* of the relevant market the Court agreed with the Commission's decision to exclude the territorial markets of France, the UK, and Italy, since they had distinguishing features, such as preferential arrangements or national systems of quota restrictions, and to instead focus on six other European states which could be considered to form a sufficiently homogeneous area.[86]

81 European Commission, 'Commission Notice on the definition of relevant market for the purposes of Community competition law' [1997] OJ C372/5, 9.12.1997, at p 5 [2], as available at <http://eur-lex.europa.eu/LexUriServ/LexUriServ.do?uri=OJ:C:1997:372:0005:0013:EN:PDF> (24 Jun 2013).

82 See generally, 'Commission Notice' (n 81).

83 Case 27/76 *United Brands Company and United Brands Continentaal BV v Commission* [1978] ECR 207 [hereafter 'Case 27/76 *United Brands Company*'].

84 For a detailed explanation by the Commission of how it determines the relevant product and geographical markets see European Commission, 'Commission Notice on the definition of relevant market for the purposes of Community competition law' [1997] OJ C372/5, 9.12.1997, as available at <http://eur-lex.europa.eu/LexUriServ/LexUriServ.do?uri=OJ:C:1997:372:0005:0013:EN:PDF> (24 Jun 2013).

85 Case 27/76 *United Brands Company* (n 83) at pp 270–3 [12]–[35].

86 Case 27/76 *United Brands Company* (n 83) pp 274–6 [44]–[57].

In determining whether United Brands occupied a *dominant position* in this market, the Court assessed a number of factors related to the *structure of UBC*, including its high degree of vertical integration which included substantial control of the banana production stage, packaging, and transportation (it owned railways and a shipping fleet).[87] UBC also possessed considerable technical knowledge as a result of continual research and imposed strict quality control standards which gave it absolute control over wholesale marketing.[88] In addition, UBC had carefully managed its product under the Chiquita label, including through large-scale repeated advertising and promotion campaigns, so as to ensure its continued status as a premier brand name on the relevant market.[89] In assessing the *competition* faced by UBC in the relevant market, the Court noted that UBC's market share was between 40 and 45 per cent, which is several times greater than the market share of its competitors.[90] Moreover, although UBC had not eliminated all opportunity for competition, it had held off its existing competitors.[91] After adding to all of these factors the practical barriers to entry of competitors, the Court concluded that UBC occupied a dominant position in the relevant market.[92]

The Court also found that UBC had *abused* its dominant position through a number of actions. UBC had prohibited the resale of green bananas by ripeners and thereby effectively frustrated cross-border trade in bananas and partitioned national markets.[93] It had punished distributors who promoted rival brands by discontinuing supply and thereby seriously interfered with their independence and continued viability.[94] It had imposed dissimilar conditions (prices) to equivalent transactions and thereby placed certain distributors/ripeners at a competitive disadvantage.[95] Interestingly, the Court disagreed with the conclusion of the Commission that UBC had directly or indirectly imposed unfair purchase or selling prices, and instead held that this allegation had not been proved.[96] The Court suggested that in order to make out such a case one would have to prove that an undertaking charged 'a price which is excessive because it has no reasonable relation to the economic value of the product supplied'.[97] Excessive pricing

[87] Case 27/76 *United Brands Company* (n 83) pp 277–9 [65]–[81].

[88] Case 27/76 *United Brands Company* (n 83) pp 279–80 [82]–[86].

[89] Case 27/76 *United Brands Company* (n 83) pp 280–1 [87]–[96].

[90] Case 27/76 *United Brands Company* (n 83) p 282 [108].

[91] Case 27/76 *United Brands Company* (n 83) pp 283–4 [113]–[120].

[92] Case 27/76 *United Brands Company* (n 83) pp 284–5 [121]–[129].

[93] Case 27/76 *United Brands Company* (n 83) p 289 [157]–[159].

[94] Case 27/76 *United Brands Company* (n 83) pp 292–3 [182]–[194]. For another example of an attempt to eliminate competition on the relevant market see Joined Cases 6 and 7/73 *Istituto Chemioterapico Italiano S.p.A. and Commercial Solvents Corporation v Commission* [1974] ECR 223, at p 251 [25]. The ECJ held that the Commercial Solvents Corporation (CSC) abused its dominant position in a market for raw materials by refusing to supply a customer with those materials. CSC justified its actions on the basis of wishing to reserve to itself the materials in order to manufacture the same derivatives as manufactured by the customer. The Court held that CSC's conduct was unlawful because it risked eliminating all competition from the customer.

[95] Case 27/76 *United Brands Company* (n 83) at pp 298–9 [227]–[234].

[96] Case 27/76 *United Brands Company* (n 83) p 303 [267].

[97] Case 27/76 *United Brands Company* (n 83) p 301 [250].

could be 'determined objectively if it were possible for it to be calculated by making a comparison between the selling price of the product in question and its cost of production, which would disclose the amount of the profit margin'.[98] The Commission had not undertaken such a comparison nor had it effectively challenged the submissions of UBC.[99]

In sum, and as illustrated by the *Chiquita Banana Case*, proof of abuse of a dominant position will require proof of dominance of, and abuse in, the relevant market. Such proof will require the marshalling of considerable evidence about the product market, the geographic market, the structure of the enterprise, the competition in the relevant market, and specific practices by which the dominant enterprise has abused its position. These practices include, but are not restricted solely to, those set out in Article 179(2) of the RTC.

Article 179(3) of the RTC sets out three exceptions to subsection (1), where abuse will not arise. Firstly, an enterprise will not be deemed to be abusing its dominant position if its behaviour is directed exclusively to increasing efficiency in the production, provision, or distribution of goods or services, or to promoting technical or economic progress, and consumers are allowed a fair share of the benefit.[100] Secondly, activity of an enterprise is excluded if it is reasonably enforcing or seeking to enforce a right related to copyright, patent, registered trade mark or design. Finally, the enterprise will be exempted if the effect or likely effect of its behaviour on the market is the result of superior competitive performance. The first and last exceptions will likely require considerable factual evidence on the part of the enterprise.[101]

11.1.4 Anti-competitive conduct by states and public undertakings

Member states also have obligations under competition rules, as we have seen in Articles 170, 174(6), and 177, described earlier. These obligations, if unfulfilled, can give rise to state liability for breaching competition law. Thus, for example, if a member state has not enacted the appropriate legislation 'to ensure consistency and compliance with the rules of competition and provide penalties for anti-competitive business conduct', as required under Article 170(1)(b)(i), another member state, CARICOM itself, or a person (under the 'correlative rights' doctrine) could bring a suit against that member state before the CCJ.[102] More strikingly,

[98] Case 27/76 *United Brands Company* (n 83) p 301 [251]. The Court summarizes the test at para [252] as follows: 'The questions therefore to be determined are whether the difference between the costs actually incurred and the price actually charged is excessive, and, if the answer to this question is in the affirmative, whether a price has been imposed which is either unfair in itself or when compared to competing products.'

[99] Case 27/76 *United Brands Company* (n 83) pp 301–3 [251]–[267].

[100] RTC Art 179(3)(a).

[101] Note the differences between RTC Arts 179(3)(a) and 177(4)(a). Technically, both sets of exceptions could be applied to the abuse of a dominant position. I thank Professor Kaczorowska-Ireland for drawing this to my attention.

[102] See RTC Arts 211 and 222 for these categories of cases, over which the Caribbean Court of Justice may take original jurisdiction. The correlative rights doctrine was established in para [32] of

the obligations under Article 177(1) and (3), which prohibit anti-competitive conduct and require the voiding of all anti-competitive agreements and decisions, fall squarely upon *member states*. This has two implications. Firstly, states must ensure that their legal systems prohibit and punish anti-competitive conduct by enterprises. Secondly, states themselves cannot engage in anti-competitive conduct with enterprises and be consistent with their obligation under Article 177(1)(c) to prohibit 'any other like conduct by enterprises whose object or effect is to frustrate the benefits expected from the establishment of the CSME'. An anti-competitive arrangement between a state and an enterprise could be squarely caught under that provision, and perhaps Article 177(1)(b) dealing with abuses of a dominant position.

From a more general perspective, a member state would be in breach of its obligations under the general undertaking provision, Article 9 of the RTC, if it either actively engaged in anti-competitive conduct or if it passively allowed such conduct to continue in its jurisdiction. For convenience, Article 9 states:

Member States shall take all appropriate measures, whether general or particular, to ensure the carrying out of obligations arising out of this Treaty or resulting from decisions taken by the Organs and Bodies of the Community. They shall facilitate the achievement of the objectives of the Community. They shall abstain from any measures which could jeopardise the attainment of the objectives of this Treaty.

Article 9 requires member states to *ensure* the carrying out of their obligations related to the RTC, and this obligation applies to state action and inaction.

Such an interpretation of Article 9 is supported by similar EU jurisprudence. As noted by Weatherill in the context of EU competition law, '[w]here the state legislates to permit or encourage a breach of the competition rules, then not only do the parties to the agreement act in breach of the Treaty, but also the State has violated its duty to co-operate in the pursuit of the objectives of the EU.'[103] This applies equally to state action and inaction, such as an approval, or tolerance, of conduct by a national authority. For example, in Case 66/86 *Ahmed Saeed Flugreisen and Silver Line Reisebüro GmbH v Zentrale zur Bekämpfung unlauteren Wettbewerbs eV*, the ECJ clearly stated that EU law prohibits state action which could render competition law ineffective.[104] In the portion of its judgment dealing with state approval of anti-competitive tariff agreements between airlines the Court noted:

48. ... [A]s the Court has consistently held, while it is true that the competition rules set out in Articles 85 and 86 [now TFEU Articles 101 and 102] concern the conduct of undertakings and not measures of the authorities in the Member States, Article 5 [now Article 4(3) of the TEU (the general undertaking provision)] of the Treaty nevertheless imposes a duty on those authorities not to adopt or maintain in force any measure which could deprive those competition rules of their effectiveness. That would be the case, in particular, if a Member State were to require or favour the adoption of agreements, decisions or concerted

the case of *Trinidad Cement Ltd and TCL Guyana Inc v Guyana*, Judgment [2009] CCJ 1 (OJ), (2009) 74 WIR 302, 15 January 2009. See further Chapter 14, on Regional Courts.

[103] Weatherill, *Cases & Materials on EU Law* (n 22) 497.

[104] [1989] ECR 803.

practices contrary to Article 85 or reinforce their effects (see, most recently, the judgment of 1 October 1987 in Case 311/85 *Vereniging van Vlaamse Reisbureaus* v *Sociaale Dienst van de plaatselijke en gewestelijke Overheidsdiensten* [1987] ECR 3801).

49 It must be concluded as a result that the approval by the aeronautical authorities of tariff agreements contrary to Article 85(1) is not compatible with Community law and in particular with Article 5 of the Treaty. It also follows that the aeronautical authorities must refrain from taking any measure which might be construed as encouraging airlines to conclude tariff agreements contrary to the Treaty.[105]

This position applies to all levels of the state. In Joined Cases C-140/94, C-141/94, and C-142/94 *DIP SpA v Comune di Bassano del Grappa, LIDL Italia Srl v Comune di Chioggia and Lingral Srl v Comune di Chiogga*, for example, the ECJ examined the licensing practices of Italian municipal committees for compatibility with competition rules.[106] The Court held that such state action was subject to the rules of Article 4(3) of the TEU and Article 101 of the TFEU:

15 The Court has held that Articles 5 and 85 [now TEU Art 4(3) and TFEU Art 101] are infringed where a Member State requires or favours the adoption of agreements, decisions or concerted practices contrary to Article 85 [TFEU Art 101] or reinforces their effects, or where it deprives its own rules of the character of legislation by delegating to private economic operators responsibility for taking decisions affecting the economic sphere (see the judgments in *Van Eycke*, paragraph 16, *Reiff*, paragraph 14 and *Delta Schiffahrts-und Speditionsgesellschaft*, paragraph 14).[107]

The Court also held that state action could give rise to a breach of Article 4(3) of the TEU and Article 102 of the TFEU, the provision dealing with abuse of a dominant position, if state laws supported that dominant position:

24 Articles 3(g), 5 [now Article 4(3) TEU] and 86 [now Article 102 TFEU] of the Treaty could apply to rules such as those contained in the Italian Law only if it were proved that that law creates a position of economic strength for an undertaking which enables it to prevent effective competition being maintained on the relevant market by affording it the power to behave to an appreciable extent independently of its competitors, its customers and, ultimately, the consumers (judgment in Case 85/76 *Hoffmann-La Roche v Commission* [1979] ECR 461, paragraph 38).[108]

As a result, if this analysis is applied to the CARICOM system member states could be held liable for breaching Articles 177 and 179 of the RTC, in conjunction with Article 9, if they engage in or tolerate anti-competitive conduct.

A second way in which CARICOM member states could violate competition law is through activities of public undertakings. Article 94(10) of the RTC defines 'public undertakings' for the purposes of that article as meaning 'central, regional, or local government authorities, public enterprises and any other organisation

[105] *Ahmed Saeed Flugreisen* (n 106) at pp 851–2 [48]–[49]. [106] [1995] ECR I-3257.

[107] *DIP SpA v Comune di Bassano* (n 107) at p I-3294 [15] [citing: Case 267/86 *Van Eycke v Aspa* [1988] ECR 4769; Case C-185/91 *Reiff* [1993] ECR 1-5801; and Case C-l53/93 *Germany v Delta Schiffahrts-und Speditionsgesellschaft* [1994] ECR 1-2517].

[108] *DIP SpA v Comune di Bassano* p I-3296 [24].

by means of which a Member State by law or in practice controls or appreciably influences imports from, or exports to any other part of the Community'. Member states have a number of obligations in relation to public undertakings under Article 94. They must ensure that public undertakings do not engage in measures which would afford protection to domestic production or practices that would constitute trade discrimination on grounds of territorial origin, as otherwise prohibited in the treaty.[109] Article 94(3) allows aggrieved member states to challenge such conduct by a public undertaking, or *anti-competitive conduct*, through consultations in the following terms:

> 3. Where a public undertaking has introduced a measure or practice which:
>   (a) is inconsistent with paragraph 1; or
>   (b) in law or in effect, results in limiting access to any market, distorts competition or fair trade, or otherwise nullifies or impairs benefits expected from the establishment of the CSME,
>
> then, in such a case, the aggrieved Member State may request consultations with the offending Member State and promptly notify COTED of the request.[110]

The remaining subsections of Article 94 set out the procedures for consultations and the subsequent referral of the matter to COTED, COTED's investigative process, its remedies, and the requirement for non-repetition.[111] Remedies available to COTED include the ability to request the offending member state to withdraw the measure or practice, or to authorize other member states to suspend their RTC obligations in relation to the offending member state. Article 94(2) also subjects Government assistance to economic development under Article 93, through public undertakings, to the same rules applicable to other enterprises.[112]

This ability to challenge anti-competitive conduct by a public undertaking, albeit textually limited under the RTC to procedures through COTED, may give rise to a broader right of challenge by member states, organs of CARICOM, and individuals (through the correlative rights doctrine), if the Caribbean Court of Justice assumes an original jurisdiction over such matters complementary to that of COTED. This practice has evolved in the EU in relation to Article 106 TFEU, which although differently worded, also subjects public undertakings to

[109] RTC Art 94(1).

[110] Note that RTC Art 94 might be subject to exceptions under Art 226(1)(c), which provides that 'Nothing in this Chapter [Treaty] shall be construed as preventing the adoption or enforcement by any Member State of measures: ... (c) necessary to secure compliance with laws or regulations relating to ... the operation of monopolies by means of state enterprises or enterprises given exclusive or special privileges.'

[111] RTC Art 94(4)–(9).

[112] The cross-reference in RTC Art 94(2) is incorrect. Instead of referring to 'Article 92' it should refer to Art 93, the provision on 'Government assistance to economic development'. See Protocol Amending the Treaty Establishing The Caribbean Community (Protocol IV: Trade Policy) (adopted 4–7 Jul 1999, not yet in force), Art XIX, which in setting out the rules on public undertakings included a cross-reference in Art 28(2) to Art XVIII of the Protocol, the latter setting out the rules on Government assistance to economic development.

competition law.[113] For example, in Case 66/86 *Ahmed Saeed Flugreisen and Silver Line Reisebüro GmbH v Zentrale zur Bekämpfung unlauteren Wettbewerbs eV* the Court held that what is now Article 106 of the TFEU prohibits member states from engaging in anti-competitive measures:

50 In the specific case of tariffs for scheduled flights that interpretation of the Treaty is borne out by Article 90(1) [now Article 106 TFEU] of the Treaty, which provides that in the case of undertakings to which Member States grant special or exclusive rights—such as rights to operate on an air route alone or with one or two other undertakings—Member States must not enact or maintain in force any measure contrary to the competition rules laid down in Articles 85 and 86 [Articles 101–102 of the TFEU].[114]

In sum, it is possible for several provisions of the RTC to regulate state conduct with the rules of competition law set out in Chapter 8. Member states cannot actively engage in anti-competitive measures, either through state organs or public undertakings, or passively support such measures through inaction by the relevant authorities.

11.1.5 Effectiveness of CARICOM competition law

Following the entry into force of the RTC on 1 January 2006, most member states have established the required national competition authorities and the CARICOM Competition Commission has been formally established, has created rules of procedure, and is covered by privileges and immunities treaties.[115] The Commission has been held by the Court to have legal personality.[116] However few member

[113] Art 106(1)–(2) of the TFEU provide:

1. In the case of public undertakings and undertakings to which Member States grant special or exclusive rights, Member States shall neither enact nor maintain in force any measure contrary to the rules contained in the Treaties, in particular to those rules provided for in Article 18 and Articles 101 to 109.
2. Undertakings entrusted with the operation of services of general economic interest or having the character of a revenue-producing monopoly shall be subject to the rules contained in the Treaties, in particular to the rules on competition, in so far as the application of such rules does not obstruct the performance, in law or in fact, of the particular tasks assigned to them. The development of trade must not be affected to such an extent as would be contrary to the interests of the Union.

Note that Art 31(2)(a) of the RTC similarly requires government monopolies to be 'subject to the agreed rules of competition established for Community economic enterprises'.

[114] [1989] ECR 803, at p 852 [50].

[115] CARICOM Secretariat, *Summary Draft Report* 26. See the section on 'Privileges and Immunities' in Chapter 6 for a brief description of the Commission's privileges and immunities framework.

[116] In *Trinidad Cement Ltd v Competition Commission*, Judgment [2012] CCJ 4 (OJ), 12 November 2012, at [11], the CCJ discussed the personality and powers accorded to the Commission:

The Commission's concession [recognizing the full juridical personality of the Commission] was rightly made. Article 174 of the Revised Treaty details quite extensive powers of the Commission to suppress anticompetitive business conduct having cross-border effects within the CSME, and Articles 175(11) and 180(3) allow the Commission in its own name and right to commence legal proceedings before this Court in furtherance of those functions and powers. Article 175(12) permits a party aggrieved by certain determinations of the Commission to apply to this Court for review of those determinations. The natural corollary is that the review proceedings are to be instituted against the Commission.

states have gone on to establish a national competition commission.[117] As a result the CARICOM Secretariat has highlighted the challenges in implementing the legal framework related to the CARICOM Competition Commission, noting that most member states not yet having put in place satisfactory domestic legislation. This has led the Secretariat to summarize that there is 'much to be done to meet the requirements of the provisions of Chapter Eight of the Revised Treaty'.[118]

11.2 CARICOM Consumer Protection

Chapter 8, dealing primarily with competition policy, integrates consumer protection into its core objectives. Article 169(2)(c) lists as a mandatory objective 'the promotion of consumer welfare and protection of consumer interests'. Several other provisions highlight the need to provide information to consumers and to protect consumer welfare.[119] The Competition Commission itself is tasked with promoting consumer welfare and protecting consumer interests. As a result consumer protection becomes crucial both for competition law and as an independent objective under the RTC.

Part Two of Chapter 8 provides obligations for both member states and the Commission in relation to consumer protection. For the purposes of Part Two the term 'consumer' is defined in Article 184(2) as follows:

> 'consumer' means any person:
> (a) to whom goods or services are supplied or intended to be supplied in the course of business carried on by a supplier or potential supplier; and
> (b) who does not receive the goods or services in the course of a business carried on by him.

Articles 184–185 impose duties on member states to promote consumer interests and to enact legislation for such purposes. The most general obligation on member states, specified in Article 184(1)(a), is to ensure that goods and services ensure the protection of the life, health, and safety of consumers. Consequential obligations include ensuring that regulations, standards, codes, and licensing requirements are created and applied.[120] The CARICOM Regional Organization for Standards and Quality (CROSQ) has an important role to play here.[121] Member states also are

> Accordingly, the Revised Treaty itself contemplates suits being brought by and against the Commission before this Court. Further, the Agreement between Suriname and the Community Establishing the Seat of the Commission states at Article II that the Commission 'shall have full juridical personality', and in particular, full capacity to institute legal proceedings. A similar provision is to be found in the Protocol on the Privileges and Immunities of the Competition Commission. [Citations omitted.]

117 CARICOM Secretariat, *Summary Draft Report* 26.

118 See also CARICOM Secretariat, *Summary Draft Report* 26 and at pp 9–10.

119 See eg RTC Arts 170(1)(a)(ii) and (1)(b)(ii), 173(2)(f).

120 RTC Art 184(1)(b)–(c).

121 See the Agreement Establishing the CARICOM Regional Organisation for Standards and Quality (CROSQ) (adopted 4 Feb 2002, provisionally applied since 5 Feb 2002, not yet in force)

obligated to: encourage ethical conduct in producers and distributors, promote effective competition, promote and ensure adequate information for consumers and suppliers, and encourage the development of independent consumer organizations.[122] Importantly, member states are further required to provide adequate redress for consumers, including in situations of discrimination against producers, suppliers, and service providers of CARICOM products and services.[123] The latter obligation integrally ties the overall operation of the CSME to consumer interests.

In terms of harmonized legislation, member states are required to enact laws to provide for, amongst other things: the fundamental terms and implied obligations of contracts; the prohibition of unconscionable contractual terms, unfair trading practices, and the production and supply of harmful and defective goods; service compliance with applicable laws; labelling requirements; regulation of distribution and consumption of hazardous and other goods; the regulation and labelling of potentially environmentally damaging goods or materials; the liability of producers and suppliers of defective goods; and sanctions for violators of consumer safety standards.[124]

The Commission has a parallel role in promoting and keeping under review these obligations and legislative requirements for member states. For example, it is required to: promote the adoption of fair contract terms; ensure the elimination of unfair trading practices; promote product safety standards and consumer education; keep under review commercial activities related to the supply of goods or services; provide consumer education and advice; engage in consumer research and data collection (including regarding legislative enactments); and promote the establishment and enforcement of quality standards and consumer protection legislation.[125] The Commission is also required to make recommendations to COTED for the enactment of legislation to enforce consumer rights, to collaborate with other CARICOM organs to promote consumer education and welfare, and to draw to the attention of COTED any business conduct adversely affecting consumer welfare.[126]

Unfortunately implementation of these requirements has not yet reached a satisfactory level. Although CROSQ is making an impact, the CARICOM Secretariat has highlighted as a concern the lack of domestic legislative implementation of the measures required under Articles 184–186.[127]

2324 UNTS 413, and Protocol on the Provisional Application of the Agreement Establishing the CARICOM Regional Organisation for Standards and Quality (CROSQ) (adopted and entered into force 5 Feb 2002) 2326 UNTS 359.

[122] RTC Art 184(1)(d)–(g) and (i). [123] RTC Art 184(1)(h) and (j).

[124] Summary of RTC Art 185. [125] Summary of RTC Art 186(1)(a)–(k).

[126] See RTC Art 186(1)(l) and (2).

[127] CARICOM Secretariat, *Summary Draft Report* 10 and 26.

12

Sectoral Development, Common Supportive Measures, and Development Policies

The present chapter completes the description of the substantive legal regimes of CARICOM and the OECS. It discusses the provisions which set out broad policy and development frameworks for the two integration movements. Most of these provisions do not establish binding obligations which would be capable of enforcement, at least not in a direct manner. However they are important because they put flesh on the bones of the institutional structures of CARICOM and the OECS, revealing the potential of both regional organizations to expand beyond trade structures and customs unions.

12.1 CARICOM Policies for Sectoral Development

Chapter 4 of the RTC sets out the broad policies for development of a number of sectors of the economies of member states and is complemented by the transport policy set out in Chapter 6.[1]

12.1.1 Industrial policy

Article 51 of the RTC sets out the broad objectives of the Community industrial policy. These objectives include cross-border cooperation and participation in industrial activities, whether through shared resources (Article 51(2)(a)), linkages among economic sectors (Article 51(2)(b)), or through the creation of regional economic enterprises (Article 51(2)(c)). The Community's role, under Article 52(1), is to promote aspects of the industrial policy, with COTED being designated

[1] Note that RTC Art 62 provides that '[t]he provisions of this Chapter [4] are without prejudice to obligations of the Member States under existing international agreements'. It will be interesting to see whether this article will be construed literally, as applying to all of the articles in Chapter 4 (Arts 51–77). The earlier draft of Art 62 RTC, is found in Art XI of Protocol Amending the Treaty Establishing The Caribbean Community (Protocol V: Agricultural Policy) (adopted 13 June 1998, not yet in force) [hereafter 'Protocol V']. The latter article sought to insert a new Art 49c into the original Treaty, and used the phrasing 'the provisions of this Protocol', not 'Chapter'. Since Protocol V primarily dealt with agriculture, fisheries, and forestry, the effect of the provision would have been more limited than Art 62 RTC.

particular responsibilities under Article 52(7). Under Article 53 the Community is required to 'adopt appropriate policy measures to encourage the development of competitive micro and small economic enterprises in the Member States'. These measures are to include developmental and technical assistance. Under Article 54 both COTED and member states assume obligations in relation to the services sector. The final provision in Part One of Chapter 4, Article 55, deals with sustainable tourism development. This reaffirms the central importance of that sector on the overall economic policy of the region.

Despite the several obligations imposed upon the Community and member states by the RTC, it is likely that the greatest role in CARICOM industrial development will be played by private enterprises. In this way it may be observed that the measures highlighted in Part I of Chapter 4 primarily serve to facilitate the role of the private sector. Such a role has already been foreshadowed by the early pronouncement of the Caribbean Court of Justice that CARICOM is to be 'private sector driven'.[2]

12.1.2 Agricultural policy

The goals of the Community's agricultural policy are ambitious, aiming to modernize and sustainably exploit the natural resources of the region. Article 56(1)(a) highlights the new perspective brought by the RTC when it describes the goal of the policy as being the 'fundamental transformation of the agricultural sector towards market-oriented, internationally competitive and environmentally sound production of agricultural products'. Article 56(1)(b) makes food security one of the goals of the agricultural policy. The importance of this goal must be emphasized given the dependence of most of the CARICOM member states upon food imports. Article 56(1)(f) highlights the range of natural resources covered by the policy. It requires the efficient management and sustainable exploitation of natural resources including the resources of the forests and exclusive economic zones of member states.

In terms of implementation of the agricultural policy, Article 57 sets out a number of responsibilities for both the Community and member states. Specific attention is paid to supporting small scale farmers and fishers, as seen in Article 57(1)(b), and the need to make agriculture more viable and attractive to persons in the Community, including the youth.[3] Importantly, given the need to transform the entire agricultural sector, Article 57(4) requires the Community, as a matter of priority, and in collaboration with other agencies and organizations, to promote and adopt measures for 'the development of infrastructure, such as port facilities, drainage, irrigation, access roads, post-harvest handling and marketing facilities'. Infrastructural development will be crucial to modernizing agriculture across the region.

[2] See *Trinidad Cement Ltd and TCL Guyana Inc v Guyana*, Judgment [2009] CCJ 1 (OJ), (2009) 74 WIR 302, 15 January 2009 [13].

[3] See RTC Art 57(1)(b), (f), (i), (j), (l), (2)(d), and (3)(b).

Article 59 supplements these requirements with others related to the marketing of agricultural products. It facilitates both regional and international marketing, and does so in a nuanced way. Marketing is seen as instrumental to both selling and creating the conditions for sale of goods. Article 59(1), for example, refers to the way in which marketing systems must 'respond to, influence and generate market demand for agricultural products of the Member States.' Article 59(3) requires the Community to adopt measures including those designed to promote: regional and national market information systems, niche marketing, regional standards and specifications, enhanced food productivity and quality, insurance coverage for primary agricultural products, and efficient distribution services for both intra- and extra-regional marketing. Article 59(4) reminds member states of their obligations in relation to the 'arrangements for marketing oils and fats set out in Schedule III'.

In terms of natural resource management, Article 58 requires the Community to adopt effective measures for the management of soil, air and all water resources, the exclusive economic zone, and other maritime areas. It also mandates the conservation of biological diversity and sustainable use of biological resources of member states. It is notable, however, that the RTC does not go further in this area. It does not expressly invoke other relevant principles of international environmental law, such as the ecosystem-based approach to environmental management, and a more general application of the principal of sustainable use. Of course such principles could be brought into play through Article 58(2), which specifically highlights the 'obligations of Member States under existing international agreements', and Article 65, which speaks to the precautionary principle.[4] Nevertheless stronger and more detailed references to international environmental standards and principles would have been desirable.[5]

In terms of management of specific natural resources, Articles 60–61 of the RTC describe obligations related to fisheries and forestry. Article 60(1) mandates the Community, 'in collaboration with competent national, regional and international agencies and organisations, [to] promote the development, management and conservation of the fisheries resources in and among the Member States on a sustainable basis'.[6] This regional and international focus is crucial in the area of fisheries,

[4] RTC Art 65(2) refers to several principles of environmental law, including use of best available scientific evidence (cf Art 65(2)(a)), the precautionary principle, and 'those principles relating to preventive action, rectification of environmental damage at source and the principle that the polluter pays' (Art 65(2)(e)).

[5] Note that in particular sectors of natural resource management these principles may be applied by regional organizations closely affiliated with CARICOM. Thus, in the area of fisheries, the Caribbean Regional Fisheries Mechanism (CRFM) is guided by these and other environmental principles. See eg Art 5 of the Agreement Establishing the Caribbean Regional Fisheries Mechanism (adopted 4 February 2002, in force 4 July 2003) 2242 UNTS 271. See also the Agreement Establishing the Caribbean Community Common Fisheries Policy [Draft] (adopted by the CRFM Ministerial Council on 20 May 2011, not yet in force) [available from CRFM Secretariat or <http://www.caricom-fisheries.com/LinkClick.aspx?fileticket=FVQaSQ%2BDh68%3D&tabid=242>] and the OECS Secretariat, 'Castries Declaration on Illegal, Unreported and Unregulated Fishing', 2nd Special Meeting of the CRFM Ministerial Council, Castries, St Lucia (28 July 2010).

[6] 'Fisheries resources' is defined in RTC Art 60(5) as 'includ[ing] all the fishable resources, natural and cultured, in the inland and internal waters, territorial seas and the exclusive economic zones of the Member States'.

since many of the key fisheries are themselves transboundary, highly migratory, or straddling stocks and are likewise influenced by international environmental factors. For such reasons Article 60(3) specifically highlights the needs to manage straddling and highly migratory fish stocks, to engage in surveillance of exclusive economic zones, to safeguard the marine environment, and to delimit maritime boundaries. The latter obligation remains important since for many CARICOM member states maritime boundaries are not fully delimited. Without such boundaries, it is especially hard to manage fisheries and the marine environment, since the management activities of one state may infringe rights of neighbouring states. Article 60(2) similarly focuses on establishing appropriate mechanisms to develop, manage, and conserve fisheries in line with the international legal obligations of member states, including by mobilizing regional representation at international fora, strengthening research and human resource capacities, developing national institutional capacities, and establishing protected aquatic habitats and associated terrestrial areas. Interestingly, perhaps in recognition of the overwhelming need for regional and international cooperation in the area of marine resources, and the insufficiency of individual state action, Article 60(4) mandates COFCOR to assume responsibility for promoting a regime for the 'effective management, conservation and utilisation of the living resources of the exclusive economic zones of the Member States'.

Article 61 requires the Community to 'in collaboration with competent national, regional and international agencies and organisations, promote the development, management and conservation of the forest resources in the member states on a sustainable basis'. The term 'forest resources' is defined broadly in Article 61(5) as including almost all potential resources associated with the forest, namely, 'those natural assets of forest lands, including timber and other forest products, biological diversity, recreation, fish and wildlife habitat, wilderness, flora and fauna, air, water and soil'. This broad definition is sensible since forest resources are crucial to such diverse sectors of the economy as lumber production, eco-tourism, and the generation of biological patents. As with fisheries, the forestry regime under the RTC focuses upon building and developing capacity, at the national and regional level, in areas such as research and human resources. Article 61 also seeks to facilitate the sustainable commercialization of forestry products, domestic and foreign investment in forestry, and the undertaking of national forest inventories.

12.1.3 Transport policy

An entire chapter of the RTC, Chapter 6, is dedicated to transport policy. This is not surprising given the broad geographical context of the Caribbean Community—spanning a region including Central America, the many islands of the Commonwealth Caribbean, and two territories on the South American mainland. This geographical context imposes significant challenges to the movement of the region's peoples, goods, and services. For this reason the Mills Report specifically identified transportation as indispensable for the achievement of integration. The Report notes that '[t]he experience of the past seventeen years...provides adequate support for the view that the establishment and effective functioning of adequate, reliable and regular sea and air transportation systems, dedicated to, and operated entirely in the interests of the people of the Caribbean Community, are among the indispensable requirements for the achievement of integration.'[7] It is for such reasons that Article 134(1), in setting out the objectives of the Community Transport Policy, provides as an overarching goal 'the provision of adequate, safe and internationally competitive transport services *for the development and consolidation of the CSME*'.[8] In fulfilment of that goal the Community is required to pursue the objectives of the organization of efficient, reliable, affordable transport services throughout the Community, the development and expansion of air and maritime transport capabilities, the promotion of cooperative arrangements for the provision of transport services, the development of efficient internationally competitive ancillary transport services, the development of human resources for the transport sector, and the implementation of transportation safety standards.[9] In implementing this transportation policy, COTED is given the primary role in promoting, amongst other things, the coordination of national transport policies; the implementation of uniform regulations and procedures for the development of an efficient multi-modal transportation system; the development of the required institutional, legal, technical, financial, and administrative support for the transport sector; the establishment of measures to ensure protection of the environment and Caribbean Sea, acquisition and transfer of technology, and human resource development; investment in the transport sector; and in removing obstacles to the provision of transport services by CARICOM nationals.[10] COTED is to achieve these objectives by developing programmes, and member states are required to coordinate their actions in support.[11] Article 136 also requires COTED to promote cooperation in air and maritime search and rescue operations.

Member states are obligated to adopt uniform standards and recommended practices for transport services. They also must notify COTED regarding any deviations from such standards, and are entitled to have recourse to dispute settlement procedures in the RTC if adversely affected by a deviation.[12] Under Article 139 member states also have obligations in relation to aircraft accidents and incidents. Both member states and COTED are required to promote the development of, and cooperate in relation to, air transport services, including registration, licensing, and certification procedures.[13]

[7] Gladstone Mills et al, *Report on a Comprehensive Review of the Programmes, Institutions and Organisations of the Caribbean Community* (Georgetown, Guyana: Caribbean Community Secretariat, 1990) 69. From close to its inception air transportation issues were placed high on the agenda at different meetings of CARICOM. For excerpts from these meetings see Kenneth Hall, *Re-Inventing CARICOM: The Road to a New Integration* (Kingston, Jamaica: Ian Randle Publishers, 2003) 79–85.

[8] Emphasis added. [9] RTC Art 134(2). [10] Summary of RTC Art 135(1).

[11] RTC Art 135(2)–(3).

[12] RTC Art 137. Note that 'standard' is defined in Art 1 in relation to transport: '"standard" means any specification for physical characteristics, configuration, material, performance, personnel or procedure, the uniform application of which is regionally or generally recognised in the international community as necessary for the efficient delivery of transport services.'

[13] RTC Art 138.

In terms of maritime transport services, Article 140 requires member states to cooperate in the development of this area of services, including by enhancing flag and port state control activities; developing and providing expertise in the shipping industry for the growth of the shipping sector; protecting the marine environment from, and combatting the effects of, vessel source pollution; and taking any other action necessary for the sustainable development of the shipping sector.[14] The Community is obligated to cooperate with national, regional, and international organizations to enable the provision of efficient and affordable maritime transport, and COTED is required to promote cooperation among member states in implementing international agreements and standards.[15] Article 141 concludes the Chapter by mandating member states to cooperate in achieving international recognition for 'the Caribbean Sea as a Special Area requiring protection from the potentially harmful effects of the transit of nuclear and other hazardous wastes, dumping, pollution by oil or by any other substance carried by sea or wastes generated through the conduct of ship operations'. The ambitions of this article have at least partly been fulfilled since the entry into force of the RTC, with the Caribbean Sea now being recognized as a special area in the context of sustainable development.[16]

12.2 Common Supportive Measures and Development Policies

12.2.1 CARICOM—common supportive measures

Part Three of Chapter 4 of the RTC mandates the establishment of a range of common supportive measures by Community organs. These include common supportive measures related to: human resource development (Article 63), research and development (Article 64), environmental protection (Article 65), protection of intellectual property rights (Article 66), standards and technical regulations (Article 67), a Community investment policy (Article 68), harmonization of investment incentives (Article 69), macro-economic policies (Article 70), financial infrastructure (Article 71), double taxation agreements (Article 72), industrial

[14] Summary of RTC Art 140(1). See also the more specific obligations of member states in Art 140(5).

[15] RTC Art 140(2)–(3). See also the additional, specific obligations of COTED in Art 140(4).

[16] See eg the two resolutions of the United National General Assembly: 'Promoting an integrated management approach to the Caribbean Sea area in the context of sustainable development', UNGA Res 230, 59th Sess, UN Doc A/RES/59/230 (16 Feb 2005), and 'Towards the sustainable development of the Caribbean Sea for present and future generations', UNGA Res 155, 65th Sess, UN Doc A/RES/65/155 (20 Dec 2010). Para 1 of the latter resolution '[r]ecognizes that the Caribbean Sea is an area of unique biodiversity and a highly fragile ecosystem that requires relevant regional and international development partners to work together to develop and implement regional initiatives to promote the sustainable conservation and management of coastal and marine resources, including the consideration of the concept of the Caribbean Sea as a special area in the context of sustainable development, including its designation as such without prejudice to relevant international law'.

relations (Article 73), legal infrastructure (Article 74), and development of social infrastructure (Article 75). Two other provisions of Part Three require COTED to play a role in modernizing government bureaucracies in the region (Article 76), and require all CARICOM organs to take into account the special needs and circumstances of less developed countries when adopting measures under Chapter 4 (Article 77).

A few points can be made about several of these common supporting measures. Firstly, most are to be achieved by CARICOM and its member states acting in coordination with third states, other regional and international organizations, and regimes.[17] Secondly, some of the articles appear to have a narrow focus, perhaps because of their drafting history. Articles 63 and 64, for example, pay specific attention to human resource development and research and development in the area of agriculture. These articles were originally conceived in the context of Protocol V: Agricultural Policy. However to the extent that these provisions can be read more broadly, as extending to other areas of human activity, they should be so read, since they form part of a Chapter focusing on a wide variety of CARICOM policies. Thirdly, otherwise generally-phrased measures in many cases contain specific provisions relevant to the needs of particular sectors of the Caribbean. For example, Article 66(c)(ii)–(ii), in protecting and promoting intellectual property, focuses expressly on the preservation of indigenous Caribbean culture and the legal protection of the expressions of folklore, other traditional knowledge, and national heritage, particularly of indigenous populations in the Community. This focus will be of particular importance to several member states which contain large indigenous communities, including Belize, Dominica, Guyana, and Suriname.

Fourthly, Part Three frames many of the measures in the context of, and to support, existing international obligations. COTED, for example, is mandated to develop a standardization programme under Article 67 RTC which is compatible with the international obligations of member states. These obligations include trade obligations, as seen in the requirement in Article 67(2) that member states not use standards, technical regulations, and conformity assessment procedures as 'barriers to trade'.[18] Article 67(5) requires the Community to establish a regional standards body. To this end the Community created the CARICOM Regional Organization for Standards and Quality (CROSQ).[19] Although some implementation problems subsist, particularly in the lack of domestic implementing legislation, CROSQ is likely to have a substantial impact upon the CSME since it will help facilitate more efficient regional and extra-regional trade.[20]

[17] See eg RTC Arts 63(5), 64(2)(b) and (6), 65(4), 66(g), 67(1). cf Art 70(3)(b).

[18] For the definitions of the terms 'technical regulations', 'standard', and 'conformity assessment procedures', see RTC Art 67(6)(a)–(c).

[19] See the Agreement Establishing the CARICOM Regional Organisation for Standards and Quality (CROSQ) (adopted 4 Feb 2002, provisionally applied since 5 Feb 2002, not yet in force) 2324 UNTS 413, and Protocol on the Provisional Application of the Agreement Establishing the CARICOM Regional Organisation for Standards and Quality (CROSQ) (adopted and entered into force 5 Feb 2002) 2326 UNTS 359.

[20] The CARICOM Secretariat, in the *Summary Draft Report on the Appraisal of the State of Implementation of the CARICOM Single Market* (September 2009) (Georgetown, Guyana: CARICOM

To implement the requirements of Article 72(1) in relation to double taxation agreements, CARICOM created a regional double taxation agreement.[21] According to a CARICOM report, however, only nine states have complied with it and Suriname's global tax system presents continuing challenges (since it provides no exemptions based on where the income is earned).[22] With respect to double taxation and third states, as mandated by Article 72(2), CARICOM is currently negotiating a regional tax position with Canada as part of a broader free trade agreement between CARICOM and Canada.[23] The common supportive measures in relation to legal infrastructure, as detailed in Article 74, are aimed at promoting investments, including cross-border investments. To this end, the Legal Affairs Committee is required to cooperate with competent CARICOM organs and member states are required to harmonize laws and administrative practices in a number of areas (Article74(2)).

12.2.2 OECS development and sectoral policies

Article 13 of the Protocol of Eastern Caribbean Economic Union sets out a wide range of development objectives and policies. The five main development objectives identified by the Authority in 2002, and for which the Authority is to set annual targets, are economic transformation, growth, employment, poverty reduction, and attainment of appropriate levels on the Human Development Indices as set by the United Nations.[24] Protocol member states are to pursue these objectives in conjunction with harmonization of a number of policy programme areas such as fiscal, monetary, trade, international economic relations, incomes, structural, social, environmental, and other programme areas as identified by the OECS Authority, as well as sectors such as agriculture, manufacturing, tourism, services, construction, information and communications technology, education, and health.[25] Protocol member states are also to coordinate policies within the Economic Union for: mobilization, development, and efficient allocation of labour; the development,

Secretariat, 2009) [hereafter '*Summary Draft Report*'] at p 8, notes that only five member states had enacted domestic legislation to transform the CROSQ Agreement into domestic law.

[21] Agreement Among the Governments of the Member States of the Caribbean Community for the Avoidance of Double Taxation and the Prevention of Fiscal Evasion with Respect to Taxes on Income, Profits or Gains and Capital Gains and for the Encouragement of Regional Trade and Investment (adopted 6 Jul 1994, in force 30 Nov 1994) 2259 UNTS 251.

[22] CARICOM Secretariat, *Summary Draft Report* 8.

[23] Canada and the Caribbean have had longstanding trade relations, from the 1925 Canada-British West Indies—Bermuda—British Guiana—British Honduras Trade Agreement (opened for signature 6 Jul 1925, in force 30 Apr 1927), available through <http://www.caricom.org/jsp/secretariat/legal_instruments/agreement_canada_britishwestindies_1925.jsp?menu=secretariat>, to the Caricom-Canada Trade and Economic Co-operation Agreement and its Protocols, including the CARICOM-Canada 1998 Protocol on Rum, to the CARIBCAN Agreement, and several bilateral investment treaties with individual member states. See generally, CARICOM Secretariat, Office of Trade Negotiations, 'CARICOM-Canada', as available at <http://www.crnm.org/index.php?option=com_content&view=article&id=51&Itemid=121&0872a8d70c6252b77261d45b4779477d=8e5e1b0314895de04ccdd0c1690fc185> (13 May 2013).

[24] Protocol Art 13.2 and 13.3.

[25] Protocol Art 13.3–13.4(a).

creation, and establishment of Research, Development, and Management Centres; and the development, integration, and regulation of money and capital markets.[26]

Articles 14–16 of the Protocol establish policies for the development of particular sectors of the Economic Union. Under Article 14 the monetary policy of the Economic Union is to be executed by the Monetary Council through the Eastern Caribbean Central Bank under the terms and conditions of the Eastern Caribbean Central Bank Agreement. Under Article 15 the Protocol member states agree to the progressive harmonization of their fiscal policies and fiscal incentives regimes, including by setting fiscal and debt benchmarks. Under Article 16 they agree to pursue employment income policies based on the principle of structured consultations between governments, the private sector, the trade unions, and other interests. Under Article 17 they agree to pursue joint policies in the area of foreign investment and other aspects of international economic relations. Subject to Economic Union competences under Article 14 of the RTB, Protocol member states also agree to establish institutional arrangements to conduct common trade policies, and to pursue a common transport policy by, amongst other things, progressively harmonizing air and maritime transport policies.[27] Article 19 of the Protocol goes into considerable detail about aspects of the OECS transport policy, including the goal of establishing a single Economic Union Area air space.[28] This may be necessary, given the tremendous importance of air and maritime transport services to tourism and the economies of the OECS.

Under Article 20.1 the Protocol member states agree to 'the development of an agriculture policy which takes into account regional and global agreements and conventions, including the St. George's Declaration and the first and eighth goals of the Millennium Development Summit and offers a strategic framework for prioritizing regional programmes that address cross border dimensions of agriculture'. In a similar manner to CARICOM member states, Protocol member states also commit to modernizing the agricultural sector, to setting benchmarks and frameworks to shape its development and integration, to adopting national policies which complement regional initiatives, and to providing mechanisms for public/private partnerships and investments.[29]

In a similar manner, under Article 21 Protocol member states agree to progressively harmonize their tourism policies, including by adoption of a common policy for tourism development which focuses on balanced growth in the entire Economic Union Area.[30] They also agree to establish mechanisms for joint marketing, promotion, and greater community participation in the tourism product.[31]

Under Article 22.1 the Protocol member states 'commit themselves to the goal of creating fair and equitable access to inclusive education and training opportunities for all citizens'. To do so they agree to harmonize the accreditation of programmes, curricula, assessments, and to establish a procurement service for educational supplies.[32] Importantly, Protocol member states also agree to implement educational

[26] Protocol Art 13.4(b)–(d). [27] Protocol Arts 18–19. [28] Protocol Art 19.8–19.9.
[29] Protocol Art 20.2. [30] Protocol Art 21.1–21.2. [31] Protocol Art 21.3.
[32] Protocol Art 22.1.

policies that, inter alia, promote human rights values such as universality, participation, non-discrimination, protection, and equality; build essential skills; support gender equality; and stimulate lifelong learning and critical thinking.[33]

Under Articles 23–24 Protocol member states commit themselves to improving human and social development and environmental sustainability. Under Article 23.1 each Protocol member state is required to 'promote sustainable social and cultural development that would ensure societies that are stable, safe and just and that are based on the promotion and protection of human rights, non-discrimination, respect for diversity, equality of opportunity, solidarity, security, and participation of all people'. Protocol member states also agree to work toward common social development policies for a wide range of areas, including policies directed to eradicating extreme hunger and poverty, achieving universal primary education, promoting gender equality and empowering women, reducing child mortality, improving maternal health, combating diseases, ensuring environmental sustainability, and facilitating broader public decision making.[34] Under Article 24.1 Protocol member states commit to implementing 'St. George's Declaration of Principles for Environmental Sustainability in the OECS to minimize environmental vulnerability, improve environmental management and protect the region's natural (including historical and cultural) resource base for optimal social and economic benefits for Member States'. They commit to do so by improving the capacity of member states and regional institutions, and by working towards the long-term protection and sustained productivity of the region's natural resource base and of the ecosystem services it provides.[35] Importantly, given the regional scope of environmental issues, under Article 24.2 the Protocol member states agree to 'collaborate with national, regional and international institutions to assist the governments and their national partners to secure and maintain the technical, financial and human resources required to achieve the goals and targets of the Declaration'.

Under Article 25.1 Protocol member states also agree to 'implement policies to facilitate the promotion of competition in the telecommunications and information technologies sector through an open, transparent and harmonised regional approach'. Each state also agrees to promote the widest possible access to telecommunications.[36]

12.3 Future Developments: CARICOM's Built-In Agenda

In addition to the existing regimes described in this Chapter, Article 239 of the RTC requires member states to expand or further define several areas of economic activity, as follows:

> The Member States undertake to elaborate a Protocol relating, *inter alia*, to:
> (a) electronic commerce;
> (b) government procurement;

[33] Protocol Art 22.2–22.5.
[34] See further Protocol Art 23.
[35] Protocol Art 24.1.
[36] Protocol Art 25.2.

(c) treatment of goods produced in free zones and similar jurisdictions;
(d) free circulation of goods in the CSME; and
(e) rights contingent on establishment, provision of services and movement of capital in the Community.

The topic on this list which has received the most attention to date is that of contingent rights. However all of these areas remain under development and will be important to ensuring the full implementation of the CSME.[37]

[37] CARICOM Secretariat, *Summary Draft Report* 53–5.

PART V

DISPUTE SETTLEMENT AND ENFORCEMENT

13

Non-Judicial Dispute Settlement Mechanisms

The legal regimes of CARICOM and the OECS, as with all regional integration movements requiring collective action of sovereign states, inevitably must produce challenges, friction, and disagreement. For example, member states experiencing difficulties in particular sectors of their economies may wish temporarily to limit their obligations under the RTC or RTB. If they seek approval for such limitations through the processes provided under the respective treaties, no controversy may arise. However if they act unilaterally, without authorization, then a dispute will likely arise regarding potential breaches of treaty obligations.

How an integration movement handles such disputes is critical to its success. All disputes between member states may be resolved through diplomatic processes, such as negotiations. They also may be resolved through the political organs of the regional organization, either formally, or on the side-lines of meetings. However if the states concerned become entrenched in their positions, a dispute may require the active intervention of a neutral third party, either to recommend a non-binding settlement, or to impose a binding settlement. For this reason both the RTC and RTB provide for a range of dispute settlement mechanisms, from dispute resolution through organs, to non-binding procedures (consultations, good offices, mediation, conciliation), to binding procedures (arbitration and adjudication). For CARICOM, Chapter 9 of the RTC sets out several dispute settlement mechanisms for member states. For the OECS, the RTB's Dispute Settlement Annex sets out a similar range of options. Both treaties also provide for the possibility of dispute settlement through organs.

Perhaps the most important standing dispute settlement mechanisms available under the RTC and RTB will be the Caribbean Court of Justice and the Eastern Caribbean Court of Appeal. As described fully in Chapter 14, the two Courts, by allowing for compulsory, legal, final, and binding dispute settlement, represent crucial developments for both CARICOM and the OECS.

13.1 Dispute Settlement through Standing Organs

Dispute settlement through standing organs, in addition to other avenues of political and personal dispute resolution, must remain important to regional integration.[1] When representatives of states gather together they may be able to amicably resolve contentious issues through both public and private discussions. Dispute settlement through organs has the benefit of being informal, allowing compromise and providing the possibility of further rule-making to resolve existing and future problems.[2] However such dispute settlement processes may be problematic because they lack several of the essential characteristics that are necessary for the kind of consistent and predictable decision making needed for economic integration. They are not transparent, not made in accordance with law, not compulsory, and may not be binding.

13.1.1 CARICOM

Historical

Under Article 19 of CARICOM's original Treaty, unless otherwise provided, the Conference had the power to determine any 'dispute concerning the interpretation or application of this Treaty'. Similarly, the Common Market Council, under Article 7(1)(b) of the Annex to the 1973 Treaty, had the responsibility of 'ensuring the efficient operation and development of the Common Market including the settlement of problems arising out of its functioning'. However the main mechanism contemplated for dispute resolution under the original Treaty and Annex was the ad hoc arbitral 'Tribunal' which could be established under Articles 11 and 12 of the Annex. This mechanism was little used during the life of the original Treaty, perhaps because the processes it contemplated were ad hoc, not compulsory, and not binding. In fact, neither the decisions of the ad hoc Article 11 arbitral tribunal, nor the subsequent recommendations of the Council, were binding.[3] Moreover the scope of dispute settlement under the original Treaty and Annex was very limited. Article 11 procedures could only be used to resolve disputes between states, not

[1] eg Kenneth Hall and Byron Blake, in 'CARICOM Administration', in Kenneth O Hall (ed), *The Caribbean Community: Beyond Survival* (Kingston, Jamaica: Ian Randle Publishers, 2001) 203–21, at 215, draw attention to the ways in which the frequent meetings of ministers and officials in CARICOM, as well as the personal contacts between national officials, allow for the resolution of conflicts at both formal and informal levels.

[2] See eg Henry G Schermers and Niels M Blokker, *International Institutional Law*, 4th edn (Boston: Martinus Nijhoff, 2003) 853 (§1355). See generally pp 852–7 (§1355–62).

[3] Hans J Geiser, Pamela Alleyne, and Carroll Gajraj, *Legal Problems of Caribbean Integration: A study of legal aspects of CARICOM* (Leyden: Sijthoff, 1976) 169–70. Art 11(3) of the Annex provided: 'If in pursuance of the foregoing provisions of this Article the Council or the Tribunal, as the case may be, finds that any benefit conferred on a Member State by this Annex or any objective of the Common Market is being or may be frustrated, the Council may, by majority vote, make to the Member State concerned such *recommendations* as it considers appropriate' (emphasis added). Art 12 does not stipulate that the decision of the Tribunal is to be binding. Nevertheless, the Common Market Council

disputes involving organs of the Community or persons.[4] As highlighted in the Mills Report, from 1973 to 1990 only once was a tribunal appointed and convened under Articles 11–12 of the *Annex*, and even then, it was not required to take a decision.[5]

Current

Under the RTC, the two main Community organs both have been accorded dispute settlement powers, the Conference under Article 12(8) and the Community Council under Article 13(4)(g).[6] On a strict textual interpretation the scope of powers of these two organs is differentiated in two ways. Firstly, the Conference is given *discretion* to consider and resolve disputes. The Community Council, in contrast, is required to receive and consider allegations of breaches. Under Article 12(8) the Conference '*may* consider and resolve disputes between Member States' whereas under Article 13(4)(g) 'the Community Council *shall*...receive and consider allegations of breaches of obligations arising under this Treaty, including disputes between Organs of the Community'. The rationale for this distinction may lie in the different outcomes envisaged by the two provisions: under Article 12 the Conference is to *resolve* such disputes. Secondly, the Conference is expressly empowered to resolve disputes between member states, whereas the Community Council can resolve disputes between organs of the Community. This distinction, however, may not be so great. The RTC does not prohibit the Conference from considering inter-organ disputes, and equally, the Community Council is not barred from considering disputes between member states. However the wording suggests a division of responsibilities between the two organs in relation to these two types of disputes, with the lower organ, the Community Council, being mandated to consider institutional disputes.

Dispute resolution by the Community Council and Conference may be binding, if expressed in the form of a binding decision. If, for example, the Conference formally resolved a dispute by means of a decision, and this decision satisfied the procedural and substantive requirements for validity imposed by the RTC, it would be binding. It would be binding upon all those addressed, including

could authorize, under Art 11(4), 'any Member State to suspend to the Member State which has not complied with the recommendation the application of such obligations under this Annex as the Council considers appropriate'.

[4] See eg Geiser, Alleyne, and Gajraj, *Legal Problems of Caribbean Integration* 166–7.

[5] Gladstone Mills et al, *Report on a Comprehensive Review of the Programmes, Institutions and Organisations of the Caribbean Community* (Georgetown, Guyana: Caribbean Community Secretariat, 1990) 23.

[6] RTC Arts 12(8) and 13(4)(g) provide, respectively:

> [12] 8. Notwithstanding any other provision of this Treaty, the Conference may consider and resolve disputes between Member States. [...]
>
> [13] 4. Without prejudice to the generality of the foregoing provisions, the Community Council shall: ...(g) receive and consider allegations of breaches of obligations arising under this Treaty, including disputes between Organs of the Community...

member states and organs of the Community, and including the party against whom the decision is made.[7] If, however, the Conference merely recommended a particular resolution to the dispute, that recommendation would not be binding.[8] Likewise, if the Conference was unable to obtain the necessary majority to pass a decision, no binding resolution of the dispute would be made. The same logic would apply to the decisions of the Community Council meant to resolve a dispute. It should equally apply to binding decisions made by any organ of CARICOM, if satisfying the procedural and substantive requirements for voting for that organ.

The latter point requires further discussion because the CCJ in its decision in the case of *Hummingbird Rice Mills Limited v Suriname and the Caribbean Community* suggests that organs of CARICOM have no power to impose sanctions unless such a power is expressly provided in the RTC.[9] Since a formal dispute resolution decision against a delinquent state would most likely involve, or could be characterized as, a sanction, the relevant passage of the Court's judgment requires analysis. The Court summarizes and evaluates the arguments of the claimant in relation to sanctions at paragraphs [49]–[51] of its judgment:

> [49] The Claimant argued that COTED and the Secretary-General should have imposed sanctions on Suriname for the non-implementation of the CET but produced no legal basis for the authority to do so. The competence of an international organization or of community actors to impose sanctions upon a sovereign state for breach of treaty obligations cannot be assumed or implied but must be stated expressly in the constituent document to which the State in question is party.
>
> [50] The Revised Treaty contains no general provisions relating to the application of sanctions for breach of treaty provisions. The schema adopted in the treaty is for Member States in certain cases to seek authorization from COTED in order that they themselves may adopt sanctions such as counter-measures or countervailing duties (Article 98), and anti-dumping measures (Article 133). COTED is rarely empowered to impose sanctions; a rather obscure provision in Paragraph 14 of Schedule III empowers the Council to apply appropriate sanctions where it is satisfied that the action taken by a Member State in relation to the Oils and Fats Sub-sector is not in compliance with the provisions of the Schedule and is likely to prejudice benefits likely to be derived by another Member State, but this is exceptional. There are certainly no express provisions granting COTED power to impose sanctions upon a Member State for breach of the obligation to impose the CET. There are no provisions permitting the Secretary-General power to impose sanctions upon Member States; indeed, the very assertion of such a power is startling given the historical development of the Community and the nature of the office of Secretary-General.
>
> [51] The Court therefore concludes that the Claimant has not established a legal basis upon which COTED or the Secretary-General could have imposed sanctions upon Suriname. It follows then that they cannot be faulted for not having imposed such sanctions.

The Court's reasoning is persuasive in relation to the lack of power of the Secretary General to impose sanctions, since the Secretary General does not possess a general, binding decision-making competence.

[7] Note that Art 28(4) of the RTC excludes parties to a dispute from voting, but does not exclude them from the binding nature of the decision. Art 28(4) states: 'Parties to a dispute or against which sanctions are being considered shall not have the right to vote on the issue falling to be determined.'

[8] See RTC Art 27(6).

[9] Judgment [2012] CCJ 1 (OJ).

However the Court's reasoning is less persuasive when discussing the powers of COTED. COTED is the organ of CARICOM which is mandated to play a key role in the implementation of the CSME. According to Article 15(2)(a) COTED is 'responsible for the promotion of trade and economic development of the Community... [and] shall... promote the development and oversee the operation of the CSME'. COTED is also expressly empowered to make binding decisions under Article 29(1) of the RTC. When these two features of COTED are combined it would appear to be at least arguable that COTED is competent to take a binding decision specifying measures necessary to ensure the successful operation of the CSME. Such a decision could require positive or negative measures. For example, COTED could require states to enact new legislation to accomplish a specific objective of the CSME. Likewise, COTED could require states, or a single state, to stop behaviour that threatens the fundamental objectives of the CSME. Such a binding decision would be supported by the state's own obligations under the general undertaking provision, Article 9 of the RTC. In order to make such a decision effective, COTED could authorize member states to suspend one or more of their obligations under the RTC in relation to a delinquent state. Such a power could be necessarily implied from the existing express powers of COTED to authorize member states to impose countermeasures, countervailing duties, or anti-dumping measures, as highlighted by the CCJ itself in the passage quoted earlier. Examples of such an implied power to sanction through exercise of discretionary powers, including by authorizing the suspension of rights and obligations, are found in general international institutional law.[10] For these reasons Community organs should be recognized as being able to take binding decisions that impose negative consequences for one or more member states.

The drawback of dispute settlement through a Community organ is that by nature it must be a highly political, and politicized, process. Individuals sitting on the Conference or Community Council are not there in an independent or personal capacity. They represent member states, with their primary duty being to represent those state interests.[11] This may be a drawback, especially where, as was the case in the original 1973 Treaty, decisions of the Conference required unanimity and did not exclude parties to a dispute.[12] Under the RTC, however, this problem has been cured, at least in relation to the Conference. Under Article 28(4), parties to a dispute or those against whom sanctions are being considered are excluded from voting.

Interestingly, it has been suggested that one of the benefits of dispute settlement through a Community organ is the same *political*, as opposed to legal, nature of the process. Because the process is political, member states are not bound to rely solely upon legal considerations. As noted by Geiser et al, states can invoke an 'element of give and take and a spirit of compromise'.[13]

[10] See eg Schermers and Blokker, *International Institutional Law* (n 2) 918 (§1454) and 929–30 (§1469).

[11] See Geiser, Alleyne, and Gajraj, *Legal Problems of Caribbean Integration* (n 4) 161.

[12] Geiser, Alleyne, and Gajraj, *Legal Problems of Caribbean Integration* (n 4) 161–2.

[13] Geiser, Alleyne, and Gajraj, *Legal Problems of Caribbean Integration* (n 4) 161.

Nevertheless, such organ-based dispute settlement processes have their limitations. For this reason a number of new, non-adversarial processes have been added in Chapter 9 of the RTC.

13.1.2 OECS

Historical

Like CARICOM, the OECS Council of Ministers established under Annex I to the 1981 Treaty was provided with an express dispute settlement function.[14] Under Article 20(1) complaints could be referred to the Council of Ministers, which was empowered to establish an 'examining committee' under Article 21 to investigate the matter. However neither the report of the examining committee nor the recommendation of the Council of Ministers to a delinquent member state was binding.[15] As with CARICOM's Common Market Council, the most that the OECS Council of Ministers could do in the event of non-compliance with a recommendation was to authorize any other member state to suspend its obligations with respect to the delinquent state.[16]

Similar to CARICOM, the main dispute settlement mechanism was to be established, on an ad hoc basis, under an annex to the Treaty. As provided by Article 14 of the 1981 Treaty, disputes were to be resolved by direct agreement or, in the event of non-resolution, through the conciliation procedure established under Annex A to the Treaty. Interestingly and perhaps uniquely, under Article 14(3) of the Treaty the conciliation commission process established under Annex A was compulsory, and its decisions and recommendations were binding:

> Member States undertake to accept the conciliation procedure referred to in the preceding paragraph as compulsory. Any decisions or recommendations of the Conciliation Commission in resolution of the dispute shall be final and binding on the Member States.[17]

The conciliation commission provided for in Annex A was to be composed of a total of five conciliators and to establish its own procedure.[18] Expenses for the commission were to be borne by the Organisation.[19] The conciliation commission

[14] Annex I—Agreement Establishing the East Caribbean Common Market, annexed to the Treaty Establishing the Organisation of Eastern Caribbean States (adopted 18 Jun 1981, in force 2 Jul 1981) 1338 UNTS 97.

[15] See Annex I (n 14) Art 20(3).

[16] Annex I Art 20(4) provides:

> 4. If a Member State does not or is unable to comply with a recommendation made in accordance with paragraph 3 of this Article and the Council of Minister finds, by majority vote, that an obligation under this Agreement has not been fulfilled, the Council of Ministers may, by majority vote, authorise any Member State to suspend as regards the Member State which has not complied with the recommendations the application of such obligations under this Agreement as the Council of Ministers, by majority vote considers appropriate.

[17] See also Art 2(a) of Annex A, which mandates that the Director General bring a dispute before the commission when he or she receives a request under Art 14 of the Treaty.

[18] Annex A Arts 2–3.

[19] Annex A Art 7.

does not appear to have been invoked frequently, if at all, during the life of the 1981 Treaty.[20]

Current

Articles 30–31 of the OECS Protocol establish a consultation and complaints procedure to resolve disputes related to the Protocol.[21] The scope of disputes, as provided in Article 30.1, includes those in which 'any Protocol Member State considers that any benefit conferred upon it by this Protocol or any objective of the Economic Union is being or may be frustrated, and [where] no satisfactory settlement is reached between the Protocol Member States concerned'. The latter phrase alludes to the possibility of dispute settlement by consultation or negotiation. In the event that consultation or negotiation fails, the dispute may be submitted to the Economic Affairs Council.

Under Article 30.2 once a matter is referred to the Economic Affairs Council, it shall arrange, by majority vote, to examine the matter. Before doing so, the Economic Affairs Council must refer the matter to the Protocol member state concerned and all Protocol member states must 'furnish all information which they can make available and shall lend their assistance to establish the facts'.[22] The Council's examination may rely upon an Examination Committee established under Article 31, which is to be composed of 'persons selected for their competence and integrity, who in the performance of their duties shall neither seek nor receive instructions from any State or territory or from any authority or organization other than the Economic Union'. Examination Committee members are appointed by the Economic Affairs Council, on such terms and conditions as may be decided by majority vote.[23]

At any time after a matter has been referred to the Economic Affairs Council, under Article 30.5 a Protocol member state may request the Economic Affairs Council to authorize, as a matter of urgency, interim measures to safeguard its position. Interim measures can only be authorized if the Economic Affairs Council finds, by a majority vote, that the circumstances are 'sufficiently serious to justify interim action'.[24] As an interim measure the Economic Affairs Council may, by majority vote, 'authorise a Protocol Member State to suspend its obligations under this Protocol to such an extent and for such a period as the Economic Affairs Council by majority vote

[20] eg A Ralph Carnegie, in 'How Exclusive is "Exclusive" in Relation to the Original Jurisdiction of the Caribbean Court of Justice? A Consideration of Recent Developments', Paper Delivered in the Faculty of Law Workshop Series 2009–2010, University of the West Indies, Cave Hill Campus, 25 November 2009, as available through <http://www.cavehill.uwi.edu/news/articles/nov2009/Conflicts_of_Jurisdiction.pdf> (12 Aug 2013), states at p 8:

> A long-standing instance of a Caribbean regional organization with its own dispute settlement provision is that of the Treaty of Basseterre, even although this writer knows of no application of its provisions. [Citations omitted.]

[21] Note that this dispute settlement procedure also applies to disputes about conflicts between rights and obligations of Protocol member states under other, prior treaties, and their rights and obligations under the OECS Protocol: Protocol Art 11.3–11.4.

[22] Protocol Art 30.2. [23] Protocol Art 31. [24] Protocol Art 30.5.

considers appropriate'.[25] Such interim measures are, however, without prejudice to any other actions taken by the Economic Affairs Council under Article 30.

After receiving the requested information from the Protocol member state and/or the report of the Examination Committee the Economic Affairs Council must assess, under Article 30.3, 'whether it has been established that an obligation under this Protocol has not been fulfilled and whether and to what extent any benefit conferred by this agreement or any objective of the Economic Union is being or may be frustrated'. As a result of such an assessment the Economic Affairs Council may, again by a majority vote, make such recommendations as it considers appropriate to any Protocol member state.[26] Such recommendations would not be binding.

However, if the delinquent Protocol member state does not or is unable to comply with a recommendation then, under Article 30.4, the Economic Affairs Council may refer the matter to the Council of Ministers. In doing so the dispute is necessarily brought to the attention of all of the member states of the Economic Union, not only the Protocol member states. This provision therefore allows for greater opportunity for informal mediation or reconciliation during, or on the side-lines of, the Council of Ministers meeting.

If, however, the Council of Ministers finds by majority vote that an obligation under this Protocol has not been fulfilled, then the Economic Affairs Council may, also by majority vote, 'authorise any Protocol Member State to suspend as regards the Protocol Member State which has not complied with the recommendations the application of such obligations under this Protocol as the Economic Affairs Council by majority vote considers appropriate'.[27] Since Protocol rights and obligations are the primary benefits for parties to the Protocol, suspension of these rights and obligations could amount to a significant sanction against a delinquent member state.

As a consequence, Article 30.6 allows for a challenge to the decision of the Economic Affairs Council to be brought to the Eastern Caribbean Court of Appeal:

> Any party aggrieved by a decision of the Economic Affairs Council under this Article may invoke the Treaty Jurisdiction of the Eastern Caribbean Court of Appeal under paragraph 1(b) of the Dispute Settlement Annex, without reference to the waiting period in Article 18.2 of the Principal Treaty, by bringing a complaint against the OECS Organisation and the other parties to the dispute. The authority of the Court in such proceeding shall be as extensive as if the dispute had been referred to it immediately after the waiting period without the intervention of the proceedings of the Economic Affairs Council. Neither conciliation nor arbitration under the Dispute Settlement Annex may be used to challenge the decision of the Economic Affairs Council.

This provision is interesting because it joins the OECS itself to the dispute and excludes dispute settlement mechanisms other than the Eastern Caribbean Court of Appeal. The Court's jurisdiction is also unaffected and unlimited by the earlier proceedings before the Economic Affairs Council. As a result it can consider the entire matter anew.

[25] Protocol Art 30.5. [26] Protocol Art 30.3. [27] Protocol Art 30.4.

In sum, the OECS Protocol Article 30 procedure reveals an interesting combination of several of the dispute settlement processes discussed in what follows. It commences with negotiation, and then proceeds to a kind of conciliation process before the Economic Affairs Council (an inquiry followed by recommendations). The Economic Affairs Council does have, however, in conjunction with the Council of Ministers, the additional power to authorize other Protocol member states to sanction a delinquent state. Such a power will give rise to legal consequences and thus an aggrieved party can refer the matter to an adjudicative process, under the treaty jurisdiction of the Eastern Caribbean Court of Appeal. In this manner the RTB both brings together a number of processes to help resolve a dispute and allows any affected Protocol member state to have recourse to the Court.

13.2 Ad Hoc Dispute Settlement Mechanisms

13.2.1 CARICOM: Chapter 9 of the RTC

Chapter 9 of the RTC provides a number of non-binding and binding methods for resolving disputes involving the interpretation and application of the RTC. The scope of disputes covered by the Chapter is set out in Article 187, which provides:

> The provisions of this Chapter shall apply to the settlement of disputes concerning the interpretation and application of the Treaty, including:
> (a) allegations that an actual or proposed measure of another Member State is, or would be, inconsistent with the objectives of the Community;
> (b) allegations of injury, serious prejudice suffered or likely to be suffered, nullification or impairment of benefits expected from the establishment and operation of the CSME;
> (c) allegations that an organ or body of the Community has acted ultra vires; or
> (d) allegations that the purpose or object of the Treaty is being frustrated or prejudiced.

Article 187(a)–(b) allows consideration of disputes about *potential* actions or injuries, as well as existing ones. Article 187(c) allows enforcement of the limitations imposed upon organs and bodies of the Community, thereby reinforcing the principles of conferral and subsidiarity.[28] Article 187(d) is very wide-ranging and could be used as a kind of catch-all provision to include most types of disputes. It should be also noted that this list in Article 187 is not exhaustive.[29] Thus a Chapter 9 dispute settlement body should be able to consider almost any type of dispute related to the RTC.

[28] See the discussion of these general principles in Chapter 8.

[29] As stated by the Caribbean Court of Justice in *Trinidad Cement Ltd v Caribbean Community*, Judgment [2009] CCJ 2 (OJ), (2009) 74 WIR 319, 5 February 2009, at para [30], 'Article 187 does not purport to present an exhaustive statement of the types of dispute that may come before this Court.'

Article 188 makes clear that the dispute settlement mechanisms in Chapter 9 are, subject to the other provisions of the RTC, exclusive in nature. Article 188(1) provides: 'Subject to the provisions of this Treaty, the disputes mentioned in Article 187 shall be settled only by recourse to any one of the following modes for the settlement of disputes, namely, good offices, mediation, consultations, conciliation, arbitration and adjudication.' The key word here is 'only'. Thus, disputes about the RTC should be settled by organs authorized to settle disputes and the listed bodies. They should not be settled by non-CARICOM dispute settlement mechanisms.

It will be interesting to see how this provision will be interpreted by the member states and organs of CARICOM. Under general international law states are allowed to resolve disputes using any resolution process existing under a treaty to which they are a party. If a dispute involving an aspect of the CSME could also be characterized as a dispute falling under another regime, such as international trade law, then in some cases it may be possible to use dispute resolution mechanisms in either regime.[30] Although some tribunals will try to give deference to more specific, localized dispute resolution mechanisms, there is no formal hierarchy of dispute settlement under international law. Thus, for example, a binding decision by an organ of the Community under Article 60 on fisheries management could give rise to a dispute between member states about applicable law of the sea rules. Depending upon the treaty commitments assumed by parties, such a dispute could properly be taken to the International Court of Justice, the International Tribunal on the Law of the Sea, or a Chapter Nine dispute settlement mechanism.[31]

Article 188(2)–(4) also make clear that parties to a dispute can use any of the modes referred to in Article 188(1), subject to the rules for each form of dispute settlement. Article 189 mandates that parties must expeditiously exchange views for the purposes of choosing a mode of settlement or method of implementation of a settlement (if applicable). Article 190(1) requires member states to notify the Secretary General of the Caribbean Community of the existence and nature of the dispute and the mode of settlement agreed upon or initiated. Similarly, member states are required under Article 190(2) to notify the Secretary General of a

[30] As seen in Chapter 10, the subsidies regime in Part Three of Chapter 5 the RTC closely parallels the regimes in the WTO Agreement and the Agreement on Subsidies and Countervailing Measures: Marrakesh Agreement Establishing the World Trade Organisation (with Final Act, Annexes and Protocol) (adopted 15 Apr 1994, in force 1 Jan 1995) 1867 UNTS 3, including the Agreement on Subsidies and Countervailing Measures (adopted 15 Apr 1994, in force 1 Jan 1995) 1869 UNTS 14. Violations of WTO law can be referred to Panels established by the Dispute Settlement Body, or to the Appellate Body. See generally, Michael Trebilcock, Robert Howse and Antonia Eliason, *The Regulation of International Trade*, 4th edn (London: Routledge, 2013) ch 5.

[31] Note that in order for a dispute to be brought to the International Court of Justice or International Tribunal on the Law of the Sea the states concerned would have to be parties to the relevant treaties and fall under the jurisdictions of the tribunals. For jurisdictional provisions see Art 36 of the Statute of the International Court of Justice (1945), Annex to the Charter of the United Nations (opened for signature 26 Jun 1945, in force 24 Oct 1945) 1 U.N.T.S. xvi, Art 21 of the Statute of the International Tribunal for the Law of the Sea, Annex VI of the United Nations Convention on the Law of the Sea (opened for signature 10 Dec 1982, in force 16 Nov 1994) 1833 UNTS 3 (UNCLOS) at 561. See also UNCLOS Arts 297–299.

settlement and the mode used to arrive at the settlement. Under Article 190(3) the Secretary General is required to notify the other CARICOM states of information received under Article 190(1)–(2) 'as soon as practicable'. These notification procedures allow CARICOM to monitor the progress of a dispute and thereby perhaps prevent its escalation. Similarly, other member states will be kept apprised of the dispute, thus allowing them to help participate in its resolution. As will be seen in Chapter 14, wide participatory rights have been accorded third parties in proceedings before the Caribbean Court of Justice, perhaps for the same reasons as well as to allow the Court to receive a wider range of submissions on matters before it.

As indicated in Article 188(1), Chapter 9 of the RTC provides six methods of dispute resolution: (1) good offices, (2) mediation, (3) consultations, (4) conciliation, (5) arbitration, and (6) adjudication. Each will be examined in what follows. Although the list in Article 188(1) sets out these methods in a particular order, and this order is repeated in the numbering of provisions of the RTC, there is no requirement to use the methods in a particular sequence. The ordering does reflect the increasing level of formality required by each dispute settlement mechanism, with good offices and mediation being less procedurally complex and formal than arbitration. A distinction can also be made between non-binding and binding dispute resolution methods, with only the latter two processes—arbitration and adjudication—being binding in nature.

One restriction that does apply to the availability of different dispute methods is that disputes, once brought to arbitration or adjudication, are subject to the jurisdiction of the arbitral tribunal or Caribbean Court of Justice and may not be removed from such jurisdiction except in accordance with the specific rules governing the tribunal or Court. For this reason if, for example, a member state commences litigation before the CCJ and subsequently changes its mind, the Court nevertheless retains the jurisdiction to continue the proceedings and decide the dispute, even in the absence of further participation by the party concerned.[32] Since CCJ judgments are binding, a state would not be wise to unilaterally cease to participate in a case.[33]

13.2.2 OECS Dispute Settlement Annex

Disputes under the RTB that are not resolved by the Economic Affairs Council are to be resolved under a combination of Article 18 and the Dispute Settlement Annex. Article 18.1 and 18.5 together set out the scope of disputes covered under the RTB, namely, disputes between full member states, associate member states,

[32] See Part 17 of the Caribbean Court of Justice (Original Jurisdiction) Rules 2006 (24 Mar 2006), as available at <http://www.caribbeancourtofjustice.org/court-instruments/rules-of-the-court> (accessed 27 Jul 2013), which allows for default judgment. Note, however, that Part 15 of the Rules allows for discontinuance of a case in certain circumstances.

[33] See Arts 215 and 221 of the RTC, which specify the requirement for mandatory compliance with judgments of the Court and the binding, precedential nature of its judgments, respectively. See also the parallel Arts XV and XXII of the Agreement Establishing the Caribbean Court of Justice (adopted 14 Feb 2001, entered into force 23 Jul 2002) 2255 UNTS 319.

and the Organisation regarding the interpretation and application of the RTB. As highlighted later, such disputes are to be 'amicably resolved by consultation' but, if this is not possible, following a waiting period of three months, they may be referred to the procedures established under the Dispute Settlement Annex.[34] These procedures include good offices, consultation, conciliation, arbitration, and adjudication.[35]

As provided in Article 18.2, Dispute Settlement Annex procedures must be invoked by means of a request to the Director General, in addition to informing the other party or parties to the dispute. In a case where the OECS itself is a party to the dispute, the request must be submitted to the Chief Registrar of the Eastern Caribbean Court of Appeal, with the Court, through the Chief Registrar, exercising the functions of the Director General.[36] If the parties are in agreement under paragraph 1(a) of the Dispute Settlement Annex, subject to Article 30 of the Protocol, they may refer their dispute to any one of the following mechanisms: good offices, consultation, conciliation, arbitration, and adjudication. If they are not in agreement, then under paragraph 1(b) the dispute must be settled 'by adjudication by the Court of Appeal of the Eastern Caribbean Supreme Court at the request of any... eligible party'. Article 18.7 provides that in the exercise of its functions under the RTB the Eastern Caribbean Court of Appeal is to be provided the necessary resources from the budget of the OECS. In the event of a shortfall, Article 18.7 authorizes the Court to require advance payment from the parties to the dispute.[37]

Article 18.6, however, excludes disputes for which the proceedings were commenced prior to the entry into force of the RTB. Such disputes are to be governed by the original 1981 Treaty until they are either resolved or discontinued.

Let us examine the particular processes set out in Chapter 9 of the RTC and the RTB's Dispute Settlement Annex, namely, good offices, mediation, consultations, conciliation, and arbitration. For each, it will be helpful to examine the nature of the process under general international law first, before analysing the particular rules and procedures established by the RTC and RTB and its Annex.

13.2.3 Good offices

The term 'good offices' is traditionally used in international law to refer to a process of non-binding conflict resolution relying upon a neutral third party to help resolve the dispute.[38] That third party may be another state, an organ of an

[34] RTB Art 18.1–18.2. The waiting period may be abbreviated in urgent circumstances by the Eastern Caribbean Court of Appeal, or exempted or shortened under the provisions of the Protocol: RTB Art 18.3–18.4.

[35] Dispute Settlement Annex (DSA) [1(a)].

[36] RTB Art 18.2.

[37] RTB Art 18.7 states that 'the Eastern Caribbean Court of Appeal may require the parties to any dispute before it to advance payment against the Court's estimated costs of the proceedings and may in its orders and judgments in the case allocate to the parties, in such shares as it considers just, the liability for those costs.'

[38] Arts 6 of both the Convention for the Pacific Settlement of Disputes (29 Jul 1899) 187 CTS 410 (hereafter '1899 Hague Convention') and the Convention for the Pacific Settlement of Disputes

international or regional organization, or an individual of high repute.[39] The third party may offer good offices, or be invited to serve such a role by the parties to the dispute; good offices may also arise as a result of treaty provisions, or on an ad hoc basis.[40] The most famous examples of the exercise of the good offices function are those associated with the United Nations Secretary General who has, amongst other things, brokered prisoner returns, troop withdrawals and secured ceasefires.[41] Speaking about this role one Secretary General has described the key ingredients for successful exercise of good offices as follows:

> In situations of confrontation, the parties to a dispute are extremely sensitive and this makes it important that they should have confidence in the impartiality or the objectivity of the United Nations and its Secretary-General. The only instrument I can use is persuasion. When successful, it is a more powerful weapon than constraint, for it makes the persuaded party an ally of the solution. But to be able to persuade, you must prove the virtues of a solution, demonstrate the need to compromise and convince the party concerned that an agreement today is much more advantageous for it than a doubtful victory tomorrow. It is here that inventiveness is essential. We have to stretch our imagination to discern points of potential agreement even where at first sight they look non-existent. Even more important is patience, the refusal to give up in the face of apparently hopeless odds.[42]

Other executive or administrative officers of international organizations have also served such a role.[43]

Good offices may entail nothing further than the provision of an additional channel of communication between disputing parties.[44] However because good offices are frequently provided by highly ranked, independent, and impartial individuals of esteemed character, additional advice or recommendations may also be sought and provided.[45] To this extent the provision of good offices may be similar

(18 Oct 1907) 205 CTS 233 (hereafter '1907 Hague Convention'), both also available through <http://pca-cpa.org/showpage.asp?pag_id=1187> (27 Jul 2013), stipulate that good offices are not binding: 'Good offices and mediation, either at the request of the parties at variance, or on the initiative of Powers strangers to the dispute, have exclusively the character of advice and never have binding force.' On good offices generally under international law see eg United Nations Office of Legal Affairs, Codification Division, *Handbook on the Peaceful Settlement of Disputes Between States* (New York: United Nations, 1992) 33–40 [hereafter 'UN *Handbook*'], Ruth Lapidoth, 'Good Offices', in R Wolfrum (ed), *The Max Planck Encyclopedia of Public International Law* (Oxford University Press, 2008–) online edition [<www.mpepil.com>].

[39] See eg Philippe Sands and Pierre Klein, *Bowett's Law of International Institutions* (London: Sweet & Maxwell, 2009) 350–2 [13-017]–[13-020].

[40] See eg UN *Handbook* (n 38) 39 [116]–[117].

[41] See eg JG Merrills, *International Dispute Settlement*, 4th edn (Cambridge: Cambridge University Press, 2005) 244–50 [hereafter 'Merrills']. Interestingly, in earlier periods on more than one occasion the United Nations set up special good offices committees: at p 241.

[42] As reproduced in the UN *Handbook* (n 38) 35–6 (citing: SG/SM/3525, pp 4 and 5).

[43] eg Merrills (n 41) at 214 and 216–19, discusses the good offices functions of the GATT Director General and the WTO Director General.

[44] Merrills 28.

[45] In the UN *Handbook* (n 38) at 33 [102], the variable nature of the good offices role is explained as follows:

> The third party exercising good offices normally seeks to encourage the parties to the dispute to resume negotiations, thus providing them with a channel of communication.

to mediation.[46] The entity providing good offices must be acceptable to all parties to the dispute.[47]

CARICOM

Article 191(1) of the RTC provides for recourse to 'good offices' of a third party, including the Secretary General, to settle a dispute. Article 191(2) allows for the termination of good offices at any time, as well as for their continued use during arbitration or adjudication, if permitted under the procedural rules of the latter processes.

OECS

Paragraph 2 of the Dispute Settlement Annex to the RTB allows the eligible parties to a dispute to rely upon good offices.[48] Good offices may be provided by a third party, including a full member state, associate member state, or the Organisation, which is not a party to the dispute.[49] Under paragraph 2(b)–(c) good offices may be commenced by agreement, or terminated unilaterally by any party to the dispute, at any time. Good offices may continue by agreement during the course of conciliation, arbitration, or adjudication under the Dispute Settlement Annex, subject to the procedural rules of the latter three processes.[50]

13.2.4 Mediation

Mediation is more formal than good offices under general international law and can be undertaken by a third state, an international organization, or a person of high repute.[51] It can be commenced before the crystallization of an international dispute, as a preventative device, or after it has fully emerged, as a settlement mechanism.[52] Mediation has been described as 'a method of peaceful settlement of an

> However, there are cases in which the third party exercising good offices is authorized to do more than merely act as a go-between and is allowed to take active part in the dispute settlement process, by making proposals for its solution and holding meetings with the parties to the dispute to discuss such proposals. In such situations, the third party in question may be considered as not only contributing his good offices but also as undertaking mediation. Accordingly, good offices may be said to share a common characterization with mediation as a method of facilitating a dialogue between parties to an international dispute, aimed, as the case may be, at scaling down hostilities and tensions and designed to bring about an amicable solution of the dispute.

[46] UN *Handbook* 33 [103]. [47] UN *Handbook* 33 [101].

[48] RTB Art 18.5 states that 'eligible parties' comprise 'the full Member States, the Associate Member States and the Organisation'.

[49] DSA [2(a)]. [50] DSA [2(d)].

[51] See eg Merrills (n 41) 29, UN *Handbook* (n 38) 43 [133]. Merrills, at pp 29–32, offers examples of mediation by such diverse actors as the International Committee of the Red Cross, highly ranked diplomats, Papal emissaries, state officials, and third states. On mediation generally under international law see eg Merrills 28–44, UN *Handbook* 40–5, Francisco Orrego Vicuña, 'Mediation', in Wolfrum (ed), *The Max Planck Encyclopedia* (n 38).

[52] UN *Handbook* (n 38) 41 [127].

international dispute where a third party intervenes to reconcile the claims of the contending parties and to advance his own proposals aimed at a mutually acceptable compromise solution'.[53] Such proposals tend to be transmitted informally by the mediator, who will keep the proceedings confidential.[54] In contrast to conciliation panels, mediators do not usually exercise an independent fact-finding role and instead rely upon information supplied by the parties.[55] Mediators are tasked with finding a solution to the dispute, one that must be acceptable to both parties.[56] In the words of Article 4 of both of the Hague Conventions of 1899 and 1907, the role of the mediator 'consists in reconciling the opposing claims and appeasing the feelings of resentment which may have arisen between the States at variance'.[57]

In finding a solution mediators must help create an atmosphere conducive to negotiation and compromise by facilitating communication, thinking of creative solutions, and in some cases, by offering inducements to parties (positive and negative).[58] Solutions proposed by the mediator, and the mediation process itself, are not binding.[59] Nevertheless mediation is valuable because it opens lines of communication, offers an honourable way out of a dispute, and has the potential to resolve it, either finally, or for a period of time.[60] Mediation proceedings are informal and confidential.[61] Mediation can be terminated by either party or the mediator, or as a result of a stipulated time period for the mediation process.[62] It is provided as a dispute resolution process in a number of international treaties.[63]

Mediation is less adversarial than other dispute settlement procedures. It may be offered by a third party, or initiated by the parties to the dispute, either on an ad hoc basis or as provided in a treaty.[64] In all cases it requires the consent of all parties to the mediation and the mediator, who should be, in most cases, neutral.[65]

[53] UN *Handbook* (n 38) 40 [123]. Likewise, according to Merrills (n 41) at 28, a mediator is 'an active participant, authorised, and indeed expected, to advance fresh proposal and to interpret, as well as to transmit, each party's proposals to the other'.

[54] Merrills (n 41) 28–9.

[55] Merrills (n 41) 28.

[56] Merrills (n 41) 36–7.

[57] 1899 and 1907 Hague Conventions, Arts 4.

[58] Merrills (n 41) 36–9.

[59] Arts 6 of both the 1899 and 1907 Hague Conventions expressly stipulate the non-binding character of mediation as follows: 'Good offices and mediation, either at the request of the parties at variance, or on the initiative of Powers strangers to the dispute, have exclusively the character of advice, and never have binding force.' See also UN *Handbook* (n 38) 44–5 [138].

[60] Merrills (n 41) 39–41 and 43.

[61] UN *Handbook* (n 38) 42 [131].

[62] Arts 5 of both the 1899 and 1907 Hague Conventions state: 'The functions of the mediator are at an end when once it is declared, either by one of the parties to the dispute, or by the mediator himself, that the means of reconciliation proposed by him are not accepted.' For examples of time periods for mediation see eg UN *Handbook* 44 [136].

[63] See eg UN *Handbook* (n 38) 40–1 [124] (listing the 1899 and 1907 Hague Conventions, the Inter-American Treaty on Good Offices and Mediation of 1936, the Charter of the United Nations, the Pact of the League of Arab States, the Charter of the Organization of American States and the American Treaty on Pacific Settlement of 1948, the Charter of the Organization of African Unity and Protocol of the Commission of Mediation, Conciliation and Arbitration of 1964, and the Antarctic Treaty of 1959).

[64] UN *Handbook* (n 38) 42 [129]–[130].

[65] For a discussion of situations in which a non-neutral mediator might also be acceptable see eg Merrills (n 41) 34–6. In discussing the components of a mediation the UN *Handbook* (n 38), at p 42 [130], summarizes:

> Components of the mediation technique, depending on the nature of the dispute, include the communication function, clarification of issues, drafting of proposals, search for areas

But mediation can be resisted because it requires both parties to admit that there is a dispute, that there are two potentially valid positions, and that that dispute requires some compromise.[66] For this reason the overall exhaustion of the parties to the dispute or the threat of escalation tend to facilitate mediation.[67]

CARICOM

Mediation under the RTC is provided for in Article 192. Member states are entitled to choose their own mediator, under Article 192(1), or may request the Secretary General to do so from persons on the list of conciliators established under Article 196. Article 192(2) provides that mediation, like good offices, can be commenced or terminated at any time, and may continue during the course of arbitration or adjudication (subject to the procedural rules of both of the latter processes). As specified in Article 192(3), mediation proceedings and the positions of parties taken therein are confidential and without prejudice to the rights of parties in further proceedings.

OECS

Mediation, except perhaps through the device of good offices, is not provided for under the Dispute Settlement Annex.

13.2.5 Consultations

Consultations may be seen as a variety of negotiations in general international law and are provided for in a number of international treaties.[68] Consultations may be used as a method to resolve a dispute, or as a pre-requisite for other dispute settlement mechanisms.[69]

of agreement between parties, elaboration of provisional arrangements to circumvent or minimize issues on which the parties remain divided as well as alternate solutions, etc., with the primary goal of an early and fundamental resolution of a dispute. It is important to demonstrate to the parties to a dispute that the prospective mediator understands their respective positions, is not biased against any of them and has the necessary skills to perform the function of mediator in the particular dispute.

[66] Merrills (n 41) 32. [67] Merrills (n 41) 42.

[68] See eg UN *Handbook* (n 38) 10 [24]–[25] (referring to the 1975 Convention on the Representation of States in their Relations with International Organizations of a Universal Character, the 1978 Convention on Succession of States in Respect of Treaties, the 1983 Convention on the Succession of State Property, Archives and Debts, the 1959 Antarctic Treaty, the 1979 Convention on the Physical Protection of Nuclear Material and the 1980 Convention on the Conservation of Antarctic Marine Living Resources).

[69] For more on the nature and role of consultations in international law (under the general rubric of negotiations) see Merrills (n 41) 9–23.

CARICOM

Articles 193–194 of the RTC provide for a kind of formalized negotiation process under the rubric of 'consultations'.[70] Interestingly, under these provisions although consultations themselves are not binding, the requirement to enter into consultations is mandatory. Article 193(1) provides that a 'Member State shall enter into consultations upon the request of another Member State where the requesting Member State alleges that an action taken by the requested Member State constitutes a breach of obligations arising from or under the provisions of this Treaty.' A request for a consultation must be in writing, must be notified to the Secretary General, and must 'state the reasons for the consultations and identify the measure at issue and the legal basis for the complaint'.[71] Article 193(2)–(3) also stipulates the timelines for the consultation process. Following receipt of the consultation request a member state must enter into consultations within a period of fourteen days or a mutually agreed period. If consultations are not commenced within this period, or if they do not settle the dispute within forty-five days from receipt of the request for consultations or from the dates mutually agreed, the requesting member state may resort to any other mode of dispute settlement including arbitration and adjudication.[72] Consultations must be confidential and are without prejudice to the rights of member states in further proceedings.[73] However, as implied by Article 193(6), a meaningful effort must be used to resolve the dispute through consultations: 'before resorting to further proceedings, the Member States shall employ their best endeavours to settle the dispute.'

Article 193(7)–(8) also provide for expedited consultation proceedings in cases of urgency, including cases involving perishable goods. The period stipulated for entering into consultations under this procedure is shortened to three days, and the period for resolution of the dispute to seven days. Failure to resolve the dispute under this expedited consultation procedure also permits resort to arbitration or adjudication.

Article 193(9) also provides a mechanism for other member states to be joined in consultations:

> Whenever a Member State, other than the consulting Member States, considers that it has a legitimate interest in consultations being held pursuant to this Article, such Member State may notify the consulting Member States and the Secretary-General, within 10 days after the date of the circulation of the request for consultations, of its desire to be joined in the consultations. Such Member State shall be joined in

[70] According to Sir Robert Jennings and Sir Arthur Watts, in *Oppenheim's International Law*, 9th edn (London: Longman, 1996) Parts 2-4, at 1181–2 (§573), consultations differ from negotiations in general international law in terms of their anticipated results:

> Consultations usually involve discussions specifically intended to import or exchange information about the matter in question, or to seek to impart views about that matter... [whereas] [n]egotiations are discussions held with a view to reaching a mutually acceptable settlement of some matter in issue between two (or more) states.

This distinction does not appear to have been incorporated into either the RTC or RTB.

[71] RTC Art 193(4)–(5). [72] RTC Art 193(3). [73] RTC Art 193(6).

> the consultations, provided that the requested Member State agrees that the claim of legitimate interest is well-founded and based on similar facts and circumstances. In that event, the Member States concerned shall notify the Secretary-General. If the request to be joined in the consultations is not granted, the applicant Member State may request consultations under paragraph 1 of this Article.

This provision is interesting for two reasons. Firstly, it sets up two tracks by which a third party can be joined in consultations. It can apply to do so under Article 193(9) if the consulting member states agree. If they refuse, it can start its own parallel consultation proceedings with the consulting states under Article 193(1). Time lines would become more complicated under the latter process, but at least it ensures that all interested states are provided with the possibility of being involved in consultations. Secondly, Article 193(9) is notable because it appears to contradict the confidential nature of consultation proceedings (as specified in Article 193(6)). Perhaps a better way of interpreting the relation of subsections (6) and (9), however, is one in which they do not conflict. The use of the words 'circulation of the request for consultations' in Article 193(9) suggests that the Secretary General has the right to disseminate basic, non-confidential information about the nature of consultations to member states following notification under Article 193(5). If read in this way, member states are put on notice about imminent consultations, and on the basis of this information may apply to intervene. But the phrase 'circulation of the request' does not necessarily imply a requirement to circulate all of the details of the consultation, including the positions taken by the parties. Such information should only be revealed in the course of the consultations, between consulting parties, and therefore retains its confidential character.

Although Article 193(9) may be unusual in the context of negotiations between states at the international level, it can serve a valuable purpose in CARICOM because it allows for widespread participation in the resolution of disputes between member states. Such a position makes sense in cases where disputes involve the interpretation or application of the provisions of the RTC governing the CSME. This is because although dispute resolution through consultation cannot create binding precedents, it will create non-binding precedents and state practice about how a particular RTC rule should be construed. State practice, as we have seen, can be used as an aid to interpretation of treaties.[74]

OECS

Consultations are provided as the default dispute resolution procedure in Article 18 of the RTB although, unlike the RTC, very little detail is provided about the nature of such consultations. Article 18.1 simply states: '[a]ny dispute that may arise regarding the interpretation and application of this Treaty shall, where parties to the dispute belong to the category of eligible parties under Article 18.5, upon

[74] See Art 31(3)(b) of the Vienna Convention on the Law of Treaties (adopted 23 May 1969, in force 27 Jan 1980) 1155 UNTS 331. See also the discussion of the role of subsequent practice in Chapter 2.

the request of any of them, be amicably resolved by consultation.'[75] Article 18.2 stipulates a waiting period of three months during which such consultations are to occur and, if they are unsuccessful, allows reference of the dispute to one of the procedures under the Dispute Settlement Annex.[76] Consultations may also be continued or reopened at any time by agreement of eligible parties to the dispute.[77]

13.2.6 Conciliation

Conciliation under general international law is distinguished from mediation both by its formality and by its increased powers.[78] Originating in the commissions of enquiry established under the Hague Conventions for the Pacific Settlement of Disputes of 1899 and 1907, conciliation has been said to have a 'semi-judicial aspect', involving panels generally empowered to investigate the facts, hear parties, and make (non-binding) proposals for settlement.[79] Conciliation thus combines elements of both enquiry and mediation.[80] Interestingly, one of the benefits of conciliation as opposed to arbitration or adjudication is that although the conciliation commission may examine and apply law in making a proposal for settlement, it need not do so.[81] The key, as with mediation, is for the commission to reach a settlement that is satisfactory to the parties.

Conciliation gained tremendous popularity in the period between the two World Wars, with nearly 200 treaties embracing this form of dispute settlement having been concluded by 1940.[82] Although conciliation is less prominent today, a number of global multilateral treaties rely upon it and the United Nations has adopted Model Rules for the Conciliation of Disputes between States.[83]

[75] Art 18.5 of the RTB provides: 'The eligible parties for the purpose of Article 18.1 comprise the full Member States, the Associate Member States and the Organisation.'

[76] The three-month waiting period may be shortened, either by the Eastern Caribbean Court of Appeal upon application by a party in cases of urgency, or as a result of the operation of the provisions of the Protocol: RTB Art 18.3-18.4. The latter Protocol may also exempt a party from the waiting period: RTB Art 18.4.

[77] DSA [3].

[78] On conciliation generally under international law see eg Merrills (n 41) 64–90, UN *Handbook* (n 38) 45–55, Jean-Pierre Cot, 'Conciliation', in Wolfrum (ed), *The Max Planck Encyclopedia* (n 38).

[79] James Crawford, *Brownlie's Principles of International Law*, 8th edn (Oxford: Oxford University Press, 2012) 719 [citations omitted]. See also Sands and Klein, *Bowett's Law of International Institutions* (n 39) 350–2 [13-017]–[13-020].

[80] UN *Handbook* (n 38) 45 [140].

[81] For examples of successful commissions that did not formally decide disputes on the basis of law see eg Merrills (n 41) 69–70.

[82] Merrills (n 41) 66. For a description of the work of some of these conciliation commissions see at 67–72.

[83] The UN *Handbook* (n 38) 46 [143], lists the following treaties: 'the 1928 Geneva General Act for the Pacific Settlement of International Disputes as revised in 1949, the 1962 Protocol Instituting a Conciliation and Good Offices Commission to be Responsible for Seeking the Settlement of Any Disputes which May Arise between States Parties to the Convention against Discrimination in Education, the 1969 Vienna Convention on the Law of Treaties, the 1969 International Convention relating to Intervention on the High Seas in Cases of Oil Pollution Casualties, the 1975 Vienna Convention on the Representation of States in their Relations with International Organizations of a Universal Character, the 1978 Vienna Convention on Succession of States in respect of Treaties, the

Negotiation may be a pre-requisite for conciliation, or conciliation itself may be a condition precedent for other forms of dispute resolution.[84] Conciliation is generally an optional third-party procedure, invoked by mutual consent and on an ad hoc basis, or convened under the provisions of a treaty.[85] In some recent cases, however, conciliation has taken on the characteristics of a compulsory process, one allowing unilateral invocation of a conciliation procedure.[86] Conciliation is usually undertaken by a conciliation commission, which traditionally is composed of three to five members, selected either by the parties to the dispute or by a neutral third party.[87] However examples also exist of commissions composed of a single conciliator.[88] Treaties providing for conciliation frequently set out extensive fact-finding powers for commissioners. As highlighted by the United Nations Office of Legal Affairs, conciliation commissions may utilize a number of procedures to accomplish their objectives:

> [I]t should be recalled that conciliation combines elements of fact-finding and that it would accordingly rely upon certain techniques for gathering and evaluating the facts giving rise to the dispute. Thus in all treaties establishing conciliation as a third-party procedure there are provisions giving the commission the right to hear the parties, to examine their claims and objections and make proposals for an amicable solution or to draw the attention of the parties to the dispute to any measures which might facilitate an amicable settlement. In carrying out its functions, the commission may also summon and hear witnesses and experts and visit, with the consent of the parties, the localities in question. Other provisions provide also the right of the parties to the dispute to be represented before the commission by agents, counsel and experts appointed by them, while also being required to supply the commission with the necessary documents and information which would facilitate its work. Some treaties provide that, unless the parties otherwise agree, the work of the commission is not to be conducted in public. If a commission is able to conclude its work, it would prepare and submit a formal report containing its recommendations. Where it has not been able to reach a settlement, the commission is still expected under certain treaties to prepare the minutes of its proceedings or procès-verbaux in which no mention shall be made as to whether the commission's decisions were taken unanimously or by a majority vote. In certain treaties, there are provisions allowing conciliators to submit separate opinions if necessary.[89]

Despite such extensive fact-finding powers, conciliation commissions have considerable discretion with regard to how comprehensive an investigation should be. In some cases a commission may decide not to explore a particular line of

1982 United Nations Convention on the Law of the Sea, the 1983 Vienna Convention on Succession of States in Respect of State Property, Archives and Debts, the 1985 Vienna Convention for the Protection of the Ozone Layer and the 1986 Vienna Convention on the Law of Treaties between States and International Organizations or between International Organizations.' See also the United Nations Model Rules for the Conciliation of Disputes between States, UNGA Res A/RES/50/50 (29 Jan 1996).

84 UN *Handbook* (n 38) 47 [146]. 85 *UN Handbook* (n 38) 51 [154].

86 eg the UN *Handbook* (n 38), at p 49 [149], refers to the conciliation provisions of the 1969 Vienna Convention on the Law of Treaties and the 1982 United Nations Convention on the Law of the Sea. See also at 51 [155].

87 UN *Handbook* (n 38) 49–50 [150]–[153]. 88 See eg Merrills (n 41) 70–1.

89 UN *Handbook* (n 38) 52 [158] (citations omitted).

enquiry if it is clear that the facts to be found may not help to resolve the dispute.[90] Treaties providing for conciliation also tend to impose fixed time limits for the conclusion of the conciliation commission's work.[91] The results of a conciliation process have traditionally been non-binding, although a few recent treaties have provided otherwise.[92] The proceedings of conciliation commissions traditionally are strictly confidential and arguments and positions may not be invoked in subsequent proceedings.[93]

Although conciliation has been provided as a dispute resolution process in a wide range and number of treaties, the quantity of cases actually heard by commissions has been small (approximately twenty in the last eighty or so years).[94] This relatively small number may be as a result of the complexity of commission processes and their cost.[95] These two factors, and the relative lack of political authority of commissions (compared to the prestige of a prominent mediator), may have discouraged the use of conciliation for both small matters and major disputes.[96] Conciliation tends to be most successful when the main issues are legal, some factual evidence is required, and yet the parties desire an equitable, rather than strictly legal compromise.[97] Nevertheless, as pointed out by Merrills, the small number of conciliation commissions may not be indicative of failure. Rather, the simple availability of conciliation as a form of dispute settlement, particularly where conciliation is required by the terms of a treaty, may have a moderating influence on the positions taken by states with respect to disputes.[98]

CARICOM

The RTC establishes a formal conciliation process. Under Article 195 this process can be unilaterally commenced by any CARICOM member state against any other member state that has agreed to submit a dispute to conciliation under the RTC. Conciliation thus requires consent, but such consent can be expressed in advance. Article 196 provides for the establishment of a List of Conciliators from which parties can draw a conciliation commission. Each member state can nominate two persons to the List, whose terms are stipulated to be five years long.[99]

Conciliation commissions under Article 197 are meant to be made up of three conciliators, one of whom is to be appointed by each party within the stipulated

[90] See eg Merrills (n 41) 73. For further examples of ways in which a commission may obtain evidence see at 73–5.

[91] UN *Handbook* (n 38) 52 [159]

[92] UN *Handbook* (n 38) 54–5 [164]–[167]. See also Merrills (n 41) 79–82 (on the conciliation processes associated with the VCLT and UNCLOS), and 83–6 (on CSCE and OSCE processes).

[93] Merrills (n 41) 75–6.

[94] Merrills (n 41) 87. A conciliation commission was convened recently under the aegis of ICSID to deal with a dispute involving a CARICOM member state: *Tesoro Petroleum Corporation v Trinidad and Tobago* (ICSID Case No CONC/83/1) (settlement agreed 27 Nov 1985), as available through <https://icsid.worldbank.org/ICSID/FrontServlet?requestType=CasesRH&actionVal=ListCases> (4 Aug 2013).

[95] Merrills (n 41) 87–8. [96] Merrills (n 41) 88. [97] Merrills (n 41) 88.

[98] Merrills (n 41) 89–90.

[99] RTC Art 196(1)–(2). Note, however, that the default position is that a conciliator's name will remain on the list until withdrawn by the relevant member state: Art 196(1). Equally, a conciliator

time limits, and both of whom are to appoint the third conciliator.[100] In the event that any party fails to appoint a conciliator, or the two conciliators fail to appoint the third conciliator, the vacant position(s) shall be appointed by the Secretary General.[101] Vacancies are to be filled in the same manner, and if two or more parties to the dispute agree, a single conciliator may be appointed.[102]

In terms of powers of the commission, under Article 198 the conciliation commission is expressly accorded the competence to suggest measures to the parties which might facilitate an amicable settlement. It thus can exercise independent initiative and is not limited to the views of the parties. The commission is also authorized under Article 199 to hear the parties to the dispute, examine their claims and objections, and make proposals to the parties with a view to reaching an amicable settlement. Under Article 200, unless the parties agree otherwise, a conciliation commission is empowered to determine its own procedure.[103] With the consent of the parties it may invite any member state to submit its views, either orally or in writing.[104] The commission is mandated to make its report, recommendations, and decisions on procedural matters by means of a majority vote.[105] Under Article 201(1), within three months of its constitution the conciliation commission is required to issue a report which 'shall record any agreements reached and, failing agreement, its conclusions on all questions of fact or law relevant to the matter in dispute and such recommendations as a conciliation commission may deem appropriate for an amicable settlement'. The conclusions or recommendations of the conciliation commission are not binding.[106] As stipulated in Article 203, the fees and expenses of the commission must be covered by the parties. The conciliation proceedings are deemed to be terminated in three circumstances: 'when a settlement has been reached, when the parties have accepted or one party has rejected the recommendations of the report by notification addressed to the Secretary General, or when a period of one month has expired from the date of transmission of the report to the parties'.[107]

serving on a commission is required to continue to serve on it until the proceedings have been completed, regardless of the maintenance of his or her name on the List: Art 196(1)–(2).

[100] RTC Art 197(a)–(d).

[101] RTC Art 197(c)–(e). Note that if the second, respondent party refuses to appoint a conciliator, the first party may simply decide to terminate the proceedings: Art 197(c). These two options for the state seeking conciliation get around the difficulties which occurred in the case of *Interpretation of Peace Treaties with Bulgaria, Hungary and Roumania* (Second Phase) (Advisory Opinion) [1950] ICJ Rep 221. In that case a dispute arose for resolution by a three-member commission. One party appointed its commissioner, but the other party refused to do so. The Secretary General was empowered under the treaty to appoint the third. The issue that arose for the International Court of Justice was whether the Secretary General could appoint both the third and the *second* commissioner. The Court held that the treaty was clear and only empowered the Secretary General to appoint the third commissioner, not the second. As a result, the commission could not be formed and the peace treaty dispute settlement process was rendered useless.

[102] RTC Art 197(f)–(g). Note that if parties do not have the same interests, or disagree about this point, the normal process for appointment of conciliators would apply: Art 197(h).

[103] Note that under RTC Art 200(2) the parties to the dispute may, 'by agreement applicable solely to that dispute, modify the procedure referred to in paragraph 1'.

[104] RTC Art 200(1). [105] RTC Art 200(1). [106] RTC Art 201(2).

[107] RTC Art 202.

OECS

The conciliation procedure under the original 1981 Treaty has been substantially continued under the Dispute Settlement Annex to the RTB. Paragraph 4 of the Dispute Settlement Annex provides for the maintenance of a list of conciliators by the Chief Registrar of the Eastern Caribbean Court of Appeal, who must be 'persons enjoying the highest reputation for fairness, competence and integrity'.[108] Each member state is entitled to nominate two conciliators to the list, with others added at the discretion of the Chief Justice of the Court.[109] The term for a conciliator nominated to the list by a member state is five years and may be renewed; the term for a conciliator nominated by the Chief Justice is decided by the Chief Justice at the time of listing, and also may be renewed.[110] A conciliator previously nominated under Annex A to the original 1981 Treaty continues until the end of his or her period of appointment under that regime.[111] A conciliator whose term has expired will nevertheless be required to fulfil any incomplete functions under the Dispute Settlement Annex.[112]

When parties agree to bring their dispute to conciliation they must notify the Director General who shall bring the dispute before a conciliation commission.[113] This commission, as stipulated under paragraph 4.7, is to be constituted by five members, two of whom are to be chosen by each party (one a citizen and one not a citizen) within thirty days of the receipt of the request by the Director General.[114] Within an additional thirty days, the four conciliators must choose the fifth conciliator from the list, who shall serve as Chairman.[115] In the event that the appointment of the Chairman or any other conciliator is not made within the time period provided, the Director General shall appoint that person within an additional thirty days, either from one of the conciliators on the list or from the membership of the International Law Commission.[116] The time periods for appointment may be extended by mutual agreement by the parties to the dispute and any vacancy is to be filled following the initial appointment procedure.[117]

Under paragraph 4.8 the conciliation commission is to decide its own procedure and 'with the consent of the parties to the dispute, may invite any Member State of the Organisation to submit to it its views orally or in writing'. Decisions and recommendations are to be made by a majority vote of the five members of the commission but, unlike its predecessor under the original Treaty, the report of the commission is not binding.[118] The commission is empowered to bring to the attention of the parties any measure which might facilitate amicable settlement and, after hearing the parties and examining the claims and objections, is to make proposals to the parties to the same end.[119] The commission is to be assisted by

[108] DSA [4.1]. [109] DSA [4.2]–[4.3]. [110] DSA [4.4]. [111] DSA [4.6].

[112] DSA [4.5].

[113] The Director General's role is subject to DSA para [5.12], which provides: 'Where the Organisation is a party to the dispute under Article 18.5, the functions of the Director-General under this Annex shall be exercised by the Chief Justice through the Chief Registrar.'

[114] DSA [4.7(a)–(b)]. [115] DSA [4.7(c)]. [116] DSA [4.7(d)].

[117] DSA [4.7(d)–(e)]. [118] DSA [4.8] and [4.11]. [119] DSA [4.10].

the Director General and its expenses borne by the Organisation and, as provided in paragraph 4.11, must submit its non-binding report within six months of its constitution:

> 4.11 The Commission shall report within six months of its constitution. Its report shall be deposited with the Director-General and transmitted to the parties to the dispute. The report of the Commission, including any conclusions stated therein regarding the facts or questions of law, shall not be binding upon the parties.

As revealed in the wording of this paragraph, the Dispute Settlement Annex appears to contemplate the conciliation commission as potentially serving a law-applying role, in a manner similar to an arbitral tribunal or court. As seen earlier, this is also the case under the RTC. However in both cases, as occurs generally under international law, it would appear that conciliation commissions need not apply law to resolve a dispute if they can otherwise amicably settle the matter to the satisfaction of all parties.

13.2.7 Arbitration

Arbitration has been a prominent dispute settlement mechanism in the international legal order since the Alabama Claims Arbitration of 1872, and is included in the Hague Conventions of 1899 and 1907.[120] Article 15 of the Hague Convention of 1899 describes international arbitration as having the objective of 'the settlement of differences between States by judges of their own choice, and on the basis of respect for law'. Article 37 of the Hague Convention of 1907 repeats these words and adds '[r]ecourse to arbitration implies an engagement to submit in good faith to the Award.' The latter phrase highlights the binding nature of arbitration under international law, a feature that distinguishes it from the other dispute settlement mechanisms discussed earlier and which it shares in common with judicial dispute settlement. As noted by the Permanent Court of International Justice in its Advisory Opinion on the Interpretation of Article 3, Paragraph 2, of the Treaty of Lausanne, arbitration involves a binding determination made by a third party, who acts judicially—deciding on the basis of respect for law—and to whom the parties have voluntarily submitted their dispute.[121]

Arbitral panels under general international law may be composed of three or five arbitrators, or a sole arbitrator.[122] Because arbitral panels generally rely upon majority

[120] *Alabama Claims Arbitration (United States v Great Britain)* Moore (1872) 1 Int Arb 495, Convention for the Pacific Settlement of Disputes (29 Jul 1899) 187 CTS 410, Convention for the Pacific Settlement of Disputes (18 Oct 1907) 205 CTS 233, both also available through <http://pca-cpa.org/showpage.asp?pag_id=1187> (27 Jul 2013). On arbitration generally under international law see eg Merrills (n 41) 91–126, UN *Handbook* (n 38) 55–65, Charles H Brower II, 'Arbitration', in Wolfrum (ed), *The Max Planck Encyclopedia* (n 38).

[121] (Advisory Opinion) [1925] PCIJ Rep, Series B, No 12, p 26. Note that because the Court emphasized the *legal* nature of arbitral awards, it could not characterize the procedure established by the Treaty of Lausanne as arbitration, properly speaking, since 'the settlement of the dispute in question depends, at all events for the most part, on considerations not of a legal character'. See p 26.

[122] See eg UN *Handbook* (n 38) 59–60 [178]. For examples of famous arbitrations involving sole arbitrators see eg Merrills (n 41) 92–4.

decision making, the selection of a neutral person to chair the panel (sometimes called the umpire), is particularly important.[123] For this reason parties often stipulate that in cases of disagreement a neutral third party, such as the President of the International Court of Justice, shall appoint the umpire.[124] Arbitral panels may be composed of individuals appointed from a pre-constituted list of arbitrators, as in the case of the Permanent Court of Arbitration, or may be selected without a list.[125]

In recent times international arbitration has been used to decide cases involving state and non-state actors. Famous mixed arbitration tribunals were formed to resolve disputes after World War I under the Treaty of Versailles and after the Iranian revolution (the Iran-US Claims Tribunal).[126] Investor-state disputes today also rely upon a number of different arbitral mechanisms.[127] State-to-state disputes resolved through arbitration are rarer, except in particular areas, such as in 'territorial and boundary disputes, disputes concerning interpretation of bilateral or multilateral treaties, and those relating to claims of violation of international law'.[128] Several boundary disputes in the Caribbean have relied upon arbitration.[129]

[123] See eg Merrills (n 41) 96. [124] Merrills (n 41) 96.

[125] See eg UN *Handbook* (n 38) 60–1 [179].

[126] See eg UN *Handbook* (n 38) 56.

[127] See eg the Convention on the Settlement of Investment Disputes Between States and Nationals of Other States (adopted 18 Mar 1965, in force 14 Oct 1966) 575 UNTS 160. A number of Caribbean cases have been filed under the ICSID rules, including: *RSM Production Corporation v Grenada* (ICSID Case No ARB/05/14); *WRB Enterprises and Grenada Private Power Limited v Grenada* (ICSID Case No ARB/97/5); *RSM Production Corporation and others v Grenada* (ICSID Case No ARB/10/6); *Booker plc v Co-operative Republic of Guyana* (ICSID Case No ARB/01/9); *Alcoa Minerals of Jamaica, Inc v Jamaica* (ICSID Case No ARB/74/2); *Reynolds Jamaica Mines Limited and Reynolds Metals Company v Jamaica* (ICSID Case No ARB/74/4); *Kaiser Bauxite Company v Jamaica* (ICSID Case No ARB/74/3); *F-W Oil Interests, Inc v Republic of Trinidad & Tobago* (ICSID Case No ARB/01/14); *Cable Television of Nevis, Ltd and Cable Television of Nevis Holdings, Ltd v Federation of St Kitts and Nevis* (ICSID Case No ARB/95/2); *RSM Production Corporation v Saint Lucia* (ICSID Case No ARB/12/10). See generally the ICSID website at <https://icsid.worldbank.org/ICSID/FrontServlet?requestType=CasesRH&actionVal=ListCases> (4 Aug 2013). Another popular set of investor-state arbitration rules is the United Nations Commission on International Trade Law, 'UNCITRAL Arbitration Rules' (as revised in 2010) (New York: United Nations, 2011). Caribbean cases filed under the UNCITRAL rules include *British Caribbean Bank Limited v The Government of Belize; Dunkeld International Investment Ltd v Belize (Number 2)*; and *Dunkeld International Investment Ltd v The Government of Belize*. For further information about these UNCITRAL proceedings see <http://www.italaw.com/> (4 Aug 2013). Other popular arbitration mechanisms, for a wide range of disputes, include the International Chamber of Commerce, 'ICC Rules of Arbitration' (in force 1 Jan 2012), as available through <http://www.iccwbo.org/Products-and-Services/Arbitration-and-ADR/Arbitration/ICC-Rules-of-Arbitration/> (4 Aug 2013), the London Court of International Arbitration, 'LCIA Arbitration Rules' (effective 1 Jan 1998), as available through <http://www.lcia.org/> (4 Aug 2013), and the Arbitration Institute of the Stockholm Chamber of Commerce, 'Arbitration Rules 2010', as available through <http://sccinstitute.com/skiljedomsregler-4.aspx> (4 Aug 2013). See also the various rules of procedure utilized by the Permanent Court of Arbitration, including the PCA's 'Arbitration Rules 2012', as available through <http://pca-cpa.org/showpage.asp?pag_id=1188> (4 Aug 2013).

[128] UN *Handbook* (n 38) 56 [172]. See also Merrills (n 41) 122. For an example of model rules see the International Law Commission, 'Model Rules on Arbitral Procedure with a general commentary' (1958) *Yearbook of the International Law Commission, 1958*, vol II.

[129] See eg the *Venezuela-British Guiana Boundary Arbitration (Venezuela v Great Britain)* [1899-1900] Vol 92, British and Foreign State Papers, p 16; *Barbados-Trinidad and Tobago Maritime*

Like judicial settlement, arbitration is a dispute settlement mechanism that relies upon law.[130] Arbitral proceedings tend to follow a similar structure to judicial proceedings, involving formal written and oral pleadings, including rules related to submission of evidence, and allowing for questioning of agents of the parties by the arbitral panel.[131] The deliberations of arbitral tribunals, like courts, are held in private and are secret, and the ultimate decision of the tribunal, which is usually arrived at by means of a majority decision, is set out in an award.[132] This award, like a judgment of a court, must set out its reasons and be based upon law.[133] It is also final.[134] The award can, however, if the parties so authorize, be subsequently interpreted, revised, rectified, appealed, or nullified.[135] The ability to appeal an award is very rare, but parties will frequently provide for subsequent interpretation of an award to resolve difficulties.[136] Revision in order to take into account new facts must be expressly authorized; but tribunals are likely to have an implied power to correct errors in the text of the award, at least until it has been executed.[137] A number of grounds could be used to nullify an award, including: the invalidity of the arbitration instrument (*compromis*), irregular appointment of an arbitrator, excess of jurisdiction, violation by the tribunal of a basic rule of judicial procedure,

Boundary Arbitration (11 Apr 2006) [2006] 45 ILM 800, also available through <http://pca-cpa.org/showpage.asp?pag_id=1152> (4 Aug 2013); *Guyana-Suriname Maritime Boundary Arbitration* (17 Sep 2007) [2008] 47 ILM 166, also available through <http://pca-cpa.org/showpage.asp?pag_id=1147> (4 Aug 2013).

130 As noted in Art 38 of the 1907 Hague Convention, '[i]n questions of a legal nature, and especially in the interpretation or application of International Conventions, arbitration is recognized by the Contracting Powers as the most effective, and, at the same time, the most equitable means of settling disputes which diplomacy has failed to settle.'

131 eg Art 63 of the 1907 Hague Convention provides:

> As a general rule, arbitration procedure comprises two distinct phases: pleadings and oral discussions.
>
> The pleadings consist in the communication by the respective agents to the members of the Tribunal and the opposite party of cases, counter-cases, and, if necessary, of replies; the parties annex thereto all papers and documents called for in the case. This communication shall be made either directly or through the intermediary of the International Bureau, in the order and within the time fixed by the 'Compromis'.
>
> The time fixed by the 'Compromis' may be extended by mutual agreement by the parties, or by the Tribunal when the latter considers it necessary for the purpose of reaching a just decision.
>
> The discussions consist in the oral development before the Tribunal of the arguments of the parties.

See also Hague Convention Art 72, which provides for the putting of questions to parties by the tribunal.

132 See eg Art 78 of the 1907 Hague Convention. The Permanent Court of International Justice, in *Interpretation of Article 3, Paragraph 2, of the Treaty of Lausanne* (Advisory Opinion) [1925] PCIJ Rep, Series B, No 12, at pp 30–1, noted that the majority principle is generally accepted for decisions of arbitral tribunals.

133 See eg Art 79 of the 1907 Hague Convention.

134 See eg Art 81 of the 1907 Hague Convention. Note that Arts 82 and 83 of the 1907 Convention allow the parties to use the same tribunal to resolve any issues of interpretation related to the award, as well as to provide for a right of revision of the award.

135 See Merrills (n 41) 110.

136 Merrills (n 41) 111.

137 Merrills (n 41) 112–13.

fundamental procedural flaws (eg, unfairness to one party or basing the award on considerations never put to the parties), failure to give reasons, fraud, corruption, or an 'essential error'.[138] Unlike judicial dispute settlement in common law legal systems, the arbitral award does not establish formal precedent.[139]

Several features distinguish arbitration from adjudication. First, like the dispute settlement mechanisms discussed earlier, arbitration is consensual in nature. Parties must agree to arbitration, either in advance or after the dispute has arisen.[140] Without such agreement one state cannot compel another state to arbitrate. Second, arbitration is ad hoc in nature. In most cases parties to the arbitration must select the arbitrators, define the scope and nature of the dispute to be considered and the tribunal's jurisdiction, and choose, amongst other things, the arbitral forum, applicable law, language of arbitration, and the method of allocation of the costs of the arbitration.[141] Similarly, the rules governing the arbitral tribunal in most cases must either be selected by the parties or the arbitrators themselves.[142] These choices tend to be set out formally in a document entitled the *compromis*.[143] This is the case even for arbitrations convened under the Permanent Court of Arbitration system, established under the Hague Conventions of 1899 and 1907 which, contrary to its name, does not set up a standing arbitral panel, but merely facilitates arbitrations through an established list of arbitrators from which parties may choose, optional arbitral rules, a default arbitral seat, and a permanent secretariat (the Bureau).[144]

A benefit that may lead to the choice of arbitration over judicial settlement is the ability of parties to choose the arbitrators. This choice allows for a level of specialization and control not usually available in a court.[145] Parties to a dispute involving principles of international trade law, for example, can choose arbitrators with acknowledged authority in that area. Similarly, the parties can define the

[138] Merrills (n 41) 113–17. Merrills notes, however, at p 126, that in most cases of state-to-state arbitral awards no formal processes exists to assess nullity claims. As a result, such claims tend to be handled diplomatically and thereby lose much of their effectiveness.

[139] See eg 1907 Hague Convention Art 84.

[140] As noted in the UN *Handbook* (n 38) at 57–8 [174], parties may rely upon bilateral or multilateral treaties specifically focused upon dispute settlement, or may include a compromissory clause in a treaty which provides for arbitration, or may invoke arbitration by means of a special agreement.

[141] eg Art 52 of the 1907 Hague Convention provides:

> The Powers which have recourse to arbitration sign a 'Compromis', in which the subject of the dispute is clearly defined, the time allowed for appointing Arbitrators, the form, order, and time in which the communication referred to in Article 63 must be made, and the amount of the sum which each party must deposit in advance to defray the expenses.
>
> The 'Compromis' likewise defines, if there is occasion, the manner of appointing Arbitrators, any special powers which may eventually belong to the Tribunal, where it shall meet, the language it shall use, and the languages the employment of which shall be authorized before it, and, generally speaking, all the conditions on which the parties are agreed.

For more on the nature of arbitral tribunals, including the applicable law, the methods of work, the seat and administrative aspects, and the apportioning of expenses, see eg UN *Handbook* (n 38) 62–4 [181]–[191].

[142] See eg UN *Handbook* (n 38) 61 [180].

[143] For more on the content of the *compromis* see eg UN *Handbook* 58–9 [175]–[177].

[144] See generally the 1899 and 1907 Hague Conventions.

[145] See eg UN *Handbook* (n 38) 55 [170].

precise scope of the arbitration, including matters over which the tribunal may take jurisdiction, the applicable law (including specific fields of international law, or municipal law, or both), the ability of the tribunal to use non-legal criteria (fairness, equitable considerations, or to decide the dispute *ex aequo et bono*), and even the ability of the tribunal to create a new legal regime to govern the future relations of the parties.[146] Arbitration also may be preferred because it can avoid the stigma associated with judicial dispute settlement, where one party (a complainant) brings a case against another party (a defendant) alleging breach by the latter of its legal obligations. Since arbitration is consensual, in principle neither party should be characterized as a defendant. Finally, by providing for the possibility of arbitration as an option for dispute settlement in a treaty parties send a clear message about the nature of the treaty. As noted by Merrills, 'a provision for compulsory arbitration, by its very existence, can discourage unreasonable behaviour, and so may be useful even if it is never invoked.'[147]

One drawback to international arbitration, however, lies in its cost. Since in most cases none of the facilities necessary for the arbitration will exist prior to the commencement of the matter, the parties will need to dedicate considerable resources to, for example, establish a secretariat, find an arbitral venue, establish rules of procedure, and pay for arbitrators. Another drawback, at least in cases of state-to-state arbitration, is related to the enforceability of the arbitral award. As noted by Merrills, '[a]lthough arbitration produces a binding decision, there is usually no guarantee that the unsuccessful party will carry out its obligation to recognise the award.'[148] This is not to say that states will not honour arbitration awards in most cases, since it is generally in their long-term interest to abide by international law. But because of potential problems with respect to enforcement, some states have sought to provide mechanisms to allow for ready execution of awards, such as by jointly creating a fund from which awards are to be paid.[149] In addition some arbitral tribunals, recognizing this difficulty, have sought to frame the award in such a way as to produce a result mutually acceptable to both parties.[150]

CARICOM

The Revised Treaty of Chaguaramas establishes a fairly elaborate process for arbitration. Arbitration under Chapter 9 may be commenced only with the consent of both member states party to a dispute.[151] Article 205 establishes a List of Arbitrators from which parties to a dispute may choose, and specifies their necessary qualifications. Under this provision arbitrators must be impartial, reliable, and possess sound judgment and

[146] See Merrills (n 41) 100, 104–10. Note that if a tribunal exceeds its jurisdiction the award can be considered a nullity: at 102.

[147] Merrills (n 41) 123. Merrills makes a similar point about optional arbitration at p 123.

[148] Merrills (n 41) 124. [149] Merrills (n 41) 125.

[150] Merrills (n 41) 125, which also argues for the creation of more formal processes to assess nullity claims as a way of ensuring that awards will be more readily enforceable.

[151] RTC Art 204.

(a) have expertise or experience in law, international trade, other matters covered by this Treaty, or the settlement of disputes arising under international trade agreements;
(b) be independent of, and not be affiliated with or take instructions from any Member State; and
(c) comply with the Code of Judicial Conduct governing the behaviour of judges of the Court.[152]

The term of an arbitrator is five years and may be renewed.[153]

The process for constituting an arbitral panel is similar to that for conciliation commissions under the RTC, albeit with much tighter time lines. Under Article 206(1), within fifteen days from the decision to arbitrate, each party to a dispute must appoint one arbitrator from the List, with the two arbitrators then having fifteen days in which to appoint the third. Arbitrators, 'as far as practicable' are not to be nationals of parties to the dispute.[154] If either party fails to appoint an arbitrator, or the two arbitrators fail to appoint a third, the Secretary General is required to appoint an arbitrator within ten days.[155] Under Article 206(3)–(4) provision is made for joint appointment of arbitrators where there are more than two parties to the dispute, and for the Secretary General to appoint an arbitrator or Chairman where the parties or arbitrators, respectively, fail to do so. In addition, if the parties agree they may consent to the Secretary General appointing a sole arbitrator from the List, who shall not be a national of a party, to decide the dispute.[156]

The arbitral tribunal is mandated to establish its own rules of procedure, although this procedure must include at least one hearing before the arbitral tribunal, as well as the opportunity to provide initial and rebuttal written submissions.[157] The tribunal's hearings, deliberations and initial report, and all written submissions to and communications with the arbitral tribunal, are confidential.[158] The tribunal is also empowered to invite any member state to submit its views either orally or in writing.[159] Similarly, under Article 209 the tribunal may, if the parties so agree and subject to any terms they impose, 'on its own initiative or on the request of a party to the dispute, seek information and technical advice from any expert or body that it considers appropriate'. Under Article 208 third parties are entitled to participate in the arbitration: they 'shall be entitled to attend all hearings and to receive written submissions of the parties to a dispute and may be permitted to make oral or written submissions to the arbitral tribunal'. This is an interesting development in the CARICOM dispute settlement system and may reflect the concern expressed earlier about the need for greater participation in dispute settlement processes that could create precedents in relation to the CSME. Although arbitration awards will only be binding upon parties to the dispute, because they represent the legal determinations of eminent jurists non-party states may be concerned about the potential effect of awards on the interpretation and application of the RTC by other bodies, including future arbitration tribunals and the CCJ.

[152] RTC Art 205(1).
[153] RTC Art 205(2).
[154] RTC Art 206(1).
[155] RTC Art 206(2).
[156] RTC Art 206(5).
[157] RTC Art 207(1)–(2).
[158] RTC Art 207(3).
[159] RTC Art 207(4).

The decision of the arbitral tribunal is to be expressed in an award, which is final and binding on the member states parties to the dispute.[160] All decisions of the tribunal, including the award, are to be taken by a majority vote.[161] The award must be confined to the subject matter of the dispute and state the reasons on which it is based.[162] Although the award is final, if a party cannot agree on the interpretation or implementation of the award, it may apply to the arbitral tribunal for a ruling within thirty days of the award.[163] The tribunal then has thirty days to make the requested ruling. The expenses of the arbitration are to be borne equally by the parties unless the tribunal determines otherwise, but with the expenses of a third party being borne by that party.[164] The termination of the tribunal is provided in Article 207(6): '[t]he term of the arbitral tribunal shall come to an end unless an application for a ruling has been received, in which case it shall continue for such reasonable time, not exceeding thirty days, as may be required to make the ruling.'

OECS

Paragraph 5 of the Dispute Settlement Annex provides a similar, fairly elaborate arbitral process for the OECS. The Chief Registrar of the Eastern Caribbean Court of Appeal is required to maintain a list of 'panelists' qualified for membership of an Arbitral Tribunal, which must consist of 'persons chosen strictly on the basis of impartiality, reliability and sound judgment, and who shall have expertise or experience in law, international trade, other matters covered by this Treaty, or the settlement of disputes arising under international trade agreements'.[165] Each member state is entitled to nominate two persons to the list, with others added at the discretion of the Chief Justice.[166] The term of a panellist nominated by a member state is five years, with that of a panellist nominated by the Chief Justice to be as decided by the Chief Justice at the time of appointment.[167] In both cases the terms of a panellist are renewable.[168] A panellist is required to continue to fulfil any on-going functions under the Dispute Settlement Annex after the expiry of his or her term.[169]

Where parties to a dispute agree to arbitration they must notify the Director General who, subject to paragraph 5.12, shall bring the dispute to an Arbitral Tribunal.[170] The Arbitral Tribunal is composed of five panellists, two of whom are to be appointed by each party to the dispute, with the four panellists within thirty days of their appointment themselves appointing the fifth who shall be Chairman.[171] If any panellist or the Chairman is not appointed within the

[160] RTC Art 207(7). [161] RTC Art 207(7). [162] RTC Art 207(5).
[163] RTC Art 207(6). [164] RTC Art 210.
[165] DSA [5.1]. Interestingly, a person may be simultaneously nominated to the list of conciliators and arbitrators: DSA [5.4].
[166] DSA [5.2]–[5.3]. [167] DSA [5.5]. [168] DSA [5.5]. [169] DSA [5.6].
[170] DSA [5.7]. DSA para [5.12] provides: 'Where the Organisation is a party to the dispute under Article 18.5, the functions of the Director-General under this Annex shall be exercised by the Chief Justice through the Chief Registrar.'
[171] DSA [5.7(a)–(b)].

specified time period, under paragraph 5.7(c) the Director General is empowered to make the appointment within thirty days following the expiry of that time period. In the case of the appointment of the Chairman, paragraph 5.7(c) provides that the Director General may choose 'either from the list or from the membership of the List of Arbitrators under the Revised Treaty of Chaguaramas'. Periods for appointment may be extended by agreement between the parties and any vacancies are to be filled in the same manner as the initial appointment.

In contrast to the Dispute Settlement Annex provision related to conciliators, which provides for a time limit of thirty days for appointment by the parties to the dispute, paragraph 5.7(a) omits a time limit for appointment of arbitral panellists by the parties. Paragraph 5.7(a) simply provides that 'each party shall appoint two members of the Tribunal from among the list of panelists.'[172] This omission could pose a serious challenge to the arbitral process, since one party could foreclose arbitration by not appointing its arbitrators. Although such a situation might seem unlikely, given that arbitration is only commenced with the consent of both parties, it could arise if one party agreed in bad faith to arbitration solely as a stalling tactic and to preclude the jurisdiction of the Eastern Caribbean Court of Appeal. As provided in paragraph 5.8, '[t]he notification by the parties to a dispute under paragraph 5.7 of this Annex terminates the right of any such party to have recourse to adjudication of the dispute by the Eastern Caribbean Court of Appeal.' Whether the Director General would be deemed to have the power to appoint the missing arbitrators, or whether a similar three-month time limit could be read into paragraph 5.7(a), remains to be seen.[173]

Under paragraph 5.9 the Arbitral Tribunal is to determine its own procedure. The Tribunal is to be assisted and provided with facilities by the Director General, and its expenses are to be borne by the Organisation.[174] The law to be applied by the Arbitral Tribunal in resolving the dispute is stipulated, under paragraph 9, to be 'public international law, including the principles of public international law governing the application and interpretation of treaties'. The Tribunal must report within six months of its constitution and this report is to be deposited with the Director General as well as transmitted to the parties.[175] According to paragraph 5.10, the 'report of the Tribunal, including any conclusions stated therein regarding the facts or questions of law, shall be binding upon the parties.' In its report (award) the Arbitral Tribunal is empowered under paragraph 10 to

(a) award monetary compensation to a complainant State;
(b) order the party complained against to take measures to comply with that party's obligations under this Treaty; [and]
(c) declare the right of a complainant state to exercise any right of redress available under international law...

[172] See DSA [4.7(b)] for the time limit for parties to appoint conciliators.

[173] In this vein, see the discussion of *Interpretation of Peace Treaties with Bulgaria, Hungary and Roumania* (Second Phase) (Advisory Opinion) [1950] ICJ Rep 221, in footnote 101.

[174] DSA [5.11]. [175] DSA [5.10].

The Tribunal is not empowered, under paragraph 10(d) to 'annul or declare void any wrongful or ultra vires act of an Organ of the Organisation'. The latter power appears to be limited to the Eastern Caribbean Court of Appeal.

13.2.8 Adjudication

The term 'adjudication' in Article 188 of the RTC refers to adjudication before the Caribbean Court of Justice in its original jurisdiction. Likewise, the same term, when used in the Dispute Settlement Annex of the RTB, refers to adjudication by the Eastern Caribbean Court of Appeal. Both of these judicial bodies—which represent standing, compulsory, authoritative, final, and binding dispute settlement mechanisms—are discussed in Chapter 14.

The CCJ and ECCA complement and complete the wide range of binding and non-binding mechanisms available under both the RTC and RTB. Taken together, the various dispute settlement mechanisms available under the two treaties allow member states to utilize whichever process is best suited to the circumstances of an individual dispute. Collectively, they represent a significant advance over the dispute resolution processes available under the original treaties which established CARICOM and the OECS.

14

Dispute Settlement through Regional Courts

14.1 Development of Regional Integration Courts

As foreshadowed in the previous chapter and in the discussions of the difficulties related to enforcement of legal obligations in Chapter 6, the need for a final and binding legal dispute resolution mechanism for regional integration is clear, and has been so for some time. Regional and sub-regional courts existed in the Caribbean in the past, including the Federal Supreme Court of the West Indies Federation and the West Indies Associated States Supreme Court. However these courts served appellate rather than treaty-interpreting functions and thus had little impact upon the legal regimes established under the original CARICOM and OECS treaties.

The need for a court with such a treaty-interpreting function was contemplated as early as 1972, in the report of the Representative Committee of the Organisation of Commonwealth Caribbean Bar Associations.[1] It was highlighted more recently in the 1992 Report of the West Indian Commission.[2] In the latter report the Commission called for the creation of a CARICOM Supreme Court, one with both an appellate and original jurisdiction.[3] In relation to its original jurisdiction, the West Indian Commission urged:

> [T]here is now another reason for establishing a court of high authority in the region, and that is the process of integration itself. Integration in its broadest economic sense—involving a Single CARICOM Market, monetary union, the movement of capital and labour and

[1] See eg Duke E Pollard, *The Caribbean Court of Justice: Closing the Circle of Independence* (Kingston, Jamaica: The Caribbean Law Publishing Company, 2004) 2.

[2] West Indian Commission, *Time for Action: Report of the West Indian Commission* (Black Rock, Barbados: The West Indian Commission, 1992) 497–501.

[3] In *Time for Action* (n 2) at p 499, when advocating for replacement of the Judicial Committee of the Privy Council the West Indian Commission stated:

> We believe that a Caribbean Supreme Court manned by distinguished West Indian jurists and in which litigants have confidence, is likely to attract a larger number of appeals from countries of the Region than the Privy Council now does. Its knowledge and understanding of regional problems, language, and culture, coupled with its identification with the very ethos of the Caribbean Community, at once invests it with intrinsic qualities which the Privy Council, despite its great learning, does not and can never hope to possess. The importance of these attributes in the judicial law-making process is not to be overlooked or underestimated.

goods, and functional cooperation in a multiplicity of fields—must have the underpinning of Community law. Integration rests on rights and duties; it requires the support of the rule of law applied regionally and uniformly. A CARICOM Supreme Court interpreting the *Treaty of Chaguaramas*, resolving disputes arising under it, including disputes between Governments parties to the Treaty, declaring and enforcing Community law, interpreting the Charter of Civil Society—all by way of the exercise of an original jurisdiction—is absolutely essential to the integration process. It represents in our recommendations one of the pillars of the CARICOM structures of unity.[4]

The call of the West Indian Commission has been answered by the creation of the Caribbean Court of Justice (CCJ), and the arrogation of a treaty-interpreting role to the Eastern Caribbean Court of Appeal (ECCA).

The potential of these two courts for the furtherance of Caribbean regional integration cannot be overemphasized. Binding, legally enforceable rules have the potential to help make CARICOM and the OECS into more efficient, predictable organizations, subject to the rule of law, and to produce greater uniformity in implementation of legal obligations. As highlighted by the impressive jurisprudence of the European Court of Justice (ECJ), and the early original jurisdiction cases of the CCJ, a treaty-interpreting court can play a vital role in furthering a regional integration project.

14.1.1 Overview of the CCJ[5]

The Caribbean Court of Justice was created by the 2001 Agreement Establishing the Caribbean Court of Justice and its inauguration was held on 16 April 2005.[6] It is empowered both by the Agreement and the RTC which, through Chapter 9, makes use of the CCJ compulsory, exclusive, final, and binding.[7] The CCJ is supported by the Agreement Establishing the Seat of the Caribbean Court of Justice and a number of other treaties related to such matters as the Court's

[4] *Time for Action* 500.

[5] For overviews of the history leading to the formation of the CCJ, see eg Pollard, *The Caribbean Court of Justice* (n 1) chs 1 and 7. For more on the CCJ generally see also the papers and speeches on the CCJ's website at <http://www.caribbeancourtofjustice.org/publications/papers-speeches> (10 August 2013), Derek O'Brien and S Foadi, 'CARICOM and Its Court of Justice' (2008) 37 *Common Law World Review* 334–55. For writings on an earlier draft of the Agreement Establishing the Caribbean Court of Justice see Hugh Rawlins, Rose-Marie Antoine, and David Berry, *Caribbean Justice for All—The Case for a Caribbean Regional Court*, Vol 3, Contemporary Legal Issues (Bridgetown, Barbados: INDI Graphics, 2000).

[6] Agreement Establishing the Caribbean Court of Justice (adopted 14 Feb 2001, entered into force 23 Jul 2002) 2255 UNTS 319.

[7] Art 188 of the RTC requires disputes to be settled through a variety of mechanisms, including 'adjudication'. The latter term refers to the Caribbean Court of Justice (CCJ) as evidenced by the definition of 'Court' in Art 1 of the RTC and the subsequent references to the Court in Arts 211–224. The Protocol Amending the Treaty Establishing the Caribbean Community (Protocol IX: Disputes Settlements) (adopted 13–14 Mar 2000, not yet in force) similarly provided for the use of judicial mechanisms, including the CCJ. The following articles of the Agreement and RTC establish the noted characteristics of the Court and is judgments: compulsory (Agreement Art XVI, RTC Arts 211(1) and 216), exclusive (Agreement Art XII(1), RTC Art 211(1)), final (Agreement Art III(2)), and binding (Agreement Arts XV and XXII, RTC Arts 215 and 221).

juridical personality, privileges and immunities, tenure of judges, etc.[8] The Court is funded from a specially established trust fund.[9]

The CCJ derives its competences from both its Agreement and the RTC. The provisions of both treaties substantially parallel one another, but in the event of conflict it is likely that the Court will prefer the RTC.[10] The Court has two basic functions, an appellate and original one. The CCJ may act as an appellate court for those contracting Caribbean states which accept that jurisdiction, and it may act as a treaty-interpreting body for all parties to the RTC. In other words, the CCJ serves as both a Court of Appeal and an international tribunal dealing with treaty law. These two functions are distinct and may lead to the development of a unique jurisprudence by the Court.

14.1.2 Caribbean Court of Justice: Composition, structure, and restriction

As specified in Article IV(1)–(2) of the Agreement, the Court is to be composed of nine judges and one President, although this number may be increased if necessary,

[8] See Agreement Establishing the Seat of the Caribbean Court of Justice and the Offices of the Regional Judicial and Legal Service Commission between the Government of Trinidad and Tobago and the Caribbean Court of Justice and the Regional Judicial and Legal Services Commission (RJLSC) (adopted and in force 23 Feb 2005) 2324 UNTS 335, Protocol to the Agreement Establishing the Caribbean Court of Justice relating to the Juridical Personality and Legal Capacity of the Court (adopted 4 Jul 2003, in force 29 Jul 2003), Protocol on the Status, Privileges and Immunities of the Caribbean Court of Justice and the Regional Judicial and Legal Services Commission (adopted and entered into force 4 Jul 2003) 2324 UNTS 171, Protocol to the Agreement Establishing the Caribbean Court of Justice relating to the Tenure of Judges, Rules of Court, Financial Arrangements and withdrawal from Agreement, as well as the relationship between Provisions on the Original Jurisdiction of the Caribbean Court of Justice and the Constitutions of States Parties (adopted 17 Feb 2005, applied provisionally from 7 Jun 2007, in force 6 Feb 2006), Protocol to the Agreement Establishing the Caribbean Court of Justice relating to Security of Tenure of Members of the Regional Judicial and Legal Services Commission (adopted and entered into force 6 Jul 2006), Protocol to the Agreement Establishing the Caribbean Court of Justice Relating to the Tenure of Office of Judges of the Court (adopted 26 May 2007, not yet in force but provisionally applied since 7 Jun 2007), Protocol for the Interfacing and Interaction of the Regional Judicial and Legal Services Commission, The Caribbean Court of Justice and the Caribbean Court of Justice Trust Fund (adopted and entered into force 25 Jan 2007), Protocol to the Revised Treaty of Chaguaramas Establishing the Caribbean Community, including the Caribbean Single Market and Economy regarding the Relationship between provisions on the Original Jurisdiction of the Caribbean Court of Justice and the Constitutions of State Parties (adopted 17 Feb 2005, in force 1 Jan 2006). The latter treaties may be obtained from the CARICOM Secretariat or the CARICOM Law website at <http://caricomlaw.org/> (10 Aug 2013).

[9] The Agreement Establishing the Caribbean Court of Justice Trust Fund (adopted 4 Jul 2003), was replaced by the Revised Agreement Establishing the Caribbean Court of Justice Trust Fund (adopted 12 Jan 2004, in force 27 Jan 2004) 2324 UNTS 231. This is supported by the Vesting Deed of the Caribbean Court of Justice Trust Fund (signed 4 Jul 2003), and the Vesting Deed of the Caribbean Court of Justice Trust Fund—Original Board of Trustees (signed between 22 Aug 2003 and 5 Sep 2003).

[10] See eg *Trinidad Cement Ltd and TCL Guyana Inc v Guyana*, Judgment [2009] CCJ 1 (OJ), (2009) 74 WIR 302, 15 January 2009, at [25]–[28], where the Court relied upon the wording of Art 222 of the RTC ('person') rather than that of Art XXIV of the Agreement ('national'). See also *Trinidad Cement Ltd and TCL Guyana Inc v Guyana*, Judgment [2009] CCJ 1 (OJ), (2009) 74 WIR 302, 15 January 2009, at [46]–[47], where the Court preferred the RTC over its own Rules, in the event of conflict.

upon recommendation of the Regional Judicial and Legal Services Commission (RJLSC).[11] As a result of the Court's initial workload, only six judges and the President have been appointed at present.[12] At least three judges of the Court are required under Article IV(1) of the Agreement to have 'expertise in international law including international trade law'. Such qualifications assist the Court to fulfil its original jurisdiction role.

In terms of the appointment process, under Article IV(6) of the Agreement the President of the CCJ is appointed by a qualified majority vote of three quarters of the contracting parties on the recommendation of the RJLSC. The other judges are appointed by a majority vote of all members of the RJLSC.[13] The President and judges are to be removed using the same processes. Since the members of the RJLSC are independent and represent a wide cross-section of the relevant legal interests of CARICOM, their role in the appointment process helps to ensure that appointments are immunised from political considerations.[14] A limited exception arises in the case of the President, whose appointment, following a recommendation from the Commission, is effectively subject to the agreement of the Heads of Government.[15]

All judicial appointments must satisfy stringent criteria including five years of judging in a court of unlimited jurisdiction in civil and criminal matters, or fifteen years of practice or the teaching of law through which the candidate has earned distinction in the legal profession.[16] Candidates may have served in a member state of the Caribbean Community, a contracting party, in some part of the Commonwealth, or in 'a State exercising civil law jurisprudence common to the Contracting Parties'.[17] Judicial candidates must also satisfy the criteria of having

[11] The Regional Judicial and Legal Services Commission (RJLSC) is established by the Agreement. Under Art VII of the Agreement the RJLSC is provided with 'full juridical personality including, in particular, full capacity to contract', privileges and immunities, and immunity from judicial scrutiny into its proceedings.

[12] For the names and qualifications of the judges and President, see Caribbean Court of Justice, 'Judges of the Caribbean Court of Justice', as available at <http://www.caribbeancourtofjustice.org/about-the-ccj/judges> (11 Aug 2013).

[13] Agreement Art IV(7).

[14] Art V(12) of the Agreement provides that '[i]n the exercise of their functions under this Agreement, the members of the Commission [RJLSC] shall neither seek nor receive instructions from any body or person external to the Commission.' As provided in Art V of the Agreement, the RJLSC is composed of eleven persons representing a wide cross-section of Caribbean society, including representatives of civil society, distinguished jurists, and the President of the CCJ. The membership of the Commission is nominated by a wide range of entities, including the Organisation of the Commonwealth Caribbean Bar Association, the Organisation of Eastern Caribbean Bar Association, national Judicial and Legal Services Commissions, national Public Service Commissions, the CARICOM Secretary General, the OECS Director General, the Dean of the Faculty of Law of the University of the West Indies, the Deans of the Faculties of Law of any of the contracting parties, the Chairman of the Council of Legal Education, and the Bar or Law Associations of the contracting parties. In making appointments the RJLSC is empowered to consult with 'associations representative of the legal profession and with other bodies and individuals that it considers appropriate': Agreement Art IV(12).

[15] Agreement Art IV(6) and (9). Note that the Heads cannot appoint the President in the absence of a recommendation from the RJLSC.

[16] Agreement Art IV(10).

[17] Agreement Art IV(10).

'high moral character, intellectual and analytical ability, sound judgment, integrity and understanding of people and society'.[18]

With respect to terms of office, under Article IX(1) of the Agreement, the office of a judge of the CCJ cannot be abolished while there is a substantive holder of that office. Under Articles IX(2)–(3) the President is appointed for a non-renewable term of seven years, or until the age of seventy-two years, whichever comes first, and judges of the court are appointed until they reach the age of seventy-two years. This compulsory retirement age was changed in 2007 to seventy-five years, for the period prior to the appointment of the full complement of judges to the bench, by means of the Protocol to the Agreement Establishing the Caribbean Court of Justice Relating to the Tenure of Office of Judges of the Court.[19] Once appointed, a judge must subscribe to the oath of office specified in Article X and Appendix I to the Agreement. In terms of termination of tenure, Article IX(4) provides that a 'Judge may be removed from office only for inability to perform the functions of his office, whether arising from illness or any other cause or for misbehaviour, and shall not be so removed except in accordance with the provisions of this Article.' The President, under Article IX(5), can only be removed by the Heads of Government upon the recommendation of the RJLSC and following the advice of a tribunal on the grounds specified in Article IX(4). The other judges of the CCJ can only be removed by the RJLSC, again on the advice of a tribunal, on the same grounds. The establishment and operation of this tribunal is governed by Article IX(6)–(7), which require the tribunal to be composed of not less than three members, who must have held judicial office, and to be governed by local rules regarding commissions of inquiry. The President, or any judge subject to enquiry by a tribunal, may be suspended during the period of operation of that tribunal.[20] The President and any judge may resign at any time.[21]

[18] Agreement Art IV(11).

[19] (Adopted 26 May 2007, not yet in force but provisionally applied since 7 Jun 2007). Art II(1) and (4) of the Protocol provide:

> 1. Notwithstanding paragraphs 2 and 3 of Article IX of the Agreement, the Commission may, if it appears to the Commission at any time during the evolutionary phase of the Court that special circumstances so require, extend the tenure in office of a Judge of the Court by a period,
>   (a) in the case of the President, that is not beyond the date on which he attains the age of seventy-five years or the date on which he completes seven years in office, whichever of those events first occurs;
>   (b) in the case of any other Judge of the Court, that is not beyond the date on which he attains the age of seventy-five years.
>
>   Where the Commission is considering an extension of the tenure of the President under this Article, the Chairman of the Commission shall take no part in any deliberations or decision of the Commission relating to the matter. [. . .]
> 4. For the purposes of paragraph 1, 'the evolutionary phase of the Court' means the period ending with the appointment of the maximum number of Judges as provided for in paragraph 1 of Article IV of the Agreement.

[20] Agreement Art IX(8).

[21] Agreement Art IX(9).

The seat of the Court is in Trinidad and Tobago but, as stipulated in Article III(3) of the Agreement, may be re-located by agreement between the contracting parties.[22] The Court may also temporarily sit in any contracting state's territory, and it has done so on several occasions in order to assist the litigants to lessen the costs of the proceeding.[23] Such costs have been an on-going concern for litigants.[24] The Court is also empowered to hold hearings by means of video conference facilities, and has done so on numerous occasions.[25] In its original jurisdiction the Court can sit in panels of three or more judges, or by a sole judge.[26]

In terms of the overall competence of the Court, the parties to the Agreement have clarified one aspect of state obligations to the Court by means of the Protocol to the Revised Treaty of Chaguaramas Establishing the Caribbean Community, including the CSME regarding the Relationship between provisions on the Original Jurisdiction of the CCJ and the Constitutions of State Parties.[27] The Protocol amends the RTC by inserting a new Article 222(*bis*), which reads:

> The provisions regarding the original jurisdiction set out in this Chapter shall not be construed to require a Contracting Party to enact legislation that is inconsistent with its constitutional structure or the nature of its legal system.

The full implications of this Article remain to be tested. Article 222(*bis*) may have been a reaction to the decision of the Judicial Committee of the Privy Council (JCPC) in the case of *Independent Jamaica Council for Human Rights (1998) Ltd and others v Marshall-Burnett and another*, discussed later.[28] This decision required

[22] See the Agreement Establishing the Seat of the Caribbean Court of Justice and the Offices of the Regional Judicial and Legal Service Commission between the Government of Trinidad and Tobago and the Caribbean Court of Justice and the Regional Judicial and Legal Services Commission (RJLSC) (adopted and in force 23 Feb 2005) 2324 UNTS 335. The Government of Trinidad and Tobago has passed legislation to incorporate the state's obligations: Caribbean Court of Justice (Headquarters) Act 2008, Laws of Trinidad and Tobago, Act No 6 of 2008 (27 May 2008).

[23] For example in the case of *Shanique Myrie v Barbados* the Court heard the evidential phases of the case in the territories of the respective parties, with Ms Myrie leading her evidence in Jamaica and the Defendant leading its evidence in Barbados. The merits of the case were argued at the seat of the Court, in Trinidad and Tobago. See *Shanique Myrie v Barbados*, Judgment [2013] CCJ 3 (OJ) [preambular paragraphs].

[24] The CARICOM Secretariat, in its *Summary Draft Report on the Appraisal of the State of Implementation of the CARICOM Single Market* (September 2009) (Georgetown, Guyana: CARICOM Secretariat, 2009) at 6, commented that some 'respondents pointed out that while it is true that the CCJ has the capacity to enforce the applicable rules under the Treaty, the vast majority of CARICOM Nationals will not be able to meet the financial costs to represent themselves before the Court.' In the *Report* it was suggested that member states or the Community could bring an advisory opinion request on behalf of such individuals 'to clarify whether a complaint is on sufficiently strong legal grounds to be pursued further'. See p 6. Nevertheless this would still require action by states or the Community on behalf of the individual, and it is questionable whether such a 'pre-review' action would be desirable.

[25] All interlocutory hearings in the case of *Shanique Myrie v Barbados* were heard by video conference. This allowed the Court, the two parties, the intervener, and the third party to participate from their respective locations, namely, Trinidad and Tobago (CCJ), Jamaica (Myrie and the attorneys representing the state of Jamaica), Barbados (the attorneys representing Barbados), and Guyana (the CARICOM Secretariat).

[26] Agreement Art XI(1) and (4).

[27] (Adopted 17 Feb 2005, in force 1 Jan 2006).

[28] [2005] 2 AC 356, [2005] UKPC 3 (PC JA).

legislation replacing the JCPC with the CCJ to be passed by the constitutional majority required for amendments to entrenched provisions of the constitution. Nevertheless Article 222(*bis*) potentially raises a number of concerns. For example, if the CCJ under its original jurisdiction decided that a party must change legislation incompatible with its obligations under the RTC, would Article 222(*bis*) render such a decision void if it had the effect of requiring constitutional changes or changes to the nature of the state's legal system?[29] Also, does Article 222(*bis*) prevent the adoption of the principle of direct effect by the Court, as an impermissible change to the nature of the legal systems of common law CARICOM member states? Such questions will need to be addressed by the Court if they arise. But they reveal the kinds of problems that will ensue from making an international treaty and an international tribunal subject to domestic law considerations.[30]

14.1.3 Eastern Caribbean Court of Appeal: Composition and structure

The Eastern Caribbean Supreme Court was established by the West Indies Associated States Supreme Court Order 1967 and is the superior court of record for Antigua and Barbuda, Dominica, Grenada, St Kitts and Nevis, St Lucia, St Vincent and the Grenadines, and the three British Overseas Territories of Anguilla, the British Virgin Islands, and Montserrat.[31] The headquarters of the Court, initially

[29] For an example of two international legal decisions requiring a CARICOM member state to change its constitution see: *Case of Boyce v Barbados* (Preliminary Objections, Merits, Reparations and Costs), I-A Ct HR, Judgment of 20 November 2007, Series C, No 169, and *Case of Da Costa Cadogan v Barbados* (Preliminary Objections, Merits, Reparations and Costs), I-A Ct HR, Judgment of 24 September 2009, Series C, No 204. For the resolution of a similar question in EU law see Case C-213/89 *R v Secretary of State for Transport, ex parte Factortame Ltd and Others* [1990] ECR I-2433. In this case the ECJ, following a decision by the House of Lords that 'under national law, the English courts had no power to grant interim relief [... which] was precluded by the old common-law rule that an interim injunction may not be granted against the Crown, that is to say against the government, in conjunction with the presumption that an Act of Parliament is in conformity with Community law until such time as a decision on its compatibility with that law has been given', was asked to assess, in the words of the Court, 'whether a national court which, in a case before it concerning Community law, considers that the sole obstacle which precludes it from granting interim relief is a rule of national law, must disapply that rule.' At pp I-2471[3] and I-2473[17]. Referring to its previous jurisprudence, the ECJ noted the requirement for uniformity of EU law, the precedence of directly applicable EU measures, and the requirement for national courts to ensure the legal protection of such directly effective provisions (including by dis-applying national law). See p I-2473[18]–[20]. Taking these features of EU law into consideration, the Court held at p I-2474[23], that 'a national court which, in a case before it concerning Community law, considers that the sole obstacle which precludes it from granting interim relief is a rule of national law must set aside that rule.' As a result, the House of Lords was required to grant interim relief in a situation where no such power existed under the common law, against an existing statute, and without further legislative authority by Parliament. Such a decision could be characterized as affecting the nature of the legal system of the UK.

[30] Perhaps the CCJ can avoid such problems by focusing on the text of Art 222(*bis*), which is concerned solely with the *enactment* of legislation. Under a strict textual analysis the decision of the ECJ in *Factortame* (n 29) need not fall under this characterization since no new legislation was needed. Rather, UK courts were required to disapply existing rules.

[31] SI 223/1967. The order was made pursuant to s 6 of the West Indies Act of 1967 (1967 c 4), and established the West Indies Associated States Supreme Court. See generally, OECS Secretariat,

located in Grenada, moved to St Lucia following the revolution in Grenada, in March 1979.[32]

The Court is composed of the Chief Justice, who is the Head of the Judiciary and is appointed by the Queen; the three Justices of Appeal, thirteen High Court Judges, and two Masters, are appointed by the Judicial and Legal Services Commission.[33] To be appointed as a Justice of Appeal, a person must be or have been a judge of a court of unlimited jurisdiction in civil and criminal matters in some part of the Commonwealth or an appellate court for at least five years, or have practised as an advocate in such a court for at least fifteen years.[34] There is no requirement for expertise in international law. The Court of Appeal is itinerant, sitting in each member state to hear appeals, and may sit in panels of three judges or one judge. Unless otherwise permitted, a judge of the Court of Appeal may hold office until the age of sixty-five years.[35] A judge can only be removed from office, under s 8(3) of the Order, 'for inability to discharge the functions of his office (whether arising from infirmity of body or mind or any other cause) or for misbehaviour'. The Chief Justice may only be removed by order of Her Majesty, and other judges of the Supreme Court by order of the Judicial and Legal Services Commission, on the advice of the Judicial Committee of the Privy Council.[36] The Chief Justice and Judges of the ECSC can only be removed after a tribunal has been constituted, under section 8(5)–(6) of the Order, to investigate the matter and has decided to refer it to the Judicial Committee of the Privy Council. During the time of the tribunal's investigations a judge may be suspended, and such suspension may be revoked if the tribunal decides not to refer the matter to the Judicial Committee of the Privy Council, or the latter advises that the judge ought not to be removed from office.[37]

Although the Court of Appeal could be argued to have treaty-interpreting jurisdiction under s 9(2) of the West Indies Associated States Supreme Court Order 1967, when read in conjunction with the RTB, the rules governing the Court of Appeal do not yet appear to embrace this jurisdiction.[38] Instead the

'Eastern Caribbean Supreme Court', as available at <http://www.oecs.org/about-the-oecs/institutions/eastern-caribbean-supreme-court-ecsc> (11 Aug 2013), and the information on the website of the Court at <http://www.eccourts.org/> (11 Aug 2013).

[32] See eg Eastern Caribbean Supreme Court, 'Brief History of the Court', as available at <http://www.eccourts.org/brief-history-of-the-court/> (11 Aug 2013).

[33] Section 5(1) of the West Indies Associated States Supreme Court Order 1976, SI 223/1967. The Judicial and Legal Services Commission was established by s 18 of the Order, for the members of the (then) West Indies Associated States, namely, (1) Antigua, (2) Dominica, (3) Grenada, (4) Saint Christopher, Nevis and Anguilla, (5) Saint Lucia, and (6) Saint Vincent. See s 2 of the Order.

[34] West Indies Associated States Supreme Court Order 1976, s 5(2)(a)–(b).

[35] West Indies Associated States Supreme Court Order 1976, s 8(1). Judges may serve an additional three years with the approval of the Judicial and Legal Services Commission and the Heads of Government of the OECS states.

[36] West Indies Associated States Supreme Court Order 1976, s 8(4).

[37] West Indies Associated States Supreme Court Order 1976, s 8(7)–(8).

[38] West Indies Associated States Supreme Court Order 1976, s 9(2) provides: 'The Court of Appeal shall have, in relation to a State, such jurisdiction to hear and determine appeals and *to exercise such powers as may be conferred upon it by* the Constitution or *any other law of the State*' (emphasis added). This provision would not apply to the RTB, per se, but could apply to domestic legislation

rules limit the Court to hearing appeals from lower courts. It is assumed that the Court of Appeal expressly will be granted a treaty-interpreting jurisdiction in the near future.

The treaty-interpreting dispute settlement function of the ECCA is to be provided for under the budget of the OECS. If these funds are insufficient, however, 'the Eastern Caribbean Court of Appeal may require the parties to any dispute before it to advance payment against the Court's estimated costs of the proceedings and may in its orders and judgments in the case allocate to the parties, in such shares as it considers just, the liability for those costs.'[39]

14.2 Appellate Jurisdictions

14.2.1 The CCJ as a regional court of appeal

The appellate jurisdictions of the CCJ and the ECCA do not fall within the scope of the present work, which is concerned with the treaty-interpreting functions of these two tribunals. However it would be remiss not to highlight three issues related to the appellate jurisdiction of the CCJ.

Firstly, the low level of acceptance by parties to the Agreement of the CCJ's appellate jurisdiction has affected the perception of the Court as a whole.[40] To date only Guyana, Barbados, and Belize have accepted the Court's appellate jurisdiction, although other states, such as St Lucia and Dominica, have expressed an intention to accept it soon.[41] It has been suggested that this low level of acceptance reflects a level of uncertainty about the Court.[42] This may partly be the case. However perhaps the stronger influence may have come from the judgment of the Judicial Committee of the Privy Council in the case of *Independent*

incorporating the RTB. For the solely appellate function of the Court's rules see eg Rule 8 of the Court of Appeal Rules, SRO 58/1968, SI 2/1970, SI 3/1973, Rule 62.1 and 62.3 of the Eastern Caribbean Supreme Court Civil Procedure Rules 2000, and Rule 62.1 of the Eastern Caribbean Supreme Court Civil Procedure (Amendment) Rules (SI 92/2011, St Lucia). These provisions are unchanged by the Eastern Caribbean Supreme Court Civil Procedure (Amendment) Rules 2013.

[39] RTB Art 18.7.

[40] This low level of acceptance is ironic because the original drafts of the CCJ Agreement vested the Court solely with an appellate jurisdiction. See eg Pollard, *The Caribbean Court of Justice* (n 1) 5.

[41] See eg 'Britain "respects" CCJ move', *Barbados Nation*, 8 August 2013, p 13. A right of appeal to the CCJ became part of the law of Barbados on 8 Apr 2005 and of Guyana on 1 Apr 2005: *Barbados Rediffusion Service Ltd v Asha Mirchandani, Ram Mirchandani and Mcdonald Farms Ltd* [2005] CCJ 1 (AJ) [20], *Brent Griffith v Guyana Revenue Authority and Attorney General of Guyana* [2006] CCJ 1391 (AJ) [10], as available on the CCJ's website at <http://www.caribbeancourtofjustice.org/judgments-proceedings/appellate-jurisdiction-judgments> (11 Aug 2013). A right of appeal to the CCJ became part of the law of Belize on 1 Jun 2010: CARICOM Secretariat, 'CARICOM Welcomes Belize's Move to CCJ', Press Release 248/2010 (2 Jun 2010) as available at <http://www.caricom.org/jsp/pressreleases/press_releases_2010/pres248_10.jsp> (11 Aug 2013).

[42] This is supported by the fact that several states made reservations in relation to Art XXV of the Agreement—the provision granting the Court an appellate jurisdiction—namely, Antigua and Barbuda, Grenada, St Vincent and the Grenadines, and Suriname. See CARICOM Secretariat, 'CARICOM Law—Agreement Establishing the Caribbean Court of Justice', as available at <http://www.caricomlaw.org/Details.aspx?EntryId=131> (27 Oct 2013).

Jamaica Council for Human Rights (1998) Ltd and others v Marshall-Burnett and another, which has had a chilling effect upon, and made more difficult, acceptance of the CCJ's appellate jurisdiction.[43] In the *Independent Jamaica Council for Human Rights* case the Judicial Committee of the Privy Council (the 'Privy Council' or 'Board') held that the three Jamaican statutes which were created to replace the Privy Council with the Caribbean Court of Justice were not passed in accordance with the constitution. According to the Privy Council, since the effect of the three Acts was to amend fundamental sections of the constitution, they required enactment under the procedure mandated for entrenched provisions. Entrenchment of the CCJ as a final court was necessary, according to the Board, because in its view the CCJ Agreement might be easily amended and those amendments could take effect under the laws of Jamaica by a simple, affirmative resolution. Ready amendment could allow for the possibility of political interference and weakening of the independence of the CCJ, and the Privy Council therefore required a higher level of constitutional protection. According to Lord Bingham of Cornhill, writing on behalf of the Board, entrenchment of the CCJ is required:

> The question is whether, consistently with the constitutional regime just described, a power to review the decisions of the higher courts of Jamaica may properly be entrusted, without adopting the procedure mandated by the Constitution for the amendment of entrenched provisions, to a new court which, whatever its other merits, does not enjoy the protection accorded by the Constitution to the higher judiciary of Jamaica. In answering this question the test is not whether the protection provided by the CCJ Agreement is stronger or weaker than that which existed before but whether, in substance, it is different, for if it is different the effect of the legislation is to alter, within the all-embracing definition in section 49(9)(b), the regime established by Chapter VII. The Board has no difficulty in accepting, and does not doubt, that the CCJ Agreement represents a serious and conscientious endeavour to create a new regional court of high quality and complete independence, enjoying all the advantages which a regional court could hope to enjoy. But Dr Barnett is correct to point out that the Agreement may be amended, and such amendment ratified, by the governments of the contracting states, and such amendment could take effect in the domestic law of Jamaica by affirmative resolution. The risk that the governments of the contracting states might amend the CCJ Agreement so as to weaken its independence is, it may be hoped, fanciful. But an important function of a constitution is to give protection against governmental misbehaviour, and the three Acts give rise to a risk which did not exist in the same way before. The Board is driven to conclude that the three Acts, taken together, do have the effect of undermining the protection given to the people of Jamaica by entrenched provisions of Chapter VII of the Constitution. From this it follows that the procedure appropriate for amendment of an entrenched provision should have been followed.[44]

As a result the Board declared the Jamaican legislation to be void.[45]

[43] [2005] 2 AC 356, [2005] UKPC 3 (PC JA).

[44] *Independent Jamaica Council* (n 43) at pp 371–2 [21].

[45] In *Independent Jamaica Council* (n 43) at p 372 [24] the Privy Council stated: 'In the result, the Board will humbly advise Her Majesty that the appeal should be allowed and a declaration made that the Judicature (Appellate Jurisdiction) (Amendment) Act 2004, the Caribbean Court of Justice

This decision by the Privy Council, which voided legislation meant to replace the Privy Council with the CCJ on grounds not satisfied by the Privy Council itself (not being entrenched in the manner required of the CCJ), has met some criticism.[46] Certainly, as a practical matter, the ability of the contracting parties to amend the CCJ Agreement to encroach upon the Court's independence or for other political reasons seems farfetched. As highlighted earlier in Chapters 2 and 3 when discussing the history of the drafting of the RTC, the ability of CARICOM member states to come together to draft, let alone amend, a significant treaty is very limited. The adoption of the Protocols preceding the RTC, and the RTC itself, took nearly five years, and the entry into force of the RTC took both the creation of another treaty and an additional five years.[47] Given these extensive delays, during which most governments in the region changed, it is highly unlikely that a future attempt to cripple the Court by such processes would be successful. In any event, the decision of the Privy Council may be argued to have had a significant negative effect upon the enthusiasm for adopting the appellate jurisdiction of the Court by most CARICOM member states.

The second issue to note about the Court's appellate jurisdiction is that it is exercised by the same judges who hear matters under the Court's original jurisdiction. The same judges fulfil two very different functions: they sit as a final domestic court of appeal, on the one hand, and as a first and last instance treaty-interpreting court on the other. Two consequences flow from this double-jurisdictional role of the CCJ. Firstly, since the same judges must consider both international legal matters and domestic appeals, unlike some domestic tribunals they should be quick to understand the international legal consequences of a case on appeal. As the Court entrusted to interpret and enforce the RTC, the CCJ should be very much alive to the harmful potential of domestic legislation which violates a state's obligations under the RTC. Thus the CCJ may, to a greater extent than many common law domestic courts, be ready to ensure the effectiveness of international legal obligations. There is some evidence supporting this position, since in several of the cases in which the Court has discussed the role of international law in the domestic sphere the Court has gone out of the way to allow international legal processes to be effective.[48]

(Constitutional Amendment) Act 2004 and the Caribbean Court of Justice Act 2004 were not passed in accordance with the procedure required by the Constitution and are accordingly void.'

[46] It is especially ironic that the operation of the CCJ, a Court that was created, in the ringing words of Pollard, in order to 'sever the last remaining vestige of a colonial condition, [and to]...signal the birth of autonomous judicial decision-making in Member States of the Caribbean Community and close the circle of independence which commenced as early as 1962', should be frustrated by the same instrument of the colonial condition it was meant to replace. Pollard, *The Caribbean Court of Justice* (n 1) 204.

[47] See Chapter 2.

[48] See eg *AG v Joseph* [2006] CCJ 3 (AJ), (2006) 69 WIR 104 (BDS) and *British Caribbean Bank v AG* [2013] CCJ 4 (AJ) (BZE). In the first case the Court found that convicted persons subject to execution had a legitimate expectation that they would be able to conclude their petitions to international human rights bodies, including the Inter-American Commission on Human Rights (which existed through unincorporated treaties), so that the Mercy Committee could consider the conclusions of those bodies in making its decision on whether to exercise the prerogative of mercy. In the case of *British Caribbean Bank* the Court looked in passing at the question of whether it could take

Of course the Court must act within its particular jurisdictional competence for each case, and thus there are limitations on its ability to aid in the enforcement of international law. It would thus be possible although very unlikely, for example, for the Court, sitting in its original jurisdiction capacity, to 'overrule' itself in relation to one of its previous appellate jurisdiction decisions.[49] As an appeal court the CCJ could, at least theoretically, find that a portion of the RTC which had not been transformed or that had been improperly transformed, as an unincorporated obligation, could not lawfully be implemented in domestic law. In such a situation, in a manner similar to the courts rendering some of the decisions discussed in Chapter 6, the CCJ acting as a final court of appeal could find itself bound to uphold the existing domestic law of a member state, even if that law led the state to be in breach of its obligations under the RTC. Although such a scenario is unlikely, it should be self-correcting. The CCJ acting in its original jurisdiction capacity would be bound to interpret and apply the RTC. Any decision of a domestic tribunal—any domestic tribunal—that resulted in a violation of the RTC would have to be identified and corrected.[50] One of the useful functions of the CCJ, in this regard, would be prevent such situations from arising by correcting improper uses, or non-uses, of the CCJ's referral jurisdiction by lower tribunals.

14.2.2 ECCA's appellate jurisdiction

The ECCA's appellate jurisdiction raises the same issues for the RTB. The ECCA, as a final court of appeal, can pronounce upon domestic legal issues. But as a treaty-interpreting tribunal with competence to interpret and apply the RTB, the

cognizance of an international arbitration process existing solely under an unincorporated treaty. The Court noted, in para [19]:

> Belize has still not passed any legislation to incorporate the 1982 BIT [bilateral investment treaty] into domestic law. The legal effect of treaties that are not incorporated into domestic law has already been examined in the decision of this Court in *Boyce and Joseph*. The orthodox view that an unincorporated treaty does not form part of the law of Belize and creates no rights or obligations which are enforceable domestically was critiqued. It is sufficient to note that the notion that an unincorporated treaty is incapable of conferring any rights on private entities in the municipal system has been rejected. At a minimum they could yield legitimate expectations cognizable under domestic law. [Citations omitted.]

The Court then went further, at [20], to suggest that a bilateral investment treaty, by resulting in an agreement to arbitrate disputes, can create a kind of 'contractual right to arbitrate…of which the courts take notice'. In sum, the doctrine of legitimate expectation was used in both cases to allow a domestic tribunal to overcome the challenges of dualism and to give effect to international treaties in the domestic legal system without their first having been transformed. For more on transformation see Chapter 6.

[49] This is not as farfetched as it might seem. There are numerous examples of cases in which UK Courts have been corrected in their interpretation of the law by decisions of the European Court of Justice, such as Case C-213/89 *R v Secretary of State for Transport, ex parte Factortame Ltd and Others* [1990] ECR I-2433, discussed at p xiv. The CCJ, in contrast, serves the roles of both the Supreme Court of the UK and the ECJ, and therefore if faced with such a situation would be required to correct itself.

[50] For an example of a hypothetical situation where the CCJ would be required, in its original jurisdiction, to overrule an appellate decision, see A Ralph Carnegie, 'How Exclusive is "Exclusive" in Relation to the Original Jurisdiction of the Caribbean Court of Justice? A Consideration of Recent

ECCA will also be required to be *au fait* with international law, specifically with the law of treaties. It is therefore likely that the ECCA will be more sensitive, perhaps sympathetic, to international legal issues.

14.3 Original Jurisdictions: Treaty Interpreting Tribunals

The treaty-interpreting jurisdictions of the CCJ and ECCA are 'original' in the sense that an applicant can file a case directly before either court without the need for a previous hearing before a national tribunal.

14.3.1 CCJ

The Court's original jurisdiction is its most important feature for Caribbean regional integration. As noted by the Court itself, under this jurisdiction it is the 'custodian' and 'Guardian' of the RTC.[51] As illustrated in Chapter 13, there are a variety of dispute settlement processes in the RTC. But the Caribbean Court of Justice is the only permanently available, standing body that will have the ability to make binding decisions. Moreover, the Court's original jurisdiction is exclusive and compulsory and its decisions are final and binding.[52] Each of these terms, however, must be subject to further discussion.

The 'exclusiveness' of the Court's jurisdiction may be limited by the ability of member states to refer legal problems which simultaneously arise under the RTC and another treaty to a tribunal empowered to interpret and apply the latter. An unlawful subsidy might, for example, simultaneously give rise to issues under the law governing the WTO and CARICOM, and each organization has its own adjudicative arm which can be invoked unilaterally by a party to a dispute.[53] Similarly, if a dispute regarding parallel obligations under the RTB and RTC, such as one regarding import duties, arose between OECS member states, it could be brought to either the ECCA or the CCJ.[54] In addition, as pointed out by Carnegie, the

Developments', paper delivered in the Faculty of Law Workshop Series 2009–2010, University of the West Indies, Cave Hill Campus, 25 November 2009, as available through <http://www.cavehill.uwi.edu/news/articles/nov2009/Conflicts_of_Jurisdiction.pdf> (12 Aug 2013) at 13.

[51] See *Trinidad Cement Ltd v Competition Commission*, Judgment [2012] CCJ 4 (OJ), 12 November 2012, at [18] and *Shanique Myrie v Barbados* (n 23), at [68].

[52] The following articles of establish these characteristics of the Court and its judgments: compulsory (Agreement Art XVI, RTC Arts 211(1) and 216), exclusive (Agreement Art XII(1), RTC Art 211(1)), final (Agreement Art III(2)), and binding (Agreement Arts XV and XXII, RTC Arts 215 and 221).

[53] See eg Carnegie (n 50) at 12–13.

[54] Carnegie (n 50) at pp 8–9, contemplates this possibility in relation to a conflict between the RTC and original OECS Treaty. However his suggested solution—applying the *lex posterior* principle so as to prioritize the RTC over the earlier, original OECS Treaty—would not work in the case of a conflict between the RTC and RTB, since the latter is the later treaty. Instead, it is submitted that as with other examples of parallel dispute settlement powers under international law, the original court of each organization would be competent to take jurisdiction over, and resolve, the dispute applying its relevant treaty. If such a case arose, it is hoped that one of the courts would stay its proceedings to allow the other to reach a conclusion prior to itself delivering judgment so as to avoid any unnecessary contradictions.

Court's original jurisdiction complements other dispute settlement mechanisms in the RTC itself, including the RTC's Chapter 9 mechanisms and the dispute resolution functions of CARICOM organs.[55] Moreover, as highlighted by Article XXIII of the Agreement and Article 223 of the RTC, alternative dispute resolution is expressly encouraged in cases of 'commercial disputes'.[56] Finally, and as discussed further later, the referral jurisdiction of the CCJ must be deemed to at least contemplate some potential for application of the RTC by domestic courts. All of these possibilities must modify our view of the 'exclusive' nature of the CCJ's original jurisdiction.

The compulsory nature of the Court's original jurisdiction is somewhat clearer, since no member state subject to the CCJ's jurisdiction can prevent the Court from hearing a matter by, for example, refusing to participate in the proceedings. As indicated in Article 216(2), the CCJ itself possesses sole competence to determine whether it has jurisdiction over a case. If a state refuses to participate in any proceedings over which the Court has jurisdiction, the Court would be entitled to render a default judgment.[57] However, as indicated earlier, states retain the sovereign competence to bring their proceedings elsewhere, even if this could lead to a breach of their obligations to the Court under the RTC.

The finality of a decision of the CCJ is only subject to the ability of the Court to entertain an application for revision of one of its decisions, as provided by Article XX of the Agreement and Article 219 of the RTC. This right of revision is severely restricted under both of these articles, however, and cannot by any means be equated to an appeal.[58] Revision can only arise within six months of the discovery of a 'fact of such a nature as to be a decisive factor, which fact was, when the judgment was given, unknown to the Court and to the party claiming revision: provided always the ignorance of that fact was not due to negligence on the part of the applicant'.[59] Revision cannot arise later than five years from the date of the CCJ's judgment.[60]

[55] See generally Carnegie (n 50). Note that Carnegie refers to the potential dispute resolution functions of the CARICOM Competition Commission and COTED in addition to those of the Conference.

[56] Note that Art XXIII of the Agreement simply uses the phrase 'international commercial disputes', without tying them to disputes between persons. Article 223 of the RTC, in contrast, uses the phrase 'private commercial disputes among Community nationals as well as among Community nationals and nationals of third States'. This difference in wording could be used to support an argument that the Agreement contemplates commercial disputes in addition to those involving persons. However given the Court's preference for the RTC it is likely that the narrower wording in Art 223 will predominate: cf *Trinidad Cement Ltd and TCL Guyana Inc v Guyana*, Judgment [2009] CCJ 1 (OJ), (2009) 74 WIR 302, 15 January 2009, at [46]–[47].

[57] See Part 17 of the Caribbean Court of Justice (Original Jurisdiction) Rules 2006 (24 Mar 2006), as available at <http://www.caribbeancourtofjustice.org/court-instruments/rules-of-the-court> (accessed 27 Jul 2013).

[58] In fact, because of the provisions stipulating that the Court is bound by the doctrine of *stare decisis*—Agreement Art XXII and RTC Art 221—the Court is arguably even more restricted with respect to reconsidering its past decisions than other international tribunals. For a formal endorsement by the Court of the applicability of *stare decisis* to its jurisprudence see *Shanique Myrie v Barbados*, Judgment [2012] CCJ 3 (OJ) at [20]–[21].

[59] RTC Art 219(2) and (5). See also Agreement Art XX(1) and (4).

[60] RTC Art 219(6) and Agreement Art XX(5).

The binding nature of the Court's original jurisdiction decisions is supported by a number of provisions of the Agreement and RTC. Article XXII of the Agreement and Article 221 of the RTC both expressly indicate that the judgments of the court are legally binding. Article XV of the Agreement and Article 215 of the RTC require all entities subject to a judgment to comply with it, the latter, for example, providing that '[t]he Member States, Organs, Bodies of the Community, entities or persons to whom a judgment of the Court applies, shall comply with that judgment promptly.' However on the related issue of enforcement of the Court's binding decisions, the treaty-based guarantees provided in Article XXVI of the Agreement and Article 224 of the RTC must be both implemented, and complied with, by the organs of each CARICOM member state.[61] The fragility of the enforcement powers of the Court is suggested by the stay of execution of judgment and contempt proceedings that followed the CCJ's judgment in the case of *Trinidad Cement Ltd and TCL Guyana Inc v Guyana*.[62]

14.3.2 ECCA

The ECCA plays an integral role in dispute settlement for the OECS. The treaty-interpreting jurisdiction of the ECCA can be invoked through Article 18 of the RTB, discussed in the previous Chapter. Paragraph 1 of the Dispute Settlement Annex provides:

> 1 The disputes mentioned in Article 18.1 of this Treaty shall be settled –
> (a) if all eligible parties to the dispute under Article 18.5 agree, and subject to Article 30 of the Economic Union Protocol, by recourse to any of the following modes for the settlement of disputes, namely, good offices, consultation, conciliation, arbitration and adjudication;
> (b) failing such agreement, by adjudication by the Court of Appeal of the Eastern Caribbean Supreme Court at the request of any such eligible party.

Paragraph 1(b) makes the ECCA the default dispute settlement mechanisms and, by allowing unilateral referral of matters to the Court, makes it compulsory. The ECCA also oversees aspects of the Dispute Settlement Annex. Under Article 18.3,

[61] Art XXVI of the Agreement provides:

> The Contracting Parties agree to take all the necessary steps, including the enactment of legislation to ensure that:
> (a) all authorities of a Contracting Party act in aid of the Court and that any judgment, decree, order or sentence of the Court given in exercise of its jurisdiction shall be enforced by all courts and authorities in any territory of the Contracting Parties as if it were a judgment, decree, order or sentence of a superior court of that Contracting Party;
> (b) the Court has power to make any order for the purpose of securing the attendance of any person, the discovery or production of any document, or the investigation or punishment of any contempt of court that any superior court of a Contracting Party has power to make as respects the area within its jurisdiction.

[62] Judgment [2009] CCJ 5 (OJ), 20 August 2009. See *Trinidad Cement Ltd and TCL Guyana Inc v Guyana*, Judgment [2009] CCJ 6 (OJ), and *Trinidad Cement Ltd and TCL Guyana Inc v Guyana*, Judgment [2010] CCJ 1 (OJ).

for example, a party to a dispute may apply to the ECCA, through the Chief Registrar, for a waiver of the three-month waiting period specified for all disputes under Article 18.2. In addition, under Article 18.2 the Chief Registrar fulfils the role of the Director General under Article 18 when the Organisation is a party to the dispute.

14.4 Advisory Proceedings

The original or treaty jurisdiction of the two Caribbean courts is divided into two general categories of cases: advisory opinions and contentious cases. Advisory opinions have been a common feature of international law since the creation of the Permanent Court of International Justice. Under this advisory role a large body of jurisprudence has been developed by the Permanent Court, and its successor, the International Court of Justice, covering many important areas of international law.

Advisory opinions may be useful precisely because they are non-binding in nature. They represent the opinion of eminent jurists, and therefore may play an important role in the development of the law. A court may be asked about any question of law that falls under its jurisdiction, even a more pointed question which has close affinity with an active dispute. But advisory opinions also do not infringe upon the right of states and international organizations to decide whether, or how, to implement them. In this sense they share some of the values of mediation or conciliation reports, discussed in Chapter 13.

The International Court of Justice has developed a kind of two-part test in deciding whether to answer an advisory request, firstly looking at whether it has jurisdiction to do so, and then considering questions which may render the request inadmissible.[63] The ICJ, however, has rarely refused to answer an advisory request and has held that it should only do so for 'compelling reasons'.[64] According to the ICJ,

> The present Court has never, in the exercise of this discretionary power, declined to respond to a request for an advisory opinion. Its decision not to give the advisory opinion on the *Legality of the Use by a State of Nuclear Weapons in Armed Conflict* requested by the World Health Organization was based on the Court's lack of jurisdiction, and not on considerations of judicial propriety (see *I.C.J. Reports 1996 (I)*, p. 235, para. 14). Only on one occasion did the Court's predecessor, the Permanent Court of International Justice, take the view that it should not reply to a question put to it (*Status of Eastern Carelia, Advisory Opinion, 1923, P.C.I.J., Series B, No. 5*), but this was due to

[63] Art 96 of the UN Charter provides:

1. The General Assembly or the Security Council may request the International Court of Justice to give an advisory opinion on any legal question.
2. Other organs of the United Nations and specialized agencies, which may at any time be so authorized by the General Assembly, may also request advisory opinions of the Court on legal questions arising within the scope of their activities.

For a concrete application of the relevant principles related to jurisdiction and admissibility see eg *Legal Consequences of the Construction of a Wall in the Occupied Palestine Territory* (Advisory Opinion) [2004] ICJ Rep 136, pp 148–64 [24]–[65].

[64] *Legal Consequences* (n 63) at p 156 [44].

'the very particular circumstances of the case, among which were that the question directly concerned an already existing dispute, one of the States parties to which was neither a party to the Statute of the Permanent Court nor a Member of the League of Nations, objected to the proceedings, and refused to take part in any way' (*Legality of the Threat or Use of Nuclear Weapons, I.C.J. Reports 1996 (I)*, pp. 235–236, para. 14).

One compelling reason for refusing advisory jurisdiction, discussed in *Legal Consequences of the Construction of a Wall in the Occupied Palestine Territory* and highlighted in this passage about the *Eastern Carelia Case*, would be if the advisory request attempted to circumvent the principle of state consent to the Court's jurisdiction.[65] The contentious jurisdiction of the ICJ is optional, and generally requires one of the following: state consent through an international agreement (specific or advance acceptance), acceptance on an ad hoc basis, acceptance *forum prorogatum* (consent *post hoc*), or formal acceptance through a declaration giving the Court jurisdiction.[66] An advisory request could circumvent this principle if, for example, it was used to allow the Court jurisdiction to scrutinize an active dispute over which it would not otherwise have had contentious jurisdiction (due to lack of acceptance by one of the states).[67] As seen in the opinion on the *Status of Eastern Carelia*, this would provide a ground for the Court to refuse to grant the advisory request.[68]

14.4.1 CCJ

Under Article XIII of the Agreement and Article 212 of the RTC, in nearly identical wording, the CCJ is granted jurisdiction to deliver advisory opinions. RTC Article 212 provides:

1. The Court shall have exclusive jurisdiction to deliver advisory opinions concerning the interpretation and application of the Treaty.
2. Advisory opinions shall be delivered only at the request of the Member States parties to a dispute or the Community.

[65] *Legal Consequences* pp 157–9 [46]–[50].

[66] See Art 36 of the Statute of the International Court of Justice (1945), Annex to the Charter of the United Nations, 26 June 1945, 1 UNTS xvi, UKTS 67 (1946). See generally James Crawford, *Brownlie's Principles of International Law*, 8th edn (Oxford: Oxford University Press, 2012) 723–8; Malcolm Shaw, *International Law* 5th edn (Cambridge: Cambridge University Press, 2003) 966–82.

[67] In *Legal Consequences* (n 63), Israel had not accepted the contentious jurisdiction of the Court and the other potential 'party', the people of Palestine, had no standing before the Court. Art 34(1) of the Statute of the International Court of Justice provides that '[o]nly states may be parties in cases before the Court.' However the Court held, at p 159 [50], that hearing the advisory request would not circumvent the principle of consent:

> The opinion is requested on a question which is of particularly acute concern to the United Nations, and one which is located in a much broader frame of reference than a bilateral dispute. In the circumstances, the Court does not consider that to give an opinion would have the effect of circumventing the principle of consent to judicial settlement, and the Court accordingly cannot, in the exercise of its discretion, decline to give an opinion on that ground.

[68] In the *Status of Eastern Carelia* (Advisory Opinion) [1923] PCIJ Series B, No 5, at pp 28–9, the Court concluded:

> The question put to the Court is not one of abstract law, but concerns directly the main point of the controversy between Finland and Russia, and can only be decided by an

As made clear in Article 212(1), the exclusivity of the jurisdiction of the CCJ over the interpretation and application of the RTC also extends to advisory interpretations. Advisory requests can only be made by member states or the Community, not by persons.

The wording of Article 212(2) of the RTC clearly authorizes the CCJ to render an advisory opinion regarding an active dispute. This role for the CCJ does not contradict the requirement for consent, a requirement which we have seen may prevent the ICJ from hearing active disputes. It is compatible with state consent because all parties to the RTC have already accepted the compulsory jurisdiction of the Court. A non-binding advisory opinion could prove valuable to states faced with an active dispute because it would allow reference of sensitive legal questions to the Court without an immediate compulsion to comply with them. In this way an advisory decision could function in a way similar to the report of a mediator or conciliation commission: it would set out the facts and law and the parties would be free to use this information in the manner they see fit. However one question that will likely arise in this context for the CCJ is whether advisory opinions fall under the Court's doctrine of *stare decisis*.[69] If they do, advisory opinions would become part of the Court's binding system of precedent. However even if they do not, an advisory opinion of the Court would still represent an authoritative statement of the law regarding a question, one from which the Court should not readily depart.

Although the wording of Article 212(2) of the RTC could give rise to different interpretations, it is assumed that advisory requests could be made by a member state even if it was not party to a dispute. This function would be very helpful since it would allow a state that is contemplating a form of action that might not be compatible with the RTC to seek advance advice, as a kind of pre-clearance, before undertaking the action. The ECJ fulfils a kind of pre-clearance role in relation to proposed treaties under Article 218 of the TFEU.[70]

Finally, advisory opinions can be used by the CCJ to resolve inter-organ disputes for CARICOM. These disputes would not fall under the Court's contentious jurisdiction under Article 211 of the RTC. Given the variety of uses of advisory opinions, Pollard predicts that 'much of the time of the Court will be taken up

> investigation into the facts underlying the case. Answering the question would be substantially equivalent to deciding the dispute between the parties. The Court, being a Court of Justice, cannot, even in giving advisory opinions, depart from the essential rules guiding their activity as a Court.

[69] See Agreement Art XXII and RTC Art 221. For a formal endorsement by the Court of the applicability of *stare decisis* to its jurisprudence see *Shanique Myrie v Barbados*, Judgment [2012] CCJ 3 (OJ) at [20]–[21]. For an earlier statement see eg *Trinidad Cement Ltd and TCL Guyana Inc v Guyana*, Judgment [2009] CCJ 1 (OJ), (2009) 74 WIR 302, 15 January 2009, at [6].

[70] See generally, TC Hartley, *The Foundations of European Community Law*, 7th edn (Oxford: Oxford University Press, 2010) ch 6. TFEU Art 218(11) provides:

1. The Court shall have exclusive jurisdiction to deliver advisory opinions concerning the interpretation and application of the Treaty.
2. Advisory opinions shall be delivered only at the request of the Member States parties to a dispute or the Community.

with the preparation and delivery of advisory opinions and with referrals from municipal courts and tribunals.'[71]

14.4.2 ECCA

Under paragraph 7 of the Dispute Settlement Annex the ECCA can issue advisory opinions in the following terms:

> 7 The Eastern Caribbean Court of Appeal shall have as part of the Treaty Jurisdiction of the Organisation the jurisdiction to give an Advisory Opinion to the OECS Authority or any other Organ of the Organisation on any matter concerning the interpretation or application of this Treaty which that Organ may refer to it for advice. An Advisory Opinion shall not be binding on the Organ requesting the same or on any Member State.

As clearly stipulated in this provision, advisory opinions may only be requested by the Authority or another organ of the Organisation, not by states or individuals. Advisory opinions are also expressly denied a binding quality.

Whether the ECCA will adopt the ICJ's consent position in relation to advisory requests related to active disputes—such as, for example, a dispute between two member states referred to the ECCA by the OECS Commission—remains to be seen. However since paragraph 1(b) of the Dispute Settlement Annex allows any eligible party to unilaterally refer a dispute to the ECCA, the issue of consent would not seem to arise for the Court. Parties to the RTB accept the compulsory jurisdiction of the ECCA. A difference between the ECCA and the CCJ, however, is that for the latter advisory requests can be made by states. The ECCA can only be referred advisory requests by the Authority or another organ of the OECS. As a result, an organ of the OECS, not one of the member states concerned, would have to make the advisory request regarding a dispute between states to the ECCA. This could raise consent issues if neither state party to the dispute was in favour of the advisory request.

In any event, such concerns would not apply to inter-organ disputes, which may be referred to the ECCA for an advisory opinion.

14.5 Contentious Proceedings

Both the CCJ and ECCA have jurisdiction over several types of contentious cases. The CCJ can hear cases between states, between states and CARICOM, referrals, and cases between persons and either states or CARICOM. Article 211 of the RTC provides:

> 1. Subject to this Treaty, the Court shall have compulsory and exclusive jurisdiction to hear and determine disputes concerning the interpretation and application of the Treaty, including:
>   (a) disputes between the Member States parties to the Agreement;

[71] Pollard, *The Caribbean Court of Justice* (n 1) 103.

(b) disputes between the Member States parties to the Agreement and the Community;
(c) referrals from national courts of the Member States parties to the Agreement;
(d) applications by persons in accordance with Article 222,
concerning the interpretation and application of this Treaty.
2. For the purpose of this Chapter, 'national courts' includes the Eastern Caribbean Supreme Court.[72]

All four categories of original jurisdiction cases must concern the interpretation and application of the RTC.[73]

The ECCA can hear cases between full member states, associate member states and the Organisation, as well as 'appeals from any internal body established to consider matters of dispute internal to any Organ of the Organisation'.[74] Let us examine each type of dispute and the potential jurisdiction of each tribunal.

14.5.1 Disputes between member states: CCJ and ECCA

Under Article 211(1) of the RTC, and Article 18 of the RTB and paragraph 6 of the Dispute Settlement Annex, respectively, the CCJ and the ECCA can hear disputes regarding the RTC and RTB between states party to those treaties. This form of jurisdiction, although common in international law, is unlikely to be of much significance to the development of regional integration jurisprudence in the Caribbean. This for the simple reason that Caribbean states, like most states globally, generally seek to avoid direct, formal state-to-state confrontations. International litigation brought by one member state against another regarding an alleged breach of an international legal obligation generally will not be conducive to smooth diplomatic relations.

The reluctance to bring direct claims against other states is illustrated by the practice of EU member states regarding a similar provision in the TFEU. Only a handful of cases have been brought under Article 259 of the TFEU (and its antecedents) since the 1950s.[75] In the CARICOM context, it should be noted that prior to the RTC not a single dispute was resolved by means of a decision of a tribunal appointed and convened under Articles 11–12 of the Annex.[76]

[72] See also Agreement Art XII.

[73] Note that the CCJ in *Trinidad Cement Ltd v Caribbean Community*, Judgment [2009] CCJ 2 (OJ), (2009) 74 WIR 319, 5 February 2009, at [30], highlighted the breadth of jurisdiction of the Court under Art 211:

> ...Article 187 does not purport to present an exhaustive statement of the types of dispute that may come before this Court. Moreover Article 211 deals with the quite different matter of jurisdiction, and when read with Article 222 gives the Court power, as a matter of procedure, to enable private entities to appear before it in all manner of disputes concerning the interpretation and application of the Revised Treaty including allegations that a body or organ of the Community acted *ultra vires*.

[74] RTB Art 18.5 and DSA [8].

[75] See eg Paul Craig and Gráinne de Búrca, *EU Law: Text, Cases and Materials*, 5th edn (Oxford: Oxford University Press, 2011) 432–3.

[76] Gladstone Mills et al, *Report on a Comprehensive Review of the Programmes, Institutions and Organisations of the Caribbean Community* (Georgetown, Guyana: Caribbean Community Secretariat, 1990), p 23.

14.5.2 Disputes between states and the Community and vice versa

Article 211(1)(b) of the RTC and Article 18 of the RTB and the paragraph 6 of the Dispute Settlement Annex provide for disputes the parties to which are CARICOM or the OECS, respectively, and their member states. The wording of these provisions does not exclude either party to a dispute from bringing the matter to the respective court. Thus, under Article 211(1)(b) of the RTC, a member state could bring a suit against the Caribbean Community, and the Caribbean Community could bring a suit against a member state.

CCJ

The jurisdiction of the CCJ over disputes between the member states and the Community (and vice versa) may prove significant. Admittedly, it has not yet been utilized: no member state has sued the Community, nor has the Community sued a member state.[77] Moreover various factors may diminish its attractiveness to both member states and the Community. For example, instead of suing the Community before the Court, a member state may wish to exert political pressure on all of the CARICOM organs on which it sits to achieve the change. Similarly, a state may choose to withhold funding in protest against actions by CARICOM rather than bring a suit against it.[78] Further, a member state seeking clarification of a legal issue may choose the less controversial route of requesting an advisory opinion of the Court.

However a situation may arise where a member state wishes to formally vindicate its rights under the RTC in a final and binding manner, and perhaps to obtain compensation for harms suffered. Such a case would best be brought against the Community under Article 211(1)(b) of the RTC. The suit must be brought against the Community, or the Competition Commission, not an organ or institution of CARICOM.[79]

[77] The Community itself has been the *respondent* in two of the Court's first original jurisdiction applications under Article 211, although both cases involved individual applications: *Trinidad Cement Ltd v Caribbean Community*, Judgment [2009] CCJ 2 (OJ), (2009) 74 WIR 319, February 5, 2009 (special leave), Judgment [2009] CCJ 4 (OJ), (2009) 75 WIR 194, August 10, 2009 (judgment), and *Hummingbird Rice Mills Limited v Suriname and the Caribbean Community*, Judgment [2011] CCJ 1 (OJ), June 27, 2011 (special leave), Judgment [2012] CCJ 1 (OJ) (judgment).

[78] This occurred in the UN context when several states refused to pay their portion of the peacekeeping expenses. The crisis that resulted was only resolved by a combination of the decision of the Court in the *Certain Expenses of the United Nations (Article 17, Paragraph 2, of the Charter)* (Advisory Opinion) [1962] ICJ Rep 151, and a decision by the UN to create an open fund for payment of peacekeeping expenses (rather than rely upon the general UN budget). See Henry G Schermers and Niels M Blokker, *International Institutional Law*, 4th edn (Boston: Martinus Nijhoff, 2003), pp 921–22 [§1459].

[79] In *Trinidad Cement Ltd v Caribbean Community*, Judgment [2009] CCJ 2 (OJ), (2009) 74 WIR 319, February 5, 2009, at [24], the Court held:

> The Community has full juridical personality (see Article 228 (1) of the Revised Treaty) and can be sued for the acts or omissions of COTED, an organ of the Community (see Article 10(2)(b) of the Revised Treaty), and those of the Secretary-General acting on behalf of COTED.

A suit brought by the Community against a member state, although theoretically attractive, may face almost insurmountable obstacles in practice. Although a very strong tradition of litigation on the part of organs of the EU is manifest in the jurisprudence of the ECJ, such a tradition may not arise in the Caribbean Community. The culture of CARICOM is not one where states are quick to resort to formal dispute resolution mechanisms. CARICOM organs, being composed of state representatives, may be unwilling to authorize a Community law suit and would in any event face challenges in obtaining the sufficient majority of votes for such a decision. Also, although the Secretariat has been granted some independent initiative, and the Secretary General is authorized to represent the Community, neither has been granted anywhere near the scope of powers, or independence, of the Commission in the EU.[80] Nowhere in the RTC is the Secretariat granted functions equivalent to those of the European Commission. The latter is required, under Article 17 of the TEU to 'promote the general interest of the Union and take appropriate initiatives to that end[,] ensure the application of the Treaties, and of measures adopted by the institutions pursuant to them, [and to] oversee the application of Union law under the control of the Court of Justice of the European Union.' Under Article 258 of the TFEU, the Commission is authorized to bring a state which has not complied with its opinion before the ECJ:

> If the Commission considers that a Member State has failed to fulfil an obligation under the Treaties, it shall deliver a reasoned opinion on the matter after giving the State concerned the opportunity to submit its observations.
>
> If the State concerned does not comply with the opinion within the period laid down by the Commission, the latter may bring the matter before the Court of Justice of the European Union.

Moreover, the CARICOM Secretariat is further constrained by the fact that it is financed by contributions from member states rather than from an independent source of income. These factors together make it less likely that Article 211(1)(b) of the RTC will be utilized by the Community to bring claims against member states.

That is not to say such suits would be impossible, or even unwelcome. In order for CARICOM to function as a Community under the rule of law breaches of the

See also ibid [33], and *Doreen Johnson v CARICAD*, Judgment [2009] CCJ 3 (OJ), March 2, 2009, at [15]. In *Trinidad Cement Ltd v Competition Commission*, Judgment [2012] CCJ 4 (OJ), November 12, 2012, at [13] the Court modified its position that only the Community could be sued by also allowing suit against the Competition Commission:

> In circumstances where the Commission was created by the Revised Treaty and has been invested by that instrument with important and far-reaching functions and powers, and expressly granted juridical personality allowing it to sue and be sued in its own name, this Court finds that original jurisdiction proceedings can properly be brought against the Commission to determine whether, in exercising or purporting to exercise those powers, it has acted in accordance with the provisions of the Revised Treaty.

[80] The Secretary General is empowered under Art 24(2)(a) of the RTC to 'represent the Community'. RTC Art 228(2) also provides that '[i]n any legal proceedings, the Community shall be represented by the Secretariat.'

law must be enforced and sanctioned. If member states, for political and diplomatic reasons, are unwilling or unable to bring suits, then the Community itself should do so. The European Commission has been a key engine of regional integration for the EU in large part because it has enforced the law. If the CARICOM Secretariat is able to assume such a role, acting on behalf of the Community to bring suits before the CCJ, then it would be advisable for the Secretariat to study the way in which the European Commission has undertaken such a role.

Comparator: Commission claims before the ECJ

In particular, it would be useful to note that the European Commission exercises considerable discretion under Article 258 of the TFEU, which lays down six steps which must be taken before a case can be brought to the ECJ: (1) the Commission must consider that a breach has been committed by a member state, (2) then it must communicate this to the member state, (3) then it must consider any observations of the member state on the matter, (4) then it must deliver a reasoned opinion, (5) then it must wait for a reasonable period to allow the member state to comply with the opinion, and (6) finally, it may bring the matter before the European Court of Justice if the member state refuses to comply. After each step the Commission may abandon a case. This capacity gives the Commission considerable scope to negotiate with member states to ensure compliance with the EU treaties. In doing so, the Commission allows member states to save face and provides room for manoeuvre where, for example, the member state wishes to implement Community law in a different manner or needs help in ascertaining how it is to do so. The Commission has resolved a large percentage of complaints in this manner.[81]

This discretion on the part of the European Commission has been upheld by the ECJ. In Case 247/87 *Star Fruit Co. v Commission*, example, involving a complaint regarding the Commission's failure to commence proceedings in a matter, the Court held:

> [I]t is clear from the scheme of Article 169 [now TFEU Article 258] of the Treaty that the Commission is not bound to commence the proceedings provided for in that provision but in this regard has a discretion which excludes the right for individuals to require that institution to adopt a specific position.
>
> 12 It is only if it considers that the Member State in question has failed to fulfil one of its obligations that the Commission delivers a reasoned opinion. Furthermore, in the event

[81] In the report of the European Commission, 'Communication from the Commission: A Europe of Results—Applying Community Law', Brussels, 5.9.2007, COM(2007) 502 final, as available at http://ec.europa.eu/eu_law/eulaw/pdf/com_2007_502_en.pdf (15 Aug 2013) at 3, the Commission highlighted:

> Relatively few of the issues arising require a ruling from the Court of Justice. Around 70% of complaints can be closed before a letter of formal notice is sent; around 85% are closed before the reasoned opinion; and around 93% are closed before a ruling from the Court. These figures confirm a high rate of agreed conformity, strengthening understanding and support for the law, increasing potential for future good application of the law and fulfilling the intentions of the EU legislator.

that the State does not comply with the opinion within the period allowed, the institution has in any event the right, but not the duty, to apply to the Court of Justice for a declaration that the alleged breach of obligations has occurred.[82]

The Court has also upheld the discretion of the Commission to bring a case in circumstances where the state has already implemented its EU obligations.[83] Such proceedings allow the Commission to: prevent 'second guessing' by member states (based upon predictions of a likely victory before the Court), catch short breaches (which may be profitable), and to provide a determination of legal liability (for use in subsequent lawsuits and legal actions).[84] In addition the Court has established that the motive of the Commission in bringing such an action, its timing, and the length of time between the breach and the bringing of the action, will in most cases be irrelevant.[85]

[82] [1989] ECR 291, at p 301 [11]–12].

[83] Note that under general international law, once a breach has been resolved a court may refuse to hear the matter. For example, in *Nuclear Tests Case (New Zealand v France)* [1974] ICJ Rep 457, at p 477 [61]–[62], the ICJ held:

> 61. The Court has in the past indicated considerations which would lead it to decline to give judgment. The present case is one in which "circumstances that have... arisen render any adjudication devoid of purpose" (*Northern Cameroons, Judgment, I.C.J. Reports 1963, p. 38*). The Court therefore sees no reason to allow the continuance of proceedings which it knows are bound to be fruitless. While judicial settlement may provide a path to international harmony in circumstances of conflict, it is none the less true that the needless continuance of litigation is an obstacle to such harmony.
>
> 62. Thus the Court finds that no further pronouncement is required in the present case. It does not enter into the adjudicatory functions of the Court to deal with issues *in abstracto*, once it has reached the conclusion that the merits of the case no longer fall to be determined. The object of the claim having clearly disappeared, there is nothing on which to give judgment.

[84] See eg Craig and de Búrca, *EU Law: Text, Cases and Materials* (n 75), pp 422–23. In Case 240/86 *Commission v Greece* [1988] ECR 1835, at pp 1855–6 [14], the Court held:

> As the Court has consistently held (see most recently the judgment of 5 June 1986 in Case 103/84 *Commission* v *Italian Republic* [1986] ECR 1759), the subject matter of an action brought under Article 169 [TFEU Art 258] is established by the Commission's reasoned opinion and even where the default has been remedied after the period laid down pursuant to the second paragraph of that article has elapsed, an interest still subsists in pursuing the action. That interest may consist in establishing the basis for a liability which a Member State may incur, by reason of its failure to fulfil its obligations, towards those to whom rights accrue as a result of that failure.

[85] In Case 416/85 *Commission v UK* [1988] ECR 3127, at p 3151 [9], the Court noted that 'it is not for the Court to consider what objectives are pursued in an action brought under Article 169 [TFEU Art 258] of the Treaty. Its role is to decide whether or not the Member State in question has failed to fulfil its obligation as alleged.' In Case 7/68 *Commission v Italy* [1968] ECR 423, at p 428, the Court noted that '[i]t is for the Commission, under Article 169 [TFEU Art 258] of the Treaty, to judge at what time it shall bring an action before the Court; the considerations which determine its choice of time cannot affect the admissibility of the action, which follows only objective rules.' In Case 7/71 *Commission v France* [1971] ECR 1003, at p 1016 [5], the Court noted that the 'action for a declaration that a State has failed to fulfil an obligation provided for by Article 141 of the Treaty, does not have to be brought within a predetermined period, since, by reason of its nature and its purpose, this procedure involves a power on the part of the Commission to consider the most appropriate means and time-limits for the purposes of putting an end to any contraventions of the Treaty.' The exception to the Commission's right to bring an action long after the breach might be if a delay by the Commission would frustrate the member state's ability to defend itself before the Court: cf Case C-96/89 *Commission v Netherlands* [1991] ECR I-2461, p I-2492 [16]. Similarly, the Commission

ECCA

By means of Article 18.2 and 18.5 of the RTB, the full member states, the associate member states, and the Organisation are all eligible parties to bring a dispute under the procedures provided in the Dispute Settlement Annex. Under paragraphs 1(b) and 6 of the Dispute Settlement Annex any eligible party may bring a dispute to the ECCA. In other words, disputes may be brought to the ECCA by any full member state, associate member state, or the Organisation against any other eligible party. As a result, as in the case of the CCJ, disputes may be brought by a member states (full or associate) against the Organisation, and vice versa, to the ECCA. The Director General, under Article 21.3 of the RTB is empowered to represent the OECS in the exercise of its legal personality.

For the reasons discussed earlier in relation to similar disputes before the CCJ, it is doubtful that OECS member states will bring claims against the Organisation, or the Organisation against its member states. As with the CARICOM Secretariat, and unlike the European Commission, under Articles 12–13 of the RTB neither the OECS Commission nor the Director General is provided with express enforcement authority. However, as noted in the context of the EU, the European Commission has played a very valuable role in implementing the legal regime of the EU. The OECS Commission may wish to assume a similar role.

14.5.3 Referrals

CCJ

The referral jurisdiction of the CCJ, described in Article XIV of the Agreement and Article 214 of the RTC, requires a national court or tribunal to refer crucial questions regarding the RTC to the CCJ for its determination. Following receipt, the CCJ will consider and answer the question, and transmit its decision back to the national judge. The national judge must then factor the CCJ's legal determination into her or his judgment, as a binding legal opinion, and decide the overall case. Article 214 of the RTC provides:

> Where a national court or tribunal of a Member State is seised of an issue whose resolution involves a question concerning the interpretation or application of this Treaty, the court or tribunal concerned shall, if it considers that a decision on the question is necessary to enable it to deliver judgment, refer the question to the Court for determination before delivering judgment.

Several points can be made about the wording of this provision. Firstly, issues can be referred by national courts and tribunals, including the Eastern Caribbean Supreme Court.[86] Secondly, national judges may only refer questions concerning

might be precluded from bringing a claim if it did not provide a reasonable period of time for the state to comply following the release of its reasoned opinion before starting the action: Case 293/85 *Commission v Belgium* [1988] ECR 305, pp 352–3 [14]–[20].

[86] See also RTC Art 211(2). The ECJ has broadly interpreted the meaning of the phrase 'court or tribunal' in its jurisprudence. For example, in the Case 246/80 *Broeckmeulen v Huisarts Registratie*

the interpretation and application of the RTC, not any other treaty. Thirdly, the national judge must be 'seised' of the issue, meaning that the issue must properly before the court for its consideration and determination. Fourthly, the national court is compelled to refer ('shall') such questions to the CCJ. But fifthly, the national judge must refer it only when he or she 'considers that a decision on the question is necessary to enable [the judge] to deliver judgment'. The fourth and fifth points give rise to the possibility for some discretion on the part of the national judge, a point returned to later in the chapter.

The referral jurisdiction simultaneously plays several valuable roles for Caribbean regional integration. It allows a national court to access the expertise of the CCJ regarding the interpretation of the RTC while at the same respecting the right of that national court to make the final decision about the entire case. By combining regional expertise with national judicial autonomy, this jurisdiction allows national courts and tribunals to work with the CCJ in implementing the regional integration project. In addition, since it removes questions concerning the RTC from the jurisdiction of national courts, the referral jurisdiction also helps to preserve the exclusive competence of the CCJ to interpret and apply the RTC. It thus strikes a delicate balance. Only the CCJ can interpret and apply the RTC; but the application of the RTC in national law (or more accurately, the dis-application of inconsistent national law) may require the assistance of national tribunals. Further, in imposing the same obligation on *all* national courts of states parties to the RTC, Article 214 helps to ensure the uniformity of CARICOM law by removing the possibility of national tribunals arriving at different interpretations of the meaning of provisions of the RTC. This will be essential to the uniform and effective implementation of the CSME.

Commissie [1981] ECR 2311, at pp 2326–8 [8]–[17], the ECJ examined whether a medical Appeals Committee could be considered a 'court or tribunal' under what is now TFEU Art 267. The ECJ noted the profound effects that could result if a person was denied the ability to register as a medical practitioner under national law and held that the Netherlands Medical Appeals Committee was entitled to ask for preliminary rulings from the Court. Several factors played a role in the Court's determination, including the following facts: the Appeals Committee acted under a degree of governmental supervision; its procedures and proceedings were similar to judicial ones; there was no right of appeal to national courts from such decisions, making the Appeals Committee final; and the actual right being asserted in the case was an EU right, which the member states were required to implement through their legal systems. Other factors that the Court may assess are explored in Case C-178/99 *Doris Saltzmann* [2001] ECR I-4421, which examined whether a preliminary reference could be made by a tribunal responsible for keeping the land register. The Court noted at p I-4442 [13]:

> In order to determine whether a referring body is a court or tribunal within the meaning of Article 177 of the Treaty, which is a question governed by Community law alone, the Court takes account of a number of factors, such as whether the body is established by law, whether it is permanent, whether its jurisdiction is compulsory, whether its procedure is *inter partes*, whether it applies rules of law and whether it is independent (see, in particular, Case C-54/96 *Dorsch Consult* [1997] ECR I-4961, paragraph 23, and the case-law cited therein, and in Joined Cases C-110/98 to C-147/98 *Gabalfrisa and Others* [2000] ECR I-1577, paragraph 33).

As illustrated in this quotation, the ECJ also established that such questions are governed by EU law, not national law.

More subtly, the referral jurisdiction gives individuals an indirect way of enforcing compliance with CARICOM obligations. As will be seen later, individuals can bring direct claims against states and the Community under Article 222 of the RTC. But these claims must be filed with the CCJ as original jurisdiction claims, with all of the challenges that may entail, including satisfaction of the requirements of Article 222 in a Special Leave application. Article 222 claims are also limited because they cannot be brought against other persons. A referral question, on the other hand, may be raised as part of ordinary domestic proceedings, including proceedings between two persons, natural or juridical (potential horizontal application of Community law), or proceedings between persons and the organs of a state (vertical application of Community law). In utilizing this form of jurisdiction a person can ensure that her or his national court understands and, following the referral decision of the CCJ, potentially enforces the correct interpretation of the RTC. Finally, and as explored later, the form of jurisdiction in EU law most similar to the CCJ's referral jurisdiction—the ECJ's preliminary reference jurisdiction—has been crucial to the development of EU law.[87] Using the preliminary reference procedure the ECJ created the principle of direct effect, one of the most revolutionary developments of the EU legal system.[88] Some of the more interesting developments in CARICOM law may similarly arise in the CCJ's referral jurisdiction, since this jurisdiction necessarily requires the Court to work simultaneously with international and domestic legal regimes. As a result, although the Court has yet to hear a single case under this jurisdiction, it is likely that referrals will play a pivotal role in deepening Caribbean regional integration.[89]

Nevertheless, two challenges to the CCJ's referral jurisdiction must be raised. Firstly, since it requires action on the part of domestic courts and tribunals, the CCJ's referral jurisdiction must be accorded a firm basis in domestic law. In order for any national court or tribunal to have the competence to act, including making a reference to the CCJ, it must have a clear legal basis for doing so. This challenge arose in the case of *Linton v Attorney General*, discussed in Chapter 6, in which a referral request by a national tribunal was frustrated by the non-transformation of the RTC.[90] Moreover the same result may obtain even in cases where the RTC has been transformed, if national tribunals are deemed to require additional specific statutory authorization to enable them to make referrals to the CCJ in their domestic law.

[87] See Art 267 of the TFEU.

[88] See Chapter 8, and the discussion of the general principle of direct effect. The seminal case in this area is Case 26/62 *NV Algemene Transport-en Expeditie Onderneming van Gend en Loos v Nederlandse Administratie der Belastingen* [1963] ECR 1.

[89] The CCJ expressly highlighted the need for national courts to use the Court's referral jurisdiction in *Shanique Myrie v Barbados* (n 23), at [82] when it held: '[i]f, in the course of a domestic proceeding, new issues arise [concerning the RTC] that have not been addressed by this Court, domestic courts and tribunals are required by Article 214 RTC to refer these new issues to this Court for determination before delivering judgment.'

[90] Antigua and Barbuda, High Court of Justice, CARILAW # AG 2009 HC 23 (Blenman J), 29 June 2009 (unreported).

A second challenge to the use of referral jurisdiction by national courts regards the exact nature of the question they are supposed to refer. Article 211 provides the Court with 'compulsory and *exclusive* jurisdiction to hear and determine disputes concerning the interpretation and application of the Treaty'. By necessary implication, other bodies, including national courts, do not have the authority to interpret and apply the RTC. Yet Article 214 only comes into play if a national court is 'seised of an issue whose resolution involves a question concerning the interpretation or application of this Treaty, [and] a decision on the question is necessary to enable it to deliver judgment'.[91] How a matter can require interpretation and application of the RTC by a national court under Article 214, when that court, under Article 211, is not allowed to interpret and apply the RTC, is puzzling to say the least. Moreover, the wording in Article 214 is more challenging when one considers that under the dualist system embraced by Commonwealth Caribbean states, treaties are never actually part of the domestic law. Rather, the statutes which transform the RTC into the domestic law of CARICOM member states, quite literally 'transform' the RTC—they convert the text of a treaty into words in a domestic statute, thereby making international law into domestic law. In doing so, they completely change the legal nature of the provisions of the RTC, which by enactment cease to be international law. As a result, domestic courts never actually apply international treaty law, and instead apply domestic legislation which contains rights and obligations that mirror those contained in the treaty.[92] Thus, the RTC, like any treaty transformed or incorporated by statute, never actually exists as a treaty in domestic law, only the domestic statute. In such circumstances, the national court would more likely be required to interpret and apply the domestic statute transforming the RTC, not the RTC itself.

Perhaps a way to overcome these challenges is to recall that national courts, when interpreting and applying national legislation which incorporates the RTC and its obligations, may be required to look to the RTC itself as an aid to interpretation of the transformation statute. The rules of statutory interpretation allow a domestic judge to examine a variety of sources to ascertain the legislative intention, including the incorporated treaty.[93] As a result, a domestic law judge might be required to interpret (but not apply) the RTC as part of the process of interpreting and applying the domestic transformation statute. Such interpretation may properly be the subject of the Court's referral jurisdiction.

[91] For a similar concern see Derek O'Brien and S Foadi, 'CARICOM and Its Court of Justice' (2008) 37 *Common Law World Review* 334–55.

[92] As summarized by Lord Hoffman in *R v Lyons* [2003] 1 AC 976 (HL) at p 992 [27]:

> Parliament may pass a law which mirrors the terms of the treaty and in that sense incorporates the treaty into English law. But even then, the metaphor of incorporation may be misleading. It is not the treaty but the statute which forms part of English law.

[93] On legislative intention see FAR Bennion, *Bennion on Statutory Interpretation: A Code*, 5th edn (London: Lexisnexis Reed Elsevier (UK), 2008) Part VIII. Bennion, at pp 685–6, argues this point strongly, suggesting that treaties can be looked to in interpreting legislation even where that legislation is unambiguous and even where the treaty is not referred to in the text of the legislation.

Comparator: ECJ and the preliminary reference procedure

In thinking about the likely shape of the CCJ's referral jurisdiction it is useful to examine the practice of the ECJ, which shares a similar, preliminary reference jurisdiction. The ECJ's jurisprudence helps us understand that the purpose of the preliminary reference procedure, at least for the EU, is to ensure the uniformity of EU law by coordinating national and EU legal systems.[94] As highlighted by Advocate-General Lagrange in his Opinion, '[a]pplied judiciously—one is tempted to say loyally—the provisions of Article 177 [now TFEU Article 267] must lead to a real and fruitful collaboration between the municipal courts and the Court of Justice of the Communities with mutual regard for their respective jurisdictions'.[95] Further, as highlighted in Case 166/73 *Rheinmühlen Düsseldorf v Einfuhr- und Vorratsstelle für Getreide und Futtermittel (No 1)*, the preliminary reference procedure ensures that there is uniformity *between* national legal systems. The Court emphasized that 'Article 177 [TFEU Article 267] is essential for the preservation of the Community character of the law established by the Treaty and has the object of ensuring that in all circumstances this law is the same in all States of the Community.'[96] Similarly, the preliminary reference procedure ensures the uniformity of interpretation of EU texts as between the different *languages* of the EU.[97] The latter function may be necessary in CARICOM if, for the benefit of Suriname and Haiti, further amendments are made to the RTC in more than one language.

Under EU law the preliminary reference procedure is strictly limited to EU law. Under Article 267(b) of the TFEU the ECJ is empowered to determine the validity of EU law and therefore can declare EU legislative acts to be void. But Article 267 does not allow the Court to rule on the validity of national law. The Court established this point clearly in the *Van Gend en Loos* case when it stated that it only has jurisdiction to interpret and apply the EU treaties, and rejected outright the request to interpret the Netherlands customs legislation as part of the preliminary reference proceeding.[98] Similarly, in Case 6/64 *Costa v ENEL*, the Court stated

[94] In Case 13/61 *De Geus en Uitdenbogerd v Bosch and Others* [1962] ECR 45, at p 51, the Court noted that 'a harmonizing of interpretation—which is the purpose of Article 177 [now TFEU Art 267]—is of particular importance in cases in which the application of the Treaty is entrusted to national authorities.'

[95] Opinion of Mr Advocate-General Lagrange, delivered on 27 February 1962, p 56, as available through <http://curia.europa.eu/jcms/jcms/j_6/> (15 Aug 2013).

[96] [1974] ECR 33, at p 38 [2].

[97] In Case C-29/69 *Stauder v Ulm* [1969] ECR 419, at p 424 [3], the Court held in relation to the interpretation of a provision of EU law:

> When a single decision is addressed to all the Member States the necessity for uniform application and accordingly for uniform interpretation makes it impossible to consider one version of the text in isolation but requires that it be interpreted on the basis of both the real intention of its author and the aim he seeks to achieve, in the light in particular of the versions in all four languages.

[98] In Case 26/62 *NV Algemene Transport-en Expeditie Onderneming van Gend en Loos v Nederlandse Administratie der Belastingen* [1963] ECR 1, at p 11, the Court clearly explained the limitation of its jurisdiction:

> [I]n this case the Court is not asked to adjudicate upon the application of the Treaty according to the principles of the national law of the Netherlands, which remains the

that the preliminary reference 'provision gives the Court no jurisdiction either to apply the Treaty to a specific case or to decide upon the validity of a provision of domestic law in relation to the Treaty, as it would be possible for it to do under Article 169 [now TFEU Article 258].'[99]

In order to discourage contrived claims, the ECJ has also rejected preliminary references when they did not involve genuine disputes. Such cases would include those created by parties simply to test laws or to challenge the validity of national systems. For example, in Case 104/79 *Foglia v Novello (No 1)* the Court observed that the two parties had inserted a clause in their contract and engaged in actions which led to the suit simply to challenge French laws. As summarized by the Court: '[i]t thus appears that the parties to the main action are concerned to obtain a ruling that the French tax system is invalid for liqueur wines by the expedient of proceedings before an Italian court between two private individuals who are in agreement as to the result to be attained and who have inserted a clause in their contract in order to induce the Italian court to give a ruling on the point.'[100] In such circumstances the Court held that it had no jurisdiction to answer the questions posed:

> The duty of the Court of Justice under Article 177 [TFEU Article 267] of the EEC Treaty is to supply all courts in the Community with the information on the interpretation of Community law which is necessary for them to settle genuine disputes which are brought before them. A situation in which the Court was obliged by the expedient of arrangements like those described above to give rulings would jeopardize the whole system of legal remedies available to private individuals to enable them to protect themselves against tax provisions which are contrary to the Treaty.[101]

The rationale behind this decision is that national litigants should challenge taxes directly, through national procedures, rather than contrive artificial questions as a kind of 'test case'.[102] The benefit of such an approach is that it respects subsidiarity by allowing challenges to domestic legislation to occur in domestic courts. In doing so, it allows states to change their own laws in response to national judgments, without the need for ECJ intervention. A similar approach may be adopted by the CCJ since a dispute regarding domestic issues can be resolved by a domestic tribunal, and one involving the RTC can be filed as an individual application under Article 222 of the RTC.

> concern of the national courts, but is asked, in conformity with subparagraph (a) of the first paragraph of Article 177 of the Treaty [now TFEU Art 267], only to interpret the scope of Article 12 of the said Treaty within the context of Community law and with reference to its effect on individuals.

See also p 14.

[99] [1964] ECR 585, at pp 592–3.

[100] [1980] ECR 745, at pp 759–60 [10].

[101] *Foglia v Novello* (n 100) at p 760 [11].

[102] Note that subsequent jurisprudence shows that the ECJ may not impose a high level of scrutiny in determining whether a dispute is genuine, and may in fact allow a suit involving some contrivance to be the subject of a preliminary reference. See eg Case 261/81 *Walter Rau v de Smedt* [1982] ECR 3961, at p 3971 [9] (Court confines its analysis to what is on the file); Case C-451/99 *Cura Anlagen GmbH v Auto Service Leasing GmbH* [2002] ECR I-3193, at p I-3227 [26]–[27] (as long as there is a genuine dispute, some contrivance will not remove the Court's jurisdiction).

The jurisprudence of the ECJ also helps us with the question of the potential effect of a referral decision by the CCJ. Although such a referral only requires the CCJ to answer the particular question posed, and therefore one might assume that its impact will be limited to the particular case before the Court, the jurisprudence of the ECJ suggests that referral decisions may have much wider application. In Case 66/80 *ICC v Amministrazione delle Finanze*, for example, the ECJ highlights the rationale behind preliminary references—to ensure the uniformity of Community law—and then explains that although, technically speaking, preliminary references can only have consequences for the particular national court that asks the question, they nevertheless must have broader impact.[103] If, for example, the ECJ declares an EU act void, that act cannot be applied by the national court that has asked for the ruling.[104] In addition, the EU act cannot be applied by any other national court without creating serious uncertainty in Community law:

> It follows therefrom that although a judgment of the Court given under Article 177 [TFEU Article 267] of the Treaty declaring an act of an institution, in particular a Council or Commission regulation, to be void is directly addressed only to the national court which brought the matter before the Court, it is sufficient reason for any other national court to regard that act as void for the purposes of a judgment which it has to give.

Nevertheless the Court also makes clear that if other national courts wish to raise further preliminary references regarding the same EU act—the one declared void—they may do so if, for example, they have questions related to the 'grounds, the scope and possibly the consequences of the invalidity' established in the earlier preliminary reference.[105] If no such questions exist, the Court makes clear that national courts can treat Community acts that have been declared void in previous references to be void for future cases.[106]

One of the most interesting questions related to the preliminary reference jurisdiction of the ECJ, given the potential for discretion in the wording of the TFEU, is whether such references are mandatory.[107] The same question must arise

[103] [1981] ECR 1191, at p 1215 [11].
[104] *ICC v Amministrazione delle Finanze* (n 103) at p 1215 [12].
[105] *ICC v Amministrazione delle Finanze* (n 103) p 1215 [14].
[106] *ICC v Amministrazione delle Finanze* (n 103) p 1216 [15].
[107] TFEU Art 267 provides:

> The Court of Justice of the European Union shall have jurisdiction to give preliminary rulings concerning:
>
> (a) the interpretation of the Treaties;
> (b) the validity and interpretation of acts of the institutions, bodies, offices or agencies of the Union;
>
> Where such a question is raised before any court or tribunal of a Member State, that court or tribunal may, if it considers that a decision on the question is necessary to enable it to give judgment, request the Court to give a ruling thereon.
>
> Where any such question is raised in a case pending before a court or tribunal of a Member State against whose decisions there is no judicial remedy under national law, that court or tribunal shall bring the matter before the Court.
>
> If such a question is raised in a case pending before a court or tribunal of a Member State with regard to a person in custody, the Court of Justice of the European Union shall act with the minimum of delay.

in the context of Article 214 of the RTC. The only CCJ decision to touch on the matter to date, *Hummingbird Rice Mills Limited v Suriname and the Caribbean Community*, suggests cryptically that a 'national court or tribunal has, of course, a measure of discretion in considering the necessity of a referral but that discretion is a limited one'.[108] This contrasts with the firm pronouncement of Pollard that national tribunals have no discretion in relation to referrals.[109] Several ECJ cases may assist us here. In Case 244/80 *Foglia v Novello (No 2)* the ECJ held that although the first assessment of the need for a preliminary reference must be made by the domestic tribunal, the ECJ itself retains the inherent right to confirm its own jurisdiction over preliminary reference proceedings.[110] Applied in the CARICOM context, this decision suggests that although national tribunals must assess whether they are required to make a referral, the legality of that decision will always be reviewable by the CCJ.[111]

There is no similar compulsory requirement in Article 214 of the RTC in relation to referrals from decisions of bodies from which there is no further right of appeal (as exists in Article 267 of the TFEU). However the same considerations may arise when referral requests are assessed by the CCJ. If a referral request is made from a final national body, then the same reasoning as applied in Case 107/76 *Hoffmann-la Roche v Centrafarm* may be relied upon by the CCJ, namely, that preliminary references are required in cases of finality in order 'to prevent a body of national case-law not in accord with the rules of Community law from coming into existence in any Member State'.[112]

The ECJ has held that a preliminary reference may not be required where the EU rule in question is absolutely clear. As noted in Case 283/81 *CILFIT*, under the doctrine of *acte clair* preliminary rulings are not required:

> [T]he correct application of Community law may be so obvious as to leave no scope for any reasonable doubt as to the manner in which the question raised is to be resolved. Before it comes to the conclusion that such is the case, the national court or tribunal must be convinced that the matter is equally obvious to the courts of the other Member States and to the Court of Justice. Only if those conditions are satisfied, may the national court or tribunal refrain from submitting the question to the Court of Justice and take upon itself the responsibility for resolving it.[113]

[108] Judgment [2012] CCJ 1 (OJ) [26].

[109] Pollard, in *The Caribbean Court of Justice* (n 1) at p 95, states:

> Article 214 of the Revised Treaty is similar to Article 177 of the Rome Treaty [now Art 267 of the TFEU] but is different in an extremely important particular. For, whereas Article 177 (2) of the Rome Treaty gives the national court or tribunal a discretion of referral to the European Court of Justice where such a court or tribunal is not a court of last resort, Article 214 of the Revised Treaty allows for no such discretion.

[110] [1981] ECR 3045, at pp 3063–4 [21].

[111] See the gently critical comments of the CCJ in *Hummingbird Rice Mills Limited v Suriname and the Caribbean Community*, Judgment [2012] CCJ 1 (OJ) at [26], regarding the lack of a referral from the High Court of Suriname regarding the unsuccessful interlocutory proceedings brought by the claimant in the latter court.

[112] [1977] ECR 957, at p 973 [5].

[113] [1982] ECR 3415, at p 3430 [16].

Nevertheless the Court also highlights that when making such determinations a national court must take into account the fact that EU law is translated into a number of different languages, entailing complex terminology, and the need to understand EU acts within the context of EU law as a whole.[114] As a result there may be need for preliminary rulings even when legal acts appear to be clear.

14.5.4 Applications by persons

CCJ

The fourth form of original jurisdiction possessed by the CCJ, not shared by either the ECCA or the ECJ, is over individual applications under Article XXIV of the Agreement and Article 222 of the RTC. In the OECS system individuals will be required to bring their claims in domestic courts (suing on the basis of the statute transforming the RTB), or must request assistance from their states of nationality to bring a suit on their behalf for breach of RTB obligations by another state. In EU law individuals can bring claims in national courts for enforcement of EU law under the principle of direct effect, and the Commission can bring claims based upon facts drawn to its attention by individuals.[115] This double competence has given rise to the expression of the 'dual vigilance' of EU law, highlighting the vigilance of EU law at both the national and EU levels. If the CCJ were to adopt the principle of direct effect, CARICOM law could be said to embody triple vigilance: vigilance at the Community level (through Article 211(b) and 222 of the RTC) and vigilance at the national level (through direct effect).

Even without direct effect, under the RTC it may be possible for an individual claim to be brought by that person's state of nationality under Article 211(a), to be brought by the Community under Article 211(b), to be referred to the Court under Article 211(c) and to be brought directly by the person under Article 211(d). Different concerns may arise in each case. A state bringing a claim on behalf of an individual may have to satisfy the general international legal requirements for claims of diplomatic protection.[116] The state would also focus on presenting

[114] In *CILFIT* at pp 3430–1 [21] the Court summarizes:

> [T]he answer to the question submitted by the Corte Suprema di Cassazione must be that the third paragraph of Article 177 [TFEU Art 267] of the EEC Treaty is to be interpreted as meaning that a court or tribunal against whose decisions there is no judicial remedy under national law is required, where a question of Community law is raised before it, to comply with its obligation to bring the matter before the Court of Justice, unless it has established that the question raised is irrelevant or that the Community provision in question has already been interpreted by the Court or that the correct application of Community law is so obvious as to leave no scope for any reasonable doubt. The existence of such a possibility must be assessed in the light of the specific characteristics of Community law, the particular difficulties to which its interpretation gives rise and the risk of divergences in judicial decisions within the Community.

[115] For more on the principle of direct effect see Chapter 8.

[116] The test and rationale for claims of diplomatic protection is succinctly summarized by the Permanent Court of International Justice in the *Mavrommatis Palestine Concessions Case (Greece v UK)* (Jurisdiction) [1924] PCIJ Rep, Series A, No 2, at p 12:

and preserving its own interests in the claim, not necessarily the interests of its national. Similarly, if the Community brings a claim it would not likely endorse all aspects of the person's claim per se, but would rather present its views about the best position for CARICOM law based upon the factual matrix. In EU law, for example, the Commission brings actions in order to ensure the general and uniform observance of Community law. A referral, in contrast, would only address the elements of the person's domestic litigation that directly raise issues requiring the interpretation of the RTC. Other aspects of the case would be considered by the domestic (referring) tribunal. For such reasons, the individual application provided for in Article 222 of the RTC is unique. It allows a person to present all aspects of a case involving CARICOM law directly to the Court, in a manner best reflecting that person's concerns.[117]

This is crucial since it appears to be self-evident that in most cases a person will be best placed to protect his, her, or its (for juridical persons) own interests.[118] The CCJ has also noted that persons must play a crucial role in the implementation of the CSME, and the individual application provided by Article 222 helps ensure this. As noted by the CCJ in the case of *Trinidad Cement Ltd and TCL Guyana Inc v Guyana*:

> From these and other paragraphs of the preamble, one deduces that, in an age of liberalisation and globalisation, the Contracting Parties are intent on transforming the CARICOM sub-region into a viable collectivity of States for the sustainable economic and social development of their peoples; that the CSME is regarded as an appropriate framework or vehicle for achieving this end and that private entities, 'and in particular the social partners', are to play a major role in fulfilling the object and goals of the RTC. The CSME is intended to be private sector driven. The question arises as to the manner in which the RTC proposes to accommodate private entities.[119]

> It is an elementary principle of international law that a State is entitled to protect its subjects, when injured by acts contrary to international law committed by another State, from whom they have been unable to obtain satisfaction through the ordinary channels. By taking up the case of one of its subjects and by resorting to diplomatic action or international judicial proceedings on his behalf, a State is in reality asserting its own rights—its right to ensure, in the person of its subjects, respect for the rules of international law.

[117] Note that the RTC and the Agreement provide other circumstances in which an individual may have locus standi before CCJ, outside of Art 222. For example, a defendant may challenge, by means of Art 175(12) of the RTC, the decision of the Competition Commission. See Part 11 of the Caribbean Court of Justice (Original Jurisdiction) Rules 2006 (24 Mar 2006), as available at <http://www.caribbeancourtofjustice.org/court-instruments/rules-of-the-court> (accessed 27 Jul 2013), and Carnegie (n 50) at 5. Also, under Article XVIII(1) of the Agreement a person may also apply to intervene if that person 'has a substantial interest of a legal nature which may be affected by a decision of the Court in the exercise of its original jurisdiction'.

[118] As noted by the Court in *Trinidad Cement Ltd and TCL Guyana Inc v Guyana* Judgment [2009] CCJ 1 (OJ), (2009) 74 WIR 302, 15 January 2009, at [20], 'Article 211 gives to "persons in accordance with Article 222", *in their own right*, qualified access to the Court' (emphasis added).

[119] *Trinidad Cement v Guyana* (n 118) [13]. The Court also notes, at [18], that '[g]iven the important role envisaged for private economic entities in achieving the objectives of the CSME, the Contracting Parties clearly intended that such entities should be important actors in the regime created by the RTC; that they should have conferred upon them and be entitled to enjoy rights capable of being enforced directly on the international plane.'

This private sector, or person-oriented, emphasis is striking. Under historic international legal doctrine states were conceived as the primary, if not exclusive, subjects of international law, with very limited recognition being given to individuals as holders of international legal rights.[120] By shifting the focus the Court emphasizes the key role of CARICOM as a framework for the lives and aspirations of the peoples of the region.

Article 222 sets out a four part, cumulative test that must be satisfied for individual applications in the following terms:

> Persons, natural or juridical, of a Contracting Party may, with the special leave of the Court, be allowed to appear as parties in proceedings before the Court where:
> (a) the Court has determined in any particular case that this Treaty intended that a right or benefit conferred by or under this Treaty on a Contracting Party shall enure to the benefit of such persons directly; and
> (b) the persons concerned have established that such persons have been prejudiced in respect of the enjoyment of the right or benefit mentioned in paragraph (a) of this Article; and
> (c) the Contracting Party entitled to espouse the claim in proceedings before the Court has:
> (i) omitted or declined to espouse the claim, or
> (ii) expressly agreed that the persons concerned may espouse the claim instead of the Contracting Party so entitled; and
> (d) the Court has found that the interest of justice requires that the persons be allowed to espouse the claim.[121]

In short, Article 222 requires that a right or benefit enure to a person directly, that prejudice to that person's right or benefit be established, that the state of nationality of the person either omits or declines to espouse the claim or expressly agrees that the person may do so in its place, and that the interests of justice support the bringing of the claim.

Article 222 has been considered by the CCJ in its early original jurisdiction decisions, particularly in the case of *Trinidad Cement Ltd and TCL Guyana Inc v Guyana*.[122] This case involved the applicants Trinidad Cement Ltd ('TCL') and TCL Guyana Inc ('TGI'), limited liability companies incorporated in Trinidad and Tobago and Guyana, whose main business was the production, packaging, sale, and distribution of cement in the common market established by the RTC. They brought a claim against Guyana alleging breach of Article 82 of the RTC for its suspension of the Common External Tariff (CET) on cement imported from third states, which caused them prejudice and damages by lessening demand for their own cement products. Guyana fully admitted the suspension and that it had not been authorized by the competent CARICOM organ, COTED.[123] In its

[120] See *Trinidad Cement v Guyana* (n 118) [14]–[15].

[121] Art XXIV of the Agreement uses nearly identical terms. One important difference is that Art XXIV refers to 'nationals' rather than 'persons'.

[122] Judgment [2009] CCJ 1 (OJ), (2009) 74 WIR 302, 15 January 2009.

[123] *Trinidad Cement v Guyana* (n 122) [3].

defence, Guyana nevertheless argued that the applicants did not have locus standi to institute proceedings before the CCJ under Article 222 of the RTC.[124] As a result, the Court was required to assess whether the applicants and their claims could fall within Article 222.

In considering the matter during the Special Leave application, the Court looked at both the RTC and the Agreement and held in relation to the different terms used in the two treaties that locus standi is to be accorded to 'persons' under Article 222, not 'nationals' (as in the Agreement).[125] In making such a determination the Court accepted a lower threshold for admissibility, since other provisions of the RTC define the term 'national' very restrictively.[126] In terms of legal persons (companies), the Court also re-formulated the general international legal test for nationality of companies (as set out in the *Barcelona Traction, Light and Power Company Case*), for the purposes of assuming jurisdiction. The Court held that it is 'sufficient for such an entity to be incorporated *or* registered in a Contracting Party'.[127]

To satisfy the requirements of Article 222(a) and (b), the applicants were required to make out an arguable case that a right under the RTC enured to them directly, and was prejudiced.[128] The challenge they faced was that the provisions regarding the CET created obligations for states, not persons. But the Court resolved this dilemma by establishing a doctrine of correlative rights arising from obligations imposed upon member states under the RTC. The Court held:

> Rights and benefits under the RTC are not always expressly conferred although some of them are, for example the rights referred to in Articles 32 and 46. Many of the rights, however, are to be derived or inferred from correlative obligations imposed upon the Contracting Parties. Unless specifically otherwise indicated, the obligations set out in the RTC are imposed on Member States (or a class of Member States) collectively. Where an obligation is thus imposed, it is capable of yielding a correlative right that enures directly to the benefit of private entities throughout the entire Community.[129]

[124] *Trinidad Cement v Guyana* (n 122) [3].

[125] *Trinidad Cement v Guyana* (n 122) [25]–[28].

[126] Art XXIV of the Agreement and Art 32 of the RTC both use the term 'nationals' and, when read together, could have significantly limited the ability of juridical applicants to access the Court.

[127] [2009] CCJ 1 (OJ) [28] (emphasis added). The test in *Barcelona Traction, Light and Power Company, Limited (Belgium v Spain)* (Second Phase) [1970] ICJ Rep 3, establishes that a company's nationality will be that of (a) the state under whose laws it is incorporated, *and* (b) in whose territory its registered office is located.

[128] The threshold for a special leave application is expressed in *Trinidad Cement v Guyana* at para [33] as follows: 'The Court holds that, at this stage, it is sufficient for the applicant merely to make out an arguable case that each of these two conditions can or will be satisfied since they are substantive requirements an applicant must in any event fully satisfy in order ultimately to obtain relief.' This threshold changes to proof on 'a balance of probabilities' when the matter is heard after the grant of Special Leave (at the merits stage): *Hummingbird Rice Mills Limited v Suriname and the Caribbean Community*, Judgment [2012] CCJ 1 (OJ) [12]. In *Trinidad Cement Ltd v Competition Commission*, Judgment [2012] CCJ 4 (OJ), 12 November 2012, at [9], the Court clarified that the burden at the merits stage is to establish the substance of the case: 'The requirement conclusively to establish what is stated in Article 222(a) and (b) has in previous cases been dealt with by this Court under the heading of jurisdiction but a better doctrinal approach might be to consider this requirement as being merged in the natural obligation of a Claimant to establish the substance of his case.' In *Shanique Myrie v Barbados* (n 23), at [12] the Court indicated that the burden of proof 'must be lower than the standard used in a criminal case'.

[129] *Trinidad Cement v Guyana* (n 122) [32].

After examining Article 82 of the RTC, the Court held that the provision could give rise to correlative individual rights, regarding which the applicants had made out an arguable case for their infringement.[130] This is a significant judicial development, one that makes the RTC potentially relevant to persons in any case where a concrete duty is imposed upon a member state.

Regarding Article 222(c)—the need for the state of nationality to omit, decline, or expressly agree to person bringing the claim—the circumstances of the suit, with a Guyanese company attempting to sue Guyana, posed additional challenges. As noted by Guyana in its defence, a state cannot omit or decline to bring a claim against itself, nor would it agree to such a suit. Thus, Guyana submitted, Article 222(c) should bar such a suit. In examining the meaning of Article 222(c) the Court adopted a teleological interpretation and held that 'it was not the intention of the Member States to prohibit a private entity from bringing proceedings against its own State.'[131] Rather, Article 222(c) was meant to prevent duplication of suits in a case where a person and that person's state of nationality would both be entitled to bring a claim.[132] As a result TGI was not required to satisfy Article 222(c). TCL did so by demonstrating that Trinidad and Tobago had decided not to participate as a party in the proceedings.[133]

In satisfaction of Article 222(d) the Court determined in the *Trinidad Cement Ltd and TCL Guyana Inc v Guyana* that it was in the interests of justice that the

[130] *Trinidad Cement v Guyana* (n 122) [34]–[35].

[131] *Trinidad Cement v Guyana* (n 122)[38] and [40]. Interestingly, Pollard, in *The Caribbean Court of Justice* (n 1) at p 101, suggests that this was the intention of the drafters of the RTC.

[132] In the words of the Court, in *Trinidad Cement v Guyana* (n 122) at [43]:

> If, as the Court has previously held, distinct and separate rights of action against a State in violation of the RTC are given to Member States and to private entities, then a means had to be found to avoid a duplication of suits. Article 222(c) is the mechanism used. It is a procedural device to avoid a State allegedly in violation being twice vexed, once by an injured private entity and again by the Contracting Party of that private entity. Article 222(c) cannot and does not apply where the State against which proceedings are to be brought is the Contracting Party of the private entity seeking to institute such proceedings. In such a case, the private entity is not required to comply with the provisions of Article 222(c).

Note that in *Shanique Myrie v Barbados*, Judgment [2012] CCJ 3 (OJ) at [26], the Court held a defendant state would not be 'twice vexed' in cases where the state of the national bringing an individual application chose to intervene in the proceedings.

[133] In *Trinidad Cement Ltd and TCL Guyana Inc v Guyana*, Interim Order [2008] CCJ 1 (OJ), 22 July 2008, at [6] the Court noted:

> The State of Trinidad and Tobago was entitled to appear and was served with a copy of the proceedings. It appeared by counsel but at the case management conference preceding the hearing it had indicated that it merely wished to observe the proceedings.

In *Trinidad Cement Ltd and TCL Guyana Inc v Guyana*, Judgment [2009] CCJ 1 (OJ), (2009) 74 WIR 302, 15 January 2009, at [44], the CCJ states: 'The Court notes that TCL has provided un-contradicted evidence of its compliance with Article 222(c).' In *Trinidad Cement Ltd v Caribbean Community*, Judgment [2009] CCJ 2 (OJ), (2009) 74 WIR 319, 5 February 2009, at [38], the Court found that the requirements of Art 222(c) were satisfied by 'the Attorney-General's reply dated December 8, 2008, which simply stated that receipt of the letter of December 2 was acknowledged and "its contents have been noted".' In *Shanique Myrie v Barbados*, Judgment [2012] CCJ 3 (OJ) at [2], it was noted that the Government had expressly agreed to Myrie bringing her claim in lieu of Jamaica bringing it on her behalf.

applicants be allowed to espouse their claim.[134] It should be noted that in no original jurisdiction case to date has the Court held that it would not be in the interest of justice for it to hear the matter. At least at present the Court's door appears to be wide open to potential applicants.[135] This is commendable, even if it may be regretted by some defendants. The widespread acceptance of original jurisdiction applications by persons will allow the Court to quickly develop its jurisprudence.

14.5.5 Appellate treaty jurisdiction of ECCA

Paragraph 8 of the Dispute Settlement Annex provides for a kind of appellate jurisdiction from decisions of tribunals in the organization as part of its treaty jurisdiction. This is unique because it combines both original and appellate forms of jurisdiction. Paragraph 8 provides:

> 8 The Eastern Caribbean Court of Appeal shall have as part of the Treaty Jurisdiction of the Organisation the jurisdiction to review or hear appeals from any internal body established to consider matters of dispute internal to any Organ of the Organisation.

Since the phrases 'any internal body' and 'dispute internal to any Organ' are not defined under the RTB, the scope of this provision could be very broad. The 'Organs' of the OECS are identified in Article 7 of the RTB as being the Authority, the Council of Ministers, the OECS Assembly, the Economic Affairs Council, and the OECS Commission.[136]

Paragraph 8 of the Dispute Settlement Annex was probably created to allow for an appeal from the dispute settlement procedures established in Articles 30–31 of the OECS Protocol, as foreshadowed by Article 30.6 of the Protocol, which allows for a challenge to the decision of the Economic Affairs Council to be brought to the Eastern Caribbean Court of Appeal. It will be interesting to see if it is more broadly construed. It is doubtful that it could be used to provide an appeal from decisions or recommendations of the other procedures established in the Dispute Settlement Annex—including good offices, consultation, conciliation, and arbitration—since those mechanisms may not be considered to be internal bodies established to consider 'matters of dispute internal to any Organ'.

[134] *Trinidad Cement v Guyana* (n 133) [45].

[135] But see the case of *Doreen Johnson v CARICAD* [2009] CCJ 3 (OJ), in which the Court refused to take jurisdiction over a suit against an Institution of the Community.

[136] Unfortunately this would seem to exclude the Institutions of the Organisation, set out in Art 6. Their inclusion would have been helpful to resolve the difficulties highlighted by the case of *Doreen Johnson* (n 135) where no legal mechanism was available to challenge employment-related decisions of an Institution of CARICOM, in the context where that Institution was immune from suit in the jurisdiction in which it was headquartered.

14.5.6 Intervention and third parties

CCJ

Article XVIII(1) of the CCJ Agreement allows a member state, the Community or persons who consider that they have 'a substantial interest of a legal nature which may be affected by a decision of the Court in the exercise of its original jurisdiction' to apply to the Court to intervene. The Court is empowered to decide the application. If the matter requires the construction of 'a convention to which Member States and persons other than those concerned in the case are parties', the Registrar must notify all such States and persons.[137] Article XVIII(3) then provides that '[e]very State or person so notified has the right to intervene in the proceedings; but if the right is exercised, the construction given by the judgment will be equally binding on all parties.' This latter provision is obscure. It is not clear whether the judgment will be equally binding upon the intervener which, technically speaking, is not a party. It also is not clear whether such judgments are binding in all cases of intervention, or only in cases of interventions regarding the construction of a convention. The latter interpretation appears to be supported by the text.[138]

Part 14 of the Caribbean Court of Justice (Original Jurisdiction) Rules 2006 provides further details about intervention and how to apply for intervener status.[139] Under Rule 14.2 an application for leave to intervene must be filed within six weeks of the applicant or the contracting party of which the applicant is a national is notified. Rule 14.2(2) specifies that the application must include details about the substantial interest of a legal nature claimed by the applicant, how that interest would be affected by a decision of the Court in the proceedings, and 'the contentions which the applicant wishes to put forward in the current proceedings'. Upon receipt of such an application the Registrar must serve it on the parties and invite them to file written submissions as to whether the applicant could be granted leave to intervene.[140] Under Rule 14.3(3) the applicant may be allowed to respond to these submissions.

The Court may determine an application for leave to intervene with or without a hearing.[141] If the Court permits the intervention, then all documents served on the other parties (except secret or confidential documents), must be served on the intervener.[142] Within twenty-eight days of receipt, according to Rule 14.4 (2), the intervener must file a statement specifying

(a) the order which the intervener wishes the Court to make in the current proceedings;

[137] Agreement Art XVIII(2).

[138] See further Rule 14.5 of the Caribbean Court of Justice (Original Jurisdiction) Rules 2006 (24 Mar 2006), as available at <http://www.caribbeancourtofjustice.org/court-instruments/rules-of-the-court> (accessed 27 Jul 2013).

[139] Note that Pollard, in *The Caribbean Court of Justice* (n 1) at pp 21–2, suggests that the Original Jurisdiction Rules were closely modelled on the Rules of the ICJ and ECJ. Even if that was the case, however, the subsequent analysis and interpretation of these rules, particularly in *Shanique Myrie v Barbados*, Judgment [2012] CCJ 3 (OJ), suggest that that Court will not be overly influenced by other jurisdictions in their application.

[140] Rule 14.3. [141] Rule 14.3(3). [142] Rule 14.4(1).

(b) any legal submissions on which the intervener relies; and
(c) where appropriate, the nature of any evidence offered in support of the intervener's contentions, annexing any documents on which it is intended to rely.

This statement is then served upon the parties who may respond. Interveners are also empowered to ask the Court to stay and resume proceedings under Rule 21.1. Finally, Rule 14.6 specifies that the 'intervener shall accept the case as he finds it at the time of his intervention so that his intervention shall have prospective effect only'.

The status of an intervener, as previously outlined, appears to lie in between that of a party and non-party. Interveners are given many of the rights of a party. They may make submissions, request orders, adduce oral and documentary evidence, cross-examine witnesses, and may be entitled to receive or be required to bear costs.[143] However interveners must take the case as they find it, and cannot introduce substantially new lines of argument. The intervener's status is also subsidiary to that of the parties in the action, who may withdraw or settle a case.[144]

There is no provision for third parties in the RTC or in the Rules, but such a status has emerged in the jurisprudence of the CCJ. The seminal decision of the Court related to both intervener status and the role of third parties is that of *Shanique Myrie v Barbados*.[145] This case involved a claim by a natural person, Ms Myrie, alleging that Barbados had breached Articles 7, 8, 9, 28(1), and 45 of the RTC in relation to alleged discriminatory and unlawful treatment, including an alleged cavity search, by Barbadian Customs and Immigration officials on 14 and 15 March 2011 at the Grantley Adams International Airport.[146] She claimed a violation of her right to free movement arising under the RTC and a 2007 Conference decision, which she argued included the right to enter Barbados and

[143] *Shanique Myrie v Barbados*, Judgment [2012] CCJ 3 (OJ) [33].

[144] See eg Justice Jacob Wit, 'The Role of the Caribbean Court of Justice (CCJ) in the Private Sector's Life', paper presented at the Regional Manufacturers' Meeting, TTMA Headquarters, Trinidad & Tobago, on 4 February 2006, available through <http://www.caribbeancourtofjustice.org/publications/papers-speeches> (21 Jul 2013) at 9–10:

> Another hidden backdoor can be found in Article XVIII of the CCJ Agreement. This provision makes it possible for a private party to intervene in current proceedings on a CSME issue if that party can show that it has a substantial interest of a legal nature which may be affected by a decision of the CCJ in that particular case. In a way this is an easier entrance than the one of article 222 of the Treaty, because no special leave is necessary. Provided that the private party can show its substantial legal interest in the outcome of the case it will be granted leave to intervene in the proceedings, which means that it will have the opportunity to side with one of the parties in the proceedings, either on the side of the applicant or on that of the defending party. As such it will be possible for that party to provide its own arguments in the current proceedings and thus to influence the outcome thereof.
>
> There is also a downside to this procedure, though. If the applicant decides not to pursue the case any further and to withdraw it before any judgment is given, the intervener may not have the right to continue the case. If he really wants a decision, the private party should try to get special leave to initiate a proceeding himself and then, if leave is granted, file his own case and then ask the court to join his case with the current one. Only then can the party be sure that he will get a decision of the court. Nevertheless: depending on the circumstances of the case, intervention alone might be a good way to enter such a proceeding.

[145] Judgment [2012] CCJ 3 (OJ).

[146] *Shanique Myrie v Barbados* (n 145) [3].

stay for six months as a CARICOM national. In fulfilling the requirements set out in Article 222 to obtain Special Leave, Myrie had presented evidence that Jamaica, her state of nationality, had expressly agreed that she should bring her claim against Barbados in lieu of Jamaica espousing it on her behalf.[147] Following her grant of Special Leave, Jamaica applied to the Court to intervene in the proceedings. This application was supported by Ms Myrie but resisted by Barbados.[148]

In deciding on the application the Court was required to assess whether Jamaica could demonstrate a substantial interest of a legal nature that would be affected by the case. In evaluating the opposing positions, the Court agreed with Jamaica that Article 221 of the RTC established a system of binding precedent and therefore that any decision in the Court's original jurisdiction could be a concern for all CARICOM member states, including Jamaica.[149] The Court held:

> It is plain that the decisions the Court reaches in these proceedings are capable of providing an authoritative precedent to guide the conduct of all Member States. The quality and extent of Jamaica's interests in these proceedings are therefore not diminished by virtue of the fact that they are shared in common with other Member States. The judgments of the Court, especially in these early years, serve to define Caribbean Community law and Community law in turn affects the obligations of Member States and the rights of Community nationals. Jamaica's interests in the outcome of these proceedings are for Jamaica not matters of general abstraction but rather matters that could, among other things, condition Jamaica's legal obligations and the rights of its citizens.[150]

The CCJ supported this interpretation by looking at the three subsections of Article XVIII of the Agreement. Article XVIII(2)–(3) gave third states and persons the right to intervene in cases involving treaties other than the RTC. Since a right existed in those treaties, according to the Court 'then conferral of a right to intervene in cases where the construction of the Revised Treaty itself is before the Court should be free from controversy.'[151] The Court also dismissed the idea that intervention in a case where a state had already expressly agreed to let an individual proceed with a claim would amount to diplomatic protection 'through the back door':

> The Court does not agree with the view that Barbados is 'twice vexed' by reason of an intervention by Jamaica. Nor does the Court agree that by intervening Jamaica is being allowed to exercise diplomatic protection 'through the back door'. An Intervener may support the claim (or defence as the case may be) of a party but it must accept the case as it is at the time of intervention. The Intervener may not expand the scope of the pleadings and may only make submissions and adduce relevant evidence in support of or in opposition to arguments made by the parties.[152]

As noted by the CCJ, the roles of a party and an intervener are distinct. A party has full rights related to the proceedings. An intervener may not expand the scope of

[147] *Shanique Myrie v Barbados* (n 145) [2].
[148] *Shanique Myrie v Barbados* (n 145) [7].
[149] *Shanique Myrie v Barbados* (n 145) [20].
[150] *Shanique Myrie v Barbados* (n 145) [22].
[151] *Shanique Myrie v Barbados* (n 145) [24].
[152] *Shanique Myrie v Barbados* (n 145) [26] (citations omitted).

the pleadings. Further, the Court expressly acknowledged its duty to monitor the intervener to prevent abuse:

> The Court will always be astute to monitor and control the nature and extent of any intervention, especially in a case like this one where Jamaica opted not to bring the proceedings itself, so that the Intervener does not widen the scope of the inquiry or cause undue material prejudice to a party and in particular the party standing in a position that is adverse to that of the Intervener. . . . The Intervener is, however, by no means a full-fledged party. The Intervener cannot expand the factual and legal framework of the case beyond that which is defined by the parties. The Intervener's position is an ancillary one. If the original case is discontinued or withdrawn or where the Originating Application is declared inadmissible, the intervention is spent.[153]

As highlighted in this passage, the CCJ is keenly aware of the need to keep the roles of interveners and parties distinct so as not to allow the former to materially prejudice the interests of a party.

In relation to the rights of third parties (as opposed to interveners), the Court summarizes the scope of participation allowed under its Rules, and notes its past practice of inviting, and receiving, submissions from states not parties to the proceedings:

> The Rules of the Court expressly permit Member States and The Community not parties in proceedings before the Court the opportunity to play some part in those proceedings or at least to make submissions on issues in dispute. In the case of referrals and proceedings for Advisory Opinions the Rules are quite explicit. In contentious proceedings too the Court has had a practice in the past of receiving submissions from States that were not parties to the case then before it. This practice was built on Part 10.3 of the Rules which requires, within fourteen days, notification to the Community and all Member States of the filing of any Originating Application.[154]

The Court draws support from the fact that it had invited third parties to make submissions in the cases of *Trinidad Cement Ltd and TCL Guyana Inc v Guyana* and *Trinidad Cement Ltd v Caribbean Community*.[155] It also highlights its power to compel member states not parties to the proceedings to supply information under Rule 23.2, as a power which implicitly could authorise the Court to invite states voluntarily to do so.[156] The CCJ contrasted the difference between a third party and an intervener, with third parties only being entitled to make oral and written submissions.[157] As a final emphatic point, the Court expressly extended 'an invitation to Member States and the Community to make submissions on the issues in dispute in these proceedings whether in relation to the relevant law or the material facts'.[158]

[153] *Shanique Myrie v Barbados* (n 145) [33]–[34].

[154] *Shanique Myrie v Barbados* (n 145) [29] (citations omitted).

[155] *Shanique Myrie v Barbados* (n 145) [30]–[31], referring to: Interim Order [2008] CCJ 1 (OJ), 22 July 2008 and Judgment [2009] CCJ 4 (OJ), (2009) 75 WIR 194, 10 August 2009, respectively. See also *Trinidad Cement Ltd and TCL Guyana Inc v Guyana*, Judgment [2010] CCJ 1 (OJ) [9].

[156] *Shanique Myrie v Barbados* (n 145) [32].

[157] *Shanique Myrie v Barbados* (n 145) [33].

[158] *Shanique Myrie v Barbados* (n 145) [35].

As can be seen, the *Myrie* case clearly supports an expansive interpretation of the Agreement, the RTC and the Rules in favour of both intervention and third-party submissions. Given the relative infancy of the jurisprudence of the Court, the CCJ's view that the interpretation of the RTC may be a matter of 'profound interest to all the Member States and the people of the Community', and the Court's express request for submissions from all member states and the Community in the *Myrie* case, it would appear very likely that intervention and third-party status will be actively encouraged in the future.[159] Although this may inconvenience parties, the additional views provided by non-parties may assist the Court in developing its original jurisdiction jurisprudence.

ECCA

There are no treaty jurisdiction rules for the ECCA and thus the issues of intervention and third-party status remain unresolved.

14.6 Developments from the Court's Original Jurisdiction Decisions

Three legal developments arising from the original jurisdiction decision of the CCJ should be briefly highlighted here.[160]

14.6.1 Treaty interpretation

Firstly, the Court has firmly embraced the public international legal rules related to treaty interpretation in its jurisprudence, including the rules of the 1969 Vienna Convention on the Law of Treaties (VCLT). Although as noted earlier in Chapter 2, technically speaking the VCLT is not applicable to the RTC or the RTB, since both treaties embrace non-states parties, the reliance upon its rules by the Court is both natural and inevitable given that many of the VCLT rules reflect customary international law. More interesting, perhaps, is how quickly the Court has moved in its jurisprudence from applying a textual interpretation of the RTC to the teleological or purposive form of interpretation. In the case of *Trinidad Cement Ltd and TCL Guyana Inc v Guyana* when the Court was required to clarify the meaning of Article 222(c) of the RTC the CCJ held that its interpretive process 'cannot cease with a literal interpretation'.[161] Rather, under the rules of treaty interpretation the

[159] *Shanique Myrie v Barbados* (n 145) [35].

[160] For further discussion of the CCJ's original jurisdiction jurisprudence see eg David S Berry, 'The Early Original Jurisdiction Jurisprudence of the Caribbean Court of Justice: Promoting Regional Integration' (2012) 61(2) *Social and Economic Studies* 27–49 and David S Berry, '*Trinidad Cement Ltd. v. Caribbean Community; Doreen Johnson v CARICAD,*' International Decisions (2009) 103 *American Journal of International Law* 561–7.

[161] Judgment [2009] CCJ 1 (OJ), (2009) 74 WIR 302, 15 January 2009 [38].

Court is permitted to 'examine the context in which the provision appears in light of the object and purpose of the *Revised Treaty* and interpret the Article in a manner that renders the *Revised Treaty* effective. In effect the Court must adopt a teleological approach'.[162] This readiness to embrace the teleological form of interpretation is notable, and should allow the Court to play a bold role in developing the regional integration law of the Caribbean Community.

14.6.2 Rule of law and judicial review

Secondly, in the case of *Trinidad Cement Ltd v Caribbean Community* the Court made the fundamental determination that the Revised Treaty establishes a new, rule of law system.[163] In response to a jurisdictional challenge by the Community, the Court held that the member states had transformed the Community from a voluntary arrangement into a rule-based system, placing the Community under the rule of law:

> By signing and ratifying the Revised Treaty and thereby conferring on this Court *ipso facto* a compulsory and exclusive jurisdiction to hear and determine disputes concerning the interpretation and application of the Revised Treaty, the Member States transformed the erstwhile voluntary arrangements in CARICOM into a rule-based system, thus creating and accepting a regional system under the rule of law. A challenge by a private party to decisions of the Community is therefore not only not precluded, but is a manifestation of such a system. Therefore it is not correct to say that by such challenge the functioning of the Community will be greatly hindered or that the exercise of state sovereignty by Member States parties to the Revised Treaty would be unduly constrained. The rule of law brings with it legal certainty and protection of rights of states and individuals alike, but at the same time of necessity it creates legal accountability. Even if such accountability imposes some constraint upon the exercise of sovereign rights of states, the very acceptance of such a constraint in a treaty is in itself an act of sovereignty.[164]

The implications of this position have already been partly spelled out in the Court's jurisprudence. In *Trinidad Cement Ltd v Caribbean Community*, for example, the Court derived a power of judicial review from the rule of law.[165] As the Court explained, there is

> a fundamental difference between the 1973 Treaty of Chaguaramas Establishing the Caribbean Community and Common Market and the RTC. While in Article 11 of the Annex the former treaty provided for States Parties only a voluntary disputes régime, the provisions of the RTC make it plain that the RTC has made available to States and to private entities, mandatory resolution of disputes by the Court in accordance with the rule of law. The RTC represented a transformation of the CARICOM Single Market and Economy 'into a rule-based system, thus creating and accepting a regional system under the rule of law': See: *TCL v The Caribbean Community* [2009] CCJ 2 (OJ) at [32]. This necessarily means that the

[162] *Trinidad Cement v* Guyana (n 161) [38].
[163] Judgment [2009] CCJ 2 (OJ), (2009) 74 WIR 319, 5 February 2009.
[164] *Trinidad Cement v Caribbean Community* (n 163) [32].
[165] Judgment [2009] CCJ 4 (OJ), (2009) 75 WIR 194, 10 August 2009.

Court has the power to scrutinise the acts of the Member States and the Community to determine whether they are in accordance with the rule of law which is a fundamental principle accepted by all the Member States of the Caribbean Community. It would be almost impossible to interpret the RTC and apply it to concrete facts unless the power of judicial review was implicit in that mandate. It is the judgment of the Court that the impugned decisions to authorise suspensions in this case are subject to judicial review by the Court.[166]

The Court has also noted that 'judicial review is a fundamental principle of law accepted by all the Member States of the Community.'[167] In exercising its competence of judicial review, the CCJ held that is has the power to strike down a decision as ultra vires and null and void.[168] Further, in *Trinidad Cement Ltd v Competition Commission* the Court defined the scope of judicial review as requiring that 'no conduct or exercise of power by a treaty created institution (especially one charged with essential functions and endowed with relevant powers under the treaty) should escape the judicial scrutiny of the Court.'[169] These are far-reaching powers.

However the CCJ also highlighted that in exercising the power of judicial review it must strike a balance between the need for legal certainty and accountability, on the one hand, and the need for flexibility in decision making on the part of organs of CARICOM, on the other. The Court held:

In carrying out such review the Court must strike a balance. The Court has to be careful not to frustrate or hinder the ability of Community organs and bodies to enjoy the necessary flexibility in their management of a fledgling Community. The decisions of such bodies will invariably be guided by an assessment of economic facts, trends and situations for which no firm standards exist. Only to a limited extent are such assessments susceptible of legal analysis and normative assessment by the Court. But equally, the Community must be accountable. It must operate within the rule of law. It must not trample on rights accorded to private entities by the RTC and, unless an overriding public interest consideration so requires, or the possibility of the adoption of a change in policy by the Community was reasonably foreseeable, it should not disappoint legitimate expectations that it has created.

The Court must seek to strike a balance between the need to preserve policy space and flexibility for adopting development policies on the one hand and the requirement for necessary and effective measures to curb the abuse of discretionary power on the other; between the maintenance of a Community based on good faith and a mutual respect for the differentiated circumstances of Member States (particularly the disadvantages faced by the LDCs) on the one hand and the requirements of predictability, consistency, transparency and fidelity to established rules and procedures on the other.[170]

The Court has elsewhere described this balancing as reserving a 'margin of discretion' to community actors.[171] In striving for this balance, the Court indicated that

[166] *Trinidad Cement v Caribbean Community* (n 165) [38].

[167] *Hummingbird Rice Mills Limited v Suriname and the Caribbean Community*, Judgment [2012] CCJ 1 (OJ) [30].

[168] *Hummingbird v Suriname* (n 167) [43].

[169] Judgment [2012] CCJ 4 (OJ), 12 November 2012, at [16].

[170] *Trinidad Cement Ltd v Caribbean Community* (n 165) [39]–[40] (citations omitted).

[171] *Hummingbird Rice Mills Limited v Suriname and the Caribbean Community*, Judgment [2012] CCJ 1 (OJ) [32].

its power of judicial review must be 'limited in circumstances where COTED has exercised a discretion'.[172]

14.7 Remedies Available to the CCJ

The Caribbean Court of Justice has started to flesh out the scope of its competence to provide remedies in some of its first original jurisdiction decisions. These remedies include interim measures, coercive orders, declarations, damages (pecuniary and non-pecuniary compensation) and the award of costs. However they exclude exemplary or punitive damages and any other remedies not available under both the common law and civil law.[173]

Interim measures

In the case of *Trinidad Cement Ltd v Caribbean Community* the Court was requested to grant interim measures under Part 12 of the Court's Rules.[174] The Court declined to do so. While affirming its power to grant interim measures the Court decided to hear the Originating Application on an expedited procedure in lieu of adjudicating the claimant's application for interim measures.[175] As a result this area remains to be developed.[176]

Coercive remedies

The Court has affirmed its power to grant coercive remedies against states and the Community. In the case of *Trinidad Cement Ltd v Caribbean Community*, the Court held that it had power to grant coercive remedies against the Community:

> Given the Court's duty to enforce the rule of law and to render the RTC effective, competence to review the legality of acts adopted by Community institutions must perforce

[172] *Trinidad Cement Ltd v Caribbean Community* (n 165) [41].

[173] In *Shanique Myrie v Barbados* (n 23), at [94] the Court held:

> Only those remedies that are known to both legal traditions of the Community can be applied in the original jurisdiction. As the civil law jurisdictions do not allow exemplary damages, these cannot form part of a legal structure that encompasses both traditions.

[174] *Trinidad Cement v Caribbean Community* (n 165) [3].

[175] *Trinidad Cement v Caribbean Community* (n 165) [4]. The Court affirmed its power to prescribe interim measures under Art 218 of the RTC and Art XIX of the Agreement at [42].

[176] It will be interesting to see whether the Court will develop its jurisprudence along the same lines as that of the ECJ related to interim measures. In Case C-246/89R *Commission v UK* [1989] ECR 3125, for example, the ECJ set out and applied the test for interim measures. The first part of the test was that the applicant must be able to show a prima facie case. On the facts, the Commission was able to demonstrate that the British fisheries measures revealed a prima facie case of discrimination on the grounds of nationality. See p 3134 [33]. The second part of the test required evidence of urgency, in other words, one had to be able to show that the order was required to prevent serious and irreparable damage. The Court found this requirement to be satisfied and therefore ordered the requested interim measures. See p 3136 [42] and operative paragraph.

include competence to award appropriate relief to private entities that have suffered and established loss as a result of an illegal act or omission on the part of the Community. If the Court were restricted to the issuance of mere declarations, none of the enforcement mechanisms referred to in the previous paragraph [interim measures, the requirement for compliance with the judgments of the Court, the requirement to enforce orders of the Court in domestic law] would have been required. In the judgment of the Court, coercive remedies are therefore available to the Court.[177]

However the Court declined to order coercive remedies in that case. In the case of *Trinidad Cement Ltd and TCL Guyana Inc v Guyana*, in contrast, the Court ordered coercive remedies against the defendant.[178] The Court required Guyana to reinstate the CET on cement from non-CARICOM sources within a period of twenty-eight days from the date of the Court's order.[179]

State liability and damages

In the case of *Trinidad Cement Ltd and TCL Guyana Inc v Guyana* the CCJ also established that member states could be liable to private persons for breaches of the RTC. However such state liability requires a high threshold of proof. As explained by the Court,

This Court holds that a similar principle [of state liability] applies under the RTC and that the new Single Market based on the rule of law implies the remedy of compensation where rights which enure to individuals and private entities under the Treaty are infringed by a Member State. But State liability in damages is not automatic. A party will have to demonstrate that the provision alleged to be breached was intended to benefit that person, that such breach is serious, that there is substantial loss and that there is a causal link between the breach by the State and the loss or damage to that person.

The reason for laying down conditions as to liability in damages is to prevent States from being harassed by claims for technical breaches or minor procedural defects. The range of potential breaches by a Member State may extend from minor breaches to flagrant and contumacious abuses of State power. The threshold for eligibility for damages is therefore a high one. It is not every infringement that would attract damages. The Court may not consider making a monetary award for minor breaches of the RTC. The breach must be sufficiently serious to warrant the award of damages.[180]

On the facts of the *Trinidad Cement* case the Court found that the breach had been sufficiently serious.[181] However, the evidence led did not prove a loss sufficiently proximate to the precise breach in question to justify an award of damages.[182]

In the subsequent case of *Hummingbird Rice Mills Limited v Suriname and the Caribbean Community*, the Court provided examples of factors that would make a breach serious, including its nature, its duration, the reasons given for

[177] Judgment [2009] CCJ 4 (OJ), (2009) 75 WIR 194, 10 August 2009 [43].

[178] *Trinidad Cement Ltd and TCL Guyana Inc v Guyana*, Judgment [2009] CCJ 5 (OJ), 20 August 2009.

[179] *Trinidad Cement v Guyana* (n 178) [45].

[180] *Trinidad Cement v Guyana* (n 178) [27]–[28].

[181] *Trinidad Cement v Guyana* (n 178) [31].

[182] *Trinidad Cement v Guyana* (n 178) [33]–[34].

non-compliance, and the importance of the obligation breached.[183] In reaching its decision in that case, the Court found itself unable to award damages, primarily because the claimant lacked evidence of loss sufficiently proximate to the breach. The evidence led did not differentiate between possible loss by the claimant, on the one hand, and its affiliates, on the other.[184] In addition, the claimant failed to make a satisfactory case for loss of profits and had not provided evidence to demonstrate that its product would have been preferred over that of its competitors.[185] As a result the Court concluded that the claimant had 'utterly failed to provide adequate evidence to maintain any claim for losses'.[186]

In *Trinidad Cement Ltd and TCL Guyana Inc v Guyana* the Court also dismissed the claim for exemplary or punitive damages on the basis that such damages were not generally recognized in international law or in EU law.[187]

However the Court did make the coercive order described earlier, requiring Guyana 'to re-impose the CET within 28 days of the date of this order and to maintain it thereafter until and unless a suspension is authorised by COTED or the Secretary-General pursuant to Article 83'.[188] Regrettably, this order was not complied with. In an effort to obtain a stay and/or variation of the Court's order, Guyana made a subsequent application to the Court.[189] The application was dismissed on the basis that Guyana had failed to make full disclosure of material facts, failed to provide a sufficient evidential basis upon which the Court could act, and had requested an unacceptable, open-ended time limit for compliance.[190]

Guyana's breach of the Court's order led to the final judgment in the case, in which the claimant requested a contempt order against the Attorney-General of Guyana.[191] Guyana had been required to reinstate the CET on cement by 17 September 2009, but only partly reinstated it on 15 October 2009.[192] On 10 January 2010, nearly four months after the time limit for complying with the Court's order, Guyana reinstated CET on all non-CARICOM origin cement.[193] In its judgment in the matter the Court rejected an oral claim for a finding of contempt against Guyana, as that claim was not properly raised.[194] However the Court held that there was no ambiguity in its original order and that Guyana's breach was unlawful.[195] In finding that Guyana had thereby breached its obligations under

183 Judgment [2012] CCJ 1 (OJ) [58].

184 In *Hummingbird v Suriname* (n 183) at [59] the Court held: 'As the juridical person bringing the claim, the Claimant is under the obligation to prove the substantial loss and damage suffered by it as distinct from Republic Grains Investments Limited with which it was affiliated. This it utterly failed to do. Each affiliated company is a juridical person legally distinct from its affiliates.'

185 *Hummingbird v Suriname* (n 183) [61] and [64].

186 *Hummingbird v Suriname* (n 183) [65].

187 Judgment [2009] CCJ 5 (OJ), 20 August 2009 [36]–[40]. See also *Shanique Myrie v Barbados* (n 23) [94].

188 *Trinidad Cement v Guyana* (n 165) [43]. See also at [45].

189 *Trinidad Cement Ltd and TCL Guyana Inc v Guyana*, Judgment [2009] CCJ 6 (OJ).

190 *Trinidad Cement v Guyana* (n 189) [14]–[15].

191 *Trinidad Cement Ltd and TCL Guyana Inc v Guyana*, Judgment [2010] CCJ 1 (OJ).

192 *Trinidad Cement v Guyana* (n 191) [5]–[6].

193 *Trinidad Cement v Guyana* (n 191) [8].

194 *Trinidad Cement v Guyana* (n 191) [13].

195 *Trinidad Cement v Guyana* (n 191) [17].

Article 215 of the RTC to comply with the judgment of the Court promptly, the Court rejected Guyana's submissions on mootness:

> The Court rejects the notion advanced by Guyana that compliance with the Order on January 8, 2010 nearly four months after the time fixed by the Order for re-imposition of the CET had passed, renders academic an inquiry into whether Guyana had complied with the Court's Order promptly. Past acts of disobedience constitute a breach of the Court's Order and consequently a breach of Guyana's obligation to obey the Court's Order promptly.[196]

The Court therefore issued a declaration 'that Guyana failed to comply promptly with the Order and so was in breach of Article 215 of the Revised Treaty'.[197]

After rejecting the arguments that the Attorney-General of Guyana could be held to be in contempt of the Court's order, on the basis that he was a non-party to the proceedings and there was no evidence of his personal responsibility, the Court turned to the question of whether it could make an order for contempt under its original jurisdiction.[198] The CCJ commenced its analysis by noting that the concept of contempt of court is a common law concept, one which has no equivalent in the civil law system.[199] The CCJ also held that Article XXVI(b) of the Agreement, although referring to contempt of court in its text, did not 'confer an express power on the Court to enforce its orders by contempt proceedings'.[200] The Court was unable to definitively conclude whether Article XXVI(b) produced an implied power of contempt, and whether that would be civil or criminal.[201] The Court also refused to express a final view on whether it had an inherent jurisdiction to make an order for contempt in a non-criminal case under international law.[202] In any event, the Court noted that significant challenges would arise in trying to enforce the common law notion of civil contempt at the international level, since it would be impossible to imprison a state, the 'writ of sequestration does not run in the international arena', and the Court possesses no enforcement machinery of its own to implement a fine.[203] The CCJ noted that instead of imposing such sanctions, a declaration of contempt or a declaration of breach of Article 215 of the RTC appeared more suitable since it would allow the other contracting parties to determine the consequences of such a finding.[204] In summary, the Court noted that

> no express power to entertain contempt proceedings is granted in Article XXVI. Further, it is by no means clear that one can extrapolate from the ad hoc international criminal tribunal cases that international courts have an inherent jurisdiction in civil contempt in

[196] *Trinidad Cement v Guyana* (n 191) [24]. See also *Hummingbird Rice Mills Limited v Suriname and the Caribbean Community*, Judgment [2012] CCJ 1 (OJ) [13].

[197] *Trinidad Cement Ltd and TCL Guyana Inc v Guyana*, Judgment [2010] CCJ 1 (OJ) [25].

[198] *Trinidad Cement v Guyana* (n 197) [29] (dismissal of contempt application).

[199] *Trinidad Cement v Guyana* (n 197) [30].

[200] *Trinidad Cement v Guyana* (n 197) [33].

[201] *Trinidad Cement v Guyana* (n 197) [36].

[202] *Trinidad Cement v Guyana* (n 197) [38].

[203] *Trinidad Cement v Guyana* (n 197) [40]–[41]. Additional challenges of course would be raised in trying to enforce civil contempt in a jurisdiction in which such a concept is completely alien, such as Suriname, a civil law contracting party.

[204] *Trinidad Cement v Guyana* (n 197) [42]–[43].

non-criminal cases. No clear authority has been cited to the Court in this regard. An argument for an implied power to deal with civil contempt might be based on the second part of Article XXVI of the CCJ Agreement. However, there are countervailing arguments against this view. On the other hand the problems outlined above and the lack of any practical value in a finding of civil contempt on the international plane in the context of the Revised Treaty and the CCJ Agreement might suggest that no such power was intended.[205]

This passage is notable because the Court is at pains not to make a final determination of the issue. In common law jurisprudence these passages would be considered *obiter dicta*. But the Court's reluctance appears to be motivated by more than judicial economy, since the Court itself highlights in paragraph [16] of its judgment that such matters might be better decided by means of a protocol amending the RTC regarding the forms and sanctions available to the Court under contempt.[206] Perhaps the strongest reason for the lack of judicial pronouncement on the issues is raised in the final section of the judgment, where the Court looks at the possible effect of domestic legislation upon its own powers. Guyana's Caribbean Court of Justice Act purported to accord to the CCJ the power to investigate and punish contempt.[207] The question therefore arose as to whether a domestic statute could add to the Court's jurisdiction or powers. The Court firmly rejected such a position, holding that '[m]unicipal law can neither confer powers on the Court in its original jurisdiction nor diminish the powers that the Court has. Municipal law may, however, recognize an international court within its national borders and give efficacy to its orders.'[208]

This determination must be correct. As a regional tribunal created by, and empowered to interpret, a regional treaty the CCJ cannot have different powers with respect to different contracting parties as a result of variations in their municipal laws. This would severely frustrate the uniformity of the effect of the obligations of the RTC, since in some states a breach would have more serious consequences than in others. As a result, in its conclusion the CCJ merely grants a declaration that Guyana is in breach of Article 215 of the RTC and dismisses the other claims.[209]

The *Trinidad Cement* saga illustrates the serious challenges that non-compliance with the RTC can pose to regional integration. These cases, and the judgments in *Hummingbird Rice Mills Limited v Suriname and the Caribbean Community*, demonstrate a wilful disregard by CARICOM member states of the requirement to either apply the CET to goods or to apply for a waiver from COTED.[210] They also reveal dissatisfaction on the part of businesses in the region with the processes by which CARICOM either decides waiver applications or acts in relation to continuing breaches of the CET obligation. Whether the decisions in the case of *Trinidad Cement Ltd and TCL Guyana Inc v Guyana* will affect public perception of the effectiveness of the Court remains to be seen.

[205] *Trinidad Cement v Guyana* (n 197) [44].
[206] See also *Trinidad Cement v Guyana* (n 197) [53].
[207] *Trinidad Cement v Guyana* (n 197) [45].
[208] *Trinidad Cement v Guyana* (n 197) [48]. See also at [49].
[209] *Trinidad Cement v Guyana* (n 197) [54].
[210] Judgment [2011] CCJ 1 (OJ), 27 June 2011, Judgment [2012] CCJ 1 (OJ) and Supplementary Judgment as to Costs [2012] CCJ 2 (OJ).

Another factor that may influence views about the Court is the nearly complete lack of damages or compensation that it has awarded to date. Only in the case of *Shanique Myrie v Barbados*, after upholding Myrie's claims to have suffered a serious breach of her right of entry into Barbados without hassle and harassment, does the Court award damages to the successful party.[211] The CCJ awarded BDS $2,240 in pecuniary damages (for an airline ticket and medical expenses) and BDS $75,000 in non-pecuniary damages (stated to be at the 'high end of the spectrum' for breach of her right of entry).[212] Unfortunately, although the Court discusses the international legal basis for non-pecuniary damages, and alludes to some of the specific treatment meriting the award (body cavity search, unsanitary detention conditions), no explanation is provided for the basis of the amount awarded.[213] No reference is made to jurisprudence from other courts or tribunals on the appropriate level of compensation for specific injuries. The Court does make clear, however, that non-pecuniary damages are only being awarded for the violation of Ms Myrie's right of entry, not for other potential violations, including those related to human or fundamental rights (ie assault or unlawful detention).[214]

Although the *Myrie* case does provide some hope for compensation for successful litigants, stronger signals may need to be sent by the Court if the original jurisdiction is to be utilized with more frequency by individual applicants. Commercial entities, which are concerned primarily with profit making, turn to litigation only if they can benefit from it. If a company incurs a substantial legal bill to pursue litigation before the CCJ in its original jurisdiction, and wins its case but receives no compensation, it may not be inclined to pursue the same route in the future. When one combines this with the apparent non-compliance by states (such as Guyana) with declaratory orders, the Court's effectiveness as a commercial dispute resolution mechanism may be thrown into doubt.[215] In this regard, it should be noted that the most the Court has done for victors financially in all of the original jurisdiction cases except the case of *Shanique Myrie v Barbados* to date is to order that some portion of their costs be paid by the defendant(s) in their favour.[216]

211 *Shanique Myrie v Barbados* (n 23).

212 *Shanique Myrie v Barbados* (n 23) [95] and [100]

213 *Shanique Myrie v Barbados* (n 23) [26] (finding of unsanitary conditions), [42] (finding of occurrence of body cavity search), [96] (international legal basis for non-pecuniary damages), [97] (entitlement to non-pecuniary damages for search and detention conditions).

214 *Shanique Myrie v Barbados* (n 23) [100].

215 Note that the Court has ordered declaratory relief against the Caribbean Community, Guyana, and Suriname: *Trinidad Cement Ltd v Caribbean Community*, Judgment [2009] CCJ 4 (OJ), (2009) 75 WIR 194, 10 August 2009 [81]; *Trinidad Cement Ltd and TCL Guyana Inc v Guyana*, Judgment [2010] CCJ 1 (OJ) [25]; and *Hummingbird Rice Mills Limited v Suriname and the Caribbean Community*, Judgment [2012] CCJ 1 (OJ) [67], respectively.

216 See eg *Trinidad Cement Ltd v Caribbean Community*, Judgment [2009] CCJ 4 (OJ), (2009) 75 WIR 194, 10 August 2009 [82] (ordering payment of one half of the costs); *Trinidad Cement Ltd and TCL Guyana Inc v Guyana*, Judgment [2009] CCJ 5 (OJ), 20 August 2009 [46] (ordering payment of two thirds of the costs); *Trinidad Cement Ltd and TCL Guyana Inc v Guyana*, Judgment [2009] CCJ 6 (OJ) [15] (ordering payment of the costs of the application); *Trinidad Cement Ltd and TCL Guyana Inc v Guyana*, Judgment [2010] CCJ 1 (OJ) [54] (ordering payment of one half of the costs); *Hummingbird Rice Mills Limited v Suriname and the Caribbean Community*, Supplementary Judgment as to Costs [2012] CCJ 2 (OJ) [8] (ordering Suriname to pay one half of the Claimant's costs, and the

Similarly, a claimant that lost an original jurisdiction case was required to pay 30 per cent of the costs of the defendant.[217] Although the Court has noted the need to take cognizance of, and perhaps ameliorate, the burden placed upon private entities at this early stage of the development of the Court's jurisprudence, it is debatable whether offsetting the costs of litigation will be sufficient to encourage persons to bring claims before the CCJ in its original jurisdiction.[218]

Despite such concerns, it should be emphasized that the high costs of litigation and the paucity of damages awarded by the Court in the majority of cases have not prevented litigants from bringing cases to the Court. In addition, the present challenges may diminish as a result of the development of the Court's jurisprudence, which will flesh out the Court's processes and procedures. Moreover, the Court to date has been limited by the evidence put forward by parties. It is hoped that in future cases claimants will lead appropriate, substantiated, and sufficiently proximate evidence of loss.

As a final point one aspect of this jurisprudence must be highlighted, namely, the CCJ's assumption of the task of assessing damages at the original jurisdiction level. Such a role is not novel under international law, since international tribunals exercising original and final jurisdiction must also decide issues related to all forms of reparation, including compensation. But when one compares the role of the CCJ to that of the ECJ, for example, clear differences emerge. As highlighted by Professor Carnegie, when the CCJ decided that the principle of state liability applied under the RTC, in some ways it went further than the ECJ.[219] In the cases referred to by the CCJ in its jurisprudence—*Francovich* and *Brasserie du Pêcheur*—state liability arose and became enforceable in national law, meaning that damages

Community to bear its own costs). But see *Shanique Myrie v Barbados* (n 23) [104] (awarding all of Ms Myrie's costs 'except to the extent unreasonably incurred').

[217] *Trinidad Cement Ltd v Competition Commission*, Judgment [2013] CCJ 2 (OJ), 29 May 2013 [11].

[218] In the case of *Hummingbird Rice Mills Limited v Suriname and the Caribbean Community*, Supplementary Judgment as to Costs [2012] CCJ 2 (OJ) at [6] the Court noted in relation to costs:

> At this nursery stage of the development of Caribbean Community law, it is important that the burden of establishing the basic principles underpinning the Single Market should not weigh too heavily and disproportionately on private entities and thus discourage the bringing of important issues of economic integration law before the Court.

In the case of *Trinidad Cement Ltd v Competition Commission*, Judgment [2013] CCJ 2 (OJ), 29 May 2013, at [8], the Court clarified that as a result of the proceedings

> the Court was able to clarify the issues relevant to this case and to review rules of the Commission. This review revealed weaknesses, in that areas of the rules were not completely consistent with the Treaty provisions and fell short of the requirement of procedural fairness. The Court made some recommendations for redress. The Court encouraged the Commission to review its rules to ensure that they are in concert with the Revised Treaty and reflect the appropriate standards of fairness. To that extent the Commission and the Community have received benefits from the litigation. To require the Claimant, a private entity to bear the full costs of the proceedings in these circumstances would not be warranted. It would be disproportionate to require it to bear the cost of clarifying the rules and procedures on this important aspect to the Single Market and Economy. At this fledgling stage of the Single Market and Economy, it is important that the private litigants are not discouraged from initiating process.

[219] See Carnegie (n 50) 14–15.

would be assessed by national tribunals.[220] The CCJ, in contrast, has determined that issues concerning state liability and its consequences must be determined by the CCJ itself, in its original jurisdiction. As a consequence, damages must be assessed by the CCJ rather than a national court. When this feature of the CCJ's jurisprudence is taken into consideration, the caution of the Court in awarding damages may be understandable.

However, as suggested in Chapter 8, one of the advantages of the adoption of the general principle of direct effect in the EU system is that it has allowed for the enforcement of EU rules by domestic tribunals. This has thereby both diminished the caseload of the ECJ and allowed litigants to access their normal, domestic tribunals to speedily and effectively enforce EU rights. The ECJ has also benefited from the addition of Article 260 to the TFEU, which expressly empowers the Court to issue lump sum and/or penalty payments against EU member states.[221] This power has proved effective and has been used to impose very serious penalties.[222] The CCJ would benefit from similar express powers.

[220] See Cases C-6/90 and C-9/90 *Francovich and Others v Italian State* [1991] ECR I-5357 and Joined Cases C-46/93 and C-48/93 *Brasserie du Pêcheur SA v Germany* and *R v Secretary of State for Transport, ex parte Factortame Ltd and Others [Factortame III]* [1996] ECR I-1029.

[221] Art 260(1)–(2) of the TFEU provide:

1. If the Court of Justice of the European Union finds that a Member State has failed to fulfil an obligation under the Treaties, the State shall be required to take the necessary measures to comply with the judgment of the Court.
2. If the Commission considers that the Member State concerned has not taken the necessary measures to comply with the judgment of the Court, it may bring the case before the Court after giving that State the opportunity to submit its observations. It shall specify the amount of the lump sum or penalty payment to be paid by the Member State concerned which it considers appropriate in the circumstances.

   If the Court finds that the Member State concerned has not complied with its judgment it may impose a lump sum or penalty payment on it.

Note that under this provision the Commission may merely recommend amounts. The Court has jurisdiction to decide whether, and to what extent (not exceeding the amount specified by the Commission), lump sum or penalty payments are required.

[222] Case C-304/02 *Commission v France* [2005] ECR I-6263 provides an example of the ECJ's powers under what is now Art 260 of the TFEU. In this case the ECJ found that France had failed to comply with an earlier judgment of the Court regarding EU rules governing fisheries conservation on its territory: at pp I-6337 [53], I-6339 [62], I-6341-43 [70], and [73]–[74]. Given its finding of an objective breach, the Court examined the question of whether under what is now Art 260 TFEU both a penalty and lump sum payment could be awarded together, or whether the wording of Art 260 must be read disjunctively. The ECJ held that recourse to both was permitted: at p I-6345 [82]. In deciding the penalties potentially applicable to the French breaches, the Court noted that the amounts specified by the Commission 'cannot bind the Court and are only a useful point of reference': at p I-6352 [103]. In exercising its discretion, the Court indicated at ibid that it must 'set the penalty payment so that it is appropriate to the circumstances and proportionate both to the breach that has been established and to the ability to pay of the Member State'. The Court held that it will weigh several factors in making such a determination, including: (1) the duration of the infringement, (2) its degree of seriousness, (3) the ability of the member state to pay, (4) the negative effect of a failure by the state to comply on private and public interests, and (5) the urgency of getting it to fulfil its obligations. See pp I-6352–3 [104]. After considering these factors, the Court assigned both lump sum and penalty payments. The Court ordered payment of a lump sum of 20 million Euros by France in reflection of the seriousness of the breach, and a penalty payment of nearly 60 million Euros for every six-month period that the breach continued. See p I-6356 (operative paragraph).

14.8 Conclusions

Both the CCJ and ECCA are likely to play significant roles in shaping the structure and content of the legal norms applicable to regional and sub-regional integration jurisprudence. The early original jurisdiction judgments of the CCJ, which have been examined in this and previous chapters, already hint at the potential of that Court. The role of the ECCA remains to be defined. But given the stronger legal regime of the RTB, which grants potentially exclusive competences to organs of the OECS and mandates direct effectiveness of OECS Acts, Regulations, and Orders of the Authority and Council of Ministers, the jurisprudence of the ECCA has an equal, if not greater, potential to increase the effectiveness of the OECS Economic Union.[223] Both courts provide original, compulsory, final, and legally binding dispute settlement mechanisms, and in doing so substantially complete the legal architectures of the two regional integration movements.

[223] See RTB Arts 5 and 14.

PART VI

THE WAY FORWARD

Conclusions and Recommendations

The present work critically assesses the significant changes that have taken place in, and the potential of, the CARICOM and OECS regional integration movements. It has located these movements within broader Caribbean and international perspectives, and has made express comparisons, where appropriate, with other regional integration developments.

Given space constraints it will not be possible to provide a comprehensive summary of the book in this chapter. However it may be useful to examine some of the more significant aspects of the historical and legal structures of these Caribbean integration movements, in an attempt both to anticipate potential future developments and to clarify the choices that will need to be made about the way forward in certain areas. In this context is may be helpful to highlight topics explored in earlier chapters.

As a preliminary point, it remains important to understand the historical, political, and economic contexts of Caribbean regional integration. As described in Chapter 2, the initiative for Caribbean integration arose in a particular colonial context, shaped by the pairing of the desire of the United Kingdom to consolidate and rationalize its colonial regime, and the desires of regional leaders to obtain greater autonomy, and independence, from the United Kingdom. The short-lived product, the West Indies Federation, owes its failure in large part to the contradictory and sometimes competing impulses underpinning integration at that time. The legacy of the Federation has been the abandonment of political integration as a serious option for both CARICOM and the OECS. Instead, the shapes of both regional organizations have been dictated by economic imperatives, both international and regional, and the desire for functional cooperation. The historical origins of CARICOM and the OECS, and the relatively recent acquisition of independent statehood by most CARICOM member states, suggest that for the immediate future regional integration will continue to be conceptualized in economic and trade terms, underpinned by functional cooperation in those and other areas.

But this does not mean that either the vision or reality of CARICOM or the OECS must be limited to regional trade. As detailed throughout this book both regional integration movements attempt to address a wide cross section of human aspirations.[1] CARICOM's Charter of Civil Society and Assembly of Caribbean Community Parliamentarians reveal the increasing tendency of the Caribbean Community to embrace other values, including human rights and democracy.

[1] See the policies for sectoral development, common supportive measures, development policies, and CARICOM's built-in agenda, described in Chapter 12. See also the objectives of the RTC and RTB, and the scope and competences of the organs of the two regional organizations, in Chapters 3–4.

In the OECS, the creation of the Assembly under the RTB represents a real attempt to extend parliamentary democracy to the sub-region. The exclusive and shared competences accorded to organs of the OECS and the creation of an OECS Commission also reveal the recognition by OECS member states of the need to devolve some aspects of their sovereignty to the broader regional structure. The creation of the CCJ, with its original jurisdiction to interpret and apply the RTC, suggests a new commitment to CARICOM as a binding legal order. All of these developments, when combined with the adoption by the CCJ of one source of regional law—general principles of law—suggest the potential for revitalization of the regional integration project. The decisions of the CCJ in its original jurisdiction may be especially instrumental in strengthening the Caribbean Community. The role of the ECCA has a similar potential.

A stronger drive for meaningful regional integration appears particularly important at this juncture in the history of the Caribbean. The developmental potential of the region's natural resources has diminished in most CARICOM territories, and all member states are facing serious economic challenges.[2] These challenges will likely increase as a result of the gradual abolition of preferential trade regimes, the increasing liberalization of the world trade system, and the lack of specialization and diversification within, and coordination between, Caribbean economies.

If strong, functional regional integration is desired, certain changes to the practices of member states and organs of both CARICOM and the OECS would appear necessary. Although it would be possible to advocate further far-reaching revisions to the two constituent documents of CARICOM and the OECS—the RTC and the RTB—such changes do not appear realistic at this time.[3] The creation of a CARICOM Commission modelled after the European Commission, for example, although potentially desirable may not be practicable at present, especially given the reluctance of member states to accord supranational authority to any organ of CARICOM and the Community's continuing financial challenges.

For these reasons the emphasis in this book has been placed upon the texts of both treaties. The texts of the RTC and RTB reveal both their meaning and potential. As explored in the previous chapters, the regimes created by the two treaties, although imperfect, are strong and capable of driving functional regional cooperation. These regimes have been analysed in the context of the wider international legal order, the comparable developments of the EU, and the economic rationales for integration. This comparative focus has been maintained both within and outside of the regional context. In each chapter the texts of the RTC and RTB have been analysed together in relation to particular topics, and then compared with other regional and international developments. Such

[2] See Chapter 2.

[3] For the historical and legal challenges that were overcome in order to create the RTC and to bring it into force see Chapters 2 and 3.

comparisons have yielded insights about the interpretive possibilities of the RTC and RTB as well as about the different choices for regional integration.

It may be helpful to recall some of the possibilities and choices suggested in earlier chapters. For example, in Chapters 3 and 4 the examination of the institutional frameworks of CARICOM and the OECS revealed several different kinds of decision-making processes, from qualified unanimity to qualified majority, each with its advantages and disadvantages. Comparisons were made between the executive rule-making structure of CARICOM, and the more participatory rule-making processes of the OECS (with its requirement for recommendations from the OECS Assembly). The latter reveals a more balanced approach to regional integration—one involving inputs from a number of different sources, including technocrats (the OECS Commission), the people (the OECS Assembly), and member states (the Authority). Chapter 5 raised questions about the personality, legal capacity, privileges, and immunities of both regional organizations, and highlighted some of the deficiencies entailed by the OECS's reliance upon the diplomatic regime of privileges and immunities.

Chapter 6 highlighted both the strengths and weaknesses of the general legal systems of CARICOM and the OECS. In particular it focused on the challenges presented by the common law requirement for transformation of treaties and treaty-based obligations, and the interpretive issues which arise under the RTC and RTB. The adoption of the doctrine of correlative rights by the CCJ—one in which obligations imposed upon states can create correlative rights for persons—may prove instrumental in ensuring compliance with CARICOM obligations. The OECS, in contrast, expressly provides exclusive and shared legislative competences to the Organisation, as well as imposes the requirement for direct effect for Acts, Regulations, and Orders of the Authority and Council of Ministers.

Chapters 7 and 8 push the analysis of the legal regimes further by introducing and providing examples of general principles of law, referring to insights on such principles from legal theory, international law, and EU law. The principle of direct effect, expressly included in the RTB, is contrasted to related principles, including direct applicability, supremacy, indirect effect, and pre-emption. The bases for these general principles under the RTC and RTB are examined, and their potentials are illustrated through comparative analysis of their meanings in EU law. General principles deserve particular attention because, as highlighted earlier, it may prove difficult to further amend or revise the RTC and RTB. As a judicially recognized source of law, at least potentially arising independently from the treaties, general principles can be used to fill in gaps, to flesh out underlying norms, and to strengthen the uniformity and effectiveness of CARICOM and OECS law.

In comparing the substantive rules and policies provided in the RTC and RTB we have started to glimpse the real potential of the CSME and the OECS Economic Union. As illustrated in Chapter 9, the articles providing free movement of persons (including the right of establishment), services, and capital may be used to strengthen the human side of regional integration. Chapter 10 deepened our understanding of the potentials of CARICOM and the OECS to facilitate regional trade, by examining their provisions regarding free movement of goods.

CARICOM's complex trade rules—including those related to the implementation Common External Tariff (CET), the abolition of duties, the restriction of discriminatory internal taxes, and the prohibition of unauthorized quantitative restrictions—were contrasted with the more succinct rules applicable to trade in the OECS Economic Union. Both sets of rules were compared to those applicable in the EU and WTO legal systems. Such comparisons yielded substantial insights about how our Caribbean regional rules can be interpreted and developed. Chapter 11 offered a brief overview of the competition and consumer protection regimes established in the two treaties, and made direct comparisons to the legal regime of the EU. Chapter 12 rounded out our understanding of both the RTC and RTB by exploring some of the future goals of each treaty, and by briefly surveying their policy regimes related to sectoral development, common supportive measures, and development.

Chapters 13 and 14 compared the wide variety of dispute settlement mechanisms existing under both treaties. Chapter 13 examined the dispute settlement functions of the central organs of CARICOM and the OECS, and the ad hoc binding and non-binding mechanisms made available in Chapter IX of the RTC and in the Dispute Settlement Annex and Protocol to the RTB. Chapter 14 focused on the two regional integration courts, the Caribbean Court of Justice and the Eastern Caribbean Court of Appeal. Its analysis of the provisions of the RTC and the early jurisprudence of the CCJ suggested that the Court may play a key role in providing uniform interpretation of, and enforcing, Community law. In sum, the tools for enhanced regional integration are available and can be used effectively.

Effective use, however, may require a number of changes. To achieve deeper and more functional regional integration, member states of CARICOM and the OECS may need to fully utilize the organs and processes of the two regional organizations. Procedures, including voting procedures, should be regularized, formalized, and become compliant with the texts of the treaties. Particularly in the context of CARICOM, where decisions of organs can give rise to binding obligations for member states and correlative rights for persons, it would be useful to record votes and finalize and publicize both the voting record and the full texts of the decisions. Where possible, decisions should expressly stipulate time limits for implementation.[4] Both regional organizations also would be advised to move towards a more transparent system of governance. They should move away from the traditions of closed door (caucus) meetings, secrecy, and the classification and restriction of most documents.

States may also need to become more tolerant of non-consensus oriented decision making, as expressly provided for in the RTC. The qualified unanimity rule applicable to decision making in CARICOM's Conference does not appear to be

[4] This suggestion was endorsed by the CCJ in the case of *Shanique Myrie v Barbados*, Judgment [2013] CCJ 3 (OJ) at [55]:

> As a matter of good practice the Community in its decision-making should stipulate a fixed time frame within which such decsions should be implemented after which the decision enters into force with the result that a delinquent State is automatically in violation of the RTC and, in principle, liable for the consequnces of such a violation.

responsive enough to allow for rapid and dynamic change. For this reason it would be useful to make more decisions in CARICOM's lower level organs, the Ministerial Councils, which generally act by qualified majority. These decisions could then be approved and prioritized by the Community Council, if necessary, and only sent to the Conference (if at all) for formal ratification.

For similar reasons, member states may need to work around the qualified unanimity voting rules employed by the main executive organs of the OECS, which may hamper the efficiency of sub-regional integration. Although such voting rules could be argued to be a necessary evil—given the authority delegated to the OECS, including exclusive and shared legislative competence, and the ability to create directly effective laws—greater effort could be made to implement a formalized legislative process to allow for more efficient rule making. For example, if the OECS Secretariat and the members of the Commission were able to consult widely when drafting Acts for the Authority, and if the OECS Assembly actively debated them, the final products would be more likely to share enough support across the states and societies of the OECS to ensure their ready adoption by the Authority.

In order to strengthen regional integration Caribbean states and territories also may need to change their attitudes about implementation of regional norms. For CARICOM, the practice of non-implementation of treaties and decisions by organs in domestic law is problematic. Although Article 240(1) of the RTC appears to reinforce the dualist system adopted by Commonwealth Caribbean territories, the requirements of Article 240(2) to 'act expeditiously' in transforming decisions of organs and of Article 9 to 'ensure' the carrying out of obligations arising from the RTC and decisions of CARICOM organs, together can provide the foundation for legal accountability. It would not be unreasonable, for example, for the CCJ to rely upon these provisions in order to find a CARICOM member state in breach of its obligations under the RTC on the basis of non-transformation of a Community obligation.

The RTB, in contrast, provides a solution to the problem of transformation. Article 5.3 of the RTB requires independent full member states to enact legislation so as to make OECS Acts, Regulations, and Orders directly effective in their legal systems. This is a significant development on the part of the OECS and, when fully implemented, would allow Economic Union rules to have effect in, and be enforced by, the domestic laws of OECS member states. Although there is no similar textual basis for direct effect in the RTC, it could be recognized as a general principle of Community law by the CCJ. This possibility is explored in some detail in Chapter 8, which recognizes the potential of a number of general principles of law, including those of direct effect, supremacy, pre-emption, state liability, and human rights. Although the Court's position is still developing, the CCJ's embrace of the general principle of state liability provides an indication that general principles of law may be an important part of CARICOM's legal architecture.

The CCJ also may assist in overcoming the challenges of transformation of CARICOM law through the active exercise of its original jurisdiction. As already developed in the early jurisprudence of the Court, the provisions of the RTC can be enforced in individual applications under Article 222. Enforcement of the RTC through the Court's original jurisdiction, including through individual applications, could overcome the problems related to transformation of Community obligations because the RTC itself would be enforced, regardless of domestic non-transformation.

In conclusion, the analysis of this book suggests that the prospects for Caribbean regional integration may be better today, despite the current harsh economic climate, than in the recent past. Both CARICOM and the OECS are underpinned by modern and potentially responsive constituent treaties, each of which is subject to the legal scrutiny of a regional court. A wide variety of binding decisions can be made today by a range of organs in CARICOM and the OECS, and compliance with these decisions can be enforced through a variety of binding and non-binding dispute settlement mechanisms. The effective use of these tools will require strong political leadership, civic commitment, and a greater understanding of the possibilities inherent in the RTC and RTB. It is hoped that this work will promote the latter.

References

BOOKS AND PAMPHLETS

Alexy, Robert, *A Theory of Constitutional Rights*, Julian Rivers (tr) (Oxford: Oxford University Press, 2002).

Arnull, Anthony, *The European Union and its Court of Justice* (Oxford: Oxford University Press, 1999).

Aust, Anthony, *Modern Treaty Law and Practice* (Cambridge: Cambridge University Press, 2000).

Balassa, Bela, *The Theory of Economic Integration* (London: George Allen and Unwin Ltd, 1961).

Barnard, Catherine, *The Substantive Law of the EU: The Four Freedoms*, 3rd edn (Oxford: Oxford University Press, 2010).

Bennion, FAR, *Bennion on Statutory Interpretation: A Code*, 5th edn (London: Lexisnexis Reed Elsevier (UK), 2008).

CARICOM Secretariat, *Annual Report of the Secretary-General 1996* (Georgetown, Guyana: CARICOM Secretariat, 1997).

CARICOM Secretariat, *Charter of Civil Society* (Georgetown, Guyana: CARICOM Secretariat, 1997).

CARICOM Secretariat, *Matrix of Agreements*, Last updated July 2012 (Georgetown, Guyana: CARICOM Secretariat, 2012).

CARICOM Secretariat, *Report of the Technical Sub Group on the Assembly of Caribbean Community Parliamentarians (ACCP)*, REP 96/1/48 ACCP, Oct 24, 2003 (Georgetown, Guyana: CARICOM Secretariat, 2003).

CARICOM Secretariat, *Restructuring of the Organs and Institutions of the Caribbean Community* (Georgetown, Guyana: CARICOM Secretariat, 1993).

CARICOM Secretariat, *Social Security in CARICOM* (Bridgetown, Barbados: CARICOM Secretariat, 2010).

CARICOM Secretariat, *Summary Draft Report on the Appraisal of the State of Implementation of the CARICOM Single Market* (September 2009) (Georgetown, Guyana: CARICOM Secretariat, 2009).

Cassese, Antonio, *International Law in a Divided World* (Oxford: Clarendon Press, 1986).

Cheng, Bin, *General Principles of Law as Applied by International Courts and Tribunals* (London: Stevens and Son Ltd, 1953).

Court of Justice of the European Union, *Annual Report 2011: Synopsis of the work of the Court of Justice, the General Court and the Civil Service Tribunal* (Luxembourg: Court of Justice, 2012).

Craig, Paul and Gráinne de Búrca, *EU Law: Text, Cases and Materials*, 5th edn (Oxford: Oxford University Press, 2011).

Crawford, James, *Brownlie's Principles of International Law*, 8th edn (Oxford: Oxford University Press, 2012).

Demas, William G, *West Indian Development and the Deepening and Widening of the Caribbean Community*, Critical Issues in Caribbean Development No 1 (Kingston, Jamaica: Ian Randle Publishers/UWI ISER, 1997).

Denza, Eileen, *Diplomatic Law: Commentary on the Vienna Convention on Diplomatic Relations*, 3rd edn (Oxford: Oxford University Press, 2008).
Dinan, Desmond, *Ever Closer Union? An Introduction to the European Community* (Boulder, Colorado: Lynne Rienner, 1994).
Dworkin, Ronald, *Taking Rights Seriously* (Guildford: Duckworth, 1977).
Dworkin, Ronald, *Law's Empire* (Cambridge, MA: Belknap Press of Harvard University, 1986).
El-Agraa, Ali M (ed) *The European Union: Economics and Policies*, 8th edn (Cambridge: Cambridge University Press, 2007).
Foster, Nigel, *Foster on EU Law*, 3rd edn (Oxford: Oxford University Press, 2011).
Gardiner, Richard, *Treaty Interpretation* (Oxford: Oxford University Press, 2008).
Geiser, Hans J, Pamela Alleyne and Carroll Gajraj, *Legal Problems of Caribbean Integration: A Study of Legal Aspects of CARICOM* (Leyden: Sijthoff, 1976).
Guest, Stephen, *Ronald Dworkin* (Edinburgh: Edinburgh University Press, 1992).
Hall, Kenneth, *Re-Inventing CARICOM: The Road to a New Integration* (Kingston, Jamaica: Ian Randle Publishers, 2003).
Hall, Kenneth, and Myrtle Chuck-A-Sang (eds), *CARICOM Single Market and Economy: Challenges, Benefits, Prospects* (Kingston, Jamaica: Ian Randle Publishers, 2007).
Hanf, Kenneth and Ben Soetendorp (eds), *Adapting to European Integration: Small States and the European Union* (London: Longman, 1998).
Hart, HLA, *The Concept of Law* (Oxford: Clarendon Press, 1961).
Hartley, TC, *The Foundations of European Union Law*, 7th edn (Oxford: Oxford University Press, 2010).
Henkin, Louis, *How Nations Behave: Law and Foreign Policy*, 1st edn (New York: FA Praeger, 1968).
Jennings, Sir Robert, and Sir Arthur Watts, *Oppenheim's International Law*, 9th edn (London: Longman, 1996).
Kaczorowska, Alina, *European Union Law*, 2nd edn (London: Routledge, 2011).
Kaczorowska-Ireland, Alina, *CSME Competition Law* (London: Routledge (forthcoming)).
Klabbers, Jan, *An Introduction to International Institutional Law* (Cambridge: Cambridge University Press, 2002).
Lange, Brenda, *Global Organizations: The Caribbean Community* (New York, NY: Chelsea House Publishers, 2009).
MacCormick, Neil, *Legal Reasoning and Legal Theory* (Oxford: Clarendon Press, 1978).
Malanczuk, Peter, *Akehurst's Modern Introduction to International Law*, 7th rev'd edn (London: Routledge, 1997).
Menon, PK, *An Introduction to the Law of Treaties* (Bridgetown, Barbados: UWI/USAID Caribbean Justice Improvement Project, 1992).
Merrills, JG, *International Dispute Settlement*, 4th edn (Cambridge: Cambridge University Press, 2005).
Mills, Gladstone et al, *Report on a Comprehensive Review of the Programmes, Institutions and Organisations of the Caribbean Community* (Georgetown, Guyana: Caribbean Community Secretariat, 1990).
Muller, AS, *International Organizations and their Host States: Aspects of their Legal Relationship* (The Hague: Kluwer Law International, 1995).
Müllerleile, Christoph, *CARICOM Integration: Progress and Hurdles—A European View* (Kingston, Jamaica: Kingston Publishers, 1996).
O'Connell, DP, *International Law*, 2nd edn (London: Stevens, 1970).

OECS Secretariat, *Economic Union Treaty—Frequently Asked Questions* (Castries, St Lucia: OECS Secretariat, 2008).

Parry, John H, Philip M Sherlock and Anthony P Maingot, *A Short History of the West Indies*, 4th edn (London: MacMillan Education, 1987).

Payne, Anthony, and Paul Sutton, *Charting Caribbean Development* (London: MacMillan Education Ltd, 2001).

Pollard, Duke E, *The Caribbean Court of Justice: Closing the Circle of Independence* (Kingston, Jamaica: The Caribbean Law Publishing Company, 2004).

Portmann, Roland, *Legal Personality in International Law* (Cambridge: Cambridge University Press, 2010).

Rawlins, Hugh, Rose-Marie Antoine, and David Berry, *Caribbean Justice for All—The Case for a Caribbean Regional Court*, Vol. 3, Contemporary Legal Issues (Bridgetown, Barbados: INDI Graphics, 2000).

Sands, Philippe QC and Pierre Klein, *Bowett's Law of International Institutions*, 6th edn (London: Thomson Reuters, 2009).

Schermers, Henry G and Niels M Blokker, *International Institutional Law*, 4th edn (Boston: Martinus Nijhoff Publishers, 2003).

Schwarzenberger, Georg, and ED Brown, *A Manual of International Law*, 6th edn (Milton, UK: Professional Books Ltd, 1976).

Shaw, Malcolm, *International Law*, 5th edn (Cambridge: Cambridge University Press, 2003).

Trebilcock, Michael, Robert Howse and Antonia Eliason, *The Regulation of International Trade*, 4th edn (London: Routledge, 2013).

Tridimas, Takis, *The General Principles of EU Law*, 2nd edn (Oxford: Oxford University Press, 2006).

UNCTAD, *Most Favoured Nation Treatment* (New York: United Nations, 2010).

United Nations Office of Legal Affairs, Codification Division, *Handbook on the Peaceful Settlement of Disputes Between States* (New York: United Nations, 1992).

Wade, HRW and CF Forsyth, *Administrative Law*, 8th edn (Oxford: Oxford University Press, 2000).

Weatherill, Stephen, *Cases and Materials on EU Law*, 9th edn (Oxford: Oxford University Press, 2010).

Weatherill, Stephen, *Cases & Materials on EU Law*, 10th edn (Oxford: Oxford University Press, 2012).

West Indian Commission, *Time for Action: Report of the West Indian Commission* (Black Rock, Barbados: The West Indian Commission, 1992).

ARTICLES AND OTHER DOCUMENTS

'Britain "respects" CCJ move', *Barbados Nation*, 8 August 2013, p 13.

'Declaration on Principles of International Law Concerning Friendly Relations and Cooperation Among States in Accordance With the Charter of the United Nations (1970)', UNGA Res 2625, GAOR, 25th Sess, Supp No 28, UN Doc A/8028 (24 Oct 1970).

'Promoting an integrated management approach to the Caribbean Sea area in the context of sustainable development', UNGA Res 230, 59th Sess, UN Doc A/RES/59/230 (16 Feb 2005).

'Towards the sustainable development of the Caribbean Sea for present and future generations', UNGA Res 155, 65th Sess, UN Doc A/RES/65/155 (20 Dec 2010).

Akehurst, Michael, 'Notes: The Hierarchy of the Sources of International Law' (1974–75) 47 *British Yearbook of International Law* 273–85.

Anderson, Winston, 'Treaty Implementation in Caribbean Law and Practice' (1998) 8 *Caribbean Law Review* 185–211.

Anderson, Winston, 'Treaty Making in Caribbean Law and Practice: The Question of Parliamentary Participation' (1998) 8 *Caribbean Law Review* 75–115.

Anthony, Kenny D, 'Caribbean Integration: The Future Relationship between Barbados and the OECS' (1998) 23(1) *Journal of Eastern Caribbean Studies* 35–50.

Arbitration Institute of the Stockholm Chamber of Commerce, 'Arbitration Rules 2010', as available through <http://sccinstitute.com/skiljedomsregler-4.aspx> (4 Aug 2013).

Arthur, Owen S, 'Prospects for Caribbean Political Unity' (1998) 23 *Journal of Eastern Caribbean Studies* 27–34.

Berry, David S, 'Interpreting Rights and Culture: Extending *Law's Empire*' (1998) 4(1) *Res Publica* 3–28.

Berry, David S, 'The New Caribbean Community: An Introduction to the Institutional Changes in the *Revised Treaty of Chaguaramas*' (2002) 7(1) *Caribbean Law Bulletin* 1–58.

Berry, David S, '*Trinidad Cement Ltd. v. Caribbean Community; Doreen Johnson v. CARICAD,*' International Decisions (2009) 103 *American Journal of International Law* 561–7.

Berry, David S, 'The Caribbean' in Bardo Fassbender et al (eds), *The Oxford Handbook of the History of International Law* (Oxford: Oxford University Press, 2012) 579–603.

Berry, David S, 'The Early Original Jurisdiction Jurisprudence of the Caribbean Court of Justice: Promoting Regional Integration' (2012) 61(2) *Social and Economic Studies* 27–49.

Berry, David S, 'The Use of International Law by Domestic Tribunals in the Caribbean in Death Penalty Cases' in DS Berry and T Robinson (eds), *Transitions in Caribbean Law: Lawmaking Constitutionalism and the Confluence of National and International Law* (Kingston, Jamaica: Ian Randle, 2013) 103–27.

Braveboy-Wagner, Jacqueline Anne, 'International Relations' in Richard S Hillman and Thomas J D'Agostino (eds), *Understanding the Contemporary Caribbean*, 2nd edn (Boulder, CO: Lynne Rienner Publishers, 2009) 161–90.

Brower II, Charles H, 'Arbitration', in R Wolfrum (ed), *The Max Planck Encyclopedia of Public International Law*, Oxford University Press, 2008–, online edition [<www.mpepil.com>].

Brown, Kathy-Ann, 'The CARICOM—"Unity for Survival"' in N Lacasse and L Perret (eds), *Le libre-échange dans les Amériques (Une perspective continentale)/Free trade in the Americas (A hemispheric approach)* (Montreal: Wilson & Lafleur, 1994) 335–68.

Byron, Jessica, 'Migration, National Identity and Regionalism in the Caribbean: A Leeward Islands Case Study' in Kenneth Hall and Dennis Benn (eds), *Contending With Destiny: The Caribbean in the 21st Century* (Kingston, Jamaica: Ian Randle Publishers, 2000) 80–90.

Caranta, Roberto, 'Government Liability after Francovich' (1993) 52 *Cambridge Law Journal* 272.

Caribbean Court of Justice, 'Judges of the Caribbean Court of Justice', as available at <http://www.caribbeancourtofjustice.org/about-the-ccj/judges> (11 Aug 2013).

CARICOM Competition Commission, 'Rules of Procedure 2011', as available at <http://www.caricomcompetitioncommission.com/images/registry/CCC-Rules-of-Procedure-2011.pdf> (31 Aug 2013).

CARICOM Secretariat, 'Administrative Arrangements and Procedures for the Free Movement of Skills Based on Successive Decisions of the Conference of Heads of

Government and Relevant Councils', as available through <http://caricom.org/jsp/single_market/single_market_index.jsp?menu=csme> (16 Mar 2013).

CARICOM Secretariat, 'Assembly of Caribbean Community Parliamentarians (ACCP)', as available at <http://www.caricom.org/jsp/community/accp.jsp?menu=community> (31 Oct 2011).

CARICOM Secretariat, 'CARICOM Law - Agreement Establishing the Caribbean Court of Justice', as available at <http://www.caricomlaw.org/Details.aspx?EntryId=131> (27 Oct 2013).

CARICOM Secretariat, 'CARICOM System', as available at <http://www.caricomlaw.org/Resources/CARICOMSystem.aspx> (3 Nov 2011).

CARICOM Secretariat, 'CARICOM Welcomes Belize's Move to CCJ', Press Release 248/2010 (2 Jun 2010) as available at <http://www.caricom.org/jsp/pressreleases/press_releases_2010/pres248_10.jsp> (11 Aug 2013).

CARICOM Secretariat, 'Communiqué Issued at the Conclusion of the Tenth Meeting of the Conference of Heads of Government of the Caribbean Community', 3–7 July 1989, Grand Anse, Grenada, as available at <http://www.caricom.org/jsp/communications/communiques/10hgc_1989_communique.jsp> (14 Sep 2013).

CARICOM Secretariat, 'Communique Issued at the Conclusion of the 13th Inter-Sessional Meeting of the Conference of Heads of Government of the Caribbean Community, Belize City, 3–5 February 2002', as available at <http://www.caricom.org/jsp/communications/communiques/13inthgc_2002_communique.jsp> (4 Mar 2013).

CARICOM Secretariat, 'Consensus of Chaguaramas', Issued at the Seventh Special Session of the Conference of Heads of Government, Chaguaramas, Trinidad and Tobago, 26–27 October 1999, as available at <http://www.caricom.org/jsp/secretariat/legal_instruments/consensuschag.jsp?menu=secretariat> (14 Sep 2013).

CARICOM Secretariat, 'Draft Report for the Twenty-Eighth Meeting of the Conference of Heads of Government of the Caribbean Community', HGC/2007/28/DR, 1–4 July 2007.

CARICOM Secretariat, 'Entry Procedures for CARICOM Nationals Exercising the Right of Establishment', as available through <http://caricom.org/jsp/single_market/single_market_index.jsp?menu=csme> (16 Mar 2013).

CARICOM Secretariat, 'Entry Procedures for CARICOM Nationals Exercising the Right to Provide Services Through Temporary Movement of Natural Persons', as available through <http://caricom.org/jsp/single_market/single_market_index.jsp?menu=csme> (16 Mar 2013).

CARICOM Secretariat, 'First Meeting of the IGTF [Inter-Governmental Task Force]', 20–22 April 1993, Georgetown, Guyana [restricted access, on file with CARICOM Secretariat].

CARICOM Secretariat, 'Free Movement in the CARICOM Single Market and Economy (CSME)' as available at <http://www.caricom.org/jsp/single_market/skill.jsp?menu=csme> (6 Oct 2011).

CARICOM Secretariat, 'Free Movement in the CARICOM Single Market and Economy (CSME)', as available at <http://www.caricom.org/jsp/single_market/skill.jsp?menu=csme> (6 Feb 2013).

CARICOM Secretariat, 'History of the Caribbean Community', as available at <http://www.caricom.org/jsp/community/history.jsp?menu=community> (3 Oct 2011).

CARICOM Secretariat, 'Model Legislation on Free Movement of Skilled Nationals', as available at <http://www.caricom.org/jsp/secretariat/legal_instruments/model_legislation_skilled_nationals_act.pdf> (6 Feb 2013).

CARICOM Secretariat, 'News Feature: Five Years On—The CARICOM Single Market and Economy' Press release NF01/2011 (28 January 2011), as available at <http://www.caricom.org/jsp/pressreleases/presnf01_11.jsp?null&prnf=1> (6 Feb 2013).

CARICOM Secretariat, 'News release 147/2006 (6 July 2006): Communique Issued at the Conclusion of the Twenty-Seventh Meeting of the Conference of Heads of Government of the Caribbean Community (CARICOM)', 3–6 July 2006, as available at <http://www.caricom.org/jsp/communications/communiques/27hgc_2006_communique.jsp> (17 Mar 2013).

CARICOM Secretariat, 'Organisational Structure' (chart, updated to 13 February 2009), as available at <http://www.caricom.org/jsp/secretariat/organigram_feb_09.pdf> (7 Oct 2011).

CARICOM Secretariat, 'Plenipotentiary Representatives of Third States Accredited to the Caribbean Community (CARICOM)', as available at <http://www.caricom.org/jsp/community/plenipotentiary_representatives.jsp?menu=community> (9 Feb 2013).

CARICOM Secretariat, 'Press Release 270/2009 (4 July 2009): Communique Issued at the Conclusion of the Thirtieth Regular Meeting of the Conference of Heads of Government of the Caribbean Community, 2–5 July 2009, Georgetown, Guyana', as available at <http://www.caricom.org/jsp/pressreleases/pres270_09.jsp> (17 Mar 2013).

CARICOM Secretariat, 'Press Release: CARICOM Studies show the CSME operating at about 64% level of compliance', No 22/20122 (23 January 2012) (Turkeyen, Guyana: CARICOM Secretariat, 2012).

CARICOM Secretariat, 'Regional Portfolios of CARICOM Heads of Government', as available at <http://www.caricom.org/jsp/community/regional_portfolios.jsp?menu=community> (5 Oct 2011).

CARICOM Secretariat, 'Report of the Sixth Meeting of the IGTF', 2–4 October 1996, Georgetown, Guyana [restricted access, on file with CARICOM Secretariat].

CARICOM Secretariat, 'Report of the Eighth Meeting of the Inter-Governmental Task Force', REP. 97/8/23 IG/TF, held in St John's, Antigua and Barbuda, 24–26 February 1997.

CARICOM Secretariat, 'Restructuring of the Organs and Institutions of the Caribbean Community' (Georgetown: CARICOM Secretariat, 26 August 1993).

CARICOM Secretariat, 'Rose Hall Declaration on Regional Governance and Integrated Development', Adopted on the Occasion of the Thirtieth Anniversary of the Caribbean Community at the Twenty-Fourth Meeting of the Conference of Heads of Government of CARICOM, 2–5 July 2003, Montego Bay, Jamaica, as available at <http://www.caricom.org/jsp/communications/meetings_statements/rose_hall_declaration.jsp?menu=communications> (14 Sep 2013).

CARICOM Secretariat, 'Rules of Procedure of the Community Council of Ministers', adopted at the Second Meeting of the Community Council of Ministers, Guyana, 15–16 May 1998, as available at <http://www.caricom.org/jsp/community_organs/rules_council.jsp?menu=cob&prnf=1> (4 Oct 2011).

CARICOM Secretariat, 'Rules of Procedure for the Council for Finance and Planning (COFAP)' adopted at the 1st Meeting of COFAP Castries, Saint Lucia, 29 June 1998, as available at <http://www.caricom.org/jsp/community_organs/rules_cofap.jsp?menu=cob> (4 Oct 2011).

CARICOM Secretariat, 'Rules of Procedure for the Council for Human and S Development (COHSOD)' [no date], as available at <http://www.caricom.c community_organs/rules_cohsod.jsp?menu=cob> (4 Oct 2011).

CARICOM Secretariat, 'Status of implementation of Six months entry Permit as Reported at April 2011 Joint Free Movement and Contingent Rights Meeting'.

CARICOM Secretariat, 'Summary of Recommendations and Conclusions of the Thirty-Second Meeting of the Council for Trade and Economic Development (COTED)', 19–20 May 2011.

CARICOM Secretariat, 'Working Document for the Thirty-Second Meeting of the Council for Trade and Economic Development (COTED)', 16–20 May 2011.

CARICOM Secretariat, Office of Trade Negotiations, 'CARICOM-Canada', as available at <http://www.crnm.org/index.php?option=com_content&view=article&id=51&Itemid=121&0872a8d70c6252b77261d45b4779477d=8e5e1b0314895de04ccdd0c1690fc185> (13 May 2013).

Carnegie, AR, 'Commonwealth Caribbean Regionalism' (1979) 33 *Year Book of World Affairs* 180–200.

Carnegie, A Ralph, 'How Exclusive is "Exclusive" in Relation to the Original Jurisdiction of the Caribbean Court of Justice? A Consideration of Recent Developments', Paper Delivered in the Faculty of Law Workshop Series 2009–2010, University of the West Indies, Cave Hill Campus, 25 November 2009, as available through <http://www.cavehill.uwi.edu/news/articles/nov2009/Conflicts_of_Jurisdiction.pdf> (12 Aug 2013).

CIA (US), *The World Factbook* 2013–14 (Washington, DC: Central Intelligence Agency, 2013), as available through <https://www.cia.gov/library/publications/the-world-factbook/index.html> (14 Sep 2013).

Corten, Olivier, 'Reasonableness in International Law', in R Wolfrum (ed), *The Max Planck Encyclopedia of Public International Law*, Oxford University Press, 2008–, online edition [<www.mpepil.com>] (accessed 23 Feb 2013).

Cot, Jean-Pierre, 'Conciliation', in R Wolfrum (ed), *The Max Planck Encyclopedia of Public International Law*, Oxford University Press, 2008– online edition [<www.mpepil.com>].

Council, 'Council Regulation (EC) No 1/2003 of 16 December 2002 on the implementation of the rules on competition laid down in Articles 81 and 82 of the Treaty (Text with EEA relevance)' [2003] OJ L1/1 (4/1/2003), as available at <http://eur-lex.europa.eu/LexUriServ/LexUriServ.do?uri=OJ:L:2003:001:0001:0025:EN:PDF> (26 Jun 2013).

Council Legal Service, 'Primacy of EC Law', 22 June 2007, 11197/07 (JUR 260).

D'Agostino, Thomas J, 'Caribbean Politics' in Richard S Hillman and Thomas J D'Agostino (eds), *Understanding the Contemporary Caribbean*, 2nd edn (Boulder, CO: Lynne Rienner Publishers, 2009) 87–132.

Davey, William, and Joost Pauwelyn, 'MFN Unconditionality: A legal analysis of the concept in view of its evolution in the GATT/WTO Jurisprudence with particular reference to "like product"' in Thomas Cottier and Petros Mavroidis (eds), *Regulatory Barriers and the Principle of Non-Discrimination* (Ann Arbor, Michigan: University of Michigan Press, 2000).

Douglas, Denzil, 'Operationalisation of OECS Economic Union' (24 January 2011) as available through <http://www.oecs.org/> (30 Sep 2011).

Dupuy, Pierre-Marie, 'International Law and Domestic (Municipal) Law' in R Wolfrum (ed), *The Max Planck Encyclopedia of Public International Law*, Oxford University Press, 2008–, online edition [<www.mpepil.com>] (accessed 17 Jul 2013).

Dworkin, Ronald, 'Is Law a System of Rules?' in Ronald M Dworkin (ed) *The Philosophy of Law* (Oxford: Oxford University, 1977) 37–65.

Dworkin, Ronald, 'Law, Philosophy and Interpretation' (1994) 80 *Archiv für Rechts-und Sozialphilosophie* 463–75.

Eastern Caribbean Supreme Court, 'Brief History of the Court', as available at <http://www.eccourts.org/brief-history-of-the-court/> (11 Aug 2013).

European Commission DG Enterprise and Industry, 'Facts and Figures', in *Single Market for Goods Information Pack* (European Union, 2007) as available through <http://bookshop.europa.eu/en/single-market-for-goods-pbNB7807452/?CatalogCategoryID=_z0KABstpR4AAAEjr5AY4e5L> (14 Sep 2013).

European Commission Internal Market and Services, *Your Single Market? Single Market Act for a highly competitive social market economy* (European Union, Luxembourg, 2010) as available at <http://ec.europa.eu/internal_market/smact/docs/brochure-web_en.pdf> (14 Sep 2013).

European Commission, 'Commission Notice on agreements of minor importance which do not appreciably restrict competition under Article 81(1) of the Treaty establishing the European Community (de minimis) (Text with EEA relevance)' OJ C368/13–15 (22.12.2001), as available at <http://eur-lex.europa.eu/LexUriServ/LexUriServ.do?uri=OJ:C:2001:368:0013:0015:EN:PDF> (23 Jun 2013).

European Commission, 'Commission Notice on Immunity from fines and reduction of fines in cartel cases (Text with EEA relevance)' [2006] OJ C298/17 (8/12/2006), as available at <http://eur-lex.europa.eu/LexUriServ/LexUriServ.do?uri=OJ:C:2006:298:0017:0022:EN:PDF> (26 Jun 2013).

European Commission, 'Commission Notice on the definition of relevant market for the purposes of Community competition law' [1997] OJ C372/5 (9.12.1997), as available at <http://eur-lex.europa.eu/LexUriServ/LexUriServ.do?uri=OJ:C:1997:372:0005:0013:EN:PDF> (24 Jun 2013).

European Commission, 'Communication from the Commission—Notice—Guidelines on the application of Article 81(3) of the Treaty', [2004] OJ C101/97–118 (27.04.2004), also available at <http://eur-lex.europa.eu/LexUriServ/LexUriServ.do?uri=CELEX:52004XC0427(07):EN:NOT> (23 Jun 2013).

European Commission, 'Communication from the Commission: A Europe of Results—Applying Community Law', Brussels, 5.9.2007, COM(2007) 502 final, as available at <http://ec.europa.eu/eu_law/eulaw/pdf/com_2007_502_en.pdf> (15 Aug 2013).

Fanning, Lucia et al, 'A large marine ecosystem governance framework' (2007) 31 *Marine Policy* 434–43.

Fitzmaurice, Sir Gerald, 'The General Principles of International Law Considered from the Standpoint of the Rule of Law' (1957-II) 92 *Recueil des Cours de l'Académie de Droit International* 5.

Gaja, Giorgio, 'General Principles of Law' in R Wolfrum (ed), *The Max Planck Encyclopedia of Public International Law*, Oxford University Press, 2008–, online edition [<www.mpepil.com>] (accessed 23 Feb 2013).

Georgetown Accord, adopted at the Eighth Conference of Heads of Government of Commonwealth Caribbean Countries, Georgetown, Guyana, 9–12 April 1973.

Girvan, Norman, 'Reinterpreting the Caribbean' in Brian Meeks and Folke Lindahl (eds), *New Caribbean Thought: A Reader* (Kingston, Jamaica: University of the West Indies Press, 2001) 3–23.

Girvan, Norman, 'Caribbean Community: The Elusive Quest for Economic Integration' in Caribbean Development Bank, *Growth and Development Strategies for the Caribbean* (St Michael, Barbados: Caribbean Development Bank, 2009) 199–218.

Grand Anse Declaration and Work Programme for the Advancement of the Integration Movement, Grand Anse, Grenada, 7 July 1989, as available at

<http://www.caricom.org/jsp/communications/meetings_statements/grand_anse_declaration.jsp?menu=communications> (14 Sep 2013).

Hall, Kenneth, and Byron Blake, 'CARICOM Administration' in Kenneth O. Hall (ed), *The Caribbean Community: Beyond Survival* (Kingston, Jamaica: Ian Randle Publishers, 2001) 203–21.

Hosein, Roger, 'Trade Policy in the Caribbean' in Caribbean Development Bank, *Growth and Development Strategies for the Caribbean* (St Michael, Barbados: Caribbean Development Bank, 2009) 151–83.

Hudec, Robert E, '"Like Products": The Differences in Meaning in GATT Articles I and III,' in Thomas Cottier and Petros Mavroidis (eds), *Regulatory Barriers and the Principle of Non-Discrimination* (Ann Arbor, Michigan: University of Michigan Press, 2000).

Huntley, Earl, 'The LDCs and CARICOM' in Kenneth O. Hall (ed), *The Caribbean Community: Beyond Survival* (Kingston, Jamaica: Ian Randle Publishers, 2001) 35–8.

International Chamber of Commerce, 'ICC Rules of Arbitration' (in force 1 January 2012), as available through <http://www.iccwbo.org/Products-and-Services/Arbitration-and-ADR/Arbitration/ICC-Rules-of-Arbitration/> (4 Aug 2013).

International Law Commission, 'Draft Articles on Most-favoured-nation Clause with Commentaries 1978' (1978) *Yearbook of the International Law Commission*, 1978, vol II, Part Two, 16–73.

International Law Commission, 'Draft Articles on Responsibility of States for Internationally Wrongful Acts with commentaries 2001' (2001) *Yearbook of the International Law Commission*, 2001, vol II, Part Two, 59–365.

International Law Commission, 'Draft Articles on the Law of Treaties with Commentaries,' (1966) *Yearbook of the International Law Commission*, 1966, Vol II, 187–274.

International Law Commission, 'Draft Articles on the Responsibility of International Organizations, with commentaries' (2011) *Yearbook of the International Law Commission*, 2011, vol II, Part Two, 2–104.

International Law Commission, 'Model Rules on Arbitral Procedure with a general commentary' (1958) *Yearbook of the International Law Commission*, 1958, vol II, 83–8.

International Monetary Fund, 'Regional Economic Outlook: Western Hemisphere', World Economic and Financial Surveys (Washington, DC: International Monetary Fund, 2013), available through <http://www.imf.org/external/pubs/ft/reo/reorepts.aspx> (11 Jul 2013).

Ishmael, Len, 'Remarks at the Signing Ceremony of the Revised Treaty of Basseterre Establishing the OECS Economic Union' (18 June 2010) as available through <http://www.oecs.org/doc-lib/addresses/cat_view/94-addresses/188-signing-ceremony-for-the-revised-treaty-of-basseterre-establishing-the-oecs> (20 Sep 2011).

Ishmael, Len, 'Remarks', Opening Ceremony of the Meeting of Leaders of the Opposition, at Gros Islet, St Lucia, on 4 May 2012 (Castries, St Lucia: OECS Secretariat, May 2012), as available through <http://www.oecs.org/doc-lib/addresses/cat_view/94-addresses/201-meeting-of-the-leaders-of-the-opposition> (3 Feb 2013).

Jamaica Information Service, 'CARICOM Member States: Observers at Meetings of the Ministerial Councils of the Caribbean Community', as available at <http://www.jis.gov.jm/special_sections/CARICOMNew/CaricomMemberStates.html> (5 Oct 2011).

Jordan, Ricky, 'Let's Put People at the Centre: New CARICOM Chief's Call', *Sunday Sun* (Barbados), 13 November 2011, 12A–13A.

Lapidoth, Ruth, 'Good Offices', in R Wolfrum (ed), *The Max Planck Encyclopedia of Public International Law*, Oxford University Press, 2008–, online edition [<www.mpepil.com>].

Lewis, Sir Arthur, 'The Agony of the Eight' (1998) 23(1) *Journal of Eastern Caribbean Studies* 6–26.

Lewis, Vaughan, 'The OECS and Closer Political Union', in Kenneth O Hall (ed), *The Caribbean Community: Beyond Survival* (Kingston, Jamaica: Ian Randle Publishers, 2001) 301–14.

Lewis, Vaughan A, 'Political Integration in the Caribbean: A Policy Approach' in Caribbean Development Bank, *Growth and Development Strategies for the Caribbean*, 219–59 (St Michael, Barbados: Caribbean Development Bank, 2009).

London Court of International Arbitration, 'LCIA Arbitration Rules' (effective 1 Jan 1998), as available through <http://www.lcia.org/> (4 Aug 2013).

Lowe, Vaughan, 'The Role of Equity in International Law' 12 *Australian Yearbook of International Law* 54–81.

Menon, PK, 'Sub-Regional Integration in the Caribbean: the OECS Experience' (unpublished paper presented at the 1995 Latin American Studies Association meeting, September 28-30, 1995 (on file at the University of the West Indies Faculty of Law Library, Cave Hill Campus).

O'Brien, Derek, 'CARICOM: Regional Integration in a Post-Colonial World' (2011) 17 *European Law Journal* 642–60.

O'Brien, Derek and S Foadi, 'CARICOM and Its Court of Justice' (2008) 37 *Common Law World Review* 334–55.

OECS Secretariat, 'Castries Declaration on Illegal, Unreported and Unregulated Fishing', 2nd Special Meeting of the CRFM Ministerial Council, Castries, St Lucia (28 July 2010).

OECS Secretariat, 'Communiqué on the 38th Meeting of the OECS Authority, Castries, 22–23 January 2004', as available through <http://www.oecs.org/doc-lib/communiques> (20 Sep 2011).

OECS Secretariat, 'Communiqué—Fifty-Sixth Meeting of the OECS Authority', Dominica, 22–23 Nov 2012 (issued 25 Nov 2012), as available at <http://www.oecs.org/news-a-events/9-secretariat/856-communique-fifty-sixth-meeting-of-the-oecs-authority> (9 Feb 2013).

OECS Secretariat, 'Eastern Caribbean Supreme Court', as available at <http://www.oecs.org/about-the-oecs/institutions/eastern-caribbean-supreme-court-ecsc> (11 Aug 2013).

OECS Secretariat, 'Milestones' as available at <http://www.oecs.org/about-the-oecs/oecs-milestones> (3 Nov 2011).

OECS Secretariat, 'Press Communiqué: Historic Signing by Antigua and Barbuda facilitates deeper OECS Economic Integration' (4 Jan 2011) as available at <http://www.oecs.org/regional-integration/press-releases/742-historic-signing-by-antigua-and-barbuda-facilitates-deeper-oecs-economic-integration> (5 Oct 2011).

OECS Secretariat, 'Press Release: OECS Economic Union Launch' (Friday, 21 Jan 2011, 14:30) as available at <http://www.oecs.org/regional-integration/press-releases/745-oecs-member-states-achieve-historic-milestone-ahead-of-52nd-authority-meeting-> (30 Sep 2011).

OECS Secretariat, 'Units & Missions' as available at <http://www.oecs.org/about-the-oecs/units-a-missions> (20 Oct 2011).

Office of Trade Negotiations, Caribbean Community (CARICOM) Secretariat, 'CARIFORUM Economic Partnership Agreement (EPA) Negotiations', as available at <http://www.crnm.org/index.php?option=com_content&view=article&id=276&Itemid=76> (14 Sep 2013).

Official Website for the Government of Antigua and Barbuda, 'Antigua and Barbuda Received Five Year Derogation from Expansion of Free Movement of Persons' (posted July 8,

2009), as available at <http://www.ab.gov.ag/article_details.php?id=50&category=34> (17 Mar 2013).

Opinion of Mr Advocate-General Lagrange, Delivered on 27 February 1962, p 56, as available through <http://curia.europa.eu/jcms/jcms/j_6/> (15 Aug 2013).

Pantin, Dennis A, and Marlene Attzs, 'The Economies of the Caribbean' in Richard S Hillman and Thomas J D'Agostino (eds), *Understanding the Contemporary Caribbean*, 2nd edn, 133–60 (Boulder, CO: Lynne Rienner Publishers, 2009).

Permanent Court of Arbitration, 'Arbitration Rules 2012', as available through <http://pca-cpa.org/showpage.asp?pag_id=1188> (4 Aug 2013).

Pollard, Duke EE, 'Amending the Treaty of Chaguaramas', in Kenneth O Hall (ed), *The Caribbean Community: Beyond Survival* (Kingston, Jamaica: Ian Randle Publishers, 2001), 252–6.

Pollard, Duke EE, 'Approaches to Regional Governance in the Caribbean Community', Appendix 3 to Richard Stoneman, Justice Duke Pollard and Hugo Inniss, 'Turning Around CARICOM: Proposals to Restructure the Secretariat', Landell Mills Ltd/Final Report/January 2012, as available at <http://www.caricom.org/jsp/communications/caricom_online_pubs/Restructuring%20the%20Secretariat%20-%20Landell%20Mills%20Final%20Report.pdf> (9 Feb 2013).

Sandiford, L Erskine, 'The Assembly of Caribbean Community Parliamentarians' (1998) 68 CARICOM Perspective, June 1998, 74.

Soetendorp, Ben and Kenneth Hanf, 'Conclusion: The Nature of National Adaptation to European Integration', in *Adapting to European Integration: Small States and the European Union*, eds K Hanf and B Soetendorp 186–94 (London: Longman, 1998).

Soetendorp, Ben and Kenneth Hanf, 'Small States and the Europeanisation of Public Policy', in *Adapting to European Integration: Small States and the European Union*, eds K Hanf and B Soetendorp 1–13 (London: Longman, 1998).

Springer, Hugh W, 'Reflections on the Failure of the First West Indian Federation,' Occasional Papers in International Affairs No 4 (Cambridge, MA: Harvard University Center for International Affairs, 1962).

Stewart, Taimoon, 'The Role of Competition Policy in Regional Integration: The Case of the Caribbean Community', paper presented at The CARICOM Single Market and Economy: Legal, Political, Economic and Social Dimensions, SALISES, UWI, St. Augustine, Trinidad and Tobago, 2004, as available at <http://sta.uwi.edu/salises/workshop/papers/tstewart.pdf> (3 Jul 2013).

Stoneman, Richard, Justice Duke Pollard and Hugo Inniss, 'Turning Around CARICOM: Proposals to Restructure the Secretariat', Landell Mills Ltd/Final Report/January 2012, as available at <http://www.caricom.org/jsp/communications/caricom_online_pubs/Restructuring%20the%20Secretariat%20-%20Landell%20Mills%20Final%20Report.pdf> (9 Feb 2013).

UNDP, *2013 Human Development Report—The Rise of the South: Human Progress in a Diverse World* (New York, NY: United Nations Development Program, 2013), as available at <http://hdr.undp.org/en/reports/global/hdr2013/download/> (14 Sep 2013).

United Nations Commission on International Trade Law, 'UNCITRAL Arbitration Rules' (as revised in 2010) (New York: United Nations, 2011).

University of the West Indies, Cave Hill Campus, 'W.I. Federal Archives Centre' [pamphlet], as available at <http://www.cavehill.uwi.edu/research/resources/FedArchives2.pdf> (10 Aug 2013).

Usher, John A, 'Variable Geometry or Concentric Circles: Patterns for the European Union' (1997) 46 ICLQ 243–73.

Vicuña, Francisco Orrego, 'Mediation', in R Wolfrum (ed), *The Max Planck Encyclopedia of Public International Law*, Oxford University Press, 2008-, online edition [<www.mpepil.com>].

Virally, Michel, 'The Sources of International Law' in Max Sørenson (ed), *Manual of Public International Law* (London: Macmillan, 1968) 116–74.

von Sydow, H Schmitt, 'Basic Strategies of the Commission's White Paper', as reproduced in Stephen Weatherill, *Cases & Materials on EU Law*, 9th edn (Oxford: Oxford University Press, 2010).

Waldock, Sir Humphrey, 'General Course on Public International Law' (1962-II) 106 *Hague Recueil des Cours* 1–252.

Walker, Neil, 'Sovereignty and Differentiated Integration in the European Union' (1998) 4 *European Law Journal* 355–88.

Wickham, Peter, 'More Shadow than Substance', in Kenneth O Hall (ed), *The Caribbean Community: Beyond Survival* (Kingston, Jamaica: Ian Randle Publishers, 2001) 234–51.

Wit, Jacob, 'The Role of the Caribbean Court Of Justice (CCJ) in the Private Sector's Life', paper presented at the Regional Manufacturers' Meeting, TTMA Headquarters, Trinidad & Tobago, on 4 February 2006, available through <http://www.caribbeancourtofjustice.org/publications/papers-speeches> (21 Jul 2013).

World Bank, 'World DataBank—World Development Indicators' database, as available through <http://databank.worldbank.org/> (14 Sep 2013).

World Trade Organization, 'Accessions—The Bahamas', as available at <http://www.wto.org/english/thewto_e/acc_e/a1_bahamas_e.htm> (26 May 2013).

World Trade Organization, 'International intergovernmental organizations granted observer status to WTO bodies', as available at <http://www.wto.org/english/thewto_e/igo_obs_e.htm> (26 May 2013).

World Trade Organization, 'WTO Analytical Index: Agreement on Agriculture', as available through <http://www.wto.org/english/res_e/booksp_e/analytic_index_e/analytic_index_e.htm> (6 June 2013).

World Trade Organization, 'WTO Analytical Index: Subsidies and Countervailing Measures', as available through <http://www.wto.org/english/res_e/booksp_e/analytic_index_e/analytic_index_e.htm> (6 Jun 2013).

INTERVIEWS AND STATEMENTS

Interview with Duke Pollard, Thelma Rodney-Edwards, and Michelle Walker at CARICOM Secretariat, Georgetown, Guyana (10 Dec 1998).

Statement by Milton Haughton, Deputy Executive Director, CRFM Secretariat (Personal communication 8 Dec 2011).

Interview with Safiya Ali, General Counsel, CARICOM Secretariat, Georgetown, Guyana (6 August 2012).

Statement by Elma Gene Isaac, Head of the OECS Regional Integration Unit (Personal communication 24 Jul 2013).

Index